Primate Behavioral Ecology

Karen B. Strier

University of Wisconsin-Madison

Allyn and Bacon

Boston ■ New York ■ San Francisco
Mexico City ■ Montreal ■ Toronto ■ London ■ Madrid ■ Munich ■ Paris
Hong Kong ■ Singapore ■ Tokyo ■ Cape Town ■ Sydney

In memory of my father, Murray Paul Strier

Series Editor: *Jennifer Jacobson*
Editor in Chief, Social Sciences: *Karen Hanson*
Editorial Assistant: *Tom Jefferies*
Marketing Manager: *Taryn Wahlquist*
Editorial-Production Service: *Whitney Acres Editorial*
Manufacturing Buyer: *JoAnne Sweeney*
Cover Administrator: *Kristina Mose-Libon*
Electronic Composition: *Omegatype Typography, Inc.*

For related titles and support materials, visit our online catalogue at www.ablongman.com

Between the time Website information is gathered and published, some sites may have closed. Also, the transcription of URLs can result in typographical errors. The publishers would appreciate notification where these occur so that they may be corrected in subsequent editions.

Library of Congress Cataloging-in-Publication Data

CIP data not available at the time of publication.

ISBN: 0-205-35236-7

Cover photo credits: Front photo by K.B. Strier; Back photos (clockwise, from top left): 1. Slender loris infant at Giritele, Sri Lanka. Photo by K.A.I. Nekaris. 2. Lowland gorilla group sitting near forest edge in Mbeli Bai, Nouabalé-Ndoki National Park, Republic of Congo; Photo by Claudia Olejniczak. 3. Male yellow baboons at Amboseli National Park, Kenya, form a coalition in a contest over meat. Photo by Ronald Noë. 4. Red colobus and Diana monkey association in the Täi National Forest, Ivory Coast. Photo by © Melanie Krebs. 5. Female patas monkeys in Laikipia, Kenya. Photo by Ron S. and Anne A. Carlson. 6. Young muriquis hanging out. Photo by Luiz G. Dias. Cover design by Bob Becker.

Printed in the United States of America

10 9 8 7 6 5 4 3 2 1   06 05 04 03 02

CONTENTS

PREFACE

I began thinking about updates for the second edition of *Primate Behavioral Ecology* not long after the first edition was published. New discoveries were being made at a remarkable rate, and I was eager for the opportunity to include them. Some, such as the comparative analyses of local behavioral traditions, were making news for what they implied about primate cultures. Others, such as the accumulation of life-long life history data and a flood of long-awaited genetic and paternity studies, have been fundamental in turning evolutionary theories of behavior into testable hypotheses. From these, new insights into patterns of behavioral diversity have emerged. The accelerated pace of discoveries in the field has been fueled as much by concerns for the world's endangered primates as by scientific curiosity. It was time to incorporate these influential advances in a second edition of this book.

This edition, like the first, is an introduction to the field of primate behavioral ecology and its applications to primate conservation. It integrates the basics of evolutionary and ecological approaches to the study of behavior with up-to-date coverage of how different primates actually behave. Examples are drawn from the "classic" primate field studies as well as more recent studies on previously neglected species to illustrate the vast behavioral variation that we now know exists, and the gaps in our knowledge that future studies will fill. Throughout the book, the interplay among theory, observations, and conservation issues is emphasized.

Readers will undoubtedly have different levels of familiarity with the genetics underlying evolutionary processes, primate evolutionary history, and basic behavioral ecology. For some, the background material covered in early chapters will be a review, but the relevance of these areas to conservation deserves to be reinforced. Subsequent chapters are organized around some of the major research themes in the field. Most begin with an overview of theoretical approaches and then examine the comparative evidence that supports or challenges evolutionary-based predictions.

Incorporating new material meant expanding several sections of the book, particularly in Chapter 3 (Primates Past to Present), where intraspecific variation is introduced, Chapter 5 (Evolution and Sex), where new insights into sexual signals and new data on male rank and reproductive success are discussed, and Chapter 6 (Food and Females), where the effects of food on shaping female reproductive patterns are elaborated. Chapter 9 (Developmental Stages Through the Life Cycle) now includes sections on puberty, adulthood and aging, and the links between life histories and conservation. Predator-prey interactions and the conservation of communities are covered in greater detail than before in Chapter 11 (Community Ecology). New topics and examples, especially from prosimians, are integrated across each of the chapters so that the flow and organization of the book are preserved; confusing topics, such as taxonomy, are clarified and a consistent classification system is used throughout. More than 200 new references, most of which appeared since the first edition went to press, reflect the extent to which updates could be made.

I took my cues for the most extensive revisions from some remarkable colleagues who cared enough about the book to send detailed comments and corrections. Irwin Bernstein, William McGrew, John Mitani, and Maria van Noodwijk were particularly influential to this edition, building on the extensive feedback that Sylvia Shepard, Murray Strier, and Jim Moore provided on the first edition's manuscript. Beth Fox, Cliff Jolly, Vincent Labbe, Michael Huffman, Cate Mitton, Jim Moore, John Oates, Alison Richard, Norman Rosen, Richard Sherwood, Patricia Wright, and Toni Ziegler made helpful suggestions and answered last minute queries. They join the long list of people to whom I am still indebted for comments on sections of the first edition, including Leslie Knapp, Jon Marks, Tom Martin, Charles Snowdon, Elliot Sober, and Robert Sussman. I also thank Sue Boinski, James Calcagno, Anne Carlson, Marina Cords, David Hill, Minna Hsu, Andreas Koenig, Andrew Klaber, Cheryl Knott, Joanna Lambert, Phyllis Lee, Sheri Morgenroth, Ronald Noë, Melisssa Panger, Martha Robbins, and Eduardo Veado for their encouragement.

It is an honor to include the photographs of many colleagues, whose hard work and research are only partially captured by their lenses. My sincerest appreciation goes to them for their generosity: Thad Bartlett, Irwin Bernstein, Carla Boe, Sue Boinski, Jean Boubli, Robert Boyd, Diane Brockman, Heather Bruce, Richard Byrne, Christina Campbell, Ron and Anne Carlson, Margaret Clarke, Marina Cords, Paulo Coutinho, Nancy DeVore/Anthro-Photo, Irven DeVore/Anthro-Photo, Robin Dunbar, Beth Erhardt, Mary Glenn, Sharon Gursky, David Haring, David Hill, Michael Huffman, Ellen Ingmanson, Robert Jeanne, Peter Kappeler, Minoru Kinoshita, Cheryl Knott, Melanie Krebs, Tim Laman, Phyllis Lee, Lois Lippold, Jessica Lynch, Katherine MacKinnon, Joe Manson, William McGrew, John Mitani, Florian Möllers, Jim Moore, Leanne Nash, Anna Nekaris, Ronald Noë, Claudio Nogueira, Marilyn Norconk, Maria van Noordwijk, John Oates, Adriana Odalia-Rímoli, Noel Rowe, Claudia Olejniczak, Deborah Overdorff, Melissa Panger, Susan Perry, Jane Phillips-Conroy, Melissa Remis, José Rímoli, Martha Robbins, Elizabeth Rogers, Carel van Schaik, Joan Silk, Meredith Small, Craig Stanford, Thomas Struhsaker, Frans de Waal, and Toni Ziegler. I am also grateful to Perry van Duijinhoven for his illustration, Cheryl Knott, Maria van Noordwijk, Alison Richard, Carel van Schaik for their help with permissions, and the individuals and publishing houses that provided the necessary approvals.

Many aspects involved in the preparation of the manuscript were facilitated thanks to others. Andreia Oliva was instrumental in compiling the initial bibliography and in cross-checking references. Bob Becker at the Wisconsin Regional Primate Research Center played a critical role in reproducing most of the photographs and in designing the cover. Larry Jacobsen, Ray Hamel, and staff at the Primate Center Library helped in locating essential reference material. Jennifer Jacobson, my editor at Allyn and Bacon, has been a pleasure and inspiration to work with. Her enthusiasm was contagious, her encouragement sustaining, and her participation in all phases of the manuscript's production essential. I would not have completed this without her. Faye Whitney-Lussier was a great help with copy editing and other details. I want to thank the following reviewers of the first edition: Wendy James Aldridge, University of Texas, Pan American; David Frayer, University of Kansas; Paul A. Garber, University of Illinois, Champaign-Urbana; John Mitani, University of Michigan, Ann Arbor; James Moore, University of California, San Diego; and Forrest D. Tierson, University of Colorado at Colorado Springs. I am equally grateful to the reviewers of the second edition for their helpful and encouraging comments and suggestions: Tibor Koertyelyessy, Ohio University; William C. McGrew, Miami University; Deborah Overdorff, University of Texas-Austin; Daniel Sellen, Emory University; and Linda L. Taylor, University of Miami.

Other friends, family members, and students were uniformly encouraging and tolerant of my concentration on this project. Tom Martin, in particular, was once again my greatest ally throughout.

But most of all, this book was possible thanks to the many primates who have continued to let us into their lives.

1 Introduction to Primate Studies

The tropical forests where most primates live are humid, shadowy places. More often than not, there is a humming in the background from the hordes of mosquitos and other insects hovering about. Fieldworkers' clothes get torn and snagged from thorny plants that thrive on the forest floor, and our skin is often covered with itchy scabs from the microscopic ticks that invariably find their way to the warmest parts of our bodies to feed on our blood. Putting up with these discomforts can be trying at times, but it is a small price to pay for the privilege of studying the world's wild primates.

Primates are special animals. Visitors flock to their exhibits at zoos, record numbers of viewers watch televised documentaries about the most intimate details of their lives, and newspaper headlines routinely cover their latest antics. This broad public appeal of primates no doubt stems from the fact that we humans count ourselves among them (Table 1.1) and see aspects of ourselves in them (Figure 1.1).

Primates are as fascinating to scholars as they are to the general public. At major colleges and universities throughout the world, primates occupy a unique niche in research and teaching curricula as examples of highly intelligent, social

TABLE 1.1 Classification of living genera in the primate order*

Common name^	Genus	Subfamily	Family	Superfamily	Infraorder	Suborder
Aye-aye Indri Sifaka Woolly lemur	*Daubentonia* *Indri* *Propithecus* *Avahi*		Daubentoniidae Indriidae	Lemuroidea	Lemuriformes	Prosimii
Sportive lemur	*Lepilemur*		Lepilemuridae			
Mouse lemur Coquerel's dwarf lemur Hairy-eared dwarf lemur Greater dwarf lemur Fork-marked lemur	*Microcebus* *Mirza* *Allocebus* *Cheirogaleus* *Phaner*		Cheirogaleidae			
Ruffed lemur Bamboo lemur Ring-tailed lemur Brown lemur	*Varecia* *Hapalemur* *Lemur* *Eulemur*		Lemuridae			
Greater bush baby Zanzibar bush baby Bush baby Needle-clawed bush baby	*Otolemur* *Galagoides* *Galago* *Euoticus*		Galagidae	Lorisoidea	(Lorisiformes)	
Potto Angwantibo Slow loris Slender loris	*Perodicticus* *Arctocebus* *Nycticebus* *Loris*		Lorisidae			
Tarsier	*Tarsius*		Tarsiidae	Tarsioidea	Tarsiiformes	
Pygmy marmoset Marmoset Goeldi's monkey Tamarin Lion tamarin	*Cebuella* *Callithrix* *Callimico* *Saguinus* *Leontopithecus*	Callitrichinae	(Callitrichidae)	Ceboidea	Platyrrhini	Anthropoidea
Squirrel monkey Capuchin monkey	*Saimiri* *Cebus*	Cebinae	Cebidae			
Night monkey	*Aotus*	Aotinae				
Titi monkey	*Callicebus*	Callicebinae	Atelidae			

Common name	Genus	Subfamily	Family	Superfamily	Infraorder
Saki	*Pithecia*	Pitheciinae			
Bearded saki	*Chiropotes*				
Uacari	*Cacajao*				
Howler monkey	*Alouatta*	Atelinae			
Woolly monkey	*Lagothrix*				
Muriqui	*Brachyteles*				
Spider monkey	*Ateles*				
Allen's swamp monkey	*Allenopithecus*	Cercopithecinae	Cercopithecidae	Cercopithecoidea	Catarrhini
Talapoin monkey	*Miopithecus*				
Patas monkey	*Erythrocebus*				
Vervet monkey	*Chlorocebus*				
Guenon	*Cercopithecus*				
Macaque	*Macaca*				
Mandrill	*Mandrillus*				
Mangabey	*Cercocebus*				
Black mangabey	*Lophocebus*				
Baboon	*Papio*				
Gelada baboon	*Theropithecus*				
Olive colobus	*Procolobus*	Colobinae			
Red colobus	*Piliocolobus*				
Black and white colobus	*Colobus*				
Hanuman langur	*Semnopithecus*				
Nilgiri langur	*Kasi*				
Capped leaf monkey	*Trachypithecus*				
Langur	*Presbytis*				
Proboscis monkey	*Nasalis*				
Pig-tailed langur	*Simias*				
Douc langur	*Pygathrix*				
Snub-nosed monkey	*Rhinopithecus*				
Gibbon	*Hylobates*		Hylobatidae	Hominoidea	
Orangutan	*Pongo*		Pongidae		
Gorilla	*Gorilla*				
Chimpanzee	*Pan*				
Human	*Homo*		Hominidae		

*Adapted from Fleagle, J. G. 1999. *Primate Adaptation and Evolution, 2nd Ed.* New York: Academic Press.
Reprinted with permission. Copyright © 1999, Academic Press. Taxa in parentheses indicate alternative classifications (e.g., Sussman, 1999a), and are discussed in Chapter 2, along with the controversial placement of the tarsiers.

^For additional common names, photographs, and taxonomic debates for some species, see Rowe, 1996.
For lists of common and Latin names, see the Appendix to this book.

FIGURE 1.1   Bipedal bonobos (*Pan paniscus*) at the San Diego Zoo. Female is on the left, male is on the right. From *Peacemaking among Primates* by Frans de Waal (1989). Photo by Frans de Waal.

animals and as members of the long evolutionary heritage to which we belong. Primatologists employed in academia are housed across departments of biology, psychology, anthropology, and anatomy, where they bring their own disciplinary perspectives to bear on uncovering and understanding the patterns that describe primate adaptations. Accumulating data from long-term studies of familiar primates and new data from recently-established field sites on rare and unfamiliar primates continue to shift our understanding of what it means to be a primate in provocative ways.

As study subjects, primates are special in two additional respects. First, because their geographic concentration to the tropics has placed many species at risk of extinction from deforestation and hunting pressures, knowledge about primates is now widely recognized as being essential to conservation efforts on their behalf. The relevance of primatology extends beyond science to its applications to mainstream societal issues, where primates are serving as flagships for their own and others' benefits, and where our discoveries about primates are being translated directly into saving endangered species and their habitats. Second, their biological similarities to humans have put primates into the position of contributing to biomedical advances (King, et al., 1988), challenging the ethical as well as biological limits of what it means to be human. Knowledge about primates is helping to determine guidelines for the use of animals in experimental research, and catalyzing public awareness and action about sensitive biomedical ethics and animal well-being. It is also stimulating greater concern with protecting wild primate populations, which may hold the keys to understanding the origins of many human diseases, including highly infectious ones such as HIV.

My own biases in this book will be immediately apparent. Trained as a biological anthropologist, my original interest in primates for what they can teach us about the evolution of human social behavior led me to study them in their natural habitats, where ecological and social pressures interact. My first field experience was as an undergraduate assistant on the Amboseli baboon project in southern Kenya (Figure 1.2). It was during this decisive six-month assignment that my early views of how nonhuman primates were supposed to behave took shape. By 1982, when I began my long-term field study of the endangered muriqui monkeys in Brazil's Atlantic forest, (Figure 1.3), I was intent on testing comparative models of primate behavioral ecology and on applying this knowledge to their conservation. Muriquis represented an ideal test case because their elusive habits had left them out of the comparisons on which the models proposed at the time were based. In addition, their endangered status meant that everything learned about them had the potential for practical as well as theoretical applications.

Although my firsthand experience on the Amboseli baboon project had given me an idea of what it took to conduct and maintain a long-term field study, I was totally unprepared for the behaviors I witnessed among muriquis. Unlike the **hierarchical** society of baboons, in which access to important resources such as food and mates are determined by **agonistic,** or aggressive and submissive interactions between females and males, muriquis maintain nonhierarchical, **egalitarian** relationships with one another. Female baboons spend their lives in their **natal,** or birth groups, and maintain strong **affiliative bonds** with their closest relatives (Figure 1.4), but in muriquis it is the males that stay in their natal groups with their mothers and other male kin, or **patrilines,** and the females that leave their kin behind to pursue their reproductive careers in other muriqui groups. The peaceful

FIGURE 1.2   Yellow baboons (*Papio cynocephalus*) at Amboseli National Park, Kenya. Mt. Kilimanjaro is in the background, the author is to the left. Photo provided by K. B. Strier.

FIGURE 1.3 Two muriquis (*Brachyteles arachnoides*) at the Estação Biologica de Caratinga, located on Fazenda Montes Claros in Minas Gerais, Brazil. Photo by A. Odalia-Rímoli.

FIGURE 1.4 Yellow baboon (*Papio cynocephalus*) mother at Amboseli National Park, Kenya, is groomed by one daughter while a younger daughter suckles. Photo by K. B. Strier.

social relationships at the core of muriqui society were an unexpected discovery that set muriquis apart not only from baboons, but also from nearly all other primates that were known at the time (Table 1.2).

Had muriquis turned the evolutionary and ecological rules that predict competitive behavior in other primates to different ends? Did they represent just one example of a previously underestimated set of behavioral options available to primates? These were some of the questions that led me to pursue my long-term research on them. My research with the muriquis inspired me to write this book on primate behavioral ecology, which examines the diverse behavioral possibilities we now know exist among primates, and emphasizes the importance of preserving this diversity in the 21st century.

TABLE 1.2   Muriqui society compared to the societies of other well-known primates, including savanna baboons

	Muriqui	Savanna baboon[1]	Chimpanzee[2]	Mountain gorilla[3]	Ringtailed lemur[4]
Group composition:	multi-male, multi-female	multi-male, multi-female	multi-male, multi-female	uni- or multi-male, multi-female	multi-male, multi-female
Grouping pattern:	cohesive, fluid	cohesive	fluid	cohesive	cohesive
Natal group dispersal:	female-biased	male-biased	female-biased	both sexes	male-biased
Female relationships:	indifferent	matrilineal, hierarchical	indifferent, weakly hierarchical	indifferent, weakly hierarchical	matrilineal, hierarchical
Male relationships:	patrilineal, egalitarian	hierarchical	patrilineal, hierarchical	hierarchical in multi-male groups	hierarchical
Male-female relationships:	egalitarian	males dominate	males dominate	males dominate	females dominate

[1]The societies of Japanese macaques, rhesus macaques, vervet monkeys, and capuchin monkeys are similar, although in contrast to baboons, among these monkeys, some females can dominate all but the highest ranking, "alpha" male. The societies of hamadryas baboons differ from those of savanna baboons, as explained in later chapters.

[2]Bonobo societies are now known to differ from those of chimpanzees in that female relationships, although not kin-based, can be highly affiliative. Male relationships are only weakly hierarchical, and females can dominate males. Spider monkey societies are more similar to those of chimpanzees.

[3]The societies of howler monkeys and Hanuman langurs are similar to those of mountain gorillas, although in Hanuman langurs natal group dispersal is male-biased. Also, female relationships tend to be hierarchical in both howler monkeys and Hanuman langurs.

[4]Although other species of lemurs live in different kinds of groups, none are known to be patrilocal.

Primates as Study Subjects

Nonhuman primates have been described as representing the "boundary" that separates humans from other animals (Haraway, 1989). Primates bear the distinction of being the group of animals to which we belong and through which we trace our **phylogenetic,** or evolutionary, history. Because other primates are the closest living links we have to our extinct ancestors, they can make excellent models for identifying our ancestral traits. But even without their connection to us, primates are interesting in their own right. As a diverse group of long-lived, socially complex animals, they provide some of the best insights into the evolutionary and ecological processes that affect behavioral variation (Rowell, 1993). In fact, studies of primates have contributed to, as well as benefited from, advances in our comparative understanding of the evolution of animal, including human, behavior (Harcourt, 1998).

Despite these continuities in behavior, deeply rooted perceptions about the similarities and differences between humans and animals have influenced the history of primate studies in significant ways. From the kinds of questions asked of primates, to the species most widely studied, to the methods employed, and interpretations of results, academic traditions in the social and biological sciences have left their distinct disciplinary marks (Richard, 1981; Strier, 1993a, 1997a).

Nowadays, many questions in primate behavioral ecology focus on efforts to understand the **ultimate,** or evolutionary, **function** of behavior. These functional approaches address the question of *why* primates have been selected to behave as they do under particular conditions. But there are other ways of posing questions about primates, and other complementary levels of explaining their behavior that many contemporary primatologists also incorporate in their research. Asking *what* are the underlying neural, chemical, physiological, or immediate causes for a particular behavior requires a **proximate** level of explanation. Discovering the developmental trajectory of *when* a particular trait or behavior emerges during an individual's lifetime involves an **ontogenetic** level of explanation. **Phylogenetic** levels of explanation describe *how* a particular trait or behavior is distributed across related species (Tinbergen, 1963).

To clarify the subtle differences between these levels of explanation, we can look at an actual example of sex differences in behavior. Consider the case of female chimpanzees at Gombe National Park, Tanzania, who use twigs to "fish" for termites that build earthy, moundlike nests (Figure 1.5). Females use these and other tools more frequently than males (McGrew, 1979). If we were interested in why these female chimpanzees are more avid tool-users, we might develop and test several predictions, such as that termites provide protein and lipids and other nutrients essential to female, but not male, reproduction. If we were concerned with what produces this sex difference in behavior, we might examine whether males and females differ in their fine-grained motor coordination or physiology to obtain an understanding of the proximate mechanisms that affect behavior. Ontogenetic approaches might lead us to explore when male and female chimpanzee behavior begins to diverge, or whether mothers provide their daughters more opportunities to observe the practice of termite-fishing than their sons. To understand this sex difference at a phylogenetic level, we might examine whether there is evidence for sex

FIGURE 1.5   Chimpanzee (*Pan troglodytes*) mother with infant fishes for termites. Photo by Jim Moore/Anthro-Photo.

differences in food procurement and object manipulation in other populations of chimpanzees and in other primate species.

Many of the questions we ask about the evolutionary function of particular behaviors require multiple levels of analyses to address. For example, in hierarchical societies like those of savanna baboons, adult males can be ranked on the basis of the outcomes of agonistic interactions among them. Fights can result in debilitating wounds, so why do they engage in this behavior? Hypotheses about the functional significance of agonistic interactions have focused on the possible reproductive advantages that high status confers on the males that manage to attain it. Yet, it has only been through the recent use of genetic paternity analyses that the hypothesized positive relationship between male rank and reproductive success could be tested. Combining different levels of analyses is the most powerful way to understand why and how different primates behave as they do.

Descriptive Studies

The early years of primate field research were characterized by descriptive, **ethnographic** type reports. Like contemporary field workers, pioneering researchers went to remote locations to find wild primates, and eventually, through hard work and persistence, succeeded in winning the trust of the primates they had gone to study. Once primates are **habituated** to the presence of an observer, they go about their business-as-usual instead of fleeing or halting their activities when humans are near (Figure 1.6). Habituation is essential for seeing how primates behave when they're not on their guard. The process can be especially challenging if the primates have already learned to avoid humans who hunt them. Of course, the transition

FIGURE 1.6   Masudi, an adult male chimpanzee (*Pan troglodytes*) at Mahale, Tanzania, and primatologist John Mitani. Masudi is fully habituated to the presence of human researchers. Photo by John Mitani.

from panic and flight to indifferent tolerance is a gradual one, and it is not always clear when human observers are fully accepted by their study subjects.

Unlike contemporary primatologists, who now collect most of their data in highly systematic ways, early primate field researchers focused on cataloging the behavioral repertories, or **ethograms,** of their subjects. These original reports continue to provide some of the most detailed descriptions of primate behavior, but comparisons across studies were difficult to make. Did one researcher's interest in aggressive behavior lead her to notice hair-raising fights more often than another researcher, whose interest in **grooming** behavior may have led him to pay closer attention to the meticulous service of removing ticks and burrs that one primate provides for another? Because standardized methods of behavioral sampling were rarely employed, no one could say for certain how much the observers' own biases and interests influenced their findings.

Anthropocentric Perspectives

The descriptive, ethnographic-type reports that characterized the early years of primate field research grew partially out of widespread **anthropocentric** interests in primates. Anthropocentric approaches, which examine primates to understand more about humans, date back to the beginning of primate field research, when curious naturalists first set out to observe wild primates. In the 1920s and 1930s, Yale University psychologist Robert Yerkes began sending students to conduct naturalistic studies of primates as part of a larger agenda in comparative psychobiology, which included chimpanzees and mountain gorillas. But in many respects, it was when Clarence Ray Carpenter went to Panama that the scientific study of wild primates got underway (Carpenter, 1934, 1964).

The howler monkeys that Carpenter studied are **arboreal,** or tree-dwelling, creatures, which, along with the other New World monkeys in Central and South America, share only a distant ancestry to humans (Figure 1.7). Nonetheless, Carpenter's depictions of their complicated family lives captured the attention of Kinjii Imanishi, a Japanese ecologist who then launched his own detailed investigations into the societies of Japanese macaques in the mid-1950s (Asquith, 1991). These macaques, along with some of the other Old World monkeys of Asia and Africa, are **semiterrestrial,** or partially ground-dwelling, monkeys (Figure 1.8). They also share more traits with humans than the howler monkeys, in part because of their adaptations to life on the ground.

In the late 1950s, U.S. physical anthropologist Sherwood Washburn recruited Irven DeVore to apply the ethnographic methods and theory employed by social anthropologists to study wild baboons, another semiterrestrial Old World monkey. Baboons had even stronger claims than macaques as possible models for human ancestors because baboons occur throughout sub-Saharan Africa, where the fossil trail of human origins begins (Figure 1.9). The baboons studied by DeVore just outside of Nairobi are found in the same types of open **woodland** and **savanna** habitats that our ancestors are thought to have occupied when they first made the transition to a **terrestrial** lifestyle (Figure 1.10). Similarities in the societies of baboons and macaques supported the idea that human sociality had been shaped by some of the same ecological pressures that influence the social behavior of these

FIGURE 1.7   Male mantled howler monkey (*Alouatta palliata*). Photo by Margaret R. Clarke.

FIGURE 1.8   Japanese macaque (*Macaca fuscata*) matriline. Three generations of females of the "Mino" lineage huddled together on a cold January afternoon at Arashiyama, Kyoto, Japan. Photo by Michael A. Huffman.

ground-dwelling monkeys. For example, primates on the ground are more vulnerable to attacks from predators such as lions and other large carnivores than their arboreal cousins, which may explain the fact that they live in large, coordinated troops (Washburn and DeVore, 1961).

Another early Washburn student, Phyllis Jay (later, Phyllis Dolhinow) conducted her research on Indian langurs, members of the other major group of Old World monkeys called colobines (Figure 1.11). Unlike baboons and macaques, langurs and other colobines are arboreal, which means they spend most of their time in the trees. Langurs have special anatomical traits that permit them to digest large quantities of leaves, which are usually found in abundance. Perhaps because of this, social relationships among members of langur troops were less hierarchical than those among macaques and baboons. Instead, Jay focused her studies on the processes of socialization and development within langur societies. Other pioneering field studies on langurs were also underway (e.g., Sugiyama, 1964), providing valuable comparative insights into the variation in langur behavior in troops that differed from one another in size and composition (Jay, 1968).

In the early 1960s, British paleontologist Louis Leakey helped establish long-term studies on three of the four great apes, the closest living primate relatives to humans. First came Jane Goodall's studies of chimpanzees, then Dian Fossey's studies of mountain gorillas (Figure 1.12), and finally, Biruté Galdikas' studies of orangutans (Figure 1.13). Japanese primatologists also expanded their work to include African apes, which they also expected would provide a deeper understanding of early human evolution (Azuma and Toyoshima, 1961/62; Imanishi,

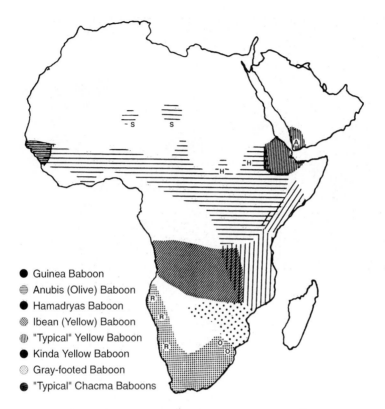

FIGURE 1.9   Distribution of baboons across Africa. Overlapping areas indicate hybrid zones (Box 3.2) or areas where different kinds of baboons integrade. S = Saharan (small) forms of olive baboons; H = sites of collections of "Heuglin's baboons"; A = Arabian forms of hamadryas; O = sites of collections of "Transvaal Chacmas"; R = general distribution of (small) Kalahari Chacmas. From Jolly, Clifford J. 1993. Species, subspecies, and baboon systematics. In Kimbel, W. H. and Martin, L. B. (eds.), *Species, Species Concepts, and Primate Evolution,* Plenum Press, New York, pp. 67–107. Reprinted with permission of the author and Plenum Press.

1966). The great apes are thought to be most similar in size, biology, and behavior to the first human ancestors, and therefore hold keys to understanding our own behavioral evolution (Moore, 1992b; Wrangham, 1987a). Comparisons among apes and other, more distantly-related primates provide perspectives on what is—and isn't—different about humans.

Comparative Biology

Biologists were equally active in the early days of primate studies, but their interest in primates extended beyond anthropocentric comparisons with humans to

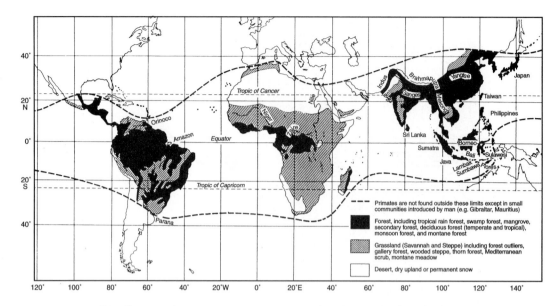

FIGURE 1.10   Distribution of major vegetation zones within the range of nonhuman primates. From Napier, J. R. and Napier, P. H., 1994. *The Natural History of the Primates,* fig. 1.2, p. 10. Cambridge: The MIT Press. Copyright © 1994, The MIT Press. Reprinted by permission of The MIT Press.

FIGURE 1.11   Hanuman langurs (*Presbytis entellus* or *Semnopithecus entellus*). Photo by Robert L. Jeanne.

FIGURE 1.12   A male mountain gorilla (*Gorilla gorilla berengei*). Photo by Martha M. Robbins.

include those with other animals. Biologists such as Stuart and Jeanne Altmann (1970) sought out the savanna-dwelling baboons for their social complexity, whose "sociobiology" could be readily observed in the open habitats they occupied. Others, such as Thelma Rowell (1966), who focused on forest-dwelling baboons, and Tom Struhsaker (1967a, 1969, 1997), who focused on semiterrestrial vervet monkeys (Figure 1.14) and their close arboreal relatives in the African rainforest, aimed to tease apart the ecological and phylogenetic determinants of social behavior. Comparisons among the same or closely related primates living in different habitats would reveal whether their behavior was responsive to the different ecological pressures they faced, or whether species-typical patterns in behavior established during their evolutionary history prevailed. Still others traced Carpenter's pioneering footsteps back to the New World to revisit howler monkeys and initiate comparative studies on other New World primates.

Early Classification Schemes

By the late 1960s, primate field research was no longer limited to the handful of monkeys and apes with clear ecological or phylogenetic connections to humans

FIGURE 1.13   A subadult male orangutan (*Pongo pygmaeus*) showing unusual limb usage. Photo by John Mitani.

FIGURE 1.14   Vervet monkeys (*Chlorocebus aethiops*) at Amboseli National Park, Kenya. Photo by P. C. Lee.

(Aldrich-Blake, 1970). Old World primates still dominated the literature, but a broader comparative framework for organizing primates had begun to take shape. Diverse species could be classified according to general ecological and social categories that clearly distinguished their lifestyles (Crook and Gartlan, 1966).

Many of these distinctions were, and still are, based on grouping primates into categories according to what the animals seem to do most of the time. As we'll see in later chapters, discrete categorical descriptions are artificial in a way, because we have no way of knowing whether our cutoffs between categories are biologically meaningful (Clutton-Brock and Harvey, 1984; Moore, 1984). Nonetheless, classifying primates helps provide a basis for comparing different species, and for identifying deviations among them that require closer scrutiny. The process of investigating unusual behavior patterns has played a major role in advancing our understanding of primate behavior diversity and the underlying evolutionary and ecological factors that shape it.

Activity Patterns.   All primates must rest, eat, and travel between food sources, and often both survival and reproduction also demand time-consuming sociality. How primates allocate their time to these essential activities, or their **activity budgets,** is highly variable among different species as well as among members of the same group. Most primates are **diurnal,** meaning that they are active during the daylight hours and inactive, or sleeping, at night. Some of the primates living on the island of Madagascar are **cathemeral,** meaning that they are active both day and night. **Nocturnal,** or night-active, primates, are thought to be the ancestral condition (Chapter 2), and are turning out to be much more numerous than was previously thought (Bearder, 1999). Primates with different activity patterns are vulnerable to different kinds of predators. Those that made the move to more conspicuous diurnal lifestyles have had to shift from being fairly solitary and inconspicuous to a more social existence, in which extra pairs of eyes and ears are necessary for detecting, and defending themselves against, predators.

All primates devote considerable portions of their active hours to resting. Many diurnal primates shift their activity patterns in dramatic ways in response to seasonal changes in day length, ambient temperature, and rainfall patterns that affect food availability. Some take long, leisurely siestas during the hottest hours of summer days, while on cold winter mornings they doze while soaking up the warmth of the sun on the tops of branches. The proportion of time different primates devote to their various activities coincides with divergent suites of behavioral and anatomical traits. For example, **energy minimizers** devote substantial proportions of their time to resting, and little time (and energy) to traveling. They rely heavily on foods such as leaves, which are relatively easy to find but are low in energy content and require both time and anatomical specializations to digest. **Energy maximizers,** by contrast, rest less and devote more of their time (and energy) to searching for and traveling between patches of foods. These foods, such as fruits, tend to be more widely dispersed than leaves, but they are also higher in easy-to-digest calories to fuel the extra energy required to find them.

Diets.   Food is necessary for survival and reproduction. As we'll see in subsequent chapters, the ways that primate foods are distributed are among the most important determinants of their social lives. All primates eat a variety of different food items to obtain the carbohydrates, fats, and proteins they need. Energy and nutrient requirements vary with body size and metabolism, and, therefore, differ among individuals and species (Sussman, 1978). Diets are generally classified based on what the primates are eating most of the time. Those that devote significant proportions of their feeding time to consuming insects are called **insectivores,** fruit-eaters are called **frugivores,** and leaf-eaters are **folivores,** but as we'll see in Chapter 6, these simplified classifications can be misleading. Most primates are considered to be either insectivore-frugivores or frugivore-folivores because, while nearly all primates consume some fruit as their primary sources of energy, they differ in whether they rely on insects or leaves for their protein. Some primates consume prey items ranging from frogs and lizards to small mammals, such as hares, small antelope, or other primates, along with their plant foods. Others supplement their diets with the gummy substance excreted by some tree species when their bark is punctured, as well as flowers and flower products such as pollen and nectar, bark, bamboo, and even dirt. The semiterrestrial primates may also include substantial quantities of grass and grass seeds or herbaceous vegetation in their diets.

Like their activity patterns, primate diets are strongly influenced by seasonal fluctuations in the availability of preferred foods. Because of the importance of nutrition to survival and reproduction, identifying primate diets is essential to understanding many aspects of their anatomy and behavior, as well as patterns in their habitat use, ranging behavior, and social organization (Figure 1.15).

Habitat Use and Ranging.   The semiterrestrial primates conduct much of their business on the ground, either feeding or traveling between their scattered food trees. Habitat use is more variable among arboreal primates depending on which level and kind of vegetation they spend most of their time in. Indeed, contrary to what it might seem like at first glance, most of the tropical and semitropical forests

FIGURE 1.15   Wild Japanese macaques (*Macaca fuscata*) warming up at a fire left by a road crew. Photo made available by Irwin Bernstein.

inhabited by primates are a three-dimensional mosaic of different kinds of vegetation. Some primates find most of their foods in the **understory,** or the area below the trees but above the ground. The understory may be overgrown with dense vegetation or fairly open depending on whether sunlight can penetrate or is blocked out by the leaf-covered branches overhead in the **canopy.** Other primates are stratified from the lower, to the main, to the upper canopy, and some even climb up into the **emergent** trees that tower above the rest of the canopy (Figure 1.16).

Primates must move through their habitats in search of food. The distance they travel each day is measured in terms of **day ranges** or **daily path lengths** and the area they utilize is called their **home range.** Both daily path lengths and home range sizes are affected by the ways that primate foods are distributed in time and space. Differences in primate **locomotor** systems determine how quickly and efficiently they are able to move about. The balance between the time and energy required to move between food resources and the nutritional quality of their foods affects primate daily path lengths.

When foods eaten over an annual cycle occur in concentrated clumps, primates can defend their food supply area from other members of their species. **Territorial** primates are those that defend the entire resource area they exploit from intrusions by other members of their species. This is usually only possible when their daily path length is roughly the equivalent of the radius of their home range (Mitani and Rodman, 1979). Nonterritorial primates have home ranges that overlap with the home ranges of other groups of their species. Some nonterritorial primates aggressively defend particular food sources, such as large fruiting trees, whenever they encounter other primates of their own or other species that compete

FIGURE 1.16   Black and white colobus monkeys (*Colobus guereza*) by the Nile River in Murchison Falls National Park, Uganda. Photo by John F. Oates.

with them for foods. But, because they require such large home ranges relative to their day ranges, they cannot keep intruders out of their home range at all times.

Territoriality is not necessarily a fixed attribute of a species. The same behavior, such as aggressive defense of food sources, may be territorial for a group of primates occupying a small home range but nonterritorial in a larger home range. Consequently, groups of the same species living under different conditions may be classified differently depending on the degree to which group home ranges overlap with one another.

Group Size. Most primates are **gregarious,** meaning that they spend most of their lives in social groups. **Solitary** primates are rarely seen with another individual except during brief periods to reproduce or during the period of infant dependency, when mothers are caring for their young. Gregarious primates form groups of various sizes made up of different age and sex compositions for a variety of reasons. One obvious advantage of a group is the increased ability to detect and defend themselves from predators. Another advantage of group versus solitary living is that groups include more individuals to participate in guarding food resources.

Groups can also be more conspicuous to predators, and competition for food can also impose limits on group sizes. Therefore, primates must balance the benefits of group living against the costs (Figure 1.17). Primate group sizes can vary tremendously between different habitats due to the effects of ecological variables, such as predator pressures and food availability, and demographic variables, such as **population density,** or the number of individuals per unit area.

Primate groups also differ from one another in their degree of **cohesiveness,** or whether group members remain together on a routine basis. Chimpanzees, for

FIGURE 1.17 Model for optimal primate group sizes based on the compromise between costs of feeding competition and enhanced safety from predators. Dotted lines indicate the point of maximum benefits relative to costs when feeding on small (S), medium (M), and large (L) resources. Note that larger groups provide greater benefits against predators, but also have greater feeding costs. From Terborgh, J. and Janson, C. H. 1986. The socioecology of primate groups. *Annual Review of Ecology and Systematics* 17:111–135. With permission from the *Annual Review of Ecology and Systematics*, Volume 17, © 1986 by Annual Reviews and the authors.

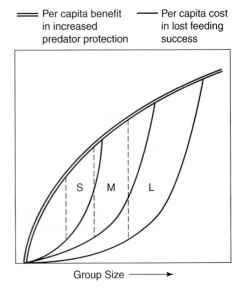

Per capita benefit in increased predator protection

Per capita cost in lost feeding success

Group Size →

example, have fluid, **fission-fusion** societies, in which group members split up into smaller parties and reunite in response to daily fluctuations in the availability and distribution of their preferred foods, whereas savanna baboons tend to stay together as a cohesive troop. Grouping patterns, like ranging and territoriality, can differ from one population to another of the same species depending on the spatial and temporal availability of their foods. In addition, different social skills are required by primates who see each other sporadically, compared to those who associate continuously. Exploring these differences provides insights into the role that sociality may have played in the evolution of primate **cognition,** as we'll see in Chapter 10.

Social and Reproductive Units.   The composition of primate groups is affected by two factors. First, patterns of **dispersal** determine whether individuals of one or both sexes leave their natal groups to join another established group or form their own groups with other members of their species. Second, the ratio of females to males of reproductive age within groups, or the **socionomic sex ratio,** has profound effects on levels of mating competition (Dunbar, 1988). This can influence the degree to which males differ from females in body size and other traits that affect male competitive ability.

Male-biased dispersal was long thought to characterize most primates because of its prevalence among the Old World macaques and baboons that were regarded as "typical" primates (Moore, 1984; Strier, 1994a). However, we now know that female-biased dispersal or dispersal by both sexes are widespread patterns among prosimians, the New World monkeys, and the apes. These varied dispersal patterns lead to very different genealogical relationships among members of primate groups. For example, in macaque and most baboon societies, females are **philopatric,** remaining in their natal groups for life. Dispersing males join groups composed of the extended, multigenerational **matrilines** formed by **matrilocal** females. When males are philopatric, like muriquis and chimpanzees, groups consist of **patrilocal** male kin that form extended **patrilines.** When both sexes disperse, groups consist largely of unrelated, or only distantly-related members. To date, there are few, if any primate species known in which neither sex disperses, a system that could lead to serious inbreeding depression (Chapter 4).

Understanding these differences in primate kinship systems is essential to understanding their social relationships, especially if familiarity affects their interactions (Altmann and Altmann, 1979; Moore, 1992a). Primates generally treat familiar individuals better than unfamiliar ones, and familiar biological relatives generally make more reliable allies than unfamiliar nonkin. Not surprisingly, whether primate societies are based on matrilineal or patrilineal relationships affects the social options available to females or males, and whether they are likely to have related allies on hand (Chapais, 2001).

The number of breeding females and males in primate groups has traditionally been used to define primate mating systems. Thus, whenever primate groups included a single adult male and female they were thought to be **monogamous.** The mating system of groups with a single male and multiple females was considered to be **polygynous,** while those with multiple males and females were thought to be

polygamous. Among a few New World monkeys, groups with a single breeding female and multiple males appeared to have a **polyandrous** mating system. These differences in the number of adult males and females in primate groups were once thought to be characteristic of different species, and indicative of species differences in their mating systems.

We now know, however, that the compositions of primate groups vary substantially in the same species living in different habitats and under different demographic conditions, and that the same groups may change in composition over time. For example, in a recent analysis of so-called monogamous primates, anthropologist Agustin Fuentes (1998) found that all but seven species exhibit variation in the composition of their groups (Chapter 5). In fact, the occurrence of single- and multi-male groups in the same populations has been documented in a variety of different species, and even groups with similar compositions, such as the multi-male, multi-female groups of chimpanzees, baboons, and capuchin monkeys can have quite different social organizations (see Table 1.2).

We also know that extrapolating from social groups to primate mating systems can be very misleading because primates don't always restrict themselves to choosing sexual partners that are members of their social groups (e.g., Cords, 1987). Behavioral observations indicate that many primates, including pair-bonded males and females, mate with individuals that are not members of their groups. In light of these findings, many of the early categorizations of primate societies must be rethought.

Field and Captive Studies

All of the aspects of primate behavior described so far, and most of the examples that follow in this book, come from studies of wild primates. But, it is important to realize that even when the first primate field studies were being conducted, there were few, if any, primate habitats that had not been altered in some way by human activities (Quiatt and Reynolds, 1993). Indeed, the effects of habitat disturbance are responsible for leading many primates to the verge of extinction. Nowadays, comparisons among primates inhabiting areas that have been subjected to different levels of disturbance are deliberately used to address questions about how primates adjust their behavior in response to the ecological and demographic variables that habitat disturbances affect (e.g., Sterck, 1998). As a result, primate studies today may reach very different conclusions than they did in the past. During the early years of primate studies, however, such distinctions about the possible effects of human interference on primate behavior were rarely made.

In addition to the relatively naturalistic conditions of human observation in the wild, there are more controlled ways of viewing primates. **Provisioned** settings have designated feeding sites where food is provided, but the primates are otherwise free to come and go, or are restricted to large enclosures or islands where they have been introduced. In **captive settings,** they may be housed in either large enclosures in social groups similar to those found in the wild, modified groups, or solitary cages.

Studies on unprovisioned primates tend to be better suited than provisioned or captive studies for exploring certain kinds of questions, such as those about the relationship between the seasonal distribution of food and primate grouping patterns. However, provisioning can stimulate primates to interact more frequently than they do in the wild, and can therefore accelerate our identification of social patterns. Once identified, these patterns can be studied more closely in unprovisioned groups where they are expressed at a slower pace. Captive studies that control and vary group membership and individual experience have been critical in calling our attention to many subtle behavioral phenomena, including the social suppression of reproduction, patterns of reconciliation after fights, and the ontogeny of vocal communication.

Captive studies also offer the advantage of better observation conditions and in many cases individual histories of the captive primates are known. However, there is always the possibility that the behaviors observed in captivity reflect extreme responses to their housing conditions instead of those that are most characteristic of them in the wild. For example, chimpanzee and bonobo males and females copulate at similar rates in the wild, but in captivity, bonobos are much more sexually active than are captive chimpanzees. Captivity clearly has a different effect on bonobo sexual behavior than it does on chimpanzees, a discovery that could only have been made when field data and captive data on both species were compared (Stanford, 1998).

Even under "natural" circumstances, we must be cautious in our observations and interpretations of primate behavior. This is particularly important when we know that their habitats have been recently altered and their behaviors may reflect recent responses to new challenges in these changed environments.

Many of our most important insights into the behavior of wild primates have come first from provisioned or captive populations. In the early years of her field study, Jane Goodall used bananas to lure the chimpanzees into her camp, where she could observe them more closely and begin to understand their social hierarchies. She also used the bananas to administer medication to chimpanzees ailing from illnesses they had acquired from the human settlements surrounding their forest (Goodall, 1971; Quiatt and Reynolds, 1993).

Providing food to primates was also employed in the original studies on Japanese macaques. Fortuitously, provisioning the monkeys led to the adoption of novel techniques used by the macaques to wash sweet potatoes and sift sand out of wheat, which have provided some of the best examples for how innovative behaviors spread through primate societies to become **local traditions** (Kawai, 1965). Attracting primates to provisioned feeding sites is a powerful way of investigating the dynamics and negotiations of social relationships, and it is still widely employed for studying primates whose ecology is already understood, or whose elusive habits make them difficult to follow.

Captive studies provide opportunities to control and experimentally vary primate social and physical environments. Field studies provide opportunities to evaluate how behavior is affected by unpredictable ecological and demographic pressures, which more closely approximate the evolutionary circumstances under which primates evolved. Integrating data from both captive and field studies of the same species is a powerful approach (Bernstein, 1972), and it has become an increasingly important source of insights into what primates are capable of doing, and what kinds of stimuli trigger varied responses (Box 1.1).

BOX 1.1
Clues from Captivity

Psychologist Charles Snowdon pursues a rare breed of primatology. Most primatologists conduct either captive or field studies, but Snowdon compares primates in both contexts. Until recently, his laboratory at the University of Wisconsin-Madison has housed colonies of two species of New World monkeys, pygmy marmosets, one of the world's smallest monkeys found throughout the Western Amazon, and the endangered cotton-top tamarin, found only in small remnant forest patches in northwest Colombia. Snowdon's students have also studied both species in the wild and continue to study the tamarins in captivity.

Marmosets and tamarins belong to the callitrichid family, a diverse group of monkeys known for their high reproductive rates. Dominant female cotton-top tamarins give birth to twins, and sometimes triplets, at seven to ten-month intervals in captivity. At birth, these twins weigh 19 percent of their mothers' weight, the equivalent of a 120-pound woman giving birth to two 11½ pound infants. Unlike most primate mothers, marmosets and tamarins get help caring for their infants from adult males and older offspring in their families. These nonmother caretakers do most of the infant carrying and provide solid food at the time of weaning (Figure B1.1). As a result, callitrichid mothers can get pregnant within two to four weeks after giving birth.

The help that mothers get in caring for their infants is critical to infant survival. Snowdon and his colleagues have found in both captive and wild populations that infant survival does not approach 100 percent unless at least four helpers are present. Experience at taking care of infants turns out to be important, too, because adults that have not been helpers prove to be poor at parenting when their own offspring are born.

Female tamarins reach puberty at 18 months of age, yet daughters living in captive groups never produce offspring of their own (Ziegler, et al., 1987). Measuring hormones from daily urine samples, Snowdon's group found that these dutiful daughters don't even ovulate. There is nothing biologically wrong with these females, because as soon as they

FIGURE B1.1   Breeding male cotton-top tamarin (*Saguinus oedipus*) carrying an infant. Photo by Carla Boe.

are removed from their family groups and paired with unfamiliar males, they ovulate and can become pregnant within eight days.

Pursuing the mechanisms behind this reproductive inhibition led Snowdon's group to discover that transfer of odors from the mother to newly paired daughters delayed the onset of ovulation and prevented pregnancy (Savage, et al., 1988). Chemical signals have recently been shown to synchronize ovulation and menstrual cycles in women (Stern and McClintock, 1998), so it is not surprising that similar cues, known as **pheromones,** influence ovulation in monkeys as well. But exposure to novel males is also an important stimulus in tamarins. Daughters removed from their families, but paired with their brothers, failed to ovulate, whereas those paired with or even housed within sight and sound of a novel male rapidly ovulated (Widowski, et al., 1990, 1992).

Recent reports from the field both support and conflict with these findings. Some wild cotton-top tamarin groups contain two pregnant females, but whether this only occurs after a novel male has joined the group is still not clear (Savage, et al., 1996a, 1997). Reproductive inhibition is often observed in captive common marmosets (Abbott, et al., 1993), but multiple pregnant females are relatively common in at least one wild population in northeastern Brazil (Digby and Ferrari, 1994). Interestingly, when two wild marmoset females gave birth close in time, the dominant female directed aggression toward the infants of the subordinate female (Digby, 1995, 2000). But, aggression toward the subordinate female's infants is rare when births are separated in time.

Multiple breeding females have also been observed in wild groups of buffy-headed marmosets (Ferrari, et al., 1996; Guimarães, 1998), buffy-tufted-ear marmosets (Coutinho and Corrêa, 1995), saddle-back tamarins (Goldizen, et al., 1996) and golden lion tamarins (Baker and Dietz, 1996; Dietz and Baker, 1993). In each case, the dominant female was the only one that reproduced routinely, but the variability in reproductive activity in subordinate females contrasts with the reproductive inhibition seen in captivity. Perhaps the suppressing effects of social or pheromonal cues communicated by dominant mothers are weaker or easier to avoid in the wild than in the closer confines of captivity. Perhaps more dispersal opportunities are available in the wild where females can locate unrelated males more readily. Evaluating hypotheses about reproductive inhibition and cooperative infant care requires multifaceted approaches that combine field and captive studies and that integrate behavioral and hormonal data on proximate mechanisms and their functional, adaptive significance.

Evolutionary Models and Problem-Oriented Studies

During the 1960s, primatology was catapulted out of its descriptive, classificatory phase into a rigorous quantitative science. This transformation was based on the explicit adoption of rigorous methodological practices, in which behavior was sampled in a **systematic,** or standardized, way in order to minimize the biases and subjective impressions of observers (Altmann, 1974). Behavioral categories were carefully defined so that different researchers could use similar criteria for scoring an interaction or a behavioral event. Observation periods, or sampling schedules, were dictated arbitrarily by time intervals instead of by the primate's behavior or the observer's attention, making it possible to reliably calculate frequencies or rates at which particular behaviors occurred. Methods of collecting systematic behavioral data now range from the use of check-sheets, to hand-written or tape-recorded descriptions, to computerized recording devices. The best ways to collect data depend on the behaviors of interest, observation conditions, and logistical considerations such as terrain and the activity patterns of the animals (Paterson, 2001). The results obtained from these methods can then be compared across individuals in a study group, across time for the same study group, and across studies of other groups and species, including nonprimates and, especially, birds (Harcourt, 1998).

The widespread adoption of systematic methods of behavioral sampling also made it possible to objectively evaluate specific questions, which could be framed in terms of testable hypotheses with comparative data. The theoretical shift of the seventies involved the incorporation of **evolutionary theory** to understand *why* individual primates behave as they do in the societies they live in, and *why* they live in their particular societies. From an evolutionary perspective, behaviors are treated like any other traits that are potentially subject to selection pressures for survival, which is a prerequisite for **reproductive success,** or an individual's direct genetic contribution to future generations. Evolution will act on social behavior if it has a **heritable,** or genetic, basis, and if it affects individual **fitness.** Individuals that behave in ways that increase their survival and reproductive success will pass on more of their genes than individuals that behave in less **adaptive** ways. For example, in contrast to solitary individuals, those that form groups in which individuals share the burden of watching for predators may be better able to avoid being eaten while also ending up with more free time for other essential activities, such as feeding, that improve their own reproductive success.

The difference in **fitness** between gregarious and solitary individuals will determine the strength of the selection pressures favorable to either type of lifestyle. The absence of predators might reduce the benefits of group living in one area, while the presence of predators might make group living highly advantageous in another area (van Schaik and van Noordwijk, 1985a). Even a shift from nocturnal to diurnal habits could be a recent response to relaxation in selection pressures from the extinction of diurnal predators (van Schaik and Kappeler, 1996).

Social skills associated with getting along in groups without being evicted, and for gaining access to the most or the best foods within groups, would also be favored by natural selection pressures (Dolhinow, 1972). And, because relatives share a proportion of their genes through common descent, individuals that choose to share vigilance and food with kin might benefit their own **inclusive fitness** indirectly through the reproductive success of their kin. Of course, keeping kin close at hand can also be risky because a catastrophe, such as a hurricane or drought, could potentially wipe out an entire genealogical line. In this case, it might be better for kin to disperse as far as possible, thereby hedging their bets in the fitness game. Indeed, many primates live in groups composed of nonkin. The trade-offs between extremes such as these are what we now think account for the patterns of behavior we observe. And, because there is no single rule that makes a particular behavior ideal under all possible circumstances, the fitness consequences of alternative behaviors can be difficult to predict and even harder to test (Bernstein, 1999a).

Evolutionary theory provided primatologists with a basis for developing predictions about primate behavior, which could then be evaluated quantitatively with data obtained systematically. The convergence of systematic methods and evolutionary theory launched primatology into a problem-oriented discipline in which comparative models could be tested and refined.

Sociobiology and Behavioral Ecology

These advances in evolutionary theory grew largely out of studies on insects, birds, and other nonprimates, which continue to exert a powerful influence on both theoretical and experimental approaches to primate behavior (Harcourt, 1998). Indeed, some of the most persuasive of these influences involved focusing on the evolution of female behavior, and how the behavior of females affects that of males (Figure 1.18). The development of evolutionary principles to understand the adaptive advantages of behavior under different ecological conditions is the basis for the field of **behavioral ecology** (Krebs and Davies, 1993), and its more controversial forerunner, **sociobiology,** or the biological study of social behavior.

When Harvard biologist E. O. Wilson (1975) compiled the principles of evolutionary theory as they apply to behavior in his comprehensive book, appropriately entitled *Sociobiology: The New Synthesis,* nonhuman and human primates were treated in sequence in the final two chapters. The idea that the evolution of human social behavior is continuous with that of other animals generated heated debate. For example, most behaviors of interest are complex traits, not simple ones controlled by single genes. The evolutionary process of **behavioral adaptation,** which is sensitive to the influence of environmental conditions, should not be confused with the concept of genetic determinism, which would mean that behavior was entirely controlled—and predestined—by genes. In fact, evolutionary theory assumes that behavior, like all other complex traits, has both a **genotype,** or genetic component, and a **phenotype,** which is the expression of an individual's genotype as it is affected by environmental influences.

What we see when we observe primates behaving is their phenotype, the product of the physical and social environment interacting with an individual's genetic makeup. In the shorthand of evolutionary theory, a behavioral phenotype is often described as if it were a **strategy,** shaped by the process of natural selection because of its advantages to individual survival and reproductive fitness. There are **feeding strategies,** behavioral patterns involved in selecting different kinds of foods, and **social strategies,** or behaviors that lead primates to live in different kinds of groups and affect how they maintain their relationships within these groups. **Reproductive strategies** include behaviors that increase the likelihood of gaining access to mates and insuring their offspring's survival. **Life history strategies** are the patterns of development from gestation length, to interbirth intervals, to age at first reproduction and lifespan, that influence the behavior of individuals at different times in their lives. Early critics of evolutionary theory challenged the implication

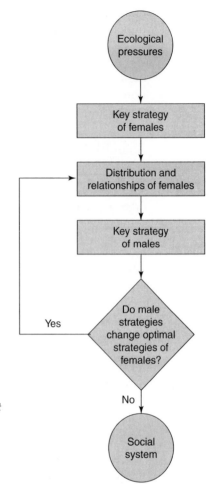

FIGURE 1.18   Female-focus view of social evolution. From Wrangham, R. W. 1982, Mutualism, kinship and social evolution. In King's College Sociobiology Group, eds., *Current Problems in Sociobiology.* Cambridge: Cambridge University Press, pp. 269–289. Reprinted with permission from the author and from Cambridge University Press. © 1982, Cambridge University Press.

that ants, baboons, or even humans make conscious decisions or thoughtful calculations about how their behavior will affect their fitness (e.g., Sahlins, 1976). However, evolutionary theory does not make assumptions about the conscious intentionality underlying behavior. Instead, behavioral patterns are referred to as *strategies* if they are the products of evolutionary selection pressures on individual fitness, and therefore have **functional,** or adaptive significance.

Testing Predictions about Behavioral Adaptations

It is important to emphasize that generating predictions about behavior based on evolutionary theory is not the same as testing or proving them. Behavioral ecologists must be wary of claims that assume all behaviors are adaptive, and, instead, focus on what our study subjects actually do. Careful observation is essential to evaluating whether behavior conforms to predictions based on what other animals do under similar circumstances. Deviations from predictions can be exceptions, or they can indicate that our underlying premises are wrong (Fuentes, 1999). It is not always possible to distinguish between these alternatives, as many of the primate examples described in this book will show.

Long-Term Field Studies and Individual Variation.   Behavioral ecology opened up primatology to the value of broader comparative studies on a wider diversity of primates and other animals, and has helped to reinforce the value of in-depth, long-term studies. Long-term studies are particularly critical when primates are involved because of their relatively long lifespans, delayed maturation, and slow reproductive rates. As a result of these **life history traits,** it takes many years to accumulate enough observations from enough individuals of different ages and sexes to be able to distinguish general behavioral patterns from individual variation. Primatologists take longer to evaluate the reproductive consequences of their study subject's behavior than scientists studying shorter lived, faster growing animals.

Collecting longitudinal data on the same study subjects is a fundamental method in ecological studies of plant and animal communities and in professions ranging from economics to epidemiology. Marketing experts, stockbrokers, and meteorologists use longitudinal data to evaluate trends in their respective areas, which then form the basis for predicting future product sales, interest rate fluctuations, or global warming. Longitudinal data about primates provide similar bases for predicting individual behavioral strategies and testing hypotheses about behavioral adaptations.

Some of the most extensive long-term data for any animals come from the continuation of primate studies begun during the 1950s and early 1960s on macaques, baboons, langurs, and apes (Wolfe, 1987). Several of the original study groups that have been followed all these years have undergone major **demographic** changes resulting from births, deaths, and immigration and emigration events. Some groups have split up as they expanded in size, others have been taken over by larger neighboring groups. Third-generation descendants of the original Gombe chimpanzees have replaced their great-grandparents as *National Geographic* stars. Research initiated more recently on other primates in other locations does not yet match these original studies in duration, but as these newer studies move into their second and third decades, they are also contributing critical comparative insights into the dynamics of primate societies.

Following recognized individuals from infancy through senescence allows us to begin to formulate answers to questions dealing with relationships among maternal kin, responses to natural ecological fluctuations, the ontogeny of social development, and demographic influences on behavior. Chronicling primate life history strategies is a challenging endeavor, nonetheless, because primates are so slow to develop relative to other animals of similar body sizes (Charnov and Berrigan, 1993). A 15 to 20 pound dog, for example, will be fully weaned within six to eight weeks of birth, and ready to give birth to her own pups within a year or two after that. A similarly sized female baboon, by contrast, will be dependent on her mother for at least six months, and won't be reproductively mature until at least four years of age.

Primates are also subjected to complex ecological conditions, such as predictable rainy season and dry season fluctuations in the availability of food and water resources, as well as even longer-term cycles in rainfall and food availability that span multiple years. Annual fluctuations in rainfall and food availability affect primate diets and reproduction, as well as their ranging, activity, and grouping behaviors. The effects of ecological fluctuations with even longer time frames require correspondingly longer periods to document. For example, when yellow baboons were first surveyed at Amboseli National Park, Kenya, in 1963–1964, there were over 2,000 individuals (Altmann and Altmann, 1970). By 1971, the area's baboon population had declined to about 200 individuals (Hausfater, 1975), and similar declines occurred in the vervet monkey population there as well (Struhsaker, 1973). These fluctuations have been attributed to alterations in the vegetation that baboons and vervets eat. Originally, shifts in underground water levels, which bring vegetation-killing salts to the surface in the volcanic soils at Amboseli, were implicated (Western and van Praet, 1973). More recently, the role of elephants in destroying the vegetation has been implicated in contributing to the decline in the primate populations here (Western, 1997).

The Amboseli monkeys, like all primates nowadays, face additional challenges as their habitats and populations are modified by increasingly intrusive human activities. As humans clear forests for agriculture, some primates, such as rhesus macaques, have been able to adjust their diets to include cultivated crops (Richard, et al., 1989). Some baboons at Amboseli now take advantage of the garbage dump from a nearby tourist hotel, gaining a constant food supply that has given females in this troop some reproductive advantages, including faster maturation and shorter interbirth intervals, compared to females in troops that rely only on the wild foods in the park (Samuels and Altmann, 1991). Still other primates, including muriquis and some lemurs, appear able to survive at higher densities in forests that have suffered human disturbances than in more pristine forests where the diversity of food choices and the quality of food may be more limited (Ganzhorn, 1995; Pinto, et al., 1993; Strier and Fonseca, 1996/97).

However, most primates rarely fare well when humans are near. Primates with highly specialized diets suffer from food shortages when their habitats are altered. Hunting and poaching pressures also plague primates, from mountain gorillas to marmosets. Often group members are slaughtered as they heroically defend prized infants from poachers who want to capture them for zoos or for sale as pets. Logging companies open roads into forests that not only alter primate habitats, but also make it easier for hunters to kill primates for food (McRae, 1997). Destruction of surrounding areas causes what habitat that does remain to become saturated with primates, leading to significant behavioral changes, such as those described for Thomas langurs, an Asian leaf-eating monkey. Female langurs usually maintain casual, egalitarian relationships with one another, but their relationships may become more aggressive and hierarchically structured when they are forced by habitat disturbances to take refuge in saturated areas where opportunities for dispersal are limited (Sterck, 1998, 1999; Sterck, et al., 1997). Documenting primate responses to both natural and human-induced changes in their habitats has become an urgent priority in primate conservation, and reinforces the importance of long-term studies that can identify the risks that habitat alterations pose for primates.

Comparisons among Species.   Comparisons among different primate species are a powerful way to evaluate the adaptive significance of behaviors under different ecological conditions (Clutton-Brock and Harvey, 1984). Early anthropocentric approaches to primates were also comparative in their focus on those species that were thought to make the best **referential models** for humans because of parallels in their ecologies or their phylogenetic proximity. Seeking the best comparative reference for humans led to vigorous debates such as whether the societies of early human ancestors were hierarchical or egalitarian, or matrilineal or patrilineal (Fedigan, 1982). Particular species, such as baboons or chimpanzees, were promoted as the most appropriate candidates depending on the prevailing preconceptions of the researchers studying them.

Some scholars have suggested that the reason aggressive competition among male primates received so much attention during the post-World War II years was a direct result of sexist attitudes about male dominance and the origins of human warfare and conflict (Haraway, 1989). Attention to the influential roles of female primates in their societies has also been attributed, in part, to the rise in feminist theory and influence in U.S. society during the late 1960s and early 1970s. However, it is important to remember that this period also coincided with the explosion of evolutionary theory in animal studies, which also recognized the importance of females and their tremendous influence on males and their societies (Eisenberg, et al., 1972; Emlen and Oring, 1977; see Figure 1.18).

Behavioral ecology helped to shift anthropocentric perspectives in primatology away from the focus on finding referential behavioral models for human social evolution (Richard, 1981). Instead, **strategic models,** which emphasized the evolutionary and ecological processes that affect behavior were developed to provide an alternative way of understanding behavioral adaptations (Tooby and DeVore, 1987). For example, instead of extrapolating from the ranging patterns of chimpanzees to those of human ancestors, we might predict that primate day range lengths increase with the proportion of fruit in their diets because fruits occur in patchy, clumped distributions compared to other foods, such as leaves, which have more even spatial distributions and can be harvested within a smaller area (Moore, 1996). Comparing the diets and day ranges of various primates provides a way to evaluate this prediction, and the underlying principle that primate ranging patterns reflect adaptations to their particular feeding strategies.

Predictions about the adaptive advantages of primate sociality under different ecological conditions can be similarly tested with comparisons among species. For example, very different kinds of societies characterize chimpanzees and their closest relatives, bonobos, which unlike chimpanzees are found only in a small portion of the Congo Basin. In chimpanzees, male contests for dominance and status are so striking and so persistent that males have been described as having "demonic" streaks (Goodall, 1986; Wrangham and Peterson, 1996). Male bonobos, by contrast, are much less excitable, in part because they spend more of their time around females, who play an active role in easing social tensions by engaging in sex (de

Waal, 1987). Differences in chimpanzee and bonobo patterns of association correspond to differences in their diets, and are largely consistent with the ways in which feeding strategies affect social relationships in other primates (Chapters 6–8).

Comparisons among primate species have become more sophisticated as predictions from behavioral ecology, often based on other animals, have become more specific and as the diversity of primates included in the comparisons has increased. Statistical methods are now used to control for the phylogenetic relationships among species so that comparisons can be made based on independent evolutionary events (Krebs and Davies, 1993; Nunn and Barton, 2001). In fact, focusing exclusively on comparisons between closely related species, such as chimpanzees or bonobos, can be misleading if the behavior patterns of interest are exhibited by other, more distantly related primates as well. For example, male bonding occurs in primates other than humans and chimpanzees, and nonreproductive sex occurs in primates other than humans and bonobos. Looking at a broader comparative sample of primates provides insights into the behavioral similarities and differences among them (Strier, 2001).

Part of the expansion in comparative primate studies has been due to explicit efforts to test existing models in primate behavioral ecology. Insights from these previously neglected primates generate new predictions, further increasing our understanding of the diversity of primate adaptations and refining our comparative perspectives.

The expansion of primate studies has also been stimulated by the increasing threats to primate survival. Elusive primates are often the ones with the most precarious futures, and learning about their adaptations is often the first essential step toward developing informed conservation management plans to protect them. As we will see in many of the examples given throughout this book, primate behavioral ecology and conservation are inextricably linked (Strier, 1997a).

Other Units of Comparison.   The common anthropomorphic practice of distinguishing individual primates instead of lumping them together was reinforced by, and contributed to, the focus on individual variation in evolutionary theory. Individual-level comparisons can involve the same individuals at different times, such as female diets during the rainy season versus dry season, or rates of social interactions among males during adolescence versus adulthood. Comparisons can also be made among individuals during the same period of time, such as male versus female diets during the rainy season of a particular year, or dominant versus subordinate female mating patterns during a particular breeding season.

The behavior of individuals in select **study groups** are then pooled to develop the comparative species models that form the basis for our understanding primate behavioral adaptations. However, it is important to remember that much of what we know about many primates still comes from single study groups, which may not be typical of a species. The question of whether one study group is representative or atypical is impossible to assess without comparative data from other groups of the same species. As more of these comparative data become available, it is increasingly clear that primates adjust many aspects of their behavior under different conditions.

Consequently, it is difficult to make informed comparisons between species without first understanding the range of behavioral variation within a species.

Group-level comparisons can involve characteristics of the group itself, such as its size and composition (Table 1.3), which can then be compared with behavioral characteristics, such as the proportion of time spent feeding on different types of food, day range length and home range size, or rates of social interactions. For example, to test the prediction that the proportion of time individuals spend feeding or fighting increases with group size, it would be ideal to compare individuals in different group sizes of the same species living in the same habitat at the same time. Such comparisons might lead to the conclusion that individuals in larger groups devote more time to feeding than those in smaller groups either because they cannot feed as efficiently due to competition or because sharing the task of watching out for predators gives them more time to feed.

Populations of primates are comprised of all individuals that could potentially interbreed. Populations are usually geographically isolated from one another, as is the case for many endangered primates whose habitats have been fragmented by human activities. Variations among different populations of the same species, just like variation in the behavior of different groups within the same population, can be highly informative. One group may devote more time to feeding each day than another group in the same population, which has a higher proportion of immatures, and therefore lower nutritional requirements. Alternatively, primate groups in habitats where the canopy is disturbed may exploit a greater range of tree heights than

TABLE 1.3   **Characteristics of primate groups**

Group characteristic	Explanation
Size	The number of individuals who associate or are observed together; highly variable.
Composition	The combined age, sex, and kinship of group members; affected by birth and death rates, population demography, and dispersal patterns.
Socionomic sex ratio	The ratio of breeding females to males in groups; highly variable except in true pair-bonded groups (see Chapter 5).
Operational sex ratio	The socionomic sex ratio weighted by the period of time during which females are actively breeding, which is affected by the degree of reproductive synchrony or seasonality among females (see Chapter 5).
Degree of cohesion	The proportion of time in which group members are found together. Cohesive groups are those in which members maintain visual and vocal contact with one another. Fluid groups are those in which members split up for hours, days, or even weeks at a time. Affected by the spatial and temporal distribution of food resources (see Chapter 6).

groups in pristine habitats where the forest canopy is more continuous. Comparisons between populations provide a way to tease apart the effects of demographic and ecological conditions on behavior.

Combining such **intraspecific,** or within species, comparisons, with **interspecific,** or between species, comparisons, can be the most reliable way of distinguishing the relative influence of phylogenetic versus environmental influences on behavior (Garland and Adolph, 1994; Sussman, 1978). For example, woolly monkeys in the Brazilian Amazon and muriquis in the southern Atlantic forest resemble the closely related spider monkeys in their highly frugivorous diets and loose, fluid, fission-fusion societies (Moraes, et al., 1998; Peres, 1994, 1996). However, woolly monkeys in Colombia and Ecuador and muriquis in the northern part of their distribution include substantial proportions of insects and leaves in their respective diets and both live in more cohesive social groups (Di Fiore and Rodman, 2001; Stevenson, et al., 1994; Strier, 1991a). The apparent role of these dietary differences in determining the variation in grouping patterns of both woolly monkeys and muriquis would not be so clear if comparisons between and within species could not be made.

Conservation Applications

Merging all sources of available data on primates has become an essential component of conservation efforts on their behalf. Indeed, in addition to the original interest in primates for comparisons with humans and other animals, primate behavioral ecology has also been influenced by practical concerns from the biomedical and conservation communities. The use of nonhuman primates in biomedical research increased during and following World War II, when vital discoveries, such as the Salk polio vaccine, were developed and tested on species like rhesus macaques. Today, most of the monkeys and apes used in biomedical research come from captive breeding programs at major primate centers and laboratories around the world, but this has not always been the case. Prior to the establishment of these breeding facilities, the demand for experimental subjects led to the capture and export of many wild primates, often with devastating effects on local primate populations. Concern about maintaining wild populations of rhesus macaques stimulated some of the early primate field studies and surveys in India. Reports of depressed populations ultimately led to the imposition of strict bans on the use of wild-caught animals, and some wild populations that had been harvested nearly to extinction have been able to recover under the protective measures that are still in place (Southwick and Siddiqi, 1988).

Rhesus macaques may have suffered from regional population pressure for biomedical research, but as a species they continue to occur over a wider geographic range than most primates. Part of the key to successful persistence for primates such as rhesus macaques across Asia, baboons in Africa, and capuchin monkeys in South and Central America, is their ability to thrive in altered habitats and in close proximity to humans. Their generalist diets permit them to feed on a variety of different foods, including agricultural crops such as rice, corn, and sugarcane.

Most other primates have more specialized dietary and habitat requirements, so their survival is threatened when their forests and key plant foods are destroyed. Habitat destruction threatens all plants and wildlife, but because primates are high on the food chain, they are important **indicator species,** which can be used as a gauge for the extent of ecological disturbance in general (Mittermeier and Cheney, 1987). And, because primates are so physically appealing (compared to snakes or spiders, for example), they are frequently used to call public attention to more general conservation concerns. As "flagship" species, primates have earned their way onto postage stamps, telephone books, and other items of daily life in many countries where they live.

Until the 1980s, research on primate behavioral ecology focused on the animals themselves, and compared to the present, relatively little public attention was paid to their conservation status or the ethics of using them in biomedical research. This is not to say that no one was concerned about the growing number of endangered species or the well-being of captive primates and their use as experimental subjects. Pioneers in these areas of conservation and bioethics were outspoken and effective even before conservation and animal rights became household topics subject to public scrutiny and political debate. But it was not so long ago that researchers could shoot an entire troop of monkeys to analyze their stomach contents just to find out what they ate. Nowadays, of course, such practices are inconceivable to most primatologists, and in many parts of the world severe penalties are imposed whenever humans kill primates for any purpose.

Almost everyone involved in primate behavioral ecology today is also simultaneously interested in, and in many cases, directly involved in, both conservation and ethical issues pertaining to primate survival and well-being. Independent of our training and background, there is widespread agreement that informed conservation and the protection of primates depends on understanding the basics of primate behavioral ecology. Many of these basics are introduced in the subsequent chapters of this book.

CHAPTER

2 Traits, Trends, and Taxonomy

There is no single trait that defines a primate or sets all of them apart from any other animals. Instead, there are trends in different suites of traits that appeared during the course of primate evolution and represent an overall primate pattern. For example, primates differ substantially from one another in their locomotor systems and manual dexterity, but for the most part, we primates have greater mobility in our hands, feet, and limbs than members of other groups of animals. Likewise, there are differences among primate brain sizes relative to body sizes, but as a group, we tend to have larger brains than other mammals of similar body sizes. The evolution and antiquity of traits such as these can be traced through the fossil record whenever skeletal or cranial material are available. In the human lineage, for example, relative cranial capacity did not begin to differentiate until about the last 2 million years, when it jumped above that of other primates. There is much speculation about the selection pressures that led to our expanded brains relative to those of other primates, and to those of other primates compared to most other animals (Box 2.1).

Behavioral traits, by contrast, leave little in the way of a fossil trail. Instead, we must rely on comparisons among living primates and on identifying anatomical

BOX 2.1

The Notable Neocortex

Primate brains are bigger, relative to their body size, than those of other animals, and human brains are bigger still. But it isn't our entire brains that are big. Instead, it is a particular part, called the **neocortex,** that is responsible for **cognitive abilities** such as reasoning and consciousness and that in primates makes up 50 to 80 percent of the total brain's volume (Finlay and Darlington, 1995). In insectivorous mammals, the neocortex is about the same size as the medulla, a primitive part of the brain that controls basic body functions such as respiration and heart rate. In prosimians, the neocortex is ten times larger than the medulla, in monkeys and apes, it is twenty to fifty times larger, and in humans, the neocortex is a whopping 105 times larger than the medulla.

In a recent comparative analysis of primate brains, primatologist Robin Dunbar (1998) explores the various hypotheses that have been advanced to explain why evolution might have led to expansions in the size of the neocortex. Usually, morphological traits that distinguish primates from other animals and that have obvious functional advantages are attributed to ecological selection pressures associated with compromises between the need to find food and mates as well as to avoid predators. However, Dunbar sees a stronger relationship between the size of the neocortex and size of primate social groups, which has led him to develop "the social brain hypothesis."

Comparing the size of the neocortex relative to the rest of the brain provides a neocortex ratio, which can then be compared across primates that differ from one another in body size, rates of development, and energetic requirements. When Dunbar and his colleagues compared primate neocortex ratios, they found three different, parallel clusters corresponding to the relationship between group size and neocortex ratios in the prosimians, monkeys, and apes. Prosimians have the smallest neocortex ratios for their social group sizes, monkeys are intermediate, and apes have the largest. Furthermore, within each of these "grades," the primates with the largest grooming networks are those with the correspondingly largest neocortex ratios. More recent analyses show that neocortical volume progressively increases from lemurs, lorises, and tarsiers, to New World monkeys, to Old World monkeys, to hominoids. However, the brain "architectures" of New World monkeys with the largest groups and most complex societies, such as squirrel monkeys, capuchin monkeys, spider monkeys, and woolly monkeys, are strikingly similar to those of Old World monkeys (Clark, et al., 2001).

Dunbar interprets the size of grooming networks to be indicative of the number of individuals that primates can maintain as reliable allies who will support them in conflicts against other individuals. Having a large neocortex ratio may provide critical advantages under a variety of ecological conditions, including remembering where food occurs over a large home range and extracting foods, such as termites, from a mound of dirt (Clutton-Brock and Harvey, 1980; Gibson, 1986; Harvey and Krebs, 1990). However, from Dunbar's perspective, the ability to maintain the social alliances that are the "crucial basis for primate sociality" was the primary selective factor in the evolution of large primate brains.

In fact, most mammals have fully developed brains by the time they are weaned, whereas much of primate brain development occurs during the long socialization period between weaning and adulthood (Joffe, 1997). Thus, primate sociality may have been as necessary to the evolution of large brains in primates as large brains have been to the evolution of primate sociality. Whether social or ecological pressures were responsible for primate brain evolution, there is no doubt about the fact that primates have social brains, or that ours are the most social brains of all.

characteristics that correlate with behavior to make inferences about the pattern of primate behavioral evolution. Differences in the diets of living primates, for example, correspond to variations in the morphology of their teeth, on the one hand, and to aspects of their social and grouping patterns, on the other hand (Chapters 6 and 7). Knowing how diet, morphology, and behavior co-vary permits us to extrapolate about the diets and aspects of the behavior of ancestral primates, whose teeth can be extracted from the fossil record.

Distinguishing Traits

The traits that distinguish primates from other animals fall into four major categories: locomotor, neural and sensory, feeding, and life histories. Each of these categories of traits affects different aspects of survival and reproduction (Jolly and White, 1995). For example, the kinds of teeth best suited for processing different kinds of foods, or the kinds of visual systems best suited for seeing in daylight versus at night, are the products of ecological selection pressures that affected primates during their evolutionary histories. Ecological, as well as social, selection pressures may have been responsible for the evolution of primate neural and sensory systems, which also affect the size of primate brains, as mentioned above.

To understand morphological adaptations that distinguish primates from other animals, it is necessary to distinguish traits that have functional advantages, which may therefore have been selected for, from traits that may differ only because they evolved in association with other functional traits. Many physical traits, such as tooth size or limb length, are scaled with body size across primates with similar feeding or locomotor systems. This simply means that larger primates have bigger teeth and longer limbs than smaller primates, but there is otherwise no functional difference between them. When a trait deviates from what is a comparatively consistent relationship with another trait, however, the deviation may be indicative of a functional difference associated with selection on that trait. For example, muriquis and their close spider monkey relatives have longer arms than other monkeys similar to them in body size, a trait that has been associated with their unusual mode of **suspensory** locomotion. Instead of traveling on four limbs like **quadrupedal** primates, muriquis, along with a few other primates that also have long arms relative to body size, travel by swinging from a suspended, hand-over-hand position. Suspensory locomotion is an energetically expensive mode of travel compared to quadrupedalism, but it has the advantage of being a fast way to travel through the trees. The ability to traverse long distances quickly cuts down on time when energy-rich fruit resources are widely dispersed (Chapter 6). Hence, the long arms of muriquis, relative to their body size, can be seen as an **adaptation.**

Allometric Scaling of Brain and Body Size

Two traits may be isometrically or allometrically related. **Isometric scaling** occurs when two variables increase or decrease in direct proportion to one another. **Allometric scaling,** or **allometry,** occurs when two variables increase or decrease at different rates. Allometric comparisons permit us to distinguish between absolute and relative effects, and to identify which are likely to be specialized adaptations as opposed to the products of natural laws that affect all animals. For example, larger (heavier) mammals have absolutely larger brain sizes (as measured by cranial volume, usually in cubic centimeters) than smaller mammals. So, an elephant's brain is roughly four times larger than our own (Martin, 1998). However, brain size generally increases at a slower rate than body size, so although the human brain is *absolutely* smaller than an elephant's in size, it is actually larger, *relative* to our body weight, than the elephant's brain is to its body weight.

Human brain size is clearly different. When we compare humans along the mammalian brain-to-body size curve, our brains stand out as being much larger *relative* to our body sizes than what we would expect from the allometric relationship that describes other mammals. Interestingly, the next largest brain-to-body size ratio is found in dolphins, not another primate. But as a group, primates tend to have larger brains relative to their body sizes than other mammals (Martin, 1996). The brain sizes of early human ancestors, or **hominids,** also fall along the brain-to-body size curve of other primates until about 2–3 million years ago, when hominid brain sizes begin to deviate from the primate pattern by becoming larger, relative to their body size, than those of other primates (Figure 2.1).

Recognizing allometric relationships is an important task because these relationships provide a basis for interpreting whether a distinguishing trait such as brain size reflects evolutionary selection pressures, or whether it is merely a consequence of selection pressures operating on a related trait, such as body size (Cartmill, 1990; Martin, 1996). The large size of an elephant's brain is a consequence of large body size. While evolutionary selection pressures may have led to the elephant's large body size, no such selection is required to explain its brain. By contrast, the relatively large size of primate brains suggests that they are not solely a consequence of body size. Something else may have been going on in their evolutionary past that gave individuals with larger brains a selective advantage.

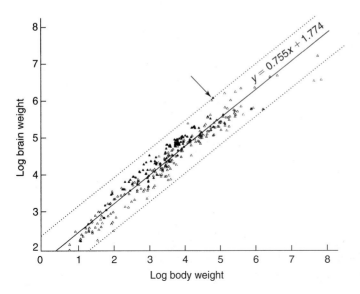

FIGURE 2.1 Allometric relationships between brain and body weights for 309 extant placental mammalian species. Primates, indicated by solid triangles, like other precocial mammals, exhibit relatively large brains. The arrow indicates humans. Figure reprinted with permission from *Nature*, from Martin, R. D. 1981. Relative brain size and basal metabolic rate in terrestrial vertebrates. *Nature* 293:220–223. Copyright © 1981. Macmillan Magazines Limited.

Effects of Diet.   Despite the larger relative brain sizes of primates overall, there is substantial variation in the brain-to-body size relationships among them. Male gorillas, for example, weigh around 350 pounds, making them the largest living primates (Rowe, 1996). Gorilla brains are similar in size to those of the much smaller-bodied, 90–130 pound chimpanzees; relative to body size, gorillas have smaller brains. This variation may be related to the different kinds of energy requirements needed to fuel their respective bodies.

As a general rule, large-bodied primates need to eat more food than smaller primates, so in absolute terms their energetic requirements are greater. But **basal metabolic rate (BMR),** which is the rate at which energy is used to maintain body function during a resting state, is allometrically related to body weight, just like brain size. As a result, large-bodied primates need less energy *per unit weight* than smaller ones. This means that large primates, like gorillas, have relatively lower BMRs, and can consume greater quantities of lower energy foods than the smaller, more frugivorous chimpanzee (Figure 2.2).

It is not entirely clear why both BMR and brain size vary similarly with body size. Metabolic rates might constrain brain size because brains require so much energy to run. In this case, the relatively slow metabolic rates of gorillas compared to chimpanzees might be responsible for their smaller relative brain sizes. The human brain, for example, constitutes only about two percent of our body weight, but it uses about 20 percent of our energy intake (Aiello and Wheeler, 1995). Constraints on maternal energy might therefore limit how much fetal brain tissue can grow, and therefore how large adult brains can become (Martin, 1981, 1996, 1998).

Alternatively, the cognitive skills required to find high energy foods, which are patchily distributed in both time and space, might necessitate bigger brains than abundant, more evenly distributed foods such as leaves (Clutton-Brock and Harvey, 1980; Harvey and Krebs, 1990). In this scenario, the relatively small brains of gorillas and large brains of chimpanzees might reflect the differences in their diets and foraging patterns.

Whether the more folivorous diets of gorillas constrain their brain development or whether the more frugivorous diets of chimpanzees select for their relatively

The Jarman-Bell Principle

	total nutrient requirement	nutrient requirement / body weight
large animal	large (abundant foods)	small (poor quality foods)
small animal	small (rare foods)	large (high quality foods)

FIGURE 2.2   Food characteristics expected from the total and relative nutrient requirements of large and small animals. From Gaulin, S. J. C. 1979. A Jarman/Bell model of primate feeding niches. *Human Ecology* 7:1–20. Reprinted with permission of Plenum Publishing Corporation.

larger brains has not been resolved. But, the relationships between body size, brain size, BMR, and diets hold up in comparisons among nearly all other closely related sets of primate species. Across these comparisons, smaller bodied primates have higher metabolic rates and consume higher energy diets, which sustain or are made possible by their relatively larger brains. The relationships between body size, metabolic rates, and diet quality, as measured by energy, are called the **Jarman/Bell principle,** which was originally identified from comparative studies of antelopes (Bell, 1970; Jarman, 1974), but applies equally well to primates (Gaulin, 1979).

Life Histories and Their Social Consequences.   Life history traits also scale allometrically with body size, brain size, and BMR across primates. As with these other allometric relationships, comparisons among closely related species indicate that the larger bodied primates tend to have *absolutely,* but not *relatively* longer gestation lengths, slower rates of postnatal development, later ages at first reproduction, longer interbirth intervals and generation lengths, and longer lifespans. Thus, despite the large size differences between chimpanzees and gorillas, they have remarkably similar life histories (Table 2.1).

Extended life history traits, like the other allometric relationships discussed so far, distinguish primates from other mammals that are similar to them in body sizes. This distinction in primate life histories may be related to the relatively large brains that primates possess. Among closely related primates, those with higher BMRs and larger brains also tend to take longer to mature and to be slower to reproduce.

Both large brains and extended life histories have significant social consequences. For example, the relatively long period of infant dependency and the overlap between generations in primates create opportunities for extensive socialization and long-term relationships between individuals. Relative to adult brain size, primate infants are born with brains that are less well developed relative to their adult brain sizes than those of other mammals. Consider the case of fawns or colts, who are **precocial,** or well developed, at birth. Soon after they are born they are able to stand and run with their mothers, although they are still dependent on their mothers for milk. The **altricial,** or undeveloped, state of primate newborns is strikingly different. Compared to other primate infants, which can cling to their mother's bodies and fur at birth, human infants are the most helpless of all.

TABLE 2.1   Ape life history traits*

	Adult female body weight	Gestation	Age at 1st birth	Birth interval
white-handed gibbon	5.34 kg (n = 66; 11.7 lbs.)	205 days	112 months	30 months
Bornean orangutan	35.8 kg (n = 13; 78.8 lbs.)	244 days	144–180 months	84–96 months
mountain gorilla	97.5 kg (n = 1; 214.5 lbs.)	??	120–144 months	36–59 months
eastern chimpanzee	37.7 kg (n = 26; 74.1 lbs.)	240 days	168–180 months	60 months
bonobo	33.2 kg (n = 6; 73.0 lbs.)	240 days	168 months	48–72 months

*Weight data from Smith and Jungers (1997). Life history data taken from Rowe, 1996.

Sexual Dimorphism. In many animals, physical differences between males and females go beyond those associated with their respective reproductive systems. In species that exhibit **sexual dimorphism,** it is almost always males that are larger, on average, than females, as we will see in Chapter 5. When males are larger than females in body size, all other traits that are allometrically related to body size differ accordingly (Figure 2.3). Larger males tend to have larger absolute brain sizes, but their brains are no larger relative to their body size. Larger males also tend to have relatively slow metabolic rates and take longer than females to mature.

The Jarman/Bell principle is applicable to sex differences in primate diets in species that are highly sexually dimorphic in body size. Just as in comparisons between different species, the relatively slow metabolic rates of sexually dimorphic males compared to females means that although larger males may require more food, they can tolerate lower energy diets (Demment, 1983). As a result, males and females may spend different amounts of time feeding and may eat different kinds of foods in different proportions, a pattern that also affects reproduction and that we'll return to in Chapter 6.

Other Morphological Traits

In addition to their relatively large brains and extended life histories, primates possess other **morphological,** or anatomical, traits that distinguish them as a group from other animals. The coordination of eyes, hands, and brain represent their primary mode of interacting with their environment.

Stereoscopic Vision. Primates have evolved a greater reliance on vision and a correspondingly reduced sense of smell compared to most other mammals. This shift in visual versus olfactory acuity is evident in the larger, more forward-facing eyes and smaller snouts of many primates (Figure 2.4). Forward-facing eye sockets allow the fields of vision from each eye to overlap, resulting in a phenomenon known as **stereoscopic vision** that makes accurate depth perception possible.

FIGURE 2.3 Patas monkeys (*Erythrocebus patas*) are the most terrestrial cercopithecines, spending nearly all of their time on the ground. Males (standing) are nearly twice as heavy as females (left). To the right of this female is a juvenile. Photo by Jim Moore/Anthro-Photo.

FIGURE 2.4   Southern red-necked night monkey (*Aotus nigriceps*). The night, or owl, monkey is the only nocturnal anthropoid. Photo © by Noel Rowe/*Pictorial Guide to Living Primates.*

To appreciate the importance of depth perception, try holding your index finger about six inches in front of your nose and closing one eye at a time. You'll notice that your finger seems to move slightly to the left or right depending on which eye is looking at it. Now look at your finger with both eyes open. You can probably see its actual position in front of your nose more accurately with both eyes than with either eye alone. Because it falls in the overlapping field of vision, your two eyes compensate in localizing your finger.

It is easy to imagine at least two possible contexts in which accurate depth perception might have been advantageous during the evolutionary history of primates (Sussman, 1999). One hypothesis emphasizes their long evolutionary history as arboreal creatures. Leaping from branch to branch in search of food or when escaping from predators can be dangerous, and even with stereoscopic vision many arboreal primates suffer from broken bones or death when they fall out of trees. The ability to gauge the precise location of the next branch and to locate small food items would have been a critical advantage for ancestral primates.

A second hypothesis, called the visual predation hypothesis, pertains to the insectivorous diet that ancestral primates are thought to have exploited (Cartmill, 1972, 1974). Depth perception to localize prey and to coordinate the hand-to-eye movements for snatching mobile insects would be a great advantage. The arboreal and visual predation hypotheses are not necessarily mutually exclusive. In other words, forward-facing eyes with stereoscopic vision could have evolved because of the dual advantages gained in navigating around the tree tops and in catching insect prey. Or, these benefits could be positive side effects of completely different selection pressures favoring depth perception (Sussman, 1999b).

Distinguishing Features of the Hands and Feet. Primates possess three traits that directly enhance both the coordination and tactile sense of hands and feet. In addition to the presence of five digits on both hands (fingers) and feet (toes), they have increased mobility of these digits, especially in the thumb and big toe, and nails that have evolved in place of the claws that primitive mammals possessed.

Not all primates have all of these traits, just as not all primates have equally well developed visual systems and diminished senses of smell. Among the New World spider monkeys and muriqui monkeys, for example, the thumb is either absent entirely or reduced to a tiny bony spur located farther up on the wrist, away from the other four long, slightly curved fingers of the hand (Figure 2.5).

An **opposable thumb,** which can reach other fingers of the hand, is another trait that is not present in all primates, yet its presence distinguishes primates from other animals. Humans have the most mobile thumbs of all primates, which you can see if you touch the tip of your thumb to your little finger on the same hand. This mobility is what gives us a **precision grip** to manipulate tiny objects (usually between our thumb and index finger), as well as to grip the handles of tools. Our big toes, however, have lost their opposability in exchange for providing a stabilizing base and adding propulsion to our bodies as we evolved our two-legged, **bipedal** mode of locomotion (Lovejoy, 1988).

Chimpanzees have opposable thumbs and big toes, which enable them to handle small objects with both hands and feet (Figure 2.6). Many primates that groom one another to remove skin parasites, such as fleas or ticks, from the fur do so by parting the fur of an associate with one hand and pulling off the foreign object with the fingers of the other (Figure 2.7). Imagine trying to pick a fleck of lint off of your

FIGURE 2.5 Muriqui (*Brachyteles arachnoides*) mother with a new infant. Note her long, curved fingers and the absence of a thumb. Photo by Claudio P. Nogueira.

FIGURE 2.6   Charlie, an adult male chimpanzee (*Pan troglodytes*) at Gombe, dips for driver ants holding the tool in his left foot while sweeping the ants off with his left hand. Adult female Flo watches from the background with her own tool in hand. Photo by J. D. Bygott, provided by W. C. McGrew.

FIGURE 2.7   Young chimpanzee (*Pan troglodytes*), Freud, grooms the ear of his mother, Fifi. Photo by W. C. McGrew.

sleeve using just your index and middle fingers. It may be possible, but it's nowhere near as precise or controlled as it is when you put your thumb to work, too.

Having nails instead of claws on fingers and toes enhances the tactile, or sense of touch, abilities of primates. With protective nails covering the digit on one side, the sensitive skin exposed on the other side can be used to feel and manipulate objects. The earliest, most ancestral primates probably retained more primitive mammalian characteristics, including claws on some digits as well as a greater reliance than their descendants on olfactory rather than visual acuity (Figure 2.8).

FIGURE 2.8 Aye-aye (*Daubentonia madagascariensis*). Note the especially long middle fingers, which are used to extract larvae from holes in tree trunks and branches. Aye-ayes tap their fingers on the wood to locate such hidden prey (Erickson et al., 1998). Photo © by Noel Rowe/*Pictorial Guide to Living Primates.*

The Collarbone and Arm Mobility.   The presence of a **clavicle,** or collar bone, is significant for its role in repositioning the upper body and in giving the arm greater mobility. The clavicle helps support the arms toward the side instead of the front of the body, and contributes to the full range of motion our upper arms have. If you think of the shape of a dog's body for comparison, you can envision how little mobility its shoulder joints have relative to its body trunk. The forelimbs of a dog move backward and forward, but a dog can't extend its forelimb from the shoulder joint above its head, nor can it rotate it sideways away from its body.

You can feel your own shoulder joint's articulation with your clavicle by slowly raising and lowering your arm in front of and to the side of your body. Greater mobility in the shoulder joint gives primates greater range of motion, an obvious benefit whenever the arms are used in climbing or holding on in the trees. This mobility is retained, though to a lesser degree, in the ground-dwelling Old World monkeys as well as ourselves, although our hominid ancestors evidently retained other traits, particularly in the wrist and ankle joints, that would have made them better equipped for climbing than we are today.

Teeth.   The last of the major anatomical trends in primates involves a reduction in the number of teeth. Primitive primates had as many as forty, whereas humans have only thirty-two. You can identify the four different tooth types that all primates share and the number of each type you have by placing your tongue along the back of your upper teeth starting at the center of your mouth and moving it slowly to the left or right. First you encounter your two **incisors,** then your **canine,** then your two **premolars.** Next you'll encounter at least two, if not three, of your **molars,** depending on whether or not you've had your third molars, or wisdom teeth, removed. Including the left side of your upper dentition and both halves of your lower dentition yields a total of thirty-two teeth, with a **dental formula** of 2–1–2–3 if you have two incisors, one canine, two premolars, and three molars. If you've had your wisdom teeth removed, you will only have two molars instead of three.

We humans share our 2–1–2–3 dental formula, and 32 teeth in total, with the Old World monkeys and apes. Other groups of living primates have up to thirty-six teeth because they possess a third premolar in each quarter of their mouth. Even three premolars represents a reduction from the four that primitive primates had (Figure 2.9). The trend toward a reduction in teeth in primate evolution may reflect

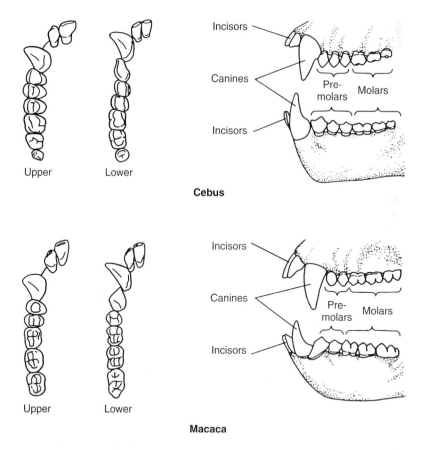

FIGURE 2.9 Comparison of platyrrhine (represented by the genus *Cebus*) and catarrhine (represented by the genus *Macaca*) teeth. From E. Staski and J. Marks, *Evolutionary Anthropology*, 1992, Harcourt Brace. Reprinted with permission of the authors.

a combination of factors, but probably the most important is related to the changes that occurred in the shape of the mouth and face along with the reduction in the snout and sense of smell. Dietary adaptations also affect the relative size and proportions of different teeth, especially the incisors relative to the molars, as we'll see when we look more closely at some of the primate feeding adaptations that marked their evolution and that are related to their diets today (Chapter 6).

Cladistic Analyses

The trends and clusters of traits that distinguish primates from other animals also distinguish them from one another. We use these distinctions in **taxonomic classifications,** which are hierarchical organizing systems based on similarities in traits due to common ancestry. Clusters of closely related taxa are considered to be members of the same **clade** because they share the same common ancestor. **Cladistic analysis** is a way of lining up traits to identify close relatives among both living and fossil primates. In contrast to other classification systems, cladistic analysis involves counting traits equally, without weighting their importance or distinguishing traits that may have adaptive evolutionary significance from those that don't. Ideally, we could distinguish between traits with and without evolutionary significance, and weight them according to the selective advantages they conferred. However, there is often no way of telling whether a trait that is adaptive today had a similar function in the past, or whether traits with no apparent function now were once adaptations that have been retained. Once clades are established based on unweighted comparisons, we can sometimes distinguish ancestral traits and begin to understand the *phylogenetic,* or evolutionary relationships among the organisms in question. We'll return to this topic, known as **systematics,** after reviewing the basics of primate taxonomy.

Taxonomic Considerations

The Linnean classification system is what most of modern primate taxonomy is based on. It runs from the largest, most encompassing taxonomic level of the kingdom, to phylum, class, order, family, genus, and species. Primates are members of the Kingdom Animalia, the Phylum Chordata, the Subphylum Vertebrata, and the class Mammalia. The mammals are subdivided into orders, with the Order Primate being one.

Below the family, and in some cases, subfamily, are the genus and species levels of classification. Species in the same genus tend to resemble each other because they descended from the same ancestor. In recognition of these ancestral lineages, the scientific literature uses the Latin genus and species names as designations. *Homo sapiens* is the scientific name for human primates. Today, our genus is **monotypic** because all humans are members of a single species, but other species of the genus *Homo* lived in the past. When there are two or more species in the same genus, like the chimpanzee (*Pan troglodytes*) and the bonobo (*Pan paniscus*), the genus is polytypic.

Among the living primates, our closest relatives are the African apes (chimpanzees, bonobos, and gorillas). Humans, the African apes, and the Asian apes (orangutans, gibbons, and siamangs) are grouped in the **hominoid** clade although some suggest extending the Hominidae family to include great apes, and grouping humans and chimpanzees in the subfamily Homininae. Humans and their hominid ancestors would then be distinguished in the tribe, Hominini (Leakey, et al., 2001). Hominoids and Old World monkeys form the **catarrhines,** which are distinct from the New World monkeys, or **platyrrhines.** Catarrhines have narrow, downward-facing nostrils, while platyrrhines have round, sideways-facing nostrils. Catarrhines and platyrrhines together form the **anthropoids,** while lemurs, lorises, and tarsiers are **prosimians** (see Table 1.1). Thus, humans are simultaneously members of the genus *Homo,* as well as hominids, hominoids, catarrhines, anthropoids, and, of course, primates (Figure 2.10).

Primates also have common names, derived from the languages of indigenous peoples or from the explorers or scientists who first described them to the rest of the scientific community. The muriquis I study in southeastern Brazil are referred to as the *mono carvoeiro,* or charcoal face monkey, by local Brazilians, and for a time, as *woolly spider monkeys* by scientists because of their physical resemblance and close phylogenetic relationships to both woolly monkeys and spider monkeys. *Muriqui* is the Tupi Indian name, which like the indigenous names of many primates, is now used in deference to the people who lived in the Brazilian Atlantic forest before they and their language were decimated by Europeans. To avoid confusion in the scientific literature, however, they are always designated by their genus and species name, *Brachyteles arachnoides,* as is the case for all other primates. In all scientific writing, the Latin genus name is always capitalized and both genus and species names are italicized or underlined.

The taxonomy of living primates is constantly being revised as new evidence, especially, but not exclusively, from molecular analyses of genetic similarities and differences among species, comes to light. In some cases, genetic data lead to dividing populations of what were previously considered to represent a single species into two. In other cases, genetic data, sometimes supplemented by morphological analyses, support new taxonomic designations at the genus level. You'll find examples of this in some of the figure legends in this book, where both traditional and revised taxonomic names are provided, and in the Appendix, where some of the controversial classifications are highlighted. As we'll see in Chapter 3, how we classify primates has important implications for how we interpret their behavior and evaluate their conservation status. Indeed, some primatologists recognize nearly 600 **taxa,** which encompass the diversity represented among species, subspecies, and genetically or morphologically distinct populations, instead of just the 240 or so different species that more traditional classifications distinguish (Mittermeier, et al., 1999; 2000).

One of the most confusing issues in primate taxonomy occurs at the level of the first major division of suborders, and involves the uncertain position of tarsiers. Traditional taxonomies put tarsiers with lemurs and lorises in the suborder **Prosimii,** as shown in Table 1.1 and Figure 2.10, but more recent taxonomies put the

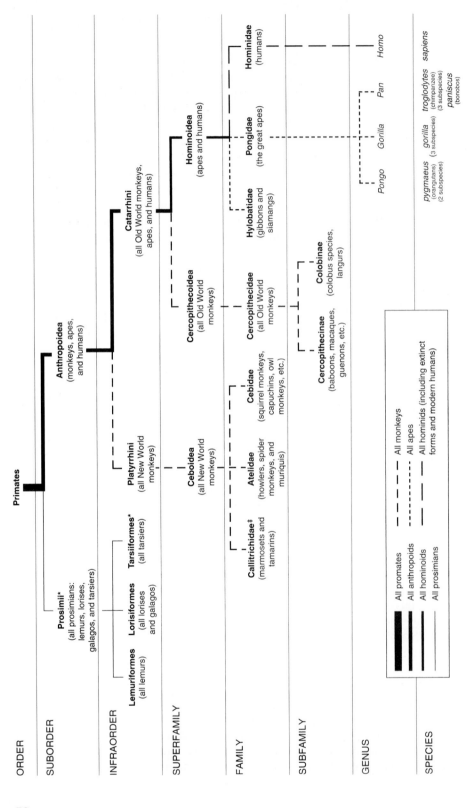

FIGURE 2.10 Except for the great apes and humans, only the more general categories are shown in this abbreviated taxonomy of the Primate Order. Taxonomies differ in some of their classifications, as can be seen by comparing this taxonomy with the one shown in Table 1.1. In particular, the position of tarsiers (*) and the family Callitrichidae (‡) are uncertain. This figure is from *Understanding Physical Anthropology & Archaeology*, 8th edition, by W. A. Turnbaugh, R. Jurmain, H. Nelson, L. Kilgore © 2002. Reprinted with permission of Wadsworth Learning, a division of Thomson Learning. Fax 800 730-2215.

tarsiers with monkeys, and hominoids, including humans, to reflect the closer phylogenetic relationship among them. In these taxonomic classifications, the primate order is divided into the suborder **Strepsirhini,** which includes only the lemurs and lorises, and the suborder **Haplorhini,** which includes tarsiers along with monkeys, apes, and humans (Figure 2.11).

The traditional division of primates into prosimians and anthropoids is adopted throughout much of the rest of this book because it is still widely employed (Fleagle, 1999; Sussman, 1999a) and because it may still be the most appropriate way to distinguish many aspects of primate behavior. Some of the figures, however, show Strepsirhini-Haplorhini comparisons. To interpret these figures, just remember that the difference is whether the tarsiers are grouped with monkeys and apes as haplorines, or with lemurs and lorises as prosimians.

Major Taxonomic Groups

Prosimians.   Today, contemporary prosimians are restricted to the Old World (Figure 2.12), but this was not true among their ancestors. Taxonomic classifications differ in whether they distinguish two or three infraorders depending on whether lorises and lemurs are separated at this level or the level of the superfamily (see Table 1.1). The most diverse superfamily, Lemuroidea, is represented by a remarkable number of species found exclusively on the island of Madagascar. Today, lemurs account for about 13 percent of all primates (Martin, 2000). As recently as 2,000 years ago, there were at least 45 species of lemur ranging in size from less than 100 grams to up to 240 kilograms, but none of today's survivors weighs more than 10 kilograms (Richard and Dewar, 1991; Tattersall, 1993). The superfamily Lorisoidea has representatives on continental Africa (the bushbaby, galago, angwantibo, and potto) and Asia (the loris; Figure 2.13).

Lemurs and lorises are the most ancient primates, and their modern-day descendants still possess many primitive traits. Most are nocturnal, and all have a

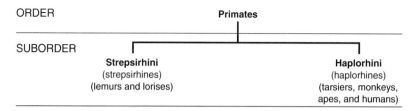

FIGURE 2.11   In this alternative classification, the suborders Prosimii and Anthropoidea are replaced by Strepsirhini and Haplorhini, respectively. Here, tarsiers are included in the same suborder with monkeys and humans to reflect a closer relationship with them than with lemurs and lorises. From *Understanding Physical Anthropology & Archaeology, 8th edition,* by W. A. Turnbaugh, R. Jurmain, H. Nelson, L. Kilgore © 2002. Reprinted with permission of Wadsworth, an imprint of the Wadsworth Group, a division of Thomson Learning. Fax 800 730–2215.

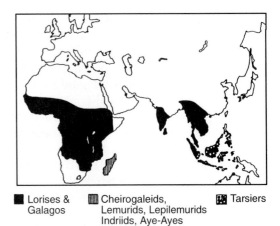

FIGURE 2.12   Geographic distribution of extant prosimians. From Fleagle, J. G. 1999. *Primate Adaptation and Evolution,* Second Edition. New York: Academic Press. Reprinted with permission of the publisher and author, © 1999 Academic Press.

■ Lorises & Galagos   ▥ Cheirogaleids, Lemurids, Lepilemurids Indriids, Aye-Ayes   ▨ Tarsiers

FIGURE 2.13   An adult female slender loris (*Loris tardigradus lydekkerianus*) at Ayyalur, Tamil Nadu, South India. Slender loris locomotion is swift and steady. Flexible limbs allow slender lorises to maneuver fluidly even through the thorn forests of south India (Nekaris, 2001). Caption and photo by K. A. I. Nekaris.

tapetum, which is a layer in the retina of the eye similar to, but independently evolved, from that of cats and other nocturnal mammals for reflecting light (Fleagle, 1999). Even diurnal and cathemeral lemurs on Madagascar have retained the tapetum (Tattersall, 1993).

Prosimians rely heavily on olfactory cues, as indicated by their relatively large nasal cavities and scent glands that, when rubbed against a substrate, leave a chemical mark (Sussman, 1992b). Although many have nails and claws, their fingers are less dextrous than those of most anthropoids. Most are arboreal, clinging vertically to tree trunks or using their powerful legs to leap through the canopy (Figure 2.14). Only one living prosimian, the ring-tailed lemur, spends much of its time on the ground.

Lemurs and lorises can have up to 36 teeth, owing to the presence of three premolars in both their upper and lower jaws, but some, such as the aye-aye (see Figure 2.8) have a greatly reduce dentition (1.0.1.3) and distinctively large, rodent-like incisors. Lemurs and lorises also possess a special set of flattened comblike lower incisors used for grooming and in some species, for feeding on tree gum. They have lower BMR and faster life histories compared to haplorhines (tarsiers and anthropoids) of similar size (Young, et al., 1990). Lemurs tend to have shorter gestation lengths, but to invest more in their offspring after birth, than lorises (Richard and Dewar, 1991). Life history comparisons among lemurs indicate tremendous variation that can be linked, in part, to body size and dietary differences (Kappeler, 1996).

The Tarsiiformes are represented by a single living genus, *Tarsius*, found only in Asia (Figure 2.15). Tarsiers get their name from the elongated tarsal region that

FIGURE 2.14   Adult male Verreaux's sifaka (*Propithecus verreauxi verreauxi*) at Beza Mahafoly. Like many other lemurs, this sifaka's powerful arms and legs make it well-equipped for vertical clinging and leaping. Photo © by Diane K. Brockman.

FIGURE 2.15   A spectral tarsier (*Tarsius spectrum*). See Gursky, 1999.
Photo by Sharon Gursky.

makes them great leapers. Although tarsiers are nocturnal, they lack the tapetums that lemurs and lorises possess. Yet, their brain architectures (Clark, et al., 2001) and relative brain sizes are more similar to those of lemurs and lorises than to anthropoids. Tarsiers have 34 teeth because although they have three premolars, they have only two (instead of four) lower incisors. Tarsiers are also unusual in their practice of parking their infants in secure, hidden tree cavities rather than carrying them on their bodies throughout their activities (MacKinnon and MacKinnon, 1980). As a result, tarsier infants may be left on their own, or in proximity to subadults, up to 50 percent of the time (Gursky, 1994).

Anthropoids.   Only one anthropoid, the New World night monkey, or owl monkey (see Figure 2.4) is habitually nocturnal. The shift to habitual diurnal lifestyles, including its greater emphasis on visual versus olfactory communication, is one of the distinctive trends among primates. The other most distinguishing feature of the anthropoids is their relatively large brains and distinctive brain architectures.

New World Monkeys.   Platyrrhines are divided into two or three families, depending on whether the Callitrichidae are recognized as distinct at this level (compare Table 1.1 and Figure 2.10). Callitrichids are a diverse set of primates known as the marmosets and tamarins, which are distinguished from all other primates by their rapid reproductive rates involving the production of twins as often as twice per year (see Box 1.1). Like many lemurs and lorises, callitrichids have 36 teeth instead of the 32 teeth found in other anthropoids. Marmosets and tamarins occur only in South America, whereas some genera from both the Cebidae and Atelidae families are distributed from Mexico in the north to Argentina in the south. Only a few (e.g., capuchin monkeys, owl monkeys, and howler monkeys) are found as far south as Argentina, and even fewer occur as far north as Mexico (e.g., howler monkeys, spider monkeys).

All New World monkeys are arboreal, but this doesn't prevent them from descending to the ground to eat, drink water, or cross gaps between trees when they need to. Their diets are diverse, with the smaller species being mainly insectivore-frugivores and the larger species being frugivore-folivores. Special incisors and guts permit marmosets to supplement their diets with gum, a dietary adaptation that may help get them through times of fruit scarcity (Ferrari, et al., 1996). Saki and bearded saki monkeys, and uacaris, have specialized teeth that give them access to fruits that are too hard for other primates to eat (Kinzey and Norconk, 1993; Norconk, 1996).

The four genera of Atelidae (Figure 2.10) or Atelinae (Table 1.1) possess a **prehensile tail,** which is strong enough to support their bodies and help in balancing along branches. Some species also occasionally use their grasping tails to carry food items. Muriquis and their spider monkey cousins are the only monkeys that habitually employ suspensory locomotion, using their arms and tails as pendulums to swing through the canopy rather than the four-limbs used by other monkeys in quadrupedal locomotion (Figure 2.16). Saki monkeys, by contrast, rely on vertical

FIGURE 2.16   Two muriquis (*Brachyteles arachnoides*) hang by one of their arms and their tails in a typical suspensory feeding posture. Photo by Claudio P. Nogueira.

clinging and leaping to get to food along the small terminal branches of trees, gaining a more diverse diet than other monkeys that share their forests but are not as agile when it comes to feeding in these spots (Walker, 1996).

Some Cebids and Atelids have extended life histories compared to Old World monkeys of similar body size as a result of their slow reproductive rates (Ross, 1991). In muriquis, spider monkeys, and woolly monkeys, for example, interbirth intervals average about three years (Strier, 1999a) compared to the one to two year interbirth intervals of most Old World monkeys whose females' weights range similarly from about two to twenty kilograms.

There is substantial variation in relative brain sizes among Platyrrhines. The most folivorous genus, *Alouatta,* or the howler monkeys, have the smallest relative brain sizes, as would be expected from their highly folivorous, low energy diet and correspondingly low BMRs (Figure 2.17). The smaller, more insectivorous capuchin monkeys (genus *Cebus*) and squirrel monkeys (genus *Saimiri*) have relatively large brains. But, whereas capuchins rely on extended postnatal development and maternal investment to grow their adult brain sizes (Figure 2.18), squirrel monkeys do most of their early brain development during an extended gestation period (Figure 2.19). Thus, in contrast to other Cebidae, which are born weighing about seven to 10 percent of their adult body weight, newborn squirrel monkeys weigh up to 17 percent of their mothers' body weight (Hartwig, 1996).

Old World Monkeys.   The Old World monkeys are grouped in a single family, which is usually divided into two subfamilies, the Colobinae and the Cercopithecinae, represented throughout Africa and Asia. Like the other catarrhines, both families of Old World monkeys have 32 teeth, but the size of their incisors relative to canines and the surfaces of their molars differ depending on their diets.

FIGURE 2.17   Mexican mantled howler monkey (*Alouatta palliata*) eating. Photo by J. W. Lynch.

FIGURE 2.18   Adult female white-faced capuchin (*Cebus capucinus*) pounding fruit against a tree branch on Barro Colorado Island, Panama. See Panger, 1998, 1999 for descriptions of this and other manipulative behavior. Photo by Melissa A. Panger.

FIGURE 2.19   Adult female Costa Rican squirrel monkey (*Saimiri oerstedii*) feeding on *Heliconia* flower nectar. Photo by Sue Boinski.

The **colobines** are unique among primates in possessing a specialized **sacculated stomach,** which is divided into pouchlike sections where leaves and in some cases, highly toxic seeds, can be digested by bacteria that live in the gut (Figure 2.20). Their folivorous adaptation also includes sharp, shearing crested molars for slicing open the tough cell walls of leaves. The **cercopithecines** include baboons in Africa and macaques in Asia, as well as mangabeys and a variety of semiterrestrial and arboreal monkeys collectively called **guenons** (Figure 2.21). Cercopithecine incisors are proportionately larger than those of the more folivorous colobines for biting into fruit, and their flatter molars are better suited for crushing and grinding hard seeds.

Cercopithecines possess cheek pouches in which they can store unripe fruits and seeds (Figure 2.22). Cheek pouches serve at least two important functions. First, they are useful to have in feeding competition because they let the monkeys grab as much food as possible before they are displaced by another monkey who is also hungry for the food (Altmann, 1998). Second, salivary enzymes help to break down toxic compounds often found in unripe fruits and seeds. Either or both of these

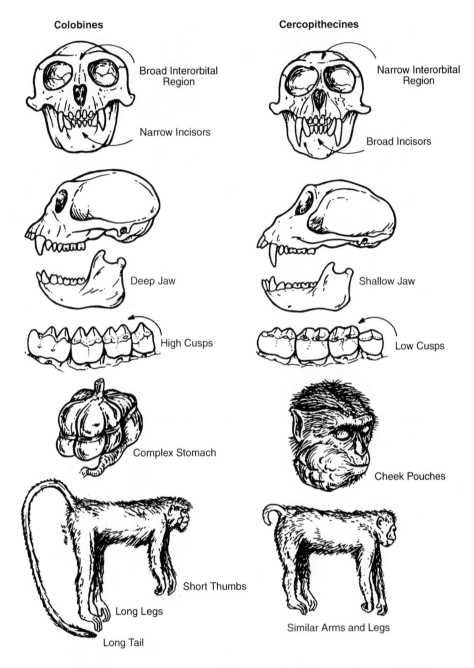

FIGURE 2.20 Characteristic anatomical features of colobines and cercopithecines. From Fleagle, J. G. 1999. *Primate Adaptation and Evolution,* Second Edition. New York: Academic Press. Reprinted with permission of the publisher and author, © 1999 Academic Press.

FIGURE 2.21   The Mona monkey (*Cercopithecus mona*) is one of the diverse species of guenons. Some were imported to the island of Grenada from 200 to 300 years ago, where they are now being studied (Glenn, 1997; Glenn and Bensen, 1998). Photo by Heather Bruce, provided by Mary E. Glenn.

FIGURE 2.22   This subadult female bonnet macaque (*Macaca radiata*) stuffed her cheekpouches with food, and then ran off to eat in peace, away from the other monkeys attracted to the food. Photo by Jim Moore/Anthro-Photo.

advantages could have been the primary selection pressure on the evolution of cheek pouches, but the trait is clearly adaptive today.

Comparisons between colobine and cercopithecine brain size and life histories are consistent with their body sizes and diets. Between families, the lower energy diets of the leaf-eating colobines generally corresponds with their relatively small brains and slower BMRs compared to cercopithecines (Figure 2.23). Within each family, larger species tend to exploit lower quality foods and have slow BMRs and small brains compared to the smaller species.

Apes.   Unlike all other primates, the hominoids, which include apes and humans, lack tails. Gibbons and siamangs, often known as the lesser apes because they weigh less than twelve kilograms compared to the much heavier thirty to one-hundred kilogram great apes, are widespread throughout tropical Asia (Figure 2.24). The other Asian ape, the orangutan, occurs only on the Indonesian islands of Borneo and Sumatra. Gibbons and siamangs, like the New World spider monkeys and muriquis, travel by suspensory locomotion, but because these apes lack tails, which the New World atelins use to propel them along, they are considered to be the only true **brachiators.** Orangutans, by contrast, use their arms and legs to hoist their heavy bodies through the canopy in a form of locomotion known as **quadrumanous** climbing (Figure 2.25).

FIGURE 2.23   Capped langur, or leaf, monkeys (*Trachypithecus pileatus*) are among the diverse species of Asian colobines. In capped langurs, natal emigration by both males and females has been observed (Stanford, 1991). Photo by Craig Stanford.

FIGURE 2.24 White-handed gibbons (*Hylobates lar*) suspended. A juvenile follows an adult female, who is carrying an infant, barely visible. Photo by Thad Bartlett.

FIGURE 2.25 An adult female orangutan (*Pongo pygmaeus*) using all four of her limbs to move through the trees. Photo by John Mitani.

Both of the African hominoid genera, *Gorilla* and *Pan*, are **knuckle-walkers.** Although they use all four limbs in their locomotion, their hands curl under so that their weight is absorbed through their knuckles instead of along the surface of their palms, as occurs in other quadrupedal primates (Figure 2.26). The fact that these African apes, like their Asian counterparts, have longer arms relative to their leg length than other primates, has been associated with a more upright posture than is typical for quadrupeds. Upright posture has been carried to its extreme in the unique bipedal stance of humans. Scientists disagree, however, about whether the common ancestors of humans and apes passed through a brachiating or knuckle-walking stage of locomotion, or whether both of these modes of locomotion are as specialized as our own (Tuttle, 1967, 1975).

Systematics

Specialized traits, such as our own bipedality, distinguish a species from its **last common ancestor.** These specializations are known as **derived traits,** which are quite different from the more **generalized,** or **primitive traits** that related species share through their common descent from the same immediate ancestor. The process of sorting out phylogenetic relationships between species based on distinguishing whether similarities or differences among them are primitive or derived is called **systematics.**

All primates possess combinations of both primitive and derived traits, and distinguishing among them requires comparisons across living, and ideally, fossil primates whose evolutionary positions are known. These comparisons can go beyond primates to include other animals. We know, for example, that the five digits primates share with other mammals is a primitive trait, whereas the anatomical modifications associated with bipedality in hominids are highly specialized, and therefore derived from the primitive, quadrupedal condition.

FIGURE 2.26   Gorillas and chimpanzees, just like the bonobos (*Pan paniscus*) shown here, walk on their knuckles. Photo by Ellen J. Ingmanson.

Making other distinctions among primates is rarely so clear-cut because different species may end up with similar traits through different routes. One route is by inheriting the same trait from their last common ancestor. In this case, the trait is called a **homology.** If the last common ancestor of modern gorillas and chimpanzees also walked on its knuckles, we would conclude that the knuckle-walking of modern chimpanzees is homologous with that of modern gorillas.

A second route by which two species can acquire the same or similar traits involves parallel or convergent evolution. In **parallel evolution,** two species that diverged from a common ancestor may nonetheless exhibit a similar novel adaptation because they faced similar ecological pressures after their divergence. In **convergent evolution,** distantly related species converge on a similar solution to the same ecological pressures. Suspensory locomotion in the New World atelins and the lesser apes is an example of such convergence. These primates did not inherit the anatomical specializations associated with suspensory travel from their last common ancestor. Instead, they each independently settled on a similar solution to the ecological problem of traveling quickly between widely dispersed patches of high quality foods.

Trichromatic vision, or the ability to discriminate red-green colors, is another example of convergence. It is known to occur in all catarrhines, but so far in only one New World primate, the howler monkey (Dominy, et al., 2001). Some suspect it may also have evolved in other species, such as ring-tailed lemurs, that rely on a wide range of diverse foods (Sauther, et al., 1999).

Similar traits that arise in two species through parallel or convergent evolution, such as supsensory locomotion in atelins and Hylobatids, or trichromatic vision in catarrhines and howler monkeys, are called **homoplasies.** In contrast to homologies, homoplasies are independently acquired instead of being inherited from a common ancestor. The only way to distinguish between homologies and homoplasies is to determine whether the trait in common was also present in the last common ancestor of the species involved. Thus, if the chimpanzee-gorilla ancestor was a brachiator instead of a knuckle-walker, knuckle-walking would have arisen independently in each lineage, and it would represent a homoplasy instead of a homology.

Homologous traits are the only ones that can be used to establish phylogenetic relationships, but differentiating between a homology and homoplasy requires knowledge about the presence or absence of the trait in the last common ancestor of the species involved. Acquiring this knowledge is difficult for a variety of reasons. First, persisting gaps in the primate fossil record mean that predictions about traits in ancestral forms can't be tested. Second, in many instances the precise phylogenetic relationships among living primates are poorly understood. Developmental biology can offer some useful clues, for when two structures look similar in an adult but differ in their ontogeny, they are unlikely to be homologous.

Recent advances in molecular genetics have also added a new dimension to phylogenetic analyses, and may help to resolve some of the major outstanding questions about shared ancestries among living primates. Genetic variation accumulates over time due to random **mutations,** or changes in the genetic code. By comparing the differences in particular genes or gene segments among species whose evolutionary relationships are known, it is possible to develop a **molecular clock,** which predicts the time it took for these random mutations to accumulate.

Results from genetic studies often vary depending on whether they are based on analyses of **mitochondrial DNA,** or **mtDNA** for short, which is only inherited through the mother, or on nuclear DNA, which is subject to **recombination** and thus reflects the genetic contributions of both parents (Chapter 4). Mutation rates in the noncoding regions of both types of DNA can be used to estimate the evolutionary distance among species, but the molecular clocks can vary with the type and region of DNA used. In addition, mutation rates are not constant over evolutionary time or under different ecological conditions (Awadalla, et al., 1999; Lenski and Mittler, 1993; Marks, 1994; Sniegowski, 1995; Strauss, 1999), and the reproductive rates and generation lengths of each species being compared can affect the rate at which mutations accumulate (Partridge and Harvey, 1988). Even very small genetic differences between species can have large effects, especially if the differences involve genes that regulate the function of others. For example, we now know that humans share more than 98 percent of our DNA with chimpanzees, which means that only some one to two percent of our respective genomes determine what makes us humans and them chimpanzees (Marks, 2002).

The most convincing, robust phylogenies are those in which results from genetic comparisons and morphological analyses agree. In some cases, systematic genetics have cleared up confusing phylogenetic relationships, but in other cases disagreements between morphological and genetic phylogenies raise new questions in primate systematics that have yet to be solved.

Finally, many of the interesting questions about primate social evolution don't leave a fossil record. This means that even if a known ancestral form is discovered, there are limits to what can be concluded about its behavior when it lived.

Phylogenetic Analyses of Behavior

Reconstructing evolutionary trends in primate behavioral adaptations depends on detailed knowledge of comparative primate behavioral ecology and how it relates to the kinds of evidence that can be found in the fossil record. Some behavioral adaptations, such as diets and feeding patterns, are closely reflected in the teeth and bony deposits where various chewing muscles insert into the skull and jaw. Other patterns of behavior, such as mating systems, can be partially inferred from the evidence of sex differences in canine size. Still others, such as dispersal patterns, can only be inferred from the distribution of their occurrence among living members of different taxonomic groups.

Evidence Related to Diet

Different kinds of primate foods require different kinds of teeth and chewing muscles. Remember that among all living primates, frugivores tend to have relatively large incisors and flat molars, whereas folivores tend to have relatively small incisors and large molars with sharp shearing crests to slice up fibrous leaves for easy digestion. You can see why this might be the case if you pay attention to how you bite into an apple or other piece of fruit compared to how you chew lettuce. Folivorous primates also tend to have well developed **temporalis** and **masseter** muscles (Figure 2.27). Although these muscles don't preserve in the fossil record, their sizes and positions relative to the teeth can be inferred from the bony deposits that build up at their points of origin and insertion into the skull and jaw.

Being able to distinguish whether an ancestral primate was more frugivorous or folivorous can tell us about other aspects of its behavioral ecology. For example, among living primates, folivores tend to have shorter day ranges and smaller home ranges than frugivores because leaves are generally more abundant and evenly distributed than fruits (Figure 2.28).

Evidence Related to Mating Systems

Among some living primates, male canines are disproportionately larger than those of females, whereas in others, male and female canines are similar in size. In some cases these differences correspond to sex differences in body size, but in others, male canines are disproportionately larger than expected for their body size. Comparisons among living primates suggest that the most pronounced examples of sexual dimorphism in canine size are found in species with intense, aggressive competition among males over access to mates. By contrast, in species with little or no **sexual dimorphism** in their canines, levels of male–male aggressive competition are usually much lower. We will get to the factors that lead to such differences in levels of male competition in Chapter 5. For now, though, let's consider what can be inferred about levels of competition among extinct primates when all we have to go on is their canines.

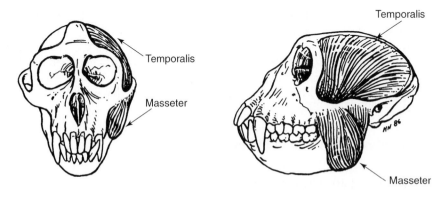

FIGURE 2.27   Location of the major chewing muscles. From Fleagle, J. G. 1999. *Primate Adaptation and Evolution,* Second Edition. New York: Academic Press. Reprinted with permission of the publisher and author, © 1999 Academic Press.

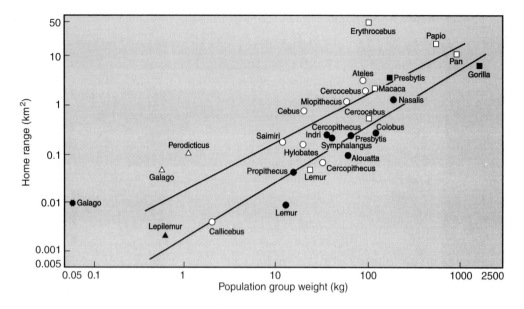

FIGURE 2.28 Relationship between primate home range size (in km²) and population group weights (kg) for different genera. Open triangles are nocturnal, arboreal frugivores; solid triangles are nocturnal, arboreal folivores; open circles are diurnal, arboreal frugivores; open squares are diurnal, terrestrial frugivores; solid circles are diurnal, arboreal folivores; solid squares are diurnal, terrestrial folivores. Lines represent regressions for folivores and frugivores separately. From Clutton-Brock, T. H. and Harvey, P. H. 1977. Primate ecology and social organization. *Journal of Zoology* 183:1–39. Reprinted with permission from Academic Press Ltd., London.

We could not conclude much about the composition of ancestral primate social groups with low canine dimorphism because among living primates, examples of such **sexual monomorphism** are found in some primates that live in multimale, multi-female societies as well as pairbonded families. We could, however, infer that highly sexually dimorphic canines reflected systems in which one or more males competed for access to multiple females because it is only among primates that live in these kinds of societies with strong mating competition that we find high levels of canine dimorphism.

Evidence Related to Dispersal Patterns

In contrast to diet and ranging patterns or male competition and canine dimorphism, whether primates live in matrilineal, patrilineal, or unrelated societies does not correlate with any morphological traits that can be discovered in the fossil record. Yet, there are patterns in how dispersal and kin-based groups are distributed across the major taxonomic divisions of living primates, from the prosimians, to the New World monkeys, to the Old World monkeys, to the apes, which are roughly consistent with their phylogenetic relationships.

All three types of dispersal systems may be represented within a taxonomic group, but usually only one or two types are expressed in the majority of genera. There are no confirmed examples of male philopatric societies among the prosimians. Male-biased dispersal with extended matrilineal groups is largely restricted to the cercopithecines. Dispersal by both sexes occurs among prosimians, callitrichids, and colobines, whereas the cebids and hominoids are roughly equally divided between patrilineal societies with female-biased dispersal and groups in which both sexes disperse. No hominoids, and only one genus of New World monkeys (capuchin monkeys), routinely form matrilineal societies (Figure 2.29).

If male-biased dispersal with female matrilocality is a primitive pattern, then the cercopithecines are among the only anthropoids that retained it, and the dispersal patterns in the other major taxonomic groups are derived. Alternatively, male-biased dispersal among the cercopithecines may be a derived condition (Di Fiore and Rendall, 1994), distinct from a more variable dispersal system that may have characterized ancestral anthropoids (Lee, 1994; Strier, 1999b).

Either phylogenetic explanation assumes that dispersal patterns have a genetic component. It may even be that dispersal and life history patterns are closely linked, with male philopatry tending to occur in the same taxonomic groups with the most

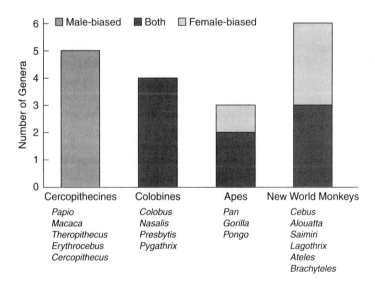

FIGURE 2.29   Dispersal patterns in anthropoid primates. Genera included in these comparisons are listed. From Strier, K. B. 1994a. Myth of the typical primate. *Yearbook of Physical Anthropology* 37:233–271. Copyright © 1994, Wiley-Liss, Inc. Reprinted by permission of Wiley-Liss, Inc., a division of John Wiley & Sons, Inc.

extended life histories and slowest reproductive rates (Strier, 1996a, 1999b). Yet, it is important to remember that dispersal patterns are not all-or-none traits. There are many examples of individuals deviating from the typical pattern for their species, and many examples of variable dispersal patterns across populations of the same species (Moore, 1984, 1992a). The availability of resources, such as food and mates, as well as local demographic conditions that affect the probability of successful dispersal, contribute to this individual and population variability. Phylogenetic analyses of behavioral traits, such as dispersal tendencies, cannot be verified from the fossil record and therefore can never be expected to reveal the whole story. Nonetheless, such analyses can provide important perspectives for interpreting primate social evolution and patterns in primate behavioral diversity.

3 Primates Past to Present

About five to seven million years ago, an unimposing primate distinguished itself as a **hominid** by adopting the peculiar habit of walking on two limbs instead of four. One group of these ancestral hominids eventually evolved into the anatomically modern, brainy humans we are today. Other hominid species, represented by their bones, teeth, and stone tool implements, eventually disappeared from the fossil record. The rest of the primates alive during these times experienced similar fates. Some evolved into what are today's modern prosimians, monkeys, and apes, just as our hominid ancestors evolved into us; others followed the more common evolutionary pathway into extinction.

Of the 240 or so species of primates recognized today, nearly half have been reduced to such small populations that they are now at risk of going extinct unless they and their diminishing habitats can be protected. Understanding the evolutionary history of contemporary species, subspecies, and populations, which are biologically meaningful ways of grouping primates, can help us to understand their behavioral adaptations and present conservation status (Harcourt and Schwartz, 2001; Purvis, et al., 2000). The evolutionary history of primates also provides clues into general principles about how anatomical features and behavior correspond to one another and reflect adaptive solutions to ecological problems. These principles can then be applied to infer the behavior of extinct primates, which are known only from their fossilized bones and teeth. Tracing such patterns gives us insights into the evolutionary and ecological pressures that have shaped the behavioral adaptations of humans and other living primates, and alerts us to the limitations on the ability of primates to adapt to new ecological pressures that human activities cause.

Evolutionary History

Primates were long thought to have made their first suspected appearance in the fossil record roughly 65 million years ago, at the time that the dinosaurs went extinct. New fossil evidence suggests that primitive primates, as well as other primitive mammals, coexisted with the dinosaurs, but it was the climatic changes, which were unhospitable to the dinosaurs, that created new habitats and opened up new **ecological niches** that primates and other mammals could fill. Taking advantage of these new opportunities, both primates and other mammals diversified in a series of **adaptive radiations,** in which multiple forms differentiated from one another and their common ancestor in close succession.

Do we have more species or fewer today than in the past? Disturbances caused by humans, especially in the last century with the world population explosion, have seriously affected primate populations and their recent evolution. Reduction of primate habitats due to deforestation and development, and the additional toll on primate populations due to hunting and poaching have had two consequences. First, diminished numbers result in threats of extinction, and the loss of diversity. Second, disruption of continuous populations may result in increased differentiation among isolated populations and ultimately reduce their ability to adapt to changing conditions. Healthy **allopatric** populations, which are geographically separated from one another, can diverge into separate species. However, many contemporary populations are already so small that their isolation is a serious threat to their survival.

The process of forming new species is called **speciation.** Most contemporary primate species owe their origins to the various adaptive radiations that have occurred within each of the major primate taxonomic groups. Adaptative radiations may occur whenever new ecological niches open up as a result of climatic fluctuations or other evolutionary events including the extinction or emergence of other species (Grant and Grant, 2002). For example, the evolution of **angiosperms,** or flowering plants, has recently been invoked to explain the extraordinary diversity of beetle species in the insect order, Coleoptera (Farrell, 1998), and may also have influenced the course of primate adaptations as new feeding niches on these plants and plant parts opened up (Sussman, 1991).

Many other natural forces unrelated to humans or our effects on the environment have impacted the course of primate evolution and the geographic distribution of species. The most obvious of these forces have been the global climate changes resulting from **continental drift,** which repositions the continents and oceans relative to one another, thereby changing ocean currents that affect air temperature and rainfall patterns. The crust of the earth is divided into plates, which are always in motion. Continents move because their land masses rest on these plates. The movement of these plates, or **plate tectonics,** causes earthquakes that lead to trenches when plates pull apart and mountain ranges when plates collide.

The results of these geological forces range from the creation of new habitats to the isolation of others. They can also lead to glaciations, or ice ages, and interglaciations, or the periods between glaciations when the earth warms up. During the evolutionary history of primates, continents that today are confined to temperate zones were much more tropical, and therefore well-suited for primates. Even after the continents reached their present positions, tropical forests contracted and expanded in response to the cooler climates of the glacial periods and the warmer interglacial respites.

In the past, as in the present, natural disturbances, such as lightning-caused fires or floods, have major impacts, but these are usually restricted to more localized areas than the global changes caused by continental drift and plate tectonics or the world-wide impact that global warming is predicted to have. Understanding broad patterns in the distribution of primates today makes more sense when the evolutionary history and biogeography of primates in the past are considered (Figure 3.1).

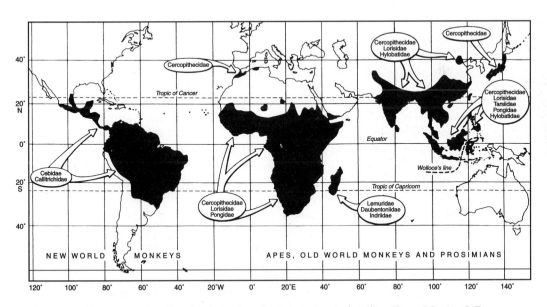

FIGURE 3.1   Contemporary distribution of nonhuman primate families. From Napier, J. R. and Napier, P. H., 1994. *The Natural History of the Primates*, Fig. 1.1, p. 9. Cambridge: The MIT Press. Copyright © 1994, The MIT Press. Reprinted by permission of The MIT Press.

Primate Diversity in the Past

The beginning of the Cenozoic Era, some 65 million years ago (mya) marked the disappearance of the dinosaurs, and the beginning of what we know about most of primate evolution (Table 3.1). There are many excellent references to consult for the latest details on new fossil discoveries and how they alter our views about primate diversity in the past. It is a fast-changing field because each new fossil find that fails to fit into the existing scenario can generate new hypotheses that only additional fossil discoveries can help to resolve (Fleagle, 1999). As we've seen, molecular data can help to resolve outstanding questions about the phylogenetic relationships among living species, but only the fossil record can provide information about the many primates that are now extinct.

Primate Origins

Until the 1990s, the first primate-like mammals were thought to belong to a group called the **plesiadapiforms,** whose fossil teeth, jaws, and skull fragments were collected from Paleocene deposits (65 to 55.5 mya) across North America and Europe, and a more recent locality in Asia. However, pleisadapiforms lost their status as ancestral primates once the first complete skull and some postcranial bones were unearthed (Rose, 1995). Nowadays, the oldest fossils definitively classified as primates are represented in the much more abundant and diverse collections from the Eocene (55.5 to 35.5 mya).

Eocene primates, like the plesiadapiforms of the Paleocene, are known mainly from fossil deposits in North America and Europe, which then resembled today's tropics in their climates. Others have also been found in North Africa and Asia, but the relationships of the Eocene primates to comtemporary species are still puzzling (Rose, 1995). Some may have been ancestral to modern lemurs and lorises, while others have been linked to modern tarsiers. Newer finds, particularly from China, provide tantalizing evidence that even the ancestors of today's anthropoids emerged during this epoch (Beard, et al., 1996; MacPhee, et al., 1995; Rose, 1995).

What is clear is that the "stem" primates of the Eocene include a diverse set of forms, which ranged from mouse-sized creatures weighing about 30 grams to fox-sized creatures weighing nearly 7 kg. Some were diurnal, others were nocturnal; some were arboreal quadrupeds, others were specialized for leaping. The smaller varieties possessed teeth for eating insects and fruits; the larger ones evidently ate leaves (Jolly and White, 1995). The diverse forms of the suspected basal anthropoid genus *Eosimias,* were estimated to have ranged in size from 300 to 1,000 grams and to have been primarily insectivore-frugivores (Kay, et al., 1997).

Primates disappeared from North America and Europe by the end of the Eocene, when the continents had shifted and their climates became cooler and more seasonal. By the Oligocene, 35.5 to 23.3 mya, a diverse set of primates with monkey-like skeletons and other anthropoid features was present in fossil deposits in the Fayum of Egypt. Somewhat later in the Oligocene, the first fossil primates, clearly

TABLE 3.1   Major events in primate evolutionary history*

Epochs (and onset)	World climate	Major evolutionary events
Holocene (12,000 years)		Essentially modern fauna
Pleistocene (1.8 mya)	Further increase in upbuilding, ice-rafting; marked climatic fluctuation; continental glaciations in the northern hemisphere	*Theropithecus* largely replaced by *Papio*; *Homo* evolves; colobines and cercopithecines in Asia but disappear from Europe (cercopithecines linger until last interglacial); New World monkeys in South America
Pliocene (5 mya)	Continued global cooling, with major glaciations; development of permanent polar icecaps in both hemispheres	*Theropithecus* baboons widespread in Africa; colobines and cercopithecines in Europe and Asia; Homininae in east and south Africa; New World monkeys in South America
Miocene (22 mya)	Cooler and drier; grasslands spread in middle latitudes; development of major icecap on east Antarctica; major increase in mountain-building, ice-rafting	Dryopithecids, sivapithecids, and (late in the epoch) colobines in Africa, Europe, and Asia; in Africa, a few fossils resembling modern prosimii; first New World monkeys (?) in South America
Oligocene (38 mya)	Sharp acceleration of cooling, and drying; unrestricted Circum-Antarctic current in Late Oligocene, with southerly retreat of warmer seas	Anthropoid primates in Africa (the Fayum); prosimians disappear from the fossil record in Europe, Asia (?), and North America; first appearance of primates in South America
Eocene (55 mya)	Continuation of Paleocene trends; more rapid cooling—seasonality occurring at high latitudes	Modern orders of mammals appear; prosimian primates in Europe, Asia, and North America
Paleocene (65 mya)	Mountain-building; gradual cooling, but tropical climates still widespread	First major mammalian radiation, including small mammals with primatelike features

*The Cenozoic era is shown. The Tertiary period encompasses the Paleocene through the Pliocene. The Quaternary period encompasses the Pleistocene. Adapted from Quiatt, D. and Reynolds, V. 1993. *Primate Behavior: Information, Social Knowledge, and the Evolution of Culture.* New York: Cambridge University Press. Reprinted with permission of the publisher and authors. Copyright © Cambridge University Press, 1993. Note that some of the evolutionary events shown here have been recently revised. For example, both prosimian-like primates and basal anthropoids are now thought to have emerged in the Eocene, and the relationships of the Miocene hominoids of Africa and Eurasia (e.g., dryopithecids and sivapithecids) to one another and as possible ancestors of contemporary hominoids are being reconsidered.

anthropoids, appeared in South America, but how they reached the New World, and who their direct ancestors were, is still a mystery (Hartwig, 1994).

Biogeography and Barriers

During the early Eocene, South America and Africa were contiguous, just as North America and Europe were. By the late Eocene-early Oligocene, however, South America and Africa had already drifted about half as far apart from one another as they are today. Whether the ancestors of contemporary New World monkeys made the journey south from North America, or west from Africa, it seems likely that they would have had to get there by sea (Figure 3.2). Recent evidence of 15 green iguanas that reached the Caribbean island of Anguilla by floating on masses of logs and uprooted trees during a hurricane shows that other vertebrates are capable of overwater dispersal (Censky, et al., 1998), and supports the possibility that Platyrrhine ancestors reached South America by rafting as well.

The Mozambique Channel must have represented a similar kind of barrier for the primates that evolved into Madagascar's tremendously diverse lemurs. The island of Madagascar was separating from continental Africa as long as 165 mya, and reached its present position, about 250 miles away, long before any of the primate radiations during the Eocene (Tattersall, 1993). New discoveries of lemur-like fossils from Pakistan are dated to be at least 30 mya old, but whether they are related to any of the modern lemurs on Madagascar is still unclear (Marivaux, et al., 2001).

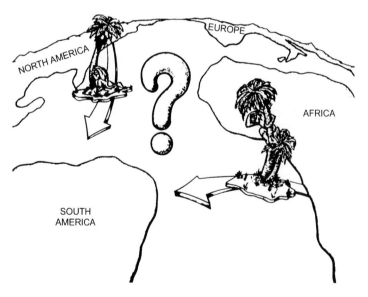

FIGURE 3.2   Alternative routes for ancestral platyrrhines. From Fleagle, J. G. 1999. *Primate Adaptation and Evolution*, Second Edition. New York: Academic Press. Reprinted with permission of the publisher and author, © 1999 Academic Press.

During much of the Miocene, which spans from 23.3 to 5.2 mya, primates could have moved more easily between Africa and Asia because the Tethyus Sea had not yet completely split into what today are the Mediterranean, Black, Caspian, and Aral Seas. Indeed, faunal exchanges between Africa and Asia are consistent with both fossil and molecular evidence for the evolution of catarrhines during this epoch (Stewart and Disotell, 1998).

Miocene Monkeys and Apes

The fossil record of Old World monkeys and apes is much more complete than it is for New World monkeys, which may have always been more restricted to forested or moist woodland habitats where fossil preservation is poor. The oldest Miocene primates have been found in Africa, but similar specimens appear in Europe and Asia a few million years later. The early Miocene (23.3 to 16.3 mya) marks the emergence of ancestral hominoids, which are distinguishable from monkeys by their uniquely five-cusped molars, referred to as a Y-5 pattern. The oldest hominoids were a diverse group that includes the genus, *Kenyapithecus,* and the newly discovered genus, *Equatorius,* which may represent an important link between the earlier African hominoids and later ones from Europe and Asia (Ward, et al., 1999). Indeed, while hominoid fossils from the middle Miocene are rare in Africa, numerous finds have been recovered in Europe and Asia. One group of Eurasian hominoids, from the genus *Sivapithecus,* is thought to be the ancestor from which orangutans diverged some 13–14 mya; another may have returned to Africa by about 10 mya (Stewart and Disotell, 1998).

The late Miocene (8 to 5.2 mya) included the last common ancestor of today's African hominoids. Climatic changes during the Miocene reduced much of what had been forest to much drier, more open habitats. The associated decline in the diversity of hominoids was followed by the appearance of a diversity of monkeys (Jablonski and Kelley, 1997; Kelley 1998). Molecular data indicate that by about 14 mya, the Old World monkeys had already split into the two major divisions, cercopithecines and colobines, we know today, but their fossils don't begin to appear until 9–10 mya. Like the Miocene hominoids before them, first some of these ancestral colobines spread to Europe and Asia, and then, about 5 mya, some of the ancestral cercopithecines followed them (Delson, 1994).

Pliocene Highlights

Colobines and cercopithecines persisted throughout the Pliocene (5.2 to 1.6 mya) in Africa, Europe, and Asia, just as the New World monkeys persisted in South America. The African savanna grasslands continued to expand and replace tropical forests, and one group of cercopithecines, ancestral to modern-day gelada baboons, became widespread. Gelada baboons are now found only in the highlands of Ethiopia (Figure 3.3), but during the Pliocene, a gigantic ancestral gelada, with huge jaws and teeth equipped for crushing and grinding grass, was more widely distributed.

The Pliocene is also the period when the first fossil evidence of bipedal primates appears in East African volcanic deposits and South African caves. Ancestral

FIGURE 3.3   Two gelada baboon (*Theropithecus gelada*) one-male units in the Simen Mountains, Ethiopia. Photo by R. I. M. Dunbar.

chimpanzees and gorillas left almost no traces, perhaps because their teeth and bones decomposed so quickly in the wetter forests they are thought to have inhabited. Indeed, what factors led our ancestors to shift to bipedal locomotion and more open habitats remains a mystery that neither the fossil record nor comparisons with living primates have yet been able to resolve (Box 3.1).

Pleistocene Glaciations

The Pleistocene (1.6 million to 12,000 years ago) was a tumultuous epoch for the evolution of primates because of the effects of the glacial and interglacial events on their habitats. During the Pleistocene glaciations, global cooling led the world's tropical forests, which depend on water, to contract in size. The result was that many large tracts of continuous forest were fragmented into smaller forest **refuges** (Figure 3.4). Areas of what is now the vast Amazon were converted to grasslands, and the Brazilian Atlantic forest was split into at least three isolated regions. Animals and plants throughout the tropics became geographically isolated from other members of their species as they withdrew into the remaining forests, or refuges, that persisted.

When the forests expanded during the interglacials, some populations had differentiated to the point that they could no longer interbreed. Other populations never reestablished contact, and have continued to evolve in isolation from one another ever since. Still others took advantage of the changing borders of the forests, thriving as specialists on the regenerating vegetation that grows along forest edges.

The concentration of primates into these refuges led to high levels of species **endemism,** or their geographic restriction in highly localized regions. Areas with many endemic species today might have served as refuges during the Pleistocene glaciations (Figure 3.5).

FIGURE 3.4 A juvenile black-headed uacari (*Cacajao melanocephalus melanocephalus*) foraging for ants on a branch. *Cacajao melanocephalus* and *C. calvus* were previously thought to have diverged during the Pleistocene fragmentation of the Amazon, but new molecular analyses using mtDNA now date the divergence of these species back to the Pliocene (Boubli and Ditchfield, 2000). Photo by Jean P. Boubli.

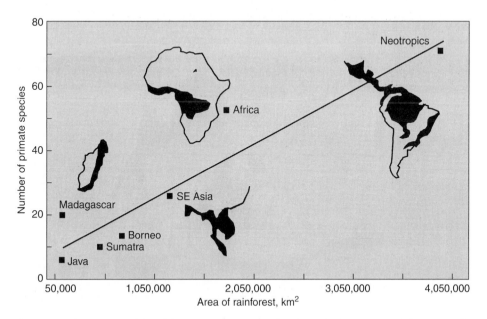

FIGURE 3.5 The number of primate species on islands and continents is a function of the area of tropical forest. From Fleagle, J. G. 1999. *Primate Adaptation and Evolution,* Second Edition. New York: Academic Press. Reprinted with permission of the publisher and author, © 1999 Academic Press.

BOX **3.1**

Mosaic Nature of Human Evolution

It is easy to distinguish modern humans from other living primates, but this is not always the case when fossilized bones and teeth are the only clues we have to go on. Confusing these distinctions even further is the fact that the three major systems we can decipher from fossils—locomotion and posture, chewing and food processing, and cranial capacity—evolved at different rates in hominids, resulting in what is called the **mosaic nature of human evolution** (McHenry, 1975).

Bipedality, with its upright stance and two-legged locomotion, has become the main distinguishing feature of early hominids (Figure B3.1). The first bipedal hominids may not have been as efficient on two legs as we are today, partly because they retained greater flexibility in their ankle joints that would be helpful in climbing. Over at least a 2 million-year period, bipedal hominids diversified into multiple species. Some became heavier, more robust creatures whose teeth and jaws imply a rough, fibrous diet. Others retained their lighter, more generalized dentition. But none of those early bipedal hominids had brains much bigger than other apes of similar body size.

This first set of bipedal hominids and their relatively small-brained descendants have been grouped into a variety of species in the *Australopithecus* genus. The traits that set the first members of our own genus, *Homo,* apart from the australopithecines are related, in part, to our bigger brain-to-body size ratio (Wood and Collard, 1999; Wood, 1992; Sherwood, et al., 2002). For example, both increased cranial capacity and shifts in the pressures and forces associated with eating cause changes in the shape of the skull.

FIGURE B3.1   Two olive baboons (*Papio anubis*) looking at a pride of lions. Most primates can stand on two legs for brief periods of time, and do so to gain a vantage point when visibility is obscure. Photo by Irven DeVore/Anthro-Photo.

Other changes associated with hominid dietary strategies inferred from the fossil record may have been direct results of locomotor shifts and either results of or causes for changes in the brain (Box 2.1).

Bipedality is not a superior mode of locomotion in every respect, and there is wide disagreement about the selective pressures that might have led to its evolution in the first place (Steudel, 1996). Some researchers believe that the benefits of traveling long distances between food resources or shelter may have provided the selective pressures that made bipedality such a successful adaptation. Others suggest that it grew out of the upright feeding postures that prehominid ancestors had begun to adopt. Still others have argued that bipedality was beneficial for cooling the body because of the greater surface area exposed for evaporation (Wheeler, 1985). Indeed, from this perspective, cool bipedality was a key factor that permitted the evolution—and cooling—of large hominid brains.

Holocene

Endemic primates are among the most endangered ones today (Table 3.2). Their restricted distributions and habitat specializations make them particularly vulnerable to ecological perturbations and hunting and logging pressures from humans. By the beginning of the Holocene, some 12,000 years ago, anatomically modern humans had penetrated most corners of the world. Some were already growing crops and raising livestock, others pursued more traditional hunting and gathering lifestyles that persist today. For the most part, however, human population densities were low enough that their impact on other primates and primate habitats was minimal. Human migrations into Australia tens of thousands of years ago have been linked to the extinctions of large mammalian and avian fauna due primarily to burning vegetation and secondarily to hunting (Miller, et al., 1999). However, it has only been during the last century, as human populations have exploded and global market economies for tropical timber and exotic animals have expanded, that our devastating effects on primates have become so evident.

Most primates today are restricted to the equatorial belt defined by the Tropic of Cancer in the north and the Tropic of Capricorn in the south, within 20° latitude of the equator (Figure 3.6). Most also occur at low altitudes. Compared to temperate and high altitude zones, the tropics are characterized by high rainfall, high plant species diversity and productivity, and low seasonality. Primate species diversity is strongly associated with annual rainfall throughout all but the Asian continent (Reed and Fleagle, 1995). The large brains and high metabolisms of primates require lots of energy compared to other kinds of mammals, and temperate climates are too seasonal for most primates to find sufficient foods to sustain themselves year-round (Figure 3.7).

Seasonality in rainfall and temperature characteristic of temperate latitudes results in discontinuous growing seasons for plants, many of which shed their leaves. Finding sufficient food in the dry, cold winters and maintaining their body temperatures are challenges that only a few kinds of primates have evolved to meet. Primates that live in seasonal temperate latitudes or at high altitudes tend to occur

TABLE 3.2 Categories for threatened taxa*

Category	Criteria
Extinct (EX)	The last individual of a taxon has died.
Extinct in the Wild (EW)	The only survivors of a taxon occur in captivity or in an introduced setting far from its natural range.
Critically Endangered (CR)	The taxon faces an extremely high risk of extinction in the wild in the immediate future. Criteria for risks include: *Population reduction:* $\geq$ 80 percent over ten years or three generations from any cause, or *Extent of distribution:* < 100 km^2 or area of occupancy < 10 km^2 (including severe fragmentation), or *Population size:* < 250 mature individuals with an estimated decline of 25 percent within three years or one generation or no subpopulation with more than fifty mature individuals, or *Total population:* < 50 mature individuals, or *Extinction probability:* $\geq$ 50 percent within ten years or three generations.
Endangered (EN)	High risk of extinction in near future. Criteria for risks include: *Population reduction:* $\geq$ 50 percent over ten years or three generations from any cause, or *Extent of distribution:* < 5,000 km^2 or area of occupancy < 500 km^2 (including severe fragmentation), or *Population size:* < 2,500 mature individuals with an estimated decline of 20 percent within five years or two generations or no subpopulation with more than 250 mature individuals, or *Total population:* < 250 mature individuals, or *Extinction probability:* $\geq$ 20 percent within ten years or five generations
Vulnerable (VU)	High risk of extinction in the medium-term future. Criteria for risks include: *Population reduction:* $\geq$ 20 percent over ten years or three generations from any cause, or *Extent of distribution:* < 20,000 km^2 or area of occupancy < 2,000 km^2 (including severe fragmentation), or *Population size:* < 10,000 mature individuals with an estimated decline of 10 percent within ten years or three generations or no subpopulation with more than 1,000 mature individuals, or *Total population:* < 1,000 mature individuals, or *Extinction probability:* $\geq$ 10 percent within one hundred years
Lower Risk (LR)	Subdivided into three categories: *Conservation dependent (cd):* Without ongoing conservation activities, the taxon would qualify for one of the threatened categories within five years; *Near threatened (nt):* Close to vulnerable category; *Least concern (lc):* Neither Conservation dependent nor Near threatened
Data Deficient (DD)	More information is required to evaluate the taxon
Not Evaluated (NE)	The criteria for classification have not been assessed

*Summarized from the IUCN (The World Conservation Union) Red List Categories, as prepared by the IUCN Species Survival Commission, 1994. See the IUCN (1994) printed version for the complete, original descriptions of categories and their criteria or the IUCN website.

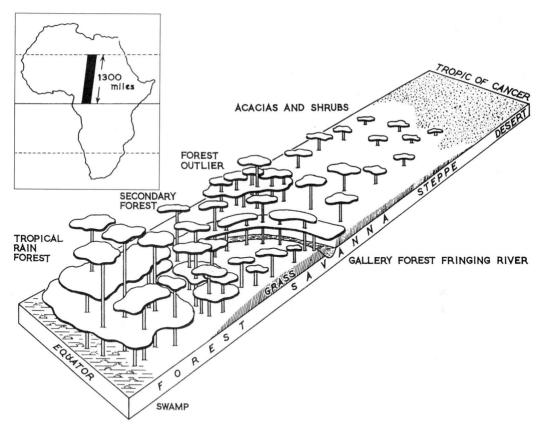

FIGURE 3.6 Vegetation zones from the equator to the Tropic of Cancer. From Napier, J. R. and Napier, P. H., 1994. *The Natural History of the Primates*, Fig. 1.3, p. 10. Cambridge: The MIT Press. Copyright © 1994, The MIT Press. Reprinted by permission of The MIT Press.

FIGURE 3.7 Japanese macaques (*Macaca fuscata*), in contrast to most primates, live at high latitudes, in highly seasonal environments. The author (*Homo sapiens*) is also shown. Photo by Jim Moore/Anthro-Photo.

at lower densities and be larger, furrier, and shorter limbed and tailed than those that occur in tropical latitudes and at lower altitudes. Within the tropics, the greatest diversity of primates is found in rainforests, where plant growth is continuous year-round and plant diversity is high. Some of the Old World primates that have adopted terrestrial lifestyles, such as ring-tailed lemurs, macaques, baboons, vervet monkeys, and patas monkeys, are found in tropical savanna and grassland biomes where annual rainfall is low and highly seasonal, while a few, such as the sportive lemur and Hamadryas baboon, inhabit desert-like biomes in Madagascar and Ethiopia, respectively (Sussman, 1999a).

Interpreting Diversity Today

Nowadays, as in past epochs, we measure the diversity of primates and particular taxonomic groups of primates by the number of species that occur. **Species** have traditionally been considered the largest "real" biological unit, defined as a set of individuals who can interbreed and produce viable offspring. But, for a variety of reasons, including natural isolation of their habitats as mountains or seas spring up, and the more rapid effects of human habitat destruction, the opportunities for interbreeding among members of the same species may be disrupted. Over time, members of isolated populations subjected to different local environmental conditions may begin to differentiate genetically, morphologically, and even behaviorally, from members of their own species in other isolated populations. The high incidence of **supernumerary,** or accessory, **nipples** found in Formosan macaques at Mt. Longevity, Taiwan compared to other macaques elsewhere may be an example of how a small, isolated population can differentiate from other members of its kind (Hsu, et al., 2000). Reductions in the body size of marine iguanas in the Galapagos Sea have been associated with recent El Niño events that have led to a reduction in their food supplies (Wikelski and Thom, 2000). With enough time, these differences may accumulate to the point that **subspecies** or **races** are recognized. With the passage of many generations, these isolated populations may diverge so much that they are no longer considered members of the same species.

The process of diversification into subspecies and even species is still occurring today. Habitat disturbances caused by humans are fragmenting the geographic distributions of primate species, and may ultimately alter their evolutionary paths. Unless small, isolated populations have opportunities to expand or exchange genes, their evolutionary futures as subspecies or new species are likely to be brief.

Intraspecific Variation

Recognizing the variation represented by nearly 600 **taxa** of primates, instead of the 240 or so traditional species, is increasingly common (Mittermeier, et al., 1999, 2000). In some cases, these subspecies represent single local populations that have been isolated for long periods, but that can nonetheless interbreed with individuals from other isolated populations of their species in captivity.

While it may seem like a trivial or semantic disagreement, distinctions between species, subspecies, or populations have important implications both for the preservation of biological diversity and for comparative models of behavior. For example, two populations of the same species living under quite different ecological conditions may differ more from one another in their diets, ranging patterns, or social organization than they differ from other closely related species. Understanding the range of **intraspecific variation,** and how it compares to **interspecific variation,** or the behavioral differences between species, provides a way of identifying behavioral traits that respond to ecological conditions as opposed to traits that are under less flexible phylogenetic control.

Scientists who emphasize variation at the level of subspecies tend to fall into the category of taxonomic **splitters,** whereas those who emphasize similarities at this level tend to fall into the category of taxonomic **lumpers.** Splitters might divide the northern and southern populations of muriquis, which are geographically isolated but can nonetheless interbreed in captivity (Pissinatti, et al., 1998) into separate subspecies or species, whereas lumpers would consider them regional varieties of the same species (Strier and Fonseca, 1996/1997; Rylands, et al., 1997).

Both splitters and lumpers rely on knowledge of variation in traits among living species, which may be morphological, genetic, or behavioral. Behavioral variation among populations is poorly understood because there are still only a small number of species that have been studied for long periods at multiple sites. Generalizations based on a single study group or population to an entire species tend to result in an underestimate of the actual degree of intraspecific variation. Comparing these narrowly based generalizations across species can lead to an overestimation of interspecific variation (Strier, 1997a). Only additional data will be able to resolve these dilemmas, and until we have the data, theoretical implications must be treated with caution.

Local Population Variability

Local selection pressures may favor a different phenotype in different environments. If populations have been geographically or reproductively isolated from one another for long periods of time, they can begin to differentiate from one another due to different selection pressures in their local environments or to random processes of **genetic drift,** in which certain genes become common in a population independent of their adaptive value to the individuals who carry them. Unlike genes with deleterious effects, which will be selected against, or those with positive effects, which are selected for, **neutral mutations,** or genetic variants that have no effects on an individual's fitness, may drift without any particular selection pressures at work.

Blood group types may be one such example of genetic drift among humans, although there is also evidence for differences in disease resistance that may reflect selection pressures as well (Molnar, 2002). Distinct styles of hand-clasping by different populations of chimpanzees (Figure 3.8) may be an example of behavioral drift among primates (McGrew, 1998; McGrew and Tutin, 1978). But, if traits affected

FIGURE 3.8   Adult female and male chimpanzees (*Pan troglodytes*) at Mahale National Park, Tanzania engage in grooming hand-clasp. The female has a sleeping infant in her groin cradle. Different populations and different groups in the same population do the grooming hand-clasp differently (McGrew, et al., 2001). Photo by W. C. McGrew.

by genetic drift were to lead to reproductive isolation between populations, the outcome might be separate species that could no longer interbreed successfully.

Many primate populations have experienced geographic isolation from one another over many generations due to natural climatic events and, more recently, to human disturbances of their habitats. How much they differentiate from one another will depend on how long they have been isolated, how large and variable their populations were at the time of isolation, and local ecological conditions that may have selected for different traits among the variations originally present in each population. When individuals from different populations subsequently encounter one another, either in the wild, if continuity in their habitats is restored, or due to human intervention in the wild or in captivity, the extent of these accumulated differences will determine whether or not they can still interbreed. Distinguishing how much population variation justifies designations as subspecies or separate species has significant consequences for conservation strategies, as well as for understanding intra- and interspecific variation in primate behavior.

Consider the case of chimpanzees and bonobos, which are taxonomically divided into two species of the genus *Pan*. Bonobos (*Pan paniscus*) occur only in a small pocket of forest, isolated by bends in the Congo River from their chimpanzee cousins, *Pan troglodytes,* which occur from western Africa, to central Africa, to eastern Africa. With their more extensive distribution, chimpanzees have now been divided into four subspecies based on geographic location and genetic, morphological, and behavioral differences among them (Gonder, et al., 1997). Recent genetic analyses have found the greatest variation *within* populations of the west African subspecies, which also are in danger of extinction (Morin, et al., 1994).

Discriminating among alternative taxonomic classifications for chimpanzees may seem like a trivial debate, but in fact, it has serious implications for their conservation. Population surveys indicate that western chimpanzees are facing greater risks of extinction, whereas the eastern subspecies is in less immediate danger although local populations are at risk. International laws on the capture and transport of endangered or threatened animals have traditionally used the species classification as the unit of protection, so technically, despite the fact that western chimpanzees are endangered, they lack special protection status under the Committee on International Trade of Endangered Species (C.I.T.E.S.) regulations. By reclassifying western chimpanzees as endangered species, distinct from the more abundant eastern chimpanzee, they can benefit by stronger protective measures.

The Status of Hybrids.   Debates about the appropriate level of classification to recognize in protective regulatory laws extend beyond species and subspecies to include **hybrids.** Hybrids are genetically unique individuals that are the product of fertile matings between two different species. Some hybrids can interbreed successfully with members of either of their parents' species if the opportunity to do so arises and may even benefit by doing so under certain conditions (Veen, et al., 2001), but the place of hybrids in both taxonomy and conservation is highly enigmatic. For example, the endangered Florida panther once belonged to a subspecies of puma (also called cougars or mountain lions) that ranged through the southern United States. Habitat destruction isolated the Florida population from others of its kind, and reduced its population to a mere fifty or so individuals, which were highly inbred. Conservation interests stimulated genetic studies, which subsequently revealed that the Florida panther had interbred with some hybrid North American and South American puma that had been released from captivity into the wild. As a hybrid, the protected status of the Florida panther was threatened for a time because the original Hybrid Policy of the U.S. Endangered Species Act did not technically include them (O'Brien and Mayr, 1991).

Naturally occurring hybrids emerge whenever the geographic ranges of different species overlap with one another and the species still recognize one another as potential mates and are capable of producing viable offspring. Among primates, the best-studied hybrid zones are in eastern Africa, where hamadryas baboons (*Papio hamadryas*) and olive baboons (*Papio anubis*) have overlapping distributions. In the Awash valley of Ethiopia, individuals from each species interbreed. Their hybrid offspring vary in appearance, and are capable of (and do) reproduce successfully themselves (Box 3.2). Neither of these baboon species is classified as endangered, and Clifford Jolly and Jane Phillips-Conroy, who have been following these hybrids

BOX **3.2**

Hybrid Baboons

In the Awash National Park, Ethiopia, two baboon species live side by side. One is the olive baboon, *Papio anubis,* which lives in cohesive, multi-male, multi-female matrilineal societies like other common savanna baboons. The other is the hamadryas baboon, *Papio hamadryas,* which has a multi-level society based on patrilineal kinship. The smallest level of their society is the one-male unit (OMU), comprised of a male who essentially collects females into his unit. Two or three related males and the females in their OMUs forage together during the daytime in a clan. Social interactions occur more frequently among clan members than between members from different clans. These clans, along with single, unattached males, form a band. Males within bands are related to one another, and females typically switch between OMUs of different bands. Bands join up at night, into troops, to sleep on rocky cliffs where they are safe from predators (Stammbach, 1987).

Male hamadryas keep their females together in their OMUs by herding them with nips on the neck. Females form attachments with the male in their unit, grooming him and following him throughout their estrous and nonestrous cycles. Female attachments last only until the male of their OMU is deposed by a younger, more vigorous male.

Most hamadryas males stick within their bands, waiting patiently until they can take over or inherit an established OMU, gain access to its females while the older male leads the group, or herd a juvenile or subadult female into their own initial OMU (Kummer, 1968, 1995). Occasionally, both young bachelor males and older deposed males may try their luck elsewhere, and as a result, end up leading very different sorts of lives. Not only do they exchange the company of the male kin in their band, they also exchange the company of their species (Figure B3.2).

The migration of hamadryas males into neighboring olive baboon troops has been part of a long-term study in this baboon hybrid zone conducted by primatologists Jane Phillips-Conroy and Cliff Jolly and their colleagues (1991, 1992). Called "cross-migrants," the behavior of these males is something of a puzzle. Their immigration into an adopted olive baboon troop is probably not too different from that of olive baboon males, who routinely disperse from their natal troops and matrilineal kin. Once in these troops, hamadryas males employ their hamadryas social skills by trying to attach themselves to females and to get the females to follow them. But olive baboon females don't respond to the same cues that their hamadryas sisters do, especially between estrous cycles when they're less interested in following males around. As a result, attachments between olive baboon males and females are short-lived compared to those that hamadryas males establish with their own kind of females. Without the cooperation of their patrilineal kin in respecting their claims on females (Bachman and Kummer, 1980; Stammbach, 1987), or the collaboration of females who are willing to follow them, cross-migrant males can't maintain their hamadryas habits.

Despite these difficulties, cross-migrant hamadryas males still manage to mate with olive baboon females. Hybrid offspring they produce behave differently from either parent, and hybrid sons look more like hamadryas while hybrid daughters look more

FIGURE B3.2   Hamadryas (*Papio hamadryas*) and olive baboon (*P. anubis*) hybrid. This male has been sedated for a physical examination, and will be monitored as part of the long-term Awash baboon project. Note the physical differences between this hybrid and the one shown in Figure 3.9. Photograph taken by Jane Phillips-Conroy.

like olive baboons (Phillips-Conroy and Jolly, 1981). The fact that these hybrids are also fertile raises questions about both species' taxonomic status. Phillips-Conroy and her colleagues (1991) are careful to point out that this hybrid zone is one of many ancient ones, in which opportunities for interbreeding between various baboon species have historically existed, and which have routinely produced fertile hybrids (Jolly, 1993). However, they also note that human ranching activities, which keep the vegetation from regenerating, may be compounding the pressures on cross-migrants and lead to increased hybridization between these species in this area.

Human activities may also be spurring a new hybrid zone, as olive baboons from the slopes of Mt. Kilimanjaro immigrate down into the yellow baboon population in Amboseli National Park (Alberts and Altmann, 2001). Like olive-hamadryas hybrids in Ethiopia, the olive-yellow baboon hybrids at Amboseli look and behave in distinctive ways. Most notable is the tendency of these hybrid males to disperse from their natal groups earlier than purebred yellow baboons, but whether this is because they are evicted sooner or have inherited a greater propensity for dispersal is not know.

during their long-term field study, think that they should be reclassified as subspecies instead of kept as two species (Phillips-Conroy, et al., 1992), despite the striking differences in their social behavior (Figure 3.9).

A very different kind of case has been made for squirrel monkeys, which are widely employed in biomedical research, often without much, if any, consideration of their taxonomic status. Yet, analyses of genetic, morphological, and behavioral variation among squirrel monkey species suggest that the use of hybrids as experimental subjects could lead to distorted results (Boinski and Cropp, 1999). In other words, taxonomic distinctions, including species and hybrid identifications, should be taken into account before interpreting research findings.

The Status of New Species.   Understanding the biological significance of population variation is also important because "new" species of primates are still being discovered. In 1987, researchers discovered a species of lemur that had been thought to be extinct in a remote tract of forest on the island of Madagascar (Box 3.3). In 1990, a new species of lion tamarin was discovered in a city park in the state of São Paulo, Brazil. Since then, at least seven new species of marmosets have been discovered in pockets of the vast Amazon rainforest (van Roosmalen, et al., 2000). Similar strides have been made in discovering new species of nocturnal primates. There are now 74 species recognized, an increase of nearly 300 percent in 30 years (Bearder, 1999).

The discovery of new primate species and remnant populations of species that were thought to be extinct is a humbling reminder of how little we know about many of the tropical forests that primates still inhabit. International politics, limited funding for systematic surveys, and the remoteness of many areas have combined to restrict where and when scientists can work. Most wild primates are unaccustomed to seeing humans as anything other than deadly predators, so finding them for scientific observations requires skill as well as time and luck. Photographing or collecting primate specimens is even more difficult, so when new findings are reported they routinely make the major newspaper headlines as well as scientific publications.

FIGURE 3.9 Hamadryas (*Papio hamadryas*) and olive baboon (*P. anubis*) hybrid. The ear-tag helps researchers to identify and monitor individuals over years. Photograph taken by Jane Phillips-Conroy.

Newly discovered primate species are often identified on the basis of morphological characteristics that distinguish them from other known species. These traits may include unique patterns of fur coloration or appendages, such as the special, bright orange labialike flesh surrounding the genitals of the Amazonian marmoset, *Callithrix saterei*, discovered in early 1996. Nocturnal species, by contrast, are most often distinguished by their vocalizations, which affect their social systems, and especially how they identify and attract mates (Bearder, 1999; Zimmermann, et al., 2000). The use of vocalizations and molecular data to distinguish cryptic species has expanded our knowledge of the diversity of nocturnal primates, including many that were previously unknown (Figure 3.10). Assigning these newly discovered primates to their own species makes sense, at least until more is learned about them and their closest relatives. As the splitters legitimately assert, it may be safer to recognize and preserve existing variation, as we now understand it, than to ignore it by lumping distinct populations in with more widely distributed species (Rylands, et al., 1995).

You may find yourself agreeing that splitting variant forms into separate species is a more cautious approach from the perspective of primate conservation, but, it is still important to appreciate that practical or political motives, however

FIGURE 3.10 The woolly lemur (*Avahi laniger*) is one of many nocturnal prosimians. Photo by David Haring.

BOX **3.3**

Lucky Lemurs

The island of Madagascar began to drift away from mainland Africa more than 165 million years ago. The primates arrived there 40 million years ago by floating on tree trunks and clumps of vegetation. Their descendants are still the only nonhuman primates on the island. By the time humans arrived, under 2,000 years ago, the ancestral lemurs had diversified into at least forty-five species (Tattersall, 1993). One-third of these species have gone extinct as a result of hunting and habitat alterations caused by humans. However, research expeditions during the 1980s have found that at least some of these supposedly extinct species can be counted as survivors.

During a 1986 expedition, Bernhard Meier and Patricia Wright independently set out to follow leads on the greater bamboo lemur, a five-pound creature that hadn't been seen in the wild since 1972 (Wright, 1988). Not only did these researchers rediscover this rare species, but they also discovered a new species, the golden bamboo lemur (Meier, et al., 1987), living side by side (Figure B3.3).

The greater bamboo lemur and the newly anointed golden bamboo lemur share a forest called Ranomafana, on the eastern coast of Madagascar, with a third species of bamboo lemur. Not surprisingly, all three of these species eat bamboo, although they focus on different parts of the plant (Wright, 1988). At first, none of the researchers were sure what they'd found. There were physical differences in fur color and markings between the greater bamboo lemur and the smaller, golden type, and subsequently, genetic differences were found (Meier, et al., 1987). There were also evident behavioral differences. The pair-bonded family groups of the golden bamboo lemur and their cathemeral habits differed

FIGURE B3.3   The elusive golden bamboo lemur (*Hapalemur aureus*). Photo by © Noel Rowe/*Pictorial Guide to Living Primates.*

from the greater bamboo lemur's uni-male and multi-male groups and more nocturnal activities (Rowe, 1996). Both species give a "raucous" call, but the greater bamboo lemur's call begins with a purr.

Finding a new species and rediscovering a rare one in the same forest makes a strong case for conserving one of their last remaining strongholds. Working closely with Malagasy scientists and conservationists, the primate researchers helped to turn Ranomafana into a National Park in 1991 where both long-term research and conservation efforts coincide (Wright, 1994).

Other lemurs have also gotten found and rediscovered. In 1987, the golden-crowned sifaka was announced to the scientific world (Simons, 1988). It had previously been seen in 1974, but was mistakenly classified as a variant on the more common diademed sifaka known to live in the area. Like the case of the bamboo lemurs, physical differences between the two sifaka species raised some suspicions. But in both cases, it was the application of chromosomal analyses that established their distinctiveness.

Chromosomal analyses are also revealing that many other lemurs previously classified as single species are actually genetically distinct enough to represent multiple species (Rowe, 1996). As a result, the diversity of living lemurs may be even higher than has commonly been thought.

Not all lemurs will be as lucky as the Ranomafana lemurs in stimulating successful efforts to get their habitats protected (Jolly, 1988). But naming a new species is a strong call to arms to conservation-minded Malagasy who, like other citizens of other primate habitat countries, are taking an increasingly active stance in protecting their natural heritage.

---

well-intentioned, are not a substitute for science. It will take a much deeper understanding of intraspecific variation in primates to make informed decisions about the diversity of primate species today, and about interpreting species diversity in the past.

Implications for Primate Behavioral Ecology

Understanding primate diversity at a taxonomic level also has important implications for how we interpret their behavioral diversity. Comparisons among primates have traditionally relied on species-level averages, in which data from different study sites, study groups, or the same study group over time are compressed into a single value. While such average values may be useful for generalized comparisons, they end up reducing the many diverse sources of behavioral variation among primates to taxonomy (Strier, 1997a). In the process, phylogenetic constraints on behavior may be emphasized at the expense of ecological or demographic determinants, even when within species differences are greater than those between or among distantly related species. Distinguishing between conservative, phylogenetically determined behaviors and more labile behavioral responses to local conditions is only possible when intra- and interspecific variation can be directly compared (Bernstein, 1999a; Fuentes, 1999).

Consider the differences between Bornean and Sumatran orangutans, which are thought to be separate subspecies (Delgado and van Schaik, 2000). Both subspecies have been studied at a variety of sites, but differences in their behavior do not follow geographic or taxonomic divisions. For example, some populations of Sumatran orangutans use tools to extract insects such as ants and termites from tree holes and edible seeds from fruits (van Schaik and Fox, 1996), but these practices are not found in all Sumatran orangutans and have never been observed in the orangutans of Borneo. Tool-using Sumatran orangutans are particularly adept at using twigs to pry the nutritious seeds of fruits in the genus *Neesia* away from the irritating hairs in which the seeds are embedded (Figure 3.11). *Neesia* seeds are also eaten by orangutans elsewhere, but without the aid of tools to extract them (van Schaik, et al., 1999; van Schaik and Knott, 2001).

Accounting for this behavioral variation has led researchers to correlate the geographic distribution of orangutan tool-use with factors other than those related to taxonomy. For example, Sumatran orangutan populations that use tools live at higher densities and are more socially tolerant toward one another than either Sumatran or Bornean orangutan populations that don't use tools. Both high population density and social tolerance could facilitate the social transmission of novel tool-using inventions, such as those associated with the extraction of *Neesia* seeds (van Schaik and Knott, 2001), independent of the subspecies in which they occur.

FIGURE 3.11   Orangutan tool use.
Illustration by Perry van Duijnhoven.

Similar cases of population variation in object-use and other social traditions have been described in chimpanzees (Whiten, et al., 1999), gorillas (Parnell and Buchanan-Smith, 2001), and capuchin monkeys (Boinski, et al., 2001; Ottoni and Mannu, 2001; Panger, 1999). Some of these behavioral traditions, such as the water splashing displays in which western lowland gorillas engage, can be attributed to the standing water and long range visibility that are found only in the swampy areas that they frequent (Parnell and Buchanan-Smith, 2001), but others, such as the tool-use associated with *Neesia* seed extraction by some orangutans, do not correspond so directly to ecological opportunities. A new area of research, known as **cultural primatology,** has developed in response to the growing evidence for intraspecific behavioral variation that may represent local traditions, or even **cultural traditions.** We'll return to this intriguing topic when we consider its implications for understanding primate learning and cognitive abilities in Chapter 10, but first let's look more closely at the theory and evidence underlying the behavioral adaptations of primates.

CHAPTER

4

Evolution and Social Behavior

It had been a typical day with the baboons. In the morning, they climbed down from the cluster of trees they had slept in that night and set out at a leisurely pace across the savanna (Figure 4.1). Along the way, they gobbled up caterpillars that were sunning themselves in the tall grass and munched on the corms, or the underground storage organs of the savanna grasses, they paused to dig up. I was with Jeffrey Stelzner, the Cornell University graduate student on whose doctoral study I had been assigned to assist.

The forty-some members of the troop were spread out, with Dogo, a young adult male, in his usual place along the periphery of the troop. Dogo was old

FIGURE 4.1   Yellow baboons (*Papio cynocephalus*) under sleeping trees at Amboseli National Park. Photo by K. B. Strier.

enough to leave his natal troop to join another troop where he would be able to begin his reproductive career. Meanwhile, he kept his distance from the older males in the troop, as if to avoid calling any unnecessary attention to his continued presence. Dogo's mother, still reproductively active herself, was occupied with keeping track of her younger offspring and finding food.

Suddenly, there was chaos. The baboons started screaming and shrieking and scrambling up the few tall trees that were growing nearby. We followed the direction of the baboons' hysteria to determine its source. What we saw in the distance was Dogo, with a hyena in close pursuit.

It seemed like the duo was running in slow motion, but it was evident that Dogo had nowhere to go. He was too far away to reach the trees where the other baboons had taken refuge and there weren't any other trees closer to him. The hyena was gaining ground and made a lunge for Dogo's flank just when one other baboon appeared on the scene, chasing the hyena and screaming in a valiant effort to buy Dogo time to escape from its predatory jaws.

It wasn't one of the large adult males, who are formidably equipped with canines, that tried to intervene on Dogo's behalf. Instead, it was an adult female, who wasn't even Dogo's mother!

At half the size of baboon males, the female was no match for the hyena, who ultimately dragged Dogo's corpse into the bushes and devoured it (Stelzner and Strier, 1981). Although her efforts were unsuccessful, by coming to Dogo's aid, this female, but not Dogo's mother, risked possible fatal injuries to herself. But why? As we'll see in this chapter, evolutionary theory provides a possible explanation for why Dogo's mother might not have been willing to risk her own life for the sake of her son's.

Natural Selection

Primate morphological and behavioral adaptations are the products of evolutionary processes that select for the traits that benefit the fitness of the individuals who carry them. By evolution's definition, the most "fit" individuals under the ecological conditions prevailing at any particular time will pass on more of their genes to future generations. Technically, this means that individuals with the highest fitness are those that produce the greatest numbers of surviving offspring, who produce more offspring themselves, and so on. Because offspring inherit 50 percent of their genes from their mothers and 50 percent from their fathers, the frequencies of parental genes passed down to each generation are a direct result of the number of offspring that parents produce. Genes that increase fitness will be increasingly represented in a population over time. Evolution is measured by the changes in these gene frequencies.

New genetic material enters populations through a variety of mechanisms, including random mutations, recombination in sexually reproducing organisms, and the immigration and subsequent interbreeding of individuals from other populations. Many people interested in primates are already well acquainted with the biology underlying the evolutionary process, and with the role Charles Darwin played in developing the theory of natural selection. However, because natural selection and its genetic basis are so fundamental to evolutionary theories of primate behavioral ecology, it is worthwhile to review some of the most basic of these principles here.

Charles Darwin knew nothing about genes or the mechanisms of genetic inheritance when he left his homeland in England to embark on a five-year voyage as the naturalist on the *H.M.S. Beagle*. Nonetheless, by the time his ship left the Galapagos Islands off the coast of Ecuador, he had begun to formulate his theory of evolution by **natural selection,** which he presented, along with another biologist, Alfred Russell Wallace, to the scientific community in 1858 and to the wider public when his book, *On the Origin of Species by Means of Natural Selection,* was published in 1859.

Darwin was fascinated by the diversity of birds he had seen on the Galapagos Islands, and was impressed by the way in which the different beaks of each species seemed distinctively well suited for the types of foods that they ate on each of the islands. Other naturalists at the time also recognized the remarkable degree to which visible differences in the structures of morphological traits, such as beaks, were matched with observed differences in their apparent functions, such as feeding on hard seeds or soft insects. What distinguished Darwin was his search for an explanatory process that could account for the consistency of these patterns.

Darwin's reasoning was strongly influenced by British economist Thomas Malthus's 1799 publication, *Essay on the Principle of Population,* which described a "struggle for existence" among individuals as populations reproduced beyond the limits of their food supplies. From Darwin's perspective, variation among individuals would lead some to fare better than others in this competitive struggle. Those that did well would leave more offspring, whose inheritance of their parents' adaptive traits would result in changes in the population over successive generations. Eventually, such changes would lead to the formation of new species that were well adapted to their respective lifestyles.

Competition over food among the descendants of the ancestral finches that arrived on the Galapagos Islands might have selected for individuals whose particular beaks permitted them to eat different kinds of food. Natural selection would favor these varieties, creating diverse species that differed from one another in their diets, and thus avoided competition with one another (Grant and Grant, 2002).

Although little was known about primate evolution during Darwin's lifetime, we can now see how the process of natural selection might explain the diversity of primate species that survive today. For example, the shift to folivory among Old World colobines like langurs, with their specialized teeth, jaws, and guts, are traits that would have permitted the ancestral colobines to reduce competition for fruit with other animals, including other anthropoids (Andrews, 1981; Delson, 1994).

Of course, we can only speculate about the past adaptive value of morphological or behavioral characteristics that living animals possess. Current adaptations may have been neutral in the past, and they tell us little about the direction that future evolutionary changes will take.

Sources of Genetic Variation

While Darwin recognized that variation within populations was necessary for natural selection to act, neither he nor the other early evolutionary theorists understood where this variation came from or how it was actually inherited. Jean Baptiste de Lamarck, for example, posited that the physical changes accumulated during an individual's lifetime could be passed on to offspring. According to Lamarck's brand of evolution, if your parents are body builders, and a muscular body was beneficial to them, then you, too, would be born with a body builder's physique. We now know, of course, that this doesn't occur. Individuals may vary in the muscle mass and definition they can develop with similar workout routines, and this propensity for muscle development may have a genetic, and therefore heritable, basis. But, even with such a propensity, exercise is still necessary to stimulate comparable muscle development.

Variation among Individuals.   Natural selection acts on the variation among individuals through the effects of variation on individual fitness. We now know that the genetic variation that distinguishes individuals comes from both random and nonrandom sources. Random **mutations,** which can occur when any genetic material is copied, create much of this essential variation. Random **recombination** of parental genetic material in the **gametes,** or sex cells, is also a critical source of genetic variation for any organism (plant or animal) that requires genetic contributions from a partner for reproduction instead of just cloning itself. In addition, nonrandom sources of genetic variation in offspring can potentially result from preferential mate choices that lead to particular combinations of inherited variation in the offspring they produce.

Mutations.   Mutations are random mistakes in the reproduction of genetic material. Mutations can occur at the level of the DNA sequences that code for particular proteins, the position of genes on a chromosome, and the total number of chromosomes, or **karyotype** of an individual. Mutations that interfere with fundamental developmental and body functions are usually so deleterious that the individuals who carry them are eliminated by natural selection, often even before birth. Chromosomal mutations, which can affect many or all of the genes located on them, are among the most severe types of mutations, and are thought to be responsible for a large proportion of spontaneous abortions and miscarriages. Even small mutations, such as those that affect a single DNA base, can have large deleterious effects on an individual's fitness if they alter the sequence of DNA in a region that codes for an important product. For example, the substitution of a single amino acid out of 146 amino acids on the beta-hemoglobin chain leads to the debilitating, and sometimes fatal, condition of sickle cell anemia.

The majority of inherited mutations are thought to be **neutral** because they have little or no effect on fitness at the time they arise. Without any functional distinctions, the fitness of the individuals who carry them is not affected. Neutral mutations are effectively invisible to natural selection. Yet, under different environmental conditions, what was originally a neutral mutation may confer some benefits to its carrier. If these benefits include improved fitness, then they will be selected for, eventually increasing in frequency in the population and possibly leading to speciation. The persistence of the mutation that causes sickling in hemoglobin is attributed to the resistance that individuals carrying one copy of the mutation gain against malaria. Without this benefit against malaria, as occurs in malaria-free environments, the carriers of the mutation are selected against.

The major adaptive radiations that have occurred throughout primate evolution are presumed to be a result of mutations that opened up opportunities for the individuals carrying them. The fact that these major adaptive radiations tend to be linked in time with major environmental changes is consistent with the idea that changing selection pressures on the available variation were responsible.

Mutations are generally assumed to occur at relatively constant rates. Those that are neutral or have minor functional effects will accumulate more rapidly than mutations that have major deleterious effects on function, and are therefore rapidly eliminated by natural selection. Mutations in genetic material that has little impact on fitness are widely used in molecular phylogeny to calibrate the length of time that separates different species and their ancestral lineages (Chapter 2).

Mechanisms of Inheritance.   While Darwin was developing his theory of evolution by natural selection, Gregor Mendel, a monk living in what is now the Czech Republic, was busy conducting experiments on peas in his garden. Mendel's work with crossing different strains of peas to understand how traits were expressed in their progeny was discovered by the scientific community in the 1900s, marking the beginning of what has come to be called **Mendelian genetics** in his honor (Henig, 2000).

We now know that every individual has two copies of each **autosomal** gene, one inherited from each parent, and that most genes have variant forms, or **alleles.** Except in the case of some social insects, such as bees and ants, all sexually reproducing animals carry one copy of each gene in their gametes. When gametes come together during fertilization, a **zygote** is formed in which each gene is represented in its **diploid** state, with one copy inherited from each of the two parents.

The position of each gene on a chromosome is called its **locus.** An individual who inherits two identical alleles is considered to be a **homozygote** at that locus, whereas a **heterozygote** inherits different alleles at that locus. Parental genes get combined in novel ways during the process of **meiosis,** which is how the diploid copy of genes we carry in other cells in our bodies gets reduced to the single copy carried in the gametes. As a result of this independent assortment of alleles during meiosis, offspring produced by the same parents end up inheriting different combinations of alleles from each parent. Thus, their **genotypes,** or genetic makeups, are unique.

It is often difficult to know from an individual's **phenotype** whether it is homozygous or heterozygous at any particular locus. This is because some alleles may be phenotypically **dominant,** meaning that they are the only alleles that are visibly expressed. When two different alleles at a locus are each equally expressed, they are considered to be **codominant.** Alleles that are only expressed in the homozygous condition are **recessive.** Many deleterious recessive alleles are transmitted to offspring and maintained in the population because their negative effects are masked by the presence of a dominant allele in the heterozygote condition.

Consider our own ABO blood group, which has three major alleles, A, B, and O. The A and B alleles are codominant with one another, which makes the AB blood group phenotype the same as its genotype. Both the A and B alleles are dominant over the recessive O allele. If you have type O blood, both your phenotype (O) and your genotype (OO) are the same. But if you have type A blood, all you can be sure of about your genotype is that you don't carry a B allele.

Now consider what happens if you reproduce with another individual who also has type A blood, and whose genotype, like yours, could also be either AA or AO. If both you and your mate have AA genotypes, your offspring will inherit one A allele from each of you, resulting in a genotype of AA at this locus and a phenotype of A. If your genotype is AA and your mate's is AO, then although your offspring can only inherit an A allele from you, it has a 50–50 chance of inheriting an A or an O allele from your mate. Its genotype may be AA or AO, but in either case, it will be phenotypically type A. If your offspring possesses type O blood, however, it can only mean that both you and your mate have AO genotypes, and that your offspring inherited an O allele from each of you. Yet, with type O blood, your offspring differs phenotypically from both you and your mate (Figure 4.2).

Because each offspring inherits one copy of each gene from each parent, it is never a carbon copy of either one. It could end up with the same phenotype and even genotype (e.g., AA by inheriting an A allele from each parent) as one parent (if one is AA), but only one of its alleles for this gene would have come from that

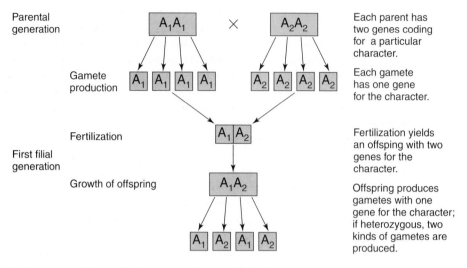

Parental generation

Each parent has two genes coding for a particular character.

Gamete production

Each gamete has one gene for the character.

Fertilization

Fertilization yields an offsping with two genes for the character.

First filial generation

Growth of offspring

Offspring produces gametes with one gene for the character; if heterozygous, two kinds of gametes are produced.

FIGURE 4.2   Mendel's First Law of segregation. Reprinted with permission from E. Staski and J. Marks, *Evolutionary Anthropology*, 1992. Harcourt Brace.

parent. If one or both parents are heterozygous for a gene, the offspring could end up with a genotype and phenotype that differ from both. Multiply this example by the 14,000 functional genes in the fruit fly genome, or by the roughly 100,000 functional genes that make up the human genome, and consider that some genes have more than ten variant forms, or alleles, and you can see why sexual reproduction is such an important source of genetic variation.

You can also see why the evolution of sexual reproduction, as opposed to asexual reproduction, or self-cloning, would have been such an important event. Sexual reproduction is costly in the sense that parents pass along only half of their genes with each offspring produced instead of all of their genes the way that clones do. However, the benefit of sexual reproduction is that new combinations of existing genetic variation are created with each successive offspring. It is this variation that gives sexually reproducing organisms a much greater opportunity to adapt to changing environmental conditions than organisms dependent on random mutations alone.

Sexual Reproduction and Mating Patterns.   There is little that individuals can do to influence how their genes get sorted out during the process of meiosis or get passed along through their gametes. Individual mate choices, however, can affect the probability that offspring will be genetically and phenotypically similar or different from their parents. Choosing a partner that is phenotypically, and therefore more than likely genotypically, different from one's self is called **negative assortative mating.** Conversely, choosing a partner that is phenotypically and genotypically similar to one's self is called **positive assortative mating.**

Blood group type is not usually a trait involved in our selection of reproductive partners. Although there may be differences in disease resistance or fertility (Molnar, 2002), we could probably say that mating is random with respect to blood group, meaning that pairings between individuals with different blood types occur in proportion to the representation of each allele in the population. But this is often not the case when complex traits such as physical appearance or intelligence or personality, which contribute to our definitions of attractiveness in a mate, are involved. Mate choices affect the genetic variation produced through sexual reproduction only to the extent that phenotypic qualities reflect genetic differences. The potential implications of primate mate choices is a topic we will look at more closely in the following chapter.

Inbreeding, or breeding between close biological relatives, can be regarded as an extreme example of positive assortative mating. Close kin will share a greater proportion of their genes through common descent from the same ancestors, including potentially deleterious recessive alleles that are masked by dominant, and functional, alleles in their heterozygote form.

Inbreeding depression results when offspring inherit two copies of a deleterious recessive allele, one through each of their related parents. Considering the genetic risks of close inbreeding, it is not surprising that some form of incest taboo exists in all known human societies. Similarly, in most animal societies, including those of primates, various dispersal and mate choice mechanisms contribute to the avoidance of inbreeding among close kin (Box 4.1). In fact, dispersal mechanisms in animals and cultural taboos in humans that promote inbreeding avoidance have been viewed as the products of strong natural selection pressures for adaptive mating patterns (van den Berghe, 1983; Gray, 1985; Packer, 1979a). Yet, although the prevalence of such mechanisms for inbreeding avoidance across human and animal societies is consistent with the potential severity of inbreeding depression, it is difficult to prove that other factors, such as competition for the same resources that lead to dispersal patterns, are not also involved (Gray, 1985; Moore and Ali, 1984; Pusey and Packer, 1987).

Primates reduced to living in small fragmented populations have limited opportunities to disperse from their natal groups. In these cases, the chances of finding unrelated mates may be severely reduced. As a result, rates of inbreeding may rise, leading to an increase in inbreeding depression through the expression of deleterious recessive alleles as well as a decrease in overall genetic variation in the population. Some animals with low genetic variation, such as cheetah, seem to be surviving. However, such closely inbred populations may be at a greater risk of going extinct because they have lost the genetic variation that is necessary for evolution to occur under changing environmental conditions (Lacy, 1983).

There is some evidence that even in small primate populations, patterns of mate choice can help to reduce the risk of close inbreeding. Among the muriquis I study, for example, mothers and their sexually mature sons do not mate with one another, and young females that have recently dispersed into a new group rarely mate with the adult males from their natal groups, where their fathers and brothers reside (Strier, 1997b). Among captive cotton-top tamarins (see Box 1.1), young females will mate with unfamiliar males, but not their fathers, when they are given similar opportunities to do so (Widowski, et al., 1990).

Variation within and between Populations.   Mutations and sexual reproduction account for individual variation, which affects the amount of genetic variation

BOX **4.1**

MHC Genes

Individuals that survive the dangers of dispersing may benefit in a variety of ways, including reducing their chances of deleterious inbreeding. But, if inbreeding is so bad, and dispersal so risky, wouldn't natural selection favor individuals that found other less dramatic ways to recognize close relatives and avoid them as mates? Recent studies, both with rodents and primates, provide evidence of mechanisms other than dispersal for distinguishing between related and unrelated mates. One of these mechanisms resides with the ability of animals to discriminate among specific odors associated with the genes that code for the **major histocompatibility complex,** known as **MHC,** for short (Brown and Eklund, 1994).

MHC molecules are critical components of all organisms' immune systems. MHC molecules recognize disease agents and hold onto them while other parts of the immune system go to work at neutralizing or destroying them. There are relatively few loci in the MHC system, but many different possible alleles associated with most of these loci. In humans, for example there are fewer than a dozen functional MHC loci, but over 200 different alleles. In mice, there are an estimated 3.6×10^9 possible phenotypes among only three different MHC loci because the number of different alleles at these loci is so high. Only when the immunological function of an MHC locus is highly specific is there evidence that natural selection pressures have conserved particular alleles and eliminated variant forms (Knapp, et al., 1998)

Individuals can end up carrying a greater diversity of MHC alleles, and therefore have greater protection from a wider variety of potential diseases, if they are heterozygous at their MHC loci instead of homozygous. Parents practicing negative assortative mating increase their offsprings' chances of inheriting different alleles at their MHC loci, and thus gaining potentially greater protection from diseases. Studies using strains of mice bred to be genetically identical in every way except their MHC alleles have shown that both sexes, but particularly females, prefer mates with different MHC alleles than their own. Evidently, each MHC genotype has a specific odor, and both males and females can discriminate these odors among potential mates (Alberts and Ober, 1993). In one study involving captive-bred mice that were released under controlled field conditions, females settled preferentially on the territories of males who carried different suites of MHC alleles than their own (Potts, et al., 1991). In addition, an unexpectedly high proportion of females who ended up on territories with MHC-similar males nonetheless mated outside their territories with males that carried different MHC genes.

The deleterious effects of reproduction among MHC similar mates have been demonstrated in captive pigtailed macaques. University of Cambridge anthropologist Leslie Knapp and her colleagues (1996) compared pregnancies resulting from pairings between males and females that were similar and different in their MHC genes. Pairs that shared the same MHC genes had significantly higher rates of spontaneous abortions, and thus produced significantly fewer offspring, than pairs with different MHC genes. Indeed, an impressive 72 percent of the pregnancy losses could be attributed to MHC sharing among parents.

Such strong differentials in reproductive success based on mate characteristics imply strong selection pressures for recognizing MHC differences. At least among mice, discriminating tastes in mates appear to be acquired through early social contact. In a natural situation, an individual raised by its mother in a litter of siblings would have ample opportunities to learn how relatives smell, and then later, to avoid mates who smell like their relatives, and presumably themselves. But, when mice are experimentally reared with individuals with different MHC alleles, they end up avoiding mates carrying those alleles even if the result is that they select mates more similar to themselves (Beauchamp, et al., 1988; Yamazaki, et al., 1988).

In the absence of experimental manipulation, learning the smell of mothers or littermates would be equivalent to learning the smell of kin, and then avoiding individuals who smell like kin when it's time to mate. The fact that these discriminations can be manipulated by different rearing conditions shows that familiarity is a critical component of kin recognition in at least some social mammals (Sherman and Holmes, 1985).

Reducing the risks of close inbreeding has beneficial consequences on parental fertility and offspring survivorship, and may occur by discriminating among familiar and unfamiliar smells, thereby avoiding the dangers of dispersal. Opportunities for maturing offspring to mate without leaving their natal groups may be limited by other factors, including competition from same-sexed adults (Moore and Ali, 1984) but when opportunities for close inbreeding do arise, it seems that females are more cautious than males (Alberts, 1999; Chapais, 2001). Recent studies in humans indicate that women prefer the odors of men with similar MHC genotypes to their own (Jacob, et al., 2002). Intriguingly, their preferences coincided only with the alleles that the women inherited from their fathers, suggesting that the olfactory cues associated with MHC genes may be an important mechanism for recognizing paternal kin, and possibly avoiding them as mates.

---

within the populations from which individuals find their mates. **Polymorphic** populations have high levels of genetic variation, as measured by the relatively high frequencies of multiple alleles for the same genes. Natural selection pressures can affect whether such polymorphisms are maintained or eliminated from populations, as well as whether different phenotypes are favored in populations living under different environmental conditions. For example, in regions where malaria is prevalent, populations tend to be polymorphic for both the normal and sickle alleles for beta-hemoglobin. Selection against the sickling allele is balanced by the benefits that heterozygote carriers gain through their greater resistance to debilitating malaria. As with the sources of variation among individuals, the genetic variation *between* populations is affected by both random and nonrandom forces (Table 4.1).

Random Genetic Drift.   We all know that we have a 50–50 probability of flipping a coin on its head or tail. But, because each flip is a random event that is independent of the previous flip, it can take a lot of flipping before we approach a 50–50 distribution of heads and tails. The same random probability applies to the frequencies of different alleles in a population. Without selection pressures or assortative mating, in a large population genes should be passed on in successive generations at the frequencies with which they occur. In small populations, however, some genes may be passed on at frequencies that are disproportionate to their actual representation, in much the same way that flipping a coin ten times is more likely to result in a heads or tails bias than when a coin is flipped 1,000 times.

TABLE 4.1   **Processes that affect genetic variation within and between populations**

Process	Genetic Variation	
	Within populations	**Between populations**
Mutation	increases	increases
Sexual reproduction	increases	increases
Assortative mating		
Negative	increases	increases
Positive	decreases	decreases
Genetic drift	decreases	increases
Gene flow	increases	decreases
Natural selection		
Directional[1]	varies	varies
Stabilizing[2]	decreases	increases, unless similar pressures
Diversifying[3]	increases	increases, unless similar pressures

[1]Directional selection leads to shifts in the population average for a particular phenotype.

[2]Stablizing selection favors the most common phenotype at the expense of extreme phenotypes.

[3]Diversifying selection favors the extreme phenotypes at the expense of the most common. If phenotypes deviate to the point that they can no longer interbreed, speciation could, theoretically, occur.

Genetic drift is the process of random fluctuations in gene frequencies over time. The size of the population affects the power of genetic drift to affect gene frequencies. In small populations, genetic drift can often lead to one allele becoming **fixed,** or present in the population at the expense of all other alleles. This happens much less frequently in large populations in which there is a lower probability of any one allele becoming fixed or being lost.

It is not entirely clear how small a population can become before the effects of genetic drift on the loss of genetic diversity become a serious concern. Populations with fewer than fifty breeding females have traditionally been regarded as being at high risk of losing sufficient genetic diversity to remain viable (Franklin, 1980), but more recent evaluations place the threshold for a minimally **viable** population size much closer to 5,000 (Lande, 1995). Small populations with high levels of genetic heterogeneity could, theoretically, be more viable than large populations with low genetic diversity. Deciphering the trade-offs between the size and genetic diversity of populations is a fundamental problem in conservation genetics, and an area of research with tremendous practical applications (Ashley, 1999).

It is often difficult to distinguish the effects of genetic drift from close inbreeding because both processes can lead to the loss of genetic variation in a population over a relatively short number of generations and both are a consequence of small population size. On the Atlantic Ocean island of Tristan da Cunha, for example, which was first colonized by the English in 1816, the entire population of 103 individuals in 1855 could be traced to only 20 ancestors (Roberts, 1968; Staski and Marks, 1992).

Such small **founder populations,** isolated for sufficiently long periods from other members of their species, can lead to speciation as well, although this obviously did not happen to the human inhabitants of Tristan da Cunha. The 800 species of fruit flies found today on the Hawaiian Islands, however, are thought to have gotten their evolutionary starts each time periodic lava flows reduced their forest habitats to small fragments. Isolated populations surviving in these forest fragments might have represented unique combinations of genetic material, which, when they subsequently recolonized regenerating forest on the lava flows, had become distinct from both their ancestral population and from one another (Butlin and Ritchie, 1994; Carson and Templeton, 1984). We encountered a similar example in Chapter 3, with the recent primate speciation events in areas such as Brazil's Atlantic forest that are thought to have occurred during the Pleistocene glaciations. Contraction of these tropical forests into small refuges isolated the primates they supported from one another. By the time the forests expanded once again, some populations had differentiated enough to justify classifying them into separate species.

Small population size is a concern in conservation biology because the effects of genetic drift and the probability of deleterious inbreeding can become severe. Mutations will constantly introduce new variation, and selection pressures associated with local environmental conditions can act on the constant accumulation of this variation. But, even without inbreeding, small population sizes mean fewer mutations can be introduced into the population. With less genetic variation, the chances for populations to adapt to changing environmental conditions are lower. The result is that small isolated populations are more vulnerable to extinction than large populations, which are more likely to be able to maintain adequate levels of genetic diversity to meet the unpredictable demands environmental changes may place on them.

Gene Flow and Dispersal.   Like Hawaiian fruit flies and Atlantic forest primates, populations that are isolated from one another can become genetically different in response to local selection pressures as well as genetic drift. The process that prevents the accumulation of genetic differences *between* populations is called **gene flow** because it involves the exchange of genes between populations. Gene flow occurs whenever an individual migrates to a new population and reproduces there. Conservation biologists estimate that it may take only a very low rate of migration, perhaps only a single migration event every three generations, to maintain enough gene flow to prevent speciation (Harcourt, 1995). Yet, when the geographic range of a primate species is disrupted by habitat destruction, populations become isolated and the opportunities for even such minimal gene flow may be eliminated entirely.

Gene flow is an extension of the dispersal patterns, discussed in Chapter 1, in which one or both sexes leave their natal groups to reproduce in others. The result of dispersal is that genetic variation *between* groups is reduced, while that within groups is increased. The distances that individuals disperse will determine the extent of these effects on genetic variation within and between groups.

The mechanisms that stimulate an individual to disperse are not always clear. As we will see in subsequent chapters, aggression from same-sexed group members, lack of breeding opportunities, or severe feeding competition within the natal group may contribute to an individual primate's decision to disperse. Yet, in pursuing their own reproductive opportunities, individuals who migrate and breed in a new group or population add their genes to the next generation's gene pool, and in doing so, contribute to the genetic variation within their population. When genes get shared between populations through the migration of breeding individuals, the genetic differences between them decline.

Genetic versus Environmental Influences

No one knows for sure how much genetic variation is necessary to maintain the adaptive **viability** of a population. Conservation biologists often assume that extinction probabilities rise steeply as levels of heterozygosity in the population drop (Figure 4.3). This creates something of a paradox, however, because natural selection, by acting on existing variation, will actually reduce variation by eliminating the genes of less fit individuals from the population.

The interacting effects of genetic and environmental influences on behavioral evolution are further confounded because we know so little about how complex

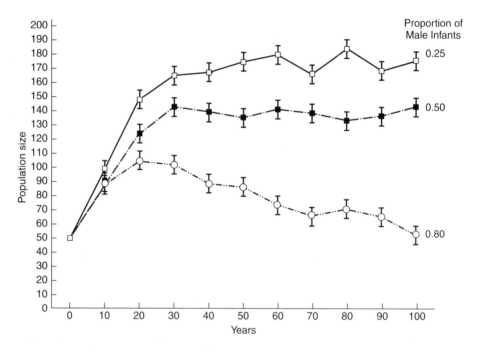

FIGURE 4.3   Sex ratios also affect extinction risks. Simulated size of one population of muriquis (*Brachyteles arachnoides*) with different proportions of male-to-female infants sex ratios based on VORTEX program (Lacy, 1993). All other demographic variables are held constant. Note that the population increases at low sex ratios, when the proportion of female infants is greater than males, and declines at high sex ratios, when the proportion of males is greater than females (Rylands, et al., 1998; Strier, 1993/1994).

traits, which include most social behaviors, are genetically coded. Species and individual differences in **temperament,** or disposition, as well as past experience, age, sex, and health are likely to have a correspondingly complex genetic component in which multiple genes that affect quantities of neurotransmitters and hormonal secretion patterns are involved (Figures 4.4, a–c).

Studies of identical human twins reared apart provide one way of distinguishing the effects of genetic inheritance versus environmental influence on diseases and behavior. However, the significance of either "nature" or "nurture" is not an all-or-nothing effect. Despite deliberate efforts to breed dogs with particular temperaments, there are still some unusually friendly pit bulls or nasty labradors. Sometimes these breed anomalies correspond to specific factors in their upbringings, but other times they seem to have more to do with the dogs' temperament than any other factor. In a unique breeding program for foxes, selection for tameness resulted in significant behavioral, morphological, and reproductive changes after 40 years (Trut, 1999). In humans, as in other animals, we still know very little about what environmental factors might trigger the expression of genetic mutations that lead to diseases such as breast cancer or alcoholism in one family member but not in another who also carries the mutation (Wilson, et al., 1994).

Even behaviors as basic as those involved in maternal care, which might be expected to evolve under strong selection pressures, are affected by environmental stimulation for their development and expression. In a series of extraordinary experiments, Harry Harlow's pioneering studies on development in primate infants

FIGURE 4.4a   Barbary macaques (*Macaca sylvanus*) are among the least aggressive of all macaques, and males frequently interact peacefully with infants independent of their paternity (Small, 1990). Photo made available by Irwin Bernstein.

FIGURE 4.4b   Celebes or crested black macaque (*Macaca nigra*). In captivity, this species exhibits low rates of aggression compared to other macaques (Bernstein and Baker, 1988). Photo made available by Irwin Bernstein.

FIGURE 4.4c   Lion-tailed macaque (*Macaca silenus*) groups exhibit one-male and multi-male, multi-female groups (Roonwal and Mohnot, 1977). Photo made available by Irwin Bernstein.

demonstrated the effects of socialization on infant rhesus macaques reared in captivity (Harlow and Zimmermann, 1959). The rhesus macaques were separated from their mothers soon after birth, and provided with surrogate wire and cloth "mothers." Infants clung to the cloth surrogate, which more closely resembled its mother's body in comfort, and left it only to suckle from the milk bottle attached to the uncomfortable wire surrogate. When these infants matured, they were less adept at caring for their own offspring than infants that were left to be reared by their mothers, indicating that experience is necessary to stimulate the expression of what has often been referred to as maternal instinct.

Harlow's experiments are controversial because of their devastating effects on the monkeys' well-being. But, the findings have had positive influences on captive breeding programs in laboratories and zoos, as well as on methods of appropriate parenting behavior in humans (Figure 4.5). More recent studies have extended these findings. For example, infant crab-eating macaques reared among their peers instead of with their mothers still grow up to be competent mothers, a finding that has been attributed to their opportunities to learn about social and physical contact through their interactions with one another (Timmermans and Vossen, 1996).

Testing Evolutionary Hypotheses for Behavior.   It is tricky to identify behavioral adaptations that have been selected for over evolutionary time. Often, behaviors make perfect sense in evolutionary terms, but the evidence for their

FIGURE 4.5   Cotton-top tamarins (*Saguinus oedipus*) at the University of Wisconsin-Madison, like many captive primates nowadays, are housed in large enclosures with branches and other stimuli. Photo by Carla Boe.

adaptive significance is difficult or impossible to obtain. Consider, for example, the occurrence of **infanticide,** or the killing of infants as a reproductive strategy. Infanticide became a hot topic in evolutionary theory when Sarah Hrdy (1974, 1976, 1977), studying Hanuman langurs in India, proposed a way of putting the pieces of this paradoxical behavioral puzzle together.

Hanuman langurs are slinky, silvery-colored colobine monkeys that live in India, often but not always, in uni-male, multi-female troops (Figure 4.6). Males leave their natal groups by the time they are sexually mature, but with all of the available females already claimed, they have limited reproductive opportunities unless they can manage to oust one of the lucky males and take his place in a female troop. Sometimes males band together in their takeover attempts, and then turn around and attack one another until a single victor emerges to claim his newly-won position as a member of the troop.

Takeover attempts create tensions in a langur troop, and not only for the male whose reign is being threatened. Females are also on their guard, because once a new male has established his sovereignty, he may direct aggression at young infants. Mothers will try to protect their offspring by avoiding a new male's approaches. But even if he succeeds in killing her infant, she is likely to turn around and mate with him as soon as she can possibly conceive again.

Hrdy (1977) interpreted both infanticidal behavior by unfamiliar males and the response of females toward infanticidal males as behavioral adaptations that have been shaped by evolution. To see how her evolutionary recipe translates into behavior, consider two possible phenotypes for males: those who commit infanticide when they take over a new troop, and those who don't. Now consider which male phenotype has higher fitness. The infanticidal male who kills nursing infants releases their mothers from **lactational amenhorrea,** the hormonal inhibition of ovulation that occurs when females nurse infants at frequent intervals. The noninfanticidal male, by contrast, waits patiently for mothers to wean their offspring and resume their ovulatory cycling without interfering.

FIGURE 4.6   Langur (*Presbytis entellus* or *Semnopithecus entellus*) male band incursion into a troop from which the resident male had vanished. An adult male copulates while two adolescents harass him. Photo by Jim Moore/Anthro-Photo.

Males of both phenotypes may gain reproductive opportunities with females eventually, but the infanticidal male stands to gain them sooner unless extrinsic factors, such as seasonal climate and food availability, prevent females that lose their infants from resuming their ovulatory cycles (Newton, 1986; Sommer and Mohnot, 1985). If a male is likely to lose his tenure before his own infants are safely weaned, then the sooner he can get his own infants started, the better chance he has of passing on his genes, and with them, his infanticidal tendencies. By contrast, if males hang onto their tenures longer, then the expected difference in fitness between infanticidal and noninfanticidal males should be minimal (Hausfater, 1984). Variation in male tenure length, among other factors, might explain why not all males in this species are infanticidal.

Evolutionary explanations for the behavioral responses of female langurs follow a similar logic. Again, consider two possible behavioral phenotypes for females: those who mate with an infanticidal male, and those who don't. If the female who cuts her reproductive losses by mating with an infanticidal male produces more surviving offspring than the female who rejects an infanticidal male after he kills her former infant, then her genes, as well as those of her infanticidal mate, will be represented at higher frequencies in the next generation. However, rates of infanticide relative to other sources of infant mortality will affect the strength of the selection pressures on females.

Infant-killing is neither unique nor ubiquitous among Hanuman langurs. Other observed cases, and many more suspected ones, have been reported in primate species ranging from lemurs, to howler and colobus monkeys, to gorillas and chimpanzees (Figure 4.7). But langurs account for a disproportionate share of these reports. Because the disappearances of infants tend to coincide closely with the appearance of new males, some researchers regard infanticide as an aberrant behavior limited largely to the crowded conditions that stimulate these takeovers (Boggess, 1984; Dohlinow, 1977; reviewed in Newton and Dunbar, 1994).

FIGURE 4.7 Adult female black and white colobus (*Colobus guereza*) with her 10-week-old infant at Kanyawara, Kibale Forest, Uganda. Photo by John F. Oates.

Other critics of the evidence for an evolutionary explanation attribute infant deaths to the incidental consequences of male aggression instead of aggression directed specifically toward infants (Bartlett, et al., 1993; Sussman et al., 1995). They have also argued that much of the evidence necessary to identify a behavioral adaptation, in an evolutionary sense, is missing. Among the most valid of these arguments is that comparisons among the lifetime fitness of infanticidal and non-infanticidal males are necessary to establish whether infanticide is an adaptive behavioral strategy (e.g., Bartlett, et al., 1993; Sussman, et al., 1995). This challenge is one that plagues most evolutionary explanations of behavior, particularly complex behaviors like aggression. And, for a variety of reasons, such comparisons among the fitnesses of individuals with different behavioral phenotypes are usually quite difficult to make.

Problems with Comparing Fitness among Primates.   Some of the obstacles to testing predictions about the adaptive value of infanticidal or other complex behaviors are more difficult to overcome with primates than with other animals. Populations of fruit flies or mice that are polymorphic in their behavioral phenotypes can be bred and crossbred through successive generations and the fitness of different phenotypes can be compared under a variety of controlled conditions. For primates, however, such breeding experiments are not feasible because of their slow rates of development and the costs and ethical questions involved. We would also have to confirm the biological parents of all offspring produced, an endeavor that is particularly difficult to undertake in the wild because even with careful behavioral observations, it is impossible to confirm male paternity without analyzing genetic data.

Advances in techniques for conducting such genetic analyses have greatly increased our ability to document paternity and evaluate evolutionary predictions about behavioral adaptations. As we'll see in Chapter 12, researchers are now employing noninvasive methods to obtain DNA from wild primates, an approach that merges both ethical and scientific concerns as well as laboratory and field approaches in behavioral ecology.

Most complex behavioral traits vary continuously across a population, and often across an individual's lifetime under different conditions. One male might always behave aggressively, another might behave aggressively in one situation but not in another, and a third might never behave aggressively. Without the ability to compare the consequences of these behavioral differences on male fitness, it is impossible to say which, if any, of these strategies is adaptive in an evolutionary sense. It is easy to develop adaptive explanations for a phenomenon like infanticide if the assumption that all observed behaviors are adaptive is not critically evaluated with relevant genetic and contextual data. The lack of these critical data does not mean that evolutionary assumptions about behaviors like infanticide are necessarily wrong, but rather, that more data are necessary to evaluate their evolutionary significance.

Recent genetic studies suggest that variation in infanticide, at least in some Hanuman langurs, conforms to evolutionary predictions. Using genetically-determined paternity data, Carola Borries and her colleagues (1999a) demonstrated that males only attacked unrelated infants, and were always the most likely fathers of the subsequent infants of mothers whose prior infants they attacked. Moreover, in multi-male groups, only genetic fathers or males that were residents in troops at the times infants were conceived intervened to protect infants from attacks initiated by other males (Borries, et al., 1999b). Male attackers, by contrast, were largely males that had joined these groups after the infants they targeted had been conceived or born (Borries, 1997).

Identifying Optimal Traits.   The adaptive value of a behavior can shift at different points in an individual's lifetime or differ among individuals, so identifying an **optimal** behavioral strategy requires knowing the relative **costs and benefits,** in terms of fitness. For example, the optimal strategy for a female langur during a takeover challenge may be to assist the father of her newborn infant so that he retains his tenure in the group and her infant will not be in jeopardy. But if a takeover is successful, her optimal strategy may shift to protecting her infant by avoiding the new male. If, despite her efforts, she nonetheless loses her infant in an attack, her optimal strategy may then be to conceive again as soon as possible.

Each of these female strategies involves potential costs and benefits to her fitness. The benefits of protecting her reproductive investment may be offset by the potential costs from risking injury to herself and her future reproductive potential. Older mothers, closer to the end of their reproductive careers and with less left of their futures to lose, may be more likely to take greater risks to protect their infants than younger mothers (Box 4.2). Yet, a young mother in her prime may be better able to protect her infant than an older mother, so the potential costs to each female of engaging in risky behaviors could be different. Without knowing the lifetime fitness consequences of these different behavioral patterns, it is difficult to evaluate how they may (or may not) have been shaped by the process of natural selection.

Evolutionary theory does not predict that individuals are infallible when it comes to assessing the fitness costs and benefits of their actions. "Bad choices" lead to a loss in fitness, and so, over evolutionary time, selection should favor individuals who, on average, make the better choices.

Generational Time Lags and Changing Environments.   An additional difficulty in distinguishing behavioral adaptations is a result of the time lag involved in evolution. Environmental changes can alter the strength and direction of selection pressures on particular traits, but the consequences of these selection pressures are only evident across generations. Thus, despite the wide range of views regarding evolutionary explanations of infanticide, nearly everyone agrees that it is a rare event. Does its rareness indicate that, compared to other sources of infant mortality, such as predation, it could never have evolved (e.g., Sussman, et al., 1995)? Or, did the benefits infanticidal males accrued in the past lead to selection favoring effective counterstrategies by females, such as confusing paternity by mating with males while still lactating or already pregnant (Hrdy, 1981), which in turn could have reduced the benefits of male infanticide, thereby lowering its prevalence in primate populations today?

BOX 4.2

Menopause

Many female mammals live beyond their reproductive years, a phenomenon that is carried to an extreme in the human menopause (Sherman, 1998). Scientists disagree about whether reproductive cessation is a by-product of the inevitable process of aging, or whether it is an adaptation to natural selection pressures that favor mothers who help their offspring to rear more of their own offspring. In between these alternatives is the hypothesis that menopause is a product of aging, but that natural selection has favored its timing so that mothers can help set their own infants on their way to independence before the end of their lifespan.

Recent studies by University of Utah anthropologist Kristen Hawkes and her colleagues on the Hadza, a group of hunters and gatherers living in Tanzania, have catapulted the "grandmother hypothesis" into front-page headlines (Hawkes, et al., 1997). Provisioning by grandmothers could increase their daughters' fertility, and therefore the propagation of more of both their daughters' and their own genes, in two ways. First, women whose mothers actively help their offspring may have shorter interbirth intervals because they can stop breast-feeding sooner. As a result, they can produce more offspring in the same time span than women without grandmotherly assistance. Second, once they are weaned, older grandchildren could fare better, in terms of weight gain, with grandmothers around to help provision them than they would if they were dependent on their mothers once a younger sibling comes along that needs to be nursed.

The evidence for grandmothers enhancing their daughters' reproductive success in other long-lived animals that experience reproductive cessation is not clear-cut, as comparative data from long-term studies of olive baboons and Serengeti lions demonstrate (Packer, et al., 1998). In both species, females live in extended kin groups where the opportunities for grandmothers to help their daughters exist. Females in both species also exhibit declines in fertility as they age. In baboons this takes the form of increasingly high rates of infant mortality when mothers reach 21 years, increasingly irregular menstrual cycles from about 21 to 23, and cessation of cycling by the time females reach 24 years of age. In female lions, the production of litters and litter size declines at around 14 years of age (Packer, et al., 1998). Yet, there was no difference in either the reproductive performance of daughters or in the survival of grandchildren when grandmothers were around to help. Older lions that were nursing their own litters may allow their grandchildren to nurse as well, but none of the hypothetical benefits of this supplementary source of nutrition were detected.

Faced with these findings, University of Minnesota biologist Craig Packer and his colleagues argue that menopause, per se, is a function of aging. The timing, however, depends upon female lifespans and the duration of infant dependency. If female baboons under two years of age are more likely to die without their mothers around, then natural selection would favor mothers that live long enough beyond having their last infant to see it safely on its way. Lion cubs need their mothers mainly during their first year of life, and few mothers older than 14 years of age, when they have their last litters, survive more than an extra 1.8 years.

The equation of declines in female fertility timed to see the last offspring to independence before death works for humans as well. As Packer and his colleagues calculate it, if human children are dependent for about 10 years, and mortality in pretechnological societies occurs between 58 to 65 years, then declines in fertility that kick in at 40 years and lead to full reproductive cessation by 50 years would make perfect evolutionary sense.

The fact that reproductive senescence is more dramatic in females than males is consistent with this hypothesis, because in most mammals, infants are more dependent on their mothers than their fathers for survival (Packer, et al., 1998). Hawkes thinks that the absence in lions and baboons of any positive effects of grandmothers on their daughters' fertility and their grandchildren's health means that something different is going on with us (Gibbons, 1998). If she's right, then maybe our children benefit longer from a larger network of relatives than other infant and juvenile mammals (Sherman, 1998). And maybe, when it comes to comparing primates, other factors, such as kinship and dispersal patterns, affect the social contributions older females make (Pavelka, 1999).

Female Japanese macaques, like female lions and baboons, are good candidates for evaluating the grandmother hypothesis because they also live in matrilineal societies where grandmothers have opportunities to assist their adult daughters and grandchildren. Yet, when Linda Fedigan and Mary Pavelka (2001) examined a large group of these females, they found no evidence that post-reproductive females had greater lifetime reproductive success than females that continued to reproduce until death. In these monkeys, females that live longer have more time to reproduce, and they certainly don't provision their grandchildren. In fact, longer lifespans with reduced fertility toward the end could be the result of selection for greater maternal investment, instead of grandmaternal investment in humans as well (Peccei, 2001). We'll take a closer look at some of the factors that contribute to variation in both female and male lifespans when we consider their development through the life cycle in Chapter 9.

We still know very little about other sources of infant mortality, such as predation rates, for most primates. Yet, without data to compare the proportion of infant deaths attributed to different factors, it is difficult to evaluate the relative strength of infanticide as a selective force in primate behavioral evolution (Treves and Chapman, 1996). And, because sources and levels of infant mortality are likely to vary across species and populations of the same species, we cannot yet evaluate all alternative explanations for this, and other, complex behavioral phenomena.

Evaluating the Role of Ecological Pressures.   Teasing apart past selection pressures from present-day conditions is complicated by the fact that the habitats of so many primates have changed dramatically in a brief period of time relative to their generation lengths. But, although comparing past and present ecological influences on behavior may be limited by a lack of prior information about both behavioral and ecological variables, comparisons among populations of the same species living in different habitats are instructive (Srivastava and Dunbar, 1996; Moore, 1999). For example, male chimpanzees studied at both the Gombe Stream National Park, Tanzania and the Taï National Park, Ivory Coast, hunt red colobus monkeys and eat them when their hunts are successful (Figure 4.8). Comparisons between these sites indicate differences in both the hunting strategies of the chimpanzees and in the defensive strategies of the red colobus monkeys. The Taï chimpanzees actively join forces to search out red colobus groups, which tend to seek refuge by hiding and to benefit from the alarms that the vigilant Diana monkey groups in their forest provide (Boesch, 1994; Noë and Bshary, 1997). The Gombe chimpanzees, by contrast, are more opportunistic and individualistic in their hunting tactics, and the red colobus monkeys at Gombe are more aggressive in their defensive tactics and don't rely on other monkeys to alert them to their danger, because there are no Diana monkeys in the forest at Gombe (Boesch, 1994; Stanford, et al., 1994).

Using a combination of behavioral observations and field playback experiments, Redouan Bshary and Ronald Noë (1997) concluded that the high, closed canopy of the Taï forest, together with the relatively large size of Taï chimpanzees and small size of Taï red colobus favor their respective strategies of cooperative hunting and active avoidance. Because red colobus can escape the chimpanzees by hiding in the canopy, the chimpanzees need to cooperate to achieve any success. At Gombe, however, the low, uneven canopy of the forest makes it more difficult for red colobus to avoid predatory chimpanzees by hiding (Wrangham and Bergmann-Riss, 1990). And, because Gombe chimpanzee males are smaller and Gombe red colobus males are larger than their respective West African cousins, red colobus males have a chance of deflecting Gombe chimpanzee predators by aggressively mobbing them (Bshary and Noë, 1997). Thus, both the hunting strategies of chimpanzees and the responses of red colobus monkeys are affected by their respective ecologies, which in each case includes not only the specific characteristics of the forest, but also the other primate species in their ecological communities (Chapter 11).

FIGURE 4.8   Male chimpanzee (*Pan troglodytes*) at Gombe National Park eating red colobus (*Procolobus badius*) meat obtained by predation. Photo by Craig Stanford.

Such comparisons are instructive because they help to establish that primates often behave in ways that are different, but nonetheless equally adaptive in their respective environments. Similar kinds of comparisons among populations of primates in which behaviors like infanticide have and have not been observed can also help to identify ecological or demographic variables that correlate with patterns of behavioral variation.

Kin Selection and Reciprocal Altruism

Behaviors that increase the survival and reproductive success of individuals should be favored by natural selection. Yet, sometimes animals, like the female baboon who tried to intervene during the hyena attack on Dogo, behave **altruistically,** in ways that appear likely to benefit the fitness of others at the expense of their own. There are many other examples of such seemingly altruistic acts among primates. For example, an alarm call given by the first individual who detects a predator will alert others in their group to take cover while possibly attracting the predator's attention to the caller. Similarly, some primates come to the aid of one another in fights against third parties, potentially risking injury or retaliation aimed at themselves.

It seems that individuals who behave in such altruistic ways should lose out in the fitness game to others who behave in more **selfish** ways to enhance their own fitness. Surely the baboon who keeps quiet when it sees a predator or stays safely in a tree when another member of its troop is attacked is more likely to survive than one who altruistically alerts its neighbors or throws herself into the fray? Likewise, the female vervet monkey who minds her own business is more likely to escape injury than the one who joins a fight in which she had no part. And why don't those marmoset and tamarin males kill other males' infants, sabotaging their competitor's reproductive interests in favor of their own, like the takeover males in Hanuman langur monkey troops do?

Altruism and the Challenge of Group Selection

How altruistic behavior could evolve through natural selection has been a puzzle to evolutionary biologists. All are in agreement that, if the individual is the unit of selection, then altruists should be selected against and selfish individuals favored. But what if the individual is not the unit of selection? What if, for example, natural selection acts at the level of groups instead of individuals? Such was the reasoning developed by V. C. Wynne-Edwards (1962) when he advanced his theory of **group selection** to account for what seemed like selfless acts.

Giving a self-sacrificial alarm call to a predator certainly increases the probability of escape for other group members, and practicing reproductive restraint, by not producing as many offspring as is biologically possible, would certainly benefit other members of the population whenever food resources are scarce. Indeed, Wynne-Edwards suggested that when animals come together, such as when starlings or geese aggregate at roosting sites, information about population size is communicated, and the birds adjust their reproductive output accordingly. Limiting reproduction at high population densities lowers competition over food among all members of their groups.

The difficulties with group selection lie with its mechanisms. For group selection to work, groups with altruists would have to have higher group fitness than groups without altruists. This might appear to be the case, for example, if we consider two groups of monkeys, one with and one without an altruist who gives an alarm call to alert others to an approaching predator. More members of the group with the altruist might escape from a predator. But, if by giving an alarm the altruist is eaten by the predator, then the group no longer has an advantage. Because individual extinction, or death, ordinarily occurs faster than the extinction of entire groups, altruistic individuals would be eliminated from the population faster than would groups without altruists.

Similar problems with group selection arise when you stop to think about how altruistic and selfish individuals fare within their groups. Selfish individuals, acting in the interests of their own fitness, will pass on more of their genes than the altruists, just as we saw in our comparison between infanticidal and noninfanticidal males. As a result, an egoist's genes end up being represented at higher frequencies in subsequent generations than those of an altruist if the egoist escapes detection by a predator whereas the altruist increases her chances of being eaten.

Many evolutionary biologists rejected group selection because of the apparently irreconcilable contradictions it posed for evolutionary theory (Box 4.3). However, to do so they had to address the puzzling, apparently altruistic behaviors that Wynne-Edwards discussed. By looking at how helping, or appearing to help, could be beneficial to an individual's fitness, many so-called altruistic behaviors turn out to have self-serving explanations.

Selfish Benefits of Helping Kin

One of the ways in which altruistic acts can actually benefit the altruist is when the recipient of the favor is a biological relative. This is because kin share some proportion of their genes through common geneaological descent. Giving an alarm call may increase the so-called altruist's own chances of being eaten, but if doing so helps enough of the altruist's relatives to survive, the fitness of the altruist is ultimately enhanced. "Helping" a biological relative in this way is proportionately the same as helping that proportion of yourself represented in your relative's genes (Table 4.2).

Kin selection essentially explains how altruistic behaviors, such as giving alarm calls that warn others while jeopardizing oneself, can evolve. Although altruistic behavior is, by definition, an act that has actual or potential costs to an individual's own fitness, these costs may be offset by the benefits to an individual's relatives. **Inclusive fitness** measures both the direct and indirect fitness effects of one's actions. Direct effects are reflected in the individual's own reproductive success. Indirect effects are reflected in the reproductive success of each of his or her relatives,

BOX **4.3**

Group Selection Revival

Despite the theoretical power of kin selection and reciprocity to explain the evolution of altruistic behavior, not all evolutionary theorists are ready to relinquish a role for group selection. According to some of the most ardent advocates, the time to reconsider multiple levels of selection is long overdue (Lewin, 1996). Philosopher Elliott Sober (1994) and biologist David Sloan Wilson (1997a, b) make a compelling point by distinguishing between individual selection, which is natural selection acting on differential fitness of individuals within groups, and group selection, which is nothing more than the same process of natural selection acting on the differential fitness of individuals between groups (Sober and Wilson, 1998). From their perspective, a single altruist must have lower fitness when surrounded by a group of selfish individuals, but individuals living in a group composed largely of altruists may have higher fitness, on average, than individuals in neighboring groups composed largely of selfish members.

The process of natural selection acts the same way at both the level of individuals and the level of groups, provided that heritable differences among each unit of selection lead to differential fitness. The process works similarly at other levels as well, from the cellular level to the population level, species level, and beyond (Gould, 1982). The result is a multilevel hierarchy of selection pressures.

To see how group selection might work, imagine two groups of the same species in a population. Within each of these respective groups, individuals that pass on more of their genes have higher fitness. One group is dominated by selfish individuals, who each reproduce as much as they can. The members of this group end up overexploiting their food resources, reducing the average fitness of all individuals if any of them manage to survive. The other group is predominantly altruists, who have lower fitness than the egoists among them. However, because the group grows more slowly, they do not run out of food, and, over time, this group persists while the selfish group goes extinct, just as Wynne-Edwards (1962) originally reasoned.

Views that are critical of group selection argue that selfish individuals would invade the altruistic group, take over through their higher reproductive success, and essentially corrupt the altruistic ethic. Supporters of group selection counter with the evidence that groups can—and do—split up or go extinct when some individuals carry their own selfishness to such extremes that the group can no longer survive. For example, group members could impose punishments on individuals whose behavior is detrimental to the group, and such punishments could be differentially administered to individuals acting in their own self-interests at the expense of others'.

Not surprisingly, the bulk of the evidence on societal rules for conformity described by group selection comes from humans, where social ostracism and punishments are routinely employed, and are highly effective methods for maintaining order. Studying these social rules in human societies whose subsistence is based on hunted and gathered foods, anthropologist Christopher Boehm (1997) emphasizes the ways in which selfish behavior is suppressed. Prized foods, such as meat, are distributed to all, and hoarders or boasters are treated with disdain. Group decisions are made through consensus, not commands, and everyone benefits from the cohesion and collective cooperation that consequently reign. There are always, of course, the perpetual freeloaders who benefit from the altruism of others in their groups without also contributing their share. But the more dependent

BOX **4.3**   **Continued**

these individuals are on others in their group, the more they have to lose if their own behavior disrupts the group's functioning. Thus, even freeloaders should be selected to keep their selfish tendencies in line.

Comparable evidence from other animal societies is not as clear-cut as the social rules that most humans abide by for their own individual benefits. For instance, field experiments with lions demonstrated that some females commonly assume leadership roles when it comes to responding to potential territorial intruders, whereas others are consistently slow to respond (Heinsohn and Packer, 1995). This sounds like a feline form of group selection. But, if prides tolerate some level of freeloading by these "laggards" because they turn out to help pull in more of their share of the meat during hunts, then reciprocity of roles, rather than group selection, would be a more parsimonious explanation for why leaders appear to tolerate laggards.

Wilson and Sober (1994) look at groups, or any other level in the organizational hierarchy of nature, as vehicles of selection. A pride of lions is a vehicle because the individuals in the pride are affected by the pride's success at both hunting and territorial defense. Indeed, they see reciprocity as a form of group selection because the "negotiation" that goes on between partners rarely impacts the fitness of each individual in identical ways (see also de Waal, 1996; Chapter 10). An affiliative relationship between two primates can therefore also be a vehicle in the sense that the participants in the relationship are mutually involved in maintaining it, and mutually affected by its consequences on their fitness. However, it is important to remember that **mutualism** can be selfish, and therefore can theoretically evolve without invoking the mechanisms of group selection to explain it.

Lion prides and many primate groups are composed of relatives, so perhaps **kin selection** suffices to account for the tolerance and cooperation members exhibit in proportion to the costs to individual fitness and the benefits to their **inclusive fitness.** Those groups of primates in which both sexes disperse, such as many howler monkey troops, might be ideal test cases for group selection because kin selection should be less of a determinant of individual behavior within them. Reconciling the role of individual selection and reciprocity may be an important next step in understanding how far group selection can go toward explaining animal behavior. The empirical tests of group selection in primates have not yet been conducted, but if the conventions that govern the societies of human primates are also identified in nonhuman primates, there could be more support for multilevel selection in the years to come.

---

weighted by the proportion of genes shared between them. The closer the relationship between you and your kin, the greater proportion of genes shared between you, and the greater the potential benefits to your own inclusive fitness when you sacrifice your own fitness to help your kin increase theirs.

A male marmoset monkey, for example, may forego reproducing to help his older brother rear offspring if by doing so the brothers can together rear more than twice the number of offspring than either one could alone. To see how this works, consider that the brothers share 50 percent of their genes because they share the same set of parents. The inclusive fitness (IF) of each brother is equal to however

TABLE 4.2   Types of interactions classified by their effects on fitness*

Type of interaction	Actor Change in reproductive potential		Recipient Change in inclusive fitness	Identity of recipient
	Short-term	*Long-term*		
Selfish	– or +	+	–	Any
Altruism, without expectation of reciprocity	–	–	+	Kin
Altruism, with expectation of reciprocity	–	+	+	Any
Mutualism	+	+	+	Any

*All interactions are expected to increase the actor's inclusive fitness in the long-term. Cells show gains (+) or losses (–) to the actor's reproductive potential and to the inclusive fitness of the recipient of the actor's action. Interactions in the lower half of the table are mutually beneficial to both individuals; those in the upper half are not.

From Wrangham, R. W. 1982, Mutualism, kinship and social evolution. In King's College Sociobiology Group, Eds., *Current Problems in Sociobiology.* Cambridge: Cambridge University Press, pp. 269–289. Reprinted with permission from the author and from Cambridge University Press. Copyright © 1982, Cambridge University Press.

many offspring he might produce if he pursued his own reproductive career (RS_{self}) plus however many offspring his brother could produce without his help ($RS_{brother, alone}$) multiplied by the proportion of genes the brothers share, or their **degree of relatedness (r),** which in this case is 0.5. In other words, each brother's IF = RS_{self} + ($RS_{brother}$ × r). The younger brother should only help if his IF is greater by helping his brother produce more offspring than if both he and his brother reproduced on their own.

Hamilton's Rule.   W. D. Hamilton (1964) developed an equation for predicting when an altruistic act toward a relative might actually be advantageous to an individual's inclusive fitness. The formula of **Hamilton's rule** requires knowing (or estimating) the values of three variables: 1) the costs (**c**) of the act to the actor's individual fitness; 2) the benefits (**b**) of the act to the recipient's individual fitness, and 3) the degree of relatedness (**r**) between the actor and recipient, or the proportion of genes shared through common descent. In the marmoset example above, the costs (**c**) to the younger brother of forfeiting his own reproduction to help his older brother are the number of offspring he and his brother could each produce alone, the benefits (**b**) are the greater number of offspring he and his brother can rear together, and their coefficient of relatedness (**r**) is 0.5, as stated.

According to Hamilton's rule, an individual will be selected to help a relative whenever **c < b × r.** Because **r** is always a fraction, except in the case of identical twins when **r** = 1 (because identical twins share 100 percent of their genes), multiplying **r** by **b** means that **b** (the fitness benefits to the recipient) must be larger than **c** (the fitness cost to the actor). In our marmoset example, in which the brothers share 50 percent of their genes, the younger brother should only help his older brother when the benefits to his IF are more than twice as high than the costs. However, if the brothers were half siblings, with only one parent in common, they would share only 25 percent of their genes and altruism would only be expected to evolve if the benefits to the younger brother were more than four times the costs to his fitness.

Evidence for Kin Selection among Primates.   Sharing some proportion of genes through common descent is not the only condition necessary for altruistic behavior toward relatives to evolve through kin selection. There must also be a genetic basis underlying the behavior, for otherwise altruism toward kin could not be transmitted across generations or among relatives. Furthermore, relatives must have opportunities to interact with one another, for how else would they be able to help each other and simultaneously benefit their own inclusive fitness?

Group living is an important requisite for kin selection and, as we have seen, primate dispersal patterns affect whether groups are comprised of female kin, male kin, or few, if any kin. As predicted, evidence of altruistic behavior toward kin is strongest among primates who live with their kin. Some of the strongest evidence of kin selection in action has been found among female Old World cercopithecine monkeys, such as baboons, macaques, and vervet monkeys, where females generally remain in their natal groups among their matrilineal relatives for life (Kawai, 1958; Sade, et al., 1976).

In Japanese macaques, for example, Jeffrey Kurland (1977) found that close female kin spend more time in close proximity with one another than they do with more distant kin (Figure 4.9). At such close range, close relatives are available to give and receive help should a male, or a female from another matriline, threaten any of them. Close kin also groom one another in proportion to the amount of time they spend in proximity, and although female kin fight more frequently with one another, their rates of fighting relative to the amount of time they spend together are disproportionately low.

Among vervet monkeys, females respond to solicitations for help in **agonistic** interactions more quickly when the distress calls come from close kin than from other group members (Seyfarth and Cheney, 1984). Interestingly, although female vervet monkeys also come to the aid of nonkin who have recently groomed them, there is no such contingency of prior affiliative behavior and subsequent assistance among kin (Figure 4.10). In other words, just sharing a high proportion of genes leads relatives to help one another, whereas others must earn the favors they receive.

Comparable forms of assistance and affiliation occur among males in the patrilineal societies of chimpanzees, where males join forces in attacks against unrelated communities of males (Goodall, 1986; Riss and Goodall, 1977; Nishida, 1979; Wrangham and Peterson, 1996). Male Peruvian squirrel monkeys, which disperse from their natal groups, form long-term alliances that help them to immigrate into new groups and find female mates (Mitchell, 1994). Among both hamadryas baboons and Venezuelan red howler monkeys, fathers may tolerate one of their sons in their

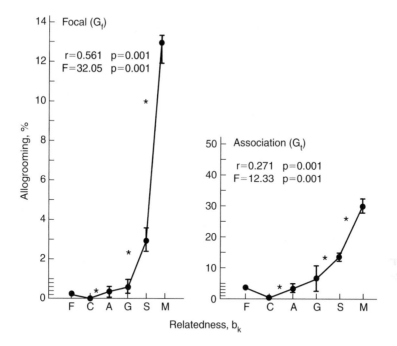

FIGURE 4.9   Percentage of time spent grooming among dyads as function of matrilineal relatedness in a group of Japanese macaques. The first graph, Focal (G_f) shows the percentage of time focal subjects groomed other individuals; the second graph, Association (G_t), shows the percentage of time two individuals groomed when they were in proximity with one another. The points plotted in both graphs are the mean and error values for each kind of dyad. Statistics show significant correlations between grooming time and kinship category (r values) and differences between kinship categories (F values). F = distant kin; C = cousins; A = aunts; G = grandmothers; S = siblings; M = mother. From Kurland, J. A. 1977. Kin selection in the Japanese monkey. *Contributions to Primatology*, vol. 12, 1977. Reproduced by permission of S. Karger AG, Basel.

troops to help them to defend females from takeover attempts by other males (Crockett and Pope, 1993; Sigg, et al., 1982). Coalitions of related male red howler monkeys last longer and are more successful than those among nonkin (Pope, 1990).

The advantages of living among kin, whose overlapping genetic interests make them more reliable allies than nonkin, may be one of the most important factors underlying dispersal patterns in primates. In fact, we would predict that female primates should remain in their natal groups when the benefits of having allies nearby and of being on hand to help a close relative outweigh the costs from competition for food or other resources (Wrangham, 1980). Similar tradeoffs between the benefits of having related allies, on the one hand, and costs of competing with

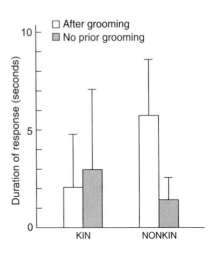

FIGURE 4.10   Vervet monkey responses to recruitment vocalizations of kin and nonkin in the presence and absence of prior grooming by the vocalizers. Means and standard deviations are shown. Grooming by nonkin led to elevated responses of subjects. Reprinted with permission from *Nature,* from R. M. Seyfarth and D. L. Cheney, 1984, Grooming, alliances, and reciprocal altruism in vervet monkeys. *Nature,* vol. 308, pp. 541–543. Copyright © 1984. Macmillian Magazines Limited.

kin for limited resources, such as access to mates, on the other hand, are likely to affect male dispersal patterns as well. We'll return to these tradeoffs, which form the basis for what we understand about the determinants of primate social organizations, later on in this and subsequent chapters.

Evaluating the Evidence for Kin Selection.   Evaluating predictions about the effects of kin selection on primate social behavior is not an easy matter. In addition to all of the problems associated with comparing the consequences of behavior on fitness in long-lived individuals, there are also the potential costs and benefits on the fitness of relatives to be considered. Calculating **r** in Hamilton's formula is complicated by the fact that without genetic tests it is impossible to confirm biological paternity or matrilineal relationships among females already present in wild primate groups when observations were initiated. Additional uncertainties arise when we try to understand how, or even if, primates recognize their kin, and whether behaviors that may appear altruist are mutually beneficial instead.

Indeed, despite the many examples of nepotistic behavior among primates, we still lack even the most rudimentary understanding of what the mechanisms of **kin recognition** may be. Primates may rely on olfactory cues or **phenotypic matching,** in which they identify traits that are genetically controlled, as is thought to occur in animals ranging from bees and guppies to mice and ground squirrels (Holmes and Sherman, 1983). However, it is also possible that primates have evolved to rely on familiarity and learned relationships during their long socialization periods, and that, when deprived of these experiences, their ability to recognize their relatives is substantially impaired (Bernstein, 1999b). Recent genetic studies suggest that yellow baboons may rely on their similarities in age to recognize paternal siblings (Alberts, 1999). Temperamental similarities among paternal sisters close in age are also thought to help female rhesus macaques recognize one another (Widdig, et al., 2001). In both studies, however, kin live in the same groups and are familiar to one another.

Distinguishing whether primates are capable of recognizing unfamiliar kin or whether they require experience is a challenging task. Captive studies have yielded mixed results, with only one study suggesting that young pigtailed macaques exhibited a preference for associating with unfamiliar paternal half siblings instead of unfamiliar nonkin (Wu, et al., 1980). The failure of other researchers to duplicate this study (e.g., Fredrickson and Sackett, 1984; Erhart, et al., 1997), however, makes it seem unlikely that primates can recognize their own kin without prior familiarity (Gouzoules and Gouzoules, 1987).

Studies of whether primates learn to recognize relationships among other members of their groups have been more compelling. For example, Dorothy Cheney and Robert Seyfarth (1985) made high-quality tape recordings of the distress calls given by wild juvenile vervet monkeys in response to social interactions with other group members. When the recordings were played back to other group members, the results were striking. Vervet monkeys responded to the distress calls based on their relationship to the juvenile's mother, indicating that they could associate the source of the distress call with its biological mother. Monkeys subordinate to the mother gave appropriate submissive gestures, as if to disclaim any responsibility for causing her offspring distress and thereby avoid any retaliation the mother might inflict. However, when the calls of juveniles from subordinate matrilines were played, monkeys dominant to the mother may have looked her way, but otherwise went about their business, as would be consistent with their higher rank and lack of concern with retaliation.

Benefits of Helping Nonkin

Most primates live in social groups with at least some unrelated individuals. Some possibly altruistic acts, such as alarm calls to predators, may have been selected for because of the inclusive fitness benefits that an altruist derives by helping its kin in the group. In this instance, the fact that other unrelated members of the group also benefit from the warning is an unavoidable consequence of kin selection. However, as with group selection arguments, it is also plausible that altruists can benefit from helping nonkin if these same individuals can be counted on to reciprocate the favor. For such **reciprocal altruism** to evolve, the costs of an act to the altruist must be offset by the benefits to be gained when the recipient reciprocates with an altruistic act of his or her own (Trivers, 1971).

Conditions for the Evolution of Reciprocity.   Like kin selection, the evolution of reciprocity requires that individuals have opportunities for repeated interactions so that a helpful act can be repaid. This generally means that reciprocity should only evolve when dispersal rates are relatively low and altruists can recognize one another (Krebs and Davies, 1993).

For an altruist to benefit from reciprocity at a later date, the recipient of any assistance must also be of more or less similar abilities so that comparable levels of help can be provided. A subordinate individual might not be able to assist a higher ranking individual in conflicts with other, more dominant group members. Thus, whereas with kin selection assistance is given preferentially to closer relatives because the inclusive fitness benefits to the altruist will be greater, with reciprocal altruism individuals in the best position to reciprocate should be favored allies.

Evidence for Reciprocity among Primates.   Many examples of cooperation among primates and other animals have been invoked as evidence for reciprocal altruism. However, it is usually difficult to measure the actual fitness costs to the altruists, or to rule out the possibility that cooperation is **mutually beneficial** to the participants, each of whom may be acting in their own self interests (Pusey and Packer, 1997). For example, **coalitions,** which involve two or more unrelated individuals forming an alliance against one or more other individuals, have frequently been regarded as an example of reciprocity. Coalitions involving unrelated male baboons against more dominant individuals were observed in the first field study of olive baboons conducted by Irven DeVore (1962; Hall and DeVore, 1965) in Nairobi National Park in Kenya. DeVore recognized that when two mid-ranking males joined forces, their **coalition rank,** or combined effort, permitted them to successfully challenge the alpha male, who could otherwise have dominated each of the males individually.

Another study of male coalitions was subsequently conducted by Craig Packer on the olive baboons at Gombe National Park, Tanzania. Packer (1977) studied eighteen adult males in three baboon troops. During his study, he observed 140 solicitations for support by adult males, and 97 resulted in the formation of coalitions. In 20 of these cases, the coalition partners challenged a more dominant male who was associating with an estrous female. In six instances, the coalition pair won the contest and the female transferred her affection—and sexual favors—to the male who, perhaps selfishly, had initiated the coalition.

Six of the 13 pairs of males formed repeated coalitions, and in all cases, a male who provided assistance subsequently received aid when he solicited it from his partner. Females and juveniles also solicited and obtained help in social conflicts from adult males who were dominant to them, but as predicted on the basis of their more symmetrical competitive abilities, adult males only solicited aid from one another.

Similar examples of cooperation have also been well-documented in the status struggles among captive chimpanzee males. In the wild, male chimpanzees remain in their natal groups, where kin selection among them could, theoretically, operate. Nevertheless, there is no evidence that males preferentially cooperate with their maternal brothers in coalitions against other males in their communities (Goldberg and Wrangham, 1997; Mitani, et al., 2000a). Either paternal kinship, or **mutualism,** which does not require altruism, are more likely explanations for why particular males form coalitions with one another.

In the captive colony at the Arnhem Zoo in the Netherlands studied by Dutch primatologist Frans de Waal, the males came from various locations and were unrelated to one another, more like the wild baboons described by DeVore and Packer. It is easy to see why de Waal's (1982) book on the Arnhem chimpanzees was entitled *Chimpanzee Politics.* In it, de Waal tells about the jockeying for dominance among three male protagonists: Yeroen, Luit, and Nikkie (Figure 4.11). At the start of his study, Yeroen was the oldest male in the colony, and also the most dominant. Luit was second in rank, followed by other adult males, with Nikkie, the youngest, most subordinate of all. The females in the colony had their own hierarchy, with the one called Mamma at the top. Support from her and the other females in the colony's social dynamics proved to be vital to the outcome of the plays for power among males.

First Luit began challenging Yeroen's supremacy. The females sided with Yeroen, and although Luit attacked them, their support helped Yeroen hang onto his rank. Then Nikkie joined up with Luit to threaten Yeroen, who returned Luit's threats but ignored the younger Nikkie. This proved to be a tactical error, for while Yeroen was distracted with repelling Luit, Nikkie established a following among the females. Within seventy-two days of the onset of the turmoil, the females had allied themselves with Nikkie, whose support for Luit forced Yeroen to submit. A short while later, the females transferred their support to Luit, who became dominant, with Nikkie second in rank, and Yeroen a humble third.

Soon Nikkie began to challenge Luit's newly attained dominance. Luit enlisted support from his old rival, Yeroen, but Yeroen would have none of that. Instead, he formed a coalition with Nikkie, despite Luit's efforts to keep the two apart. With Yeroen's support, Nikkie rose to the alpha position.

The colony managers believed that Nikkie was too young to be dominant, and isolated him for a brief period of time. Once he was gone, Luit abandoned his efforts to recruit Yeroen to his side, and the contest for dominance between Luit and Yeroen resumed. When Nikkie was subsequently reintroduced, Yeroen re-established his support and Nikkie once again became dominant.

Nikkie was a real tyrant. He castigated females who failed to support him, and eventually they stopped taking sides with Luit against him. He also tried to

FIGURE 4.11   Chimpanzee (*Pan troglodytes*) coalition at Arnhem Zoo, Netherlands. Three adults in the background together chase Dandy, the male on the right. From *Chimpanzee Politics* by Frans de Waal (1982). Photo courtesy of Frans de Waal.

keep Luit and Yeroen apart, for his own precarious position depended on Yeroen's support. Yeroen still had some support among the females, who he encouraged to help him keep Nikkie in line. Nikkie was able to monopolize copulations with females, but it was Yeroen's support that determined Nikkie's success.

De Waal (1982) interpreted the shifting coalitions among the three male protagonists and the influential females as evidence of **triadic awareness,** in which each chimpanzee understood the risks that a coalition among rivals posed to his own position. Thus, although Luit became individually dominant, he could not sustain his position when Nikkie and Yeroen joined forces against him. Nikkie used Yeroen to dominate Luit, and Yeroen regained his status over Luit with Nikkie's help. In the end, Nikkie and Yeroen formed what de Waal (1982) called a "collective leadership" because neither male could retain his own position without the support of the other.

Evaluating the Evidence for Reciprocity.   Coalitions, which could be evidence of reciprocal altruism or mutually exploitative relationships, should have positive consequences for the fitness of the individuals who help one another. Yet, as in the case of evaluating the consequences of kin selection, it is usually difficult to obtain the necessary genetic data to evaluate the predicted consequences of behavior on individual fitness. Distinguishing between the evolution of seemingly altruistic acts through kin selection versus reciprocal altruism requires knowledge of the genetic relationships among actors and recipients and the genetic consequences of the behavior for the actors. For example, giving alarm calls that alert other group members to the presence of a predator could evolve through kin selection if at least some of the beneficiaries are related, or through reciprocal altruism if the warnings are reciprocated by unrelated group members. Alarm calls could also arise through individual selection if they alert others, who mob the predator or whose own calls alert the predator to the fact that it has been spotted.

Knowledge of paternity would also be necessary to assess whether unrelated male baboons achieve higher reproductive success through their coalitions than they do on their own. Among the Arnhem chimpanzees, the fitness consequences are even more difficult to evaluate because Yeroen was infertile due to a prior injury, and therefore incapable of enhancing his fitness through his coalitionary support. Presumably, he was unaware of his own infertility, suggesting that his willingness to risk injury by taking sides in the power struggles between Nikkie and Luit, and his reluctance to relinquish his own dominance position to Luit's challenge, represents a complex set of behaviors that might link male status and reproductive success in chimpanzees (Wrangham and Peterson, 1996).

With reciprocal altruism, as with the predicted effects of kin selection and natural selection on behavior, there is no need to assume that the animals are conscious of their motives or the reproductive consequences of their behavior. Instead, we predict that fitness-enhancing actions will be selected for, and then seek ways of testing our predictions by comparing our observations of behavior—what the animals actually do—against our predictions.

A recipient of an altruistic act who fails to reciprocate is a cheater. Cheaters may gain in the short run by receiving aid without any costs to their own fitness, but if reciprocity is a requisite for future support, then in the long run their fitness should suffer compared to individuals who reciprocate. An altruist should likewise be selected for the ability to distinguish between cheaters and noncheaters, and to remember and deny help to those who have failed to reciprocate in the past. Engaging in affiliative interactions, such as grooming, may be one of the ways in which primates develop reputations as worthwhile allies (Henzi and Barrett, 1999). The fact that vervet monkeys are more responsive to solicitations for support from individuals who have recently groomed them than they are to solicitations from nonkin who haven't may be an example of how the favor of being groomed is reciprocated (Seyfarth and Cheney, 1984). However, it is still necessary to demonstrate that grooming is costly, and therefore meets the criteria for reciprocal altruism to evolve (Pusey and Packer, 1997).

Testing or reaffirming one another's commitment to reciprocate support may also be why male baboon coalitionary partners engage in ritualized greetings before coordinating their joint assaults against third parties. These ritualized greetings include the potentially risky act of grasping one another's testicles, essentially putting their reproductive future in their coalitionary partner's hands (Smuts and Watanabe, 1990). A male unwilling to submit to such familiarity could be signaling that he will be equally unwilling to support his partner when the going gets rough whether or not he is conscious of his intentions.

Establishing the behavioral rules for evaluating whether another individual will come through as an ally or behave as a traitor has occupied an area of evolutionary theory called **game theory,** in which the optimal behavior of one individual is dependent on the behavior of the other (or others). The **Prisoner's dilemma** is a classic example of how the costs and benefits of an individual's behavior will vary depending on the behavior of others. In its original rendition, two prisoners are questioned separately about their own and each other's culpability in committing a crime. Each prisoner has the opportunity to "cooperate" by saying nothing and accepting punishment, or to "defect" by blaming the other and claiming innocence for themselves. Neither is aware of the other's response, yet the consequences vary depending on whether both cooperate, both defect, or one cooperates while the other defects. Theoretical values are assigned to their responses, with both individuals faring better if each of them cooperates by refusing to blame the other than if both of them defect by blaming the other and claiming innocence for themselves. But, if only one of them defects, that individual fares best of all (Figure 4.12).

Given these payoffs, what should they do? The most **evolutionary stable strategy,** or **ESS,** is one in which both participants follow the rule of tit-for-tat by adjusting their responses according to what the other did in the preceding trial. As long as one individual cooperates, the other should follow suit, as predicted if reciprocal altruism has evolved (Axelrod and Hamilton, 1981).

The limitations of the tit-for-tat rule are that cooperation among animals is rarely an all-or-nothing event (Keller and Reeve, 1998) There is a continuum of cooperation ranging from minimal to enthusiastic cooperation, and presumably evolution would favor those individuals that manage to cooperate as little as possible to ensure that their cooperation is reciprocated. More recent analyses have emphasized that animals are sensitive to subtle adjustments in the degree of cooperation an ally exhibits. Overcompensating by offering more help than needed, as

Player B

	C Cooperation	D Defection
Player A C Cooperation	R=3 Reward for mutual cooperation	S=0 Sucker's payoff
D Defection	T=5 Temptation to defect	P=1 Punishment for mutual defection

FIGURE 4.12   The Prisoner's Dilemma game. The numerical payoff to player A is shown. The game is defined by $T > R > P > S$ and $R > (S + T)/2$. Thus, although player A gains the most or least if player B does the opposite ($T = 5$ or $S = 0$), both players fare better by cooperating ($R = 3$) than by defecting ($R = 1$). Reprinted with permission from Axelrod, R. and Hamilton, W. D. 1981. The evolution of cooperation. *Science* 211:1390–1396. Copyright © 1981, American Association for the Advancement of Science.

well as testing the minimum threshold of cooperation that is necessary to elicit cooperation, are the ways in which these sensitivities get expressed. Familiarity and opportunities to interact repeatedly permit individuals to constantly adjust their behavior according to more flexible rules than the original tit-for-tat scenario depicts (Roberts and Sherratt, 1998).

Translating these rules of behavior to primates makes sense when the asymmetry that characterizes many primate social interactions is taken into account. For example, low ranking primates often groom their higher ranking partners longer than they are groomed themselves. Subordinates may do this because high-ranking individuals are in a better position to help them than they are to help their superiors in the hierarchy. Low-ranking female baboons and capuchin monkeys groom high-ranking males in their groups more often and for longer durations than the males groom them (Smuts, 1987a). In gibbons, by contrast, males groom females more than females groom males, suggesting a different kind of asymmetry in which males are more interested than females in maintaining their relationships (Palombit, 1999).

Failure to reciprocate may result in retaliation. Retaliation among individuals that are similar in size and strength may take the form of direct attacks. Among individuals that differ in their abilities, retaliation may involve the withholding of support, grooming, or most important of all, mating opportunities, as we'll see in the following chapters.

Individual Strategies and Social Organizations

We have come a long way in this chapter on evolutionary processes, from the basic genetics of evolution, to complex behaviors that we attribute to evolutionary selection pressures. More often than not, these attributions take the form of predictions that are consistent with evolutionary theory, but that nonetheless must still be tested by comparing the long-term fitness consequences of individual behavior. As we've seen, advances in genetic analyses are beginning to provide the critical evidence needed to evaluate the effects of male behavior on paternity success, and of both maternal and paternal kinship on patterns of social relationships. But many predictions still remain to be tested.

Individual behavioral strategies also interact with one another, resulting in the diversity of social and mating systems we observe. For example, individuals should form groups whenever group living is advantageous to them. As we saw in Chapter 1, living in a group may be advantageous to individuals that can share in the distracting, but necessary, burden of detecting predators in environments where predators pose threats to their individual survival. When kin comprise groups, giving alarm calls that help relatives escape from predators will benefit an individual's inclusive fitness, but even among nonkin, reciprocity in alarm calls should be mutually advantageous.

If there were no costs to fitness associated with group living, then we would expect primate groups to grow in size without limits. The fact that groups don't do this implies that counteracting selection pressures, or fitness costs, are also involved when groups become too large. Usually these fitness costs can be attributed to competition for access to essential resources, such as food or mates, which must be balanced against the benefits of living in groups as well as both the costs and benefits of dispersing (Hill and Lee, 1998; Treves, 1999a).

Conflict and Cooperation among Same-Sexed Individuals

The tradeoff between the benefits and costs of group living on the fitness of group members leads to selection pressures for **optimal** group sizes (see Figure 1.17). Groups increase in size by retaining offspring and recruiting outsiders. They decrease in size through the eviction of offspring and repulsion of outsiders attempting to join them. The optimal group size should vary in different environments depending on the intensity of predator pressures and the ways in which food and mates are distributed (Janson, 1992). Some primates, like ring-tailed lemurs, adjust their home range sizes instead of their group sizes in response to habitat differences (Sussman, 1992a), but in other primates, group sizes within a population are highly variable. Thus, a young female marmoset may be permitted to stay in her natal group as a nonreproductive helper to her mother because the benefits of having her daughter's assistance outweigh the costs of competing for food with her daughter. Conversely, a daughter should only accept such a nonreproductive, subordinate position when her options of dispersing and finding her own mate in an area with sufficient food resources are limited compared to the gains to her inclusive fitness by helping her mother, or to her individual fitness by gaining parenting experience.

Wild marmosets living at high population densities have lower chances of successfully dispersing and establishing their own breeding groups, and therefore may be more likely to occur in extended family groups than marmosets living at lower population densities where dispersal opportunities are greater (Ferrari and Digby, 1996). Similar factors could be involved in the evolution of helping among the male marmosets we considered earlier in this chapter, but the genetic tests of these predictions still need to be done.

The "decision" to disperse is an individual "strategy," but as we have seen, it can have profound effects on the genetic composition of primate groups and therefore affect the social interactions among group members. Evolutionary approaches to behavior tend to focus on individuals. However, primate social groups take on lives of their own that aren't always so easily predicted from their individual members. Reducing such complex dynamic relationships into their individual components can oversimplify the dynamics that result from the interacting effects of individual strategies in such groups (Mason and Mendoza, 1993; Rowell, 1993).

Dispersing individuals may adjust their membership in groups in ways that enhance their fitness. Male ring-tailed lemurs, for instance, will move from group to group in search of a group whose favorable sex ratio affords them the greatest reproductive opportunities (Sussman, 1992a). The advantages of seeking such a group, however, are offset by the risks of dispersing, which include vulnerability to predators, difficulties of finding and defending food, and aggression from resident males in the groups they attempt to join.

Whenever one sex is philopatric, random demographic events, such as skewed infant sex ratios and survival, may interfere with the ability of individuals to maintain optimal group sizes (Strier, 2000a). Macaque and baboon matrilines may become so large, for example, that within-group competition among females for food outweighs the benefits of cooperation among female kin in defending food resources against other groups of related females (Figure 4.13). Similarly, chimpanzee or muriqui patrilines could potentially become so large that within-group competition among males for mates outweighs the benefits of cooperation among male kin in defending access to females against other groups of related males. In these cases, factions of kin should split from their relatives to establish smaller groups where they can increase their fitness.

This seemed to be what happened when a faction of male chimpanzees at Gombe National Park split off from the growing Kasakela community. However, instead of benefiting from their move, they were systematically exterminated during aggressive encounters with their former associates (Figure 4.14). Evidently, their decision to strike off on their own had lethal consequences, which could not have been anticipated by evolutionary theory.

Resident group members usually attempt to repel the immigration attempts of others of their own sex because immigrants raise the competitive stakes. If cooperating in finding and defending food or reproductive resources is beneficial, kin should be preferred allies over nonkin because of their shared genetic interests, and sex-biased philopatry should occur. Thus, when allies are important in defending food resources, female primates are expected to live in matrilineal societies. Conversely, when allies are important in defending access to mates, male primates are expected

FIGURE 4.13   White-faced capuchin monkey (*Cebus capucinus*) alpha- and beta-ranking females threaten the alpha male. By joining forces, females can keep males in their place. Photo by Susan Perry.

FIGURE 4.14   A male chimpanzee (*Pan troglodytes*) from the Kahama community at Gombe was fatally wounded during an attack by males from the Kasakela community. This photo was taken about six weeks after the attack; he died soon after it was taken. Photo by Jim Moore/Anthro-Photo.

to live in patrilines. Evaluating these predictions requires data on the degree to which food and mates are defensible resources for different primates in different habitats. As we'll see in Chapters 6–8, the available data are largely consistent with predictions about the relationships between cooperative resource defense and patterns of philopatry.

There are limits, however, to how far an individual will go toward repelling an unrelated competitor. These limits, like those affecting optimal group size, are based on the tradeoffs between the costs, in terms of time, energy, and risk of injury, of repelling an intruder and the benefits, in terms of reduced competition, if an intruder is successfully deterred. The benefits are significant in the case of primates such as Hanuman langurs, where males stand to lose not only their own position in a female troop but also their offspring to a takeover by an infanticidal competitor. For males in the multi-male groups of olive baboons or macaques, however, the costs of deflecting males attempting to immigrate may outweigh the benefits of doing so. Of course, it is also possible that males may simply fail at their efforts to repel an immigrant, and therefore suffer the fitness consequences.

I have witnessed shifts in the behavior of female muriquis toward other females attempting to immigrate into the study group. At first, resident females chase and threaten the young intruders, who end up tagging along well behind the main body of the group for up to months at a time. Eventually, however, the resident females relax their vigilance, and the new immigrants begin to establish friendly relationships with the offspring of these females and with young males, who also turn out to be their future mates (Strier, 1993b).

Establishing affiliative bonds with members of the opposite sex as a way to integrate into a new group has been well-documented in olive baboons, where males instead of females disperse (Strum, 1982). By recruiting female "friends," immigrant males slowly ease their way into baboon society and may even gain preferred status when their female friends are ready to mate (Smuts, 1985). Females participate in these friendships because males can be influential allies in their hierarchical societies (Smuts, 1987b).

Conflicts between the Sexes

Reconciling male and female interests is not always as clear-cut as the example of baboon friendships implies because the resources that affect male and female reproductive success are usually different. Food has more direct effects on the reproductive success of females than of males. A number of field and captive studies on a variety of primates have shown that better-fed females begin reproducing at an earlier age, produce healthier offspring, have shorter interbirth intervals, and live longer to reproduce (Altmann, et al., 1985; Mori, 1979; Small, 1981). Males, too, need to eat to survive, and healthy males have reproductive advantages over hungry ones. However, the number of females that can be fertilized is also a key determinant of male reproductive success. These fundamental differences between the sexes are critical to understanding the diversity and flexibility of primate social and mating systems, and how these arise from conflicts and compromises among individual behavioral strategies (Eisenberg, et al., 1972; Emlen and Oring, 1977).

5

Evolution and Sex

Many male primates look different from females. The differences range from the bright blue testicles of vervet monkeys, to the thick beards covering the protruding throat sacs of howler monkeys (and some human chins), to the razor-sharp canines that a baboon's lips can barely conceal (Figure 5.1). Such flashy signs of primate maleness seem like cumbersome attachments to the more svelte, streamlined forms that females take (Figure 5.2). Whenever the sexes differ from one another in body size or form, it is almost always the males that are larger, brighter, or more elaborately endowed (Figure 5.3). Why do the males of some species carry such excess baggage around with them, while others blend in with females so well that their sex can only be visibly distinguished by their telltale, but otherwise unremarkable, genitals?

    Showy male attributes more often than not evolved in response to competition from other males, which can escalate from ritualized displays into brutal fights with

FIGURE 5.1 Olive baboon (*Papio anubis*) male displaying his canines. Photo by Irven DeVore/Anthro-Photo.

FIGURE 5.2 Male mandrills (*Mandrillus sphinx*) are larger and their faces much more vibrantly marked than females. Photo by Dr. M. E. Rogers, I. C. A. P. B., University of Edinburgh, Scotland.

fatal consequences. If greater size, strength, or toothy weaponry gives males advantages over their competitors, then these traits will be selected for over evolutionary time. Consequently, a great deal of research has focused on trying to test predictions about the relationship between morphological and behavioral traits that affect the fitness of males relative to their competitors.

FIGURE 5.3   An adult red-tailed guenon (*Cercopithecus ascanius*) male weighs about two pounds more than an adult female. Photo by Marina Cords.

A secondary benefit of being bigger in body size or canine size is that males gain some advantages over females, who can be bullied or coerced into compliant behaviors through aggression or the threat of aggression. Females may directly or indirectly perpetuate the system if, by choice or in self-defense, they mate with the showiest or most aggressive males (Small, 1992; Smuts and Smuts, 1993). And, if their sons inherit the same traits that contributed to their fathers' success, mothers should also benefit through higher inclusive fitness from their sons' success. As with predictions about male competitive abilities and fitness, those associated with the fitness consequences of female mate choices are among the hottest topics in behavioral ecology.

It is no coincidence that when males and females are similar in size and strength, relationships between the sexes also tend to be more egalitarian. If pronounced sexual dimorphism reflects one extreme on a continuum of male reproductive competition and dominance over females, sexual monomorphism, associated with greater sexual equality, represents the other extreme.

Sexual monomorphism is not rare among primates. Prosimians, many New World monkeys, some Old World monkeys, and gibbons are sexually monomorphic, even though males with size on their side have a competitive edge. In lemurs, sexual monomorphism and its effects on female dominance over males has been linked to the harsh and unpredictable ecology of Madagascar (Wright, 1999). But, whatever the reason, when male competition is constrained, or when females prefer mates possessing other attributes, such as their willingness to help care for offspring, then the benefits of size or showiness are reduced.

Sexual Selection

The legacy of male reproductive competition, and the patterning of sexual dimorphism across primates and other animals, is rooted in fundamental and irrefutable biological differences between the sexes. In his 1871 follow-up volume to natural selection, entitled *The Descent of Man and Selection in Relation to Sex*, Darwin attributed the widespread occurrence of **secondary sexual characteristics**, which are traits that serve no purpose in survival or the mechanical process of reproduction, to **intrasexual competition** driven by a process he called **sexual selection.** Sexual selection is more specific than natural selection because sexual selection acts on traits that affect differential reproduction among individuals of *the same sex.*

Sexual selection, as proposed by Darwin and expanded upon by Robert Trivers (1972) and other evolutionary biologists, involves two processes: selection for competition over access to mates, which is usually stronger among males; and selection for choice of mates, which is usually stronger among females. Brightly colored faces or fur, or larger bodies or larger canines should contribute to fitness among males if these characteristics confer benefits in their competition with other males for mates or in enhancing their attractiveness to females. Male competition for access to mates may also explain why many male primates take longer to mature than females, and why males of many species engage in more brutal aggressive competition, which results in higher mortality rates among males than females.

Females, on the other hand, appear to be more discriminating about their mates than males. This is because compared to males, the **reproductive potential** of females is more limited. Females are born with a finite number of large sex cells, or ova, which subsequently develop once a female begins to ovulate. Females are only capable of conceiving when an ovum reaches maturity and is released from the ovaries during ovulation. Male sex cells, or sperm, are smaller and more numerous than the female sex cells, and are constantly being replenished during spermatogenesis throughout adulthood. Males are biologically capable of fertilization whenever they have produced enough viable sperm.

Once fertilization has occurred, female primates, like all female mammals, bear the time and energetic costs of gestation. During pregnancy, a female cannot conceive again, whereas the male who fertilized her is technically free to pursue other reproductive opportunities with additional females. Mothers also expend energy in lactation when an infant is finally born. In most species, hormonal feedback mechanisms inhibit ovulation for an extended period, resulting in lactation amenorrhea. Except in the case of callitrichids (see Box 1.1), the biology of internal reproduction and lactation constrains mothers, but not fathers, from pursuing new reproductive opportunities from the moment they conceive until the time they wean their current offspring (Figure 5.4).

The consequences of these basic inequalities between the sexes lead to two predictions. First, ovulating females should become limiting resources for male reproduction. Unlike males, females are out of the immediate reproductive picture during the intervals between their ovulations, as well as when they are not ovulating during pregnancy or lactation. As a result, male–male competition for access to ovulating females should be much higher than female–female competition for access to males, who are usually biologically capable of pursuing any additional reproductive opportunities that come their way.

Second, reproductive mistakes should be more costly for females than they are for males. A female who loses a fetus early on in its development must still wait

FIGURE 5.4   An adult female long-tailed macaque (*Macaca fascicularis*) with her first infant eating a *Ficus* fruit. Photo by Maria van Noordwijk and Carel van Schaik.

for her hormones to kick in before she can resume ovulating and possibly conceive again, whereas a male's reproductive capacity is independent of the success or failure of his prior copulations. If the fetus spontaneously aborts or the infant dies at birth or afterward, the mother is the parent who has irrevocably lost time and energy that instead could have been invested in a more successful reproductive effort. Considering that a single error in reproduction can result in months or years of wasted female investment, at virtually no cost to her male counterpart, it is no wonder that sexual selection would favor females who are finicky about their mates, but not so choosey that they miss out on chances to reproduce.

The intensity of male competition is directly affected by what females, as well as what other males, are doing. It is easy to envision how the solitary habits of many female orangutans or tarsiers could present very different sets of challenges to males of their species than the large, cohesive groups of female Hanuman langurs or the even larger groups of female olive baboons, which, in turn, present different challenges than the fluid and unpredictable associations that female chimpanzees or spider monkeys maintain. Likewise, the brief, two- to three-week-long annual breeding season of female lemurs clearly creates quite different reproductive opportunities for males than the aseasonal resumption of estrus associated with the three–six year **interbirth intervals** of female mountain gorillas.

Another way of looking at these differences among primates is to consider the effects of life histories on male competition. For example, mountain gorillas and olive baboons resemble one another in having breeding group sex ratios of roughly two females for every male. Yet, female baboons give birth at two-year intervals, whereas female gorillas give birth at three–six year intervals. As a result of these differences in reproductive rates, a male baboon encounters estrous females roughly two to three times as often as a male gorilla does. Thus, despite their similar sex ratios, there are clearly substantial differences in the number of fertile females available to males in each species at any point in time (Mitani, et al., 1996b).

Interbirth intervals are just one of the reproductive variables that are expected to affect the availability of fertile females to males. Breeding seasonality, as mentioned above and breeding synchrony among females in the same group (Nunn, 1999a) are other such variables that should affect the **variance in** male **reproductive success,** or the degree to which some males gain a disproportionate number of fertilizations than other males at different times in their lives.

Reproductive monopolies that result in high variance, or highly skewed reproductive success among males, are not easy to maintain, particularly if females spatially segregate themselves apart from one another or if female **estrous** cycles, when ovulation occurs, are tightly synchronized. After all, not even the most fit male primate can be in more than one place at the same time (Strum and Latour, 1991). The more synchronized that reproduction is among females, the more ovulating females there will be at any one time, and the more difficult it will be for a single male to monopolize mates. When males can't monopolize multiple females, the variance in male reproductive success tends to be lower than when males can. Over the long term, the variance in male reproductive success may not be as great as reproductive monopolies imply. Males move up and down in their hierarchies and in the degree to which they are preferred by females as mates (Altmann, et al., 1996; Berard, 1999; Dunbar, 1984; Hausfater, 1975; Takahata, et al., 1999).

The **operational sex ratio** takes into account the availability of ovulating females as well as the number of breeding females and males in a group (Table 5.1). Consequently, it provides a more accurate index of the intensity of primate male competition at any particular time than the sex ratios of primate groups (Emlen and

---

TABLE 5.1   The operational sex ratio*

Variables involved in calculating OSR (based on 365 days per year for both sexes)

---

f = the number of females

m = the number of males

S_f = the period when females are ready to mate (should include the sum of estrous cycles of c days of duration prior to conception, divided by the birth interval, B.

S_m = the period when males are ready to mate. For seasonal breeders, this is the product of B multiplied by the duration of the breeding season; for aseasonal breeders, this is the product of B multiplied by 365 days.

m multiplied by S_m = the expected number of reproductively active males

f multiplied by S_f = the expected number of reproductively available females

The OSR is the ratio of the expected number of reproductively active males to females.

---

*As calculated by Mitani, et al., 1996b.

Oring, 1977). Because operational sex ratios are also a more accurate predictor of the potential variance in male reproductive success, they can also explain more about the range of variation in levels of sexual dimorphism that tend to distinguish primates living in pairbonds, uni-male, or multi-male groups (Mitani, et al., 1996b).

Sexual Dimorphism

Sexual selection explains why the spatial and temporal distributions of estrous females affect the intensity of male competition, and why **female choice** can alter the outcome of aggressive competition among males. Sexual selection also produces a tension between female mate choice and male competition whenever sexually dimorphic males, who are larger and stronger than females, can employ coercion to override or influence female mate choices. Comparing levels of sexual dimorphism provides an indirect measure for assessing the degree of competition among males over mates, and therefore for evaluating the male competition component of the sexual selection equation. However, other factors, such as phylogenetic and ecological constraints, may affect the ways in which sexual selection is expressed in primates.

Phylogenetic Constraints

Sexual selection, like natural selection, can only act on the variation present in a population. In other words, sexual selection can only lead to high levels of sexual dimorphism if secondary sexual characteristics vary with individual fitness and have a heritable component. The last common ancestors of closely related species often determine the expression of morphological and behavioral patterns in descendant species unless one or both are subjected to vastly different selection pressures. This is why closely related species that share similar lifestyles also tend to resemble one another in their life history strategies and their degree of sexual dimorphism.

The effects of phylogeny can provide insights into how sexual dimorphism is distributed across primates, just as phylogenetic analyses demonstrated that male-biased dispersal with female philopatry among anthropoid primates are prevalent only in cercopithecines (Di Fiore and Rendall, 1994; Chapter 2). For example, lemurs are sexually monomorphic in body size and canine size, yet males clearly compete for mates, and females, who are dominant over males, clearly assert their mate choices (Kappeler, 1997a; Richard, 1992; Richard and Dewar, 1991).

Ecological Constraints

The mechanics associated with eating place upper limits on male canine size, and canine size is often, but not always, allometrically scaled with body size (see Chapter 2). Larger males should have proportionately larger canines than females because of these scaling effects between tooth size and body size.

The ecological constraints on body size dimorphism are even more complex because body size is inextricably related to the energetics of diet and locomotion.

Although larger bodies require more food to sustain, their metabolic requirements are lower per unit body weight than smaller bodies (Chapter 2). As a result, male and female diets in sexually dimorphic species differ in predictable ways, with smaller females consuming smaller quantities of high-energy foods and larger males consuming larger quantities of lower-energy foods.

The energetics of locomotion and the need for agility also affect sexual dimorphism in expected ways. Larger males may be able to travel longer distances efficiently, but they would also be at a severe disadvantage in mate competition if their size interfered with their ability to maneuver through the canopy. In some of the larger bodied arboreal primates, such as spider monkeys and muriquis, the necessity of rapidly traversing long distances between widely spaced fruit resources offset other advantages to large body size. Despite these constraints, the sexually dimorphic canines of spider monkeys and the large testes of muriquis reflect differences in the intensity of competition between and within communities of male kin (Strier, 1994b).

Large male orangutans reconcile the loss of agility that comes with their size by descending to the ground whenever speed matters, although even then, their bodies are not well-suited for terrestrial travel. Indeed, the energetics associated with their quadrumanous mode of locomotion may be one reason why male orangutans can't adopt the chimpanzee male strategy of cooperating with one another to patrol a larger area supporting more females (Rodman, 1984). The more versatile knuckle-walking mode of chimpanzee travel that makes their cooperative community patrols so feasible also influences some of the differences in the competitive regimes between them and their orangutan cousins.

Comparisons among most other primates with similar levels of male competition, as estimated by operational sex ratios, are consistent in showing that sexual dimorphism in body size is more pronounced in terrestrial species than in arboreal ones. Indeed, secondary sexual characteristics, including body and canine size dimorphism and other physical attributes, such as striking colors on their faces or genitals, are more prevalent in terrestrial primates than in arboreal primates (Mitani, et al., 1996b). Of course, being out in the open on the ground also means that males can't slip easily behind foliage to avoid confrontations, and that females can't conveniently go off unnoticed with preferred suitors. As a result of these environmental factors, the dynamics of male competition and female mate choice are likely to be different for primates that spend considerable time in the open on the ground compared to those that live mainly in the trees. Sexual selection has capitalized on the greater visibility of life on the ground in the fantastically colored muzzles and male genitalia, as well as impossible-to-conceal sexual swellings on females, that advertise competitive ability in males and attractiveness in both males and females.

Mating Patterns

Being a limiting resource puts female primates in an influential position when it comes to males. From how they distribute themselves in relation to their food resources, to how frequently they are capable of reproducing, to how they assert their mate choices, female primates determine the behavioral options and reproductive opportunities available to males (see Figure 1.18). Primate mating patterns reflect the compromises between female and male strategies to gain access to mates, food, and other resources that they and their offspring need to survive. These compromises are constrained by life history and physiology, and vary with ecological and demographic conditions.

Mating Patterns When Females Are Solitary

Consider the four options available to males when females distribute themselves to avoid one another and the intragroup competition for food that would arise if they were to live together: (1) A male can either join up with a single female on a shared and mutually defended territory from which together they exclude intruders of both sexes; or (2) he can try to repel competitors from a territory that encompasses the smaller **core areas** used by a few solitary females; or (3) he can join forces with other males to help raise a female's offspring; or (4) he can join forces with other males in defending several scattered females from other groups of males. Each alternative affects the intensity of male competition and degree of sexual dimorphism in predictable ways. But, in all cases, the range of male options is established by the distribution of ovulating females in space and time.

The Case of Monogamy.   When a male establishes a longterm bond with a female, he essentially ties his reproductive fate to hers. By foregoing his higher reproductive potential, he can increase his ability to monitor the fidelity of his mate, and therefore gain some measure of **paternity certainty** about any offspring she produces. The female of such pairs gains an ally in defending her food resources against other females and, because his reproductive success is tied to hers, she can exact high levels of male investment. In some pair-bonded gibbons and siamangs, male investment takes a variety of forms, including deference to females at food sources (Leighton, 1987). In owl monkeys and callitrichids, male investment also involves significant contributions to infant carrying, which appears to improve infant survival as well as to allow unencumbered mothers to replenish the energy reserves they need to reproduce again (Wright, 1990).

   If the male and the female reproduce exclusively with one another, the variance in reproductive success among monogamously mated males should be comparable to that among females. The relaxation of sexual selection pressures on monogamous primates is evident from the absence of secondary sexual characteristics (Figure 5.5). Sexual monomorphism characterizes all pair-bonded primates, which include representatives from each of the major taxonomic groups (prosimians, New World monkeys, Old World monkeys, and apes). But, not all sexually monomorphic primates are monogamous. And, even more striking, few primates that typically live in pair-bonded societies turn out to practice monogamy when it comes to mating (Box 5.1).

An Extreme Form of Polygyny.   In some species, a male who attempts to single-handedly monopolize access to more than one solitary female is taking big risks,

FIGURE 5.5   Bolivian gray titi monkeys (*Callicebus donacophilus*) are one of the few monogamously pair-bonded primates. Photo by © Noel Rowe/*Pictorial Guide To Living Primates.*

presumably in exchange for potentially big gains. Neighboring territorial males and males who lack territories of their own pose constant threats to his vigilance. While he is off feeding or reconnoitering with a female in one part of his territory, the other females in other parts of his territory are vulnerable to incursions from outsiders. The possibility of increasing his reproductive success beyond what it would be with a single mate must be compelling, indeed, for otherwise why would a male ever sacrifice the security of a stable pair-bond and its presumably higher paternity certainty?

Polygyny, in which a single male monopolizes access to multiple females, is widespread across primates, and usually occurs when a single male either joins an established female group or succeeds in attracting dispersing females into new groups. Polygyny resulting from a male patrolling multiple solitary females is common among nocturnal prosimians, but among the diurnal primates it occurs only in some populations of orangutans. For both historical reasons (Chapter 1) and practical ones involving the greater difficulty of observing small, nocturnal primates compared to large, diurnal ones, orangutans have received more attention than the nocturnal prosimians, but the similarities between them are quite striking.

Female orangutans are thought to avoid exclusive associations with a single male because of the greater energy and time expenditure they would incur in finding sufficient food with another adult around. Perhaps the greatest assistance a male could provide her is to prevent other males from harassing her? Perhaps females reinforce and reward their territorial mates by screaming loudly to attract their attention and struggling to resist any mating attempts by intruding males?

In orangutans, the potential variance in male reproductive success is high if a successful male's territory includes the core areas of two or more females (Rodman and Mitani, 1987). The extreme level of sexual dimorphism that orangutans exhibit is consistent with the strength of male–male competition (Figure 5.6). At more than twice the size of a female, full grown males weighing over 80 kilograms (compared to females, which weigh less than 40 kg) can barely manage to climb through the canopy. Branches are constantly in danger of snapping under these heavy weights, and nearly all male orangutan long-distance travel occurs on the ground (Rodman, 1984).

The large adult male orangutans are also endowed with large canines and huge fleshy cheek pads, and throat sacs to blast their long-distance calls. The air stored in their throat sacs resonates so that their warning vocalizations can be heard for up to a kilometer (Mitani, 1985a). Males use their impressive bulk, intimidating canines, and cheeky armaments to compete with one another in establishing and defending their territories. Encounters between large males can be avoided because they announce their presence with long territorial spacing calls, but when a territorial male discovers an adult male intruder, he becomes a fierce aggressor (Knott, 1999; Rodman and Mitani, 1987).

With territorial males keeping tabs on more than their equal share of females, there is a surplus of less fortunate males in the population. For many years, researchers encountered these solitary males ranging widely throughout the forest.

FIGURE 5.6   A fully adult male orangutan (*Pongo pygmaeus*). Photo by Tim Laman.

BOX **5.1**

Gibbon Games and Tarsier Tactics

Technically, monogamy means mating with just one partner. Lots of birds were long thought to be monogamous based on the strong pair-bonds that individual males and females established with one another, their joint territorial defense against intruders, and their mutual investment in the offspring that were sure to inherit half of each paired-up parent's genes. However, this view of pair-bonded birds began to blur when molecular techniques to confirm partner paternity were put to the test. Researchers occasionally observed pair-bonded partners of many bird species mating with members of the opposite sex other than their mates, but no one imagined that up to 35 percent of the chicks raised by established pairs would turn out to be fathered by these extra-pair males (Birkhead and Moller, 1992). Birds differ in the degree to which **extra-pair copulations,** and **extra-pair fertilizations** occur, but the bases for these differences, both among species and within species, are not yet known (Petrie and Kempenaers, 1998).

So-called monogamous primates show similar infidelity (Bartlett, 1999). During a two and one-half year study at the Ketambe Research Station in Sumatra, Ryne Palombit (1994) observed five extra-pair copulations by a pair-bonded female siamang. Three of these extra-pair copulations involved a young male from a neighboring group, two involved different adult males. In Thailand's Khao Yai National Park, eight extra-pair copulations were observed by white-handed gibbons (Reichard, 1995). All occurred during or after hostile clashes at the territorial boundaries, when the female stuck around a little longer than her mate. It wasn't the female who initiated these liaisons, but neither did she take evasive actions to avoid or discourage this male's advances. Her mate intervened when he was nearby, but when he'd already moved off, his competitor could copulate.

Why gibbons cheat on their partners is anyone's guess. Extra-pair copulations may give both males and females an opportunity to assess one another as a future potential mate. Any possible fertilization resulting from an extra-pair copulation might be beneficial to the female, particularly if she has fertility problems with her own mate, as well as the male (Palombit, 1994, 1995). In other words, females may be practicing a risk-aversive strategy to maximize their reproductive success (Palombit, 1999). Fertilizations resulting from extra-pair copulations would also clearly be beneficial to the fathers as well. But a pairbonded male must balance these potential gains against the risks of losing his mate, or at least his paternity if his mate conceives with another male while he is off looking for an extra partner for himself (Reichard, 1995).

Warren Brockelman and his colleagues (Brockelman, et al., 1998), who have studied the gibbons in Khao Yai National Park for years, are peeling back yet another layer of the secret sociality of these lesser apes. In addition to the hostility that usually occurs between territorial groups of gibbons, a high percentage of their encounters are friendly and relaxed. Juveniles play with and groom their peers from neighboring families, and have interacted peacefully with an adult male who might have been their uncle.

These findings are consistent with prior observations that prolonged interactions and associations characterize many encounters between neighboring groups of white-handed gibbons in this region (Reichard and Sommer, 1997). If male gibbons in the neighborhood are related to one another, they may be more likely to affiliate than to fight with one another. Highly aggressive fights, involving lethal wounds in one known case, have also been reported between males in this species (Palombit, 1993; Reichard and Sommer, 1997), but whether variation in the social and genetic relationships among males in adjacent groups explains the different degrees of tolerance they display will require genetic studies similar to those that confirmed extra-pair paternity in birds (Brockelman, et al., 1998). In fact, new genetic data from gibbons in Indonesia indicate that subadult males and females sometimes join family groups other than their own (Oka and Takenaka, 2001).

Deviations from purported pair-bonding take a different, but no less significant, form in Indonesian spectral tarsiers, which are nocturnal creatures weighing a mere four ounces. In many other small bodied nocturnal primates, individual females avoid one another in their nonoverlapping ranges, and mate exclusively with the male whose larger home range overlaps with their own (Bearder, 1987). In tarsiers, however, some groups contain more than one adult male and others contain multiple females (Gursky, 1995; MacKinnon and MacKinnon, 1980).

Working with a flashlight to find her way through the forest at night, primatologist Sharon Gursky (1995, 1998) used the tarsiers' distinctive wake-up vocalizations and radio telemetry to locate groups and determine their composition and ranging habits. She discovered that up to 14 percent of spectral tarsier groups in northern Suluwesi included two adult females and a single adult male, and that the home ranges of females, which are just about 50 percent smaller than the 3.1 hectare ranges of males, often overlapped.

This variation in group composition and the nonexclusivity of female home ranges led Gursky to suspect that male tarsiers may have tactics other than monogamy in mind. For starters, female tarsiers get no help from their mates in caring for their infants (Gursky, 1994). Mothers put their infants in their mouths to move them around, and deposit them in trees while they go out to eat unencumbered. In other pair-bonded primates, male participation in either occasional infant care or routine range defense is part of the game in gaining female fidelity, and even then, as with gibbons, there are no guarantees.

Variation in habitat quality and population density may explain why some female tarsiers tolerate one another, and why some male tarsiers can monitor more than one female. For example, in habitats that support high population densities, female tarsiers encounter one another more often and might therefore be expected to be more tolerant than at lower densities, where encounters can be more easily avoided. In this case, higher female density would also facilitate males' monitoring multiple females.

Similar ecological variables could also account for why some male gibbons stay close to home (Brockelman, et al., 1998) and why both male and female gibbons take advantage of extra-pair mating opportunities to assess the local mate market. Deciphering the ways in which ecological variables affect monogamy, extra-pair copulations, and facultative, or opportunistic, polygamy, will require further comparative investigations among populations of primates in which individuals spend most of their time alone or with a mate (Fuentes, 1998).

Because they were smaller in body size, and lacked the secondary sexual characteristics of territorial males, they were at first assumed to be immatures. However, as these vagrant males became known to observers as individuals, it was clear that some of them were well beyond the age at which secondary sexual characteristics typically develop (te Boekhorst, et al., 1990). Unable to compete for territories themselves, these undeveloped males have few options other than to adopt transient lifestyles. They slip in and out of female core areas and cross the territorial boundaries staked out by larger males. Some of these transient males seem to be on reconnaissance, looking for unoccupied places where they can set up their own territorial bases. Others are undoubtedly sons who come back periodically to visit their mothers, and, perhaps, to ascertain whether a vacancy as the territorial male in the area has opened up. Still others may be looking for estrous females that are unattended by a territorial male, and thus vulnerable to stealing an opportunity to mate.

Female orangutans generally resist the sexual advances made by transient males. The ferocity of their resistance has led researchers to label them victims of forced copulations, or even rape (Galdikas, 1981, 1985; MacKinnon, 1974; Mitani, 1985b). The loud screams of a female victim will bring the territorial male, if he is close enough to hear, racing to the scene to interrupt the assault. If intervention is too far away, and the female cannot escape from her attacker, the transient male may get reproductively lucky. In fact, many copulations observed in orangutans have involved these males, which females try to resist (Galdikas, 1995a; Knott, 1999).

Little else is known about transient males. The elusive habits they maintain to avoid the wrath of territorial males make monitoring them as difficult for researchers as it is for other orangutans (van Schaik and van Hooff, 1996). Apparently there are two phenotypes among male orangutans, just as there are among some species of frogs and fish. Among mammals, however, staying small and undeveloped is a most unusual solution to the problem of intense male competition. It is assumed that a transient male who discovers a vacant area to set up his own territory will develop the phenotype of other territorial males, but what causes the hormonal switches that trigger development of these secondary sexual characteristics is still unclear. In captivity, some young males begin to develop secondary sexual characteristics from about seven years of age, while others fail to do so. Although both types of males are believed to be fertile, those that are **developmentally arrested** have lower levels of testosterone and other hormones than fully mature males (Maggioncalda et al., 1999, 2000). Sexual selection, and the effects of male competition, must be powerful, indeed, for such extraordinary mechanisms to have evolved.

A similar phenomenon of two male phenotypes has also been observed in the Zanzibar bushbaby (Figure 5.7). In one population studied in Kenya by anthropologist Leanne Nash (1986), the males fell into two distinct classes: small males, who weighed less than 141 grams, and large males, who weighed at least 145 grams. The small males had larger ranges than the large males, whose more restricted ranges put them into more direct association with females. As in the early orangutan studies, Nash couldn't be sure whether the small males in her study were younger than the large males. And, as is also still true for orangutans, we don't know yet whether differences in male size and ranging patterns correlate with differences in their reproductive success.

Polyandry.   It is common for female primates to mate with multiple males, but it is rare for males to be tolerant of it. Callitrichids may be an exception, for in some populations multiple males associate with a single breeding female, and cooperate in caring for the infants she produces. It is common to find polyandrous groups of

FIGURE 5.7   An adult Zanzibar galago (*Galagoides zanzibaricus*) from Gedi, Kenya, poised in a tree near a trap. Photo by Leanne T. Nash.

tamarins living alongside monogamous groups, but usually relationships among males in polyandrous groups are distinctly hierarchical. The alpha male monopolizes most, if not all, copulations, even if the males living together are related to one another (Baker, et al., 1993). Low ranking brothers will leave if opportunities to find mates elsewhere exist, but while they are members of these groups they also help with infant care. The rapid reproductive rates of female callitrichids may require mothers to have help in caring for and carrying their infants (see Box 1.1). Alpha males may therefore tolerate subordinate males because of the help they provide, and subordinate males may provide help in exchange for being tolerated in these groups when opportunities to associate with females elsewhere are limited.

Ambivalent Polygamy.   The fourth option for a male confronted with independent females is to form cooperative alliances with other males in defending an area occupied by several females. By coordinating their activities, each male in an alliance has a competitive advantage over solitary males or those in smaller alliances. Recruitment into these male alliances typically comes through kinship because, as we saw in Chapter 4, the genetic interests relatives share tend to make them preferred, more reliable allies. Chimpanzees and spider monkeys are two examples of species in which male kin form cooperative alliances to defend a collective territory containing females from unrelated males belonging to other **communities.**

Competition among males in these patrilineal societies may be as intense as it is among unrelated males, but it is configured differently in these species than in the other primates considered so far. The benefits of cooperating with their kin in competition against other groups puts patrilocal males in an awkward position when it comes to conflicts amongst themselves for access to estrous females. Losing out on an opportunity to fertilize a female may not be as bad when the winner carries some of the loser's genes as it is when there is no genetic relationship between competitors. But, because it's still genetically better to be the father of an offspring than related to the father, even within these kin groups, males compete over mates.

With hair-raising charges, bites, kicks, and screams, male chimpanzees challenge their brothers and uncles for dominance and the advantages that high rank confers. The alpha male can keep subordinates away from an estrous female through threats or aggressive attacks, but usually he isn't the only male who ends up mating (Tutin, 1979). Female chimpanzees, like many other female primates, mate **promiscuously** with multiple partners, especially at times just before and after their actual ovulations, when there may still be some chance of fertilization. And, if more than one female is in estrus simultaneously, the alpha male is unlikely to be able to keep track of both (Watts, 1998).

Subordinate males sometimes pressure ovulating females into accompanying them on **safari,** in which the pair moves stealthily off to a remote part of the community's territory to feed and rest and mate together for days on end. Being so isolated, the **consorting** pair is potentially vulnerable to lethal attacks by male kin of neighboring communities patrolling the boundaries of their ranges. Females are often reluctant to take such risks, but by refusing to cooperate they risk inciting male attacks (Smuts and Smuts, 1993; Wrangham and Peterson, 1996). Subordinate males are evidently willing to risk attacks from neighboring communities if going on safari is the only way they can mate without interference from more dominant males in their own communities. High-ranking males fear little in the way of intervention from other males in their community, and can therefore mate more openly without incurring the risks of being attacked by males from adjacent communities, against which one is no match on his own.

The chimpanzee mating system is a polygamous one because both sexes mate with multiple partners. By definition it differs from polygyny, where only a few fortunate males monopolize reproductive access to multiple females and from polyandry, where it is the female that mates with multiple partners. The variance in male reproductive success in polygamous mating systems is higher than in monogamous mating systems because some males have more reproductive opportunities than others with a larger number of females.

As might be expected, levels of sexual dimorphism among primates with polygamous mating systems also fall somewhere in between those among monogamous pair-bonds and uni-male polygynous systems (Figure 5.8). For example, greater terrestriality in chimpanzees may explain why males weigh about 25 percent more than females, and also have disproportionately larger canines. But the degree of sexual dimorphism is lower among chimpanzees and other primates in which males stay in their natal groups and compete against their kin than it is among primates in which males disperse and compete against nonkin. Nonetheless, in these polygamous patrilines, males have large testes relative to body size, suggesting that at least some of their competition for fertilization occurs at the level of sperm instead of through direct aggressive challenges against their relatives (Figure 5.9).

Male chimpanzees, spider monkeys, and muriquis need their kin for cooperative intergroup defense, and kinship has an inhibitory effect on aggression. The costs of wounding or killing a relative extend beyond the loss of an ally important in intergroup competition to include the losses to male inclusive fitness. **Sperm competition** offers an alternative to aggression whenever monopolies on mating are hard to achieve (Harcourt, 1996). Between males who mate with the same female, the one with the greatest production of sperm or the most viable (or long-lived) sperm might have a higher probability of fertilization success. To the extent that

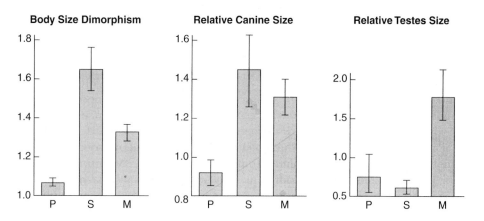

P–Pair living or monogamous; S–Single-male; M–Multi-male

FIGURE 5.8   Body size dimorphism, relative canine size and relative testes size for primate genera belonging to different breeding systems. Bars indicate one standard error from the mean. Values of 1.0 indicate no sexual dimorphism in body size, or no deviation in canine size and testes size from body size allometry. From Harvey, P. H. and Harcourt, A. H. 1984. Sperm competition, testes size, and breeding systems in primates. In R. L. Smith, Ed., *Sperm Competition and the Evolution of Animal Breeding Systems,* Chapter 18, pp. 589–600. New York: Academic Press. Reprinted with permission from the authors and the publisher. Copyright © Academic Press, 1984.

FIGURE 5.9   Muriqui (*Brachyteles arachnoides*) males in an embrace huddle. Note their disproportionately large testes, which may be a way of competing for fertilizations through sperm instead of access to mates. Photo by Paulo Coutinho.

large testes confer advantages in male competition through sperm production, large testes size relative to body size is another indication, along with sexual dimorphism in canine size, of the strength of sexual selection.

Mating Patterns When Females Live in Groups

Many female primates live in stable groups with other females. In some cases, females in these groups are members of one or more extended matrilines, who remain with their mothers, older sisters, and other female relatives for their entire lifetimes (Figure 5.10). In other cases, these groups consist of females who left their natal groups as adolescents to join unfamiliar females away from their mothers and fathers.

Independent of their composition, cohesive groups of females represent a different set of reproductive opportunities for males than females who actively avoid one another. Females who form groups may do so for their own protection from predators or aggressive males, or in pursuit of their own optimal feeding strategies, as we'll see in the following chapters. But, whatever the underlying cause of female groups, the best strategy for males is the obvious one: join the group with the most females and try to keep all other males away (Alberts and Altmann, 1995). The problem, of course, is that all males have the same strategy, so male competition for membership in female groups can be intense.

Gregarious females affect the intensity of male competition in two related ways. First, the size and cohesiveness of a group of females affects whether a single

FIGURE 5.10   Japanese macaques (*Macaca fuscata*) huddling.
Photo by Minoru Kinoshita, Technician, Kyoto University,
Primate Research Institute.

male can maintain exclusive access to the group. In a uni-male group, the residing male must constantly repel efforts by unattached males to take over the group. If females are too numerous, or if they spread out too far while feeding, a single male may not be able to prevent other males from joining the group. In the multi-male groups that form as a result, males will fight to try to prevent additional competitors from entering the group, and compete for reproductive opportunities with those males whose immigrations are successful.

As we saw earlier, group-living females also affect male competition when they experience high levels of **reproductive synchrony** because it is difficult for one male to keep track of multiple estrous females at once. Ecological factors, and, in particular, the seasonal availability of important food resources, are usually at least partially responsible for **reproductive seasonality** both within and between groups (Lindburg, 1987). Predator pressures (Boinski, 1987a) or social factors may also lead to synchronized reproduction within, but not between, groups (Clarke, et al., 1992). The more restricted and synchronized that estrus is in time, the more difficult it should be for a single male to monopolize multiple mates. An increase in reproductive opportunities for multiple males potentially lowers the variance in male reproductive success. If females come into estrus at different times, however, each estrous female becomes a potentially monopolizable resource, and the variance in male reproductive success can be greater.

Single-Male Female Groups.   The size and cohesion of female groups determines the number of males that can join them (Mitani, et al., 1996a). The relationship between female group size and male group size appears to be strong, even when the potentially confounding effects of phylogeny, in which related species have a tendency to share similar ancestral conditions for sexual dimorphism and behavior, and possibly even the effects of breeding seasonality (Ridley, 1986), are controlled. Nonetheless, the number of males in a female group is only an imperfect predictor of male competition because a male's membership or exclusion from a group does not always predict his lifetime reproductive success.

This seems like an implausible contradiction. After all, the mating system of a female group with a single adult male looks like a polygynous one, while that of a multi-male group looks like polygamy. Male competition in polygynous mating systems should be more intense than in polygamous mating systems because the variance in male reproductive success should be greater in the former than in the latter. Yet, when data from long-term studies are taken into account, the differences between single- and multi-male groups of primates end up looking more similar to one another than the differences in their compositions imply.

In Hanuman langurs, for example, there is tremendous variation in how long males manage to single-handedly monopolize groups. Some males hold their tenures for nearly ten years, but many are fortunate if they manage to stick with a female group long enough to see the offspring they sire survive beyond weaning age. The challenges from other males, who are unattached to female groups and have little to lose, are just too severe to resist for very long. Constant vigilance and the threat of aggression take their tolls on even the strongest and healthiest of males, and violent attacks from roving all-male bands or solitary males can leave debilitating wounds that weaken a male's resistance to future assaults (Figure 5.11). Thus, the tenure of the breeding male in a troop of females may be barely long enough to see any offspring sired through their vulnerable period of dependency (Hrdy and Hausfater, 1984; Moore, 1993).

In some primates, including Hanuman langurs, red howler monkeys, and mountain gorillas, both uni-male and multi-male groups are observed in the same population even though females in these species may live in groups for different reasons. It is easy to see how strong takeover pressures from male outsiders might make it advantageous for a male to permit one of his sons to remain with him in the group as a sort of bodyguard. Theory predicts that the son should help his father repel attempted attacks, even if he is denied breeding opportunities himself, if one day he stands to inherit his father's position with the females and if his opportunities to establish his own breeding group are limited. A father, in turn, might stay on to help his son once his own breeding career is over (Figure 5.12).

Such an **age-graded** system is difficult to distinguish from a multi-male group without knowledge of the kinship between males or the ways in which reproductive opportunities are allocated among them. Genetic paternity exclusion studies have shown, for example, that infants born in multi-male groups of Venezuelan red

FIGURE 5.11   A juvenile male langur (*Presbytis entellus* or *Semnopithecus entellus*) grooms a serious abdominal wound he received during a fight with a competing male band. Incredibly, this male survived. Photo by Jim Moore/Anthro-Photo.

howler monkeys are typically sired by a single male in each (Pope, 1990). Behavioral studies indicating that only the dominant male copulates with estrous females in the group have also been found in the dominant and subordinate male partnerships of golden-lion tamarins (Baker, et al., 1993).

Considering the reproductive uncertainties of being a single male in a group of females, why do males put themselves through the struggle? The answer, as is so often the case when puzzling over male primates, seems to lie with the females. In pursuit of their own optimal reproductive strategies, female primates contribute to the pressure on males to attain and defend their reproductive sovereignty. Additional males accompanying the group may mean more mouths to feed. Finding enough food efficiently is usually hard enough as it is, and any extra time or energy spent locating and traveling between food sources means that much less time and energy that can be allocated to reproduction. So, if one male can keep other males from bothering females and their infants, it is in the females' best interests to support him in competitive challenges against other males, or to follow a male challenger into a new group if he demonstrates his superior ability to defend her (Watts, 1989, 1996; Yamagiwa, 1983).

Multi-Male Female Groups.   There are circumstances when having more than one male around can be advantageous to females, and then it becomes virtually impossible for a single male to prevent other males from joining the group. Large groups of females are more difficult for a single male to monopolize because

FIGURE 5.12   Mountain gorilla (*Gorilla gorilla berengei*) group. Note the silver back visible on the standing male. Photo by Martha M. Robbins.

the females are likely to spread out more to feed even if they travel together as a cohesive group. In addition, as the number of females concentrated in one group increases, the number of males seeking females will correspondingly increase.

Having more than one male around may not be so bad if there is plenty of food to go around at the time. It could even be a benefit if the additional eyes and ears help females detect predators, or if males also help females in defending their food resources from other groups of females. Indeed, females generally don't form large cohesive groups unless the advantages of numbers in defending resources from other groups of females or in predator detection outweigh the disadvantages of competing with one another for access to food (see Chapter 6).

Males in multi-male groups of matrilocal females face three basic challenges. First, they must overcome the determined resistance from those males already present, who rightly regard them as future competitors for reproductive opportunities. If they manage to fight their way into the group, they will still face stiff competition with each other as reproductive opportunities arise. Sometimes these male contests occur directly over access to estrous females; sometimes they occur without any obvious reason other than that their position in the **dominance hierarchy** is affected by the outcome. A male who achieves a high-ranking position must be on constant alert to challenges to his rank from other males. **Rank reversals** resulting from these challenges may be frequent occurrences, and in many species, ranging from capuchin monkeys to gorillas, alpha males depend on support from females to hold onto their positions (Fedigan, 1993; Janson, 1984; Watts, 1996).

High rank presumably confers some reproductive advantages, or else why would males compete for it? Yet, as we'll see later in this and other chapters, evidence supporting the predicted relationship between male rank and reproductive success has been mixed. One reason for this is that female cooperation is often essential to males, especially if they can't win direct aggressive contests against other males by themselves. Monopolizing an estrous female comes with foraging costs to males (Alberts, et al., 1996), which cooperative females can help keep down. Examples of female cooperation in male mating consortships have been reported in olive baboons (Bercovitch, 1995; Smuts, 1985) and both Japanese and rhesus macaques (Berard, et al., 1994; Huffman, 1992; Manson, 1996; Soltis, et al., 1997a,b).

Intergroup encounters tend to occur at food or water sources utilized by both groups, and females may play an active role in defending these resources from other groups of females. Males also go on alert, presumably to protect their interests in keeping nongroup males away. And, if any estrous females are present in either group, chaos is likely to break out as males from the other group attempt to mate. Females have their own reproductive interests at heart when they join forces to defend the resources at stake, but a female's interests don't necessarily include fidelity to the males in her group. Often, in fact, females mate with nongroup males during these encounters in what appear to be deliberate ways (Sprague, 1991).

Extra-Group Copulations.   Apart from competing for admission to a group and for access to estrous females once in it, males in multi-male groups, like those in uni-male groups, have the problem of incursions from nongroup or extra-group males.

These extra-group males may already be members of other multi-male groups, or they may be solitary males in the process of trying to immigrate themselves.

Females in both uni- and multi-male groups mate with extra-group males who roam as solitaries or in all-male bands in search of reproductive opportunities (Carlson and Isbell, 2001). The prevalence of extra-group male matings has led researchers to question the legitimacy of inferring primate mating systems from the composition of their social groups (Cords, 1987; Rowell, 1993; Strier, 1994a). Indeed, if female primates associate in groups with one or more males, but mate with males from outside their groups, then why do male primates go to such lengths to join groups of females at all?

Presumably, a male's chances of copulating are higher as a group member than they would be as an outsider. Copulations with extra-group males are clearly important at an evolutionary level if they result in conceptions, but there can also be other, more indirect benefits involved. For example, mating between outsider males and group females could help establish relationships that make it easier for the outsider to subsequently immigrate.

In fact, many extra-group liaisons, observed in diverse species ranging from the uni-male patas monkeys (Figure 5.13) to the multi-male macaques (Soltis, et al., 2001), take place when females are in estrus (and mating with group males as well). Extra-pair copulations leading to fertilization are common among many so-called monogamous birds (Petrie and Kempenaers, 1998; Westneat and Sherman, 1997) and may even result in greater disease resistance in their offspring (Johnsen, et al., 2000). Paternity studies of chimpanzees at the Taï National Forest in Ivory Coast

FIGURE 5.13   Patas monkeys (*Erythrocebus patas*) drinking at a water hole. Patas monkeys are generally found in one-male, multi-female groups, except during the brief breeding season, when influxes of extra-group males join up to compete for copulations with females (Harding and Olson, 1986; Chism and Rogers, 1997; Carlson and Isbell, 2001). Photo by Ron S. and Anne A. Carlson.

suggest that although much rarer than previously thought (Gagneux, et al., 1997), extra-group paternities may occasionally occur (Vigilant, et al., 2001).

Seasonal versus Aseasonal Breeders.   Extra-group males are especially problematic for males in both uni-male and multi-male groups whenever female estrus is a seasonal occurrence. In some uni-male matrilineal groups of patas monkeys, influxes of surplus males are a constant distraction during the two-month-long breeding season (Harding and Olson, 1986). A female who fails to conceive during this breeding season will have to wait for the next year's breeding season to try again. Losing a year will contribute to the lowering of her reproductive success relative to other females, a loss that few female patas monkeys, or any other female animals with restricted breeding seasons, voluntarily take (Cox and Le Boeuf, 1977). Mating with extra-group males is a form of insurance against losing a year of her reproductive career (Carlson and Isbell, 2001).

The multi-male groups of the matrilineal ring-tailed lemurs are similarly inundated with extra-group males during the even more restricted two- to three-week-long annual breeding season (Figure 5.14). Male ring-tailed lemurs often use the confusion that sets in during the breeding season to transfer between groups, leaving ones with few females for those with more promising sex ratios (Sussman, 1992a). Female ring-tailed lemurs vary in their mating preferences, sometimes choosing familiar males and other times choosing extra-group males, who subsequently succeed in joining the group.

FIGURE 5.14   Ring-tailed lemurs (*Lemur catta*), like other species of lemurs, have a two- to three-week breeding season, during which time competition among males for mates is pronounced. Photo by K. B. Strier.

There is little competition among the males in these multi-male groups most of the time because there is little for them to compete over except during the brief period each year when females are in estrus. In Verreaux's sifaka, elevations in the testosterone levels of resident males have been associated with the social disruption and increased competition caused by incursions of other males during the brief annual breeding season (Brockman, et al., 2001). Yet, like all other lemurs, which also have restricted breeding seasons and are sexually monomorphic in body and canine size, females are liberated from the threat of male aggression and therefore capable of asserting their choices of mates (Richard, 1992; Richard and Dewar, 1991).

In primates like lemurs, where the ability of males to monopolize matings is low, as well as primates like muriquis and chimpanzees, where the benefits of male competition are ambiguous or offset by the benefits of cooperation within patri-lines, reproductive competition among males may occur through their sperm. Large testes relative to body size give lemurs in multi-male groups ways to compete for fertilizations during the brief breeding season when females are avidly mating with both group and extra-group males (Kappeler, 1997b). It is not necessary for females to prefer males with large testes for sperm competition to evolve. Instead, males that achieve higher reproductive success as a result of having more or higher quality sperm will pass on their genes for these attributes to their sons.

The breeding season of multi-male groups of Central American squirrel monkeys is more similar in duration to that of the single-male groups of patas monkeys. Except for the few months each year that female squirrel monkeys are in estrus, related males live peacefully with one another in groups comprised of unrelated females, without any evidence of aggressive competition or dominance hierarchies among them (Boinski, 1987b). At the onset of the breeding season, however, males undergo a physical metamorphosis. They begin to put on fat due to testosterone and cortisol build-ups (Bercovitch, 1992), puffing out until some males are visibly larger than other males as well as females (Figure 5.15). Males also begin to challenge one

FIGURE 5.15   Adult male Costa Rican squirrel monkey (*Saimiri oerstedii*) feeding on fruit in a "fattened" state while a six-month old-youngster looks on. Photo by Sue Boinski.

another with threats and displays. The fattest of these "fatted males" becomes the alpha male for the breeding season, and it is he who may account for over 70 percent of all copulations with estrous females through a combination of deferrals by his subordinates and female choice (Boinski, 1987b).

Male competition is restricted to the breeding season in these squirrel monkeys, and even then, because males are patrilocal, the higher reproductive success of the dominant male contributes to the inclusive fitness of his subordinate relatives. Kinship among males also mitigates the fitness costs of losing reproductive opportunities, resulting in the relaxation or inhibition of the sexual selection pressures that lead to sexual dimorphism.

If female estrus is not tightly seasonal, competition among males will be less limited in time. In such cases, it should behoove males to avoid competing with their kin for the sake of their inclusive fitness. The intensity of male competition and levels of sexual dimorphism in these multi-male groups should be similar to those in uni-male groups because, in both instances, asynchronous estrus means that individual males can potentially monopolize a disproportionate number of reproductive opportunities.

Seasonally-induced differences in male mating patterns and corresponding testosterone levels like those seen in sifaka have also been detected in brown capuchin monkeys in southeastern Brazil. During a year-long study, primatologist Jessica Lynch observed the capuchin monkeys copulating throughout most of the year. Although females focused on copulating with the alpha male during the conception season, they mated with both him and other males at other times. There may be little point for males to compete aggressively when female fertility, and female mate choice, are so seasonally restricted (Lynch, et al., 2002).

The Influence of Males on Females.   As limiting resources, female primates determine the behavioral options and competitive strategies available to males. Whenever the temporal and spatial distribution of female resources permits, male primate strategies tend toward monopolizing access to the maximum number of females. We have discussed how, through their patterns of avoidance or association with one another, and through the timing of estrus, female strategies could preclude or facilitate such male monopolies. When females are indifferent toward one another, the opportunities for males to impose their own reproductive strategies are determined only by the competitive abilities and attractiveness of males. Thus, sexual dimorphism in these primates is extreme.

Hamadryas baboons and mountain gorillas are two examples of primates in which male influence on females is pronounced. This may be due, in part, to the fact that females in these species are indifferent toward each other (Watts, 2001). Hamadryas baboons live in a comparatively unproductive habitat, where defensible food resources are rare. Mountain gorillas feed on abundant foods that are easy to find and not worth defending. In both cases, though for different reasons, these female primates have little cause either to avoid or to seek one another's company. Their indifference makes them prime targets for male reproductive monopolies.

Male hamadryas baboons and mountain gorillas employ somewhat different tactics. A hamadryas baboon male begins to collect females either by challenging a male who already possesses a harem, attaching himself to his father's or another male's unit until he can inherit it, or by enticing young females, who are still sexually immature, away from their natal groups. By maneuvering himself into proximity and steering a wandering female back to the other females he has collected, and by giving her bites to the back of her neck, a male hamadryas baboon can "herd" indifferent females into a group that he then defends against challenges from other males trying to steal mates.

Mountain gorilla males in search of females may shadow the older, most dominant male, who is usually visible by the silver coloring of the fur on his back. It may take months, but when the moment is right, this male shadow rushes into the center of the group to challenge the resident silverback male. In the process of these aggressive displays, infants in the group may be wounded or killed. Even if a marauding male is ultimately repelled, one or more of the resident females may disappear from the group, only to turn up a few days later elsewhere with him (Sicotte, 2001). Other mountain gorilla males stay in their natal groups or integrate into new groups as younger, subordinate, black-backed adults. These black-backed males, which have not yet acquired the silver coloring of their elders, are subordinate to the resident silverback and rarely mate, though they do help the silverback repel attacks. When mountain gorilla groups contain more than one silverback male, dominance relationships established between them provide the higher-ranking male with more mating opportunities (Robbins, 1995; 2001).

Considering the high variance in male mating success in both of these species, it is not surprising that male competition and sexual dimorphism are so pronounced. It is also not surprising that females need protection from the aggression that these large males are capable of directing toward them and, in the case of gorillas, toward their infants. When females live in groups with their relatives, female kin provide some protection against attacks by larger males. Without their relatives to intervene, female hamadryas baboons and mountain gorillas rely on males who demonstrate their capacity to provide such protection (Stewart, 2001).

Females can be very fickle. Unattached to particular feeding areas or extended matrilineal networks, females in these species are free to follow the male who proves himself the best protector. Deterring marauding males from harassing females and their offspring, and intervening on behalf of a female against an assailant are some of the benefits to females of following a particular male. Through **mate guarding** males maintain their female monopolies and keep their female companions from wandering away (Watts, 1996). Harassment from outsider males interferes with female feeding activities and can harm her dependents directly, through infanticide, or indirectly, through the melee of a takeover challenge. However, if an intruding male manages to penetrate the defenses of a female's guard, it may indicate that he would be a better protector against future interference than her current associate, and therefore worthwhile to a female's future reproduction to switch her loyalties by following him.

Female Mating Strategies

Protection for themselves and their offspring is not the only basis for female mate choices, and clearly fidelity is not always the best reproductive strategy. In fact, sometimes promiscuity is the safest, most reliable strategy, particularly when the priority is getting pregnant with the best possible male. There may be costs to being promiscuous, including greater risks of contracting sexually-transmitted diseases (Nunn, et al., 2000). Yet, in many primates, females seek out or accept multiple partners, either during the same cycle or from one conception cycle to the next (Gust, et al., 1998). Studies of female primate mate choices are abundant and inconclusive, in part because it is so difficult to distinguish social from reproductive strategies when sex is involved (Wolfe, 1991), and in part because females may shift their mate choices at different times in their lives and in response to the options available to them. To understand these alternatives, consider the different concerns females must juggle to maximize their reproductive potential (Small, 1992).

Sperm and Fertilization

Females should be selected to copulate so that they conceive when they can. Technically, fertilization requires just one male at the right time, but some males are more fertile than others, particularly if some have temporarily depleted their sperm supplies by mating with other females. In these cases, which are more likely to occur when breeding is seasonal or female estrus is synchronized, mating with multiple males can provide insurance against missed reproductive opportunities.

Food and Safety from Predators

Females need resources for themselves and their offspring, and males can help acquire two of the main resources, food and safety. For most primates, male contributions to female food supplies involve defending an area where food can be found. In birds, for example, the quality of the territory that a male can defend by himself is often a determinant of how many females he can attract to it. The **polygyny threshold** (Figure 5.16) is based on the conditions that might lead a female to fare better as a second mate on a good territory than as an only mate on a poor quality territory. Although derived for birds, a similar principle may be operating in primates, but it has not yet been demonstrated with data.

Allies against Aggression

Males can be useful allies in a female's aggressive interactions with other females, as well as protectors from aggression directed toward females by other males. In sexually monomorphic primates, females are capable of defending themselves against other females or males, who lack the advantages of size, strength, or dental weaponry. Yet, even in sexually monomorphic rufous lemurs, females feeding near male partners often have higher feeding rates than when feeding near others (Overdorff,

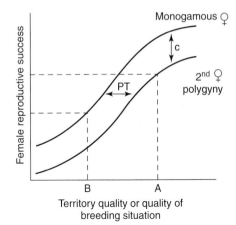

FIGURE 5.16   The polygyny threshold (PT) in birds. The first female to arrive on the breeding grounds should select the male holding the highest quality territory. The second female to arrive should opt to become the second female on a high-quality territory instead of the first female on a low-quality territory if her reproductive success in the former situation is higher. The differential between these options is the polygyny threshold. From Davies, N. B. 1991. Mating systems. In J. R. Krebs and N. B. Davies, eds., *Behavioural Ecology*, Third Edition, Oxford: Blackwell Scientific Ltd. pp. 263–294. Reprinted by permission of the publisher.

1998). In sexually dimorphic primates, a male ally can be even more useful for a female to have. If he associates regularly with her, his presence may deter other males from threatening her even if they are his superiors in the male hierarchy. He may also deter or actively intervene on her behalf against threats from other females. In exchange for his support, a female may reward him with mating opportunities he would otherwise miss if his success depended solely on his ranking among males (Smuts, 1985; Strum, 1984).

Parental Investment

Females sometimes need males to contribute toward infant care. Male contributions may vary from actively carrying infants to relieve mothers from this heavy energetic burden, to baby-sitting infants while mothers are resting or feeding, to protecting infants from the threats of aggression posed by other males or females (Figure 5.17). In many primates, male investment in infant care is proportional to how confident he can be of his or his relatives' paternity. After all, a male who helped care for an infant sired by a competitor would be undermining his own fitness unless, of course, the infant's biological father is his brother or another close relative. Theoretically, females can assure a male of his paternity by mating monogamously. Or, females can confuse males about their paternity by mating promiscuously. A male unsure of his paternity should be less likely to harm—and more likely to help care for—an infant he may have sired than one he did not (Hrdy, 1995). As we saw earlier, the evidence from Hanuman langurs is consistent with these predictions about males that protect or harm infants (Borries, et al., 1999b).

Good Genes

Finally, females may choose males for the genes that their offspring will inherit (see Box 4.1). However antisocial a male's behavior may be, from severe aggression

FIGURE 5.17   The alpha male of a brown capuchin (*Cebus apella*) group, shown in proximity to an infant in his group. Photo by J. W. Lynch.

toward other males, females, or infants sired by a competitor, if it increases a male's reproductive success, it should benefit a female's fitness if her sons inherit it. Male genes may be why a female mountain gorilla abandons her current group to join a male who has just killed her infant, and why a female Hanuman langur mates with a male who has just taken over her group.

Choosing unfamiliar males as mates may also be a way that many females unconsciously hedge their bets in assuring genetically variable offspring (Takahata, et al., 1999). Unfamiliar males are also, sometimes, more attractive to females than familiar males, who may also be their kin. Indeed, long-term familiarity and the sexual disinterest it engenders may be one of the proximate mechanisms that leads to inbreeding avoidance (Zumpe and Michael, 1996).

Sexual Signals

Deciphering the basis of female primate mate choices is a complicated task because of the multiciplicity of factors that contribute to them. Even if we could ask our primate sisters why they mate with some males and not others, it's unlikely we'd get anything like a consistent answer. The mate choices a solitary female makes may be as different from those of a group-living female as the choices that the same female makes at different times in her life. Ontogeny, learning, and genetic factors are all likely to affect the variation in criteria involved in female mate choices both across and within a species.

The opportunities to express their mate choices also differ between species. Females who are equal to males in size and strength can take more liberties than females who must navigate their own reproductive interests through the threats of aggression from larger males (Smuts and Smuts, 1993). In sexually dimorphic species, females may mate with preferred males in seclusion or even at night (Soltis, et al., 1997a, b). Female choice is a powerful selection pressure, however, and even the females in sexually dimorphic species have found devious ways to assert their preferences. Confusing males about their estrus is one way; advertising it is another.

Female Choice and the Unpredictability of Ovulation.   Female primates are most attractive to males when they act, smell, or look as if they are ovulating. When a female is **sexually receptive,** she may solicit a male's sexual interest through behaviors she shows at no other times. Presenting her hindquarters to a male's face can be a potent aphrodisiac. Striking exposed postures with a special, come-hither looking facial expression, or calling in a seductive shriek or twitter are some of the other behavioral signals female employ to attract a favored male, or any males near enough to see or hear them (Figure 5.18). Some females transmit information about their ovulatory cycles through their urine, which they distribute by wiping it along branches or by washing it into their fur. Males have to be on alert for these signals, which can be subtle indeed. This isn't to say that males never check out a female on their own initiative, but males have to eat and they have to watch out for predators and for other males. If there are lots of females around, it is hard to constantly monitor the conditions of each.

Females can't fake how they smell at different times in their cycles, but they can alter their behavior when it suits them. Feigning sexual receptivity is one of the

FIGURE 5.18   Red-tailed guenon (*Cercopithecus ascanius*) female solicits grooming from an adult male, who complies. Photo by Marina Cords.

most powerful ways to manipulate males, and not surprisingly, it is one that many females employ. A male who would otherwise pose a potential threat to an unrelated infant may be duped into behaving as if he is the father if a pregnant female has persuaded him to mate before the infant was born, or if a female has mated with so many different males throughout her ovulatory cycle that none of them can be sure whose infant is whose.

Encouraging such nonreproductive sex can only work, however, if males have no way of verifying that a female's behavioral solicitations correspond to her hormonal condition. This appears to be the case among white-faced capuchin monkeys. In this species, males and females engage in an elaborate courtship ritual that includes making "duck faces" by sticking their lips out while staring, grunting, and squeaking, dancing about, and chasing one another. Pregnant and lactating females are as likely to copulate as females that are cycling, and therefore potentially fertile, which suggests that nonreproductive matings are a strategy to confuse paternity in this species (Manson, et al., 1997).

There may be limits to a female's ability to confuse males about their paternity, especially if she is already pregnant. Postconceptive matings occur in many different species (van Schaik, et al., 1999b; van Noordwijk and van Schaik, 2000), including Hanuman langurs living in multi-male groups. Male Hanuman langurs do not protect infants if they joined the groups or mated with the infants' mothers after the infants were conceived (Borries, et al., 1999b). At least in this species, males appear to adjust their behavior in response to temporal cues, such as the timing of copulations relative to births, instead of on the basis of their mating histories *per se.*

Theoretically, the fewer honest indications of female ovulation a male has to go on, the easier he should be to trick into mating at an unlikely or impossible time for fertilization. Yet, in some 10 percent of Old World monkeys and apes, female sexual signals are carried to an unusual extreme.

Sexual Swellings and the Female Dilemma.   Some female primates, like baboons and chimpanzees, have patches of skin on their rumps that inflate and deflate like balloons in response to the ovarian hormones circulating in their blood. During the menstrual phase of a baboon female's 30- to 35-day cycle, the **sex skin** around the vulva is flat and pale. Rising levels of progesterone and estrogen during the two to three weeks or so leading up to ovulation trigger the color of the sex skin to brighten and the connective tissue to swell up. The sex skin reaches its maximum tumescence near the day of ovulation, and remains at its peak size and color for two to three days. Within a week of conception, the tumescence ordinarily deflates while the sex skin becomes an even brighter reddish pink. If a female fails to conceive, the sex skin returns to its anovulatory appearance by her next menstruation, only to begin to swell and brighten as another ovulatory cycle begins (Hrdy and Whitten, 1987). During maximum tumescence, female body weights can increase by 14 percent in baboons (Bierlert and Busse, 1983) to as much as 25 percent in red colobus monkeys (Strusaker, 1975), but whether there are energetic or other costs to carrying this extra weight around is not known (Dunbar, 2001).

Sex skins have evolved independently at least three times, from cerco-pithecines to colobines to hominoids (Dixson, 1998). Species in which females have sex skins tend to live in multi-male, multi-female social groups and usually breed year-round. Both of these conditions provide females with a ready supply of males from which to choose their mates. Sexual swellings, which advertise to males when copulations will count most, can help females to make the best choices.

Having a sexual swelling is a bit like wearing your reproductive condition on your sleeve (Figure 5.19). Everyone can see it, and there is absolutely nothing a female can do, short of disappearing, to hide it. But they are not completely reliable signals of fertility because the timing of maximum tumescence and ovulation do not always perfectly coincide (Dixson, 1998; Nunn, 1999b; van Schaik, et al., 1999b). In female chimpanzees, for example, ovulation and maximum swelling can take place up to nine days apart (Dahl, et al., 1991). Male chimpanzees—and human observers—can be fooled about which copulations really count.

As **graded signals,** sexual swellings provide information about the probabil-ity of ovulation, instead of its actual timing (Nunn, 1999b). Males monitoring fe-male sexual swellings can judge from afar when fighting for females should have the highest reproductive pay offs. Predictably, male aggressive competition and mate guarding are most intense when a female is maximally tumescent, and more relaxed when the probability of fertilization is low. Males that win contests against other males are good bets for good genes, on top of the protection and access to resources that high ranking males have the power to provide.

Females with sexual swellings turn the cyclical fluctuations in their attrac-tiveness to males to their advantage in ways that females with less visible behinds cannot. Inciting competition at the most fertile times helps females to bias their off-spring's paternity in favor of winners, while mating with other males when the odds for conception are slim helps confuse paternity. Not surprisingly, in species in which confusing paternity might matter, females tend to mate over a longer period

FIGURE 5.19   Female yellow baboon (*Papio cynocephalus*) with a sexual swelling is being groomed by her male consort. Note the size differences between them. Photo by K. B. Strier.

and with more partners than in species in which males pose fewer potential threats (van Schaik, et al., 1999b, 2000). Extended mating periods, including post-conceptive matings, are how some females solve the dilemma of both chosing and confusing paternity for their infants (van Noordwijk and van Schaik, 2000).

Male Rank and Reproductive Success

The dilemma of paternity uncertainty is shared by all male primates, including primatologists. Internal fertilization means that the only way a primate male can be sure of his paternity is to be the only male to mate with a female. As we have seen, monopolizing mating opportunities is difficult unless fidelity with her partner is also in a female's interests. It may be impossible in large multi-male and female groups because no male can possibly monitor all males and females at all times.

Contemporary primatologists have an advantage over their predecessors and over their study subjects. New methods of genetic testing have increased the tool kit of the primatologist who, with a drop of blood, a piece of hair, or a cell from a spoor of their subjects, can determine paternity, or at least exclude a substantial number of males as possible fathers. The noninvasive methods to extract genes from feces are still relatively new and expensive, and getting hair or blood from the majority of primates still requires darting or capturing them (Chapter 12). Those using blood from wild primates that are captured and then released, or hair samples taken from nests made and subsequently vacated by chimpanzees, confirm that variance in male reproductive success can be high.

Male paternity often, but not always, corresponds to behavioral predictors such as a male's social rank. In what is known as the **priority-of-access** model, high rank should lead to high reproductive success (Altmann, 1962). Without results from genetic paternity tests, researchers have relied on their observations of male mating success to infer the effects of male rank on male reproductive success (Cowlishaw and Dunbar, 1991). In one of the first systematic inquiries into the relationship between male rank and reproductive success, Glenn Hausfater (1975) looked at the copulation frequencies of fourteen yellow baboon males at Amboseli National Park in Kenya. He found that dominant males mated more often than subordinates, and that the top three ranking males accounted for most of the copulations that occurred around the time of female ovulation. Similar rank and mating success correlations have been found in many other primates, including olive baboons in Gombe National Park, Tanzania (Packer, 1979b) and Peruvian brown capuchin monkeys (Janson, 1984).

More recently, genetic and behavioral data in multi-male groups of primates ranging from brown lemurs (Gachot-Neveu, et al., 1999), to red howler monkeys (Pope, 1990), to yellow baboons (Altmann, et al., 1996), to long-tailed macaques (de Ruiter and van Hooff, 1993; de Ruiter and Geffen, 1998) have revealed strong correlations between male rank and reproductive success. This could be attributed to the alpha male's higher mating success during female fertile periods (de Ruiter, et al., 1994). In Hausfater's study, for example, the alpha male mated only about a third as often as the second ranking male, and only half as often as the third ranking male. Even then, rank reversals among high ranking males made it difficult to estimate male lifetime reproductive success.

More recent paternity studies of the Amboseli baboons confirmed that alpha males can sire over 80 percent of the infants conceived, but their priority of access to fertile females only lasts as long as they can hold their place at the top of the male hierarchy (Altmann, et al., 1996). During years of social instability, frequent rank reversals shorten the tenures of alpha males, and therefore reduce the variance in male paternity success over time.

Differences in the quality of females can have impacts on male reproductive success as well. For example, in a recent study of olive baboons at Gombe National Park, Tanzania, Domb and Pagel (2001) found that males fought more ferociously with one another to consort with females with the largest sexual swellings. Males also spent more time grooming these females than those whose maximum swellings were less pronounced. Whether the relative size of a female's maximum swelling is an **honest advertisement** of her fitness is still unclear, but male primates do seem to make decisions about allocating their **mating effort** based on how fertile a female is during her cycle. High ranking males that can monopolize the most fertile females at their most fertile times can achieve higher reproductive success than males who mate with less fertile females as suboptimal times.

The relationship between male rank and mating or reproductive success is not always a perfect one because males can employ alternative reproductive strategies when they can't win in one-on-one contests against a more powerful competitor. As we saw earlier, coalitions among lower-ranking male baboons can interfere with the mating activities of a higher ranking male. While one member of the coalition attracts the consorting male's attention, the other member can mate with the temporarily abandoned female consort (Packer, 1977; Noë, 1990; Noë and Sluijter, 1995). Coalitions among male chimpanzees in the Ngogo community at Kibale National Park, Uganda, permit two or three allies to guard a desirable female and gain greater mating privileges with her than any of them would have by themselves (Watts, 1998).

In addition to coalitions, some males are careful to discriminate among the contexts in which they initiate or respond to aggressive challenges (Popp and DeVore, 1979). A male may submit to a contender when the contest is over food, but fight to win when the resource is an estrous female whose sex skin is approaching maximum tumescence. The outcome of agonistic interactions among males can be quite different when contests over mates are distinguished from contests over other resources (Rowell, 1974).

Finally, older males often seem to have some advantages with females independent of their rank in the male hierarchy. This phenomenon attracted the attention of researchers studying the olive baboons at Gilgil Ranch in Kenya. Shirley Strum (1982), who has maintained a long-term study on the Gilgil baboons, noticed that males attempting to immigrate into the troop often formed affiliative relationships with females, and that these female allies helped the males integrate. Barbara Smuts (1985) noticed that these male–female "friendships" extended beyond the sensitive period of male immigration, and persisted well beyond a female's estrous period. Smuts described cuddly males nuzzling and grooming their female friends, and tolerating the annoying antics of infants even though, in many instances, the males' recent arrival in the troop meant that these infants could not possibly have been their own. When the female began cycling again, she might choose her friend, often an older male, as a mate independent of his rank in the male hierarchy. Smuts found that male friends accounted for 40 percent of the copulations by estrous females, suggesting that befriending a female is a strategy used by some males to curry favor as mates.

The male chimpanzees who coerce estrous females into accompanying them on safaris may also be the same ones who shower friendly attention on the females before they come into estrus (Tutin, 1979). Baboons and macaques don't take safaris, but females can cooperate in sustaining a sexual consortship with a preferred partner (Manson, 1997). In both chimpanzees and baboons, female choice of their male friends as mates can offset some of the consequences of competition incited by female sexual swellings and the priority-of-access that high-ranking males would otherwise gain. In rhesus macaques, however, female preferences for male friends is highly variable among individuals and can switch from year to year (Manson, 1994).

Males may vary in their ability to cultivate female friends, just as they vary in their ability to compete against one another aggressively (Figure 5.20). Young males may lack the patience or social skills essential to establishing long-term friendships with females that older, more socially experienced males have acquired. Or, older males may resort to friendships because they are no match in fights against younger males in the prime of their lives. Whatever the reason, female choice for different types of males and different male attributes can influence the outcome of male competition and therefore determine the degree to which a male's rank affects his reproductive success.

FIGURE 5.20   This old male langur (*Presbytis entellus* or *Semnopithecus entellus*) has a facial scar and nearly absent incisors. He has evidently survived some battles, but may no longer be able to hold his own against more robust male competitors in their prime. Photo by Jim Moore/Anthro-Photo.

6

Food and Females

Winter mornings are dry and cold in the Atlantic forest of southeastern Brazil. Overnight temperatures drop to as low as 5°C (that's just 41°F), and at 6:30 a.m., when my students and I set out to find the muriquis, the sun was just beginning to burn off the mist rising up through the treetops. The screeches of parrots sliced crisply through the air as we climbed up a trail speckled with leaf-filtered sunlight. Near the top of the ridge, we stopped hiking and turned around. Scanning the canopies of the tallest trees, we spotted the muriquis' golden bodies scattered about. Some were still curled up in furry huddles, their identities concealed from view. Others were sprawled precariously along the uppermost branches, soaking up the warmth. Nearby, Princessa, a young juvenile female, about four years of age, slid down the trunk of the tree where her mother and a friend, barely recognizable in a bundle of intertwined arms, legs, and tails, were still sleeping.

　　Princessa jumped into an understory tree full of small, white berrylike fruits, uttered a soft chirp, and began to eat, pulling the pliant branch tips toward her mouth with one hand while balancing from a branch overhead with her other hand and prehensile tail. About ten minutes passed before she swung off to nibble on some new leaves sprouting from one of the many lianas weaving its way through the branches of supporting trees (Figure 6.1). The sounds of other swishes coming from nearby indicated that Princessa was not the only member of the group who had woken up hungry. Within the hour, the other sixty members of our study group dropped from their sleeping spots and began their daily quest of filling up their bellies.

Muriquis, like all other animals, need to eat to survive. Wild primates also need to locate food in addition to getting it into their mouths. **Foraging,** which includes looking for, handling, and actually eating food, can occupy more than 50 percent of a primate's waking hours. It is difficult to measure exactly how much time primates devote to foraging for plant foods because we can usually only relate their movements to foraging when specific activities are followed by eating. For example, if the muriquis take twenty minutes to travel to a new feeding tree, we can't include that time in their foraging budget because we can't be sure they were aiming for that tree as a feeding spot. Unless they are clearly searching for food along the way, for most primates it is the proportion of time devoted to feeding on different types of food that is used to characterize their diets.

At different times of the year, the same individuals may vary both the proportion of time they devote to food-related activities and their daily feeding patterns (Strier, 1987a). Usually these seasonal differences in diet and feeding behavior reflect primate adjustments to seasonal differences in available foods. Primates also adjust their diets and behavior to the spatial distribution of their food resources. Together, differences in the temporal availability and spatial distribution of food resources can account for much of the dietary variation observed across populations of the same species.

Many of the anatomical specializations that distinguish primate species are attributed to their adaptations to particular dietary niches over evolutionary time (Chapter 2). In addition, nearly all aspects of primate social organization, from the size, composition, and cohesiveness of their groups, to the social relationships they

FIGURE 6.1 Muriqui monkeys (*Brachyteles arachnoides*) devote an average of about 50 percent of their annual feeding time to leaves, yet compared to sympatric brown howler monkeys (*Alouatta fusca*), muriquis are more frugivorous and their births are more seasonal (Strier, 1992b; Strier, et al., 2001). Photo by K. B. Strier.

maintain within and between groups, are affected by the distribution of their foods in time and space.

Food is especially important to female primates because of the high metabolic costs associated with gestation and, especially, lactation (Lee, 1996). Toward the end of their pregnancy, female primates must eat enough food to nourish both themselves and the fetuses developing in their womb, as well as maintaining the body fat that they'll need to support nursing infants. With the exception of tarsiers and some other prosimians, who park their infants in safe crooks and crannies while they forage unencumbered, and owl monkeys, marmosets, and tamarins, who get high levels of help carrying their infants from their mates and other group members (see Box 1.1), most primate mothers bear the sole responsibility of caring for their infants until they are able to find their own food and move about on their own.

Manufacturing milk is even more energetically costly, and lactating females need to compensate for the energy they divert from their own maintenance into milk. Energy requirements can be two to five times higher during lactation than at other times (Lee, 1996). To meet these requirements, lactating females spend more time feeding and feeding on foods with higher energy contents. The quality of milk female primates produce varies tremendously across species and is affected by diet (Lee, et al., 1991, Power, 1999). In general, prosimian mothers who "park" their infants produce milk that is higher in fat content than prosimian and anthropoid mothers who carry their infants during lactation, but the adaptive significance of these differences and the variation in maternal energetic demands are still unclear (Tilden and Oftedal, 1997). The added weight of carrying infants while lactating clearly increases maternal energy requirements, much like carrying a heavy backpack increases our own (Figure 6.2).

Both in the field and in captivity, female reproductive success has been linked to female nutritional condition. As a rule, better-fed females begin reproducing at an earlier age, produce healthier offspring, have shorter interbirth intervals, and live longer to reproduce. As we saw in Chapter 5, life history strategies constrain

FIGURE 6.2   Vervet monkey (*Chlorocebus aethiops*) mother carrying her nursing infant while she climbs into a feeding tree. Photo by P. C. Lee.

the actual number of offspring that even the healthiest female can produce in her lifetime. Female muriquis, for example, typically give birth to their first infants at about ten years of age. If they live to be about thirty to thirty-five years of age, they have a reproductive lifespan of about twenty to twenty-five years. With an average interbirth interval of three years, females can produce no more than seven to eight offspring in their lifetimes.

Not all female primates achieve their full reproductive potential, however, and oftentimes the differences in female reproductive success come down to measurable individual differences in their diets. The variance in female primate reproductive success is greatest, however, whenever food resources are especially scarce. Because of this relationship between female nutrition and reproductive success, many aspects of female primate behavior can be related to strategies associated with balancing their intake of the most nutritious foods against the time, energy, and risks associated with gaining access to these foods (Koenig, 2000).

Access to food is as important to female reproductive success as access to fertile females is to male reproductive success (Chapter 5). The importance of food to females applies to nonprimates as well. In fact, many of our ideas about food and female primates can be traced to theoretical and empirical studies conducted on other organisms (reviewed in Krebs and Davies, 1993).

There are three key variables that affect female feeding strategies: **food quality; food distribution;** and seasonal **food availability.** And, because females are limiting resources for male reproduction, we can trace many of the differences in primate societies to how these characteristics of primate foods affect the ways that females distribute themselves in space and how female fertility is distributed over time. In the following chapter we will take a closer look at the social side of female primate behavioral ecology. This chapter focuses on how the quality, distribution, and seasonality of primate foods affect their diets, ranging, grouping, and reproductive patterns.

Food Quality

All primates eat a wide variety of foods to meet their basic nutritional requirements. **High-quality diets** are those that are rich in easily digestible energy and protein; **low-quality diets** are those that are poor in these nutrients. When given a choice, most primates prefer high-quality diets, balancing their intake of energy, digestible protein sources, and essential vitamins and minerals. High-quality diets are also sometimes referred to as **growth diets,** because they permit reproduction (Wrangham, 1980). In the wild, there are rarely sources of high quality foods available at all times, and most primate diets also include some proportion of alternative, lower-quality, **subsistence foods** to fall back on for survival at least some of the time.

Primates have different nutritional requirements and digestive abilities, so what constitutes a high-quality diet for one primate may not be sufficient for another (Richard, 1985). Knowledge about primate nutritional requirements is critical for maintaining healthy, reproductively viable populations of primates in zoos and laboratories (Sussman, 1978). Consequently, studies of what different primates eat in the wild have important practical applications in addition to their contributions to understanding primate behavioral ecology. An active area of research in primatology involves the biochemical analysis of the wild plant foods primates exploit. New methods of measuring the physical and chemical characteristics of primate foods are also helping to standardize data collection, and thus increase the power of comparisons (Lucas, et al., 2001).

Energy and Nutrients

As we saw in Chapter 1, fruits are a basic source of caloric energy, whether in easy-to-digest **carbohydrates** or in oily, **lipid,** or fat-rich form. Consider the differences between blueberries, peaches, apples, and avocados, and you have some idea of the range of sizes, caloric content, and digestibility of primate fruits. These fruits, like the ones that primates eat, also contain varying quantities of vitamins, minerals, and water.

Nearly all primates include some fruits in their diets, but none could survive without other foods, such as insects and leaves, that provide essential **proteins,** as well as other vitamins and minerals often lacking or present in only small quantities in fruit. Proteins are the building blocks for growth, reproduction, and regulating bodily functions, but they need to be broken down in the body before their amino acid components can be absorbed and utilized (Richard, 1985).

Many primates obtain essential fats and starches from seeds. Flowers are also good sources of carbohydrates, with nectar, in particular, providing soluble sugars. Pollen is also high in protein, but because it is difficult to digest, it is unlikely to contribute much to primate diets. The exudates, or gums, eaten by many marmosets and tamarins are key sources of calcium in their diets (Smith, 2000). Calcium is essential for proper skeletal development in all primates, but the requirements of female callitrichids may be especially high during the later stages of gestation and lactation when producing twins depletes their own supplies.

Digestibility and Edibility

The stage of maturity of primate plant foods is an important determinant of an item's nutrient content and its digestibility, and, thus, its attractiveness as a food resource. Mature leaves and grasses that are high in cellulose and dietary fiber are difficult to break down during the digestive process. Sharp, shearing molars and strong chewing muscles are specializations that help folivorous primates break open plant cell walls (Figure 6.3). Elongated gastrointestinal tracts, which are proportionately larger in large-bodied primates, generally provide more time for nutrients to be absorbed as they pass through the gut (Demment, 1983). Primates such as howler monkeys, which include a high proportion of leaves in their diets, have even longer large intestines and colons than expected from their body size, giving them longer food passage rates to absorb the nutrients from leaves, which are generally more difficult to digest than fruit (Milton, 1984a). The sacculated stomachs of the Old World

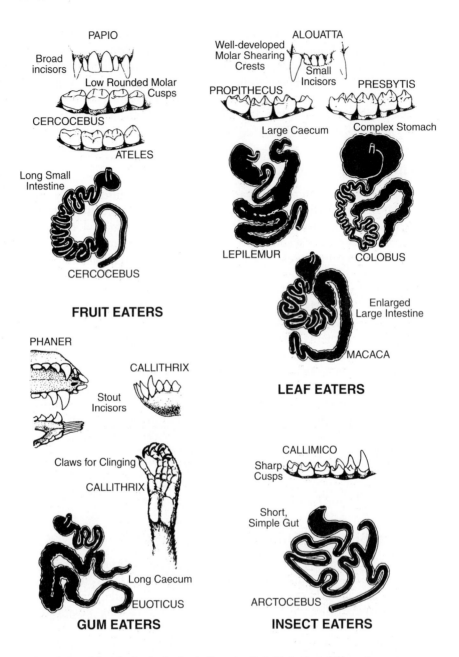

FIGURE 6.3   Morphological adaptations to diet. Note that different genera, shown in capital letters, are compared by diet. From Fleagle, J. G. 1999. *Primate Adaptation and Evolution*, Second Edition. New York: Academic Press. Reprinted with permission of the publisher and author, © 1999 Academic Press.

colobine monkeys that provide opportunities for microbial action to break down leaves are part of their evolutionarily successful specialization for folivory. And, perhaps because this specialization requires the maintenance of an ionic balance in their guts, many (but not all) colobines tend to avoid mature, sugar-rich fruits (Kay and Davies, 1994; Waterman and Kool, 1994). The unusual trichromatic vision found in howler monkeys and catarrhines (Chapter 2) is now thought to be an adaptation for detecting leaves that are high in protein content and low in fiber (Dominy and Lucas, 2001).

Physical Deterrents.   Some plants suffer when parts of them are eaten by primates or other animals. Protective husks and spines are some of the physical defenses that plants have evolved to protect their fruits and seeds from primates that prey on them (Kinzey and Norconk, 1990, 1993). To break through these defenses, some primates have evolved strong jaws and teeth and powerful biting muscles that enable them to crack open hard fruits and crush their seeds (Figure 6.4).

Other plants depend on animals, including primates, to disperse their seeds. The fruits of these species are typically soft and fleshy, inviting animals to swallow them, and their seeds, whole. The pulp of the fruit gets digested, but the seeds, usually smoothly coated, pass intact through the digestive tract, and are deposited elsewhere when the primate next defecates. These seeds can be surprisingly large relative to the size of the primates that ingest them. Panamanian tamarins, for example, weigh less than 500 grams, yet some of the seeds they swallow are three and

FIGURE 6.4   Selection of pods from the Bignoniaceae family eaten by bearded saki monkeys (*Chiropotes satanas*). Photo by M. A. Norconk.

one-half inches in length (Garber and Kitron, 1997). The ecological role that these and many other primates play in dispersing the seeds of their important fruit sources will be examined further when we look at primate ecological communities (Chapter 11).

Chemical Deterrents.   Plants also produce **secondary compounds,** or chemical deterrents that can range from unpalatable to toxic. Plant secondary compounds can be divided into two major classes, **tannins,** which bind with plant proteins in the gut to make them difficult to digest, and **alkaloids,** which disrupt metabolism inside the cells of a primate's body. Levels of secondary compounds differ between plant species, as well as between plant parts growing in different habitats and at different stages of maturity (Waterman and Kool, 1994). Compared to mature leaves, for example, young leaves are lower in both alkaloids and in the protein-binding tannins that interfere with digestion. Not surprisingly, most primates prefer young leaves over mature ones. Primates such as Japanese macaques are thought to vary their consumption of particular leaf species to avoid consuming too much of any particular type (Hill, 1997).

Primates differ in their ability to combat plant chemical defenses, so foods that are edible to one primate may be inedible to another. Some of the leaves eaten by black colobus monkeys, for example, would be lethal in a primate that lacked this species' extraordinary capacity for detoxifying alkaloids (McKey, et al., 1981). Red colobus monkeys on the African island of Zanzibar have adopted the practice of eating charcoal from burned trees and human cooking kilns to detoxify the secondary plant compounds in the almond and mango leaves in their diet (Cooney and Struhsaker, 1997; Struhsaker, et al., 1997; Figure 6.5). The golden bamboo lemur relies on a species of bamboo that contains lethal levels of cyanide with no ill effects (Glander, et al., 1989). Parrotlike red and green macaws in Venezuela are thought to detoxify some of the seed species in their diets by eating clay, which neutralizes tannins (Norconk, et al., 1997). Eating claylike soil, a practice known as **geophagy,** may be one of the ways in which primates that lack such digestive specializations can neutralize the toxic compounds in their plant foods (Box 6.1).

Body Size Energetics and Turnover Rates

Digesting food utilizes energy. Extracting the energy and nutrients stored in plant and animal matter into units that can be utilized after consumption also takes time. As we saw in Chapter 2, the energetics of body size dictate how much energy a species requires and which types of protein sources they exploit. Smaller primates (<10 kg) are typically frugivore-insectivores and larger primates (>10 kg) are typically frugivore-folivores (Figure 6.6). The relatively high metabolic turnovers of small-bodied primates restrict them to insects that can be digested more rapidly than leaves. Larger-bodied primates, with their relatively slow metabolic turnover rates, can tolerate the long lag between ingestion and digestion that leaves require, and might also have difficulty finding sufficient quantities of insects on a regular basis (Figure 6.7).

FIGURE 6.5   Juvenile Zanzibar red colobus (*Procolobus kirkii*) eating charcoal to detoxify plant secondary compounds. Photo by Thomas T. Struhsaker.

While these body size–diet relationships generally apply, they are weaker among platyrrhines than among catarrhines (Ford and Davis, 1992). For the most part, the smallest of primates (<500 grams) eat gum instead of fruit for their carbohydrates, while the largest primates within each of the major taxonomic groups may also rely on herbaceous vegetation, grasses, and, in the case of the semiterrestrial cercopithecines, the underground storage organs of grasses, called corms, which are rich in carbohydrates as well as high in protein and water (Figure 6.8a,b). Some primates, including marmosets, capuchin monkeys, baboons, and chimpanzees also include vertebrate prey, such as frogs, lizards, birds, or small mammals, in their diets (Figure 6.9a-c).

The diet of savanna-dwelling patas monkeys is an exception to these general body size rules. Patas monkeys get more than two thirds of their food from gum and insects, yet adult females may weigh over four and one-half kilograms (Figure 6.10). Patas monkeys also have one of the shortest interbirth intervals (one year) and earliest ages of reproduction (three years) among the cercopithecines, suggesting that their high-quality diets and high reproductive rates are related (Isbell, 1998).

BOX **6.1**

Forest Pharmacy

For over a decade, Michael Huffman has been interested in what primates put into their mouths. He also monitors what comes out in their dung. But what distinguishes Huffman from most other primatologists studying primate feeding behavior and diet is his fascination with why primates sometimes go out of their way to swallow things that have little or no nutritional value. Merging meticulous behavioral observations in the field with chemical and parasitological analyses in the laboratory, Huffman has become an authority on what is now known as **zoopharmacognosy,** or more simply, self-medication by wild animals (Huffman, 1997).

For over a decade, Huffman's own research has focused on the chimpanzees at the Mahale Mountain National Park in Tanzania, where Japanese researchers established a long-term field study that has been going on since the early 1960s (Nishida, 1990). During his second field season at Mahale, Huffman and his Tanzanian counterpart, game officer/medicine man Mohamedi Seifu Kalunde, first saw an adult female chimpanzee behave oddly while she was suffering from severe malaise and constipation (Figure B6.1). Instead of following the group's route that day foraging on patches of preferred fruits, she slept more than usual and sought out a particular species of plant whose leaves and roots are used widely across Africa to treat gastrointestinal distress, parasite infection, and more than a dozen other major ailments. Since then, Huffman has observed other similar cases. One species, *Vernonia amygdalina,* a member of the Compositae, or daisy family, contains unpalatable, bitter pith. Huffman noticed that the condition of ailing chimpanzees seemed to improve after they had chewed the pith and, curious as to why, he collected some samples

FIGURE B6.1   Michael Huffman (right), Mohamedi Seifu Kalunde (center) and a colleague in the field at Mahale, Tanzania. Photo by Daisuke Izutsu, provided by Michael A. Huffman.

for his collaborators to analyze. Sure enough, *Vernonia* pith contains **anthelminthic** properties that cause parasites living in chimpanzees and humans to decline in activity, in some
instances making it easier to expunge the parasites from the gut. Some of these parasites
have little, if any deleterious effects on their primate hosts. Others, however, can lead to
weight loss, reduced immunity to other infections, and, in severe cases, death.

Antimalarial and antibilharzia activities have also been isolated from *Vernonia* and
other plant species used by chimpanzees. Across Africa, chimpanzees, bonobos, and eastern lowland gorillas ingest the pith and fruit of wild ginger, *Afromomum* species, which
has been proven to have significant antimicrobial activity (Berry, et al., 1995). The same
fruits that these apes eat in the wild are sold by people at local markets for treating bacterial and fungal, as well as parasitic, infections. Baboons in the Awash Valley of Ethiopia
eat berries from *Balanites aegyptiaca* trees, which may provide protection against bilharzia
in both human and nonhuman primates (Phillips-Conroy, 1986). Many primates eat clays
that contain kaolinite, the active ingredient in products such as Kaopectate™. Recently,
Huffman and his collaborators have found that clays eaten by chimpanzees, Japanese
macaques, orangutans, and humans absorb toxic plant alkaloids at highly effective rates.
Absorption of water and bacteria are other important properties effective at combating
diarrhea and bacterial infections.

Huffman's investigations seek to tease apart the medicinal benefits that primates
may gain incidentally in the process of eating foods for nutritional purposes (Glander,
1994; Janzen, 1978) from those that seem to be directly and exclusively used as medicine.
For example, another self-medicative behavior is the ingestion of rough, bristly leaves from
at least 34 different species of plants found in the ranges of chimpanzees, bonobos, and
both eastern and western lowland gorillas. Swallowing these leaves decreases transit
times for foods, helping the animals to physically expel intestinal nematodes and tape
worms from their bodies (Huffman and Caton, 2001).

How have chimpanzees and other primates figured out these methods of medicat-
ing themselves? It's easy to see how eating a fruit rich in carbohydrates that also happens
to make an animal feel better might become a common practice, but it is more difficult to
fathom the mechanisms by which practices such as swallowing whole leaves or chewing
bitter pith by sick animals become established, particularly when recovery lags behind the
act itself. Furthermore, Huffman has recently found in controlled captive chimpanzee
studies that social learning is an important element of acquiring self-medicating behaviors. Is it mere coincidence that the *Citrus* leaves Costa Rican capuchin monkeys rub
against their fur during the rainy season repel insects and provide relief against bacterial
and fungal infections (Baker, 1996)? Or, do these primates—and other animals, such as
bears and coatis—selectively use a diverse variety of naturally occurring products to med-
icate themselves? Huffman (1997, p. 195) is convinced by "the obvious adaptive significance of self-medicating behavior," and predicts that more research on the subject will
turn up more evidence of its widespread occurrence not only in primates, but throughout
the animal kingdom.

Reproductive Energetics

In nearly all primates studied, females have higher-quality diets than the males of
their species. In other words, females are pickier about what they eat, and focus
their diets as much as possible on foods that contain the highest digestible energy,
protein, and other essential nutrients available.

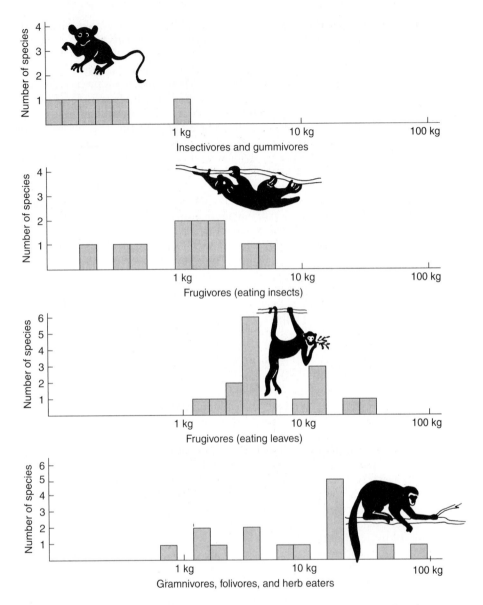

FIGURE 6.6   Range of body sizes in the major dietary categories. Note that frugivore–insectivores tend to be lighter in weight than frugivore–folivores. Reprinted from Primates in Nature by Alison F. Richard © 1985 by W. H. Freeman and Company. Used with permission from the author.

Some of these sex differences in diets can be explained by the smaller body sizes of females relative to males in sexually dimorphic species (Chapter 2). Larger males may be unable to find enough high-quality food to meet their absolute energy

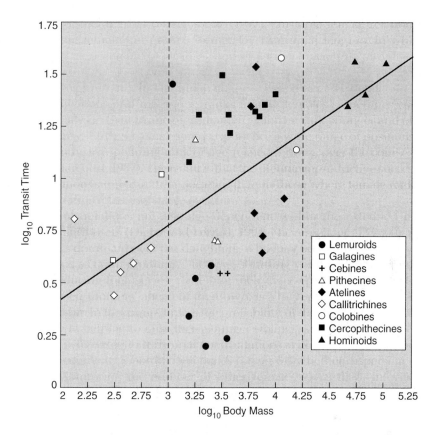

FIGURE 6.7 Relationship between body mass and digestive transit times. Note that there is only a slight positive relationship between the two variables. Lambert (1998) suggests additional factors, including diet or absorption and processing constraints, influence primate transit times. From Lambert, J. E. 1998. Primate digestion: Interactions among anatomy, physiology, and feeding ecology. *Evolutionary Anthropology* 7:8–20. Copyright © 1998 Wiley-Liss, Inc. Reprinted by permission of Wiley-Liss, Inc., a division of John Wiley & Sons, Inc.

requirements, and their proportionately larger digestive tracts mean that they have more time than smaller females for absorption. Larger males may engage in more strenuous foraging than females, and may forage lower in the canopy, where thicker branches can support their weight, as occurs in white-faced capuchin monkeys, among whom males, who weigh about 3.2 kilograms, are 25 to 35 percent heavier than females (Rose, 1994).

Such sex differences in diet are very compelling in highly dimorphic primates. In fact, some researchers have suggested that sexual dimorphism in body size reflects ecological selection pressures favoring the avoidance of feeding competition

FIGURE 6.8a A mountain baboon (*Papio ursinus*) forages in the dead grass of late winter in the Drakensberg highlands of Natal, South Africa. A principal food at this time is the underground storage organs of monocot plants, such as orchids, gladioli, and irises (Byrne, Whiten, Henzi, and McCulloch, 1993). Photo by Richard W. Byrne.

FIGURE 6.8b The rhizome of the orchid *Eulophia foliosa* is large and rich in starch. However, the only clue to its presence underground is the narrow stem, shown crossing the knife blade nearest the hilt; this is the same pale brown color as the dead blades of grass, and is remarkably difficult for humans to detect. Photo by Richard W. Byrne.

between the sexes (Demment, 1983; Selander, 1972). However, although sex differences in diet are clearly associated with sex differences in size, the sexual selection hypothesis would interpret these associations as consequences rather than causes of body size differences (Rodman and Mitani, 1987; Rose, 1994).

Even among primates that are sexually monomorphic in body size, female diets are generally better than those of males. In the family groups of sexually monomorphic marmosets, tamarins, and gibbons, for example, breeding females are dominant over males, and therefore get priority of access to the most preferred foods. This may be important when female energy needs are high (Wright, 1999). In the multi-male, multi-female egalitarian society of sexually monomorphic muriquis, female diets during some months include higher proportions of fruit, flowers, and new leaves than male diets (Strier, 1991a).

There are few data on the exact energetic demands of pregnancy and lactation in nonhuman primates. Baboon and macaque mothers are thought to have difficulty maintaining their own body weights while nursing infants older than about five to six months of age (Altmann, 1980; van Noordwijk and van Schaik, 1987; van

FIGURE 6.9b Adult male grabs the coati pup. Photo by Katherine C. MacKinnon.

FIGURE 6.9a Costa Rican white-faced capuchin (*Cebus capucinus*) adult male and large juvenile male descending a tree to nab a coati pup (*Nasua narica*) on the ground. Photo by Katherine C. MacKinnon.

FIGURE 6.9c Adult male returns to the safety of the trees with his prey in hand (see MacKinnon, 1995; Rose, 1997). Photo by Katherine C. MacKinnon.

Schaik and van Noordwijk, 1985b). The absence of body weight differences in reproductive and nonreproductive common marmosets may reflect the costs of reproduction on high ranking females and the costs of low rank on females not burdened by reproduction (Araujo, et al., 2000). Indeed, the time and energetic costs of reproduction for females may be one of the factors that affects weaning age (Lee, 1996), while recovering their energy reserves may be why most wild primate mothers don't immediately conceive after weaning.

FIGURE 6.10 Patas monkey (*Erythrocebus patas*) feeding on gum from *Acacia drepanalobium* tree. Photo by Ron S. and Anne A. Carlson.

The Spatial Distribution of Food

The tradeoffs between the nutritional content of potential foods and individual nutritional requirements are not the only factors that influence primate diets. There is also the tradeoff between the time and energy primates expend in finding and eating foods relative to the nutritional value of the foods they obtain. In the equations of foraging economics, time and energy expenditures for locating food and handling food are the costs, and the energy and other nutrients obtained from these foods are the benefits. From an evolutionary perspective, primates should be selected to behave in ways that either minimize their costs or maximize their benefits (Oates, 1987). In other words, they should forage in an optimal way.

Many primate food resources may occur in discrete clumps, or **food patches** (Figure 6.11). A single fruiting tree of a particular species may be separated from others of its kind by several hundred meters, or clumps of the same tree species may grow so close together that their canopies overlap and moving from one tree to another is no different than moving within the same tree. As a rule, high-quality foods such as fruits have patchier distributions than low-quality foods such as leaves. However, even leaves, which may appear to be ubiquitous in a tropical forest, occur in patches that differ from one another in quality depending on their stage of maturity and the lighting and soil conditions that affect them (Glander, 1978;

FIGURE 6.11   A female red-bellied lemur (*Eulemur rubriventer*) feeding on a berry from the Psychotria family. Feeding competition can lead to daughters being evicted from their natal groups. Photo by © Deborah Overdorff.

Waterman and Kool, 1994). Folivorous primates are selective about which leaves they eat, generally preferring those with the lowest tannin and highest protein contents, and with the fewest secondary compounds (Figure 6.12).

Patch Size and Feeding Efficiency

The size of food patches places physical limits on the number of individuals that can feed together at the same time. The density of food items within a patch determines **foraging efficiency,** or how much energy and protein an individual can eat before expending time and energy to move to another feeding site within a patch or to another patch altogether. Food patches that can feed multiple individuals before they are depleted may be worth the time, energy, and risks necessary to defend them, just as differences in feeding efficiency associated with feeding sites within a patch may be worth competing for. As a result, the size of food patches and the distribution of items within them affect female grouping patterns and patterns of cooperation and competition within and between groups (Figure 6.13).

Nearly all primates adjust the size of their feeding groups, or **feeding parties,** in response to the size of their food patches (Chapman, 1990; Leighton and Leighton, 1982; Overdorff, 1996; White and Wrangham, 1988). Primates with fluid grouping patterns, such as chimpanzees and spider monkeys, routinely split up into smaller feeding parties when their preferred fruit resources occur in small patches, and solitary females are frequently sighted foraging alone. They come together into larger feeding aggregates whenever large fruit patches, which can accommodate

FIGURE 6.12 Adult female diademed sifaka (*Propithecus diadema edwardsi*) feeding on new leaves at Vatoharanana study site, Ranomafana National Park, Madagascar. Note the infant, whose head is barely visible, on her left side. Photo by E. M. Erhart © 1998.

FIGURE 6.13 The influence of the spatial distribution of resources on the ability of individuals to monopolize them. Dots indicate resources (e.g., food or mates); circles are the defended areas. From Krebs, J. R. and Davies, N. B. 1993. *An Introduction to Behavioural Ecology*, Third Edition. Oxford: Blackwell Scientific Ltd. Reprinted with permission of the publisher.

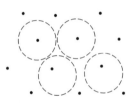

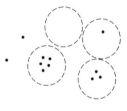

Even distribution.
Little polygamy potential

Patchy distribution.
High polygamy potential

more individuals without competition, are available, resulting in their fission–fusion social system (Chapman, et al., 1994, 1995; Symington, 1990). Muriquis also adjust their feeding party sizes in response to the size of their preferred fruit patches, but not in response to the size of less preferred leaf patches (Moraes, et al., 1998; Strier, 1989). Even orangutans, which are often described as solitary because they are so rarely encountered together, aggregate at large patches of ripe fruit (van Schaik, 1999). Within these fruiting trees, however, competition for the best feeding sites reigns, and individuals vary in their foraging efficiency depending on their ability to dominate others (Utami, et al., 1997).

Female orangutans, chimpanzees, spider monkeys, and muriquis maintain fluid associations because there are not enough large patches of their preferred fruits to make cooperative resource defense economical. Subordinate individuals, which would lose out to dominant members of their groups in contests over access to fruit in small patches, are better off on their own than they would be by helping one another to defend a few large fruit patches from other groups. In other words, the costs of competing with members of their own groups, or *within group competition,* are greater for these females than the benefits of cooperating with group members in competitive contests against other groups.

All primates face some levels of within- and between-group feeding competition, but not all types of competition involve direct **contests** because not all resources can be monopolized by dominant individuals or groups. When resources either cannot be defended or are not worth the costs of defending because they are too low in quality, the form of competition is described as **scramble.** Social relationships among female primates that maintain cohesive groups differ from one another depending on whether within-group feeding competition is of the contest or scramble variety, as well as whether within-group or between-group contest competition is greater (Chapter 7). For example, the preferred fruits of Peruvian squirrel monkeys occur in large patches that can be defended, whereas those of Costa Rican squirrel monkeys occur in small, undefensible patches. As expected, only female Peruvian squirrel monkeys live in extended matrilines and cooperate in defending their fruit patches in between group competition (Mitchell, et al., 1991).

Female primates should form cohesive groups when the benefits of doing so outweigh the costs. Food-related benefits include cooperative defense of food resources in between-group competition (Wrangham, 1980, 1987b), but, as we have discussed, there are other benefits, including protection from predators or male harassment (Janson and Goldsmith, 1995), that may affect both the optimal size of female groups and the relationships among females and between females and males within these groups (Chapter 7).

Effects of Patch Density

The density of food patches in space affects the time and energy economics of traveling between these patches and defending them from other individuals or groups with similar tastes. Consequently, the density of their foods affects primate ranging and grouping patterns. In contrast to either Peruvian or Costa Rican squirrel monkey foods, the fruits eaten by squirrel monkeys in Suriname occur in small, dense patches. Because they can be monopolized by individuals, intra-group feeding competition is much higher here than it is for squirrel monkeys elsewhere (Boinski, 1999). If food patches occur at high densities relative to a primate's daily travel path, the entire food supply area becomes potentially defensible (Mitani and Rodman, 1979). If preferred patches are too spread out to monitor daily, however, then territoriality is not an economical option. Instead, groups will have overlapping home ranges, and compete with one another to monopolize access to high-quality food patches when they are encountered.

The relationship between primate diets and their ranging patterns comes down to a basic distinction between the intake and expenditure of time and energy. Primates with higher-quality, more frugivorous diets obtain more energy than primates with lower-quality, more folivorous diets. However, obtaining fruit also typically requires greater energy expenditure because edible fruits are more patchily distributed than leaves. Consequently, across most primates, the degree of frugivory generally correlates positively with time spent traveling, daily path lengths, and home range size. Conversely, as the proportion of leaves in the diet increases, both travel requirements for finding leaves and the time and energy available for traveling decrease. Sympatric L'Hoest's monkeys and blue monkeys in the Nyungwe Forest Reserve of Uganda seem to deviate from this general pattern. Here, L'Hoest's monkeys have longer day ranges although they are more folivorous than blue monkeys. The blue monkeys spend most of their time in mature forests where their preferred fruits occur in large patches and at high densities, and evidently don't need to travel as far in search of food as the L'Hoest's monkeys, which spend most of their time in secondary forest habitats where foods are more widely dispersed (Kaplin, 2001).

Small home ranges might appear to be ideally suited to territorial defense. However, low-quality foods such as mature leaves or grasses rarely inspire territorial behavior because they aren't worth the time, energy, or risk of injury to defend. Mature leaves and grasses also tend to be more abundantly and evenly distributed than patchy, high-quality foods such as fruits. As a result, food resource defense among folivorous primates like colobines and howler monkeys tends to be targeted mainly to high-quality food patches, such as fruiting trees, within what is otherwise a relatively small home range by comparison to the more frugivorous primates that share their habitats.

Patches of high-quality fruits are worth defending when intruders can be monitored and deterred during the course of other daily activities. At low population densities, primate groups may encounter one another infrequently, and between-group competition will be rare. Habitats become increasingly saturated as population density increases, however, resulting in more intense levels of between-group competition. Females in large groups that can monopolize contested patches of high-quality foods in their home ranges or territories containing the best foods should have higher reproductive rates than females in smaller groups (Cheney, 1987). In Venezuelan wedge-capped capuchin monkeys, the breeding male in large female groups not only has higher reproductive success than the breeding male in smaller female groups because there are more potential female mates, but also and because these females have higher fertility (Robinson, 1988a). Thus, the distribution of high-quality foods affects female grouping patterns and both female and male reproductive success within these groups.

The Temporal Availability of Food Resources

The high-quality foods that many primates prefer are not uniformly available throughout the year. As one moves away from the equator, day length becomes increasingly seasonal, affecting patterns of plant photosynthesis, growth, and reproduction. Seasonal variation in temperature and rainfall also affects the availability of edible plant parts (Oates, 1987; Richard, 1985). In fact, the past and present geographical restriction of primates to tropical and subtropical habitats is attributed to the increasingly seasonal scarcity of high-quality foods in temperate climates (Figure 6.14).

FIGURE 6.14 Japanese macaques (*Macaca fuscata*) inhabit one of the most seasonal habitats of any living primate. In the winter, they consume large quantities of low-quality tree bark to sustain themselves. Photo by Minoru Kinoshita.

For some primates, the rainy season is a time of comparative plenty. When high-quality fruits, flowers, and new leaves are scarce, primates typically include high proportions of less preferred, lower-quality, subsistence foods in their diets. Their diets also tend to be more diverse, including a larger number of different species, during times of the year when preferred foods are scarce (Hill, 1997; Olupot, et al., 1997). What we know about the food preferences of wild primates is based largely on field studies that document which foods are included or excluded from primate diets relative to the availability of these foods, and how many different foods are included at different times of the year.

Behavioral Adjustments to Food Seasonality

Primates vary both intra- and interspecifically in the degree to which they adjust their diets, as opposed to their ranging and grouping patterns, in response to seasonal shortages in their preferred foods. For example, although the muriquis I study devote an average of 51 percent of their annual feeding time to leaves, the proportion of mature leaves in their diet increased during the dry season when new fruits, flowers, and new leaves were scarce, and decreased to virtually nothing during the rainy season when these more preferred food items were more abundant (Strier, 1991a). Like other primates, muriqui daily ranging patterns also shift in response to their seasonal diets. During the dry season, when low-energy leaves comprise the bulk of their diets, their daily path lengths are about half as long as during the rainy season, when high-energy, but patchy fruits and flowers are available (Strier, 1987b). By contrast, in habitats with more stable climatic conditions and more constant supplies of fruit, muriquis maintain more frugivorous diets throughout the year (Moraes, et al., 1998).

Other highly frugivorous primates, such as chimpanzees and spider monkeys, increase the proportion of leaves and other low-quality foods in their diets during times of the years when fruits are scarce (Castellanos and Chanin, 1996; Doran, 1997; Wrangham, 1977). Conversely, folivorous primates, such as howler monkeys and gorillas, increase the proportion of high-quality fruits and flowers in their diets whenever they can be economically found (Chapman, 1988; Remis, 1997a; Struhsaker, 1978; Watts, 1985; Yamagiwa, et al., 1994).

Chimpanzees and spider monkeys differ from other primates, however, in their fidelity to maintaining as high a quality diet as seasonal fruit shortages permit. The fluid grouping patterns that females in these species maintain in response to the size and spatial distribution of their fruit patches are also affected by seasonal fluctuations in the size of fruit patches (Symington, 1990). These primates live in extended patrilineal societies in which relationships among females are only weakly defined. Females don't establish rigid hierarchical relationships because they can avoid feeding competition throughout the year by going off on their own. The more cohesive groups of bonobos, compared to chimpanzees, have been attributed both to the greater temporal stability in their preferred food resources and to the more even distribution of the terrestrial herbaceous vegetation they consume (Chapman, et al., 1994).

Variation in the temporal stability of preferred fruit resource availability may account for differences in the diets and grouping patterns of other primates as well. In habitats where fruit is more evenly distributed across the year, muriquis maintain both more frugivorous diets and smaller feeding party sizes than when fruit availability is strongly seasonal (Moraes, et al., 1998). Differences in the diets, ranging, and grouping patterns of Brazilian and Colombian woolly monkeys may also be related to differences in the availability of their preferred fruits. Brazilian woolly monkeys, for example, disappeared from their home range for weeks at a time during a period of seasonal fruit scarcity. When fruit was plentiful, however, they formed small feeding parties of variable composition in response to the size of their fruit patches (Peres, 1994, 1996). Their Colombian cousins, by contrast, stick together in a cohesive group year-round, perhaps because they include higher proportions of insects in their diets (Stevenson, et al., 1994).

In contrast to Old World monkeys, many New World monkeys appear to adjust their grouping patterns, as well as their diets, in response to fluctuations in the availability of their preferred fruit resources (Kinzey and Cunningham, 1994). Perhaps their more flexible grouping patterns account for why matrilineal societies, which facilitate cooperation among females in between group competition, are so rare among platyrrhines (Strier, 1999b). Among wedge-capped capuchin monkeys, which do live in cohesive matrilineal groups, seasonality in the availability of preferred foods affected small and large groups differently. During the rainy season, when preferred fruits were more abundant, females in smaller groups had higher feeding rates than females in large groups. During the dry season, however, the tables were turned because large groups of females could displace smaller groups at food patches (Miller, 1996).

Many cercopithecines shift their diets and ranging patterns to include higher proportions of fall-back foods when preferred high-quality foods are seasonally scarce (Wasser, 1977b). By doing so, their groups tend to remain together as cohesive units. Struck by the comparison with species that shift their grouping patterns to maintain a more stable, specialized diet of fruit, Richard Wrangham (1980) hypothesized that dietary shifts that permitted females to stay together would be advantageous whenever a cohesive group of females gained a competitive advantage in cooperatively defending whatever high-quality food patches persisted during times of scarcity (Figure 6.15). These primates tend to live in extended matrilineal societies. Females maintain hierarchical relationships that affect the outcome of contests over food within groups, but the advantages of cooperating with kin in between-group competition were thought to outweigh the costs of competing against kin within their group because of their ability to include subsistence foods in their diets.

The climatic and rainfall conditions that lead to seasonal fluctuations in primate food availability may also lead to substantial year-to-year variation (Tutin and Fernandez, 1993). Years of heavier than usual rainfall may permit primates to sustain high-quality diets for much or all of the year. Conversely, years of low rainfall that affect fruiting and flowering cycles can lead to declines in the quality of primate diets. Thus, from one annual rainy or dry season to another, the same individuals may have dramatically different diets (Box 6.2). In cases of extreme drought, the effects of limited food and water take their toll on primate reproduction and survivorship, as we'll see in the following chapter.

	Rank order of competitive abilities	Individuals occupying feeding sites	Individuals excluded
No cooperation	A > B > C > D	 A B	C,D
Cooperation between C and D	(C > D) > A > B	 C D	A,B
Cooperation between A and B, C and D	(A > B) > (C > D)	 A B	C,D

FIGURE 6.15   The advantage of cooperating at a food patch containing a limited number of feeding sites. If none of the four individuals shown cooperates, individuals C and D are excluded due to their lower-ranking competitive abilities. If C and D cooperate, they can exclude A and B. This forces A and B to also cooperate. From Wrangham, R. W. 1980. An ecological model of female-bonded primate groups. *Behaviour* 75:262–300. Reprinted with permission from E. J. Brill Publishers and the author.

BOX **6.2**
The Power of Food

One of the most exciting new techniques for evaluating the impact of seasonal fluctuations in food availability on primate diets involves the analysis of **ketones,** which are produced when the body metabolizes fat. Ketone values can be measured in urine that has been collected noninvasively from wild primates (Chapter 12). The presence of ketones in the urine indicates that stored fat is being mobilized, which only occurs when the energy expended by an individual exceeds the energy obtained from food. In a pioneering study of caloric intake and ketones, Cheryl Knott (1998) demonstrated the effects of fruit availability on orangutan diets and ketones at the Gunung Palung National Park in West Kalimantan, Indonesia.

The availability of fruit in this forest, as in many others throughout the tropics, fluctuates annually as well as seasonally. Knott found that orangutans are well-suited to take advantage of **mast fruiting** events, when many species of trees flower and then fruit in synchrony, because they can consume many more calories than they need, and then store these calories as fat, for later use, when they need it. During January, the peak month of fruit availability, fruit accounted for a whopping one hundred percent of the orangutans' diets. Despite their size differences, males and females had nearly comparable caloric intakes (an average 8,422 kilocalories, or kcals, and 7,404 kcals per day, respectively), and the absence of urinary ketones in either sex indicated that both were probably gaining weight. By May, however, fruit availability had declined to the point that only twenty-one percent of the orangutans' diets consisted of fruit and they had to fall back on low quality foods, such as bark, to survive. Although they devoted the same amount of time to feeding in fruit-poor months as in fruit-rich months, caloric intake was significantly reduced, and now females were consuming significantly fewer calories (1,793 kcals per day) than males (3,824 kcals per day). The presence of urinary ketones in both males and females during the fruit-poor periods confirmed that their energy balances were negative and that they were losing weight. Females had significantly higher levels of urinary ketones than males, implying that they suffered greater energetic stress.

If female orangutans show measurable energetic stress in fruit-poor periods during a year of mast fruiting, imagine how much harder it must be on them in other years when the opportunities to accumulate stored fat are more limited. As Knott (1998) notes, the challenges of coping with negative energy balances may be why orangutans reproduce as slowly as they do. Their eight-year interbirth intervals, which are longer than those of other great apes, may be a consequence of reconciling the energetic demands associated with reproduction while meeting their own energetic needs when fruits are scarce.

Orangutans are not the only primates that have adapted to cope with extreme fluctuations in food availability. Lemurs, for example, represent a diverse group of primates that are united by a unique suite of traits associated with scarce and unpredictable food. In a recent review, Patricia Wright (1999) found that most lemur behavioral oddities, including female dominance and weaning synchrony, could be attributed to adaptations for maximizing the use of scarce and unpredictable food resources (Figure B6.2). Lemur habitats in Madagascar are known for their poor soils, and cyclones and storms frequently, but unpredictably, bombard the island, wreaking ecological havoc on the vegetation and the animal populations alike. Poor soils make poor growing conditions for the kinds of high quality foods that primates elsewhere enjoy, and at any time, what food there is can be lost or damaged by catastrophic climatic events (Gould, et al., 1999).

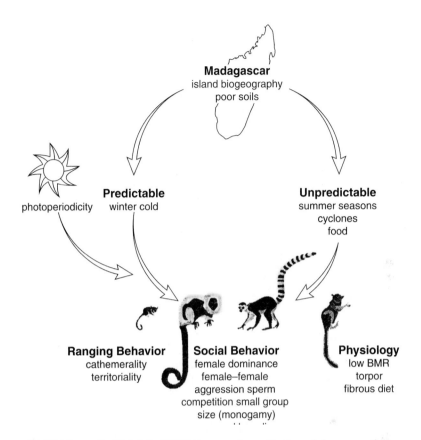

FIGURE B6.2   In Wright's (1999) "energy frugality" model, poor soils and island climate result in scarce and unpredictable food resources for the lemurs of Madagascar. Many of their adaptations can be explained in terms of how they permit lemurs to conserve energy. Only photoperiod and winter season are predictable here, and cold winters at Madagascar's southern latitude contribute to the importance of energy conservation. From Wright, P. C. 1999. Lemur traits and Madagascar ecology: Coping with an island environment. *Yearbook of Physical Anthropology* 42:31–72. Copyright © 1999, Wiley-Liss, Inc. Reprinted with permission of Wiley-Liss, Inc., a division of John Wiley & Sons, Inc.

Staying alive under these kinds of conditions can be problematic enough, but for females, reproducing also means meeting extra energetic needs. Lemurs have evolved a number of physiological responses to conserving energy such as maintaining low BMRs (Chapter 2), which some species, like gray mouse lemurs, carry to an extreme by entering into daily **torpor** and hibernation (Schmid, 1998). Other species can digest and detoxify highly fibrous or toxic foods (Glander, et al., 1989). But, just as striking as their abilities to hibernate or ingest cyanide is the way that females of different species with

(continued)

BOX **6.2**   **Continued**

varying gestation and lactation lengths nonetheless all manage to time weaning to coincide with the peak months when food availability is most reliable.

Twelve species of lemur live side by side in the rainforest at Ranomafana National Park, where Wright and her colleagues work (Box 3.3). Gestation lengths in the eight studied species range from about 60 to 70 days in the tiny brown mouse lemur and greater dwarf lemur, which weigh no more than 1–2 lbs each, to six months in the 12–16 lb diademed sifaka. Births occur from June through December, depending on the species, and seemed to be timed so that, despite lactation lengths lasting from two to three months in the smallest species to nearly nine months in the largest, all eight species wean their infants at once.

It is odd to find such strict weaning synchrony in different species, even when they occur sympatrically and overlap in their diets like these lemurs do. But if, as Wright suggests, it helps to keep infants alive under unpredictable ecological conditions, it may be one of the keys to understanding the lemurs' impressive evolutionary success.

Reproductive Seasonality

In many primates, births are concentrated during particular times of the year as opposed to occurring throughout the year (Lindburg, 1987). Reproductive seasonality is generally more pronounced in primates that face strong seasonal fluctuations in the availability of preferred high-quality food resources. In extreme seasonal habitats, such as northern Japan and the Himalayan mountains, macaque births are confined to a two-month period, whereas in more moderate climates, births occur over a four-month period (Melnick and Pearl, 1987). Across the geographic distribution of langurs, the degree of reproductive seasonality correlates with latitude and climate (Borries, et al., 2001; Koenig, et al., 1997; Newton and Dunbar, 1994). The short, two- to three-week-long breeding seasons and associated birth seasons of lemurs have also been attributed to their highly seasonal food supplies (Kappeler, 1996), and the timing of weaning (Box 6.2).

Sympatric primates often differ in their response to seasonality. For example, vervet monkey births are restricted to a three-month period (Cheney, et al., 1988), but there is no corresponding birth seasonality among sympatric baboons (Altmann, et al., 1977). Among sympatric capuchin monkeys, howler monkeys, and spider monkeys in Costa Rica, births are concentrated during the dry season months (Fedigan and Rose, 1995), but in the Brazilian Atlantic forest, where muriqui births are also concentrated in the dry season (Strier, 1996b), sympatric capuchins give birth during the rainy season, while howler monkeys give birth year round (Lynch, et al., 2002; Strier, et al., 2001).

Why the timing of reproduction differs across sympatric primates is not entirely clear. Reproductive seasonality associated with food availability may be advantageous to mothers and their offspring alike, so primates with different diets may be affected by seasonal differences in food availability. The seasonal abundance of high quality foods should benefit mothers most when the energetic costs of carrying developing infants while lactating reach their peak, and infants most when they are being weaned (Altmann, 1980). Muriqui mothers who give birth during the dry season meet their greatest energetic demands during the rainy season, when high quality fruits, flowers, and new leaves are most abundant. They do not wean their infants until the rainy season the following year, when high-quality foods are once again available (Strier, 1991b).

Female primates that conceive too early or late during the breeding season may have difficulty in carrying their fetuses to term and their infants may suffer higher mortality if they are unable to produce sufficient quantities or qualities of milk or if weaning occurs at a suboptimal time. In Hanuman langurs, females in good physical condition resulting from better nutrition are more likely to conceive during the ecologically most favorable times of year (Koenig, et al., 1997).

The **proximate** mechanisms that lead to reproductive seasonality are still poorly understood. Changes in day length have been shown to stimulate ovulation and spermatogenesis in some captive studies, but most primates appear to exhibit flexibility in fine-tuning the timing of their reproduction to nutritional and social cues (Lindburg, 1987). How this fine-tuning works, however, is difficult to understand (Strier, et al., 1999; Wallis, 1995). Cues that trigger the onset of the breeding or conception season may not be accurate indicators of ecological conditions during the subsequent birth season, lactation, or weaning periods (Crockett and Rudran, 1987). Indeed, there may be social advantages to synchronizing reproduction that have little or nothing to do with ecology (Clarke, et al., 1992).

Interpreting Diets and Their Behavioral Correlates

Despite the general patterns in how ranging, grouping, reproductive, and social patterns vary with primate diets that we have reviewed so far, there are still many questions about these relationships that remain to be resolved. For example, do selection pressures reflect how primates behave most of the time, or how they behave during critical times when their survival is at stake, and how well do the diets of primates that nowadays survive in variably altered habitats reflect their dietary adaptations in the past? Additionally, the compromises between selection pressures associated with optimal feeding strategies and those associated with predators and social variables are difficult to sort out.

Evaluating "Critical Functions"

In an analysis of primate dentition, Alphie Rosenberger and the late Warren Kinzey (1976) emphasized the importance of distinguishing between what primates use their teeth to eat most of the time versus what they rely on their teeth to do during critical times of food scarcity, when survival depends on the ability to subsist on a particular kind of food. In introducing the question of a tooth's **critical function** during these life-or-death crunch periods, Rosenberger and Kinzey inadvertently opened up a Pandora's box for functional morphologists and behavioral ecologists alike.

The muriquis I study can help illustrate this quandary. On the one hand, their large body sizes and the dental and masticatory systems they possess permit them to rely heavily on leaves. On the other hand, their rapid suspensory mode of locomotion permits them to minimize travel time between widely dispersed fruit patches. Based on the high (>50 percent) annual proportion of feeding time some populations devote to leaves, they have been characterized as facultative, or non-obligatory, folivores (Milton, 1984b). Yet, in their ranging and grouping patterns, and for some populations, dietary proportions, they resemble frugivorous spider monkeys more closely than folivorous howler monkeys (Moraes, et al., 1998; Strier, 1992b).

It may be appropriate to classify muriqui diets as folivorous based on their demonstrated ability to subsist on a highly leafy diet, but classifying their behavior presents more of a paradox. While their morphological adaptations for folivory may be a product of evolutionary selection pressures for this critical function during times of seasonal fruit scarcity, their ranging and social behavioral patterns are more consistent with exploiting high-quality fruits whenever possible. A similar paradox arises when the frugivorous diets and frugivore-like grouping and ranging patterns of Western lowland gorillas are compared to those of the herbivorous mountain gorillas (Figure 6.16), on the one hand, and more frugivorous chimpanzees on the other hand (Tutin and Fernandez, 1984, 1994; Remis, 1997b). However, it is important to remember that dietary classifications based on the proportion of feeding time devoted to different food types are arbitrary ones (Chapter 1). Consider that two species that devote 60 percent and 80 percent of their feeding time to leaves are labeled as folivores, whereas if 40 percent and 60 percent of their diets were leaves, one would be labeled a frugivore. Comparing multiple populations with the same

FIGURE 6.16 Lowland gorillas (*Gorilla gorilla gorilla*) in the Central African Republic consume a higher proportion of fruit than their mountain gorilla cousins (Remis, 1997a, b). During lean seasons, they shift their diets to include fruits that are high in fiber and secondary compounds (Remis, et al., 2001). Like the silverback male shown, they also spend a greater proportion of their time in the trees than the more terrestrial mountain gorilla. Photo by Melissa Remis.

sets of sympatric species might provide a better indication of the range of each species' dietary flexibility than absolute dietary proportions alone.

Effects of Altered Habitats

Morphological traits might be expected to change more slowly than behavior, and therefore reflect more about the selection pressures that operated in a species' evolutionary past. As a result, primates with specialized feeding strategies are more vulnerable to extinction than generalists whenever alterations in their habitats disrupt the availability of key foods in their diets (Yamagiwa, 1999). Conversely, primates that are capable of expanding or shifting their diets in response to changes in food availability will also have a competitive advantage over specialists when ecological conditions are unstable.

Because the habitats of so many primates nowadays have been altered, diets and behavior may not always match up in predicted ways. Comparisons between provisioned versus unprovisioned Japanese macaques (Hill and Okayasu, 1995, 1996), yellow baboons that feed at trash dumps versus those that obtain all of their food from the wild (Muruthi, et al., 1991), populations of Thomas langurs living in fragmented versus continuous habitats (Sterck, 1998), or muriquis living in disturbed or pristine forests (Moraes, et al., 1998) provide insights into the ways in which variation in feeding, ranging, grouping, and social behavior are affected by differences in dietary quality and levels of feeding competition. However, it is often difficult to reconstruct the ecological conditions under which primates evolved with sufficient specificity to distinguish what their ancestral behavioral adaptations were like (Chapter 1).

Changes in predator populations and population densities resulting from habitat alterations further confound our ability to interpret how primates adjust their diets and behavior in response to food availability, as has been hypothesized for a wide range of primates, from lemurs (van Schaik and Kappeler, 1996) and langurs (Sterck, 1997), to gorillas (Remis, 1997a; Yamagiwa, et al., 1996) and other apes (Boesch, 1996; Sakura, 1994; Tutin, et al., 1983). However, we can use comparisons between primates occupying different habitats as natural experiments into their flexibility and facultative responses to measurable ecological variables. Thus, understanding the effects of habitat alterations on primate diets is a methodological, rather than a conceptual, challenge.

7

Female Strategies

Most female primates are pregnant or lactating for most of their adult lives. It may seem remarkable that they devote so much time and energy to reproduction, but if you stop to consider the long gestation periods followed by long periods of infant dependency that characterize most primate *life histories,* it is easy to see how producing one offspring translates into months of investment, and how with each successive offspring these months quickly add up to years (Figure 7.1). Avoiding predators to stay alive and finding enough water and food to sustain themselves, reproduce, and give their dependents a good start in life is nearly a fulltime job for females.

Most female primates must also negotiate complex social relationships with other members of their groups. For females that remain in their natal groups for life, these negotiations begin long before the onset of their reproductive careers and persist throughout the duration of their adult lives. Effective negotiations may bring direct benefits, in terms of access to resources essential for reproduction, and indi-

FIGURE 7.1 Mother olive baboon (*Papio anubis*) secures her infant while nursing. Photo by Ron S. and Anne A. Carlson.

rect benefits, in terms of being left alone, without harassment, to pursue activities that affect their reproductive success. When females disperse from their natal groups, their ability to integrate into established social networks with other females may determine their success or failure at gaining membership in a new group, and thus whether they survive to reproduce at all.

Social relationships among female primates are not merely pleasurable ways to pass the brief daily interludes between the essential tasks of avoiding predators, finding and consuming food, resting, and caring for infants. Regardless of whether females live among kin or unrelated females, their relationships reflect a complex combination of competitive and cooperative strategies. These strategies vary across species, among populations of the same species living in different habitats under different ecological and demographic conditions, and among individual females over the course of their lifetimes.

Ecology of Female Relationships

The variation in female primate relationships can be examined at multiple levels, ranging from their ecological determinants to their social correlates. Phylogenetic trends are also evident within the major taxonomic groups, which presumably reflect similarities in their ecological and social adaptations. Comparisons among different populations of the same species provide insights into the degree to which female social and reproductive strategies correspond with and affect the demography of their groups and populations.

Types of Relationships

Relationships among female primates can be categorized according to the types of competition females face and the intensity of their competition (van Schaik, 1989). Hierarchical relationships develop whenever competition among females involves contests over access to essential resources, and are usually maintained by frequent aggressive and affiliative interactions that result in the formation and maintenance of dominance hierarchies (Rowell, 1974). Females invest in these interactions because the benefits of high rank include priority of access to limited resources, such as food, water, protected sleeping sites, and mates. Compared to subordinates, high ranking females should achieve higher reproductive success, though this may only be apparent when critical resources are most limited.

Egalitarian relationships develop when competition among females is indirect. For example, instead of engaging in direct contests for the best food or feeding sites, females may scramble for resources in more or less autonomous ways. The depletion of a food resource by one female before a second female arrives is an example of this form of **scramble competition** because although the late arriving female may lose out on the food, there is no opportunity for her to contest access to it. Under these circumstances, social relationships among females are weak. They have little to gain by interacting with one another, and their relationships tend to be based on indifference, or such infrequent encounters that opportunities to develop and maintain stable relationships are minimal.

Unlike female relationships in hierarchical societies (Figure 7.2), there are no consistent alliances among females, and little of the affiliative grooming or hugging that hierarchical females engage in to cement their alliances, reconcile their disputes, or reassure one another of their benign intentions (Cords and Aureli, 1993, 1996; Silk, 1996; Silk, et al., 1996). Strong alliances are not necessary when resources are rarely contested and competition is instead of the scramble variety, and because contests are infrequent, there is little, if any, advantage to developing social mechanisms for **postconflict resolution** (van Schaik and Aureli, 2000).

Across primates, it is the relative importance of **contest competition** within-groups versus contest competition between-groups that distinguishes the kinds of social relationships maintained by female kin. The balance between levels of contest competition and scramble competition within- and between-groups also affects whether females stay in or disperse from their natal groups. In the absence of contest competition, females tend to disperse.

Within- and Between-Group Competition

Dutch primatologist Elisabeth Sterck and her colleagues (1997) have distinguished four categories of female relationships that correspond to each of the four combinations of within- and between-group contest competition (Table 7.1). Their classification represents the latest in a succession of ecological models for the variation in female primate relationships. As we saw in Chapter 6, pioneering efforts to

FIGURE 7.2   Matrilineal gelada baboons (*Theropithecus gelada*) live in one-male groups. In gelada baboons, female matrilines are powerful enough to influence the outcome of male competition for membership. Photo by R. I. M. Dunbar.

TABLE 7.1   Competitive regimes and categories of female social relationships*

Social category	Competitive regime		Social response		Examples
	Within-group contest	*Between-group contest*	*Female philopatry*	*Female ranking*	
Dispersal-Egalitarian	Low	Low	No	Egalitarian	brown lemurs, muriquis
Resident-Egalitarian	Low	High	Yes	Egalitarian	patas monkeys, most guenons
Resident-Nepotistic	High	Low	Yes	Nepotistic & despotic	vervets, capuchins, most baboons and macaques
Resident-Nepotistic-Tolerant	High (Potentially)	High	Yes	Nepotistic but tolerant	Sulawesi macaques

*Categories based on diurnal gregarious primates. Reprinted with permission from E. H. M. Sterck, D. P. Watts, and C. P. van Schaik, 1997, The evolution of female social relationships in nonhuman primates. *Behavioral Ecology and Sociobiology* 41:291–309, Table 1. Copyright © 1997 Springer-Verlag.

model the ecology of female relationships focused on the costs of contest competition within-groups versus the benefits of cooperation among group members to win contests against other female groups (Wrangham, 1980). In these early models, female primate relationships were dichotomized into those that were **female-bonded** and *nonfemale-bonded* based on the relative strength of within- versus between-group contest competition. Female-bonded primates, like most cercopithecines, live in extended matrilines in which close kin differentially groom and provide agonistic support for one another. They were thought to cooperate with one another in resource defense because of the benefits that large female groups gain in contests against other female kin groups (Figure 7.3). Competition within-groups over the highest quality, preferred foods or the best places to eat were thought to lead to the maintenance of stable hierarchies among individual females within their matrilines, and among different matrilines within these groups.

Subsequent modifications of this model extended the bonded-nonbonded dichotomy to account for a third category of females, which include patas monkeys and some guenons (Figure 7.4). These females face minimal within-group competition, but nonetheless stay with their kin because they need their cooperation to defend resources against other groups of females (van Schaik, 1989). In the absence of within-group feeding competition, day range length does not increase with group size, and there are no advantages to maintaining hierarchical relationships (Isbell, 1991). As a result, female kin in these groups maintain weaker, less differentiated relationships than they do in the original characterization of female-bonded groups where both within- and between-group competition play a role.

Sterck and her colleagues (1997) take these distinctions one further step by distinguishing among the kinds of relationships that females maintain in their groups. For example, female Sulawesi and stump-tailed macaques are more tolerant toward one another in their hierarchical matrilineal societies than most other

FIGURE 7.3 The dynamic relationship between group size and group growth rate in social primates. Within-group competition increases with group size. Groups above the minimum size and below the equilibrium size will grow. Reprinted with permission from E. H. M. Sterck, D. P. Watts, and C. P. van Schaik, 1997, The evolution of female social relationships in nonhuman primates. *Behavioral Ecology and Sociobiology* 41: 291–309, Figure 3. Copyright © 1997 Springer-Verlag.

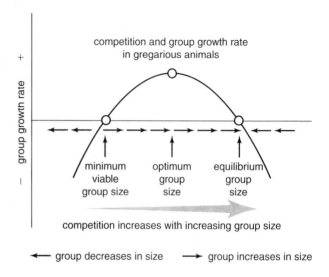

FIGURE 7.4   Members of a wild patas monkey (*Erythrocebus patas*) matrilineal group survey the field. Photo by Ron S. and Anne A. Carlson.

macaques (Figure 7.5). The greater tolerance of dominant females has been attributed to the fact that they rely on support from other females when it comes to defending food resources in between-group contests, and thus, would suffer in terms of fitness if subordinates were to disperse. This balance between competition and cooperation was originally recognized and developed into a model for birds (Vehrencamp, 1983), but it should apply equally well to primates under conditions of high between-group competition. Such tolerance, which takes the form of comparatively low rates of within-group aggression and high rates of postconflict reconciliation, is less prevalent when low levels of between-group contests reduce the

FIGURE 7.5   Stump-tailed macaques (*Macaca arctoides*) engage in a grooming session. Females in this species have more relaxed relationships than most other macaques. Photo made available by Irwin Bernstein.

need for extended cooperation among female matrilines over food. In these cases, groups can simply split up.

As long as the fitness of a subordinate is higher than what it would be if she left her group, she is likely to stay put no matter how badly she's treated (Cheney, 1992). For example, when habitats are saturated so that there is no place for a female to go, hierarchical relationships can become more linear, as they appear to do in some langurs (Borries, et al., 1991; Koenig, et al., 1998). Under these conditions, subordinates may even postpone reproduction altogether (Ferrari and Digby, 1996), like some subordinate female marmosets and tamarins apparently do (see Box 1.1).

Because of the ecological differences between habitats, females of the same species can end up living in very different kinds of groups, with different kinds of relationships among themselves and leading to different kinds of options for males. In fact, intraspecific variation in female grouping patterns has been observed in most primates for which data from multiple populations are available (Moore, 1984). It is precisely these sorts of comparisons between intraspecific and interspecific patterns that help us to distinguish between the ecological and phylogenetic correlates of behavior (Chapter 1).

Social Dynamics in Female Groups

Matrilocal Societies

Probably more is known about female relationships among baboons and macaques than about those of any other primates (Box 7.1). With the sole exception of hamadryas baboons, females in these species typically remain in their natal groups for life, so daughters mature with their mothers and sometimes even grandmothers, as well as sisters, aunts, and cousins. Groups may split up when they become so large that feeding competition within the group outweighs the benefits of living with kin for their cooperation in between-group competition, but even then, members of matrilines usually tend to stick together (Chepko-Sade and Sade, 1979; Dunbar, 1987b; Sade, et al., 1976).

Social relationships among most female baboons and macaques are organized around stable dominance hierarchies in which rank reversals are usually rare (Samuels, et al., 1987). Although Sulawesi and stump-tailed macaques exhibit more tolerance toward one another than other macaques, they still maintain kin-based hierarchies like most other Old World cercopithecines and many species of colobines.

Just as with the males, the relationship between female rank and reproductive success is not nearly as clear-cut as evolutionary models of behavior would predict (Fedigan, 1983). Dominant yellow baboon females at Amboseli National Park don't have higher birth rates than subordinates, but they begin their reproductive careers roughly 200 days earlier, giving some of them a chance to produce an extra infant during their reproductive lifespan (Altmann, et al., 1988). Among olive baboons in Tanzania, high-ranking females have shorter interbirth intervals and higher infant survival, and their daughters mature faster than low-ranking females. However, these high-ranking females also appear to have a higher probability of miscarriages, and some high-ranking matrilines have inexplicably low fertility (Packer, et al., 1995).

Once again we find a parallel with male primates in the hypothesis that stress associated with maintaining high rank may take its toll. If stress offsets some of the benefits of better nutrition, then the variance in reproductive success between high- and low-ranking females may be lower than expected, and selection pressures favoring aggression by high ranking females toward subordinates might be balanced by the costs of being hyperaggressive. This hypothesis is controversial, however, because although aggression has been associated with establishing dominance, it is not associated with the maintenance of dominance (Altmann, et al., 1995).

It may be that the benefits of high rank to female reproductive success are most apparent when critical resources are severely limited. For example, in a long-term study of toque macaques, rank-related differences in the probability of survivorship increased sharply during a period in which drought resulted in food shortages (Dittus, 1979). Similar rank-related effects have been documented in vervet monkeys in southern Kenya during a severe drought (Wrangham, 1981).

Female vervet monkeys live in matrilines and defend territories (Figure 7.6). During a severe drought, only two of the three study groups (B and C) had standing water on their territories, and females in these groups repulsed the efforts of females from the third group (A) to enter their territories to drink. Within group A, high-ranking females were able to find some water in their own territory by licking dew off of trees, but low-ranking females were forced to search for alternative water sources outside of their territories. More than half of the females and immatures in group A died during this drought, and all of the mortalities were low-ranking females and their offspring (Cheney, et al., 1988).

At another field site in northern Kenya, high-ranking vervet monkeys have priority of access to the best feeding sites, and therefore higher feeding rates, than low-ranking females throughout the year. The high-ranking mothers also produce more surviving offspring than low-ranking mothers, but only when preferred food resources occur in clumped, patchy distributions (Whitten, 1983).

FIGURE 7.6 Vervet monkeys (*Chlorocebus aethiops*) in Amboseli National Park, Kenya. Individual in the foreground stands bipedally to survey the area. Photo by P. C. Lee.

BOX **7.1**

Mysterious Matrilines

Cracking the code of kinship among female baboons was not one of his objectives when, in 1959, American anthropologist Irven DeVore conducted the first systematic study of olive baboons at Nairobi Park (Figure B7.1). By this time, Japanese macaque studies had already been underway for several years, and the importance of kinship in these macaque societies was well-established (e.g., Kawai, 1958; Kawamura, 1958). But, deciphering baboon society during the 10-month period that DeVore had for his fieldwork was another matter altogether.

For starters, no one at that time had any idea how similar baboons and macaques would turn out to be. Hamilton's (1964) pivotal publication demonstrating the significant role that kin selection could play in the evolution of animal social relationships and their societies had not yet been published, so the theoretical basis for a longer-term study that would identify matrilineal kinship was not so apparent then as it is today (Chapter 4). Ten months did not give DeVore enough time to follow the fate of the infants born in his study troop as they matured and either left or were integrated into adult society.

Additionally, by coincidence, there were only seven adult females in DeVore's main study group, an unusually small number compared to the 12 to 20 adult females found in most other baboon troops (Melnick and Pearl, 1987). With so few females, there was little competition among females, and therefore few of the agonistic interactions that researchers depend on to detect the patterns in their dominance relationships. Subsequent studies, conducted elsewhere and over longer periods on baboons and other primates, have demonstrated that troop size and composition affect the types and rates of social

FIGURE B7.1   Irven DeVore watching olive baboons (*Papio anubis*) during his original field study in Nairobi National Park. Photo by Nancy DeVore/Anthro-Photo.

interactions, and that the number of females and their matrilineal relatedness influence the stability of female hierarchies (Altmann and Altmann, 1979; Dunbar, 1979, 1987b; Samuels, et al., 1987). Even among Japanese macaques, females in small, unprovisioned groups rarely engage in aggression because they avoid one another by maintaining their distance while feeding (Takahata, et al., 1994).

Despite these constraints on what DeVore could discern, at least three of his original depictions of female baboons have since been substantiated. For example, in contrast to females, throwing food to the troop promptly triggered males to reveal their ranks. With their convincing canine displays and comprehensible coalitions (Chapter 5), the approach of male superiors always led subordinates to yield. Low-ranking females seemed fearless by comparison, perhaps because high-ranking females were less likely to attack them (DeVore, 1962, p. 83).

The failure of the small number of females in his study troop to respond to these food tests in consistent ways meant that their relationships with one another remained enigmatic. But, when the females did engage in aggression, their interactions were less severe than those among males. This sex difference in the severity of male and female aggression may be a consequence of the differences in their body and canine sizes, as well as one of style. It has since been confirmed in baboons and other primates in which females, but not males, live with their kin (Smuts, 1987a).

DeVore was also quick to catch on to the ways in which female relationships fluctuated throughout their reproductive cycles. Female "bickering" was frequent during the intervals between estrus and after an infant was weaned. DeVore witnessed, however, that when females were in estrus or nursing newborns, the protective proximity of their male consorts gave them special status. Individual females passed in and out of these protected positions during the course of his study, making it difficult to identify among females anything like the coalition alliances that give the male hierarchy its structure (Chapter 5). Instead, it appeared "impossible to build the male kind of power structure on the shifting sands of female physiology" (DeVore, 1962, p. 85). Subsequent advances in evolutionary theory have since put into perspective the power of females as limiting resources to males (Trivers, 1972) and the influential role that male "friends" (Smuts, 1985; Smuts and Smuts, 1993) play in female social dynamics (Chapter 5).

Subsequent research has also built on the foundations of DeVore's (1962, p. 93) descriptions of individual temperaments in "predicting a female's position within the structure of the troop." He noted such traits as "short-tempered" "hyperactive," "very aggressive," "placid," and "retiring" to describe individual females and explain their relative ranks. DeVore's successors, employing more rigorous approaches to quantifying individual variation, such as rates of aggression, that are now standard in the field (Chapter 1), have since found support for these kinds of temperamental differences, both across species with differences in dominance styles (de Waal and Luttrell, 1989), and among individuals within groups (e.g., Altmann, 1980).

Nowadays, the study of individual temperament and its social consequences has become one of the fastest growing areas of primate research (Clarke and Boinski, 1995; Clarke and Mason, 1988; Moore, 1992a). When I recently asked him about female matrilines, DeVore insisted that he "missed the main point" (14 May 1997). But, in other respects, from his descriptions of female styles of aggression compared to those of males, to his suspicions about the roles of males in mediating female relationships, to his appreciation of individual female personalities, DeVore's pioneering observations helped frame the questions about female baboons that longer-term studies, evolutionary perspectives, and systematic methods have been able to explore.

Rank Inheritance.   In the matrilineal societies of most baboons, macaques, and vervet monkeys, a female's position in the hierarchy is inherited from her mother. Daughters of high-ranking females become high-ranking themselves, while daughters of low-ranking females remain subordinate. Females in low-ranking matrilines can rise above their birth rights by splitting off from the group, staging a coup, or if higher-ranking matrilines completely die off. But even in these cases, the relative ranking of surviving matrilines tends to persist (Samuels, et al., 1987). Presumably, low-ranking matrilines stick with their groups because they benefit by being part of the larger group in between-group contests or in predator detection. Over time, it is possible for high-ranking matrilines to be reduced in size due to reproductive pathologies (Packer, et al., 1995), but more typically, high rank confers greater survivorship, which can result in higher reproductive success (Altmann, et al., 1995; Fedigan, 1997; van Noordwijk and van Schaik, 1999).

One of the mechanisms that maintains this system of matrilineal rank inheritance is the differential ability of high- and low-ranking mothers to come to the aid of their daughters in agonistic encounters against other females in their groups. Daughters see their mothers' interactions with other females, and they experience the benefits of maternal assistance corresponding to their mothers' ranks. However, daughters born to mothers high in the hierarchy are not totally dependent on their mothers to claim their inheritance. Other females in the group apparently recognize their birth rights, and support them in fights when, as adolescents, they begin to assert themselves.

Japanese primatologists were the first to identify the two phases in this system of female rank acquisition (Kawai, 1958, 1965). The first, termed **dependent rank,** involves maternal help during the transitional period when females begin to assert themselves in agonistic contests against other, often older and larger, females. The second phase, termed **basic rank,** occurs when females reach adult size and can assert their dominance on their own.

During a systematic study of yellow baboons at Amboseli National Park, Jeffrey Walters (1980) found that adolescent females only focused their challenges on adult females that were subordinate to their mothers or other maternal kin. During her transitional period of rank assertion, a young female begins to shift her behavior toward lower-ranking adults from exclusively submissive, to a mixture of aggressive and submissive displays, to exclusively aggressive. The older female may exhibit only aggressive behavior at first, but eventually she will add submissive gestures to her aggressive responses. Once the older female gives her first indication of submission, the younger female never reverts to submissive displays and the older female eases into the submissive responses appropriate to her lower position in the hierarchy.

One of the most extraordinary features of this process is that females seem to understand their ranks and the ranks of other females relative to one another. Maternal kin, other adolescents, and even unrelated adult females will come to an adolescent's aid when she begins to assert her rank, but only if she has chosen an adult whose rank is lower than what her inherited rank should be (Figure 7.7).

FIGURE 7.7　Amboseli yellow baboons (*Papio cynocephalus*) in a triadic interaction. The raised tail of the individual in the center is a submissive gesture, given in response to the baboon she is facing, who has threatened her. Her screams attracted a supporter, standing behind her. Photo by K. B. Strier.

The ability of young females to correctly target their inherited positions in the hierarchy and the involvement of other females in these assertions have been tested through ingenious playback experiments with wild vervet monkeys. Dorothy Cheney and Robert Seyfarth (1990) tape-recorded distress cries given by the daughters of dominant and subordinate mothers. They then played back these taped recordings to other females, whose responses they monitored. They found that listeners' responses to the recorded distress cries were appropriate to their own ranks relative to the infants' mothers. Female test subjects responded with anxious, submissive gestures when the distress call came from an infant whose mother was dominant to her. Playbacks of distress calls from an infant whose matriline was subordinate to the subject failed to elicit submissive responses.

One consequence of maternal rank inheritance is that the status of all females drops with each successive daughter that is born into a higher-ranking matriline. In general, daughters assume the rank directly below that of their mothers, and younger daughters displace their older sisters just below their mothers in the hierarchy. In yellow baboons, there are some caveats in the system based on differences in female size and age, which affect their competitive abilities. Daughters attain the rank above their mothers if their mothers are over fifteen years of age, and younger sisters only outrank their older sisters if there is less than a two year age difference between them (Altmann, et al., 1985).

Until very recently, these "rules" of youngest daughter ascendancy seemed remarkably straightforward. However, new analyses have thrown a monkey wrench into our understanding of this system, at least as it is practiced among Japanese macaques. Comparisons of populations of Japanese macaques at naturally occurring low densities and provisioned, high density populations indicated that it was only the provisioned, high density macaques that appeared to conform. Female Japanese macaques living at lower densities are less limited by their matrilineal birth order, perhaps because the distribution of their naturally occurring foods relative to their group sizes means that females can avoid direct contests over food by spreading out to feed. Females don't need—or get—as much support from kin when disputes are rare, and as a result, the youngest ascendancy rules are relaxed (Hill and Okayasu, 1995, 1996; Takahata, et al., 1994) or nonexistant in nonprovisioned groups (Hill, 1999). This emphasizes that "rules" of behavior are not genetically specified, but instead, stem from the predictable interaction of learning not to fight individuals whose mothers and other kin defend them.

Relations among Females.   Females that benefit by living with their kin walk a thin line between the costs of competing with their kin over food and the benefits of cooperating with kin against nonkin. Affiliative interactions and close spatial associations may be beneficial when it comes to having allies, but the rest of the time they risk getting in each other's ways. This leads to conflicts, which can have a disruptive effect on individual feeding efficiency, social cohesion, and ultimately on reproductive success. Not surprisingly, it is precisely in these cohesive, matrilineal societies, where both aggressors and victims stand to lose the most if conflict keeps them apart, that **reconciliation,** or peaceful postconflict interactions, are most evident (de Waal and van Roosmalen, 1979).

Peaceful postconflict interactions have been described for more than twenty species of primates (Silk, 1997). Most of these examples come from captive or provisioned studies, where observation conditions make it possible to monitor interactions among the same individuals both following conflicts and in the absence of conflicts at the same time each day. This controls for day-to-day or diurnal variability in social interactions so that the potential effects of conflicts can be measured.

In reconciliation, rates of grooming or other affiliative interactions increase after a conflict, apparently with the result of restoring, or repairing, the relationship between opponents. In one of the few field studies on reconciliation, high-ranking female baboons approached infant carrying lower-ranking females after an agonistic interaction, and grunted. These grunts have been interpreted as a form of reassurance that high-ranking females provide to communicate their peaceful intentions to the victim in the conflict (Silk, et al., 1996). Female baboons are attracted to new infants, and are eager to handle them, but if they've just had a fight, mothers rarely relinquish their infants to other females willingly (Figure 7.8). Grunting increases a female's opportunities to handle another female's infant, even without prior conflict (Cheney, et al., 1995), so grunting may signal appeasement as well as reconciliation intentions after a conflict (Cords and Aureli, 1996).

Researchers disagree about whether such peaceful postconflict interactions serve the function of repairing relationships that are important over the long-term (Cords and Aureli, 1996; de Waal, 1996) or whether they serve as more immediate, short-term signals of an opponent's intention to "stop fighting and behave peacefully" (Silk, 1996). Either interpretation makes sense from an evolutionary perspective because all individuals benefit from resolving their conflicts (Mason, 1993). Nonetheless, distinguishing between the long-term and short-term consequences of reconciliation on female reproductive success requires data that are not yet available.

Female primates vary in the frequency of their peaceful postconflict contacts, in part because of the differences in their dominance relationships. In rhesus ma-

FIGURE 7.8   An adult female yellow baboon (*Papio cynocephalus*) handles the infant of another female at Amboseli National Park, Kenya. Photo by Joan Silk.

caques, for example, dominance relationships are rigidly defined, and subordinate females rarely direct aggression, or reconciliation, toward higher-ranking females. In stump-tailed macaques, by contrast, reversals in female dominance relationships are more common, and subordinate females both direct aggression toward their higher-ranking colleagues and initiate friendly postconflict interactions more frequently (de Waal and Luttrell, 1989).

Following a conflict, the victim's anxiety levels typically increase. These anxiety levels are evident from displacement activities, such as self-scratching. Among long-tailed macaques, these displacement activities returned to baseline levels sooner if the victim and its opponent reconciled than if they didn't (Aureli, 1992; Aureli and van Schaik, 1991). Furthermore, females with higher affiliation frequencies were also more likely than "nonfriends" to reconcile after their conflicts (Aureli, 1997). Evidently, the benefits of maintaining strong affiliations among females in some species of primates have led to the evolution of mechanisms that reduce postconflict tension, thereby facilitating the ability of females to return to their preconflict relationships (Cords and Aureli, 2000).

It is important to remember that females living in matrilocal societies may also have paternal kin present. This is especially true when alpha males can monopolize access to more than one fertile female, and therefore be the father of multiple offspring in a cohort (Chapter 5). Genetic and behavioral data in rhesus macaques show that while the most affiliative relationships among females involve close maternal kin, females are also more affiliative toward their paternal sisters than they are toward nonkin (Widdig, et al., 2001). Whether they can recognize their paternal sisters by their physical or behavioral attributes is not entirely clear, although familiarity is undoubtedly important (Bernstein, 1999b; Chapais, 2001).

Relations with Males.   Females in matrilineal societies also establish nonsexual affiliative relationships with males. As we saw in Chapter 5, these heterosexual friendships are beneficial to males, both because associating with a female helps male immigrants to integrate into the group and because females may choose their male friends as mates (Smuts, 1985; Strum, 1982). Male friends also intervene on behalf of their female friends if another male or female threatens them or their infants, so females benefit directly from their alliances with males (Smuts, 1987a; Smuts and Smuts, 1993). Trusted males can also provide babysitting services (Figure 7.9) freeing females to feed and forage without the burden of carrying or watching out for their infants.

In the multilevel societies of gelada baboons, however, female relationships are focused more exclusively on one another than on the single male that associates with female units, which form larger bands, which in turn form the even larger troop. Female geladas remain with their kin and form strong bonds with one another (Dunbar, 1983, 1984). Males compete with one another for access to female units, and rely on female support for their membership as well as their mating monopolies. Within these units, high-ranking females may reduce the fertility of low-ranking females by interfering with their mating attempts. Males can't assert their greater size and strength to protect low-ranking females, however, because doing so may jeopardize the female support that males need to maintain their membership in the group (Dunbar, 1988).

Age-Related Rank.   The stability of inherited hierarchical relationships is undermined when female ranks are based on age. Indeed, female ranks may be so unstable and so inconsistently asserted that they are difficult to detect, giving female relationships in these age-graded societies the appearance of being egalitarian

FIGURE 7.9   Adult male Barbary macaques (*Macaca sylvanus*) also frequently engage in allomothering, independent of their paternity (Small, 1990). Photo by Meredith F. Small.

instead of hierarchical (Sterck, et al., 1997). Unstable female relationships occur within the female kin groups formed by Hanuman langurs, in which younger females can dominate older ones, and other colobines (except red colobus monkeys), most guenon species (except vervet monkeys), and some group-living lemurs (Figure 7.10). In Hanuman langurs, which live in extended matrilines like yellow baboons and macaques, ranks among females sometimes correspond to age. Females in their prime reproductive years outrank younger and older females alike (Hrdy, 1977), so females may experience a wide range of positions in the hierarchy, and corresponding rank or age-related fertility, over the course of their lifetimes (Harcourt, 1987). The result is that the lifetime reproductive success of females may be more similar in these societies than in those where female ranks are inherited, and thus relatively stable over time.

Rank relations are also age-dependent within the extended matrilines of female marmosets (Digby and Ferrari, 1994; Nievergelt, et al., 2000). A marmoset mother is dominant over her daughters, who may be permitted to stay in their natal groups as nonreproductive helpers, shuttling younger siblings around instead of reproducing themselves. Forfeiting their own reproduction, or at least putting that of their mothers' ahead of their own, is a high price to pay for retaining their membership in the group, unless the probability of dispersing successfully is low. In addition to helping to raise their younger siblings, subordinate female marmosets play an active role in territorial confrontations with neighboring groups. During these encounters, subordinate females can assess whether dispersing might make sense. Monitoring the number of other females gives them information about whether the breeding opportunities in other groups might be better than they are in their own (Lazaro-Perea, 2001; Lazaro-Perea, et al., 2000).

FIGURE 7.10   A troop of black and white colobus monkeys (*Colobus guereza*). Troop members other than mothers and their infants rarely interact with one another (Oates, 1977). Photo by John F. Oates.

Relations among Females. Without inherited ranks to maintain the stability of female relationships with one another, there is little in the way of coalitionary support. Female affiliative bonds are weak in these species, and among the group-living lemurs, female kin may be evicted when resources are scarce (Kappeler, 1997a). Lemur fruit patches tend to be smaller than those of many group-living anthropoids (Ganzhorn, 1988; Kappeler, 1997a), so within-group feeding competition tends to be high and there is little communal defense of food patches in between-group encounters. Evicting female kin is one way that female lemurs, and presumably other non-female-bonded primates, including many platyrrhines, keep their group sizes small and their levels of within-group feeding competition low. Both ring-tailed and brown lemurs, for example, will target aggression against other females, which sometimes results in the victims being expelled from their groups (Vick and Pereira, 1989). Splitting up into smaller subgroups during times of resource scarcity is another solution to the problems of within-group feeding competition that many lemurs and other group-living primates employ (Chapter 6). Attacking and killing infants may be another way (Digby, 2000; Jolly, et al., 2000).

Relations with Males. A second characteristic of female primates that live in age-ranked matrilines is their tendency to maintain strong affiliative bonds with particular males (Figure 7.11). Female white-faced capuchin monkeys live in cohesive matrilineal groups, and there is some evidence that mothers support their daughters in agonistic interactions, affecting the ranks their daughters ultimately attain (Fedigan, 1993; O'Brien, T. G., 1991; O'Brien and Robinson, 1993; Robinson, 1988b; Robinson and Janson, 1987). However, in brown capuchins and wedge-capped capuchins, females gain little, if any, third-party support from any group members except the highest-ranking male. Females maintain proximity and groom the alpha male, and mate preferentially with him. In exchange for these favors, females gain protection from aggression by other group members and increased access to food

FIGURE 7.11 A male red-tailed guenon (*Cercopithecus ascanius*) presents his hindquarters in a grooming solicitation, with which a female complies. Female guenons like these live in resident-egalitarian societies. Photo by Marina Cords.

for themselves and their offspring (Janson, 1985; O'Brien, T. G., 1991). Female white-faced capuchins mate with multiple partners and do not show the same preference for the alpha male in their groups that brown and wedge-capped capuchin monkeys do (Fragazy, et al., in press).

The "cross-sex bonds" that characterize female relationships with the highest-ranking male in these species of matrilineal capuchin monkeys also occur in mountain baboons of southern Africa (Byrne, et al., 1990). In contrast to their more equatorial cousins, mountain baboons live at low densities in a harsh climate. Instead of forming coalitionary alliances with one another, female mountain baboons form their strongest affiliative bonds with the dominant male in their group. Females mate almost exclusively with him, and in return, he protects their offspring from aggression by other group members. Lactating females compete with one another for access to alpha males, and it is usually the younger, higher ranking females that succeed in gaining more time near their male protectors (Palombit, et al., 2001). In some baboons, the special support males provide is contingent on the infant's survival (Palombit, et al., 1997).

Some female lemurs also form bonds with particular males, which has been interpreted as a strategy to prevent infanticidal assaults (van Schaik and Kappeler, 1997). However, unlike brown- and wedge-capped capuchin monkeys or mountain baboons, dominant male lemurs do not enjoy mating monopolies in exchange for their potential protection. For starters, female lemurs are individually dominant over males, and both sexes are similar in body size (Figure 7.12). As a result, male lemurs can't bully females into copulating with them, and female lemurs are free to assert their preferences for new immigrant males (Erhart and Overdorff, 1998) or

FIGURE 7.12   Ring-tailed lemurs (*Lemur catta*), like other lemurs, are sexually monomorphic in body size and females are dominant over males. These individuals are wearing identifying collars. Photo by Peter M. Kappeler.

unfamiliar mates from one breeding season to the next. And, because female lemurs come into estrus during their brief annual breeding season, no single male can consistently keep other males away (Pereira, 1991; van Schaik and Kappeler, 1993).

Life without Kin

In most New World monkeys, many prosimians, and all of the apes, females have the option of establishing their reproductive careers in groups without kin. Dispersing females rarely base their social relationships with one another on nepotism, although nowadays, the small number of groups in many fragmented populations may mean that females disperse into a limited number of groups, which quickly consist of other females from the same natal groups. Even in undisturbed habitats with large continuous populations, dispersing females may end up in adjacent groups unless they disperse over long distances.

In some species, including many lemurs and howler monkeys, daughters are evicted from their natal groups by their mothers (Figure 7.13). By kicking out their daughters, adult females keep their group sizes close to the optimal size for protection from predators without increasing the number of potential food competitors or the attractiveness of groups to infanticidal males (e.g., Crockett, 1984, 1996; Kappeler, 1997a). In other species, like muriquis, daughters seem to take leave at their own initiative, but the possibility that subtle methods of eviction are practiced cannot be ruled out (Printes and Strier, 1999; Strier, 1991b). In still others, such as Thomas langurs and mountain gorillas, females may change groups whenever a marauding male demonstrates his ability to protect them from harassment better than the resident male in their current group (Sterck, 1997; Watts, 1996).

FIGURE 7.13   A troop of brown howler monkeys (*Alouatta fusca*) takes a break. Photo by J. W. Lynch.

Dispersal patterns vary a great deal within species. For example, although male chimpanzees are philopatric, only some females leave their natal communities (Pusey, et al., 1997). Conversely, in matrilineal baboon and macaque societies, females occasionally transfer out of their natal groups (Hsu and Lin, 2001). These "exceptions" are often ignored in the face of what seem to be larger, more general patterns, but as anthropologist Jim Moore (1984, 1992a) has repeatedly noted, different sets of patterns begin to emerge when these exceptions are pooled. His comparative analyses provide a strong cautionary reminder that primates are highly variable in their behavior. Ignoring this variation can lead to oversimplified, and even inaccurate depictions of species differences (Figure 7.14).

It is also important to remember that different processes and mechanisms can lead to similar behavioral outcomes. For example, a variety of factors can result in female natal group transfers, ranging from downright evictions by their mothers to overt attractions toward unfamiliar males. Understanding these mechanisms is a necessary step in deciphering the patterns underlying primate behavioral variation (Moore, 1999).

Gaining Group Membership.   Whatever the stimulus that prompts daughters to disperse, leaving home is almost always a risky endeavor. Dispersing individuals are more vulnerable to predators during the period they are without the safety of a group. Dispersing leads females into unfamiliar areas where the location of food

FIGURE 7.14   A rare muriqui (*Brachyteles arachnoides*) matriline. Although males are philopatric and females typically disperse in this species, in this case a daughter (center) remained in her natal group with her mother (right). Both the mother and her mature daughter are reproductively active. Thus, an infant, her mother, and her grandmother can embrace. Photo by Claudio P. Nogueira.

and other resources is not known and therefore less predictable. In addition, dispersing females are rarely accepted into new groups by other females without resistance. Indeed, if females stood to gain by recruiting one another as allies, presumably they would preferentially recruit among kin in their natal groups as red howler monkey females seem to do (Pope, 2000).

In female mantled howler monkeys, an immigrant female fighting her way into an established troop may attain the top-ranking position in the process (Jones, 1980). However, the stresses of immigration and fighting to the top seem to take a reproductive toll. Ken Glander (1980) found that none of the firstborn infants of these young "alpha" females survived through infancy. As the alpha females dropped in rank with each successive female that subsequently immigrated, a higher proportion of their infants survived. Only very old or low-ranking females experienced infant mortality levels that approximated those of young alpha females.

New immigrants constantly shake up these female howler monkey hierarchies. But, in contrast to the effects of maturing daughters in matrilineal societies, rank reversals are not entirely predictable in mantled howler monkeys. Evan Zucker and Margaret Clarke (1998) found that female age and rank were not significantly related to one another in the mantled howler troops they observed during a four-year field study. Instead, some young immigrants started out as low-ranking, and only later, when they began to fight their way up the hierarchy, did the rates of aggression among females increase. It seems that there are at least two different ways to immigrate in this species, each of which has a different set of consequences.

Independent of their mothers' ranks, Zucker and Clarke (1998) found that young infants were always attractive to other females, and that the birth of infants led to changes in female social relationships with one another. In fact, hierarchical relationships among females also changed in response to immigrations by new females and males, resulting in a much more dynamic society than was previously thought to occur in this species.

Despite their egalitarian relationships, dispersing female muriquis initially encounter resistance from longer-term residents in the groups they seek to join. Their integration seems to go more smoothly if they immigrate with a peer, but the process can take months for females immigrating on their own. Lone female immigrants tend to stick to the periphery of their new group, following their movements and occasionally, getting lost. If they get too close too soon to the main part of the group, older females will chase them away. Gradually, the immigrants are included in playful interactions with juveniles and adolescent or young adult males, and eventually their presence is tolerated by other females (Strier, 1993b).

Muriqui females disperse between five and eight years of age, before they have begun to show any signs of being sexually attractive or receptive to males and prior to undergoing puberty (Strier and Ziegler, 2000). There may be a two- to ten-year lag between when a female immigrates and when her first infant is born (Strier, 1996b), but immigrant females appear to achieve complete integration, as measured by their activites and patterns of association with other females, within months after joining their new group (Printes and Strier, 1999).

The situation with female chimpanzees differs from that of howler monkeys and muriquis. Female chimpanzees often leave their natal communities when they are sporting the prominent sexual swellings that signal their estrus (Goodall, 1986). Such a "passport" may be necessary for solitary female chimpanzees to make the dangerous crossing between the borders separating their natal community's range and another community because males patrolling these borders are less likely to attack a visibly estrous female than one that may already be pregnant with another male's offspring (Nishida, 1990). Once she makes it past the males into a new community, she still has to watch out for hostile females, who regard her as a future competitor for food.

At Gombe National Park, only about half of all adolescent females leave their natal community. The fortunate females who are able to establish their own feeding areas near those of their mothers' seem to get a head start on their reproductive careers compared to females that emigrate from their natal communities (Pusey, et al., 1997). However, the situation for females at Gombe may be unique, because so far, it is the only place known where some females stay home. Limited dispersal opportunities lead to female philopatry, and may therefore reflect recent environmental conditions instead of an adaptive, evolutionary strategy (Kano, 1997; Nishida, 1997).

Autonomous Interests.   When females avoid one another's company, as is the case in the fission–fusion societies of chimpanzees and spider monkeys, they have few opportunities to establish and maintain defined dominance hierarchies or affiliative alliances with one another, and presumably, derive few benefits from doing so. Their relationships with one another are constantly in flux because they adjust the size of their feeding parties in response to the size of their fruit patches. And, because their food patches are not defensible, they should not need to curry favor with allies they are not likely to ever need.

However, the undifferentiated, egalitarian-like relationships that these autonomous females were thought to maintain have turned out to be more complicated than was previously thought. For example, despite their general avoidance policies, when female chimpanzees do encounter one another, they exhibit consistent patterns in their aggressive and submissive responses. Dominant females give pant hoots and subordinates move away, but these patterns of interacting were hard to recognize because female encounters happen so rarely. Only recently, when more than thirty years of behavioral data from the Gombe chimpanzees were examined, did the significance of these subtle interactions begin to make sense (Pusey, et al., 1997).

Female chimpanzees could not be classified in a rigid, linear hierarchy. However, they could be classified by their relatively high, intermediate, and low ranks. Female ranks were positively related to reproductive success, with high-ranking females producing more surviving offspring and living longer than their low-ranking counterparts, similar to the effects of dominance on female reproductive success in matrilineal societies (Fedigan, 1997; van Noordwijk and van Schaik, 1999). Daughters of high-ranking females reach sexual maturity and give birth to their first infants up to four years earlier than daughters of low-ranking females. High-ranking female chimpanzees are thought to have access to higher quality foods in their core areas and to the best feeding sites in patches where females aggregate.

Aggregations around Males.   Weak social relationships among unrelated females make them particularly vulnerable to manipulations by males whenever the costs of associating with one another are low (Figure 7.15). In the multilevel societies of hamadryas baboons, for example, subadult females are herded by a male into his one-male-unit (Kummer, 1968; Stammbach, 1987). In both howler monkeys and mountain gorillas, abundant, evenly distributed food resources mean that although females gain few, if any, benefits from associating with one another, they also suffer few, if any feeding costs (Watts, 1985, 1990). Both mountain gorilla and howler monkey males intervene to settle conflicts among females, and defend females and their infants from incursions by male outsiders (Watts, 1996; Zucker and Clarke, 1998). When a female mountain gorilla, howler monkey, or hamadryas baboon switches groups, it is almost always associated with the appearance of a new male on the scene.

Avoidance of Males.   The basis for indifference among female chimpanzees, spider monkeys, or orangutans differs from that among hamadryas baboons, mountain gorillas, or howler monkeys, and therefore affects their relationships with males. For example, whereas mountain gorillas don't suffer much in the way of feeding costs when they voluntarily join up with males, female chimpanzees, spider monkeys, and orangutans do (Watts, 2001). Female chimpanzees associating in feeding parties with males have lower rates of feeding than they do by themselves (Wrangham and Smuts, 1980), and female orangutans feeding in large patches of ripe figs have lower feeding efficiencies than the males in their parties (Utami, et al., 1997). Because females in these species seem to distribute themselves in response to the spatial distribution of their preferred fruit resources, males cannot single-handedly attract them into units or aggregations that can be defended for any length of time. As we saw in Chapter 5, male chimpanzees and spider monkeys adopt the strategy of joining forces with their brothers to patrol a community range that includes

FIGURE 7.15   An anubis-like female baboon (*Papio anubis*) grooms the hybrid male of her unit. Photograph taken by Jane Phillips-Conroy.

independent females (Wrangham, 1979). Male orangutans, by contrast, monitor solitary females on their own.

Males defend resources in each one of these systems, but the resources they defend seem to be fundamentally different. In the case of Hamadryas baboons, mountain gorillas, and howler monkeys, males defend females, whose foraging interests are unaffected by the groups in which they live. In the case of patrilocal chimpanzees or solitary orangutans, males defend the feeding areas that females exploit, and therefore, indirectly affect female reproductive success. Differences between **female-defense polygyny** and **resource-defense polygyny** have been described in a variety of other animal species, where the attractiveness of males is determined by their ability to either provide females with protection against harassment by other males, which interferes with female feeding efficiency, or provide females with access to food and other essential resources (Figure 7.16).

Managing Males.   Female alliances against other groups of females are restricted to matrilineal societies. After all, it would be highly self-defeating to a female's own reproductive fitness if she were to ally herself with nonkin against her own relatives living in neighboring groups. But, while kinship facilitates cooperation and may inhibit direct competition among females, it is not a precondition for the development of affiliative relationships among females that serve other, nonfeeding related social functions.

Alliances among female kin affect heterosexual relationships, particularly in sexually dimorphic species where larger males may pose serious threats to females and their offspring (Chapter 5). Yet, when it is in female self-interest to keep peace in their groups, they may form affiliations with one another independently of kinship.

Bonobos illustrate the potential effectiveness of alliances among unrelated females at mediating male social behavior and the relationships between males and females (Hashimoto, et al., 1996; Gerloff, et al., 1999). Like chimpanzees, bonobos

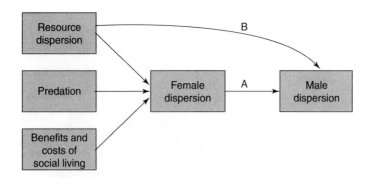

FIGURE 7.16   Influences on mating systems. Males may compete directly for females (A), which can lead to female-defense polygyny, or indirectly (B) for resource-rich areas that will attract females, leading to resource-defense pologyny. From Krebs, J. R. and Davies, N. B. 1993. *An Introduction to Behavioural Ecology,* Third Edition. Oxford: Blackwell Scientific Ltd. Reprinted with permission of the publisher.

live in large, multi-male, multi-female communities in which males remain in their natal groups and females disperse before or after reproduction. Bonobos also resemble chimpanzees in their fluid patterns of association, but the species differ markedly in the size and composition of their parties. Female chimpanzees spend most of their time alone or with their dependent offspring in individual core areas, and come together with other adults only when large patches of preferred fruits are available. Male chimpanzees associate with one another more frequently, but when united at large food resources or during a female's estrous period, the sexes are generally segregated.

Female bonobos, by contrast, travel in larger parties, which often include males as well as other females. The bonobos' inclusion of herbaceous vegetation in their diets, in addition to their preferred patchy fruits, reduces the costs of feeding together compared to chimpanzees. Within bonobo communities, females are codominant with males, and young males rely on their mothers to rise in rank in much the same way that adolescent female baboons rely on their mothers to assert their inherited ranks (Furuichi, 1997).

Male bonobos don't dominate females the way that male chimpanzees dominate females because female bonobos establish and maintain strong affiliative alliances with one another that help keep the males in line. These female alliances are also apparently important to the successful immigration of young females into their new communities (Kano, 1996). For example, immigrant females typically follow in the shadow of an older, longer-term female resident until invited to participate in an explicitly sexual interaction that involves females rubbing their genitals against one another's while facing each other (Figure 7.17). Once a new immigrant female engages in "genital–genital (or g–g) rubbing," she becomes a steady companion to her new friend (Figure 7.18).

G–g rubbing is not limited to newfound friends during female immigration events. It takes place in a variety of other contexts, including whenever potential

FIGURE 7.17 Wild female bonobos (*Pan paniscus*) engage in genital–genital, or g–g, rubbing. Photo by Ellen J. Ingmanson.

FIGURE 7.18   Although female bonobos (*Pan paniscus*) typically
disperse from their natal communities, g–g rubbing helps them
to establish strong social bonds with one another. Photo by
Ellen J. Ingmanson.

tensions arise over access to food, and as a form of reconciliation after a rare aggressive interaction (de Waal, 1987). The alliances that female bonobos establish with one another are effective in subduing male aggressive outbursts and thereby contribute to the influential position of females in bonobo society.

Wild chimpanzee females have no comparable affiliative interactions that strengthen bonds among them, perhaps because their autonomous feeding strategies mean that they are more likely to avoid than encounter one another. But their ability to form alliances against males has been demonstrated in captivity. When housed in close and constant company, female chimpanzees may take advantage of the opportunities for the repeated interactions necessary to establish and maintain long-term alliances that permit them to mediate among males as well (de Waal, 1982).

Population Consequences of Female Strategies

The ecology of female primate social relationships affects the variance in female reproductive success within- and between-groups and across different species. Because female fertility directly affects population growth rates, female strategies to increase their fitness have implications for the probability of recovery or extinction of small populations isolated in fragmented, altered habitats. Understanding the variation in female primate behavioral strategies is thus a necessary step in developing informed conservation management plans on behalf of endangered and threatened populations, and in predicting and monitoring the effects of habitat disturbance on fertility.

Habitat Fragmentation and Saturation

We have seen how female primate grouping patterns, the composition of female groups, and the social relationships among females in these groups reflect compromises between the types of within- and between-group competition for access to preferred foods, and the risks of predation and male aggression against themselves and their offspring. When Japanese macaques are provisioned or yellow baboons have access to garbage dumps, the increases in food availability are associated with reduced feeding competition and corresponding increases in female fertility (Asquith, 1989; Harcourt, 1987; Muruthi, et al., 1991). Likewise, when risks of predation are reduced or eliminated, female lemurs may alter their activity patterns (van Schaik and Kappeler, 1996) and long-tailed macaques adjust their groups to be smaller and less cohesive, and more directly related to the spatial and temporal distribution of their food resources (van Schaik, et al., 1983).

What happens to female behavioral strategies when their food supplies are permanently disturbed is equally significant. Naturally occurring seasonal food shortages or drought lead to higher mortality rates due to illness and starvation, especially among young, low-ranking individuals within groups and among smaller, lower-ranking groups that are excluded from access to the critical food or water resources (Cheney, et al., 1988). Insufficient nutritional intake also reduces fertility, and again, it is low-ranking females that are likely to suffer the most severe consequences. The age structure of primate groups may become unbalanced, and with fewer reproductively active females, the genetic variation in a population can decline (Packer, et al., 1995). Whether natural fluctuations in population sizes have long-term consequences depends on the severity of mortality and whether the population is still large enough to recover over time.

When habitat fragmentation causes primates to crowd together in a limited area, their population density may be initially high. High population density can be exaggerated by the elimination of natural predators, whose large hunting areas mean that they are usually among the first animals to disappear from disturbed areas. High population density will alter the effects of within- and between-group feeding competition on female behavior, but the social and reproductive consequences of these effects are manifested in different ways depending on the dietary adaptations and behavioral strategies of different kinds of primates.

Effects on Philopatric Females.   In saturated habitats of Hanuman langurs, rates of within-group aggression among females increase and female hierarchies become more rigidly defined than they are in groups living at lower population densities with more abundant food supplies (Borries, et al., 1991). When high-quality foods occur in small, clumped patches, high-ranking female vervet monkeys can defend them, and therefore achieve higher feeding rates (Whitten, 1983). By contrast, when preferred foods occur in small, undefensible patches, the benefits of maintaining cohesive, matrilineal societies are reduced, and smaller groups may form, as has been proposed to explain the lack of female kin groups among Costa Rican squirrel monkeys compared to their occurrence among squirrel monkeys in Peru (Mitchell, et al., 1991). In the absence of predators, groups may also become less cohesive, as reported for long-tailed macaques (van Schaik and van Noordwijk, 1985a).

Primate diets may also be altered by the changes in vegetation structure and composition that occur when economically valuable trees are selectively harvested. The loss of large fruit patches may change the dynamics of within- versus between-group feeding competition, and lead to adjustments in grouping patterns that affect the rates and types of social interactions among females and between females and males (Figure 7.19). For example, unprovisioned Japanese macaques living in strongly seasonal habitats reduce within-group feeding competition both by shifting their diets to include lower quality foods (Hill, 1997) and by maintaining greater distances from one another while feeding (Hill and Okayasu, 1995, 1996; Takahata, et al., 1994). As a result, rates of both affiliative and aggressive interactions among females decline.

Effects on Groups of Unrelated Females. Females that avoid one another because of the high costs of within-group contest competition generally have low rates of interactions to start with. If the availability of high-quality foods becomes absolutely limited, they shift their diets to include a greater reliance on more abundant, low-quality foods. As a result, groups may become either more or less cohesive depending on their diets and levels of within-group feeding competition (Chapter 6). Expanding cultivation from human population pressure has pushed remaining populations of mountain gorillas into a few patches of high altitude forest, where they are forced to rely more on herbaceous vegetation than the more frugivorous populations of eastern and western lowland gorillas (Doran and

FIGURE 7.19   Barbary macaques (*Macaca sylvanus*) engaged in a mutual grooming bout reinforce social bonds. Photo by Meredith F. Small.

McNeilage, 1998). Mountain gorilla groups may be more cohesive compared to some lowland gorilla groups, which adjust their party sizes in response to the size of preferred fruit patches, because their more herbaceous diets lead to scramble instead of contest competition among females (Remis, 1997b; Tutin and Fernandez, 1993; Watts, 1996; Yamagiwa, et al., 1996).

Similarly, muriqui populations living in disturbed forests have more folivorous diets than those in undisturbed, pristine areas. The muriquis' ability to include high quantities of regenerating foliage in their diets may permit their populations to expand because immature foliage tends to be lower in secondary compounds than mature foliage (Chapter 6). Lower levels of feeding competition permit the formation of more cohesive groups, and high population densities may lead to the formation of larger groups (Moraes, et al., 1998; Strier, 1992b).

Red howler monkeys appear to have a different response to high population densities in saturated habitats. During the early phases of population expansion, red howler monkey troops increase in size as daughters of high ranking females are permitted to remain in their natal groups (Pope, 1992, 1998). However, as their habitats become increasingly saturated, rates of female eviction increase so that there are rarely more than four adult females in any troop. Evicted females join up with dispersing males to form new troops, resulting in a higher density of troops instead of larger troop sizes (Crockett, 1996). Indeed, female red howlers may disperse up to six kilometers from their natal troops in saturated habitats (Crockett, 1998).

Mantled howler monkey troop sizes and compositions are also affected by habitat alteration, as well as hunting, disease, and annual fluctuations in high-quality food availability (Chapman and Balcomb, 1998). At high population densities, troops increase in size because female mantled howler monkeys are more likely to remain in their natal troops than female red howlers (Fedigan, et al., 1998).

We can't yet account for why mantled howlers living at high populations increase their troop sizes instead of troop densities the way that red howler monkeys do. It is possible that these two species are less ecologically similar than was previously thought (Crockett and Eisenberg, 1987), or that differences in demographic variables are affecting their responses. Comparative long-term data from additional populations of both species would provide the necessary insights into what's going on.

Reproductive Implications

Changes in the size and composition of primate groups can alter competitive strategies among females within groups and the risks of aggression from males. Harassment from other females or males can be reduced by dispersing, but dispersal can be costly for females. At high population densities, both within- and between-group competition to establish a new territory or join an existing group on their home range may be severe. And at low population densities, a female encounters risks traveling long distances to locate a new group to join (Dunbar, 1987a).

We have seen how dominant female callitrichids can suppress reproduction in their subordinate daughters when opportunities for dispersal are limited. Evictions may only occur in these circumstances when all the adult males in a group are related to them (Dietz and Baker, 1993). Other forms of female harassment include interfering with feeding and mating, which ultimately affect female fertility (Dunbar, 1988). Among Tanzanian yellow baboons, coalitions of females routinely attacked other females just before and after they gave birth, leading to delayed conception and longer interbirth intervals (Wasser and Starling, 1988). Dispersing female chimpanzees and Thomas langurs tend to be older when they give birth to their first infants than females that remain in their natal groups (Pusey, et al., 1997; Sterck, 1997), but habitat fragmentation may also limit dispersal opportunities altogether (Nishida, et al., 1990). When **local resource competition** leads to higher rates of female dispersal, populations may grow more slowly, or not at all.

Female red howler monkeys limit the number of females in their troops by evicting their daughters. This would be advantageous if small female groups are less likely to attract infanticidal males than large ones (Crockett, 1996). As a result, in saturated habitats, troop sizes remain constant but the density of troops increases as more dispersing females establish new troops. Females also become more related to one another in troops where daughters are not evicted, which can translate into higher reproductive success (Pope, 2000). In langurs, the opportunities for females to disperse may be more limited in saturated habitats where they occur at high densities than in unsaturated habitats (Sterck, 1998, 1999), where males also hold onto their tenures longer and therefore the risks of infanticide are comparatively low (Chapter 5).

Female muriquis may also disperse to avoid the risks of close inbreeding (Strier, 1997b). However, because muriqui females typically disperse during or following intergroup encounters, which occur more frequently at high population densities, females living at high densities may have greater opportunities to disperse, and thus avoid inbreeding, than females living at low densities where intergroup encounters are rare (Strier, 2000b).

Manipulating Sex Ratios

Female primates may alter levels of within-group feeding competition, as well as their lifetime fitness, by manipulating the sex of their infants as well as by adjusting the sex ratios in their groups. No one is sure of the mechanisms that lead to sex-biased infant sex ratios in primates or other mammals, but the variation in patterns is consistent with reproductive strategies that correspond with the ability of mothers to invest in their offspring under different social and ecological conditions (Clutton-Brock and Iason, 1986; Frank 1990; Hiraiwa-Hasegawa, 1993; Johnson, 1988; Trivers and Willard, 1973).

Consider the case of daughters born to low-ranking females in matrilineal societies, who rarely have a chance to improve their lots in life. From a mother's point of view, giving birth to daughters means perpetuating her destiny, so perhaps it is not so surprising that dominant and subordinate mothers might be selected to produce daughters and sons in different proportions (Altmann, 1980; Clark, 1978; van Schaik and Hrdy, 1991; Silk, 1983). In both baboons and macaques, subordinate mothers sometimes give birth to higher proportions of sons, which disperse from their natal groups and establish their own ranks as they fight their ways into new groups. Unfettered by their matrilines, they may achieve high ranks and repro- ductive success. Dominant mothers, by contrast, have position to pass on to their daughters, and consistent with evolutionary predictions (Trivers and Willard, 1973), they tend to produce them in equal or greater numbers as sons. By doing so, their matrilines tend to increase in size faster than subordinate matrilines, further perpetuating their influence and the differential advantages that high rank confers.

In the patrilineal societies of spider monkeys, the effects of maternal rank on infant sex ratios are reversed. Over a six-year study of spider monkeys at Manu National Park in Peru, Meg Symington (1987a) found that low-ranking mothers gave birth exclusively to daughters, whereas high-ranking mothers produced off- spring of both sexes. This pattern of differential son and daughter production is exactly the opposite from that seen in matrilineal baboons and macaques, and is consistent with what might be expected in a patrilineal society where philopatric sons born to low-ranking mothers bear the marks of their mothers' ranks for life.

The basis for spider monkey rank acquisition is still poorly understood. If young immigrants achieve high rank when they join new groups and drop in rank as they age, then the differential production of sons and daughters by particular mothers should change over time with age-related shifts in maternal ranks (Strier, 1996b). Alternatively, the manipulation of infant sex ratios may be a response to local resource and demographic conditions (Nunes and Chapman, 1997; Strier, 1999c).

It makes evolutionary sense for mothers to bias their production of daughters or sons depending on whether the benefits of increasing the number of kin in their groups outweigh the costs of competing with their kin, as has been described for red-cockaded woodpeckers (Gowaty and Lennartz, 1985), red deer (Gomendio, et al., 1990), spotted hyenas (Holekamp and Smale, 1995) and Seychelles warblers (Komdeur, 1996). Biasing infant sex ratios in favor of the philopatric sex should occur when increases in the number of kin in a group give females an advantage in obtaining access to resources through cooperation in between-group competition (Nunn and Pereira, 2000). Such **local resource enhancement** is more likely to occur in expanding populations when levels of within-group contest competition are comparatively low (Emlen, et al., 1986; Gowaty and Lennartz, 1985).

However, as levels of within-group contest competition increase with group size, low-ranking females may shift to producing more offspring of the dispersing sex to avoid **local resource competition** (Komdeur 1996; Silk, 1983; van Schaik and Hrdy, 1991). As habitats become saturated, even high-ranking females will be af- fected by the costs of within-group feeding competition, and therefore they, too, will shift to producing more offspring of the dispersing sex (Holekamp and Smale, 1995).

The theoretical rationale for why natural selection might favor females that can adjust the sex of their infants to different kinds of social and ecological condi- tions is compelling. But, as is true for many evolutionary hypotheses, there is still cause for caution in how we interpret the available data. Consider, for example, the demographic data on muriquis that my students and I have amassed. Over the first 18 years of the study, infant sex ratios were significantly and consistently female-biased. No more than seven infants were born in any year, but the number of sons never exceeded the number of daughters. Then, during the nineteenth year, eight infants were born, and only three of them were females. Was this year an anomaly? Or were ecological conditions changing so that mechanisms to stabilize the growth of what had been an expanding population had begun to kick in? Or, were the sex ratios in each of the 19 years merely random deviations from what is otherwise a 50:50 infant sex ratio?

To answer questions like these for muriquis—and other primates—requires many more years of data than we have, and an understanding of how the process of biasing infant sex ratios might be regulated. Solving this puzzle has important implications for estimating the viability of endangered primate populations (Figure 4.3) as well as for integrating their behavioral ecology and demography. For example, primates with different dispersal regimes that employ similar strategies of infant sex ratio manipulation under high or low population densities will have very different trajectories of population growth. If female primates produce more offspring of the dispersing sex to avoid local resource competition at high densities, then matrilocal societies should exhibit slower growth rates than patrilocal societies (Strier, 2000b). One of the consequences of these predictions for small populations of endangered species is that those with female-biased dispersal should have very different recovery trajectories than those with male-biased dispersal.

Of course, differential mortality on male and female primates may counteract the effects of sex-biased infant sex ratios on population growth rates. For example, Nunes and Chapman (1997) found that high levels of male mortality in groups of Brazilian spider monkeys offset their male-biased infant sex ratios, resulting in the maintenance of both a constant number of males in their study groups and a female bias in adult sex ratios.

As we've seen in this and previous chapters (Chapter 5), adult sex ratios have important implications for male reproductive strategies because, along with levels of reproductive synchrony, they affect both within- and between-group competition for access to fertile females. Thus, understanding the variation in female reproductive strategies under different ecological and dispersal regimes is critical to understanding male behavior as well as population dynamics.

8 Male Strategies

At first glance, male primates, like all male mammals, seem to have it easy compared to females. Males don't get pregnant or bear the energetic burden of lactation; basically, all that they need to worry about is staying alive and gaining access to mates. And yet, in nearly all primate species known, fewer males than females survive to old age (Figure 8.1). Evidently, males pay a high price for their otherwise liberated lots in life.

Some males tie their fates to those of their kin, either by remaining in their natal groups or dispersing together. Other males are more or less left to their own devices from the time that they're weaned. Unrelated or distantly related males who transfer together into the same group could theoretically form mutually beneficial coalitions against other males if doing so means gaining better reproductive opportunities than they would on their own. However, the nature of their bonds differs from those among related males because there are no inclusive fitness benefits to be gained (Chapter 4).

Independent of kinship, males are always at least partially at odds with each other over access to limited reproductive opportunities (Chapter 5). Even when

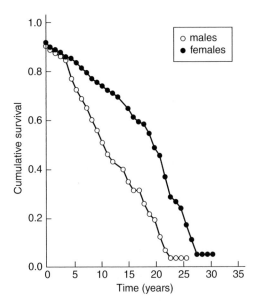

FIGURE 8.1 Survival curves for male and female Japanese macaques (*Macaca fuscata*), including all causes of death and disappearances. From Fedigan, L. M. and Zohar, S. 1997. Sex differences in mortality of Japanese monkeys. *American Journal of Physical Anthropology* 102: 161–175. Copyright © 1997 Wiley-Liss, Inc. Reprinted by permission of Wiley-Liss, Inc., a division of John Wiley & Sons, Inc.

cooperating helps male allies compete against other males or male factions, the fact that an estrous female can only be fertilized by one of them makes the costs and benefits of male bonds quite different from those of females (van Hooff and van Schaik, 1992, 1994).

Complicating male strategies even further is the fact that their relationships with females also influence their reproductive opportunities. Sometimes female preferences coincide with the outcomes of male competition, so winning fights and achieving high rank have clear-cut payoffs. Other times, female preferences can be carefully cultivated with subtle and not-so-subtle social skills, shifting the focus of male competition away from one another and toward their ability to befriend future mates (Chapter 5). Often, however, there is no way for a male to "know" what a female prefers in a mate, or of deterring her from pursuing copulations with multiple males. And, because males can never be certain of their paternity, they can easily be fooled by what seem like signs of female fidelity.

We don't assume that male primates make conscious calculations about their relationships or reproductive strategies any more than females do about theirs. But we can compare how males behave against how evolutionary theory predicts they should. From affiliation and cooperation, to aggression and competition, male reproductive strategies vary across species, among populations of the same species living in different habitats under different ecological and demographic conditions, and over the course of an individual male's lifetime. This variation, and the evolutionary principles underlying it, are perhaps the only aspects of male reproductive strategies that resemble those of females.

Ecology of Male Relationships

Females represent the resources that most strongly affect male reproductive success, in much the same way that survival and access to high quality food resources affect female reproductive success (Chapter 6). Male social strategies are affected by the spatial and temporal distribution of estrous females, just as female social strategies are affected by the spatial and temporal distribution of high quality food resources. Consequently, much of the variation in male primate relationships comes down to the differences in the relative strength of the competition males face within and between groups over access to females (Hill and van Hooff, 1994; van Hooff and van Schaik, 1992). The grouping patterns, degree of reproductive seasonality, reproductive rates, and mate choices of females affect the costs and benefits of cooperation and competition among males, and thus, their relationships with one another (van Hooff, 2000).

Types of Relationships

Every estrous female is a potentially monopolizable resource, and therefore a potential object of strong contest competition for males. Male primates, like females, establish and maintain hierarchical relationships based on the outcomes of aggressive and submissive interactions whenever high-ranking individuals are likely to benefit from priority of access to contested resources (Fedigan, 1983).

Aggressive interactions among males may be more violent than those among females because males should be willing to take greater risks when access to estrous females is at stake (Smuts, 1987a). Mating with an estrous female has potentially greater consequences for male fitness than access to a preferred food resource does for female fitness. As a result, a male that defers to others at feeding sites may not be so easygoing when an opportunity to fertilize a female is at stake (Popp and DeVore, 1979). Asymmetries between male fighting abilities, effects on male kin, and the probability of gaining access to contested resources with aggressive versus nonaggressive tactics are expected to correspond with differences in how males compete overtly over access to mates (Box 8.1).

Males of some species also establish affiliations with one another by grooming, embracing, and providing other reassuring contact. Some provide mutually beneficial coalitionary support for one another in competitive interactions against their common opponents (Chapter 5). In primates with rigid hierarchies, like baboons or chimpanzees, a male's position in the pecking order and his access to mates can be partially dependent on his ability to maintain coalitionary support through mutual assistance and affiliative interactions with other males.

Affiliations differ from associations, in which males spend time together, because affiliations also involve support in agonistic contexts (Hill and van Hooff, 1994). Establishing and maintaining affiliations almost always involves associations, during which time grooming, embracing, or other affiliative interactions occur, but associations do not always imply affiliative support. For example, although philopatric male bonobos exhibit tolerant associations, they rarely form affiliations with one another that lead to coalitionary support (Furuichi and Ihobe, 1994). Conversely, male affiliations with coalitionary support have been described among related males that either live in patrilocal societies, like chimpanzees, or disperse together, like Peruvian squirrel monkeys, and among unrelated male savanna baboons. Thus, kinship is not as good at predicting affiliative relationships among males as it is among females.

Within- and Between-Group Competition

Differences in male relationships, like those in females, can be explained by the relative tradeoffs of competition between and within groups. Males that form unimale groups by evicting young natal males and preventing dispersing males from joining them reduce *within-group competition* for access to estrous females. However, these males may face strong *between-group competition* from unattached males attempting to oust them from their positions.

Males that live in multi-male groups must contend with competitors both within their own groups and outside of their groups. Philopatric males sometimes form coalitions against other groups of male kin, but there are at least two other contexts in which male alliances are routinely observed. Dispersing males can form kin-based coalitions, either by migrating together or by dispersing into groups that their older male kin have also previously joined. In ring-tailed lemurs (Sussman, 1992a), Peruvian squirrel monkeys (Mitchell, 1994), long-tailed macaques (van Noordwijk and van Schaik, 1985), and vervet monkeys (Cheney and Seyfarth, 1983), pairs of males disperse together from their natal groups. Familiar coalition partners increase male success at joining established female groups where unfamiliar males, already established in these groups, would benefit by keeping additional competitors out (Figure 8.2).

FIGURE 8.2   Male long-tailed macaques (*Macaca fascicularis*) on a river bank. At first, young males of this species often disperse short distances from their natal groups in cohorts. Photo by Maria van Noordwijk and Carel van Schaik.

BOX **8.1**

Using and Abusing Infants

Aggressive interactions between adult males in baboon and other cercopithecine societies can escalate into ugly, down-and-out fights. Usually this happens when hierarchical relationships between the two males are ambiguous, such as when a newcomer challenges a troop member and neither one is willing to back down. All other members in the baboon troop go on alert, watching the turmoil with evident interest while doing everything they can to stay out of the way. Females caring for dependent infants are particularly attentive, but sometimes they comply with a male's solicitation to carry their infants into combat (Figure B8.1).

Carrying infants in the context of fights is a strategic maneuver that male baboons make use of often enough to stimulate interest in their underlying motives (Whitten, 1987). Sometimes the males are potential fathers known to have mated with the female months before when the infant in question was conceived (Busse, 1984; Busse and Hamilton, 1981; Smuts, 1985). Other times, the males are recent immigrants to the troop or long-standing group members with no possible genetic interests in the infants' fate (Paul, 1999; Stein, 1984; Strum, 1984). But even with such varied histories, males are not indiscriminate about which infants they enlist in their episodes of infant carrying.

Two strategies are thought to be working at once, and have been framed in terms of alternative hypotheses depending on the identity of the male who grabs the infant and his prior relationship to the infant's mother. In the protection hypothesis, a male grabs an infant before his opponent in what seems like an attempt to get the infant out of harm's way (Busse and Hamilton, 1981). A male protector may be the infant's father guarding his own genetic stakes. Or, he may be the mother's friend demonstrating his willingness and

FIGURE B8.1   Adult male gelada baboon (*Theropithecus gelada*) carries a yearling on his back after being threatened by another male. Photo by R. I. M. Dunbar.

ability to protect future infants that the two might produce by guarding her current inter-ests (Smuts, 1985). In the agonistic buffering hypothesis, the male grabs an infant to protect himself from his opponent's attacks (Deag and Crook, 1971). In this scenario, the opponent is a possible father to the infant and the infant is used against him as a sort of living shield.

Without knowing actual paternity relationships, researchers must rely on a combina-tion of their knowledge of the relationships and reactions among the parties involved to interpret these events. A male protecting his own or his female friend's infant elicits a calmer response from both mother and infant than a male who is using the infant as a buffer for himself. These males tend to handle infants carefully, and neither the infant nor its mother exhibit signs of distress (Busse, 1984; Stein, 1984; Strum, 1984). Infants also respond differ-ently when they are carried by familiar males with whom they and their mothers have previously had peaceful interactions compared to unfamiliar males, and resistance from mothers and infants alike can thwart a male trying to enlist their support (Whitten, 1987).

Carrying an infant against an opponent almost always leads to reduction in hostilities. Faced with the prospects of injuring his own offspring, an attacker is more likely to back off than persist. But even if it isn't his own infant at stake, an opponent protecting an infant sig-nals a higher level of commitment to a conflict than most males are inclined to make.

The effectiveness with which infants are used by males in their competitive contests reinforces female counter-strategies to confuse male paternity and contributes incentives to mothers to form friendships with protective males (Chapter 5). Philopatric male primates don't carry infants into combat, nor do they usually threaten the well-being of infants in other ways when they share kinship and common genetic interests with the other males in their group (Chapter 4). Male competition under these conditions may take other forms, but infants are typically left out of their conflicts.

Males that disperse from their natal groups with age peers are likely to be paternal kin in societies in which alpha males can monopolize fertile females (Chapter 5). If they disperse into groups where older males from their natal groups have previously gone, their chances of being paternal kin will be determined by how long alpha males can hold onto their reproductive monopolies. Instead, they may end up following their maternal brothers, or other males from their extended matrilines (de Ruiter and Geffen, 1998). Whether these males recognize one another as kin is not clear, but they will be familiar to one another if they are close enough in age to have overlapped with one another in their natal group.

Unrelated males that wind up dispersing into the same groups, as well as close kin in patrilineal societies, also form coalitions in response to high levels of within-group competition. However, like females, males don't form coalitions with nonkin for between-group competition.

There are several situations in which even the highest ranking individuals or coalitions can't monopolize access to females within their groups. For example, when female grouping patterns are fluid, as in the case of chimpanzees and spider monkeys, males can't keep close track of every female's reproductive condition at all times. Likewise, when female reproduction is tightly synchronized, as is the case in lemurs, some langurs and cercopithecines, and squirrel monkeys, one male may not have enough stamina or sperm to spare (Small, 1988). Among lemurs and

Costa Rican squirrel monkeys, the frequency of aggression among males living in multi-male groups is low or nonexistent for much of the year. Competitive reproductive strategies are manifested when male lemurs kill or attempt to kill infants sired by their competitors (Erhart and Overdorff, 1998; Hood, 1994; Jolly, et al., 2000; van Schaik and Kappeler, 1997; Wright, 1995), but direct, male–male hostilities are largely restricted to the brief breeding season, when access to estrous females is at stake (Boinski, 1994; Gould, 1997).

Male competition is more indirect when females are not defensible resources, and therefore resembles the scramble competition that females face when they feed on undefendable foods (van Hooff and van Schaik, 1994). This indirect competition among males may be expressed through sperm competition, which involves competing for fertilizations instead of for exclusive mating privileges (Chapter 5).

Male–male competition may also relax when female choice can override the reproductive consequences of male social strategies. When females can dominate males in aggressive interactions, as in lemurs, or are deferred to by males, as in muriquis and bonobos, males gain less by striving for rank amongst themselves and more by cultivating female preference. Likewise, when females rely on male participation in infant care, as in callitrichids, males may gain female choice by demonstrating their caregiving commitment (Garber, 1997). As a result, male relationships with one another tend to be more tolerant and less hierarchical than when males dominate females.

High-ranking males are able to keep competitors at bay through the use of threats and if necessary, brute force. However, maintaining a consortship with an uncooperative female can wear down a male's most determined defenses (Figure 8.3). Sneaking off to mate with a preferred partner, advertising their availability, or blatantly beckoning to male outsiders are just a few of the ways that female choices can undermine the effects of rank and coalitions on male reproductive success. Nonetheless, in nearly all primates for which paternity data are available, high ranking males father more offspring than lower-ranking males at any particular time (Chapter 5). The disparity between high- and low-ranking male paternity success varies between species and between groups of the same species at different times. And, because males don't maintain their positions at the top of their hierarchies for life, their lifetime reproductive success may not be as variable as has previously been thought (Altmann, et al., 1996).

Female primates opt to live alone or in groups in response to the spatial and temporal distribution of their food resources (Chapter 7). However, although dispersing females may also lead solitary lives until they join up with a male or an established heterosexual group (Glander, 1992), there is no female equivalent to all-male bachelor bands that dispersing males of some primate species, like Hanuman langurs and mountain gorillas, often form (Moore, 1999; Robbins, 1995, 2001). Whether alone or in association with one another, unattached males represent a constant threat to the reproductive sovereignty of other males' associations with females. As a result, males that manage to eliminate within-group competition by evicting young males or maintaining higher ranks than them are nonetheless faced with a form of between-group competition from male outsiders that group-living females generally lack.

FIGURE 8.3   Rhesus macaque (*Macaca mulatta*) consort. The female's "ground slap" is a proceptive signal. Photo by Joe Manson and Susan Perry.

Social Dynamics among Males

The ability of males to network with one another and with females (Bernstein, 1981; Smuts, 1985) and the length of male residency in a group (Strum, 1982) are known to contribute to differences in male reproductive opportunities to varying degrees at different times in their lives. The effects of *life histories* on male social dynamics transcend differences in whether males remain in their natal groups or disperse. This occurs because male fighting abilities, social skills, and the presence of allies change during the course of their lifetimes.

In most hierarchical male societies, young adult males strive to best one another whereas older males, who are established residents of their groups, rely on their social networks with coalition partners or with individual females to maintain their ranks or secure mating opportunities (Figure 8.4). However, when dominance hierarchies are either weakly defined or nonexistent, as occurs in the male philopatric societies of bonobos and muriquis, male reproductive opportunities may be more strongly affected by factors such as maternal support, individual initiative, and female preferences, than by rank. In these cases, there is little to be gained from forming coalitions with related males against other male relatives in their groups.

Patrilocal Societies

Males that remain in their natal groups have two advantages over males that disperse. For starters, there aren't unattached, surplus males looking for female groups

FIGURE 8.4   Rhesus macaques (*Macaca mulatta*) mating in a secluded treetop. This may reduce interruptions from higher-ranking males. Photo by Susan Perry.

to join or takeover. Male kin groups face competition from other groups of male kin to attract the same females, but their closed group membership alleviates the pressure of male invasions. In addition, patrilocal males don't face the problem of gaining access to groups containing females (Strier, 2000a). They must compete with other groups of male kin for the best habitats to attract dispersing females, but they don't need to contend with the dangers of dispersal themselves.

There may be differences in the degree to which male chimpanzees need one another's support against neighboring communities. For example, the distribution of food sources, which females follow, may affect the frequency with which encounters with other communities occur, and therefore influence male relationships with one another as well as with females (Boesch and Boesch-Achermann, 2000; Herbinger, et al., 2001).

Relationships among males in patrilocal societies also differ from those among dispersing males because kinship facilitates cooperation among them in competition against other groups of male kin. This cooperation can be entirely mutualistic, because all males benefit if, by cooperating with one another, they increase their own access to mates (Watts and Mitani, 2001; Wilson, et al., 2001; Wrangham, 1999). Within their groups, however, male relationships are variable depending on the degree to which they can monopolize reproductive opportunities (Vehrencamp, 1983). Among matrilocal females, levels of within-group competition fluctuate with the availability and defendability of preferred, high quality foods. Similarly, among philopatric males, contest competition over access to estrous females depends on the availability and defendability of fertile females.

When males can monopolize access to estrous females, they establish and maintain hierarchical relationships through aggressive interactions. Behavioral observations indicate that high-ranking male chimpanzees have higher mating success than subordinates, particularly during the times when females are most likely to conceive (Hasegawa and Hiraiwa-Hasegawa, 1983; Nishida and Hosaka, 1996; Tutin, 1979). Paternity studies of chimpanzees at Gombe National Park, Tanzania and the Taï National Forest, Ivory Coast, provide confirmation that long-term, high-ranking males father more offspring than lower-ranking males within their communities (Constable, et al., 2001; Morin, et al., 1994).

However, even these high-ranking males don't monopolize all fertilizations because they can't completely override the effects of female choice. Conceptions can occur when female chimpanzees go on safaris with low-ranking male consorts (Tutin, 1979), or conceivably if females sneak off to mate with males from other communities (Gagneux, et al., 1997). Genetic data now indicate that such extra-community fertilizations occur rarely, if at all (Vigilant, et al., 2001), at least in the patrilocal societies of chimpanzees.

Male hierarchies are rarely as stable as the hierarchies among and within matrilines because challenges from lower-ranking males, often in coalitions, and the rank reversals that result from challenges, are comparatively common. Extended patrilineal hierarchies also differ from matrilineal ones because there is no evidence that males inherit their fathers' ranks the way that daughters in many matrilineal societies inherit the ranks of their mothers. Indeed, maternal assistance appears to be a decisive factor affecting male rank and mating success in the patrilineal societies of bonobos, where the social equality between females and males means that mothers can be strong allies for sons with social ambitions (Furuichi, 1997; Furuichi and Ihobe, 1994). Moreover, among males, uncertain paternity should limit the degree to which mechanisms of rank inheritance operate.

Female bonobos are sexually active throughout much of their cycles, which may confuse the cues males use to assess female ovulation (Kano, 1996). Males never know exactly when a female is ovulating, and there is usually more than one sexually receptive female around. Both factors interfere with a male's ability to figure out when the costs of contesting a female might be worth taking. Indeed, although aggressive interactions occur more frequently among male bonobos than among unrelated females, they rarely escalate into the kinds of violent attacks that have been reported among philopatric male chimpanzees (Furuichi, 1997).

The effects of female freedom from male domination on male relationships are carried to an extreme in muriquis, which lack any evidence of agonistically-based hierarchies (Strier, 1990, 1992c). Like bonobos, male muriquis can't monopolize females because the sexes are socially equal. When a female muriqui is ready to mate, she emits a vocalization called a "mating twitter" (Milton, 1985a) and everyone nearby is immediately clued in. Females also solicit and tolerate male-initiated inspections of their genitals, which, judging from the amount of sniffing and tasting that goes on, appear to transmit pheromonal cues about their reproductive conditions (Strier, 1992a).

A stimulated male need not be obliged. If a female opts out of mating with a particular male, she can move away without the threat of being pursued or harassed into submission. Alternatively, she can choose to mate with multiple males in close succession, and there's nothing that any male can do about it except to wait in line for his turn and hope that it will be one of his sperm in the copious ejaculate he emits that will succeed at fertilization (Milton, 1985a; Strier, 1992a). In either case, there's no point in males competing for status if female mate preferences are based on other attributes unrelated to rank, such as long-term familiarity and inbreeding avoidance (Strier, 1997b).

Male muriquis exhibit high variance in mating success that appears to be independent of their age or popularity as associates to other males (Strier, 1997c). Young males seek out older, more central males by approaching them and embracing (Strier, 1993b). Although their reproductive opportunities seem to be largely up to females, males that associate with one another may gain more copulations by sharing access to the same females (Strier, et al., in press).

Spider monkeys have hierarchical societies that are more similar to those of chimpanzees than their closer muriqui relatives. Male spider monkeys in Guatemala and Peru, and male muriquis, spend more time associating and grooming or embracing one another than females (Fedigan and Baxter, 1984; Strier, 1992a, 1994b; Symington, 1990). However, in contrast to muriquis, male spider monkeys, like male chimpanzees, also interact aggressively with one another, and with females, at sufficient frequencies for dominance hierarchies to be discerned (Fedigan and Baxter, 1984). Alpha male spider monkeys, like alpha male chimpanzees, appear to have mating privileges that are consistent with their high rank (Symington, 1987b). Furthermore, coalitions of male spider monkeys gang up to chase individual females (Fedigan and Baxter, 1984; Symington, 1987b) in ways that male muriquis, with their more egalitarian relationships, almost never do (Figure 8.5).

FIGURE 8.5   Muriquis (*Brachyteles arachnoides*) mate in full view of other group members. Because of their egalitarian relationships with males, females can assert their preferences for particular mating partners. Photo by Paulo Coutinho.

Rank Acquisition and Coalitions.   Male chimpanzees don't inherit their ranks from their fathers, but this doesn't prevent brothers or other males in their communities from forming coalitions against higher-ranking opponents (Nishida and Hosaka, 1996; Riss and Goodall, 1977). Most chimpanzee coalitions involve partnerships between two males, but it's not uncommon for a coalition partner to shift his allegiance between two closely matched males, who are themselves opponents. Indeed, males seem to evaluate the advantages and disadvantages to themselves before they lend another male coalitionary support, and do so only when their opportunities to mate increase as a result (Watts, 1998). There is no indication that maternal kinship among males increases their attractiveness as coalition partners (Goldberg and Wrangham, 1997; Mitani, et al., 2000a).

Both in captivity (de Waal, 1982) and in the wild (Nishida and Hosaka, 1996), most social striving among chimpanzees occurs at the top of the male hierarchy. The alpha and beta males may have consistent, dominant–subordinate interactions on their own, but the alpha male's position can be easily upset if the beta male establishes a strong alliance with another male in the community. Consequently, much of the social negotiating that goes on among male chimpanzees involves cultivating their own alliances and intervening in the formation of alliances between other males. Grooming one another, maintaining close proximity, providing third-party support for a partner against another male opponent, and sharing meat are just some of the ways in which male chimpanzees cultivate their allies. Interfering with these interactions, or offering more benefits, may prevent the formation of coalitions involving lower-ranking opponents.

Young males need allies to rise in rank. Fortunately for the social climbers, not every male exhibits the same interest in gaining power for himself by challenging other males. Some of the closest associations and strongest affiliations among the nine males in one community at Mahale National Park, Tanzania, involve combinations of these two complementary types of males (Nishida and Hosaka, 1996).

Relationships with Females.   In captivity, female chimpanzees can play pivotal roles in male rank relationships by actively intervening on behalf of preferred males against their opponents and by attempting to reconcile males that have recently fought by luring them with grooming into proximity and eventual contact with one another (Chapter 5). In the wild, however, females don't get so involved in male power struggles (Nishida and Hosaka, 1996). This may be because females have enough to worry about just finding food in the wild, or because it is easier for females to make themselves scarce, and thereby avoid becoming victims of redirected aggression from frustrated males. In captivity, where food is provided and females are confined alongside males, there is both the time and perhaps, a greater need, to reconcile male conflicts.

Relationships among Males.   When males depend on each other for cooperation against other male kin groups, there are good reasons for them to reconcile their differences after the ruckus caused by challenges to ranks and successful rank reversals. In chimpanzees, reconciliations among related males take similar forms to those among female primates living in hierarchical, matrilineal societies (Chapter 7).

Maternal Rank Inheritance.   Unlike chimpanzees, male bonobos rarely form coalitions with one another, and therefore rarely require reconciliation (Furuichi, 1997; Kano, 1996). Male bonobos don't have consistently hostile relationships with males from other groups, so they don't need to stay on one another's good sides like male chimpanzees, who rely on solidarity for their success in between-group competition. Within-group competition is also more relaxed in bonobos than it is in chimpanzees, in large part because of the influence of females.

Male bonobos at Wamba, in the Democratic Republic of Congo (formerly, Zaire) lack a strict linear hierarchy. However, three rank classes corresponding with male age and the presence or absence of their mothers have been distinguished (Furuichi, 1997). Males born to young mothers, who can assist them in aggressive interactions with other males, attain higher ranks than males born to older mothers whose ability to provide support is limited. In bonobo society, adult females are not uniformly subordinate to males. High-ranking mothers who outrank adult males are therefore useful allies against their sons' male opponents. With their mothers nearby to help, they are less likely to be challenged by other males (Figure 8.6).

The main advantage that high rank confers on male bonobos appears to be the ability to associate with the central part of the group, where the majority of matings take place. Thus, whether it is their higher rank or their greater access to the central part of the group, male bonobos achieve higher mating success when they can count on their mothers' support (Furuichi, 1997; Kano, 1996).

More frequent and extended estrus in bonobos compared to chimpanzees (Table 8.1) is also thought to lower competition among male bonobos for access to mates (Ihobe, 1992; Kano, 1996). By one calculation, female bonobos experience eight times as many estrous cycles in their lifetimes as female chimpanzees (Furuichi, 1989; Kano, 1996). Yet, paternity studies have shown that high-ranking males have higher fertilization success than low-ranking males (Gerloff, et al., 1999).

Ranks in Age-Graded Groups.   In some primates, such as red howler monkeys, hamadryas baboons, mountain gorillas, and marmosets and tamarins, some males are philopatric while others disperse from their natal groups. When male philopatry

FIGURE 8.6   Possible patterns of age-related change of dominance status of male bonobos (*Pan paniscus*). From Furuichi, T. 1997. Agonistic interactions and matrifocal dominance rank of wild bonobos (*Pan paniscus*). *International Journal of Primatology* 18: 855–875. Reprinted with permission of the author and Plenum Publishing Corporation. Copyright © Plenum Publishing Corporation.

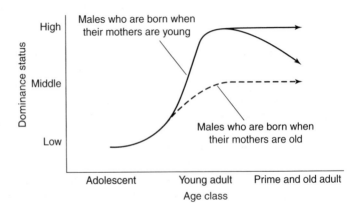

TABLE 8.1   **Characteristics of female bonobo (*Pan paniscus*) and chimpanzee (*Pan troglodytes*) cycles**

	Bonobos	Chimpanzees
Cycle length[1]	32.8–42 days	31.5–36 days
Maximum or semi-maximum sexual swelling[2]	> 20 days	9.6–12.5 days
Time to resuming postpartum swelling[2]	≤ 1 year	3–5.5 years

[1]From data summarized in Stanford (1998a).

[2]From data summarized in Kano (1996).

occurs in these societies, it is sometimes because a dominant father permits one of his sons to stay in the group as his subordinate instead of evicting him when he reaches sexual maturity. These special sons may eventually assume their father's position in their age-graded societies, permitting deposed fathers, if they are still alive, to stay on as subordinate followers in their newly claimed domain.

The arrangement works well for both males when levels of between-group competition are high. The dominant male gains a related ally in defending females from male outsiders, and the subordinate male can avoid the risks and rigors of dispersing into a population where access to females is limited. Genetic and behavioral studies indicate that paternity is clearly skewed in favor of the dominant male in the multi-male groups of red howler monkeys (Pope, 1990) and golden lion tamarins (Baker, et al., 1993). And, when they are related, cooperative endeavors improve the inclusive fitness of both father and son.

Not all sons are tolerated by their fathers, however, which means that there can be different kinds of groups within the same population. For example, both uni-male and multi-male groups occur in populations of Rwandan mountain gorillas and Venezuelan red howler monkeys, and in marmosets and tamarins throughout their geographic distributions (Crockett and Pope, 1993; Robbins, 1995; Rylands, 1996). In mountain gorillas and Hanuman langurs, evicted males may succeed at joining or establishing new groups with females, or they may join up with other unfortunate outcasts in all-male groups. In hamadryas baboons, males may remain as unattached bachelors in their patrilineal bands until they can establish their own one-male unit (see Box 3.2).

Relationships among Males.   Multi-male groups may be more attractive to females than single male groups because of the greater protection that multiple males provide against male outsiders. Mountain gorilla males living in multi-male heterosexual groups tend to avoid social interactions by maintaining their distance (Robbins, 1995; Watts, 1996). Nonetheless, males in these groups exhibit higher rates of wounding and more consistent dominance relationships than males living in all-male groups, where friendly interactions are more common and aggression takes milder forms (Robbins, 1996; Yamagiwa, 1987).

Nearly all of the affiliative interactions between mountain gorilla males in multi-male groups occur among close kin, in contrast to those in the all-male groups, where kinship does not affect male affiliations (Robbins, 1996). Kinship among males seems to be similarly unimportant in the affiliative relationships in all-male groups of langurs as well (Rajpurohit and Sommer, 1993). This may be because males join all-male groups instead of living alone, for the mutual benefits that group-living provides (Figure 8.7).

Because males in multi-male gorilla groups avoid one another, there is little evidence, and probably little need, for mechanisms to reduce aggression. Thus, these males don't reconcile after their occasional fights, and don't greet one another the way that baboon coalition partners do (Robbins, 1996). Subordinate males redirect aggression at females after confrontations with dominant males (Watts, 1995a, 1995b), and consequently, wild female mountain gorillas sometimes intervene in male conflicts the way that wild female bonobos and captive female chimpanzees do (Sicotte, 1995).

In hamadryas baboons, sons that are permitted to stay in their natal units do so as subordinate followers, but there are also young bachelor males, who have been evicted from their natal units, and older, deposed unit leaders, in the population (Kummer, 1968; Phillips-Conroy, et al., 1992; Stammbach, 1987). Males typically stay in their patrilineal bands, although some may migrate out if opportunities to establish their own female units or follow established units are scarce (Figure 8.8). In captive and field experimental situations, subordinate males recognize female preferences for particular males, and only high ranking males attempt to intervene (Bachman and Kummer, 1980).

Relationships with Females.   Despite the fact that the males in multi-male, heterosexual groups of mountain gorillas, hamadryas baboons, or red howler monkeys may be related to one another, they maintain stronger social relationships with females than they do amongst themselves. In these species, adult females spend more time grooming and in proximity with adult males than with one another (Stammbach,

FIGURE 8.7   Young male mountain gorillas (*Gorilla gorilla berengei*) at play. Photo by Martha M. Robbins.

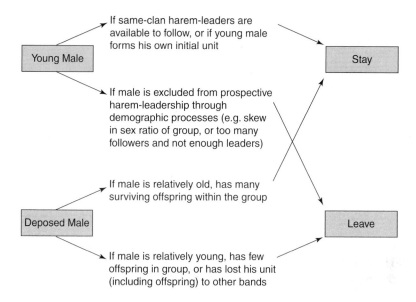

FIGURE 8.8   Possible decision rules for emigration of hamadryas male baboons (*Papio hamadryas*). From Phillips-Conroy, J. E., Jolly, C. J., Nystrom, P., and Memmalin, H. A. 1992. Migration of male hamadryas baboons into anubis groups in the Awash National Park, Ethiopia. *International Journal of Primatology* 13: 455–476. Reprinted with permission of the author and Plenum Publishing Corporation. Copyright © Plenum Publishing Corporation.

1987; Watts, 1996; Zucker and Clarke, 1998). In mountain gorillas, females usually initiate associations with the dominant male in preference to subordinate males, while younger, subordinate males initiate associations with females (Watts, 1996). Older males may also show strong affiliative behavior toward daughters and grand-daughters, and support them in agonistic conflicts against other females or males.

When Males Disperse

Relationships among males that disperse from their natal groups differ from those among dispersing females because during the process of male dispersal, within- and between-group competition are one and the same. Adult males get rid of potential competitors within their groups by evicting young males, but threats to their reproductive sovereignty come from outsiders attempting to join their groups, take over their groups, or infiltrate their defenses to mate with estrous females.

Within-group competition for access to mates leads inevitably to hierarchical relationships among males (Hill and van Hooff, 1994). This differs from the ecological conditions of scramble competition that may coincide with female dispersal and weak, undifferentiated relationships among female immigrants (Chapter 7).

Hierarchical Relationships.   The ranks of unrelated males in multi-male groups of primates such as Japanese macaques tend to be associated with male age. Among Japanese macaques, length of tenure in a group also influences male rank unless frequent group transfers prohibit males from establishing long-term relationships with other males and females in their groups. Males in smaller groups found in unprovisioned populations are less likely to form coalitions because their tenure tends to be briefer than it is for males in larger groups (Sprague, et al., 1996). However, greater male movement between smaller groups also leads to more balanced sex ratios, and as a result, males are more likely to groom one another in these groups than they are in larger groups with more potential female grooming partners (Hill, 1994).

Coalitions among unrelated males can have decisive effects on male hierarchical relationships (Chapter 5), but the payoffs of coalitions vary greatly among males (Figure 8.9). For example, the highest-ranking males in savanna baboon troops rarely form coalitions because they don't need them to maintain their rank. High-ranking males have lower basal cortisol levels than subordinates, suggesting that they are also better able at coping with, and controlling, socially stressful situations (Sapolsky and Ray, 1989). The lowest-ranking males rarely form coalitions because their support is not sufficient to effect rank reversals (Noë and Sluijter, 1995). Instead, coalitions are most likely to develop among males in the middle of the hierarchy where the benefits are likely to be greatest (Bercovitch, 1988).

A male's fighting ability relative to that of his opponents and that of his affiliates determines how useful a coalition will be (Noë, 1994). Males who rank close to one another in the hierarchy can reciprocate support more than males with widely disparate ranks. And, because male rank generally corresponds to male age

FIGURE 8.9   A coalition of two males of one faction in a male band of Hanuman langurs (*Presbytis entellus* or *Semnopithecus entellus*) harass a member of the other faction, who is retreating to one of his allies. Note the perfect synchrony of the coalition partners, who are in step with one another and shoulder-to-shoulder. Photo by Jim Moore/Anthro-Photo.

and length of residency in baboon troops, coalitions are more likely to form between males of similar age and length of residency than between long-term residents and new immigrants (Bercovitch, 1988; Noë and Sluijter, 1995).

Male ring-tailed lemurs also exhibit affiliations with one another, but, in contrast to baboons, their affiliations are not related to rank or age and are comparatively short-lived. Frequent fluctuations in the male hierarchy occur in part because
the membership of males in ring-tailed lemur groups changes much more often.
Furthermore, female dominance over males and tight breeding seasonality mean
that males have little to gain or to offer one another in exchange for their coalition
support (Gould, 1997).

Baboon coalitions have often been described as examples of male cooperation
(Chapter 4), but coalition partners do not always share equally when access to
estrous females is involved (Packer, 1977). This is especially true when there are
subtle asymmetries in the contributions made by male allies (van Hooff and van
Schaik, 1994; Noë, 1990).

Coalitions also occur among related males that disperse together from their
natal groups. In Peruvian squirrel monkeys, for example, male cohorts of similar
ages transfer together into new groups, where they provide one another coalitionary support in contests against other male coalitions (Mitchell, 1994). In other
species, however, help from related or familiar males is particularly influential in
their first, natal dispersals, but less so in subsequent dispersal endeavors unless
they have had opportunities to interact with males from other groups without hostilities (Perry, 1996).

Gaining Group Membership.   Dispersing males may change groups several times
in the course of their lives (Figure 8.10). Natal dispersal typically occurs before males
are physically fully adult, and, therefore, before they are capable of winning fights
with larger, stronger males (Figure 8.11). Young males dispersing for the first time
typically enter groups at the bottom of the male hierarchy (Cheney and Seyfarth,
1983; van Noordwijk and van Schaik, 1985; Sprague, et al., 1996). How long they
stay in these groups depends on their reproductive prospects, which are a product
of adult sex ratios, their ability to rise in rank on their own or with coalitionary support, and their attractiveness to females when it comes to being chosen as a mate
(Alberts and Altmann, 1995; Sussman, 1992a).

Multi-male groups of Hanuman langurs typically contain more females than
uni-male groups. As a result, males that can attain alpha status in the larger multi-
male groups can father nearly 50 percent more offspring than males in uni-male
groups. However, because competition for alpha status is correspondingly stiffer in
multi-male groups, striving for status in these groups is a risky strategy, with both
higher costs and higher potential gains (Launhardt, et al., 2001).

Secondary dispersal typically occurs after a male has reached the physical
maturity needed to hold his own in challenges with longer-term resident males
and after he has acquired some of the requisite social skills that appeal to females.
Male ring-tailed lemurs switch groups repeatedly in search of more favorable sex
ratios, where their chances of success during the brief mating season are improved

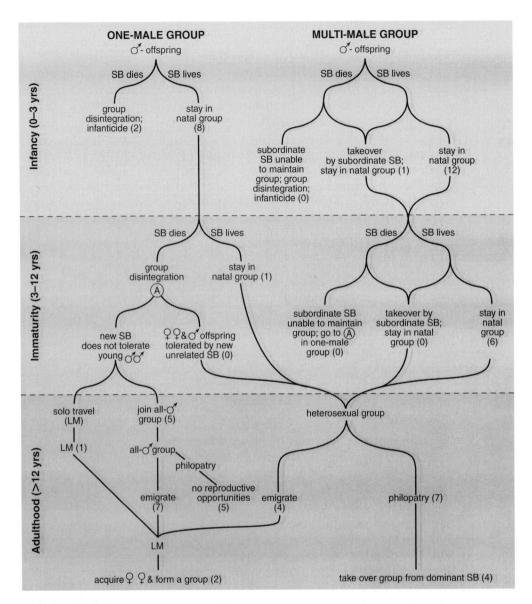

FIGURE 8.10 Male mountain gorilla (*Gorilla gorilla berengei*) life history patterns in one-male and multi-male groups. The numbers in parentheses indicate the number of males who pursued each option. Each age-class represents a different subgroup of males due to the incompletely known life histories of most males. LM = lone male; SB = silverback male. From Robbins, M. M. 1995. A demographic analysis of male life history and social structure of mountain gorillas. *Behaviour* 132: 21–47. Reprinted with permission from E. J. Brill Publishers and the author.

FIGURE 8.11   Juvenile white-faced capuchins (*Cebus capucinus*) fight near the alpha male of their group. Note size differences. Photo by Susan Perry.

(Sussman, 1992a). Young male vervet monkeys (Cheney and Seyfarth, 1983) and long-tailed macaques (van Noordwijk and van Schaik, 1985) are more likely to disperse with cohorts into groups adjacent to their natal groups. By contrast, secondary dispersal by older males is more likely to be solitary and to take them further away from home.

In unprovisioned troops of Japanese macaques, males disperse from their natal troops at around five years of age, and spend an average of three years in a new troop. Young Japanese macaque males also join their new troops at the bottom of the hierarchy, but opportunities to climb the social ladder are limited unless they disperse again. As they mature, however, their chances of transferring into troops higher up in the male hierarchy increase (Sprague, et al., 1998; Suzuki, et al., 1998).

White-faced capuchin monkeys typically disperse alone (Perry, 1996), although occasionally cohorts of males are successful at ousting an alpha male through their coordinated efforts (Fedigan, 1983). The alpha male relies on coalitionary support from females to protect his status in the group, but female coalitions aren't effective at keeping new males from immigrating (Perry, 1998a). When groups encounter one another, the subordinate males sometimes engage in a display called a "wheeze dance" because of the distinctive vocalization used only in this context (Perry, 1998b). These dances, which are nonaggressive interactions, are thought to be one of the ways that subordinate males test and establish relationships that might facilitate their future prospects of transferring into other groups (Perry, 1996).

There is no doubt that dispersal is stressful for males, particularly when low population densities make it difficult to find new groups containing females (Alberts and Altmann, 1995a). Hormonal analyses of yellow baboons during the immigration of an aggressive adult male indicated that, compared to other adult males, the immigrant male had higher cortisol levels and lower lymphocyte counts, both of which are indicative of stress (Alberts, et al., 1992). High cortisol levels and low lymphocyte counts were also detected in adult females who were targets of aggression from this immigrant male.

One way that females can reduce the risks of being targets of male aggression during immigrations is to form affiliative bonds with the new males in their groups (Strum, 1982). Bonds with females help new males to integrate into their new groups, and may lead to greater reproductive opportunities for middle- and low-ranking males if females also later choose these "friends" as mates (Gould, 1997; Noë and Sluijter, 1995; Smuts, 1985).

Unattached Males.   To maintain a monopoly over a group of females, either alone or with help from a related male "follower," a reigning male must defend his position against takeover attempts by unattached males in the population (Figure 8.12). In Hanuman langurs, up to 25 percent of all males never gain access to female groups, and males that do rarely have more than one chance at it in their lifetimes (Sommer and Rajpurohit, 1989). In the population at Jodhpur, males that manage to gain a foothold in a female group hold onto their tenure for an average of 26.5 months. This is longer than the average interbirth interval of 16.7 months, and therefore, theoretically, long enough for an average male to see his offspring weaned before he loses his position in the group.

In these langurs, fewer than five percent of conceptions involve extra-troop males, and the strongest determinant of male reproductive success is how long a male manages to hold onto his tenure in a female group (Sommer and Rajpurohit, 1989). In other primates, however, male associations with female groups do not always coincide with their access to mates, even though male dispersal presumably reflects strategies to increase their reproductive opportunities (Alberts and Altmann, 1995a). In unprovisioned Japanese macaques, for example, 41 percent of all

FIGURE 8.12   An adolescent male Hanuman langur (*Presbytis entelles* or *Semnopithecus entellus*) extends his hand toward the ankle of an unfamiliar adult male who he had been threatening while the adult male was copulating. This gesture could be an effort at reconciliation initiated by the adolescent male. Photo by Jim Moore/Anthro-Photo.

copulations involve extra-troop males (Sprague, et al., 1998) and at least some of these copulations lead to fertilizations (Soltis, et al., 2001). Adult male outsiders display at the periphery of the troop, and wait for females to approach them to mate. Troop males will try to restrict female movements, but their efforts to intervene in these extra-troop matings don't always succeed. Among the rhesus macaques imported to the island of Cayo Santiago, Puerto Rico, sneaky matings by subordinate males often lead to fertilizations, making the relationship between male rank and reproductive success an imperfect one (Berard, et al., 1994).

Other male outsiders take advantage of the breeding season to immigrate into established groups (Jack and Pavelka, 1997). Female Japanese macaques, as well as Barbary macaques and ring-tailed lemurs, sometimes exhibit mating preferences for unfamiliar males, who may be short-term, ephemeral visitors or new immigrants into their groups (Small, 1989; Sussman, 1992a; Sauther and Sussman, 1993). In one study, six of the seven female red howler monkeys that copulated with extra-troop males had lost their previous infants to male aggression (Agoramoorthy and Hsu, 2000). Unfamiliar male advantages may result from a combination of female reproductive strategies that include confusing paternity among hostile or potentially friendly males (Figure 8.13), increasing their probability of conception (Chapter 5), or even gaining greater disease resistance for their offspring (see Box 4.1).

In birds, the frequencies of extra-pair copulations and fertilizations are highly variable both within and between populations of the same and different species (Petrie and Kempanaers, 1998). We do not yet have sufficient data on paternity in different primates to compare with birds, but the widespread observations of extra-group copulations across diverse primates suggest that similar variation in the rate

FIGURE 8.13   Two male Barbary macaques (*Macaca sylvanus*) play with an infant on the grass. Photo by Meredith F. Small.

of extra-group fertilizations may occur. Whatever the ecological or demographic bases for these differences are, extra-group males who succeed in reproducing affect the genetic composition of primate groups and populations.

Males in Pairbonded Societies

Pressure from outsiders is more comparable for males and females that form pair-bonds. Not surprisingly, in these species both sexes are more aggressive toward same-sexed competitors, and more responsive to the presence of individuals of the opposite sex (Buchanan-Smith and Jordan, 1992). Extra-pair copulations may provide females with opportunities to evaluate their own mate relative to other potential mates in the vicinity, or to confuse paternity (see Box 5.1). Although evidence that infanticide occurs in gibbons is still lacking, in the monogamous, nocturnal Milne-Edwards' sportive lemur, the infant of a female whose mate had deserted her was killed by the new male that subsequently joined her (Rasoloharijaona, et al., 2001).

Whatever the reason, the possibility of female infidelity puts pairbonded males in a dilemma (Sommer and Reichard, 2000). Should they pursue extra-pair copulations, and possibly fertilizations, when the opportunity to do so arises? Or, should they resist these temptations, and instead guard their own mate and protect their own infants (Figure 8.14)?

In fact, pairbonded gibbon and siamang males are more attentive toward their mates than their mates are toward them, a pattern that stands in sharp contrast to species such as chacma baboons, where it is the females that curry protection from males (Figure 8.15). But, the possibility of pursuing their own extra-pair mating opportunities may also be why at high densities, where pressure from extra-group males and access to extra-group females may be great, they may be more likely to tolerate sons or other males on their territories, where the younger males can serve as back-up bodyguards for their mates (Reichard and Sommer, 1997; Palombit, 1999, 2000).

FIGURE 8.14   A pair of nonmatrilineal white-handed gibbons (*Hylobates lar*). The darker adult male is grooming a juvenile. Photo by Thad Bartlett.

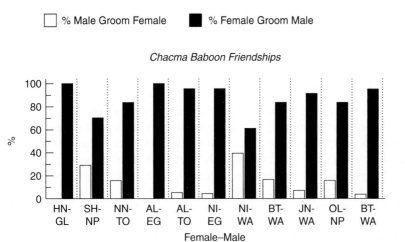

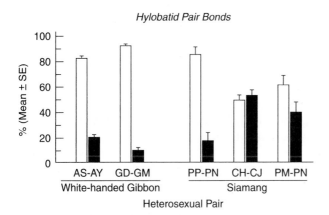

FIGURE 8.15   Male and female contribution to grooming exchanges differ across species. In chacma baboons, females groom males more than males groom them, whereas in pairbonded gibbons and siamangs, males usually do most of the grooming. Initials under each graph indicate the individuals involved in each dyad. From Palombit, R. A. 1999. Infanticide and the evolution of pair bonds in nonhuman primates. *Evolutionary Anthropology* 7:739–760. Copyright © 1999 Wiley-Liss, Inc. Reprinted by permission of Wiley-Liss, Inc., a division of John Wiley & Sons, Inc.

Population Dynamics

Male behavioral strategies are strongly influenced by those of females, and therefore are indirectly influenced by ecological and demographic variables that affect levels of within- and between-group competition for resources. For example, clumped food resources that permit females to form larger groups may increase levels of competition for males seeking to join or retain breeding positions in these groups. Male social strategies to increase their access to estrous females have consequences for the genetic structure of their population, as well as for their individual and inclusive fitness. And, their optimal strategies change throughout their lifetimes.

Genetic and Demographic Correlates

Consider the different genetic consequences when a few males monopolize a majority of fertilizations, or when male kin versus nonkin form cooperative alliances that include sharing fertilizations. The more that reproductive opportunities can be monopolized by individual males or by closely related males, the lower the genetic variation within groups, and the greater the genetic variation between groups, will be (Pope, 1992, 1998). By contrast, frequent dispersal or extra-group fertilizations will have the dual effects of maintaining high genetic variation within groups while reducing the genetic differences between groups. For example, from 92 to 97 percent of the genetic variation within populations of three species of macaques is represented in particular social groups because of the effects of male dispersal (Melnick and Hoelzer, 1992).

Nonrandom natal dispersal by young vervet monkey males actually facilitates the avoidance of close inbreeding while increasing the incidence of slight inbreeding (Cheney and Seyfarth, 1983). When population densities are low, opportunities for male dispersal will be restricted, and as a result, a higher proportion of males may remain in their natal groups (Alberts and Altmann, 1995a). The isolation of primate populations in fragmented or severely altered habitats can further restrict male dispersal opportunities, leading to both higher levels of inbreeding within groups and higher levels of both within- and between-group competition.

High population densities, which can result from either habitat fragmentation or from an abundance of food resources in undisturbed habitats, should also lead to higher levels of between-group competition among philopatric males. We've seen how increases in group size and population densities favor the formation of multi-male groups over uni-male groups in primates such as mountain gorillas, black howler monkeys and Hanuman langurs (Borries, 2000; Ostro, et al., 2000; Robbins, 1995). Similar demographic pressures have increased levels of between-group competition for muriquis as well (Strier, 1997b). In the patrilocal societies of muriquis, however, high densities also promote greater opportunities for inbreeding avoidance because females have greater opportunities to mate with extra-group males (Chapter 7). Understanding how dispersal patterns, population densities, and effective population sizes interact have important implications for the long-term viabilities of these and other primates.

In their search for females, some males disperse into groups of closely related species (see Box 3.2). Hamadryas baboon males disperse into troops of olive baboons when reproductive opportunities with hamadryas females are limited and olive baboon males disperse into groups of yellow baboon males. Group transfers and matings also occur in hybrid zones of squirrel monkeys and of marmosets, as well as among sympatric species of Old World guenons (Chapter 11). Such drastic dispersal strategies raise questions about the genetic implications of taxonomic classifications based on differences in physical appearance and behavior (Alberts and Altmann, 2001; Boinski and Cropp, 1999; Jolly, 1993), but there is little doubt that cross-migrants maintain gene flow within and between hybrid populations.

The effects of male social and reproductive strategies take on increasing significance as more and more primate populations become fragmented by human activities. For example, gorillas living at high densities have more frequent rates of inter-group conflicts and violent competition between males compared to gorillas living at lower densities (Yamagiwa, 1999). Similarly, male dispersal in an isolated chimpanzee community in Bossou, Guinea, is thought to be comparable to female dispersal because the costs of within-group competition for mates are high relative to the absence of between-group competition that makes male philopatry advantageous in other chimpanzee populations (Sugiyama, 1999). Clearly, ecological conditions, whether natural or human-caused, affect different primate species in different ways and with different implications for their conservation (Yamagiwa, 1999; Strier, 2000b).

Male Life Histories

Deciphering the genetic and demographic correlates of male social strategies is complicated by the changing options males experience during their lifetimes (Strum, 1994). Male Hanuman langurs may have a brief, two to four year period during which they are in good enough condition to compete for and maintain alpha status. Before and after this window of time during their prime, the best they can do is to maximize their access to cycling females by residing in bi-sexual groups, as opposed to all-male groups, and dispersing into other bi-sexual groups whenever better mating opportunities elsewhere appear (Borries, 2000).

As we've seen, dispersal is costly for males, especially in habitats where predators represent major threats to the survival of solitary individuals or when population densities, and thus the chances of locating another group to join, are low (Alberts and Altmann, 1995b). The trade-offs between staying alive and maximizing their reproductive success are more sharply defined for males than for females, whose lifetime reproductive success is more closely linked to longevity than to reproductive opportunities (Pavelka and Fedigan, 1999). These trade-offs may be why male strategies seem to change so much during their lifetimes. As we'll see in the following chapter, however, the differences in male and female life histories do not usually become so evident until they reach reproductive age.

9 Developmental Stages Through the Life Cycle

Differences in the behavior of male and female primates don't emerge overnight. From the time that an X- or Y-bearing sperm fertilizes an egg, the chromosomes of a female zygote differ from those of a male. Females inherit one X chromosome from each of their parents, whereas males inherit one of their mother's X chromosomes and a copy of their father's single Y chromosome. Genes on the Y chromosome stimulate a fetus to develop testes, which secrete hormones called **androgens** that lead to the formation of male external genitalia and internal organs. Without these testicular hormones, the fetus will develop into an anatomical and physiological female. Genetic anomalies that prevent male fetuses from being exposed to testicular hormones in sufficient quantities lead to the development of feminized males, whereas those that result in female fetuses being exposed to inordinately high levels of these androgens lead to the development of masculinized females (Snowdon, 1997).

Once they are born, male and female primates in the same social group grow up in different ways. For starters, males and females often have different rates of development, and different probabilities of dying at different times in their lives. Their mothers and other group members treat male and female offspring differently, especially once they have passed through the period of infant dependency and are independent juveniles. The births of younger siblings affect immature male and female primates similarly because for both sexes the birth of a younger sibling typically signals their complete physical independence from their mothers. After weaning, sons and daughters receive different kinds and levels of assistance from their mothers, if they receive any help at all. By the time they reach sexual maturity and either disperse from their natal groups or remain to begin their reproductive careers, male and female reproductive strategies have already been shaped by the biological and social influences in their lives.

Fertilization to Birth

How individual sex is determined varies widely across the animal kingdom (Snowdon, 1997). In reptiles and amphibians, offspring sex is determined by the incubation temperature of eggs, and in many fish, individuals pass through sequential life stages as males or females. In primates, as in other mammals, males are **heterogametic,** which means that their sperm carry either an X or a Y chromosome, whereas females are **homogametic** because their ova carry only an X chromosome. In birds, however, females are the heterogametic sex, with W or Z chromosomes, and therefore are responsible for determining offspring sex. Male birds, with only Z chromosomes, are homogametic.

What determines the probability of a union between an X-bearing ovum and an X- or Y-bearing sperm? Many human couples would like to know the answer to this question because they value sons and daughters differently for social and economic reasons (Nicolson, 1991). However, the mechanisms involved are still elusive, and probably a consequence of many factors. For example, X- and Y-bearing sperm are thought to have differential mortality or mobility, and XX or XY zygotes can have differential survival once they are formed (Clutton-Brock and Iason, 1986). In the first case, the probability of conceiving a male or a female is at stake, whereas in the latter case, postconception mechanisms influence the probability of spontaneously aborting or carrying a male or female offspring to term (Symington, 1987a).

We have no way of knowing whether primate **secondary sex ratios,** or the proportion of sons and daughters that are born (Chapter 7), are accurate reflections of the **primary sex ratios,** or the proportion of sons and daughters that are conceived. Embryos and fetuses of different sexes may suffer differential mortality, or they may have equal probabilities of being carried to term. There is some evidence that male fetuses place greater energetic demands on their mothers during gestation than female fetuses, and mothers sensitive to these differences might adjust their prenatal investment in sons and daughters according to their own nutritional condition (Trivers and Willard, 1973). For example, in zebra finches, mothers produce more sons when their food intake is experimentally restricted, a phenomenon that makes evolutionary sense if food scarcity during rearing in these birds affects the variance in the reproductive success of daughters more severely than that of sons (Oddie, 1998).

Primates are notorious among mammals for their slow rates of development. Primates have relatively long gestations, which is the period from conception to birth (Chapter 2), and during lactation, increasing energetic demands require mothers to shift their behavior to increase their energy intake and reduce their energy expenditures (Chapter 6). Primates also have relatively long infancies, which encompass the interval from birth through weaning (Figure 9.1).

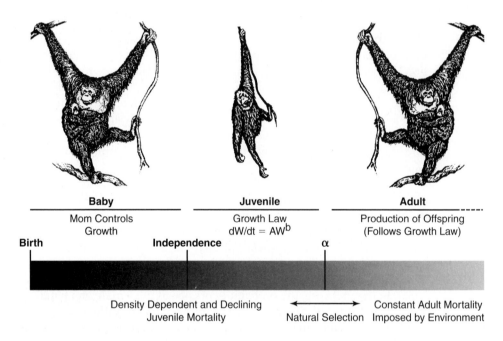

FIGURE 9.1 Life history model for generating predictions about the role of production. Maternal body size (W) determines the rate of energy delivery, and therefore growth rates, of infants. By adulthood, growth ceases and maternal energy is devoted to reproduction. The Growth Law indicates that dW/dt, or the rate at which weight increases over time, is equal to the degree to which energy is allocated toward growth as a function of weight. The alpha value is measured from weaning to age at first birth. Charnov, E. L. and Berrigan, D. 1993. Why do female primates have such long lifespans and so few babies? *Or life in the slow lane. Evolutionary Anthropology* 1: 191–194. Copyright © 1993 Wiley-Liss, Inc. Reprinted by permission of Wiley-Liss, Inc., a division of John Wiley & Sons, Inc.

Infancy

The length of the infancy phase varies across primates with body size and taxonomy. In general, lemurs and lorises are more altricial, or helpless at birth, than tarsiers, monkeys, apes, and humans, which are born weighing proportionately more relative to their mothers' weights (Figure 9.2). Like all mammals, primate infants depend on their mothers to meet their nutritional needs. But, unlike many other mammals, some primate infants are also dependent on others for their transportation needs. Substantial energetic investments are made by whoever is nursing and carrying them.

Prosimian mothers who "park" their infants produce milk that is high in fat content compared to other prosimian and anthropoid mothers whose infants travel on them or on other group members until they are able to keep up on their own (Tilden and Oftedal, 1997). However, it isn't clear whether the energetic cost of producing high-quality milk is a tradeoff that leads to conserving energy expenditure by parking instead of carrying infants, or whether parking an infant requires mothers to produce high-quality milk to sustain their offspring during the intervals they are left on their own while their mothers are off feeding (Chapter 6). For example, small-bodied lorises produce more concentrated milk than larger lemurs, but the energy content of pygmy marmoset and common marmoset milk may be lower than that of prosimians similar to them in body size (Figure 9.3). Differences in the energetic costs of producing energy-rich milk, as well as differences in nursing patterns, might be involved, but how they operate is not yet known (Power, 1999).

In still other primates, such as the monogamous owl monkeys and titi monkeys, and the callitrichids, males and older siblings take on much of the energetic burden of carrying infants. By about two weeks of age, infants in some of these

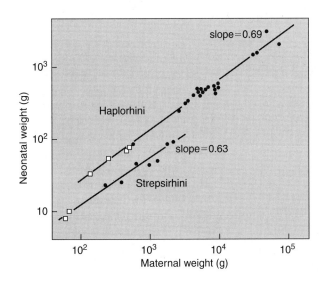

FIGURE 9.2 Relationship between neonatal weight and maternal weight. Solid circles = single births; open squares = multiple births. Haplorhines (n = 25 species) tend to be born heavier, relative to maternal weight, than strepsirhines (n = 9 species), indicative of great maternal prenatal investment. From Leutenegger, W. 1979. The evolution of litter size in primates. *American Naturalist* 114: 525–531. Reprinted with permission from the author and the publisher, The University of Chicago Press. Copyright © 1979 by The University of Chicago.

FIGURE 9.3   A male infant slender loris (*Loris tardigradus nordicus*) at Giritele, Sri Lanka. After the first two months of life, slender loris babies are parked throughout the night while their mothers forage. Unlike many species of nocturnal prosimians, they are visited by many members of their sleeping group. Not only their mothers, but also adult and juvenile males may play and travel with them. Caption and photo by K. A. I. Nekaris.

species may spend up to 50 to 90 percent of their time away from their mothers, whose primary postnatal investment in their infants is to nurse them (Snowdon, 1997; Wright, 1990). Carrying infants comes with costs, in terms of later weaning and breeding ages, but may reduce mortality compared to infants that are parked (Ross, 2001).

Caregivers also provide thermoregulation, grooming, and defense against predators and aggression (Nicolson, 1991). These needs are comparable in male and female infants, and caregivers do not appear to discriminate their investment based on infant sex (Nicolson, 1987). Male infants may be more likely to be victims of infanticide in Hanuman langurs, but mortality from other causes is still higher in female infants (Rajpurohit and Sommer, 1991). In some populations of spider monkeys, males experience higher infant mortality than females due to aggression from females other than their mothers (Nunes and Chapman, 1997). However, in most nonhuman primates, it is not until weaning that clear sex differences in maternal investment emerge, and even then, patterns of maternal investment in daughters and sons are highly variable (Nicolson, 1987).

Stochastic, or random, demographic events, can also affect infant survivorship. For example, the number of males and females that die of predation should be proportionate to their representation in particular groups. However, the chances of a predator "sampling" male and female infants in perfect proportion to their presence is similar to the chances of flipping a coin on its head or tail. Each time the coin is flipped, it has an equal chance of landing on its head or tail, but it can take many trials before these probabilities are realized. Infrequent predation events are subject to similar random effects, and as a result, a disproportionate number of male or female infants might die in any particular year. Successive years of such randomly determined, female-biased mortality could lead to an adult cohort with few females, and therefore slower group and population growth rates, and more intense competition among males for access to scarce females.

Maternal Care

In all nonhuman primates, mothers bear the burden of nursing their own offspring. Unlike other mammals that live in extended matrilineal societies, such as lions, primate infants are rarely nursed by anyone other than their mothers (see Box 4.2). This puts a premium on maternal survival until an infant is weaned. Nonetheless, mothers differ from one another in the duration of maternal care they provide, and in the degree to which they rely on other group members to contribute to their infants' survival (Nicolson, 1991).

Mother–infant bonds start out strong in all primates. Mothers appear to be capable of recognizing their infants within days of giving birth using visual, olfactory, and auditory cues. For example, vervet monkey mothers respond to their own infants' distress calls more than to distress calls given by other infants (Cheney and Seyfarth, 1985), and both mother and infant squirrel monkeys get stressed out, as indicated by the high cortisol levels they register, if they are separated for brief periods of time in captivity (Coe, et al., 1983). Wild baboon mothers will search for their infants if they become lost and will carry dead infants for days (Nicolson, 1991). For these reasons, infant mix-ups are generally rare. In a few species, however, kidnapping and adoptions may be a part of everyday life. In a study of captive hamadryas baboons, for example, genetic data revealed that 14 out of 25 infants were being carried and cared for by mothers other than their own (Smith, et al., 1999). Some had been sired by extra-group males, but others were kidnapped by lactating mothers whose own offspring had been kidnapped by others.

Primate mothers also groom their infants, and sometimes play with them in quite individualistic ways. For example, the Gombe chimpanzee, Flo, and her daughter, Fifi, had the same special way of dangling their respective infants with their feet (Fagen, 1993). Different maternal styles of interacting with infants can have life-long effects on infant social development because infants are likely to be more familiar with their mothers' closest associates than with other members of their groups (Berman and Kapsalis, 1999).

Paternal Care

Males who can be confident of their paternity are expected to invest more in their infants than males who cannot. This difference arises because any contributions that a father makes toward increasing his infants' chances at surviving will enhance his own reproductive success (Chapter 4). As we've discussed, one of the consequences of female promiscuity is that male paternity is uncertain. Mating with multiple partners could be a female strategy that not only inhibits males from harming infants, but also increases male tolerance and even investment in infants that they might have sired. Among many so-called monogamous primates, females engage in extra-pair copulations, some of which may lead to fertilization (see Box 5.1). Consequently, even in pairbonded societies the relationship between male infant care and paternity is confounded more often than not (Snowdon, 1997).

High metabolic stress on both mothers and their infants may favor high levels of male infant care to increase both maternal and infant survival. Males play an active role in infant care in many, but not all, small-bodied primates (Wright, 1990) and in some larger primates, such as Barbary macaques, that experience severe seasonal thermal stress due to low temperatures (Small, 1990).

Male investment in infants can be divided into direct and indirect forms of care. Infant carrying, grooming, food sharing, and agonistic aid are forms of direct care that males provide their actual or putative offspring (Figure 9.4). Indirect forms of male care include tolerance, detection and defense against predators or other threats to infants, and resource defense (Snowdon, 1997; Taub and Mehlman, 1991; Whitten, 1987).

Male mantled howler monkeys carry only those infants that they may have sired (Clarke, et al., 1998), and male Barbary macaques form strong affiliations, which include protection, with particular infants that may be their own (Taub and Mehlman, 1991; Paul, 1999). Silverback mountain gorilla males provide protection against extra-group males that is critical to infant survival (Robbins, 1995). And, as

FIGURE 9.4 Adult male chacma baboon (*Papio ursinus* or *P. hamadryas ursinus*) holds an infant during a fight with another male at Okavango Crater. Photo by Rob Boyd-Okavango, provided by Joan Silk.

we've seen, Hanuman langur males neither attack their own infants nor protect infants other than those that are, or could be, their own (Borries, 1999a,b).

In both captive and wild cotton-top tamarins, increases in group size lead to decreases in both the amount of time mothers spend carrying their infants and in levels of infant mortality (Garber, 1997; Snowdon, 1997). In wild cotton-top tamarins, for example, about 40 percent of infants survive in groups with three caretakers. However, as the number of caretakers increases to up to six individuals, infant survivorship jumps to a whopping 87 to 100 percent (Savage, et al., 1997). A decline in infant carrying by mothers is the most obvious effect of multiple nonmaternal caretakers (Savage, et al., 1996b) but the presence of more group members also means that males can redistribute their time and energy to other beneficial activities, including watching for predators and finding and sharing food with infants who are close to being weaned by their mothers (Figure 9.5).

Alloparental Care

Alloparental care refers to infant care provided by individuals other than the parents. By this definition, much of the so-called paternal care provided by male primates may actually be alloparental care unless these males are the biological fathers of the infants they help. Male primates may invest in offspring if they have mated with the mothers, and therefore are potential fathers. Or, males may invest in offspring sired by other males as a means to establishing affiliations that may lead to future preferential access to the mothers when they next mate. Alloparenting can help males gain valuable experience at caring for infants that will help them take care of their own offspring in the future. In callitrichids, alloparental care may even

FIGURE 9.5   Adult male buffy-headed marmoset (*Callithrix flaviceps*) shares gum with an infant. Photo by J. W. Lynch.

be the commodity that maturing offspring of both sexes use to "buy" their parents' permission to remain in their natal groups (Snowdon, 1990a).

In other primates, older siblings of either sex, and more distantly related or unrelated juvenile and adolescent females, also participate in infant care (Figure 9.6). Both male and female red howler monkeys will adopt younger siblings whose mothers die or neglect them. But even infants that are carried by their kin will die if they are orphaned before they are weaned (Pope, 2000). Allomothering is more common in patas monkeys and other guenons than it is among most baboons and macaques. More relaxed female social relationships, breeding seasonality, relatively short interbirth intervals, and relatively rapid infant development in many guenons may contribute to their greater tolerance toward other group members that show an interest in their infants (Chism, 2000; Mitani and Watts, 1997).

Usually, female juvenile and adolescent primates are more interested in infants than immature males, except when it comes to seeking play partners (Chism, 1991). This sex difference may be linked to an "inhibition of attraction toward infants in males," (Nicolson, 1991). The hormone **prolactin,** which is produced by both females and males, sometimes even before an infant is born, also suppresses male testosterone levels, and both may result in increased parental care (Box 9.1).

Mothers may also send behavioral signals that inhibit unrelated males from trying to interact with their infants. By contrast, mothers seeking to enlist male investment in offspring must take pains to make their tolerance toward these males known (Snowdon, 1997).

Why immature females are attracted to other females' infants is not entirely clear. One explanation is that immature females have been selected to seek out infants

FIGURE 9.6   Juvenile female Barbary macaque (*Macaca sylvanus*) allomothering an infant. Photo by Meredith F. Small.

to prepare for their own roles as future mothers (Chism, 1991). Among solitary prosimians, there is no evidence that females need prior exposure to infants to become adequate mothers themselves (Nash, 1993). By contrast, infant baboons, tamarins, and mantled howler monkeys born to **primiparous,** or first-time, mothers, suffer higher mortality than those born to **multiparous,** or reproductively experienced, mothers (Clarke, et al., 1998; Nicolson, 1991; Snowdon, 1997), suggesting that prior experience in infant care may be very important. Indeed, immature females may be so awkward in their handling of other females' infants that they have been accused of "aunting to death" (Hrdy, 1976) the infants that capture their attention (Figure 9.7).

Mothers differ in their degree of permissiveness toward infants and in their tolerance of other group members' interest in handling their infants (McKenna, 1979). Interestingly, kinship seems to have little bearing on these variations in mothering styles (Paul, 1999). Females living in despotic hierarchical societies are reluctant to hand over their infants to other females, including kin (Moore, 1984, 1992a). Among unrelated females in mantled howler monkey troops, mothers try, but often fail, to prevent other troop members from handling their infants (Clarke, et al., 1998). In the matrilineal societies of baboons, high-ranking and low-ranking mothers behave differently. Low-ranking mothers are more protective toward their infants, keeping them nearby and avoiding contact with other group members as much as possible. By contrast, high-ranking mothers are much more laid back, allowing their infants to wander freely and be handled and carried by others. Their high rank gives these "laissez-faire" baboon moms the ability to retaliate against other females who might inadvertently pose a threat to their infants, whereas low-ranking mothers, who are less able to help, need to keep a tighter reign on their infants to keep them out of trouble (Altmann, 1980). Females less concerned with their power differences, like most guenons, may be more relaxed about who handles their infants in the same way that high-ranking baboon females are (Chism, 2000).

FIGURE 9.7   An adolescent female yellow baboon (*Papio cynocephalus*) awkwardly carries an infant she has "borrowed" from the mother, who is a member of her extended matriline. Photo by K. B. Strier.

BOX **9.1**

Parental Prolactin

The hormone **prolactin** has hundreds of metabolic functions in mammals, as well as in birds, amphibians, and fish (Ziegler, 2000). Its most widely known function is to stimulate the mammary glands of mammalian mothers to make and secrete milk for dependent offspring. But, prolactin affects males as well as females through its inhibitory effects on other hormones, such as testosterone, and on sexual and parental behavior. In an elaborate set of studies on cotton-top tamarins, reproductive endocrinologist Toni Ziegler and her colleagues (Ziegler, et al., 1996; Ziegler and Snowdon, 2000) have investigated how patterns in levels of urinary prolactin affect both maternal and paternal caretaking behavior alike.

Ziegler knew that elevated levels of prolactin and low levels of testosterone had been reported in male common marmosets who carried ten- to thirty-day-old infants (Dixson and George, 1982). She didn't know how prolactin levels in male caretakers in the closely related cotton-top tamarin compared to pregnant and nonpregnant females, or how variable the timing and degree of prolactin elevations were in these males. Collecting near daily urine samples from males and females housed in family groups in Charles Snowdon's captive cotton-top colony (see Box 1.1), Ziegler first confirmed that males carrying infants had higher levels of prolactin compared to males paired with nonpregnant females, similar to what had been reported for common marmosets. The actual levels of prolactin in nursing females were similar to those of infant carrying fathers, and in both parents, prolactin levels remained high up to two weeks after infants died (Figure B9.1).

Older sons in these family groups exhibited higher prolactin levels within two weeks after the birth of their younger siblings compared to nonfathers. However, it wasn't clear from these results whether male caretaking behavior is responsible for stimulating elevations in prolactin or whether high levels of prolactin stimulate these males to participate in infant care. To distinguish between these alternative causal scenarios, Ziegler and her colleagues examined male and female prolactin levels beginning before their infants were born. Sure enough, compared to males paired with nonpregnant females, paternal prolactin levels turned out to be significantly higher by at least two weeks prior to the births of their offspring. Evidently, paternal prolactin levels respond to hormonal or behavioral cues from females approaching their parturition dates. Fathers are effectively hormonally "primed" to care for their infants even before they arrive.

Yet another intriguing discovery from Ziegler's study is the finding that experienced fathers have higher prolactin levels than inexperienced fathers. Indeed, prolactin levels were positively related to paternal reproductive history, with the most reproductively experienced fathers having the highest levels of prolactin of all. This may be why reproductively inexperienced older siblings exhibit elevations in their prolactin after, but not before, new infants are born.

Exactly how reproductive experience might affect paternal prolactin levels is still not entirely clear. The fact that infant survivorship increases with both maternal and paternal reproductive experience suggests that elevations in prolactin may facilitate parental care, and therefore increase their offsprings' chances of survival. Prolactin also has an inhibitory effect on testosterone, and thus on sexual and aggressive behavior. If females can detect male prolactin levels through olfactory or behavioral cues, they may be

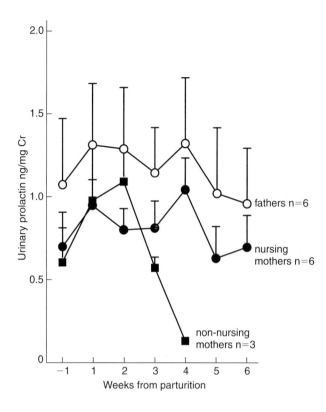

FIGURE B9.1 Mean urinary prolactin levels in six paired male and female cotton-top tamarins (*Saguinus oedipus*) during the week before (–1) and the six weeks following parturition. Prolactin levels declined in females who lost their infants and stopped suckling. From Ziegler, T. E. 2000. Hormones associated with non-maternal infant care: A review of mammalian and avian studies. *Folia Primatologica.* Reproduced with permission of author and S. Karger AG, Basel.

more likely to entrust infants to their care. In primates like these, where male reproductive success hinges on reducing the energetic costs of reproduction to females so they can ovulate and conceive again, both male infant care and communication between mates should be under strong selection pressures. Indeed, understanding the hormonal mechanisms underlying male parental behavior is a necessary step in testing evolutionary hypotheses about behavioral adaptations.

Ziegler's long-standing quest to decipher how hormones and behavior interact is not limited to prolactin and parenting. Nor is it limited to cotton-top tamarins in captivity. She is one of a handful of pioneering reproductive endocrinologists committed to developing noninvasive techniques for getting hormonal information from wild and captive primates alike. Prolactin, like many other hormones, gets metabolized into unrecognizable forms in primate feces, and can therefore only be measured in blood or urine. However, a few of the key hormones produced by the gonads (testes and ovaries), such as testosterone, estrogen, and progesterone, and by the adrenal glands, such as cortisol, can also be measured in feces. Thanks to scientists like Ziegler, these gonadal and adrenal hormones are now being monitored in a wide range of wild primates (Chapter 12). Results from these studies provide crucial information on the interactions between the proximate and ultimate mechanisms involved in regulating behavior.

Even among close female kin, entrusting an infant to an inexperienced female can imperil the infant's well-being. High-ranking mothers can afford to take these risks with their infants because they are better situated to retrieve a distressed infant from mishandling than low-ranking mothers. When adult female baboons seek permission to handle another's infant, they give conciliatory grunts as an indication of their harmless intentions (Chapter 7).

Weaning Conflict

Primate parents and their offspring don't always see eye to eye. The discord begins once an infant is capable of taking care of itself, and reaches a crisis that culminates in weaning. With the exception of marmoset and tamarin mothers, female primates stop ovulating while they are nursing dependent offspring (Chapter 5). The sooner that her offspring can find food on its own, the sooner a mother can stop lactating, resume ovulating, and reproduce again. Because a mother is equally related to each of her offspring, any unnecessary time or energy expended on a current offspring comes at the expense of her future offspring.

An infant's perspective on the timing of weaning is entirely different. In the first place, an infant is 100 percent related to itself. Thus, although an infant will share at least a quarter of its genes with each of its mothers' future offspring, it is still in an infant's best interests to capture more of its mother's investment than a mother is prepared to make. The difference between a mother's genetic relatedness to each of her offspring, on the one hand, and an offspring's genetic relatedness to itself versus future siblings, on the other hand, leads to what evolutionary biologist Robert Trivers (1974) called **parent–offspring conflict** (Figure 9.8).

In Trivers's model of parent–offspring conflict, a parent's inclusive fitness is maximized by halting its investment in a current offspring sooner than when that

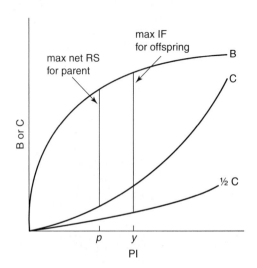

FIGURE 9.8 The benefit, cost, and half the cost of an act of parental investment (PI) toward an offspring. The parent's fitness is maximized (B-C) at p; the offspring's inclusive fitness (IF) is maximized (B-C/2) at y assuming the offspring's future siblings will be full siblings. From: Figure 2 (p. 252) of R. L. Trivers, 1974, Parent–offspring conflict. *American Zoologist* 14: 249–264, reprinted with permission.

offspring's inclusive fitness is maximized. Mothers should therefore be selected to stop investing in an offspring sooner than the offspring should be selected to accept it. Nursing is a major source of maternal investment, and the disparity between mothers and their infants over the optimal time for weaning leads to conflict.

Primate infants resist being weaned by following their mothers, attempting to suckle, and screaming when their attempts are thwarted by a mother who turns away or threatens her infant. Many even learn to accommodate maternal resistance by waiting until mothers have fed themselves, and are therefore less likely to rebuff an infant's appeals (Nicolson, 1987). But even among the most peaceful of primates, like the muriquis, the cries of an infant whose mother steadfastly refuses to nurse can go on for more than half an hour without pause.

Muriqui infants also try to hitch rides on their mothers' backs during long-distance excursions or at difficult tree crossings, where gaps in the canopy require courageous leaps of faith (Figure 9.9). Muriqui mothers use their bodies and limbs to form bridges across wide gaps, but if a mother fails to provide assistance to her infant before the infant is ready to go it alone, shrieks and cries of distress from the abandoned youth echo through the forest (Strier, 1992a). For terrestrial primates, jumping on and off a mother's back can interfere with the mother's foraging efficiency (Figure 9.10). Baboon infants throw tantrums when their mothers refuse to

FIGURE 9.9 Muriqui (*Brachyteles arachnoides*) flings herself across a gap in the canopy. She is carrying a small infant, just barely visible, on her side. Photo by K. B. Strier.

FIGURE 9.10 Infant yellow baboons (*Papio cyncocephalus*) ride jockey-style while their mothers forage. Photo by K. B. Strier.

carry them, just as they do when their mothers refuse to let them nurse. Infants that figure out how to hitch rides without disrupting their mothers' activities may eventually win out in these battles of wills (Altmann, 1980).

Weaning is a gradual process in most primates (Lee, 1996; Koenig, et al., 1997), and may not be fully completed until the birth of an infant's younger sibling (Nicolson, 1987). Weaning is also highly variable within species, and reflects individual growth rates dictated, in part, by the quality of mothers' milk (Lee, 1996). Patterns of dental eruption indicate that folivores develop faster than frugivores, a difference that makes sense considering the importance of shearing molars to breaking down the cell walls of leaves compared to chewing softer fruits (Godfrey, et al., 2001).

For many primates, the weaning period coincides with times of the year when high-quality foods are most abundant, and as a result, reproductive seasonality is timed to the availability of weaning foods (Altmann, 1980; Nicolson, 1991). The remarkable degree of weaning synchrony exhibited by sympatric lemurs with quite different life histories can be explained by the greater availability of foods at this time (see Box 6.2). In callitrichids, the frequency of food sharing by male caretakers also increases during the weaning period (Snowdon, 1997), and may continue for up to 50 percent of their extended growth period, months after immatures are entirely self-sufficient for locomotion (Garber, 1997).

Sex differences in the timing of weaning are not very obvious in wild primates (Nicolson, 1991). It may be that individual styles of mothering and variation in maternal temperament, or maternal rank in hierarchical societies, age, or prior reproductive experience swamp any effects that infant sex might have on weaning age (Altmann, 1980; Nicolson, 1991). For example, mothers might be expected to wean sons later than daughters if the extra investment translated into higher maternal inclusive fitness as a result of the higher reproductive potential of sons compared to daughters (Trivers and Willard, 1973). High-ranking female chimpanzees from the Taï population evidently follow this strategy by investing more in their sons, whose survival is improved (Boesch, 1997). Until about eighteen months of age, Hanuman langur female infants have higher mortality than male infants. It is not until males begin to disperse from their natal troops that their mortality rates exceed those of females (Rajpurohit and Sommer, 1991, 1993), so it is possible that the initial sex differences in mortality in this species reflect greater maternal investment in sons.

In species such as savanna baboons and bonnet macaques, high-ranking mothers tend to adopt more relaxed mothering styles, and are better at intervening on behalf of their infants in agonistic conflicts, than low-ranking mothers. These dual correlates of maternal rank make it difficult to disentangle the effects of maternal rank and mothering style from investment in infants. Older mothers also tend to invest more in offspring than younger mothers (Pavelka, 1999), a trend that culminates in postreproductive senescence, or menopause in humans (see Box 4.2).

Mothers might also be expected to wean offspring of the dispersing sex later than offspring of the philopatric sex if the extra investment translates into higher probabilities that their offspring will survive the ordeal of dispersal to reproduce. In other words, because they won't be around in the group for long, mothers might benefit their inclusive fitness by making sure their progeny are well-nourished before they must face the world on their own. However, in most primates, weaning takes place years before offspring reach maturity and leave their natal groups. Because of this long time lag, we don't yet know whether variations in weaning patterns affect the fitness of offspring that disperse from their natal groups.

Juvenile Challenges

Compared to other mammals, primates have the longest juvenile periods for their body size (Pereira and Fairbanks, 1993). The juvenile phase, which spans the period from weaning to sexual maturity, has been referred to as a period of "phenotypic limbo" because juveniles are too old to be treated like infants and too small to behave like adults (Pagel and Harvey, 1993). In contrast to infants, juveniles are likely to survive the death of their primary caretakers (Pereira, 1993a), but even then they are extremely vulnerable to both starvation and predation because of their small body size (Janson and van Schaik, 1993). Their higher vulnerability may also be why rates of play decline as juveniles mature (Fagen, 1993).

Several hypotheses have been advanced to explain the long juvenile periods of primates. One hypothesis emphasizes the complexity of primate social systems, which may have selected for larger brains that take a long time to develop (Janson and van Schaik, 1993; see Box 2.1). Other hypotheses revolve around growth laws associated with adult body size and age at first reproduction (Pagel and Harvey, 1993). Whatever the cause, the small body sizes of juvenile primates should put them at an ecological disadvantage compared to adults when it comes to competing for access to food and avoiding predators.

Staying Alive

There are two possible strategies to reduce the ecological risks that juveniles face. One is to minimize the amount of time spent as a juvenile, as might be expected in species in which juveniles occupy distinct nonadult niches. Compared to monkeys and apes, lemurs grow rapidly over a short period of time. High infant mortality in their highly seasonal and unpredictable habitats may make more rapid growth rates one of the keys to their survival. It may also offset the sexual selection pressures that lead to **bimaturism,** or sex-specific growth periods, in other primates (Leigh and Terranova, 1998).

The other strategy for juveniles is to grow slowly, and thereby reduce metabolic needs and the amount of food required even if doing so means spending more time as a juvenile. According to comparative analyses by Charles Janson and Carel van Schaik (1993), this "risk averse policy" is the one that most anthropoids appear to follow. It minimizes the probability of dying from starvation or predation while in the vulnerable position of being a juvenile in an adult world. The essence of this strategy is that juvenile primates sacrifice rapid growth to stay alive longer.

Age, Size, and Sex.   Anthropoids grow slowly during the early juvenile period although even among them there are striking species and sex differences (Figure 9.11). Being small, juveniles can feed on terminal branch tips that are too small to support

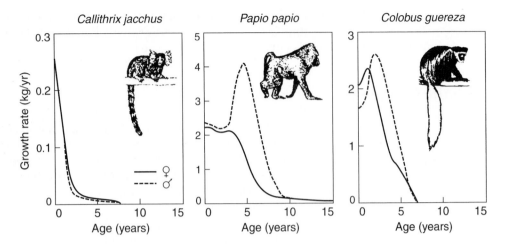

FIGURE 9.11   Primate species differ in their patterns of somatic growth. Some (e.g., marmosets) show no growth spurt; others have growth spurts that are either sexually dimorphic (baboons) or occur in both sexes (colobus monkeys). From Leigh, S. 1994. Growing up to be a primate. *Evolutionary Anthropology* 3: 106–108. Copyright © 1994 Wiley-Liss, Inc. Reprinted by permission of Wiley-Liss, Inc., a division of John Wiley & Sons, Inc.

an adult's body weight. This can lead to niche separation in diets, and thus reduced levels of feeding competition between juveniles and larger, more dominant adults. Nonetheless, there are still disadvantages associated with small size. For example, although juveniles may be only 50 to 70 percent the size of adult females, they devote 105 percent of the time that adults do to feeding because their efficiency is so much lower. Janson and van Schaik (1993) found that juvenile primates had only 80 to 90 percent of adult foraging success when feeding on invertebrates, and spent about twice as long as adults feeding on fruits. As a result, juveniles are more vulnerable to starvation than adults, even though their smaller body size means that their absolute food requirements are lower.

Nutritional and especially energy shortfalls during their early years of life can have life-long and life-determining consequences. The diets of yearling yellow baboons, for example, affected their chances of surviving to reproductive maturity and the longevity of those that survived (Altmann, 1998). Juvenile females, in particular, with energy-poor diets not only had shorter reproductive lifespans as adults, but also produced fewer offspring, of which fewer survived, compared to females that met their energy needs when they were young. Early diet seems to have less of an effect on the age at which males reach sexual maturity (Bercovitch, 2000).

Juveniles are also more vulnerable than adults to predators. They may be less adept at detecting predators or at responding to alarms given by other group members in the presence of potential predators. If predator pressures are high, juveniles will benefit from the greater protection that living in large groups provides against predators even though in large groups they may face higher levels of feeding competition. Growing slowly can mitigate the problems of competing with adults for food when group living is advantageous for any reason (Janson and van Schaik, 1993).

In sexually dimorphic species, males tend to mature later than females (see Figure 9.11). Juvenile females may also be the targets of more aggression from unrelated females or distant relatives than juvenile males because females will be future reproductive competitors. Agonistic interactions lower juvenile female food intake and further increase their mortality risks (Janson and van Schaik, 1993). By the time most primates reach their juvenile years, the same sex differences—or lack of sex differences—that characterize adult diets are usually evident (Watts and Pusey, 1993). Therefore, it is also possible that females compete more amongst themselves because they are feeding on the same types of foods.

Experience.   If primates require an extended period as juveniles to gain their adult body size, there should be strong selection pressures on them to make the most of this most vulnerable time in their lives (Pagel and Harvey, 1993). Juveniles can increase their foraging success by observing adults and trying different foods and feeding styles (Figure 9.12). They may also gain experience at detecting predators and responding to alarms. And, of course, they can hone their social skills and fighting abilities through play (Figure 9.13).

Social Skills

Natal groups are the social groups of all primates through puberty, but they will only be the future social groups of the philopatric sex (Walters, 1987). Not surprisingly, then, sex differences in the social relationships that juvenile primates develop,

FIGURE 9.12   An infant langur (*Presbytis entellus* or *Semnopithecus entellus*) inspects the food that her mother is eating. The close contact most infants maintain with their mothers provides primates with extended opportunities to learn. Photo by Jim Moore/ Anthro-Photo.

FIGURE 9.13 Vervet monkeys (*Chlorocebus aethiops*) playing. Photo by P. C. Lee.

both with one another and with other members of their groups, generally correspond both to where and with whom they will be in the future, and to the presence of same-sexed or opposite-sexed siblings and peers (Altmann, et al., 1977).

Juveniles develop and practice social skills as well as motor coordination through play (Dolhinow, 1999). Rough contact games, which involve hitting, biting, and wrestling tend to be more common among juveniles who have grown up together (Figure 9.14). Play permits juveniles to establish affiliative relationships with peers who may be useful allies during dispersal or during life-long social negotiations in their natal groups. The play partners juveniles choose are determined by whether same-sexed peers are likely to be important social allies later on (Fagen, 1993), but the presence of same-aged peers can vary widely from cohort to cohort, and thus the social experiences of juveniles can be quite different from one another.

Skewed sex ratios can result in skews in the number of same-sexed playmates (Chapter 7), and the degree to which alpha or high-ranking males can monopolize fertilizations will determine the number of paternal siblings in a cohort (Chapter 8). Unusually high infant mortality, such as that experienced by ring-tailed lemurs during successive drought years (Gould, et al., 1999) can wipe out entire cohorts

FIGURE 9.14 Two adolescent male langurs (*Presbytis entellus* or *Semnopithecus entellus*) play-fight in a tree. Photo by Jim Moore/Anthro-Photo.

altogether. All of these demographic conditions influence the social environments in which juveniles mature.

Long-Term Bonds.   As juvenile males in patrilocal societies mature, they shift their affiliations from their mothers and peers to adult males. They do this by following, sitting next to, and embracing one another and older males as a way of integrating themselves into the adult male network, while females become increasingly peripheral (Strier, 1993b). The opposite pattern occurs in matrilocal societies, where juvenile males become increasingly peripheral while their female peers become increasingly integrated into adult female networks. In many Old World monkeys, orphaned males leave their natal groups earlier than males whose mothers are still alive (Alberts and Altmann, 1995a,b; Fairbanks, 2000).

Juvenile females differ in whether they socialize primarily with one another or with adult females in their groups. These differences depend, in large part, on whether they will rely more on peers or on adults for social support. In the matrilineal societies of Japanese and rhesus macaques, where juvenile females inherit their mothers' ranks, integration into the adult hierarchy through social interactions begins at an early age, and is reinforced through the support they receive from their mothers and other female kin throughout their lives (Chapais and Gauthier, 1993; de Waal, 1993). As they become independent, their relationships with other maternal kin may begin to deviate from those of their mothers (Berman and Kapsalis, 1999). They also begin to include paternal siblings, with whom their mothers are unrelated, among their close associates (Widdig, et al., 2001). Among matrilineal Hanuman langurs, where female ranks are inversely related to age, peers are more likely to make better future allies than adult females, who will drop in rank as they age. Thus, juvenile female langurs socialize more with one another than they do with older females in their troops (Nikolei and Borries, 1997). In ring-tailed lemurs, juvenile females neither inherit their mothers' ranks nor receive coalitionary support from their mothers. Instead, they rely on their own competitive abilities in fights with other juvenile females and adults to attain their place in the hierarchy (Pereira, 1993b).

In the matrilocal societies of wedge-capped capuchin monkeys, both peers and older females can be helpful. Juvenile female capuchins form strong affiliative relationships with one another and with adult females in their groups that often persist into adulthood (O'Brien and Robinson, 1993). By contrast, juvenile female vervet monkeys initiate affiliative interactions preferentially with high-ranking adults of both sexes. They restrict their interactions with one another primarily to play partners, but affiliative relationships among playmates dissolve as they mature (Fairbanks, 1993).

Sex-Biased Dispersal.   Sex differences in development, which begin early on, are evident by the time that males or females leave their natal groups. In solitary species, where both sexes disperse, daughters are more likely than sons to establish overlapping or continuous territories with those of their mothers, and receive more tolerant treatment from their mothers (Nash, 1993). In group-living primates, such as red howler monkeys, daughters may be expelled from their natal troops when they are only two years old, long before they are sexually mature and younger than when their brothers typically leave (Crockett and Pope, 1993). Female muriquis are not overtly evicted from their natal groups, but they nonetheless spend less time in proximity to other group members than philopatric male cohorts (Strier, 1993b; Printes and Strier, 1999).

In long-tailed macaques, where males disperse with their natal cohorts, post-conflict reconciliations are more common among juvenile males than among male–female or female–female peers in captivity (Cords and Aureli, 1993). One explanation for this sex difference is that males need to maintain affiliative bonds with members of their natal cohort for dispersing together (Chapter 8). The same differences between the sexes in reconciliation behavior among juveniles have also been observed in captive chimpanzees, a species in which females disperse and males remain in their natal groups and cooperate with their male kin for life (de Waal, 1984). Indeed, juvenile male primates may benefit more from resolving conflicts amongst themselves quickly because their conflicts are more likely to escalate into serious aggressive interactions than those involving females (Cords and Aureli, 1993).

Puberty

Sexual maturation, or **puberty,** is a deceptively long process during which hormonally-induced physiological, morphological, and behavioral changes occur (Bronson and Rissman, 1986; Plant, 1994). Gonadal maturation is triggered by hormones secreted by the hypothalamus, which is located in the brain. These hormones, mainly gonadotropin-releasing hormone, or GnRH, activate the pituitary gland to secrete luteinizing hormone, or LH, and follicle-stimulating hormone, or FSH, which then affect the gonads. In males, these are the testes, which are stimulated to produce the testosterone required for spermatogenesis, or the production of sperm, as well as for the development of secondary sexual characteristics in the species that have them (Chapter 5). In females, LH and FSH trigger the production of progesterone and estrogens in the ovaries. These lead to the maturation of oocytes, which then burst from their follicles at ovulation. As in males, female secondary sexual characteristics, like the sexual swellings of baboons or the breasts of humans, develop in response to these hormonal changes. The establishment of a cyclical pattern, in which progesterone and estrogen levels rise and fall, is the hallmark of puberty in females, and female weight is a critical component.

The timing of puberty and its implications for fertility is highly variable, even in the same species living in the same populations. In male yellow baboons, for example, testicular enlargement occurs when most males are five to six years old, but sons of high-ranking mothers tend to undergo puberty earlier than sons of low-ranking mothers (Alberts and Altmann, 1995b). Although males usually don't attain their adult ranks or first sexual consortships for at least another year, whether they become sexually active before or after they disperse seems to depend on a variety of other factors, such as the presence and rank of their mothers and their access to females, including paternal sisters, in their natal groups (Alberts, 1999).

Variation in the timing of puberty in male orangutans is even more pronounced, with some males showing arrested development of their secondary sexual traits (Chapter 5). Although levels of testosterone, LH, and growth hormone in "arrested" males are significantly lower than they are in fully developed males, these males nonetheless have sufficient levels of FSH, LH, and testicular hormones to be sexually functional and fertile. Staying small without forfeiting the possibility for fertilizations may help males to avoid direct competition with fully developed males at high population densities, but the social cues that trigger different developmental pathways in different males at different densities are not yet fully understood (Maggioncalda, et al., 1999, 2000).

Arrested development of secondary sexual characteristics has also been documented in male mandrills. Fully developed, or "fatted" male mandrills are more social, and have more brightly colored sex skins, fatter rumps, larger testes, and higher testosterone levels than "nonfatted," developmentally arrested adult males (Setchell and Dixson, 2001). As in orangutans, differences in male developmental pathways are thought to be a way in which subordinate males avoid the risks of competing for mates with higher-ranking males that are fully developed.

When males are larger than females, they tend to take longer to reach sexual maturity. Fully developed male mandrills, for example, weigh nearly three and a half times more, and can take up to four years longer to mature, than females (Setchell, et al., 2001). In species that are sexually monomorphic in body size, by contrast, age at sexual maturation for males and females is more comparable. Nonetheless, ecological, demographic, and social factors also influence the timing of puberty in female primates. We have seen how the onset of ovulation in female callitrichids can be inhibited by pheromonal, behavioral, and social cues (see Box 1.1), and there is now evidence from wild common marmosets that the inhibitions on ovulation in subordinate females may be stronger when the dominant female is lactating than when she is pregnant (Albuquerque, et al., 2001).

Some female chimpanzees undergo puberty, and even conceive, prior to transferring out of their natal groups (Wallis, 1997), but others, like female muriquis, disperse long before they begin to ovulate or become sexually active (Strier and Ziegler, 2000). Female muriquis do not usually become sexually active until at least their second year in a new group, corresponding to a delay in the onset of ovarian cycling. Even then, like many cercopithecines and great apes, their cycles can take awhile to become regular, and their fertility is correspondingly delayed. Dispersing females are usually older when they give birth to their first infants than females that remain in their natal groups, both across species in which females are similar to one another in body size and within the same species. The energetic costs of dispersing, as well as risks associated with greater vulnerability to predators or difficulties of finding sufficient food, could make it advantageous for females to postpone puberty, and the risks of conception, until they are settled into new groups. Alternatively, delayed or inhibited puberty could be what activates some female callitrichids, or even muriquis, to leave their natal groups, in the same way that access to fertile females seems to influence the different ages at which male yellow baboons ultimately disperse, or the alternative development pathways that some male orangutans and mandrills follow.

Adulthood and Aging

Primates mature later and live longer than other mammals of similar body sizes, which contribute to their comparatively slower life histories (Figure 9.15). Both age at maturation and longevity affect the length of time available for reproduction, or the **reproductive lifespans,** of both males and females alike. Reproductive lifespans can be remarkably similar despite differences in age at first reproduction if greater longevity compensates for delayed maturation, or conversely, if early maturation results in shorter life expectancies. The kinds of life history trade-offs that primates have been selected to make often fit with predictions based on the predictability of food and the pressure from predators in the habitats in which they have evolved (Borries, et al., 2001; Ross, 1991; Wright, 1999), but fluctuations in social and demographic conditions can also be involved (Jones, 1999; Strier, In preparation).

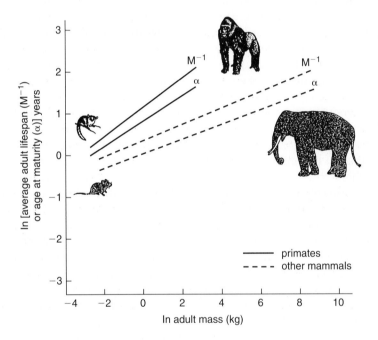

FIGURE 9.15   Primates have long lifespans and late maturity. Allometric relationships between age at first reproduction and adult lifespan for primates versus other mammals. Alpha measured from weaning to age at first birth; M^{-1} is the inverse of the average adult instanteous mortality. From Charnov, E. L. and Berrigan, D. 1993. Why do female primates have such long lifespans and so few babies? *Or* life in the slow lane. *Evolutionary Anthropology* 1:191–194. Copyright © 1993 Wiley-Liss, Inc. Reprinted by permission of Wiley-Liss, Inc., a division of John Wiley & Sons, Inc.

Accumulating data on longevity in wild primate populations is complicated by the long lifespans of most primates relative to the duration of most field studies and by the difficulties of monitoring dispersing individuals for the duration of their lives. Consequently, comparative data are still only available for a small number of species, but nearly all of them indicate that females live longer, on average, than males. Sex differences in survivorship may not emerge until males and females reach sexual maturity, but their persistence throughout adulthood can be dramatic (see Figure 8.1). Even in wild chimpanzees, where males remain in their natal groups and so are buffered from the higher risks of mortality associated with dispersal in other species, adult males have a lower probability of surviving than females. Forty one percent of female chimpanzees, but only 27 percent of all males born, survive to 15 years of age, and it is more common to find 40-year old females than 40-year old males (Hill, et al., 2001). Chimpanzees can live into their fifties in captivity, but very few live this long in the wild.

Explanations for the differences in male and female primate lifespans revolve around the costs associated with their respective reproductive strategies (Chapter 5). Indeed, there is some evidence that the greater survival of females relative to males corresponds to their differential contributions to parental care. At least in captivity, species in which males outlive females are those, such as marmosets, tamarins, owl monkeys, titi monkeys, and siamangs, in which males make substantial and direct contributions to infant care (Allman, et al., 1998). However, these findings do not take into account the potential effects of dispersal and intrasexual competition that are known to affect sex-specific survivorship of males and females in other species for which data from wild populations are available (Altmann, 2000; Fedigan and Zohar, 1997; Robbins, 2001).

Causes of mortality can be different for adults than for immatures of the same sex. For example, mortality among adult female ring-tailed lemurs rose from just 3.1 percent to more than 20 percent following a prolonged drought. All of the females that died during the drought were lactating, and therefore under severe energetic stress at the time (Gould, et al., 1999). Infectious disease is a more common cause of death in younger, reproductively active female Japanese macaques than it is in older, post-reproductive females in the same population (Fedigan and Zohar, 1997), while mortality among dispersing adult male yellow baboons, presumably from predators, can be up to ten times higher than it is during their residence in groups (Alberts and Altmann, 1995a,b).

We might expect that individual variation in longevity would be correlated with rank, especially among females for which rank translates into better feeding opportunities. Yet, while high-ranking females have higher fertility, they do not necessarily live longer lives. Among Japanese macaques, for example, longer-lived females produced more offspring, on average, than shorter-lived females independent of their ranks (Fedigan and Pavelka, 2001). Living longer gives females more time to reproduce. Longevity can compensate for slower reproductive rates along the way, especially if long-lived females continue to reproduce and survive long enough to bring their last infants safely through weaning (see Box 4.2).

Even the longest-lived females may not be able to compensate for the effects of physiological changes that occur as their bodies age. During pregnancy, for example, middle-aged mice have lower levels of estrogens circulating in their blood than younger females in their reproductive primes. Middle-aged mothers produced daughters that weighed less at birth and underwent puberty later than young mothers, and their sons had smaller reproductive organs (Wang and vom Saal, 2000). In mandrills, however, both high-ranking and older females give birth to heavier offspring than low-ranking or younger females. Heavier babies mature faster than light babies, but whether mothers that produce them also live longer is not yet clear (Setchell, et al., 2001). Female rhesus macaques in their twenties are in generally poor health and become increasingly acyclic (Johnson and Kapsalis, 1998).

The effects of longevity on male reproductive lifespans are even more complicated to calculate than they are for females without paternity data to compare with male behavior. Highly competitive, high risk strategies can have high payoffs, but they can also lead to higher risks of injury or death. Perhaps because of this, males are more likely than females to adjust their behavior in response to the ways their competitive abilities change with age (Chapter 8). Pronounced transformations in the behavior of males as they age have been described in species ranging from yellow and olive baboons, to Japanese macaques, to hamadryas baboons, to Hanuman langurs, and mountain gorillas. Although no single pattern rules, males generally shift from being aggressive challengers toward other males during their prime, to social benefactors toward females during mid-life, to allies of their sons or restless, unthreatening transients that take whatever rare mating opportunities come their way later in life.

Population Consequences of Life Histories

We have seen how infant sex ratios at birth and sex differences in survivorship and maturation can impact the size and composition of populations. Demographic conditions can fluctuate during an individual's lifetime, and they influence the social and reproductive options of males and females differently. Primates are clearly sensitive to unfavorable demographic conditions, as is evident from the kinds of dispersal decisions they make. Dispersal patterns, in turn, have consequences on populations because of their effects on the number and distribution of adult males and females that survive. For example, high mortality among dispersing males might reduce the number of males in the population competing for membership and reproductive access in female groups. High mortality among dispersing females, by contrast, has more serious effects on population growth rates because the number of fertile females in a population affects whether and how fast the population can grow.

Fluctuations in female numbers can have long lasting effects depending on female maturation and reproductive rates (Struhsaker, 1997). For example, mantled howler monkeys recolonized regenerating forest in Costa Rica faster than sympatric capuchin monkeys because the howlers have faster life histories (Fedigan and Jack, 2001). Populations can show signs of recovering from catastrophic events, such as epidemics or severe drought, within a few years in species like ring-tailed lemurs, which reach sexual maturity by two to three years of age (Gould, et al., 1999). Muriqui or chimpanzee populations would take many more years to recover from comparable losses of lactating females because females in these species take so much longer than lemurs to mature, and the rates at which they reproduce are so much slower. But, they might also be more buffered from temporary shortfalls in food because they can sacrifice reproduction for the sake of survival more easily than lemurs and other primates with faster life histories.

The life histories we see in living primates today reflect adaptations to the ecological conditions that prevailed during their evolutionary past (Ross, 1991). Fast life histories make more sense in unpredictable habitats, where secure sources of food and life expectancies are limited. Slow life histories make more sense in more ecologically stable, predictable habitats, especially if staying alive longer means living longer to reproduce. The interactions between life history strategies, which are constrained by phylogeny, and demography and ecology can profoundly affect the **viability** of endangered primate populations as we'll see in later chapters.

Communication and Cognition

Baboons grunt like pigs, muriquis neigh like horses, and howler monkeys roar so loudly that they can be heard for over a kilometer under the right ambient conditions. Describing the sounds primates make is a simple process compared to the challenge of deciphering what exactly it is they are saying to each other (Figure 10.1). Add to the difficulties of interpreting their complex vocal repertoires a host of bizarre facial expressions, genital displays, and urine washing rituals, and you begin to get an idea of what constitutes primate communication.

Understanding primate communication is a necessary component of understanding their social diversity. For example, if we're interested in understanding patterns in the effect of social rank, we need to know how different primates signal their status to one another. The eyelid flash of a male baboon (Figure 10.2) may convey the same warning message as the head-wagging display of brown capuchin monkeys to other members of their respective species. And, it appears that at certain times of the month associated with ovulation, many female primates present their genital regions to males, who sniff, jab, and visually inspect them.

FIGURE 10.1   An adult male Hanuman langur (*Presbytis entellus* or *Semnopithecus entellus*) "whoops," a display or intergroup call. Note his visibly distended throat. Photo by Jim Moore/Anthro-Photo.

FIGURE 10.2   An adult male yellow baboon (*Papio cynocephalus*) flashes his eyelids in an aggressive display. Photo by K. B. Strier.

Vocalizations, facial expressions, body postures, temporary anatomical distortions, and smells represent some of the most striking ways in which primates communicate information about themselves and their environments, in some, but not all, of the same ways we humans use language (Figure 10.3). Deciphering what each signal means, and whether it is intentional, like when we tell a lie or reassure a lost child with soothing words and gentle caresses, or an uncontrollable emotional reaction, like our own embarrassed blushing response, requires repeated observations

FIGURE 10.3 Begging hand gesture and screaming by a juvenile chimpanzee (*Pan troglodytes*) from whom food was just taken away by a dominant. Photo provided by Frans B. M. de Waal from *Chimpanzee Politics* by Frans de Waal (1982).

of the contexts in which signals are given, the identities of the signalers and the receivers, and the response of receivers once a signal has been offered.

Communication systems are a prerequisite for maintaining the complex social lives that primates lead, and are vital components of the learning and sharing of ecological information about the location of food resources or predators that affect survival. Human language, with its ability to refer to abstract concepts, is the most complex communication system known among primates, and probably reflects the highly developed **cognitive abilities** that are associated with our disproportionately large neocortexes (see Box 2.1). But, even though other primates lack language, they all need some form of communication system.

No other primates possess the vocal apparatus, including the mobile position of the tongue and larynx, necessary for the formation of the sounds that comprise human languages. Early efforts to train our close chimpanzee relatives to speak the way we do were doomed to fail—and did. But the inability to speak, in humans as well as other primates, does not imply a comparable inability to think or communicate. Training chimpanzees to work with American Sign Language (Fouts and Fouts, 1999) and computers, and conducting field experiments monitoring primate responses to tape-recorded vocalizations, offer alternative ways of finding out what goes on in the minds of other primates.

In fact, communication systems serve as windows into their cognitive processes, where the cost and benefit assessments that are so central to evolutionary theories of behavior take place (Shettleworth, 1984). To understand primate cognitive abilities and information-processing systems, we must begin with their communication. And, as appreciation for primate cognitive abilities has grown, so, too, has concern about their well-being in captivity and the ethical practices involved in the use of primates in biomedical and other invasive forms of research.

Components of Communication Systems

Communication is a two-way street. There must be at least one actor and one receiver in each interaction, but in primate groups other members may also play active roles. Communication systems can be divided into four interrelated components: signal, motivation, meaning, and function (Smith, 1977). The **signal** is the form that the act of communication takes. Signals may involve vocalizations, facial expressions, body postures or movements, odors, or touch. Each species has its own repertory of reassuring and threatening signals, which are usually identified by matching them with contexts and the reactions of others. A juvenile primate may crouch, pull its lips back, and utter soft grunts when an unrelated adult of either sex approaches (Figure 10.4). If the adult returns the grunt, or lightly clasps the juvenile on the shoulder, the juvenile may resume its prior activity, apparently reassured that no threat is imminent. A juvenile that fails to acknowledge its subordinate status initially may be targeted for a more direct threat until it yields. Observing these exchanges, we can piece together the signals that primates use to mediate their social relationships and maintain the integrity of their societies.

Motivation refers to the internal state of the actor who is sending the signal. Fear, aggression, sexual interest, appeasement, alarm, and excitement are among the many states that motivate individuals to emit signals. Motivational states need not be conscious, and except in highly controlled laboratory or field settings where physiological measures can be taken, we must rely on the prior and subsequent behavior of the actor to infer its motivational state at the time of signaling. When

FIGURE 10.4   Immature yellow baboon (*Papio cynocephalus*) cowers and moves aside as an adult male approaches with his head down. Photo by K. B. Strier.

physiological data are available, they indicate corresponding heart rates and hormonal and neurotransmitter levels that are thought to stimulate the behavior. Drug therapies prescribed for treating human behavioral disorders rely on these insights to target the biochemical processes underlying motivational states.

Meaning refers to the message that is received by the recipients of a signal. A signal given by one individual may be received differently than the same signal given by another individual, or by the original individual in a different context. By observing context-specific patterns in the reactions of recipients, it is possible to assess how primates evaluate the meaning of a signal. Recipients that differ from one another in age, experience, history, and relationship to the actor may respond differently to the same signal received at the same time. Thus, when vervet monkey mothers respond more strongly to distress cries given by their own offspring than they do toward the same cries given by nonkin, we attribute the difference to the monkey's ability to identify their respective relationship to the caller. Likewise, when mothers respond differently depending on whether the distress call is given by an individual from a higher or lower ranking matriline than their own, we attribute it to their ability to evaluate their respective positions based on who they can and cannot successfully challenge (Cheney and Seyfarth, 1990).

The **function** of communication describes its evolutionary advantage. Vocalizations and odors that distinguish among closely related species increase the probability of finding appropriate mates. Ritualized aggression, territorial scent marking, and vocalizations are mutually beneficial to both the actors and the recipients because these signals allow individuals to avoid the risks of actual fights. Indeed, such displays only escalate into direct combat when neither party signals their subordination in the appropriate, species-specific, and in some cases, locally acceptable, way. A group of monkeys that moves away from an area on hearing the long distance vocalizations of a neighboring group avoids provoking an unnecessary confrontation with the group that has signaled its presence in the vicinity. There are usually distance thresholds to these avoidance responses, such that calls judged to be coming from far away may signal the absence of any immediate threat, and therefore the absence of a need for avoidance tactics (Waser, 1977a).

Modes of Primate Communication

Primates depend on their ability to communicate information about a variety of subjects, including the identification of mates of the appropriate species, sex, and reproductive condition, the avoidance of predators, the maintenance of social relationships, and the defense of their territories. The four main modes of communication used by primates are tactile, visual, olfactory, and vocal. They can be used singly or in combination, depending on the different levels of proximity and familiarity each mode requires. For example, primates can detect auditory signals at greater distances than visual signals, particularly when dense vegetation obscures their ability to see one another. Visual displays do not require the same degree of proximity that physical contact requires, and some chemical cues can be detected by the recipient long after the signaler has left her mark in an area.

The modes of sensory perception that primates use to locate and process foods provide a good model for organizing their modes of communication with one another. Nate Dominy and his colleagues (2001) describe a series of boundaries radiating outward from an individual, that moves from touching, to seeing, to smelling, to hearing. We can think about the different kinds of communication that are possible within the same sensory boundaries.

Tactile Communication

Primates are highly physical creatures. Except for the primates that "park" their infants, most primate infants are carried by their mothers, or other group members, for extended periods of time that may extend up to, or even beyond, weaning (Chapter 9). Juveniles grapple with one another during play, and except for the most solitary of primates, group members either groom one another with their hands and mouths or give their friends reassuring touches or hugs when they meet up with one another or during threatening situations (Figure 10.5). Unrelated male baboons permit their coalition partners to grasp their testicles (Smuts and Watanabe, 1990; Colmenares, 1991), a strong measure of trust and solidarity that I have also seen among related male muriquis when they take a united stance against an intruder in their midst.

Physical contact is obviously a prerequisite for sexual interactions. Male hamadryas baboons give their mates gentle bites on the neck, and male bonobos may push or pull parts of their partner's bodies into more comfortable or effective positions (Savage-Rumbaugh, et al., 1977; Stammbach, 1987; Zeller, 1987). The degree of affiliation between mating partners, and the duration of their contact, is

FIGURE 10.5   Adult male Yakushima Japanese macaque (*Macaca fuscata yakui*) grooms another adult male. Photo by David A. Hill.

highly variable both within and between species (Figure 10.6a–d). When the risks of being interrupted by competitors are high, mating tends to be quicker than when the risks of interruptions are low. Low-ranking macaque and capuchin monkey males sneak copulations whenever females comply to avoid attracting the attention of high-ranking males (Chapter 8), and subordinate male chimpanzees sequester females on safaris, away from the presence of higher-ranking males, who might otherwise interfere with their liaisons (Chapter 5).

Reassuring physical contact can also be used to avoid aggression (Colmenares, 1991) and in reconciliation interactions following conflicts between opponents, even when the conflict itself has been restricted to nonphysical displays and threats (Chapter 7). Conflicts that escalate into physical violence can have serious

FIGURE 10.6a   Stage one of a courtship sequence in bonnet macaques (*Macaca radiata*). Here, the male (left) and female (right) grimace face-to-face. Photo by Jim Moore/Anthro-Photo.

FIGURE 10.6b   Male grimaces. Photo by Jim Moore/Anthro-Photo.

FIGURE 10.6c   The male extends his arm; the female appears to be threatening him. Photo by Jim Moore/Anthro-Photo.

FIGURE 10.6d   The pair copulate. The entire courtship sequence took about one minute, and was clearly a conceptually "single" interaction, illustrating the complexity and social aspects of sexual solicitations in this species. Photo by Jim Moore/Anthro-Photo.

repercussions because even minor wounds may become infected and lead to death in the humid tropics most primates inhabit. However, affiliative contact, from infancy through adulthood, is something that most social primates seek.

Visual Communication

Enhanced visual acuity is one of the distinguishing characteristics of primates compared to many other mammals, associated in part with the forward-facing eyes that create overlapping fields of vision for depth perception and the differentiation of rods and cones with variable abilities to perceive colors (Chapter 2). Body postures are used in the visual communication of all primates, but facial signaling is largely restricted to monkeys and apes (Figure 10.7). Prosimians have a more limited repertory of facial expressions because their lips are attached to their gums, and are therefore less mobile, and they have fewer nerves enervating the facial muscles that are used by anthropoids in their more expressive countenances (Zeller, 1987).

Eyes, eyebrows, and mouths are important in the facial expressions of monkeys and apes (Figure 10.8). In Barbary macaques, and probably other primates, many of the same facial expressions involving the eyes and eyebrows are used in both aggressive and friendly interactions (Figure 10.9), whereas the mouth seems to be specially reserved for less ambiguous signals (Zeller, 1987). Captive chimpanzees shown two-dimensional, black-and-white images of unfamiliar chimpanzee faces discriminated a wide variety of facial expressions almost immediately by choosing the same expression in a subsequent choice experiment (Parr, et al., 1998). Only the "relaxed-lip face," an expression with low signal value, failed to elicit such rapid discrimination in the test chimpanzees.

Individuals differ in their abilities to send and "read" one another's facial expressions. These differences in expressive communication were demonstrated in a series of experiments involving captive rhesus macaques. Individual monkeys

FIGURE 10.7   Ventro-ventral copulation between bonobos (*Pan paniscus*) at the San Diego Zoo facilitates face-to-face visual contact. Photo provided by Frans B. M. de Waal from *Peacemaking among Primates* by Frans de Waal (1989).

FIGURE 10.8 Frederico, a subadult male brown capuchin monkey (*Cebus apella*), displays his canines. Photo by J. W. Lynch.

FIGURE 10.9 Female rhesus macaque (*Macaca mulatta*) looks at her mating partner. Photo by Joe Manson and Susan Perry.

learned quickly to respond to two stimuli by pulling or pushing a bar. Failures were punished with mild shocks; correct responses were rewarded with food. Once all individuals had learned the appropriate response to each stimulus, they were paired up with another individual in separate cages where they could see each other on closed circuit T.V. One monkey in each pair was presented with the stimulus, but did not have access to bars. The other monkey was in control of the bars, but could see only the face of its partner instead of the stimulus. Both partners received food rewards when a correct response was given, and mild shocks for incorrect responses. Subordinates proved to be better at sending appropriate expressions, intermediate-ranked monkeys were better at responding, and dominant individuals were adequate at both in these studies of "cooperative conditioning" (Miller, 1971, 1975).

Although visual communication transmits information about the emotional state of the signaler, at least some primates are able to send deceptive signals. A male chimpanzee at the Arnhem Zoo used his hands to cover the fear grimace that had settled on his mouth so as not to signal his submission to a challenger, a remarkable effort at concealment that implies the voluntary control of an involuntary response. Another subordinate male, who had become aroused while flirting with a female chimpanzee, used his hands to conceal his erect penis from a higher-ranking male. One adult female even used conciliatory gestures to get close enough to other chimpanzees in the enclosure so that she could bite them (de Waal, 1982).

Visual cues may also be important in kin recognition, although it has been difficult to demonstrate that such phenotypic matching is responsible for the different ways in which kin and nonkin interact (Alberts, 1999; Chapais, 2001; Widdig, et al., 2001). In captivity, for example, yellow baboons reared apart from their paternal siblings did not appear to recognize them when they were given the opportunity to interact (Erhart, et al., 1997). Remarkably, however, chimpanzees trained to match similar images they viewed on a computer screen were evidently using visual cues when they matched unfamiliar mother-son pairs of chimpanzees, but not other combinations of kin and nonkin (Parr and de Waal, 1999).

Olfactory Communication

Despite their visual acuity, all living primates, including humans, use and respond to odors (Jacob, et al., 2002). In contrast to tactile and visual communication, olfactory communication involves smells that can be detected directly in the presence of the signaler or indirectly from the odors that the signaler leaves behind. The odors involved in olfactory communication are volatile fatty acids produced by bacteria. They are secreted from glands located at different positions of the body in different primates, including, but not limited to, the ano-genital region (Figure 10.10). These chemical emissions, or **pheromones,** are best known for the information they transmit about female reproductive conditions (Hrdy and Whitten, 1987), but they may also be involved in communicating information about the identity, age, and sex of an individual (Zeller, 1987).

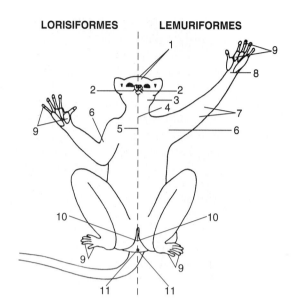

LORISIFORMES   LEMURIFORMES

FIGURE 10.10   Topography of the known cutaneous glands in prosimians. 1 = Nonspecialized glands of the crown and forehead; 2 = glands of the lips; 3 = submaxillar glands; 4 = neck glands; 5 = chest glands; 6 = brachial glands; 7 = glands of the elbow region; 8 = antebrachial glands; 9 = nonspecialized glands of the palmar and plantar regions; 10 = glands of the external genitalia; 11 = glands of the anal region. From Schilling, A., 1979. Olfactory communication in prosimians. In G. A. Doyle and R. D. Martin, eds., *The Study of Prosimian Behavior.* New York: Academic Press. Reprinted with permission of the author and publisher. Copyright © Academic Press, 1979.

Olfactory communication can involve passive signals given off by individuals going about their everyday business, in much the same way that sweaty people unintentionally leave a smelly trail as they walk down the street, or the way that an estrous female primate—of any kind—leaves a scent trail as she passes. Captive cotton-top tamarin males presented with different olfactory stimuli demonstrated that they could discriminate between familiar and unfamiliar females that were ovulatory and nonovulatory in the absence of the females themselves by their greater attraction to the scents of ovulating females (Washabaugh and Snowdon, 1998). There is now evidence that these cues elicit emotional responses in the brain. In a fascinating study, male common marmosets were lightly anesthetized so that their brains could be imaged by a magnetic resonance spectrometer. When the males were presented with odors from an ovulating female marmoset, their brains signaled sexual arousal, but when presented with an ovarectimized female's odor, their brains did not respond (Ferris, et al., 2001).

Olfactory cues can also be transmitted with more active deliberation, such as when a male ring-tailed lemur rubs his upper arm and wrist against a branch in an area where his group's range overlaps the range of a neighboring group or when males competing for mates during the breeding season engage in ritualized stink-fighting (Zeller, 1987; Gould, 1999). Both male and female black-handed spider monkeys chew on the leaves of three species of Rutaceae and then rub the saliva and chewed up leaves into their chests (Figure 10.11). The fact that they then rub their leaf-coated chests against tree trunks and branches raises the possibility that the behavior serves a social function (Campbell, 2000), in contrast to the urine washing behavior of slender lorises to protect them while they feed on toxic and stinging insects (Nekaris, 2002).

FIGURE 10.11   A female black-handed spider monkey (*Ateles geoffroyi*) climbing a tree trunk. The fur rubbing, in which these spider monkeys engage, resembles the medicinal plant use of white-faced capuchin monkeys (see Box 6.1), but may serve social function instead (Campbell, 2000). Photo by Christina J. Campbell.

When females present their genitals for a male to inspect by sniffing and licking, they are providing olfactory or pheromonal cues about their ovulatory condition (Michael, et al., 1972). In wild common marmosets, both males and females leave scent marks during their daily feeding and traveling activities. Ordinarily, subordinate females scent mark as much as dominant females, but when they have the chance to signal their presence to males from other groups during territorial confrontations, subordinate females do it even more (Lazaro-Perea, et al., 1999).

Urine washing is another ritual practiced by many primates. It differs from urination because it involves coating one or both hands and feet with urine and then either rubbing the soaked appendages on vegetation, the way that squirrel monkeys and owl monkeys do, or on themselves, the way capuchin monkeys do (Zeller, 1987). Urine washing may be a particularly effective way for females to alert males in the vicinity to their sexual receptivity if they do not ordinarily associate together where more continuous surveillance is possible (Milton, 1985b).

Vocal Communication

Deciphering primate vocalizations falls into an intermediate realm between the more obvious interpretations of postures, gestures, and facial expressions and the more subtle interpretations of olfactory communication. As with tactile and visual signals, we humans can discriminate many primate calls and associate them with particular contexts just by using our own ears and eyes. As with chemical cues, however, our perceptions may differ from those of other primates. For example, nocturnal prosimians have such acute hearing that they can localize and catch their insect prey by sound alone (Dominy, et al., 2001). We can, however, analyze high-quality tape recordings with sensitive **sound spectrograms,** for characterizing and comparing the distinguishing acoustic features of primate calls (Figure 10.12).

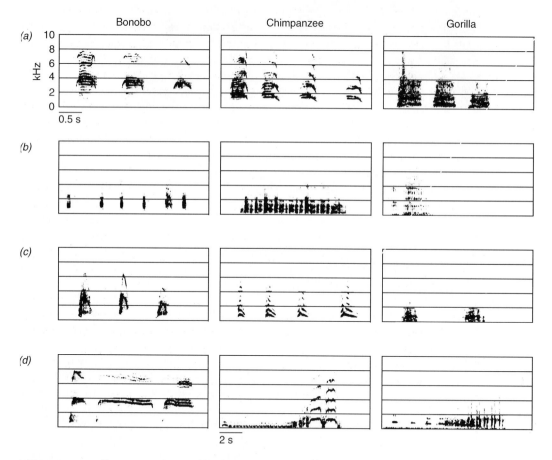

FIGURE 10.12 Representative audiospectrograms of calls produced by bonobos, chimpanzees, and gorillas: (a) = adult female screams; (b) = adult male grunts; (c) = adult male barks; (d) = adult male hoots. From Mitani, J. C. 1996. Comparative studies of African ape vocal behavior. In W. C. McGrew, L. F. Marchant, and T. Nishida, Eds., *Great Ape Societies.* New York: Cambridge University Press. Reprinted with permission of the author and publisher. Copyright © Cambridge University Press, 1996.

Species Recognition.   The vocalizations of different species vary from one another in ways that permit primates to distinguish members of their own kind from others. It is easy to see how the ability to discriminate one's own species from another would be advantageous when it comes to finding appropriate mates, and therefore such species-specific recognition would be under strong evolutionary selection pressures. Closely related species may have unique types of vocalizations, such as the high-pitched "peeps" of bonobos versus the "humming" of mountain gorillas, as well as similar types of vocalizations, such as loud calls or screams (Mitani, 1996; Mitani and Gros-Louis, 1995).

Spectrographic analyses of vocalizations used by closely related primates indicate distinguishing features in their acoustical structures that correspond to taxonomic classifications. For example, comparisons among the loud calls given by five species of African bushbabies show species-specific characteristics. Greater similarities were found in the vocalizations of two species of greater bushbabies and of three species of lesser bushbabies than between the lesser bushbabies and the greater bushbabies, which corresponds with their phylogenetic proximity and possibly other anatomical traits, such as body size (Zimmermann, 1990). Similarly, chimpanzee screams are given at lower frequencies than the higher-pitched screams of the closely related bonobo, a difference that has been attributed to the anatomical differences in the size of their respective vocal tracts (Mitani and Gros-Louis, 1995).

In a field experiment, primatologist John Mitani (1987) tape-recorded the territorial songs sung by males from two populations of agile gibbons, one living in West Kalimantan and another in South Sumatra, Indonesia. He also recorded the same type of call given by one population of the closely related Müller's gibbon from East Kalimantan. Species differences were evident from comparisons of the acoustical features of agile gibbons and Müller's gibbons, while the calls of agile gibbons from the West Kalimantan population differed from those of agile gibbons from South Sumatra in their duration and maximum frequencies.

To determine whether agile gibbons from West Kalimantan could discriminate between unfamiliar gibbons of their own species and gibbons of another species, Mitani observed their responses to tape recordings played from concealed speakers placed at the periphery of their territories. In nearly every trial in which the West Kalimantan agile gibbons heard recordings of agile gibbon songs from both their own and South Sumatran populations, they responded by moving toward the area that the songs were coming from to engage in their own territorial duets. By contrast, only about half of the trials using recordings of Müller's gibbons elicited similar approach responses. The reactions of the West Kalimantan agile gibbons indicate that the vocalization differences between the species were greater than those within their own species.

Analyses of advertisement calls given by two species of nocturnal mouse lemurs revealed high variability in the alarm whistles they gave in response to predators. By contrast, calls given in mating contexts were highly species-specific. The "vocal fingerprints" of their mating calls help the lemurs to recognize their appropriate mates, and researchers to distinguish between morphologically similar species (Zimmermann, et al., 2000).

Within- and Between-Group Distinctions. The ability to distinguish vocalizations made by members from one's own or another social group would also clearly have advantages when it comes to defending territories or resources, avoiding competitors, and finding unrelated mates. Many primates use long-distance vocalizations to communicate their whereabouts, permitting members of different groups to avoid or approach one another according to who is calling and where they are. For example, large male orangutans give long-distance calls to warn intruder males away and to attract estrous females. Gray-cheeked mangabeys, an African forest-dwelling cercopithecine, approach the "whoop-gobble" calls given by a male from their own group, but leave the area upon hearing a recording of the same call made by a male from another group closer than 400 meters. The same call from an unfamiliar male played at greater distances was ignored, suggesting that these monkeys take identity as well as risk into account in their responses (Waser, 1977a). Male titi monkeys, like gibbons, respond with a loud call and move to the border of their territories, where they sing a duet with their mates, on hearing another male calling (Kinzey and Robinson, 1983).

Long-Distance Calls. Long calls of ring-tailed lemurs, like howler monkey roars, can carry one kilometer or more (Sauther, et al., 1999). Low frequency sounds (500–2,500 hertz) carry farther than high frequency sounds in tropical forests because they are less affected by the distorting scattering and degradation effects of vegetation. Not surprisingly, all of the long-distance calls primates use are in this low frequency range (Seyfarth, 1987). Additionally, sounds carry farthest in the early mornings in tropical forests, intermediate distances in the evenings, and have the shortest transmission distances during midday owing to the ways in which temperature and humidity absorb and attenuate sound. As a result, most primates that rely on long-distance vocalizations as a mechanism to maintain spacing between their groups vocalize most in the mornings when their long-distance calls are more likely to be heard (Seyfarth, 1987).

Some populations of howler monkeys sing dawn choruses as a routine matter, but any signs of other troops or nontroop members can lead to roars throughout the day (Horwich and Gebhard, 1983). Male and female howler monkeys sound different from one another because of the differences in their body size and the corresponding size of the **hyoid** bone, which resonates and amplifies their long calls (Figure 10.13). As a result, their choruses can communicate as much about the size and composition of their troops as they do about their location (Crockett and Eisenberg, 1987). Long-distance neighs are exchanged between groups of muriquis living at high densities on a regular basis whenever more than one group is in the same vicinity, but at low densities, these long-distance neighs are rarely heard.

Close-Range Calls. The varying degrees to which primates employ long-distance and short-range vocalizations coincide with differences in their social systems, even among closely related species. For example, chimpanzees, with their fluid grouping patterns, employ long-distance calls, primarily to recruit allies, more than mountain gorillas, whose more stable, cohesive groups lead to a greater emphasis on

FIGURE 10.13   Male mantled howler monkey (*Alouatta palliata*) in forward threat. Note the thick growth of hair covering his throat. The hyoid is just below. Photo by Margaret R. Clarke.

short-range "grunts" in their vocal repertoire (Mitani, 1996). Just as vervet monkey mothers give more frequent alarm calls when their offspring are nearby than in the presence of nonkin (Cheney and Seyfarth, 1990), group size and composition influence the rates and types of vocalizations that other primates employ (Mitani, 1996).

Vocal communication among group members also differs depending on the circumstances. For example, pygmy marmosets make one kind of "trill" when group members are spread out, and another kind of trill when they are close together (Snowdon and Hodun, 1981; Snowdon and Pola, 1978). Group members trill in sequence, waiting for all members to indicate their presence before any one member trills a second time as if they are holding polite conversations (Snowdon and Cleveland, 1984).

Japanese macaques have a variety of "coos" that vary in their peak frequencies and acoustic patterns depending on the identity of the caller. Infants make one kind of "coo" when they are out of contact with their mothers, while estrous females make another kind of "coo" to attract potential mates (Green, 1975b).

Consistent patterns of individual "signature" calls have been identified in a variety of primates, including pygmy marmosets, squirrel monkeys, stump-tailed macaques, gibbons, gorillas, and chimpanzees (Clark and Wrangham, 1994; Lillehei and Snowdon, 1978; Marler and Hobbett, 1975; Mitani and Nishida, 1993; Seyfarth, et al., 1994; Smith, et al., 1982; Snowdon and Cleveland, 1980; Tenaza, 1976; also reviewed in Seyfarth, 1987; Snowdon, 1986). In addition, many primates are capable of associating individual calls with their rank and kinship relationships. In field experiments, Dorothy Cheney and Robert Seyfarth (1980, 1982) played tape recordings of two-year-old juvenile vervet monkey screams to two unrelated adult females and the juvenile's mothers. Mothers responded more strongly to the screams of their own offspring than to those of unrelated juveniles, and unrelated females looked at the juvenile's mother even before responding themselves. Rhesus macaque mothers exhibit similar discrimination capabilities in response to whichever one of the four types of noisy screams their offspring give when they are in physical contact or interacting with related or unrelated individuals who are higher- or lower-ranking than them (Gouzoules, 1984; Gouzoules, et al., 1984). Indeed, whereas the "pant-hoots" used by chimpanzees in their long-distance calls are highly specific to individuals, the "pant-grunts" they use in their social interactions at close range are much more variable (Mitani, 1996).

Ontogeny.   Like the variation detected in the songs of agile gibbons from different populations, chimpanzee vocalizations recorded from populations living in Gombe National Park and Mahale National Park, Tanzania, exhibit identifiable acoustical differences (Mitani, et al., 1992). Population differences like these imply that at least some aspects of primate vocal communication are influenced by social circumstances instead of being under tight species-specific genetic programming (Green, 1975a; Mitani, 1996).

Despite the suspected role of social influence on primate vocalizations, evidence of vocal learning in primates has been difficult to obtain (Snowdon, 1990). The "babbling" that immature pygmy marmosets engage in resembles the babbling that human infants use as they begin to practice producing the sounds used in language (Snowdon, 1988). However, without isolation experiments, we cannot be sure whether learning is involved (Seyfarth, 1987; Snowdon, 1990b). In some early studies in which squirrel monkeys were deafened or housed in isolation, their vocalizations nonetheless developed normally (Talmage-Riggs, et al., 1972; Winter, et al., 1973). **Cross-fostering** experiments, in which infants of one species are reared by members of another species, have yielded inconclusive results using closely related rhesus and Japanese macaques (Masataka and Fujita, 1989; Snowdon, 1990b). Comparisons between the acoustic properties of pant hoots given by chimpanzees in Tanzania and Uganda point to the effects of ecological factors rather than social conditions (Mitani, et al., 1999).

The role of learning is much more strongly implicated in how primates acquire the appropriate uses of and responses to vocalizations than it is in vocal production per se (Snowdon, 1990b). For example, in contrast to adults, infant vervet monkeys indiscriminately give alarm calls to both harmless and predatory birds (Seyfarth and Cheney, 1986). Reinforcement from adults may be one of the ways in which infants learn when to give the specific alarm calls associated with aerial and terrestrial predators. Adult vervet monkeys look up and take cover in bushes in response to avian alarm calls. They climb into trees in response to leopard alarm calls, and check out the grass around them in response to snake alarm calls (Seyfarth, et al., 1980; Struhsaker, 1967b). Immatures do not exhibit the appropriate alarm-specific responses until they are twenty-four to thirty weeks of age, after having had repeated opportunities to learn their cues from more experienced adults (Seyfarth and Cheney, 1986). Pygmy marmosets require similar experience in the appropriate uses of and responses to different trill vocalizations, and are nearly adults by the time that they demonstrate adult competency levels with these calls (Elowson, et al., 1992; Snowdon, 1988).

Intentional or Involuntary Information Sharing.   We humans use language, the most distinct component of our vocal communication, in intentional ways. We may involuntarily gasp in surprise or scream in fear, but we are more deliberate in our use of words to describe objects and events in the abstract, and in our use of grammar to situate our descriptions relative to time, place, ourselves, and others (Seyfarth, 1987). We also decide whether or not to speak, and whether to be honest about what we say.

Other primates, too, are evidently capable of exhibiting some voluntary control over their vocalizations. For example, low-ranking chimpanzees refrained from vocalizing at a feeding station originally set up to facilitate studying them at Gombe National Park, thereby avoiding attracting higher-ranking chimpanzees to the food. Males also maintain uncommon silence amongst themselves when they are on a patrol of their community's boundaries, simultaneously increasing their ability to detect the presence of chimpanzees from adjacent communities and reducing the chances of attracting attention to themselves (Goodall, 1986). They are especially careful about not making noise when traveling in small parties, perhaps because confrontations with larger parties from other communities can be lethal for the chimpanzees that are outnumbered (Wilson, et al., 2001). Thus, as with human language, the voluntary control of vocal communication may be beneficial in both ecological and social contexts.

Many primates have distinctive vocalizations associated with food and predators. A group of Japanese macaques, known as the Arashiyama A—and later West—troop, transferred to a 20-hectare ranch in southern Texas, developed a new alarm call to the rattlesnakes that they encountered for the first time (Pavelka, 1993). The alarm calls of ring-tailed lemurs also signal the class of predators involved (Pereira and Macedonia, 1991). We have seen how vervet monkeys discriminate among predatory birds, leopards, and snakes in both the alarm calls they give and their responses to alarms given by others. The ability of vervet monkeys to respond appropriately to tape-recorded playbacks of different alarm calls without directly viewing the particular predator themselves is indicative of the referential role of these calls in their behavioral repertory (Cheney and Seyfarth, 1990).

Investigations into primate food calls have not provided comparable evidence for their referential functions. Instead, it appears that at least in their rates of food calling, primates communicate more about their own affective state than about the food per se (Snowdon, 1990b), calling at higher or lower rates depending on how much food is available (Hauser, et al., 1993). Social factors may also mediate vocal communication in the context of food. For example, female chimpanzees vocalize more frequently when they are traveling in large parties than when they are alone (Clark, 1993), and subadult males "pant-hoot" more often when they approach a large fruit tree that adult males have already entered than when no one else is present (Clark and Wrangham, 1994). Withholding information about the location of food in experimental studies and distracting high-ranking individuals from discovering a monopolizable food resource by looking or running in the wrong direction are additional ways in which communicating ecological information is tempered by social considerations (Goodall, 1986; Seyfarth, 1987).

Despite the differences in the social systems of chimpanzees and gorillas, in both species high-ranking adult males do most of the vocalizing (Clark, 1993; Harcourt, et al., 1993; Mitani and Nishida, 1993). High-ranking males may have much to gain in terms of attracting estrous females and allies, whereas low-ranking males and females may be better off by not attracting the attention of competitors who can displace them from feeding sites (Mitani, 1996).

It is easy to envision why vocal communication, including the ability to recognize individuals by their calls, would be especially advantageous in large groups where shorter-range forms of communication, such as visual signals, would be more difficult to maintain (Mitani, et al., 1992). It is also clear that learning to discriminate between honest and dishonest signals would be beneficial in societies in which attending to reliable information about the presence of predators could mean survival. Not surprisingly, primates such as vervet monkeys ignore the calls of individuals who repeatedly give false alarm calls to predators or the presence of other groups, while continuing to attend to the same alarm calls of more reliable colleagues (Cheney and Seyfarth, 1988). The benefits of giving deceptive signals, such as false alarms to predators that cause high-ranking group members to pause while the low-ranking caller enters a feeding area, would last only so long as their deceptive tactics worked.

Cognition

The step from primate communication to cognition is a short one, particularly if vocal communication and gestures can be voluntarily controlled in ways that olfactory signals cannot. The complexity of primate communication, and especially the demonstrated ability of some primates to practice deception, provide insights into the extent of their cognitive abilities that shed light on the differences and similarities between what humans and other primates do.

Investigations into primate cognition have focused on experiments conducted in both captivity and the field, and fall into three general categories. One approach involves the mechanisms by which primates develop their cognitive abilities, which have been most intensively studied from the perspective of vocal learning. The second involves the ecological selection pressures associated with both spatial memory and tool use, both of which increase primate access to food resources, and therefore have important potential impacts on their reproductive success. The third involves the social advantages of maintaining, manipulating, and deceiving allies, all of which require that an individual primate possess some understanding of its social position and own emotive state relative to others. In each case, apes demonstrate abilities that prosimians and monkeys evidently lack.

Learning and Imitation

There's little doubt that primates learn, or that learning is influenced by social opportunities. Young primates have ample opportunities to observe their mothers, and in most species, other group members. Yet, there is little evidence of active teaching among any primates except humans (King, 1991) and possibly chimpanzees (Boesch, 1991a). There is also, somewhat surprisingly, little evidence that nonhuman primates learn by imitating one another, despite the advantages that **imitation** would have compared to the time required for practice and experience (Boesch and Tomasello, 1998; King, 1991; Visalberghi and Fragaszy, 1990).

Play may be an exception to this pattern of nonimitation, because during social play, young primates exhibit tremendous improvisation and accommodations instead of taking their cues from adult role models (Fagen, 1993). They may develop original games, such as covering their eyes, and experiment with novel signals, movements, and activities in the nonthreatening context of play. When immature primates play with members from different species or different social groups (Chapter 11), the stimulus of social facilitation seems to lead them to cooperate in adjusting their style of play to accommodate their partners and can appear imitative (Fagen, 1993).

Social facilitation may increase a primate's interest in an activity or performance of a task, but imitation requires a level of representational thought that no monkey has yet demonstrated (Cheney and Seyfarth, 1990). For example, if imitation was responsible for the spread of innovative practices such as potato washing among Japanese macaques, some researchers question why it took as long as it did—three years—before nearly half of the 25 members of the study group caught on (Nishida, 1987; Visalberghi and Fragaszy, 1990).

Imitation is assumed to be a shortcut to learning, but it requires an ability to understand a cause–effect relationship without actually experiencing it. In a series of experiments with captive capuchin monkeys, which are the most adept primate tool-users next to hominoids (Panger, 1999) individuals observed a tool-using cagemate. They may have learned from observation that a relationship existed between the tool and the task, but they failed to learn the necessary actions required to get the food with the tool just by watching. In other words, these monkeys could not "ape" each other (Visalberghi and Fragaszy, 1990).

Apes also require practice and experience to benefit from social learning, but they show some indications of being able to figure things out in ways monkeys cannot (Byrne, 1998). Unlike monkeys, apes can infer where a hand has hidden an object if they are able to watch the hand doing the hiding (Visilberghi and Fragaszy, 1990). In the wild, chimpanzees carry tools from one location to another, where the food to be acquired is found (Boesch and Boesch, 1984; Goodall, 1986; Matsuzawa, 1996). In at least this respect, apes seem to be capable of understanding object–task relationships that even capuchin monkeys cannot (Byrne, 1997b; Jalles-Filho, et al., 2001).

These differences between the cognitive abilities of monkeys and apes, including questions about the processes involved in learning, are important ones in behavioral ecology. For example, we might expect species with greater cognitive abilities to be more flexible in their responses to novel ecological and social situations, which ultimately affect the fitness costs and benefits of their actions (Shettleworth, 1984). Different species have evolved in response to different ecological and social challenges, so it is to ecology and sociality that we turn for insights into the kinds of selection pressures that have shaped primate cognition.

Ecological Intelligence

Ecological models for the evolution of primate intelligence attribute species differences in cognition to the relative strength of selection pressures for abilities such as remembering where food can be found or following birds to food sources. Theoretically, individuals possessing skills that permit them to locate and harvest high quality foods should have higher fitness than individuals whose abilities are more limited. In captive studies, most primates perform remarkably well at novel tasks that reward them with food, but only some, such as capuchin monkeys and apes, can tackle problem-solving tasks that involve extracting food from concealed sources (Parker and Gibson, 1977, 1990). Both observational and experimental studies in the wild yield a comparable diversity of skills that have been linked in ecological models of primate intelligence.

Spatial Memory.   The ability to remember the location of important food resources is a considerable advantage to any primate because any increase in foraging efficiency saves time and energy for other activities (Chapter 6). Good spatial memories would presumably be more advantageous to primates that rely on food resources with patchy distributions, such as fruits, than to primates whose food resources are more evenly and abundantly available, such as leaves and grasses. Thus, the fact that frugivorous primates have larger brains for their body sizes than folivores could be attributed to the stronger ecological selection pressures on cognitive abilities that fruit-eaters face (Milton, 1981; see Box 2.1).

Despite the obvious logic of these arguments, it is almost impossible to evaluate the extent of primate spatial memories without experimentally manipulating the location of their food resources and then monitoring their ability to locate them (Janson, 1996). Emil Menzel (1974) conducted some of the earliest tests of chimpanzee "mental maps" by hiding pieces of food around a large enclosure while the chimpanzees watched. The chimpanzees were not only quick to retrieve the hidden morsels, but they also often took the shortest routes between hiding places (Menzel, 1991).

Recent field and lab studies have extended these experiments to further understand the decision-making processes of brown capuchin monkeys in Argentina and moustached tamarins in Peru. After observing capuchin monkeys for over a year in Argentina's Iguazu National Park, ecologist Charles Janson (1998) and his collaborators set up feeding platforms during the dry season, when fruits are scarce. They hauled loads of tangerines, which the capuchin monkeys love, into the forest on a regular basis, varying which platforms were provisioned with fruit, and the amount of fruit in each experimental "patch."

The capuchins were quick to discover that platforms sometimes contained delicious fruits. Provisioned platforms were detected at greater distances by the group than by individual members, confirming that group-living has benefits when it comes to locating food (Chapter 6). Provisioned platforms were also more likely to be spotted when the group was traveling at a leisurely pace than when the group was moving quickly through the forest, and at any travel speed, large "patches" had a greater probability of being spotted than small ones (Janson and Di Bitetti, 1997).

Insights into the foraging decisions and cognitive abilities of moustached tamarins come from the experimental feeding platforms that Garber and Dolins (1996) set up in a Peruvian forest. Platforms were provisioned with real and artificial bananas on an alternating schedule so that patches with real bananas in the morning would not have them in the afternoon and vice versa. The tamarins were quick to figure out the system. When the platform closest to them in the morning had food, they sought out a different platform later in the day, using the decision rule of WIN–SHIFT. Conversely, if the platform closest to them had not been provisioned, they returned to it later in the day for their reward, using the decision rule of LOSE–RETURN. The decision rules did not appear to carry over from day-to-day because the tamarins treated each new day as if it were the start of a new experimental trial. Within a single day, however, the tamarins incorporated their earlier experience into their later foraging decisions.

Tool Use.   Many animals manipulate objects in their natural environments to achieve a desired goal, and as such, conform to the classic definition of tool use (Beck, 1980). Birds and insects build nests. Sea otters use rocks to crack open shellfish on their chests. Yet, no one doubts that the kind of tool-use long thought to be a hallmark of humanity (see Box 3.1) implies a different sort of cognitive capacity than what other animals possess (Parker and Gibson, 1977). The varied tools and tool-related behaviors of nonhuman primates represent cognitive abilities somewhere in-between what other animals and humans possess.

All of the great apes construct sleeping and resting nests from suitable twigs, branches, and leaves wherever they are when they are ready to settle down (Fruth and Hohmann, 1996). Chimpanzees, bonobos, and orangutans sometimes fashion shelters from leaves to shield themselves during heavy rainstorms or take refuge under protective branches (Ingmanson, 1996; van Schaik and Fox, 1996). Some orangutans use twigs to extract insects from bark and seeds embedded in fruit (Chapter 3). Chimpanzees also scrunch up leaves to soak up drinking water, modify twigs to probe termite mounds, and transport stones to use as hammers and anvils for cracking open the hard shells of nutritious nuts (Boesch and Boesch, 1984; Sugiyama, 1997).

The use of hammers and anvils or **tool-composites** are defined by primatologist Yukimaru Sugiyama (1997) as "two or more tools having different functions that are used sequentially and in association to achieve a single goal" (Table 10.1). Chimpanzees don't use one tool to make another, a more sophisticated procedure that so far appears to be restricted to humans.

TABLE 10.1   Reported observations of tool-composite use by wild chimpanzees*

Activity	Tool-Composite
Ant-nest dipping and ant catching	Digging stick, Dipping wand
Mound perforating and termite catching	Perforating stick, Frayed dipping stick
Mound digging and termite catching	Digging stick, Fishing stick
Water drinking	Crumpled leaf "sponge," Pushing–pulling stick
Palm-sap collecting	Branch "pestle," Tree fiber sponge
Hard nut cracking	Stone or wood hammer, Stone or root anvil
Nut picking	Hammer and anvil, Twigs
Propping anvil	Stone anvil, Small stone prop

*See Sugiyama (1997) for localities and references. Adapted from Sugiyama, Y. 1997. Social tradition and the use of tool-composites by wild chimpanzees. *Evolutionary Anthropology* 6: 23–27. Copyright © 1997 Wiley-Liss, Inc. Reprinted by permission of Wiley-Liss, Inc., a division of John Wiley & Sons, Inc.

Tool-use and tool-related behaviors are not limited to achieving shelter or food-related goals. Many arboreal monkeys break and throw branches as part of their threatening or defensive displays, as many human observers can attest. Silverback western lowland gorillas use water in their social displays (Parnell and Buchanan-Smith, 2001). The rise in rank of a subordinate male chimpanzee, named Mike, at Gombe National Park was facilitated by his innovative dragging of the researchers' five gallon tins in his aggressive display toward other chimpanzees (Goodall, 1986). Primatologist Ellen Ingmanson (1996) has discovered that young bonobos hold sticks during social play and adult bonobos sometimes drag leafy branches, which seem to signal their travel direction to others (Figure 10.14).

Neither chimpanzees nor orangutans are uniform about their tool-using behaviors. Populations differ in their respective tool traditions, even when similar materials and foods are available to them (McGrew, 1992, 1993; Sugiyama, 1997; van Schaik and Knott, 2001; Whiten, et al., 1999). Chimpanzees living in Bossou, Guinea, rely heavily at times of fruit scarcity on just a few types of food, including oil-palm nuts, which must be cracked open with stones, and oil-palm pith, which must be

FIGURE 10.14   Wild bonobo (*Pan paniscus*) dragging a branch. Photo by Ellen J. Ingmanson.

pounded with a pestle (Yamakoshi, 1998). By contrast, wild chimpanzees in Gabon's Lopé Reserve lack this technological knowledge despite the availability of appropriate stones and nuts in their habitat (McGrew, et al., 1997). Orangutans living at high densities use twigs to extract *Neesia* seeds, while those living at low densities, where they also eat these seeds, have not developed this tradition (van Schaik and Knott, 2001). Bonobos in captivity demonstrate an adeptness with tools that in the wild is more restricted to social contexts, such as displays and group movements, than for procuring food (Ingmanson, 1996). Different tool-using practices seem to become established and maintained through local social or **cultural traditions** (Boesch and Tomasello, 1998; McGrew, 1992; McGrew, et al., 1997; Sugiyama, 1997; Whiten, et al., 1999; Whiten and Boesch, 2001). Social tolerance, related to local ecological conditions, may facilitate the social transmission of novel behaviors, accounting for the variation in behaviors across populations (van Schaik, et al., 1999a).

Among all primates, including provisioned Japanese macaques that play with stones (Figure 10.15), it is almost always the immatures or adult females that develop tool-related innovations first (Huffman, 1984; Quiatt and Reynolds, 1993; Sugiyama, 1997; Whiten, et al., 1999; Whiten and Boesch, 2001). Whenever sex differences in tool-use related to food are observed, it is almost always the case that females are more technologically facile than males (Boesch and Boesch, 1984; McGrew, 1979; Sugiyama, 1997). Whether these sex differences reflect differences in motor skills, patience, or cognitive abilities remains unclear.

Mountain gorillas, which rely on abundant herbaceous vegetation for their survival, neither hunt nor use tools in the wild. Yet, they employ complex food-processing techniques to break through the physical defenses that might otherwise

FIGURE 10.15 A Japanese macaque (*Macaca fuscata*) at Arashiyama stone rubbing (Huffman and Quiatt, 1986). Photo by Michael A. Huffman.

protect their foods from less adept foragers (Figure 10.16a,b). These abilities may have developed from a more frugivorous adaptation, which lowland gorillas and other apes still exhibit. Or, they may reflect cognitive abilities that were shaped by social pressures.

Social Intelligence

Mountain gorillas, like the more technologically sophisticated chimpanzees, demonstrate many forms of deception, such as concealment of their actions, inhibition of their vocalizations, and distraction of others' attention, in their social lives (Byrne, 1996a, b). The benefits of possessing a good memory may be of comparable, or even greater, importance as spatial memory when it comes to keeping track of their social relationships (Byrne, 1996a, b; Cheney, et al., 1986; de Waal, 1996) and may even set a cognitive limit on group size (Dunbar, 1996).

Alliances.   Most of us know from our own experiences that social skills are important when it comes to getting along with others. From our families, to friends, lovers, or colleagues at work, numerous opportunities for competitive conflicts, as well as

FIGURE 10.16a   Nettles (*Laportea*) are rich in protein and low in secondary compounds, but protected by powerful stings. These are most numerous on the plant's stem and leaf petiole (shown here), and least on the underside of leaves. Photo by Richard W. Byrne.

FIGURE 10.16b   A juvenile gorilla processes a nettle stem. Gorillas' elaborate technique enables leaf blades from one or several plants to be detached and their petioles removed, while minimizing contact between soft parts of the hands and the painful stings (Byrne and Byrne, 1993). The resulting bundle of leaf blades is then folded in two, to encase the food in a single leaf underside, before putting into the mouth. Photo by Richard W. Byrne.

cooperation, routinely arise. Resolving conflicts to maintain alliances appears to be an ongoing challenge for at least some social primates, as well. Like our own dealings with one another, other primates make social decisions about the value of establishing and maintaining relationships with one another (Figure 10.17). Understanding how primates negotiate their social relationships provides insights into the ways in which sociality has shaped primate cognitive abilities just as understanding their foraging decisions and technological innovations provides insights into ecological influences on cognition (Cheney, et al., 1986; Essock-Vitale and Seyfarth, 1987; de Waal, 1996, 2000).

Many of the field studies reviewed in this and previous chapters provide evidence for complex levels of primate social negotiations. For example, various studies of vervet monkeys, baboons, and macaques demonstrate their abilities to distinguish among familiar kin, higher- and lower-ranking individuals, recent grooming partners, and long-term allies. In captive experiments, brown capuchin monkeys were more likely to share food rewards obtained by joint efforts than when only one of the monkey's efforts was required (de Waal and Berger, 2000). Comparative analyses indicate that apes possess more sophisticated social skills than even the most diplomatic of monkeys, a distinction that is consistent with the better performance of apes on other types of cognitive tasks (Byrne, 1998; de Waal, 1996; de Waal and Luttrell, 1988).

As we've seen, stump-tailed macaques have more relaxed social relationships with one another than rhesus macaques (Chapter 7). Yet in both of these closely

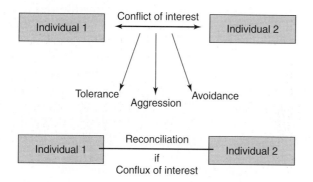

FIGURE 10.17   The "relational model" for resolving conflicts, described by de Waal (1996). Tolerance, aggression, and avoidance are different ways of settling conflicts of interest. Reconciliation should occur when both individuals share a strong mutual interest in maintaining their relationship, which goes through cycles of conflict and reconciliation. From de Waal, F. B. M. 1996. Conflict as negotiation. In W. C. McGrew, L. F. Marchant, and T. Nishida, Eds., *Great Ape Societies*. New York: Cambridge University Press. Reprinted with permission of the author and publisher. Copyright © Cambridge University Press, 1996.

related monkey species, alliances among high-ranking individuals are directed down in the hierarchy, which keeps lower-ranking group members in their places. By contrast, high-ranking chimpanzees are not only tolerant toward subordinates, but are also kept in line by subordinates, who form powerful alliances with one another (de Waal and Luttrell, 1988, 1989). Greater social symmetry occurs in chimpanzee societies because the positions of high-ranking "despots" are always vulnerable to being toppled through the collective actions of subordinates (de Waal, 1982). Asserting their dominance while simultaneously appeasing subordinates requires tremendous negotiating skills and underlying expectations that no other primates, except humans, have been shown to possess (de Waal, 1996).

Tactical Deception.   The flip side of the social cognition coin is a darker, but no less intriguing, one. Championed by primatologists Richard Byrne and Andrew Whiten (1988), it focuses on the cognitive implications of **tactical deception,** which they define as "acts from the normal repertoire of the agent, deployed such that another individual is likely to misinterpret what the acts signify, to the advantage of the agent" (Bryne, 1997a; Byrne and Whiten, 1988).

Byrne and Whiten pooled their own observations of wild primates with those of other primatologists (e.g., Humphrey, 1976; Jolly, 1966, 1991; Mitchell and Thompson, 1986; de Waal,1982) and came up with an unexpectedly large number of examples, often anecdotal, about ways in which many primate species deceive one another in both social and ecological contexts. Giving false alarm calls to divert the attention of others or concealing their facial expressions by turning away are just a few of the many anecdotes that observers have described. The number of examples from a wide diversity of primates continues to grow (Byrne, 1997a; Byrne and Whiten, 1990; Whiten and Byrne, 1997), firmly planting the idea that primates have evolved varying degrees of **Machiavellian intelligence,** named for the strategic advice about the value of deception that Machiavelli espoused.

Effective deception requires the possession of a **theory of mind** (Premack and Woodruff, 1978), in which an individual can perceive the mental perspective of another rather than responding solely to its overt behavior (Byrne and Whiten, 1997; Cheney and Seyfarth, 1990). As with other measures of cognition, apes prove to be more adept in their mental perspectives than monkeys. For instance, pairs of rhesus macaques learn to cooperate with one another in experimental set-ups to obtain a food reward, but they are unable to switch roles in the task without additional learning trials the way that chimpanzees can (Povinelli, et al., 1992a, b). Likewise, individual chimpanzees, gorillas, and orangutans recognize themselves in mirrors, as others would "see" them, whereas monkeys do not (reviewed in Byrne and Whiten, 1997).

Without a theory of mind, monkeys are capable of deceiving one another, but they don't really understand how their deceptions lead others to hold false beliefs (Byrne, 1997a; Cheney and Seyfarth, 1990). Put another way, "whereas monkey abilities seem tied to the social world, in a number of ways great apes seem to understand "how things work' " (Byrne and Whiten, 1997, p. 22), and therefore possess not only greater social, but also greater technological complexity (Figure 10.18).

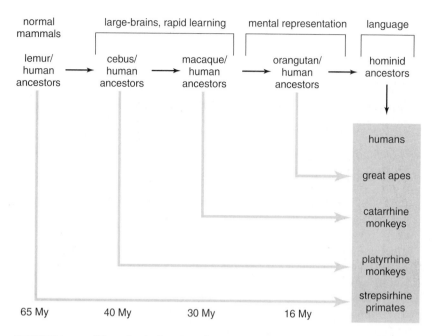

FIGURE 10.18 Hypothetical series of ancestor species, whose cognitive adaptations led to the human minds, in relation to their modern descendants. From Byrne, R. W. 1996c. Machiavellian intelligence. *Evolutionary Anthropology* 5: 172–180. Copyright © 1996 Wiley-Liss, Inc. Reprinted by permission of Wiley-Liss, Inc. a division of John Wiley and Sons, Inc.

Implications for the Ethical Treatment of Primates

Growing appreciation for the cognitive abilities of nonhuman primates, and especially the apes, has prompted intensive scrutiny over their ethical treatment in captivity. Insights into their perception, mental processes, and social awareness have helped to raise questions about our responsible and respectful treatment of them. Whether primates serve as ambassadors for their species in zoos, or as subjects in biomedical research, improved standards of living in their housing, maintenance, and general well-being are now enforced by federal laws. Many professional societies in the United States, Europe, and elsewhere have developed guidelines for the ethical treatment of animals, including primates, as research subjects (e.g., the Animal Behavior Society and the American Society of Primatologists). Most journals will not publish research results without signed declarations that ethical protocols have been followed, and universities require appropriately elaborate protocol approvals to conduct animal research. Federal funding agencies, such as the National Science Foundation (NSF) and National Institutes of Health (NIH), require evidence of protocol approval before releasing research funds.

Improvements in primate standards of living in captivity and general well-being have practical, as well as ethical, value (Blum, 1994). Housing naturally social primates in social groups instead of in isolation reduces the risks of abnormal behavioral developments and impaired cognitive performance that can be self-destructive to the animals as well as lead to distorted experimental results (Chapter 1). Adhering to the guidelines established from field studies about the size and composition of groups in the wild has reduced aggression and increased the success of captive breeding efforts. According to a recent (1997) National Research Council report, even minor adjustments, such as providing hiding spaces, climbing structures, and objects for play, reduce primate stress, and therefore stress-induced health problems. Stress can lower resistance to disease, impair fertility, and increase mortality in both captive and wild primates (Creel, 2001; King, et al., 1988).

Ethical and practical questions persist about the fate of long-lived primates such as chimpanzees, who are retired from their careers as biomedical or space program research subjects. Releasing them back into their natural habitats is only sometimes a viable option. Infants rescued from illegal hunting or collecting expeditions are usually too young to survive without their mothers, and may require extensive care with low prospects for recovery from the trauma and poor conditions following their capture. Those that were born or reared in captivity lack essential survival skills in the wild, although intensive training periods and monitored social integration have proven successful in at least one case (Box 10.1). Primates used in biomedical research may carry infectious diseases, such as hepatitis or HIV, to which they are resistant, but which could be transmitted to local humans and wildlife with far-reaching, lethal results.

Sanctuaries for primates recovered from illegal trade activities or healthy retirees have sprouted up throughout the world, including parts of the tropics where the primates are from. They are essentially rehabilitation centers, but many of the primates lucky enough to land in them never fully recover their independence. And, there is not enough space or resources in these sanctuaries for all of the primates that need care. Most of these sanctuaries are operated by volunteers or nonprofit organizations. They often rely on private donations, which further limits the number of places for primates to go. Such **reintroductions,** together with **translocations,** which involve moving primates to new areas either to increase gene flow, or more commonly, as emergency rescues from habitat destruction, are costly to conduct and don't always succeed (Yeager and Silver, 1999). Yet, sometimes they are the last hopes for the primates, especially if their habitats will be completely destroyed by development projects such as the flooding created by hydroelectric dams (Thoisy, et al., 2001).

Nearly all practicing primatologists face ethical choices when deciding how and under what conditions to conduct their research. All primatologists must be careful about transmitting diseases to their study subjects, which can become infected from contact with contaminated food or human waste, or even from the close proximity observers establish with habituated primates (Wallis and Lee, 1999). Some become hardened to the problems primates face, and others mortgage their homes to care for orphans or retired research subjects. There is no single "right answer" to be found in science, but we can no longer evade these difficult questions.

BOX **10.1**

Rehabilitation, Reintroduction, and Sanctuary

Figuring out what to do with primates retired from biomedical and space research programs is a problem. Most people would agree that these primates deserve some reward for their contributions to science, but few of them are capable of coping with the rigors of release into the wild without extensive rehabilitation. Even then, many primates carry infectious diseases that could put local humans and other wildlife in jeopardy.

This dilemma is particularly poignant for some 1,500 chimpanzees, which are the product of breeding programs initiated by the National Institutes of Health (NIH) in 1986 to meet what was expected to be a demand for nonhuman subjects for studies on AIDS. Despite their close genetic similarities to humans, only one of about 200 chimpanzees infected with HIV has exhibited AIDS-like symptoms, challenging their suitability as models for the research programs for which they were bred.

In early 1999, however, the origin of HIV-1, the strain responsible for most human infections, was traced to the central African subspecies, *Pan troglodytes troglodytes* (Gao, et al., 1999). This discovery has triggered a wave of concern about the highly endangered status of this subspecies in the wild (Weiss and Wrangham, 1999).

Maintaining a colony of 200 chimpanzees costs about a million dollars a year. In July 1997, a National Research Council panel commissioned to evaluate the future of these chimpanzees rejected the option of euthanasia as an unethical one. Instead, the panel recommended that the NIH create a management program to shelter these retired chimpanzees for the duration of their lives (Roush, 1997). Similar sanctuaries, funded in at least one case by an animal rights group, are springing up to support other chimpanzee retirees used in other kinds of research, including NASA's space program.

A very different solution has been implemented for the golden lion tamarin, one of the endemic Atlantic forest primates, which like muriquis, has been pushed toward extinction. In the 1970s, the Rio de Janeiro Primate Center and the National Zoo in Washington, D.C. initiated golden lion tamarin breeding programs with tremendous success. After a decade, there were over 400 golden lion tamarins, known as GLTs for short, housed in 60 zoos across North America and Europe (Beck, et al., 1986). This surplus of GLTs made them prime candidates for what has become a pioneering project to **reintroduce** captive-born monkeys to their natural habitat.

Where to release them was not problematic. A 12,500 acre forest less than 100 miles from Rio de Janeiro had been set aside for GLTs in 1974 (Kleiman, et al., 1988). Known as the National Biological Reserve of Poça das Antas, about 40 percent of the area contained suitable habitat for what in 1980 was estimated to be a small population of only about 75–150 GLTs (Dietz, et al., 1986). The protected status of the area and the density of GLTs there, which was low relative to the population size that the forest could potentially support, along with good records on the family and medical histories of the captive monkeys, met other criteria for responsible reintroduction programs (Kleiman, 1996). In 1983, the first 15 GLTs, representing four social groups, were targeted for release and flown from the National Zoo back to their Brazilian homeland.

These pioneering primates spent their first months in Brazil at the Rio de Janeiro Primate Center. They had to be quarantined to make sure they wouldn't introduce new diseases to their wild cousins, and acclimatized to the Brazilian climate. They also had to learn how to survive in the wild. They had never had to search for their own food, for example,

(continued)

and had never had to navigate anything as complicated as the branches and trees that would be their substrates in the forest. Putting novel configurations of branches in their cages gave them practice at locomotion. Replacing the bowl of food to which they were accustomed with hidden foods located in different places helped them learn how to forage (Beck, et al., 1986). The researchers hoped to create opportunities for the monkeys to learn in captivity the skills they would have acquired, and would soon require, to survive in the wild.

The first of the GLTs were brought to the Poço das Antas forest reserve about six months after their arrival in Brazil. At first, they were kept in large enclosures where they could still be provisioned and improvements in their foraging and locomotor skills could be monitored. Meanwhile, studies of wild GLTs were underway, and experiments involving translocating individuals and following them with radiotelemetry were conducted (Dietz, et al., 1986). The translocation studies indicated that the monkeys would need supplementary provisioning before they could find enough food on their own in a new area of the forest, and that it was important to move whole groups together instead of individuals and to avoid releasing groups too close to the territories of established groups (Pinder, 1986).

Even following these recommendations, only two of the four original groups were intact by the second month of freedom in the forest. Some died from attacks by feral dogs, some died or disappeared from aggressive social encounters with GLTs whose territories they inadvertently invaded. But the surviving groups succeeded in setting up their own territories and in one case, reproducing in what was only a year or so after arriving back in Brazil (Beck, et al., 1986).

Despite the early setbacks, the reintroduction program has persisted. There were no pre-established guidelines or protocols for reintroducing GLTs, or any other primates, so the learning curve for the researchers has been steep (Kleiman, 1996). Nonetheless, by 1996, the population of reintroduced GLTs numbered around 200, with high survivorship and reproductive rates among them. Many reintroduced monkeys have reproduced with wild-born mates, increasing the genetic variation in their surviving offspring. At the same time, active conservation education programs to increase public awareness, and reforestation programs to stimulate the recovery of degenerated areas within and around the reserve have progressed (Kleiman, et al., 1988).

GLTs are neither the only primates nor the only animals that have been rehabilitated and reintroduced to wild sanctuaries (Box, 1991; Kleiman, 1996). From chimpanzees and orangutans (Borner, 1985; Hannah and McGrew, 1991; Rijksen, 1974) to the Arabian oryx (Stanley Price, 1986, 1989), captive populations can be returned to the wild. As the GLT reintroduction program shows, these management efforts take years to establish, and cost a great deal to implement and monitor responsibly. Reintroductions may only be feasible for endangered animals that breed well in captivity, and for whom protected wild habitats still exist.

Community Ecology

So far, we have focused on behavioral comparisons of individual primates within their groups and between groups of their own species. We have not yet considered how different species of primates interact with one another, or how interspecific competition for food and mutual interests in avoiding common predators can lead different species of primates to associate with one another.

We have also taken an approach to primates that examines the ways in which they respond, on a day-to-day or seasonal basis, and over evolutionary time, to these natural selection pressures. We have not yet considered in any detail how primates affect their ecological communities (see Chapter 6), or whether the extinction of local populations of primates or entire primate communities might affect the functioning of the ecosystems to which they belong (Box 11.1). To understand the full significance of primate conservation efforts, and the long-term effects of primate extinctions, it is necessary to appreciate how different species of primates manage to live side by side and with other organisms in their ecological communities.

Primate Communities

Humans are unique among primates because members of our species have penetrated nearly all corners of the earth. We have found ways to live in nearly all habitats on the planet, and with these technological modifications, we are often the only

BOX **11.1**

Primates and Parasites

Primates, including humans, serve as hosts for many **parasites,** which are organisms that live in or on another organism. Many of these parasites are perfectly harmless, but some can compromise fitness in times of stress or be downright pathogenic to the health of the host. When their effects are pathogenic, parasites represent a potentially powerful set of selection pressures on primates, favoring behaviors that reduce their risks of becoming infected (Freeland, 1976; Hart, 1990). For example, living in large groups, using the same travel routes or sleeping sites, and direct social contact, including grooming and mating, can increase the opportunities for infectious parasites to spread. As a result, the effects of parasites on primates are important to understanding the costs and benefits of their group sizes, ranging patterns, and social interactions.

Yellow fever, schistomiasis, and malaria are among the diseases that blood parasites can bring on in both humans and other primates (Carpenter, 1964; Davies, et al., 1991; Phillips-Conroy, 1986). Skin parasites include botflies, which lay their eggs in flesh that the developing larva can feed on. Left undisturbed, they will turn into full-fledged flies, which break through the skin when they're fully mature. Scratching the itchy, irritating swellings can lead to skin infections that may be responsible for high mortality among primates such as the mantled howler monkeys living on Barro Colorado Island in Panama (Milton, 1982).

Much more common among primates are the **endoparasites,** such as hookworms, that pass through their guts. Though rarely fatal, these parasites can make primates ill, and lead to behavioral remedies, including dietary accommodations (see Box 6.1) as well as shifts in primate grouping and ranging patterns (Freeland, 1976, 1980; Hart, 1990). The finding of higher incidences of parasitic infections among dominant male and lactating female baboons has been attributed to their more frequent social interactions with a wider variety of partners than subordinate males or nonlactating females (Hausfater and Watson, 1976).

Infectious gut parasites can be transmitted in a variety of manners, including eating contaminated foods, like the insects, which carry parasites, that are eaten by callitrichids (Araújo Santos, et al., 1995), or vegetation that has been soiled by infected feces (Eilenberger, 1997). Switching sleeping sites and feeding areas are ways by which primates, including humans, can reduce their chances of becoming infected. Both nomadic human populations that change their camps often, and mantled howler monkeys that avoid repeated use of arboreal pathways, have lower prevalences of parasites than sedentary humans and monkeys that traverse contaminated areas (Chernela and Thatcher, 1989; Stuart, et al., 1990). These findings are consistent with the higher prevalence of infectious parasites found in chimpanzees (McGrew, et al., 1989) and red howler monkeys (Gilbert, 1994) living at high population densities.

Wet conditions appear to favor the survival of parasite ova and larvae excreted in primate dung (Hausfater and Meade, 1982). This may account for the higher prevalence of parasites in Kenyan yellow baboons during the rainy season versus dry season (Hausfater and Meade, 1982) and in both Costa Rican mantled howler monkeys living in riparian forests (versus drier, deciduous forests) at Hacienda La Pacifica (Jones, 1994) and muriqui populations in humid (versus dry) habitats (Stuart, et al., 1993). In addition, dietary differences and patterns of habitat use can affect primate parasite loads. For example, primates such as tamarins and lowland gorillas that feed or travel in the understory or on the ground are especially vulnerable to becoming infected by parasites transmitted through humans (Araújo Santos, et al., 1995; Eilenberger, 1997). Increasing encroachment of humans into primate habitats can bring primates into contact with parasites with which they have no prior experience, and therefore no resistance to. Indeed, greater contact with humans was one of the hypotheses advanced to account for the higher incidence of parasite infections found among Gombe chimpanzees compared to the more isolated chimpanzee population at Mt. Asserik, Senegal (McGrew, et al., 1989).

But equally disconcerting are the more subtle effects of habitat disturbance on the complex ecological communities to which primates, parasites, and their intermediate hosts belong. Disruptions in these ecological communities can be difficult to detect, but the absence of any parasites in a primate's dung may be a subtle indication that a delicate ecological balance between parasites and their hosts has been disturbed (Stuart and Strier, 1995).

---

primates around. Almost the opposite is true among our nonhuman relatives, where it is rare to find only a single species at a time. Except in extreme parts of their geographic distributions, such as in Japan, or in marginal habitats at high altitudes or in arid regions around the tropics, whenever there is one species of nonhuman primate there are usually others as well.

Sympatric primates are those found in the same ecological communities, and as a result, end up sharing to various degrees their space, shelters, predators, parasites, water sources, and food resources with one another and, often, with other nonprimate animals as well. No two primates, or any other organisms, have identical *ecological niches,* which include every aspect of the space, time, and resources they utilize. The requirements of different species may overlap substantially with one another, or hardly at all, but competition between species will lead, over evolutionary time, to at least some degree of differentiation, or divergence, in their niches.

Niche Divergence

Niche divergence among sympatric primates can be extremely subtle. For example, five sympatric lorisids, along with eleven other primate species, are found in the Makokou forests of northeastern Gabon (Richard, 1985). The lorises and galagos are all nocturnal, and are similar to one another in their body sizes, metabolic requirements, and diets. They differ from one another in the details of their locomotor behavior, which affects the levels of the canopy and the types of structural supports they use (Charles-Dominique, 1977).

The ten diurnal monkey species found in this forest range in size from the 2-kilogram talapoin monkey to the 12-kilogram female mandrill. In contrast to the lorisids, talapoin monkeys, crested mangabeys, and DeBrazza monkeys all use the same canopy levels but differ from one another in their diets and ranging patterns. The smaller talapoins consume more insects, and forage over a wider variety of habitat types. DeBrazza monkeys live in small groups on home ranges that are roughly one fourth the size of the home ranges of crested mangabey groups. These species feed on many of the same kinds of foods, but the smaller home range that the DeBrazza monkeys use is consistent with the lower diversity of food species in their diets (Gautier-Hion, 1978).

Elsewhere, sympatric red colobus monkeys and black and white colobus monkeys devote different proportions of their feeding time to leaves and seeds. Red colobus monkeys also have a much more diverse diet, which includes at least eighty different plant species, than the much more selective black-and-white colobus monkeys, which have been seen to eat only forty-six different plant species to date (Maisels, et al., 1994).

There are other classic examples of niche divergence among sympatric communities of primates from around the world (Janson and Chapman, 1999; Richard, 1985; Terborgh, 1983). In each of these communities, the sympatric primates differ from one another in size, diet, or habitat use (Figure 11.1). In general, the smaller-bodied species tend to use smaller branches to support themselves while feeding than the larger-bodied primates (Fleagle and Mittermeier, 1980). Other behavioral differences, such as where primates position themselves in the canopy, can vary more within a single species than between species in the community (Gebo and Chapman, 1995). Nonetheless, the ways in which shared resources are partitioned among sympatric primates affects both the costs of interspecific competition and the possible benefits of **polyspecific,** or mixed-species, **associations.**

Polyspecific Associations

With as many as sixteen different primate species living side by side in some tropical forests, encounters between species are an inevitable occurrence. This is especially true whenever groups of different species converge at food resources that each species exploits. Having common food resources creates opportunities for interspecific competition similar to those between **conspecifics,** or members of the same species. Usually, larger-bodied species can dominate the smaller-bodied species, and can therefore displace them or exclude them from food patches. But small-bodied primates may have other advantages. For example, if they form large groups, smaller-bodied primates can achieve a high **biomass,** or total group weight, and therefore manage to swarm through a food patch occupied by larger primates as a result of their grouping patterns. Their greater agility and the strength of their numbers can make it difficult for a smaller number of larger, less agile primates to evict them.

In the Brazilian Atlantic forest, it is not unusual for a subgroup of four to five of the large-bodied muriquis to expel a similar sized troop of smaller brown howler monkeys from a fruit tree, only to be swarmed by a group of twenty or so frenetic, but much smaller-bodied brown capuchin monkeys. The muriquis and capuchin monkeys may feed together, and only after both of these species have gone their separate ways will the howler monkeys return to the fruit tree to resume their meal of whatever their competitors left or overlooked (Dias and Strier, 2000). Relations between red howler monkeys and capuchin monkeys are different on Maracá Island, in the northern Brazilian Amazon. There, when the howlers approach a fruiting tree, the capuchins retreat (Mendes Pontes, 1997), but the reasons for these different patterns are not clear.

Clumped resources may attract aggregations or **assemblages** of species, but in these assemblages there is no evidence for any coordinated activities among the

FIGURE 11.1   A Suriname rainforest showing forest levels with different kinds of substrates and the primates that occupy them. From Fleagle, J. G. 1999. *Primate Adaptation and Evolution*, Second Edition. New York: Academic Press. Reprinted with permission of the publisher and author, © 1999 Academic Press.

different species (Mendes Pontes, 1997). It is an entirely different matter when members of one or more species modify their behavior to accompany members of another species in what are mixed-species or polyspecific associations.

Occasionally, one or a few individuals will join up with and travel alongside a group of primates of a species different than their own (Figure 11.2). Sometimes, single male guenon monkeys will associate with groups of a different guenon species, resulting in interbreeding and the production of hybrid offspring (Struhsaker, et al., 1988; Tutin, 1999; see Box 3.2).

We assume that when species associate, the one that alters its behavior while accompanying the other is the one that benefits the most. Detailed observations indicate that one male crowned guenon, who spent nearly a third of his time traveling with three different troops of black colobus monkeys, matched his own behavior to that of his associates whenever he joined them (Figure 11.3). This male participated in grooming bouts and vocal exchanges with the colobus monkeys, and ate many, but

FIGURE 11.2   A subadult female nilgiri langur (*Presbytis johnii* or *Trachypithecus* or *Kasi johnii*) sitting next to a juvenile Hanuman langur (*Presbytis entellus* or *Semnopithecus entellus*), in the group that the subadult has joined. Photo by Jim Moore/Anthro-Photo.

FIGURE 11.3   Blue monkey (*Cercopithecus mitis*) and red-tailed monkey (*C. ascanius*) play chase while a second red-tailed monkey watches in another type of polyspecific association. Photo by Marina Cords.

not all, of the colobus monkeys' foods. Presumably he would have joined a group of his own species if he had been able to find one that would accept him or overcome the resistance of resident males against a potential reproductive competitor. But, the benefits of being in a group made it preferable to hang out with the colobus monkeys than to spend his time alone (Fleury and Gautier-Hion, 1997). Similar associations have been observed in fragmented forests, where finding groups of conspecifics can be difficult for dispersing individuals (Tutin, 1999).

The most common variety of polyspecific associations involve entire groups of two or three different species that meet up and travel together for variable lengths of time, ranging from less than an hour, to part or all of a day, to days. In this respect, these mixed-species groups resemble the fluid, fission–fusion patterns of associations found in groups of chimpanzees or spider monkeys because, like chimpanzees or spider monkeys, members of polyspecific groups join up and split apart when it is advantageous to do so (Chapman and Chapman, 1996a).

Polyspecific associations may be initiated and maintained by one or all of the species involved, and may be mutually beneficial or only beneficial to one of the species (Figure 11.4). Polyspecific associations provide ways for primates to benefit from increasing their group sizes while avoiding the costs of increasing group size

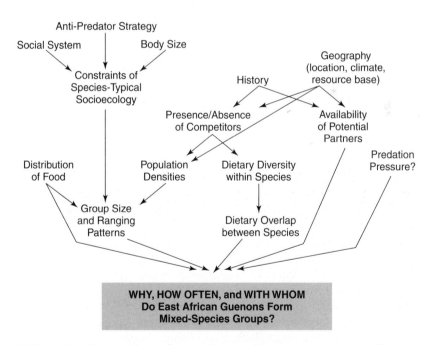

FIGURE 11.4   Factors that influence the mixed-species associations of East African guenons. From Cords, M. A. 1990. Mixed-species associations of East African guenons: General patterns or specific examples? *American Journal of Primatology* 21: 101–114. Copyright © 1990 Wiley-Liss, Inc. Reprinted by permission of Wiley-Liss, Inc., a division of John Wiley & Sons, Inc.

with conspecifics. For instance, participating species in mixed-species groups are less likely to compete with one another for the same mates. And, because they exhibit at least some degree of niche separation, the levels of feeding competition between species should be lower than those between groups of their own respective species.

Two categories of benefits have been invoked to explain the occurrence of polyspecific associations. One set of benefits pertains to the potential increased foraging efficiency that species with overlapping diets gain by associating together; the other set pertains to the potential advantages of large groups when it comes to avoiding predators.

Foraging Benefits. Participating members of polyspecific associations may exhibit higher feeding rates because the need for individual vigilance is more relaxed in larger groups. Associating with other species can also increase the ability of primates to locate and defend common resources. Shared resources can also be used more efficiently because each species can avoid visiting food patches that have already been depleted (Chapman and Chapman, 1996a; Terborgh, 1983). Grey-cheeked mangabeys in Kibale National Park, Uganda, share their fig trees with both hornbills and chimpanzees. The mangabeys are not deterred by hornbill vocalizations, but they avoid associating with chimpanzees in the fig trees (Olupot, et al., 1998).

In some polyspecific associations, one species gains access to foods that might otherwise be inaccessible if it was on its own. For example, in Manu National Park, Peru, squirrel monkeys often maintain associations with brown capuchin monkeys, which are larger and can supplant the squirrel monkeys at contested resources. Nevertheless, squirrel monkeys maintain these associations because the capuchins have strong jaws, which they use to crack open hard palm nuts that the squirrel monkeys lack the strength to open by themselves. At times of the year when more accessible fruits are scarce, these palm nuts become a staple in the brown capuchin monkeys' diets. By associating with the capuchins, the squirrel monkeys gain access to the nuts that the capuchins have opened and then dropped or discarded (Terborgh, 1983).

Mixed-species associations are rare among lemurs, but in northern Madagascar, crowned lemurs and Sanford's lemurs associate for hours during the rainy season. Sanford's lemurs typically feed in the main canopy, while crowned lemurs feed in the understory. By joining up, both species can increase their ability to find food when resources are scarce (Freed, 1999).

In Manu National Park, as well as throughout their distribution elsewhere in Peru and the Amazon, saddle-back tamarins and moustached tamarins form permanent polyspecific associations. Single groups of each species share and defend a common range, and forage together throughout the day (Heymann, 1995; Peres, 1992; Terborgh, 1983). The long-term stability of saddle-backed tamarin associations with other tamarin species are attributed to the niche separation they exhibit when it comes to locomotor style, substrate and habitat preferences, and the types of insects each species eats (Buchanan-Smith, 1999; Heymann, 1995). During a twelve-month study in northeastern Peru, saddle-back and moustached tamarins associating with one another ate only three of the same species of insects, and, even then, the saddleback tamarins spent most of their time in the understory, less than four meters off the ground, while the moustached tamarins stuck to the lower and middle canopy levels, from four to fifteen meters in height (Nickle and Heymann, 1996). Sometimes insects such as katydids escaped from moustached tamarins only to be captured by the saddle-back tamarins foraging below. In one study in Brazilian Amazonia, over 40 percent of the insect prey captured by saddle-back tamarins had been flushed out by the moustached tamarins overhead (Peres, 1992).

In Bolivia, tamarins are often accompanied by sympatric Goeldi's monkeys, especially during the rainy season when fruit is abundant and the Goeldi's monkeys can follow the tamarins to fruit sources. During the dry season, however, the diets of Goeldi's monkeys diverge from those of tamarins, and they are rarely found in association (Porter, 2001).

Predator Protection.   Some polyspecific associations have nothing to do with foraging efficiencies. In fact, species that associate may forage less efficiently together than when they are alone. In detailed comparisons among five sympatric monkeys in Kibale National Park, Uganda, there were no consistent differences in the feeding rates of individuals when they were in monospecific and polyspecific groups (Chapman and Chapman, 1996a; Cords, 1990). Although red-tailed monkeys and blue monkeys had higher feeding rates when they associated together, red colobus feeding rates were lower when they associated with blue monkeys and mangabey feeding rates declined when they associated with red-tailed monkeys. Similarly, although the feeding rates of both red colobus and black-and-white colobus monkeys increased when their groups associated with one another, whenever a group of red-tailed monkeys joined them, their feeding rates dropped.

Polyspecific associations formed by red colobus monkeys and Diana monkeys in the Täi National Park, Ivory Coast, where these two species spend roughly 62 percent of their time together, lead to alterations in the behavior of both of them (Holenweg, et al., 1996). Red colobus and Diana monkeys have low dietary overlap. Nonetheless, in polyspecific associations, the smaller Diana monkeys altered their diets to include more insect prey (Wachter, et al., 1997), and the red colobus monkey groups altered their grouping patterns by spreading out more like the Diana monkeys (Höner, et al., 1997). These dietary and behavioral shifts, as well as the fidelity of particular partner groups, in which the same groups of each species share a common range, suggest that both species benefit from their associations in ways that are unrelated, if not costly, to their foraging efficiencies.

In fact, the polyspecific associations between red colobus and Diana monkeys in the Täi National Forest have been attributed to the benefits that both species gain in avoiding predators. Polyspecific associations between these primates are more common in this forest than they are in nearby forests where there are fewer predators (Holenweg, et al., 1996). With more members, there are more eyes and ears to detect predators, greater opportunities to confuse predators, and a lower probability that any one individual will be captured by a predator (Chapman and Chapman, 1996a).

Diana monkeys travel lower in the canopy than red colobus monkeys, which are thought to serve as a shield against the Diana monkeys' aerial predators (Holenweg, et al., 1996). At the same time, Diana monkeys spend more time foraging on the terminal ends of branches, and may therefore serve as sentinels for terrestrial or arboreal predators that tend to prey on red colobus monkeys (Höner, et al., 1997).

One of the most serious predators on red colobus monkeys are chimpanzees, which may account for up to a third of all red colobus monkey mortality in some forests. In the Täi National Forest, the chimpanzees do most of their hunting during the rainy season when other preferred food resources in this forest are scarce (Boesch and Boesch, 1989; Boesch and Boesch-Acherman, 2000). This is also the time of year when polyspecific associations between red colobus and Diana monkeys are most common, and when red colobus monkeys take the initiative of joining up with the Diana monkeys (Noë and Bshary, 1997).

Tape recordings of chimpanzee vocalizations played back to red colobus monkeys provide strong evidence that their polyspecific associations are related to avoiding predators. Hearing chimpanzee vocalizations during the daytime led red colobus and Diana monkey groups that were over one hundred meters apart to converge into mixed-species associations. Hearing chimpanzee vocalizations when the two species were already associating with one another kept them in association longer the following morning than when no playbacks were used (Noë and Bshary, 1997). The only remaining question about the relationship between the threat of chimpanzee predators and the polyspecific associations that red colobus monkeys form is whether associating with Diana monkeys actually reduces the success rate of chimpanzees preying on red colobus (Dunbar, 1997).

Other efforts to investigate the potential benefits that polyspecific associations bring to one or more species against predators have involved comparing how much time individuals of each species spend scanning their environment when they are traveling with conspecifics versus when they are associating in a mixed-species group. In Kibale National Park, Uganda, red colobus monkeys were the only species whose vigilance rates declined in polyspecific associations. The other monkeys behaved similarly, independent of whether or not they were associating with other species, except for red-tailed monkeys, who became more vigilant in polyspecific associations (Chapman and Chapman, 1996a). The fact that it is only adult male red-tailed monkeys who increase their vigilance rates when red colobus are associating suggests that the interactions between group size and predation pressures may be more complex (Treves, 1999a) and species-specific (Treves, 1999b) than previously thought (Chapter 1).

Predator-Prey Interactions

We have seen how predatory chimpanzees can affect the behavior of their red colobus monkey prey. However, chimpanzees are neither the only predatory primates nor the only potential predators that primates must watch out for. Predators play critical roles in ecological communities through their effects on the feeding, grouping, and reproductive patterns of their prey, as we've seen. Predators can also have large impacts on the populations of their primate prey (Box 11.2).

BOX **11.2**

Chimpanzee Hunters

Primates do many things to protect themselves from predators. They tolerate feeding competition with other members of their groups or form polyspecific associations that reduce their feeding efficiency because there is safety in numbers when predators are near (Isbell, 1994; van Schaik, 1983; Terborgh and Janson, 1986). With such strong selection pressures, one would think that predator attacks on primates would be routine occurrences. Yet, for many primates studied in habitats known to support resident predators, observations of predation have typically been rare (Boesch 1991b; Cheney and Wrangham, 1987). In fact, there is evidence suggesting that the presence of researchers may inhibit unhabituated predators from striking primate prey (Isbell and Young, 1993).

No such inhibition interferes with the predatory activities of chimpanzees at Gombe National Park, Tanzania (Busse, 1978; Goodall, 1968, 1986; Teleki, 1973; Wrangham and Bergmann-Riss, 1990). From 1974–1991, one well-studied community of Gombe chimpanzees is known to have killed 744 mammals, including 577 individual monkeys (Stanford, 1998b; Stanford, et al., 1994). Red colobus monkeys accounted for over 95 percent of the monkeys that fell prey to the chimpanzees.

Chimpanzee predation on red colobus monkeys is not limited to the Gombe population (Boesch, 1996; Boesch and Boesch, 1989; Chapter 4). Nor is the frequency of Gombe chimpanzee hunting consistent across the year or from year-to-year. The Gombe chimpanzees appear to hunt more during the dry season months when their preferred fruit resources tend to be scarce. They also tend to kill more in years when there are large cohorts of males, who are the primary predators, because the success rate of their hunts increases with hunting party size (Stanford, et al., 1994). Indeed, during 1982–1992, over 50 percent of chimpanzee hunts resulted in at least one colobus killed (Stanford, 1995).

Such heavy hunting pressure takes a tremendous toll on the red colobus monkeys. Roughly 75 percent of the red colobus victims are immatures, with juveniles accounting for the bulk of them, and up to 35 percent of all red colobus mortalities can be attributed to chimpanzee predators (Stanford, et al., 1994). The result is that predation by chimpanzees has a significant effect on the red colobus monkeys' population dynamics and demography, as well as on their behavior (Stanford, 1995; Chapter 4).

Red colobus living in the main hunting areas of the Gombe chimpanzees are found in groups that are nearly half the size of those living farther away, where the risks of predation from chimpanzees are lower (Stanford, 1995). Other primates eaten by other kinds of predators make similar behavioral adjustments when necessary. South American tamarins may monitor the vicinity of their sleeping holes for up to an hour before entering them to insure that no predators are lurking nearby (Caine, 1993), and may reduce their chances of being discovered by predators by avoiding returning to the same sleeping sites on more than a few consecutive nights (Heymann, 1995). Costa Rican squirrel monkeys may even synchronize their births to reduce their vulnerability as prey, a common strategy among ungulates and other animals (Boinski, 1987a).

Despite these examples, it is difficult to measure the real predation risks most primates face because predator populations, like those of their prey, have been altered by human encroachment on their habitats (Boinski and Chapman, 1995). Even the Gombe chimpanzees, which live in an isolated forest surrounded by farmland, may be hunting more red colobus today than before because of changes in the ecological communities of both predators and prey.

Primates as Predators

Many primates that rely on insects or other invertebrates for any measurable part of their diets also prey on other animals, including snails, eggs and nestlings, and even mammals smaller than themselves (Chapter 6). In contrast to the deliberate hunting parties of some chimpanzee communities, most primates consume prey they encounter opportunistically. The savanna baboon that grabs an African hare darting across its path, or the capuchin monkey that comes across unattended eggs or nestlings while foraging along a branch are examples of such opportunistic predation.

Predation of one sort or another has been observed in all species of capuchin monkeys, but so far it has only been studied intensively in the white-faced capuchins at Santa Rosa National Park, Costa Rica (Rose, 1997, 2001). Unlike Taï chimpanzees, capuchin monkeys hunt more often during the dry season, when their favorite fruits are scarce, than during the rainy season. Male white-faced capuchin monkeys, like male chimpanzees, account for most of the mammalian prey taken. Intriguingly, these capuchin monkeys sometimes "collaborate" with one another to capture adult squirrel monkeys and coati pups (see Figure 6.8a–c). Successful kills of any large prey attract other group members, who gather to grab a piece or scrap for themselves (Figure 11.5).

Predation by primates, such as white-faced capuchin monkeys, seems to be a part of the behavioral repertories of intelligent, opportunistic foragers. In other words, the prey they consume is another form of food. Predation by chimpanzees, however, may serve an additional or entirely different function. For starters, chimpanzees hunt in parties. Hunting parties vary in size from site to site and from season to season, and the main participants are always males. Red colobus monkeys are their primary targets, and their kills are reciprocally shared.

FIGURE 11.5   Two subadult male white-faced capuchins (*Cebus capucinus*) with a magpie jay hen. Primates are both prey and, as in this photo, predators, in their communities. Photo by Katherine C. MacKinnon.

There is no doubt that the meat chimpanzees eat represents a valued dietary supplement, but if their hunting behavior was solely food-driven, they would concentrate on hunting during those times of the year when major fruit sources are scarce, as white-faced capuchin monkeys seem to do. The fact that chimpanzees hunt most often when other foods are readily available led primatologists John Mitani and David Watts (2001) to consider the social benefits of hunting and sharing meat instead.

Among the many males in the Ngogo community at Kibale National Park, Uganda, party size and composition predicted whether the chimpanzees hunted the red colobus monkeys they encountered as well as their hunting success (Mitani and Watts, 1999). Success rates were nearly twice as high as those of chimpanzees at other sites, including Gombe (Box 11.2). The Ngogo males did not engage in more hunting episodes when estrous females were around, and there was no evidence that sharing meat with females gave males any kind of mating advantages. Instead, these males seem to hunt and share meat reciprocally with one another in accord with their social alliances (Mitani and Watts, 2001).

Primates as Prey

While the Ngogo chimpanzees may hunt and exchange meat for agonistic support, their predatory behavior nonetheless takes a toll on the red colobus monkey population in this forest. Ngogo chimpanzees consume an estimated three percent of the red colobus population each year (Mitani and Watts, 1999). At other sites, such as Gombe, red colobus monkeys suffer even more. Craig Stanford (1998b) estimated that the Gombe red colobus monkey population would nearly double in size in just one decade if the chimpanzees were to suddenly cease hunting or disappear. By Stanford's calculations, some 30 percent of red colobus monkeys at Gombe die during their first six months of life, and more than half of the mortality can be attributed to predators.

Milne-Edward's sifaka also suffer high levels of predation in Ranomanfana National Park, but their main predator is a cat-like creature known as a fossa (Wright, 1995, 1998). During a nine year period, from five to seven sifaka of all age and sex classes are known or suspected to have fallen prey to the fossa. Remains of other species of diurnal lemurs have been found in fossa feces, and lemur losses due to predators tend to be higher than those of most other primates elsewhere (Wright, 1999).

Accurate accounts of the toll that predators take on primate population can be hard to obtain, especially if predators avoid habituated primates that are accompanied by human observers (Isbell and Young, 1993). The role of primates in the diets of large avian predators is somewhat easier to calculate because droppings around their nests can be monitored systematically. During one such study, involving two nests of crowned hawk-eagles at Kibale National Park, monkeys emerged as a major portion of the birds' diets. These eagles were estimated to have taken about two percent of the monkey population in the area, including one percent of the red-tailed monkeys (Mitani, et al., 2001).

Estimating the impact of predators on primate populations involves more than just numbers because, as we saw in Chapter 9, mortalities of males and females have very different effects on demography. Nonetheless, extreme predation on any age or sex class can disrupt social groups so severely that they dissolve or go extinct. Disturbances that reduce the size of a predator's hunting range can lead to concentrated hunting in whatever suitable habitat remains (Wright, 1995). In undisturbed ecological communities, however, predators contribute to the stability of their prey population sizes.

Primate-Plant Interactions

Plants represent another major component of primate ecological communities, and the interactions between primates and plants have been influential in their respective evolutionary histories. It may be more than coincidence that the diversification of primates and other groups of animals during the late Paleocene and early Eocene (Chapter 3) was contemporaneous with the diversification of the angiosperms, or flowering plants (Sussman and Raven, 1978). Primatologist Robert Sussman (1991) has proposed that the key adaptations of the earliest primates led to an enhanced ability to feed on the reproductive parts (e.g., flowers, fruits, and seeds) of these plants. He further suggests that primates (and other vertebrates, such as bats) may have played a more direct role in angiosperm evolution than is generally assumed (Chapter 3).

Primates and other animals that feed on plants can both help and hinder a plant's own reproductive success. For example, primates can destroy flowers by consuming them or damaging them while feeding on other plant parts or just by passing through a tree. But primates can also act as pollinators if, when eating nectar or passing by a flower, the flower's pollen collects on their hands, face, or fur and gets inadvertently transmitted to another flower (Figure 11.6). Likewise, primates can destroy a plant's seeds by chewing them up, along with the protective fruit surrounding them, or aid in dispersing the seeds away from the mother plant by swallowing them whole, and excreting them in their dung elsewhere in the forest. If the seeds land in an area where conditions are favorable for their germination and development, the seeds may actually be more successful than those that fall closer to their parent, where seeds are in direct competition with one another and their parents.

FIGURE 11.6 Male muriquis (*Brachyteles arachnoides*) feeding on nectar from *Mabea fistulifera*, a member of the Euphorbiaceae family. Their faces and hands become covered with the yellow pollen, which they carry as they move from flower to flower. Photo by Paulo Coutinho.

It is difficult to demonstrate that plants and primates have **coevolved,** or evolved traits as a result of a mutual interdependence on one another (Lambert and Garber, 1998). Indeed, one of the only convincing examples of coevolution between primates and plants involves lowland gorillas, which are the only animal of any kind known to disperse the seeds of the *Cola lizae* fruit in Gabon (Tutin, et al., 1991). Far more commonly, animals other than primates, including insects, birds, and bats, can be more reliable at pollinating plants and dispersing their seeds. For example, whereas birds tend to exploit juicy fruits resembling cherries, which lack thick husks, mammals, including primates, exploit both unhusked and husked fruits, which are harder to process (Janson, 1983). Thus, plants protecting their seeds from potential predators would be hard-pressed to simultaneously increase the accessibility of their seeds to potential dispersers (Chapman, 1995; Lambert and Garber, 1998).

Independent of their evolutionary effects on one another, there is no disputing the fact that primates play a vital role in perpetuating the reproduction of the plants they exploit, with important implications for both primates and plants in ecological communities. Habitat disturbances that affect the availability of plant species important to primate diets will affect primate populations. Conversely, in habitats where primates account for a large component of the frugivorous biomass, reductions in primate numbers or their local extinction can lead to reductions in the number of seedlings that grow, and therefore interfere with forest regeneration (Chapman and Chapman, 1996b; Chapman and Onderdonk, 1998).

Pollination

From the point of view of most flowers, the approach of a primate means being eaten or destroyed. Unlike nectivorous insects, birds, and bats, primates usually do more harm than good because primates are often messier and clumsier. Flower-visiting birds are generally active during the day, while bats and marsupials are generally active at night. But in places such as Madagascar, where bats and marsupials are rare, the nocturnal lemurs have the flowers more or less to themselves (Sussman and Raven, 1978).

Flowers that rely on nocturnal pollinators like bats tend to be dull in color, suspended downward, and present in small numbers at a time. They tend to have strong odors so that nocturnal visitors can locate them by smell instead of sight. By contrast, flowers that rely on diurnal, nonflying mammals have a different suite of traits. They need to be tough with long stamens so that their nectar and pollen are accessible and to grow upright on branches where they can be reached. They also need to be visually conspicuous, either in their color or by flowering at times when leafy foliage will not interfere with a pollinator's ability to detect them. There also must be many flowers in bloom at a time so that they represent a sufficiently large nutritional patch to attract the attention of potential pollinators with high energy requirements, such as primates (Janson, et al., 1981).

Many flowering plants possess these attributes, which attract primates as well as other nonflying mammals. At Manu National Park in southeastern Peru, six species of diurnal monkeys, including the tiny 100-gram pygmy marmoset and the large, seven to eight-kilogram spider monkey, as well as nocturnal owl monkeys, visit these kinds of flowers. The evidence suggesting that these primates pollinate the flowers is based on the observations that the flowers are rarely damaged when primates feed on their nectar, and that pollen accumulations are visible on the primates' facial fur as they move from tree to tree (Janson, et al., 1981). In the Brazilian Atlantic forest, at least three species of primates, including the buffy-headed marmoset, the brown capuchin monkey, and the muriqui, feed on the nectar of the same species of flower, a member of the Euphorbiaceae family (Ferrari and Strier, 1992; Torres de Assumpção, 1981). Like their Peruvian counterparts, these flowers are not damaged and the faces of the monkeys look like they've been powdered with the pale yellow pollen as they move from one flower to the next.

Nectar is nutritionally similar to fruit, whereas flowers are more similar to leaves (Ferrari and Strier, 1992; Janson, et al., 1981). Not surprisingly, nectar represents an important source of energy for primates and other frugivorous animals when fruits are seasonally scarce (Janson, et al., 1981). Among primates, it is generally the smaller-bodied species that exhibit nectivory, and therefore have opportunities to act as pollinators (Sussman and Raven, 1978; Terborgh, 1983).

The absence of reports of nectivory among catarrhine monkeys and diurnal lemurs implies that other nectivorous animals, which may include nocturnal prosimians, already fill this niche (Sussman and Raven, 1978). When they can, primates take advantage of opportunities to feed on nectar, and in the process, may act as pollinators, too.

Seed Dispersal

Most primates include at least some fruits in their diets, a practice that puts them into direct contact with seeds (Lambert and Garber, 1998). However, what different primates do with and to the seeds they encounter is highly variable. Primates masticate, drop, spit, and swallow seeds, and it is probably most appropriate to view primate–seed interactions as a continuum in which seed predation and seed dispersal represent opposite extremes (Norconk, et al., 1998).

To discourage primate and other seed predators, plants protect their seeds with toxic secondary compounds or physically resistant seed coats or fruit husks (Figure 11.7). To encourage seed dispersers, plants surround their seeds with nutritious and easy-to-access fruity flesh. Traits that insulate seeds or facilitate their dispersal by one species of animal may offer little resistance or incentive to another. For example, primates that have developed physiological mechanisms for coping with secondary plant compounds or anatomical mechanisms for breaking through physical barriers erected by plants will not be dissuaded from including seeds in their diets (Chapter 6). Conversely, primates with small mouths that can only take small bites may be incapable of swallowing large seeds that other animals, including larger primates, disperse.

Seed predators typically destroy seeds by chewing them up. Primates that eat seeds for their high nutritional content tend to do so primarily when other alternative foods, which require less detoxification, are scarce. For example, sympatric red colobus

FIGURE 11.7   Open ripe fruit of *Micrandra spruceana* (Euphorbiaceae), the most important fruit in the diet of black-headed uacaris. The fruits are protected by especially hard husks, which these monkeys can open with their specialized teeth. Large, dense clumps of these trees in the Pico da Neblina National Park, Brazil, may explain why the uacaris there can form large groups with some 70 individuals (Boubli, 1999). Photo by Jean P. Boubli.

monkeys and black-and-white colobus monkeys are both equipped to detoxify and eat seeds. However, both species also include higher proportions of seeds in their diets in forests with poor, acidic, sandy soils than in forests with richer soils where plants with higher quality foliage occur (Maisels, et al., 1994). Other primates, such as saki and bearded saki monkeys, masticate seeds in the process of eating the surrounding fruit, but if the seeds are small enough they may escape mastication and survive intact to be defecated elsewhere in the forest (Norconk, et al., 1998).

Seed predators that manipulate seeds to remove the pericarp or seed coats before ingesting them end up dropping substantial numbers of them on the ground, where they may survive to germinate (Chapman, 1995; Norconk, et al., 1998). Landing close to the parent tree, however, is rarely the ideal location for seeds to establish themselves because of high levels of competition with one another and their parents.

Seeds that get carried away from their parents by wind or animal dispersers face a different set of challenges. One benefit of long-distance dispersal is that seeds are less likely to suffer from conspecific competition. One disadvantage is that there is no telling whether or not they will land in a place with suitable soil, moisture, and light conditions for their development (Figure 11.8). Wild primates rarely carry fruits or seeds away from their feeding sites in their hands. As a result, the most common way for primates to disperse seeds is to swallow them. When and where

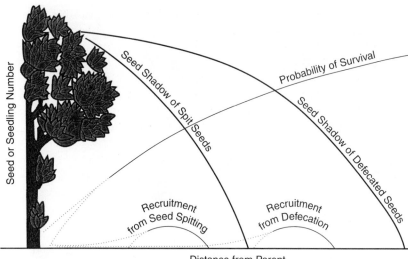

Distance from Parent

FIGURE 11.8   Hypothetical illustration of the seed shadow beneath a parent tree, the probability of seed survival, and the effects of different mechanisms of dispersal. From Chapman, C. A. 1995. Primate seed dispersal: Coevolution and conservation implications. *Evolutionary Anthropology* 4: 74–82. Copyright © 1995 Wiley-Liss, Inc. Reprinted by permission of Wiley-Liss, Inc., a division of John Wiley & Sons, Inc.

any seeds that have managed to stay intact emerge again depends on the gut passage rates and ranging patterns of the primates that swallowed them.

The Old World cercopithecine monkeys are exceptions to the more common pattern of dispersing seeds by swallowing them because cercopithecines have cheek pouches in which they can transport as much food as their stomachs can hold. Red-tailed monkeys spit out seeds they have stored in their cheeks only thirty to fifty meters from the parent tree, whereas New World monkeys without cheek pouches, like the white-faced capuchins, defecate seeds from 200 to 1,000 meters away from their source (Rowell and Mitchell, 1991). Long-tailed macaques in the Bukit Timah Nature Reserve in Singapore use different methods of expelling seeds depending on seed size. Seeds smaller than three millimeters in width are swallowed whole, while larger seeds are spit out when the fruit is being processed (Lucas and Corlett, 1998).

The success of seeds that primates drop, spit out, or swallow intact is by no means assured. A number of studies on a variety of primates indicate that seeds that pass through primate guts and emerge in their own fertilizing heap of dung have higher germination success than control seeds (e.g., Chapman, 1989; Kaplan and Moermond, 1998; Rogers, et al., 1998).

Other animals extract seeds from primate dung, either to eat themselves or to disperse secondarily. For example, roughly 90 percent of the seeds dispersed by mantled howler monkeys at Los Tuxtlas, Mexico, were destroyed by rodents or secondarily dispersed by dung beetles (Estrada and Coates-Estrada, 1991). Similarly, over 50 percent of seeds dispersed by the three sympatric monkeys at Santa Rosa National Park, Costa Rica, were removed by secondary dispersers or destroyed by seed predators within a few days (Chapman, 1989).

Among sympatric primates, one species may be a seed predator on the same species of plant that another species disperses (Gautier-Hion, et al., 1993), exerting different selection pressures on the plants. As Colin Chapman and Linda Fedigan (1990) discovered, groups of white-faced capuchin monkeys living just a few hundred kilometers apart have significantly different diets despite the similarities in fruit species available to them.

Conservation of Communities

In some tropical habitats today, primates account for as much as 25 to 40 percent of the frugivore biomass present (Chapman, 1995; Terborgh, 1983). In their capacity as frugivores, primates can play a critical role in the regeneration and maintenance of the tropical forests on which they also depend (Chapman, 1995; Terborgh, 1983; Wrangham, et al., 1994). For example, at Kibale National Park, Uganda, chimpanzees account for 1.4 percent of the primate frugivores by number, 14.2 percent of primate frugivores by biomass, and over 45 percent of the seeds primates defecate. More than 800 large seeds are defecated per square kilometer each day by the chimpanzees and other monkeys in this community (Wrangham, et al, 1994).

Forest fragments with reduced primate populations have much lower seedling densities and many fewer seedling species than forest patches with their primate communities intact (Chapman and Chapman, 1996b; Chapman and Onderdonk, 1998). Take away their fruit sources, either through direct harvesting of the trees for timber or through other forms of habitat disturbance, and primates with specialized diets will surely suffer. Eliminate the primates, or reduce their population numbers to minimal levels through hunting, and the regeneration of plant species whose seeds primates disperse will be severely compromised (Chapman and Onderdonk, 1998).

The contributions primates make to maintaining their ecological communities vary tremendously depending on each species' diets and habitat specializations. For example, frugivorous primates that range widely across habitats dispersing seeds are expected to have a greater impact on their ecosystems than largely folivorous primates with more restricted ranges. Comparisons among endangered primate communities on Madagascar and in Africa, Asia, and South America indicate that their extinctions would have different levels of impact on their ecological communities depending on the degree of each species' specialization (Jernvall and Wright, 1998). Because primates account for a higher proportion of nonflying, terrestrial mammals on Madagascar (44 percent) than elsewhere in the tropics (8 to 12 percent), the extinction of lemurs is projected to have severe effects on Malagasy ecosystems. Similarly devastating effects of primate extinctions on ecosystems are projected for the Brazilian Atlantic forest, where primates represent a large proportion of the mammalian biomass.

Clearly, primates are an integral part of their tropical communities, and conservation efforts to protect primate species diversity must take these larger ecological considerations into account.

Specialists, Generalists, and Social Responses

Niche separation among species in communities can affect the abilities of different species to adapt to or recover from environmental changes. Species with specializations for particular foods or microhabitats are most vulnerable to local disturbances that affect their narrow food or habitat requirements. Generalists, by contrast, can more easily adjust their diets or shift their ranging patterns as long as there is still some suitable habitat available nearby (Channell and Lomolino, 2000; Cowlishaw and Dunbar, 2000). In the process, however, they may displace other species that occupy the niches into which they move.

Local disturbances created by human activities, such as logging, can have long-term effects on primate communities that persist for decades after the disturbances have ceased. For example, red colobus monkey population densities in areas of Kibale National Park that had been logged declined to about one third of what they were in unlogged areas (Struhsaker, 1997). The frequency with which red colobus participated in polyspecific associations also declined, presumably because the costs of foraging in disturbed habitats outweighed the benefits of associating with other species for predator detection in undisturbed habitats. While the populations of some of the other primates in the Kibale community seem to have recovered from the effects of logging, nearly 25 years later, the red colobus population was still depressed (Mitani, et al., 2000b).

One of the most sinister examples of the long-term consequences of temporary habitat disturbances on primates comes from the Lopé Reserve in Gabon (White and Tutin, 2001). Comparisons of chimpanzee densities before and after low scale logging in different parts of the forest indicate that it can take as much as 15–25 years for their populations to recover, but here it is lethal aggression from other chimpanzees that is thought to be the cause.

Chimpanzees, like other primates, move out of an area when loggers move in. Although the loggers left chimpanzee food trees more or less alone, the noise and disruption they generated led the chimpanzees to flee, like refugees, into the ranges of neighboring communities. At first, the density of chimpanzee nests increased in the areas where the displaced communities had gone. Loud pant hooting, screaming, and drumming on tree buttresses by chimpanzees was often heard, and large groups of excited chimpanzees were often seen. Five months later, however, the number of nests, along with chimpanzee sightings and sounds, mysteriously decreased, and stayed down long after the loggers had left.

Sympatric western lowland gorillas, which feed on many of the same foods as chimpanzees in this region, also moved out when the loggers arrived. But, perhaps because gorilla groups are less territorial and more tolerant toward one another than chimpanzee communities, their populations did not show the same long-term effects from the distrubances that the chimpanzees' did.

Preserving Diversity

The diversity of an ecological community, or its **species richness,** reflects a combination of factors including the number of different species and their respective population densities, and the number of endemic species present (Cowlishaw and Dunbar, 2000; Eeley and Lawes, 1999; Reed, 1999). Recall that endemic species are those with limited biogeographical distributions, usually restricted to particular ecosystems found nowhere else in the world. Modern lemurs are endemic to Madagascar, and muriquis and lion tamarins are endemic to the Atlantic forest of Brazil. By contrast, baboons are found throughout much of Africa in a variety of ecological settings, and brown capuchin monkeys are present in at least 50 percent of all known neotropical primate communities (Peres and Janson, 1999). Primates with broad, generalized niches, like those of baboons, capuchin monkeys, and macaques, are more widespread than those with narrower, more specialized niches. Specialists are therefore more vulnerable than generalists, not only to habitat disturbances within their communities, as we've seen, but also to the risks of extinction on a global scale because of their more limited geographic and ecological distributions.

Whether you look at plants or primates, the number of endemic species that an area supports is a good indication of its species richness, and therefore of the species diversity that can be preserved if the area can be effectively protected. Using data on plant endemism and the proportion of vegetation loss that has already occurred, conservationists concerned with protecting the world's biological diversity have identified 25 **hotspots,** or regions of the world that are priorities for protection (Myers, et al., 2000). These 25 hotspots represent a small fraction of the Earth's land surfaces, yet they support 44 percent of all species of plants and 35 percent of all vertebrate species. Not surprisingly, 15 of the 25 hotspots are tropical forests, and two of the five "hottest" hotspots are Madagascar and the Atlantic forest, where primates also play pivotal roles in their ecological communities (Jernvall and Wright, 1998; Wright and Jernvall, 1999).

Identifying biodiversity hotspots is a way to prioritize the parts of the world where conservation efforts can have the greatest impact. Yet, there is no telling how these ecosystems will change with global warming, and some projections estimate that up to 18 percent of the species that hotspots support will be lost even if what still remains of them can be saved (Cowlishaw and Dunbar, 2000; Pimm and Raven, 2000).

CHAPTER

12 Conservati

The living descendants of ancestral primates evolved during millions of years of natural environmental changes. Shifting continents altered global temperatures and rainfall patterns, creating and eliminating ecological niches. The more recent Pleistocene glaciations and interglaciations, dating back nearly two million years, led tropical forests to contract and expand, confining and then extending primate habitats. Yet, in less than a century, the devastating effects of exploding human populations have brought about the greatest challenge yet for primates. Unless human activities undergo dramatic changes, there is little doubt that many primates now classified as endangered will soon become extinct, or that other threatened and vulnerable primates will follow in their footsteps (see Table 3.2). More stringent policies to protect primates and their ecological communities are clearly needed if we are to save them from extinction. For those primates whose populations have already been reduced to critically low levels, concomitant management programs will play an increasingly vital role.

The future risks of extinction of the world's threatened and endangered primates are more than an aesthetic concern. As we discussed in previous chapters, primates hold the keys to understanding and combating infectious diseases, like HIV, that plague modern humans (see Box 10.1) and play vital roles in their ecological communities (Chapter 11). With stakes as high as these, understanding the diversity of lifestyles that characterize the primate order is much more than an interesting intellectual endeavor from which insights into their behavior, and our own, can be gained.

It is almost impossible nowadays to study primates without also being simultaneously involved with their conservation. Conversely, informed conservation strategies depend on detailed knowledge of primate behavior and ecology because extinction risks vary greatly with the biology of each species. There is no single solution that applies to all endangered primates, or even to populations of a particular species subject to different natural or human-imposed disturbances. Instead, conservation efforts must be custom-tailored to specific populations if they are to have any chance of success.

Many of the details about primate populations described in previous chapters in this book have direct implications for primate conservation. From taxonomy and biogeography, to population genetics, dispersal patterns, mating systems, and diets, the more we learn about primates, the more they show us what it will take just to keep them alive. Primate behavioral ecology and conservation biology are converging disciplines at both theoretical and methodological levels (Gosling and Sutherland, 2000; Strier, 1997a). It is not surprising, therefore, that some of the most compelling questions for future generations of primatologists to pursue are those that link basic research and conservation agendas in a unified and mutually reinforcing way.

Threats to Primates

Among the forces that conspire to threaten primate futures, none has a more devastating, irreversible impact than the destruction of their habitats (Mittermeier and Cheney, 1987; Oats, 1994). Despite widespread concern about the effects of deforestation on global climate patterns and international treaties designed to prevent it, clear-cutting and burning continue to destroy significant areas of the world's remaining tropical forests (Figure 12.1). The deleterious effects of human activities compound natural climatic fluctuations, with the result of destroying, instead of altering, primate habitats (Figure 12.2).

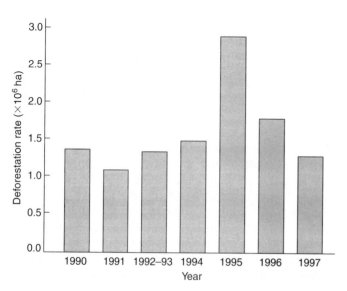

FIGURE 12.1   Rates of Amazonian deforestation. Reprinted from *Trends in Ecology and Evolution*, Volume 13, W. F. Laurence, A crisis in the making: Responses of Amazonian forests to land use and climate change, pp. 411–415, Copyright © 1998, with permission from Elsevier Science.

FIGURE 12.2   A fire, originally set to burn trash, spread into adjacent forest. Local farmers joined forces to bring the fire under control, thereby minimizing the forest it destroyed. Much greater devastation of some of the Indonesian forests that support primates like orangutans occurred when fires set to clear scrubland for cultivation spread uncontrollably. Photo by K. B. Strier.

Other threats to primate survival are more subtle, and therefore more difficult to monitor. These threats range from selective logging, in which particularly valuable trees are removed (Figure 12.3), to hunting pressures, which increase as development or logging operations make remote areas more accessible. Activities involving the capture of wild primates for biomedical research or zoological exhibitions are rare nowadays thanks to captive breeding initiatives and stringent international regulations on the importation of primates. However, some populations that were subjected to intensive harvesting for these purposes in the past have not yet recovered and may never do so without direct intervention (Figure 12.4).

Habitat Disturbances

Both the fragmentation of continuous forest into isolated pockets and selective logging operations affect primate populations and the forests that support them in both predictable and unanticipated ways (Figure 12.5). For example, despite the genetic risks of inbreeding depression in small, isolated populations (Chapter 4), some primates compressed into small forest fragments actually experience increases in population growth because their natural predators have disappeared or have been eliminated.

Selective, low-intensity logging has even more variable effects on primate populations (Johns, 1992; Johns and Skorupa, 1987; Moraes, et al., 1998; Pinto, et al.,

FIGURE 12.3 The lumber from a large tropical hardwood tree, such as the one shown here, can be worth tens of thousands of dollars. The selective logging of such valuable trees creates huge gaps in the forest's canopy where secondary vegetation can grow. With enough time, the open patch can theoretically regenerate, but replacing a tree like this one can take hundreds of years, and requires that sufficient seeds of the species are available and survive. Photo by K. B. Strier.

FIGURE 12.4 Rhesus macaques (*Macaca mulatta*) were heavily imported into the United States from India for biomedical research, and contributed to important medical discoveries such as the Salk polio vaccine. When surveys demonstrated that wild populations were locally threatened, greater regulation on exportation was imposed. Photo by Jim Moore/Anthro Photo.

1993; Struhsaker, 1997; Wilson and Wilson, 1975). For instance, Sulawesi crested black macaques living in logged forests occur at lower densities than those living in undisturbed, primary forests (Rosenbaum, et al., 1998). Densities of specialized African frugivores also decline in disturbed forests, whereas those of folivores are actually higher in mildly disturbed forests than undisturbed ones (Oates, 1996).

FIGURE 12.5   Most of the Atlantic forest of southeastern Brazil, the only part of the world where primates like muriquis and golden lion tamarins occur, has been cleared for agriculture and ranching purposes. Many of the remaining forest fragments, like those shown here, are too small and disturbed to support primates anymore. Photo by K. B. Strier.

Logging operations that are limited to particular tree species may have little or no impact on primates if these tree species are not important components in their diets. Moreover, selective logging creates gaps in the canopy where heterogeneous vegetation can grow. Early successional growth, which includes leaves with high protein-to-fiber ratios, can provide higher quality or more diverse food options to opportunistic primates that have evolved generalist feeding strategies than mature, unlogged forest, with its more homogeneous composition and correspondingly lower primate densities (Ganzhorn, 1995). In fact, some Indonesian forests that have been selectively logged contain high levels of tree species diversity, and are therefore important areas to protect for their primate inhabitants (Cannon, et al., 1998; Chazdon, 1998). In the dry deciduous forests of western Madagascar, low-intensity logging, which removed less than 10 percent of the forest cover, led to higher fruit productivity and leaf quality (as measured by protein-to-fiber ratios). An increase in lemur sightings in these areas was attributed, in part, to the greater productivity of their foods (Ganzhorn, 1995; Ganzhorn, et al., 1999).

Hunting Pressures

Hunting pressures on primates also vary by region and affect primate species to different degrees. Orangutans, for example, are not eaten by indigenous people because they are considered so similar to humans (Galdikas, 1995b). Local taboos against hunting primates also offer some protection to less humanlike monkeys, such as a few populations of the critically endangered Nigerian Sclater's guenon (Oates, et al., 1992), but these taboos can be violated if the need for meat is high and not all populations are protected by taboos (Figure 12.6). In many parts of the world, primates ranging from chimpanzees to spider monkeys are hunted for their meat, skins, or purported medicinal properties (Mittermeier, 1987). On top of these local pressures is the international demand for trophy species, such as mountain gorillas (Fossey, 1983), which continue to bring high prices in the illegal wildlife trade.

Hunting is thought to pose a greater threat than habitat disturbances for folivorous primates (Figure 12.7), which also tend to be large in body size, and therefore particularly prized by hunters for their meat (Oates, 1996). By one calculation, a single family of rubber tappers in the Brazilian Amazon killed nearly 500 large primates, including woolly monkeys, spider monkeys, and howler monkeys in less than two years (Peres, 1990). At local markets in the interior of Surinam, 25 percent of the available meat may come from primates (Mittermeier and Cheney, 1987). In Gabon and other parts of Africa, red colobus are particularly vulnerable to hunting because not only are they larger than most sympatric monkeys, but also because their large, noisy groups in the upper levels of the canopy make them comparatively easy targets for human hunters (Oates, 1994). Great apes, such as chimpanzees and gorillas, also have slow reproductive rates, so even moderate hunting can

FIGURE 12.6   An endangered Sclater's guenon (*Cercopithecus sclateri*), victim of a hunter. Photo by John F. Oates.

FIGURE 12.7   A Yanomami Indian holding a smoked howler monkey. Hunting pressures are increasing as the people shift from their traditional nomadic ways of life to become more sedentary. Photo by Jean P. Boubli.

cause a steady reduction in population sizes whenever annual losses fall below replacement levels (Harcourt, et al., 1989).

Hunting persists in many parts of the world despite laws that prohibit it and the enforcement of steep penalties against perpetrators unlucky enough to be caught. Hunters periodically make forays into protected parks in the Brazilian Atlantic forest, where endangered primates, including muriquis, have been found among their victims. Hunting pressures have also increased in areas of West Africa and Malaysia where logging operations are underway (Bennett, 1991; Wilkie, et al., 1992). First, there is increased demand from the workers for meat, which is acquired by hiring local hunters to provide it (Johns and Skorupa, 1987; Oates, 1996). Second, logging roads make remote forests more accessible to hunters seeking meat to sell in local markets. In central and West African **bushmeat** markets, prices range from the equivalent of $5 for small monkey carcasses such as guenons, to $20 for chimpanzees, to $40 for gorillas (McRae, 1997) to $10 for two gorilla arms (McNeil, 1999).

The effects of the bushmeat market on wild populations of primates and other animals are similar to the effects that guns and expanding human populations had on North American buffalo populations (Figure 12.8). Traditional hunters had minimal, if any impact on the buffalo, but when hunting techniques changed and human demand for meat and hides rose, the buffaloes were nearly exterminated.

Primate behavioral responses to new or intensified hunting pressures can be rapid. For example, within a decade of widespread use of shotguns, guenons in the Conkouati Reserve, Congo, shifted from their usual response of fleeing through the

FIGURE 12.8   Guenons (*Cercopithecus erythrotis*) and (*C. preussi*) in the bushmeat market in Malabo, Bioko Island. Photo by John F. Oates.

canopy in the presence of terrestrial predators, to dropping to the ground to hide in the dense undergrowth (Tutin and White, 1999). Nonetheless, the slow reproductive rates of most primates make it difficult for their populations to recover if human hunting pressure are persistent and severe.

Conservation Policies

Efforts to protect remaining primate populations and their habitats require cooperation at all levels of society, from local people living in or near nonhuman primate communities, to regional, national, and international governments (Figure 12.9). Yet, conservation interests, commitments, and compliance levels are often widely disparate among and within these groups, particularly when individual livelihoods and economic or political gains or losses are involved.

Economic Incentives

There is widespread agreement that local participation is a necessary condition for conservation efforts of any kind to succeed, but strategies for how to most effectively recruit the local people who live in proximity to wild primate populations into conservation causes vary widely. Some conservationists argue that it is necessary to make forests and their inhabitants, including the primates, economically profitable to the local people. Profits and conservation can potentially be reconciled through **sustainable forest management,** which involves the use of the forest or

FIGURE 12.9 Hanuman langurs (*Presbytis entellus* or *Semnopithecus entellus*) are one of the few primates that are commensal with humans, who regard these monkeys as sacred and leave food for them at temples. Photo by Jim Moore/Anthro-Photo.

forest products in a way that either avoids overexploitation or replaces what is taken through planting. However, recent analyses of such so-called sustainable use projects indicate that most are doomed to fail because they cost much more to implement and maintain than they can expect to earn back in profits. One such project in Bolivia cost nearly $20 million to implement, a huge sum to invest considering that one-time, unsustainable logging yields profits up to 450 percent higher than those predicted for sustainable logging operations (Bowles, et al., 1998a, b).

Eco-tourism, which can theoretically bring in large sums of money, has worked in the short-term for some charismatic primates, such as mountain gorillas, particularly in accessible habitats where study groups have been habituated by researchers. However, tourism is an unreliable source of long-term revenue because the tourist industry is determined as much by economic and political upheavals as by conservation objectives. Armed conflicts in Rwanda, Sierra Leone, and Liberia have made primate conservation sites, like the mountain gorilla sanctuary in the Virunga Volcanos of Rwanda, inaccessible to tourists and conservation groups alike (Oates, 1996). These conflicts, like the Colombian drug wars, Brazilian inflation levels, or terrorist bombings, are not aimed at primates, but their effect on deterring tourism can undermine conservation programs dependent on tourist income. Even in politically safe regions, tourism brings people, who can transmit infectious diseases to primates whose immune systems are unable to cope (Wallis and Lee, 1999).

Some conservationists argue that the only solution to protecting primates and their habitats is to set aside large blocks of protected lands and enforce hunting prohibitions (e.g., Bowles, et al., 1998a; Oates, 1994). Doing so requires the countries inhabited by primates to voluntarily forego potential profits from foreign logging, ranching, and other development enterprises, sacrificing their own economic gains in the process. International incentives have been made in the form of debt-for-nature swaps, but only in countries, such as Costa Rica, that are deemed to be politically stable. Even then, commitments to protecting forests rarely include sufficient funds to defray the costs of hunting enforcement or conservation education programs. Recent assessments of conservation efforts in 93 protected areas in 22 tropical countries are promising, as long as restrictions on human impacts can be enforced and local communities can be compensated (Bruner, et al., 2001). This requires careful management and funding, especially in and around the biodiversity hotspots (Chapter 11) where human population densities are high and still growing (Cincotta, et al., 2000).

Increasing Public Awareness

Despite the economic and political obstacles, efforts to conserve primates and their habitats have continued to grow. In fact, there is no evidence that any primate taxon went extinct during the twentieth century (Mittermeier and Konstant, 1996/97) although the prospects for at least one, known as Miss Waldron's red colobus, are looking increasingly grim (Mittermeier, et al., 1999, 2000). Education programs have increased local and international awareness about conservation issues, and have stimulated research interest and provided training opportunities for the next generation of conservation leaders in primate habitat countries (Lippold, 1995, 1999).

Educational campaigns require that great care be taken to avoid misinterpretations of the conservation message. For example, the recent discovery that HIV-1 originated in central African chimpanzees and spread to humans through **zoonoses,** or inter-species transmission, has reinvigorated long-standing concerns over the hunting of chimpanzees for food (Gao, et al., 1999). Educating people about the medical hazards of eating chimpanzee meat could have a positive effect on populations by reducing hunting pressures, but there is also the danger that fears of infection could stimulate intensive slaughtering campaigns to eliminate the hazard (Weiss and Wrangham, 1999).

Similarly, evidence that some primates survive, and even appear to thrive, in forests that have undergone low-intensity logging can be misrepresented in the popular media. Most of us interpret the practical significance of these scientific findings as concrete reinforcement for the value of protecting all remaining primate habitats, including those that have been disturbed. However, they have also been used to make misguided declarations about the acceptability and, more incredibly, the beneficial consequences, of cutting trees in tropical forests.

Nongovernmental Organizations

The establishment of **nongovernmental organizations,** known simply as **NGOs,** serve important roles as mediators between international and national funding sources, policymakers, researchers, and the primates themselves (Box 12.1).

BOX **12.1**

The Primates' People

Every field has its heroes, those men and women whose dedication, hard work, and skills at motivating others result in long-lasting contributions with far-reaching consequences. In the world of primate conservation, there are many such people who have made life-long commitments to promoting primate survival. The majority of them persevere quietly behind the scenes, and often under difficult conditions, to keep primates and their habitats from being destroyed. Their names are known locally in the regions where they work and often also in the scientific literature. In fact, the authors of the references cited in this book and the photographers whose work illustrates it are among the heroes of primatology.

A notable few have gained more widespread fame, as much for their own scientific accomplishments as for their effectiveness at bringing the plights of endangered primates into the public domain. One of these prominent "primate people" is Russell Mittermeier, president of the NGO, Conservation International, or CI, which is based in Washington, D.C., and chair of the International Union for the Conservation of Nature and Species Survival Commission's (IUCN/SSC) Primate Specialist Group. Trained as an anthropologist, Mittermeier established his scientific credentials with his doctoral dissertation on the primates of Suriname. But instead of specializing on a single species or region of the world, he took on the more general challenge of becoming one of the leaders in the global primate conservation campaign.

Nowadays, it is hard to find primatologists anywhere in the world whose work with endangered species has not brought them some form of contact with Mittermeier or his associates. Some pioneers in the primate conservation movement were already hard at work before Mittermeier joined the scene, but many of us owe our introductions to endangered primates to him and the groundwork for collaborations he has helped to lay.

Mittermeier is responsible for introducing me to muriquis, and to the many Brazilian primatologists and conservationists who have been my guides, field companions, and lifelong friends. Collaborations between CI and Brazilian conservationists were successful in creating the Biological Station of Caratinga, the field site at which I work, and for negotiating its recent transformation from a privately-owned forest to a full-fledged protected reserve. Now recognized by the Brazilian government, the Biological Station of Caratinga is a sanctuary for one of the largest, most viable populations of muriquis currently known, along with three other species of primates, including two others, the brown howler monkey and the buffy-headed marmoset, that, along with muriquis, are endemic to the Atlantic forest.

Saving this site was a major accomplishment for conservation. It is also a testimony to the power of international collaborations among NGOs, individuals like Mittermeier and his Brazilian counterparts, and researchers. One of the best ways to find out about who is working on what species and where is to look at the Primate Information Net, or PIN website, at www.primate.wisc.edu/pin/index.html. Listings of primatologists and their affiliations, primate research and educational opportunities, and conservation activities around the world can be found at this site.

NGOs sponsor opportunities for basic researchers and policymakers to interact. For example, the Conservation Breeding Specialist Group (CBSG) of the International Union for the Conservation of Nature (IUCN) conducts Population and Habitat Viability Assessment workshops, or PHVAs, on behalf of endangered and threatened primate species, including orangutans, golden lion tamarins, and, more recently, muriquis (e.g., Rylands, et al., 1998). One of the most constructive features of these workshops is that they include among their participants researchers, conservationists, and policymakers from those countries in which primates and their habitats represent natural resources.

Another critical component of these workshops is the pooling of information about endangered primates from every available source. Inevitably, large gaps in our knowledge emerge, even among the best-studied of the endangered primates. Identifying these gaps in knowledge serves the crucial function of establishing research priorities to address questions that must be resolved before informed conservation plans can be developed. In these workshops, and throughout the conservation community, the vital role of basic research to the future of primates is invariably acknowledged (Figure 12.10).

Noninvasive Research

Tremendous advances have been made in our understanding of primate behavioral diversity over the past half century. As with any field of knowledge, new discoveries about primates have raised new questions, which we can now begin to address with newly available techniques. Nonetheless, there are still many primates for which even the most basic behavioral and ecological information has yet to be

FIGURE 12.10 Some of the many dedicated Brazilian students who have worked with me on the muriqui project. They, like their contemporaries in other countries throughout the world, represent the future hope for the world's endangered primates. From left to right: Cristiane Coelho, Luiz Dias, and Claudio P. Nogueira. Photo by K. B. Strier.

obtained. Some of these neglected primates are highly endangered, others are more common, but have eluded scientific scrutiny. Still other primates are known from single populations or single study groups, which, however intensively they are studied, can provide only a glimpse into the range of variation that may exist within their species. Think about how biased our perceptions on chimpanzee or orangutan tool use and other local social traditions would be if only a single population had been studied. Then, consider the cultural traditions, and enormous behavioral diversity, that will be lost if any of these or other primate populations go extinct.

Theoretical developments have helped situate what we now know about primates into broader, more comparative perspectives than were previously possible when data from only a handful of species were available to contrast (Strier, 1994a). The replacement of descriptive, anecdotal ethnographies of primate behavior with systematic behavioral and ecological sampling methods to test evolutionary hypotheses represented one of the first of these major leaps, but in recent years primate studies have moved in other productive directions as well. For example, the widespread inclusion of proximate, ontogenetic, and phylogenetic approaches has begun to provide insights into how physiological mechanisms, developmental patterns, and evolutionary history affect primate behavioral adaptations. Moreover, the increase in the number of long-term studies, in which the life histories of individuals, groups, and, in some cases, populations have been monitored, are contributing to the growing recognition that both predictable and unpredictable demographic events can have profound effects on primate behavior (Altmann and Altmann, 1979; Dunbar, 1979; Moore, 1992a, 1999; Strier, 1999c).

Like the historical processes that have shaped primate studies, identifying future research priorities for primates is a highly subjective endeavor. It is unlikely that any two primatologists would produce identical lists, but most would agree that areas in which basic research can make its most direct contributions to primate conservation deserve special consideration. The conservation significance of many of these research areas has been mentioned in earlier chapters of this book. For example, understanding species diversity and past and present distributions plays a critical role in identifying conservation priorities (Chapter 3), while understanding how evolutionary processes such as gene flow and inbreeding operate in small populations (Chapter 4) helps us to estimate population viabilities and extinction risks. Similarly, insights into primate cognition have fueled concerns about the well-being of captive primates (Chapter 10), while knowledge about primate interactions within their communities provides a basis for assessing the broader ecological impacts of declining populations (Chapter 11).

Despite these advances, some important questions in primate behavioral ecology have been difficult to pursue. For example, until recently, information about the historical habitats of primates was restricted to what could be gleaned from the often vague locality references attached to museum specimens or to what primates local people remember having seen or heard about from others. Now, however, advances in the application of stable isotope analyses make it possible to distinguish between foods eaten by primates in open versus closed forest canopies. These analyses use hair samples obtained from a variety of primates ranging from galagos, to spider monkeys, to chimpanzees (Schoeninger, et al., 1997, 1998, 1999). Because these data can be derived from hair, there is now the potential to decipher what kinds of diets, in what kinds of habitats, primates represented in museum collections ate when they were alive. Comparing these data with living populations of the same species can provide insights into ways in which primate diets and their habitats have changed.

The development of noninvasive methods is also revolutionizing investigations into the reproductive biology of wild primates and the genetic composition of their populations. In the past, the only way to obtain these data from wild primates required the use of invasive methods to take blood samples. Nowadays, the development of noninvasive techniques for obtaining genetic and hormonal data from both captive and wild primates make it possible to obtain answers to some of the most fundamental questions about reproduction and genetics in primate behavioral ecology that also have tremendous conservation significance.

Reproductive Biology

Throughout this book, we have seen the importance of reproduction to understanding primate behavior. Yet, even the most basic questions about primate reproductive biology, such as gestation lengths, can be elusive without successive hormone samples from the same individuals to distinguish between the phases of the ovulatory cycle and conception cycles (Figure 12.11). Extrapolating gestation lengths from observations of mating and subsequent births is highly unreliable because many primates copulate at times when the probability of conception is low and because even under the most ideal observation conditions it is impossible to be certain that all copulations have been witnessed.

Traditional approaches to measuring primate hormone levels required capturing the primates to obtain blood samples, which still provide the most reliable indicators of hormone levels circulating at the time they are taken. But blood samples cannot be collected from wild subjects with sufficient regularity to construct profiles of the ways in which hormone levels fluctuate in response to ecological, social, and reproductive conditions. Additionally, many researchers are reluctant to use such invasive methods out of concern for the animals and for the potential impact that repetitive captures could have on the same behaviors that are being studied.

This dilemma has been solved now that techniques to measure both female and male steroid levels in wild primates from their urine (e.g., Andelman, 1986; Knott, 1998; Robbins and Czekala, 1997) and feces (e.g., Brockman, 1999; Brockman and Whitten, 1996; Brockman, et al., 1995, 1998; Campbell, et al., 2001; Strier and Ziegler, 1994, 1997, 2000; Strier, et al., 1999; Wasser, et al., 1988, 1991) have been developed. These noninvasive methods are opening new paths to exploring the endocrinological correlates of reproduction and stress in wild primates. Fecal steroid assays, in particular, are rapidly becoming a standard component of many field studies because many arboreal primates live in social groups that make it unfeasible to collect urine samples from specific individuals (Figure 12.12).

Fecal steroids must be calibrated with serum or urinary steroids because it can take longer for hormones to be excreted into feces (Heistermann, et al., 1993; Pryce,

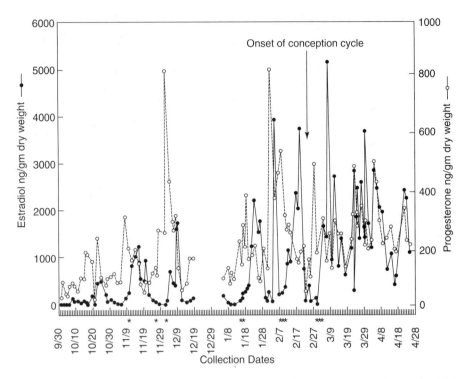

FIGURE 12.11   Hormonal profile from a wild female muriqui (*Brachyteles arachnoides*) showing ovarian cycling, the onset of the conception cycle, and days on which copulations were observed (asterisks right above dates). The profile was developed from analyses of steroid levels measured in feces collected on a near-daily basis (except during the brief gap shown) by following the female throughout the forest until she defecated during the course of her normal activities. From Strier, K. B. and Ziegler, T. E., 1997. Behavioral and endocrine characteristics of the reproductive cycle in wild muriqui monkeys, *Brachyteles arachnoides*. *American Journal of Primatology* 42: 299–310. Copyright © 1997 Wiley-Liss, Inc. Reprinted by permission of Wiley-Liss, Inc., a division of John Wiley & Sons, Inc.

et al., 1994; Shideler, et al., 1993; Wasser, et al., 1988; Ziegler, et al., 1997), but these calibrations can be done with captive subjects and then applied more widely to a larger sample of individuals in the wild. Different species exhibit different lag times for different hormones, so it is necessary to discover what these times are before attempting to integrate fecal steroid and behavioral data.

Fecal steroid levels may also undergo large fluctuations during the course of a day, so diurnal variation in their levels must be documented to determine the most appropriate collection times (Sousa and Ziegler, 1998). In addition, preservation procedures need to be established so that the hormones of interest don't deteriorate during the interval between when the samples are collected and analyzed. And, of course, appropriate permits for transporting fecal samples must be obtained from the countries in which the collections are made and the samples are analyzed.

FIGURE 12.12 An example of dung from a wild muriqui (*Brachyteles arachnoides*) collected for subsequent fecal steroid analyses. This sample was obtained during the dry season, when muriquis feed mainly on leaves. Photo by K. B. Strier.

Working out the various details for fecal hormone studies takes time, energy, and funding. But these are worthwhile investments to make considering the insights to be gained from hormonal data. Monitoring the complex interactions among individual life histories, diets, social relationships, and reproductive strategies is particularly important for endangered primates whose fertility may be compromised by habitat disturbances or small population sizes.

From Paternity to Population Genetics

Evaluating questions ranging from the genetic composition of wild primate populations to paternity requires access to cells containing individual DNA (Ashley, 1999). Collecting this material from most primates has traditionally involved tranquilizing primates to obtain blood or tissue samples. Some of the smaller-bodied primates, like callitrichids and galagos are fairly easy to entice into cages with food (see Figure 5.7), and the terrestriality of primates like baboons facilitates their periodic capture for long-term monitoring (see Figure B3.2). For most primates, however, obtaining the samples necessary for group or populationwide genetic analyses has been problematic.

Now, however, advances in the development of noninvasive techniques for obtaining DNA from wild primates are yielding results. Hair samples collected from chimpanzee nests (Figure 12.13) have provided the genetic data needed to evaluate questions about paternity, the fitness consequences of chimpanzee behavior, and population variability, and the evolutionary relatedness among populations

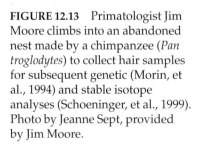

FIGURE 12.13   Primatologist Jim Moore climbs into an abandoned nest made by a chimpanzee (*Pan troglodytes*) to collect hair samples for subsequent genetic (Morin, et al., 1994) and stable isotope analyses (Schoeninger, et al., 1999). Photo by Jeanne Sept, provided by Jim Moore.

and their current viability (Constable, et al., 2001; Inagaki and Tsukahara, 1993; Morin and Woodruff, 1992; Morin, et al., 1994; Takasaki and Takenaka, 1991; Vigilant, et al., 2001). And, because few primates other than the great apes construct nests, investigators are also making promising advances in extracting DNA from cheek cells, which adhere to the chewed-up food primates drop, and from intestinal cells, which are excreted in their feces (Launhardt, et al., 2001; Takenaka, et al., 1993; Takasaki and Takenaka, 1991).

Developing noninvasive techniques for extracting DNA, like those for extracting hormones, requires significant expertise and expense (Kohn and Wayne, 1997; Taberlet, et al., 1999). Genetic primers must be identified so that the primate DNA can be distinguished from the DNA of the plants, insects, or other animal matter that has been ingested. The quantity of DNA in extracts must be carefully evaluated (Morin, et al., 2001; Vigilant, et al., 2001). In contrast to hormone studies, not all primates are suited to all types of genetic investigations (Melnick and Hoelzer, 1992). For example, paternity studies may be difficult to conduct in primate populations with low levels of genetic variability (Martin, 1992; Martin, et al., 1992; Rogers, 1992), and at least some colobines have such low genetic variability that the possibilities for discriminating paternity are limited (Turner, et al., 1992). Callitrichid twins share the same placenta, which can confound identifying their individual DNA for paternity studies (Anzenberger, 1992; Dixson, et al., 1992) although maternal genetic studies can still be done (Nievergelt, et al., 2000).

Obtaining genetic data will not resolve all of our questions about how to best manage endangered primate populations to ensure their viability because it is difficult to distinguish differences in the extent of genetic variability due to historical, phylogenetic factors, more recent effects associated with the isolation of small populations, or the mating and dispersal patterns of the primates (Pope, 1996). Nonetheless, comparative genetic studies can help to identify populations in which the loss of heterozygosity has put them at such high risks of extinction that interventions, such as the reintroductions underway for the golden lion tamarins in south-eastern Brazil (see Box 10.1), might make sense.

The Next Millennium

Basic research on primates, like primate conservation efforts, cannot be decoupled from the constraints imposed by economic realities. It costs money to conduct even the most basic surveys and observational studies. These costs escalate dramatically when state-of-the-art laboratory components are added to analyze the genetic or hormonal data so urgently needed for evaluating the status of endangered populations. Typically, the funds to cover these costs come from competitive grants administered by governmental agencies, such as the U.S. National Science Foundation (NSF), and NGOs, zoos, and professional societies, which raise money from their donors and members. But, even with increases in federal research spending and new commitments from NGOs, financial support is always in short supply compared to the need for funds from primate researchers and conservationists.

Despite these constraints, scientific and public interest in primates continues to grow. With this growing interest has come greater concern for and commitment to studying primates and ensuring their future survival. The Great Ape Conservation Act of 2000, which authorizes $5 million annually toward ape conservation, is an example of the kind of commitment that wealthy countries will need to make for other primates as well.

There is little doubt that the next generation of primatologists will inherit the tragic legacy of living through the extinction of some of the world's most endangered primates, whose plights were recognized too late to save them (Figure 12.14). But primatologists of the 21st century will also inherit the urgent and incredibly exciting challenge of learning more about the vast diversity of adaptations that characterize other primates, whose continued survival holds the clues to understanding our own.

FIGURE 12.14   Sclater's guenons (*Cerecopithecus sclateri*), the most endangered of Africa's guenons (Oates, et al., 1992). Photo by © Noel Rowe/Pictorial Guide to Living Primates.

A P P E N D I X : Primate Names

The tables in this appendix are divided into the Prosimians, New World Monkeys, Old World Monkeys, and Apes. The common names of groups and the genus and species names are compiled from Nowak (2000); some common names are from Rowe (1996). Some of the major discrepancies between these sources are noted. Details on controversial taxonomies can be found in these sources, and the references therein.

Prosimians

Common Name of Group	Common Name (Notes)	Genus	Species
golden potto or angwantibo	golden potto or angwantibo (1)	*Arctocebus*	*aureus*
	potto or angwantibo	*Arctocebus*	*calibarensis*
slender loris	slender loris	*Loris*	*tardigradus*
slow loris	slow loris	*Nycticebus*	*coucang*
	pygmy loris	*Nycticebus*	*pygmaeus*
potto	potto	*Perodicticus*	*potto*
needle-clawed bush baby	southern needle-clawed bush baby	*Euoticus*	*elegantulus*
	northern needle-clawed bush baby	*Euoticus*	*pallidus*
	Matschie's (or needle-clawed) bush baby (2)	*Euoticus*	*matschiei*
lesser bush baby	Somalia bush baby	*Galago*	*gallarum*
	southern lesser bush baby	*Galago*	*moholi*
	northern lesser bush baby	*Galago*	*senegalensis*
dwarf galago	Allen's bush baby	*Galagoides*	*alleni*
	Demidoff's bush baby	*Galagoides*	*demidoff*
	Thomas's bush baby	*Galagoides*	*thomasi*
	Zanzibar bush baby	*Galagoides*	*zanzibaricus*
greater bush baby	thick-tailed greater bush baby	*Otolemur*	*crassicaudatus*
	Garnett's greater bush baby	*Otolemur*	*garnettii*
hairy-eared dwarf lemur	hairy-eared dwarf lemur	*Allocebus*	*trichotis*
dwarf lemur	greater dwarf lemur	*Cheirogaleus*	*major*
	fat-tailed dwarf lemur	*Cheirogaleus*	*medius*
Coquerel's dwarf lemur	Coquerel's dwarf lemur	*Mirza*	*coquereli*

Prosimians *(continued)*

Common Name of Group	Common Name (Notes)	Genus	Species
mouse lemur	gray mouse lemur	*Microcebus*	*murinus*
	pygmy mouse lemur	*Microcebus*	*myoxinus*
	brown mouse lemur	*Microcebus*	*rufus*
fork-marked dwarf lemur	fork-marked lemur	*Phaner*	*furcifer*
sportive or weasel lemur	gray-backed sportive lemur	*Lepilemur*	*dorsalis*
	Milne-Edwards' sportive lemur	*Lepilemur*	*edwardsi*
	white-footed sportive lemur	*Lepilemur*	*leucopus*
	small-toothed sportive lemur	*Lepilemur*	*microdon*
	weasel sportive lemur	*Lepilemur*	*mustelinus*
	red-tailed sportive lemur	*Lepilemur*	*ruficaudatus*
	northern sportive lemur	*Lepilemur*	*septentrionalis*
ring-tailed lemur	ring-tailed lemur	*Lemur*	*catta*
lemur	crowned lemur	*Eulemur*	*coronatus*
	brown lemur	*Eulemur*	*fulvus*
	black lemur	*Eulemur*	*macaco*
	mongoose lemur	*Eulemur*	*mongoz*
	red-bellied lemur	*Eulemur*	*rubriventer*
variegated or ruffed lemur	ruffed lemur	*Varecia*	*variegata*
bamboo (or gentle) lemur	golden bamboo lemur	*Hapalemur*	*aureus*
	lesser bamboo lemur	*Hapalemur*	*griseus*
	greater bamboo lemur	*Hapalemur*	*simus*
avahi or woolly lemur	woolly lemur	*Avahi*	*laniger*
sifaka	diademed sifaka	*Propithecus*	*diadema*
	golden-crowned sifaka	*Propithecus*	*tattersalli*
	Verreaux's sifaka	*Propithecus*	*verreauxi*
indri	indri	*Indri*	*indri*
aye-aye	aye-aye	*Daubentonia*	*madagascariensis*
tarsier	western tarsier	*Tarsius*	*bancanus*
	Dian's tarsier	*Tarsius*	*dianae*
	pygmy tarsier	*Tarsius*	*pumilus*
	spectral tarsier	*Tarsius*	*spectrum*
	Philippine tarsier	*Tarsius*	*syrichta*

Notes:
1. Some recognize a single species, *A.calibarensis*
2. Some include in genus Galago

New World Monkeys

Common Name of Group	Common Name (Notes)	Genus	Species
Goeldi's monkey	Goeldi's monkey	*Callimico*	*goeldii*
marmoset	bare-ear marmoset	*Callithrix*	*argentata*
	buffy tufted-eared marmoset	*Callithrix*	*aurita*
	buffy-headed marmoset	*Callithrix*	*flaviceps*
	Geoffroy's tufted-ear marmoset	*Callithrix*	*geoffroyi*
	tassel-eared marmoset	*Callithrix*	*humeralifer*
	common marmoset	*Callithrix*	*jacchus*
	Wied's tufted-eared marmoset	*Callithrix*	*kuhli*
	Maues marmosest	*Callithrix*	*mauesi*
	black-headed marmoset	*Callithrix*	*nigriceps*
	black tufted-eared marmoset	*Callithrix*	*penicillata*
	newly recognized	*Callithrix*	*chrysoleuca*
	newly recognized	*Callithrix*	*emiliae*
	newly recognized	*Callithrix*	*intermedia*
	newly recognized	*Callithrix*	*leucippe*
	newly recognized	*Callithrix*	*marcai*
	newly recognized	*Callithrix*	*melanura*
	newly recognized	*Callithrix*	*satarei*
pygmy marmoset	pygmy marmoset	*Cebuella*	*pygmaea*
tamarin	bare-faced tamarin	*Saguinus*	*bicolor*
	saddleback tamarin	*Saguinus*	*fuscicollis*
	red-crested tamarin	*Saguinus*	*geoffroyi*
	emperor tamarin	*Saguinus*	*imperator*
	mottled-faced tamarin	*Saguinus*	*inustus*
	red-bellied tamarin	*Saguinus*	*labiatus*
	silvery-brown bare-faced tamarin	*Saguinus*	*leucopus*
	golden-handed tamarin	*Saguinus*	*midas*
	mustached tamarin	*Saguinus*	*mystax*
	Spix's black-mantled tamarin	*Saguinus*	*nigricollis*
	cotton-top tamarin	*Saguinus*	*oedipus*
	golden-mantled saddleback tamarin	*Saguinus*	*tripartitus*
lion tamarin	black-faced lion tamarin	*Leontopithecus*	*caissara*
	golden-headed lion tamarin	*Leontopithecus*	*chrysomelas*
	black lion tamarin	*Leontopithecus*	*chrysopygus*
	golden lion tamarin	*Leontopithecus*	*rosalia*
night or owl monkey	southern red-necked night monkey (1)	*Aotus*	*nigriceps*
	northern gray-necked owl monkey (1)	*Aotus*	*trivirgatus*

New World Monkeys *(continued)*

Common Name of Group	Common Name (Notes)	Genus	Species
titi monkey	brown titi monkey	*Callicebus*	*brunneus*
	chestnut-bellied titi monkey	*Callicebus*	*caligatus*
	ashy titi monkey	*Callicebus*	*cinerascens*
	red titi monkey	*Callicebus*	*cupreus*
	Bolivian gray titi monkey	*Callicebus*	*donacophilus*
	titi monkey	*Callicebus*	*dubius*
	Hoffmann's titi monkey	*Callicebus*	*hoffmannsi*
	titi monkey	*Callicebus*	*modestus*
	dusky titi monkey	*Callicebus*	*moloch*
	Andean titi monkey	*Callicebus*	*oenanthe*
	Beni titi monkey	*Callicebus*	*olallae*
	masked titi monkey	*Callicebus*	*personatus*
	collared titi monkey	*Callicebus*	*torquatus*
capuchin monkey	white-fronted capuchin monkey	*Cebus*	*albifrons*
	brown (or tufted) capuchin monkey	*Cebus*	*apella*
	white-faced (or throated) capuchin monkey	*Cebus*	*capucinus*
	wedge-capped capuchin monkey	*Cebus*	*olivaceus*
	newly recognized	*Cebus*	*xanthosternos*
	newly recognized	*Cebus*	*kaapori*
squirrel monkey	Bolivian squirrel monkey	*Saimiri*	*boliviensus*
	red-backed squirrel monkey	*Saimiri*	*oerstedii*
	common squirrel monkey	*Saimiri*	*sciureus*
	golden-backed squirrel monkey	*Saimiri*	*ustus*
	black squirrel monkey	*Saimiri*	*vanzolinii*
saki	equatorial saki	*Pithecia*	*aequatorialis*
	buffy saki	*Pithecia*	*albicans*
	bald-faced saki	*Pithecia*	*irrorata*
	monk saki	*Pithecia*	*monachus*
	white-faced saki	*Pithecia*	*pithecia*
bearded saki	white-nosed bearded saki	*Chiropotes*	*albinasus*
	bearded saki	*Chiropotes*	*satanus*
uacari	bald uacari	*Cacajao*	*calvus*
	black-headed uacari	*Cacajao*	*melanocephalus*
howler monkey	red-handed howler monkey	*Alouatta*	*belzebul*
	black-and-gold howler monkey	*Alouatta*	*caraya*
	Coiba island howler monkey	*Alouatta*	*coibensis*
	brown howler monkey	*Alouatta*	*fusca*
	mantled howler monkey	*Alouatta*	*palliata*
	black howler monkey	*Alouatta*	*pigra*
	Bolivian red howler monkey	*Alouatta*	*sara*
	red howler monkey (2)	*Alouatta*	*seniculus*

(continued)

New World Monkeys *(continued)*

Common Name of Group	Common Name (Notes)	Genus	Species
spider monkey	white-bellied spider monkey	*Ateles*	*belzebuth*
	black-faced black spider monkey	*Ateles*	*chamek*
	brown-headed spider monkey	*Ateles*	*fusciceps*
	black-handed spider monkey	*Ateles*	*geoffroyi*
	white-whiskered spider monkey	*Ateles*	*marginatus*
	black spider monkey	*Ateles*	*paniscus*
woolly monkey	yellow-tailed woolly monkey	*Lagothrix*	*flavicauda*
	woolly monkey	*Lagothrix*	*lagotricha*
muriqui	muriqui (3)	*Brachyteles*	*arachnoides*

Notes:
1. May include five species
2. Some separate *A. arctoidea*
3. Some split the two subspecies, *B. arachnoides arachnoides* and *B. a. hypoxanthus*, into separate species

Old World Monkeys

Common Name of Group	Common Name (Notes)	Genus (Subgenus)	Species
macaque			
—*arctoides* group	stump-tailed macaque	*Macaca*	*arctoides*
—*fascicularis* group	Formosan rock macaque	*Macaca*	*cyclopsis*
	long-tailed (or crab-eating) macaque	*Macaca*	*fascicularis*
	Japanese macaque	*Macaca*	*fuscata*
	rhesus macaque	*Macaca*	*mulatta*
—*silenus* group	Celebes moor macaque	*Macaca*	*maura*
	pig-tailed macaque (1)	*Macaca*	*nemestrina*
	Celebes (or crested) macaque (2)	*Macaca*	*nigra*
	booted macaque (3)	*Macaca*	*ochreata*
	lion-tailed macaque	*Macaca*	*silenus*
	Tonkean macaque (4)	*Macaca*	*tonkeana*
—*sinica* group	Assamese macaque	*Macaca*	*assamensis*
	bonnet macaque	*Macaca*	*radiata*
	toque macaque	*Macaca*	*sinica*
	Tibetan macaque	*Macaca*	*thibetana*
—*sylvanus* group	Barbary macaque	*Macaca*	*sylvanus*

Old World Monkeys *(continued)*

Common Name of Group	Common Name (Notes)	Genus (Subgenus)	Species
baboon	olive baboon	*Papio*	*anubis*
	yellow baboon	*Papio*	*cynocephalus*
	hamadryas baboon	*Papio*	*hamadryas*
	Guinea (or western) baboon	*Papio*	*papio*
	chacma baboon	*Papio*	*ursinus*
drill	drill	*Mandrillus*	*leucophaeus*
mandrill	mandrill	*Mandrillus*	*sphinx*
gelada baboon	gelada baboon	*Theropithecus*	*gelada*
mangabey	agile mangabey	*Cercocebus*	*agilis*
	Tana River mangabey	*Cercocebus*	*galeritus*
	white-collared mangabey	*Cercocebus*	*torquatus*
	sooty mangabey (5)	*Cercocebus*	*atys*
black mangabey	gray-cheeked mangabey	*Lophocebus*	*albigena*
	black mangabey	*Lophocebus*	*aterrimus*
Allen's monkey	Allen's swamp monkey	*Allenopithecus*	*nigroviridis*
talopoin	dwarf guenon (or southern talopoin monkey)	*Miopithecus*	*talapoin*
patas monkey	patas monkey	*Erythrocebus*	*patas*
savanna guenon	vervet (or grivet or green) monkey (6)	*Chlorocebus*	*aethiops*
guenon	red-tailed guenon	*Cercopithecus*	*ascanius*
	Campbell's guenon	*Cercopithecus*	*campbelli*
	mustached guenon	*Cercopithecus*	*cephus*
	Diana monkey	*Cercopithecus*	*diana*
	dryas guenon	*Cercopithecus*	*dryas*
	white-throated guenon	*Cercopithecus*	*erythrogaster*
	red-eared guenon	*Cercopithecus*	*erythrotis*
	owl-faced monkey	*Cercopithecus*	*hamlyni*
	L'hoest's monkey	*Cercopithecus*	*lhoesti*
	blue monkey (7)	*Cercopithecus*	*mitis*
	Mona monkey	*Cercopithecus*	*mona*
	De Brazza's monkey	*Cercopithecus*	*neglectus*
	putty-nosed (or greater spot-nosed) guenon	*Cercopithecus*	*nictitans*
	lesser spot-nosed guenon	*Cercopithecus*	*petaurista*
	crowned guenon	*Cercopithecus*	*pogonias*
	Presuss's monkey	*Cercopithecus*	*preussi*
	Sclater's guenon	*Cercopithecus*	*sclateri*
	sun-tailed guenon	*Cercopithecus*	*solatus*
	Wolf's guenon	*Cercopithecus*	*wolfi*

(continued)

Old World Monkeys *(continued)*

Common Name of Group	Common Name (Notes)	Genus (Subgenus)	Species
black-and-white colobus monkey	Angolan black-and-white colobus	*Colobus*	*angolensis*
	Abyssinian or eastern black-and-white colobus	*Colobus*	*guereza*
	king (or western black-and-white) colobus	*Colobus*	*polykomos*
	black colobus	*Colobus*	*satanas*
	Geoffroy's or white-thighed black-and-white colobus	*Colobus*	*vellerosus*
red colobus monkey	western red colobus	*Procolobus (Piliocolobus)*	*badius*
	Pennant's red colobus	*Procolobus (Piliocolobus)*	*pennantii*
	Preuss's red colobus (8)	*Procolobus (Piliocolobus)*	*preussi*
	Tana River red colobus	*Procolobus (Piliocolobus)*	*rufomitratus*
	newly recognized (8)	*Procolobus (Piliocolobus)*	*gordonorum*
	newly recognized (9)	*Procolobus (Piliocolobus)*	*kirkii*
olive colobus monkey	olive colobus	*Procolobus*	*verus*
langur or leaf monkey	grizzled leaf monkey	*Presbytis*	*comata*
	banded leaf monkey	*Presbytis*	*femoralis*
	white-fronted leaf monkey	*Presbytis*	*frontata*
	Hose's leaf monkey	*Presbytis*	*hosei*
	mitered leaf monkey	*Presbytis*	*melalophus*
	Mentarawai Island leaf monkey	*Presbytis*	*potenziani*
	maroon leaf monkey	*Presbytis*	*rubicunda*
	Thomas's leaf monkey	*Presbytis*	*thomasi*
Hanuman langur	Hanuman langur	*Semnopithecus*	*entellus*

Old World Monkeys *(continued)*

Common Name of Group	Common Name (Notes)	Genus (Subgenus)	Species
brow-ridged langur or leaf monkey	ebony langur	*Trachypithecus (Trachypithecus)*	*auratus*
	silvered langur	*Trachypithecus (Trachypithecus)*	*cristatus*
	Delacour's langur (10)	*Trachypithecus (Trachypithecus)*	*delacouri*
	Francois's langur	*Trachypithecus (Trachypithecus)*	*francoisi*
	golden langur	*Trachypithecus (Trachypithecus)*	*geei*
	dusky (or spectacled) leaf monkey	*Trachypithecus (Trachypithecus)*	*obscurus*
	Phayre's leaf monkey	*Trachypithecus (Trachypithecus)*	*phayrei*
	capped leaf monkey	*Trachypithecus (Trachypithecus)*	*pileatus*
	Nilgiri langur	*Trachypithecus (Kasi)*	*johnii*
	purple-faced leaf monkey	*Trachypithecus (Kasi)*	*vetulus*
Douc langur	red-shanked Douc langur	*Pygathrix (Pygathrix)*	*nemaeus*
	black-shanked Douc langur (11)	*Pygathrix (Pygathrix)*	*nigripes*
snub-nosed langur	Tonkin snub-nosed monkey	*Rhinopithecus (Presbytiscus)*	*avunculus*
	black (or Yunan) snub-nosed monkey	*Rhinopithecus (Rhinopithecus)*	*bieti*
	Guizhou snub-nosed monkey	*Rhinopithecus (Rhinopithecus)*	*brelichi*
	Sichuan golden s nub-nosed monkey	*Rhinopithecus (Rhinopithecus)*	*roxellana*
proboscis monkey	proboscis monkey	*Nasalis*	*larvatus*
pig-tailed langur	pig-tailed langur (12)	*Simias*	*concolor*

Notes:

1. Some separate *M. pagensis*
2. Some separate *M. nigrescens*
3. Some separate *M. brunnescens*
4. Some separate *M. hecki*
5. Some put in *C. torquatus*
6. Some recognize four species
7. Some separate *C. albogularis*
8. Some include in *P. pennatii*
9. Some include in *P. badius*
10. Some include in *T. francoisi*
11. Some include in *P. nemaeus*
12. Some include in *Nasalis*

Apes

Common Name of Group	Common Name (Notes)	Genus (Subgenus)	Species
gibbon	hoolock (or white-browed) gibbon	*Hylobates (Bunopithecus)*	*hoolock*
	dark-handed (or agile) gibbon	*Hylobates (Hylobates)*	*agilis*
	Kloss's gibbon	*Hylobates (Hylobates)*	*klossii*
	white-handed gibbon	*Hylobates (Hylobates)*	*lar*
	silvery Javan gibbon	*Hylobates (Hylobates)*	*moloch*
	Mueller's Bornean gray gibbon	*Hylobates (Hylobates)*	*muelleri*
	pileated (or capped) gibbon	*Hylobates (Hylobates)*	*pileatus*
	black gibbon	*Hylobates (Nomascus)*	*concolor*
	golden-cheeked gibbon	*Hylobates (Nomascus)*	*gabriellae*
	Chinese white-cheeked gibbon	*Hylobates (Nomascus)*	*leucogenys*
siamang	siamang	*Hylobates (Symphalangus)*	*syndactylus*
orangutan	Sumatran orangutan (1)	*Pongo*	*pygmaeus*
	Borneo orangutan (2)	*Pongo*	*pygmaeus*
gorilla	mountain gorilla (3)	*Gorilla*	*gorilla*
	western lowland gorilla (4)	*Gorilla*	*gorilla*
	eastern lowland gorilla (5)	*Gorilla*	*gorilla*
chimpanzee	bonobo	*Pan*	*paniscus*
	western chimpanzee (6)	*Pan*	*troglodytes*
	eastern chimpanzee (7)	*Pan*	*troglodytes*
	central chimpanzee (8)	*Pan*	*troglodytes*
	Nigerian chimpanzee (9)	*Pan*	*troglodytes*

Notes:
1. *P. p. abelii*
2. *P. p. pygmaeus*
3. *G. g. beringei*
4. *G. g. gorilla*
5. *G. g. graueri*
6. *P. t. verus*
7. *P. t. schweinfurthii*
8. *P. t. troglodytes*
9. *P. t. vellerosus*

BIBLIOGRAPHY

Abbott, D. H., Barrett, J., and George, L. M. (1993). Comparative aspects of the social suppression of reproduction in female marmosets and tamarins. In Rylands, A. B. (ed.), *Marmosets and Tamarins: Systematics, Ecology and Behavior,* Oxford University Press, Oxford, pp. 152–163.

Agoramoorthy, G. and Rudran, R. (1995). Infanticide by adult and subadult males in free-ranging red howler monkeys, *Alouatta seniculus,* in Venezuela. *Ethology* 99: 75–88.

Agoramoorthy, G. and Hsu, M. J. (2000). Extragroup copulation among wild red howler monkeys in Venezuela. *Folia Primatologica* 71: 147–151.

Aiello, L. C. and Wheeler, P. (1995). The expensive tissue hypothesis. *Current Anthropology* 36: 184–193.

Alberts, S. C. (1999). Paternal kin discrimination in wild baboons. *Proceedings of the Royal Society of London, Series B* 266: 1501–1506.

Alberts, S. C. and Altmann, J. (1995a). Balancing costs and opportunities: Dispersal in male baboons. *American Naturalist* 145: 279–306.

Alberts, S. C. and Altmann, J. (1995b). Preparation and activation: Determinants of age at reproductive maturity in male baboons. *Behavioral Ecology and Sociobiology* 36: 397–406.

Alberts, S. C. and Altmann, J. (2001). Immigration and hybridization of yellow and anubis baboons in and around Amboseli, Kenya. *American Journal of Primatology* 53: 139–154.

Alberts, S. C., Altmann, J., and Wilson, M. L. (1996). Mate guarding constrains foraging activity of male baboons. *Animal Behaviour* 51: 1269–1277.

Alberts, S. C. and Ober, C. (1993). Genetic variability in the major histocompatibility complex: A review of non-pathogen-mediated selective mechanisms. *Yearbook of Physical Anthropology* 36: 71–89.

Alberts, S. C., Sapolsky, R. M., and Altmann, J. (1992). Behavioral, endocrine, and immunological correlates of immigration by an aggressive male into a natural primate group. *Hormones and Behavior* 26: 167–178.

Albuquerque, A. C., S. R., Sousa, M. B. C., Santos, H. M., and Ziegler, T. E. (2001). Behavioral and hormonal analysis of social relationships between oldest females in a wild monogamous group of common marmosets (*Callithrix jacchus*). *International Journal of Primatology* 22: 631–645.

Aldrich-Blake, F. P. G. (1970). Problems of social structure in forest monkeys. In Crook, J. H. (ed.), *Social Behavior in Birds and Mammals,* Academic Press, New York, pp. 79–101.

Allman, J., Rosin, A., Kumar, R., and Hasenstaub, A. (1998). Parenting and survival in anthropoid primates: Caretakers live longer. *Proceedings of the National Academy of Sciences USA* 95: 6866–6869.

Altmann, J. (1974). Observational study of behavior: Sampling methods. *Behaviour* 49: 227–267.

Altmann, J. (1980). *Baboon Mothers and Infants.* Harvard University Press, Cambridge.

Altmann, J. (2000). Models of outcome and process: predicting the number of males in primate groups. In Kappeler, P. M. (ed.), *Primate males: Causes and consequences of variation in group composition,* Cambridge University Press, Cambridge, pp. 236–247.

Altmann, S. A. (1962). A field study of the sociobiology of rhesus monkeys, *Macaca mulatta. Annals of the New York Academy of Sciences* 102: 338–435.

Altmann, S. A. (1998). *Foraging for Survival.* The University of Chicago Press, Chicago.

Altmann, S. A. and Altmann, J. (1970). *Baboon Ecology.* University of Chicago Press, Chicago.

Altmann, S. A. and Altmann, J. (1979). Demographic constraints on behavior and social organization. In Bernstein, I. S. and Smith, E. O. (eds.), *Primate Ecology and Human Origins,* Garland Press, New York, pp. 47–64.

Altmann, J., Alberts, S. C., Haines, S. A., Dubach, J., Muruthi, P., Coote, T., Geffen, E., Cheesman, D. J., Mututua, R. S., Saiyalele, S. N., Wayne, R. K., Lacy, R. C., and Bruford, M. W. (1996). Behavior predicts genetic structure in a wild primate group. *Proceedings of the National Academy of Sciences USA* 93: 5797–5801.

Altmann, J., Altmann, S. A., Hausfater, G., and McCusky, S. (1977). Life history of yellow baboons: Physical development, reproductive parameters, and infant mortality. *Primates* 18: 315–330.

Altmann, J., Hausfater, G., and Altmann, S. A. (1985). Demography of Amboseli baboons. *American Journal of Primatology* 8: 114–125.

Altmann, J., Hausfater, G., and Altmann, S. A. (1988). Determinants of reproductive success in savannah baboons, *Papio cynocephalus.* In Clutton-rock,

T. H. (ed.), *Reproductive Success,* University of Chicago Press, Chicago, pp. 403–418.

Altmann, J., Sapolsky, R., and Licht, A. (1995). Baboon fertility and social status. *Nature* 377: 688–689.

Andelman, S. J. (1986). Ecological and social determinants of cercopithecine mating patterns. In Rubenstein, D. I. and Wrangham, R. W. (eds.), *Ecological Aspects of Social Evolution,* Princeton University Press, Princeton, pp. 201–216.

Andrews, P. (1981). Species diversity and diet in monkeys and apes during the Miocene. In Stringer, C. B. (ed.), *Aspects of Human Evolution,* Taylor and Francis, London, pp. 25–61.

Anzenberger, G. (1992). Monogamous social systems and paternity in primates. In Martin, R. D., Dixson, A. F., and Wickings, E. J. (eds.), *Paternity in Primates: Genetic Tests and Theories,* Karger, Basel, pp. 203–224.

Araújo, A., Arruda, M. F., Alencar, A. I., Albuquerque, F., Nascimento, M. C., and Yamamoto, M. E. (2000). Body weight of wild and captive common marmosets (*Callithrix jacchus*). *International Journal of Primatology* 21: 317–324.

Araujo Santos, F. G., Bicca-Marques, J. C., Calegaro-Marques, C., de Farias, E. M. P., and Azevedo, M. A. O. (1995). On the occurrence of parasites in free-ranging callitrichids. *Neotropical Primates* 3: 46–47.

Asquith, P. J. (1989). Provisioning and the study of free-ranging primates: History, effects, and prospects. *Yearbook of Physical Anthropology* 32: 129–158.

Asquith, P. J. (1991). Primate research groups in Japan: Orientations and east-west differences. In Fedigan, L. M. and Asquith, P. J. (eds.), *The Monkeys of Arashiyama: Thirty-Five Years of Research in Japan and in the West,* SUNY Press, Albany, pp. 81–98.

Ashley, M. V. (1999). Molecular conservation genetics. *American Scientist* 87: 28–35.

Aureli, F. (1992). Post-conflict behaviour among wild long-tailed macaques (*Macaca fascicularis*). *Behavioral Ecology and Sociobiology* 31: 329–337.

Aureli, F. (1997). Post-conflict anxiety in nonhuman primates: The mediating role of emotion in conflict resolution. *Aggressive Behavior* 23: 315–328.

Aureli, F. and van Schaik, C. P. (1991). Post-conflict behaviour in long-tailed macaques (*Macaca fascicularis*): II. Coping with the uncertainty. *Ethology* 89: 101–114.

Awadalla, P., Eyre-Walker, A., and Maynard Smith, J. (1999). Linkage disequilibrium and recombination in hominid mitochondrial DNA. *Science* 286: 2524–2525.

Axelrod, R. and Hamilton, W. D. (1981). The evolution of cooperation. *Science* 211: 1390–1396.

Azuma, S. and Toyoshima, A. (1961–1962). Progress report of the survey of chimpanzees in their natural habitat, Kabogo Point area, Tanganyika. *Primates* 3: 61–70.

Bachmann, C. and Kummer, H. (1980). Male assessment of female choice in hamadryas baboons. *Behavioral Ecology and Sociobiology* 6: 315–321.

Baker, A. J. and Dietz, J. M. (1996). Immigration in wild groups of golden lion tamarins (*Leontopithecus rosalia*). *American Journal of Primatology* 38: 47–56.

Baker, A. J., Dietz, J. M., and Kleiman, D. G. (1993). Behavioural evidence for monopolization of paternity in multi-male groups of golden lion tamarins. *Animal Behaviour* 46: 1091–1103.

Baker, M. (1996). Fur rubbing: Use of medicinal plants by capuchin monkeys (*Cebus capucinus*). *American Journal of Primatology* 38: 263–270.

Bartlett, T. (1999). The gibbons. In Dolhinow, P. and Fuentes, A. (eds.), *The Nonhuman Primates,* Mayfield Publishers, Mountain Valley, California, pp. 44–49.

Bartlett, T. Q., Sussman, R. W., and Cheverud, J. M. (1993). Infant killing in primates: A review of observed cases with specific reference to the sexual selection hypothesis. *American Anthropologist* 95: 958–990.

Beard, K. C., Tong, Y., Dawson, M. R., Wang, J., and Huang, X. (1996). Earliest complete dentition of an anthropoid primate from the late middle Eocene of Shanxi Province, China. *Science* 272: 82–85.

Bearder, S. K. (1987). Lorises, bushbabies, and tarsiers: Diverse societies in solitary foragers. In Smuts, B. B., Cheney, D. L., Seyfarth, R. M., Wrangham, R. W., and Struhsaker, T. T. (eds.), *Primate Societies,* University of Chicago Press, Chicago, pp. 11–24.

Bearder, S. K. (1999). Physical and social diversity among nocturnal primates: A new view based on long term research. *Primates* 40: 267–282.

Beauchamp, G. K., Yamazaki, K., Bard, J., and Boyse, E. A. (1988). Preweaning experience in the control of mating preferences by genes in the major histocompatibility complex of the mouse. *Behavior Genetics* 18: 537–547.

Beck, B. B. (1980). *Animal Tool Behavior: The Use and Manufacture of Tools by Animals.* Garland STPM Press, New York.

Beck, B. B., Dietz, J. M., Kleiman, D. G., Castro, M. I. C., Lemos de Sa, R. M., and Luz, V. L. F. (1986). Projeto mico-leao. IV. Reintroducao de mico-leoes-dourados (*Leontopithecus rosalia* Linnaeus, 1776) (Callitrichidae, Primates) de cativeiro para seu ambiente natural. In Thiago de

Mello, M. (ed.), *A Primatologia no Brasil—2*, Sociedade Brasileira de Primatologia, Campinas, pp. 243–248.

Bell, R. H. V. (1970). The use of the herb layer by grazing ungulates in the Serengeti. In Watson, A. (ed.), *Animal Populations in Relation to Their Food Resources*, Blackwell Scientific Publications, Oxford, pp. 111–124.

Bennett, E. L. (1991). Diurnal primates. In Kiew, R. (ed.), *The State of Nature Conservation in Malaysia*, Malayan Nature Society, Kuala Lumpur, pp. 150–172.

Berard, J. (1999). A four-year study of the association between male dominance rank, residency status, and reproductive activity in rhesus macaques (*Macaca mulatta*). *Primates* 40: 159–175.

Berard, J. D., Nurnberg, P., Epplen, J. T., and Schmidtke, J. (1994). Alternative reproductive tactics and reproductive success in male rhesus macaques. *Behaviour* 129: 177–201.

Bercovitch, F. B. (1988). Coalitions, cooperation and reproductive tactics among adult male baboons. *Animal Behaviour* 36: 1198–1209.

Bercovitch, F. B. (1992). Estradiol concentrations, fat deposits, and reproductive strategies in male rhesus macaques. *Hormones and Behavior* 26: 272–282.

Bercovitch, F. B. (1995). Female cooperation, consortship maintenance, and male mating success in savanna baboons. *Animal Behaviour* 50: 137–149.

Bercovitch, F. B. (2000). Behavioral ecology and socioendocrinology of reproductive maturation in cercopithecine monkeys. In Whitehead, P. F. and Jolly, C. J. (eds.), *Old World Monkeys*, Cambridge University Press, Cambridge, pp. 298–320.

van den Berghe, P. L. (1983). Human inbreeding avoidance: Culture in nature. *Behavioral and Brain Sciences* 6: 91–123.

Berman, C. M. and Kapsalis, E. (1999). Development of kin bias among rhesus monkeys: Maternal transmission or individual learning? *Animal Behaviour* 58: 883–894.

Bernstein, I. S. (1972). The organization of primate societies: longitudinal studies of captive groups. In Tuttle, R. (ed.), *The Functional and Evolutionary Biology of Primates*, Aldine-Atherton, Chicago, pp. 399–414.

Bernstein, I. S. (1981). Dominance: The baby and the bathwater. *Behavioral and Brain Sciences* 4: 419–467.

Bernstein, I. S. (1999a). The Study of Behavior. In Dolhinow, P. and Fuentes, A. (eds.), *The Nonhuman Primates*, Mayfield Publishing Company, Mountain View, California, pp. 176–180.

Bernstein, I. S. (1999b). Kinship and the behavior of nonhuman primates. In Dolhinow, P. and Fuentes, A. (eds.), *The Nonhuman Primates*, Mayfield Publishing Company, Mountain View, California, pp. 202–205.

Bernstein, I. S. and Baker, S. (1988). Activity pattern in a captive group of Celebes black apes (*Macaca nigra*). *Folia Primatologia* 51: 61–75.

Berry, J. P., McFarren, M. A., and Rodriguez, E. (1995). Zoopharmacognosy: A "biorational" strategy for phytochemical prospecting. In Gustine, D. L. and Flores, H. E. (eds.), *Phytochemicals and Health*, American Society of Plant Physiologist, Rockville, Maryland, pp. 165–178.

Bielert, C. and Busse, C. (1983). Influence of ovarian hormones on the food intake and feeding of captive wild female chacma baboons (*Papio ursinus*). *Physiology and Behavior* 30: 103–111.

Birkhead, T. R. and Moller, A. P. (1992). *Sperm Competition in Birds: Evolutionary Causes and Consequences*. Academic Press, London.

Blum, D. (1994). *The Monkey Wars*. Oxford University Press, New York.

Boehm, C. (1997). Impact of the human egalitarian syndrome on Darwinian selection mechanics. *American Naturalist* (Supplement) 150: 100–121.

te Boekhorst, I. J. A., Schurmann, C. L., and Sugardjito, J. (1990). Residential status and seasonal movements of wild orangutans in the Gunung Leuser Reserve (Sumatra, Indonesia). *Animal Behaviour* 39: 1098–1109.

Boesch, C. (1991a). Teaching among wild chimpanzees. *Animal Behaviour* 41: 530–532.

Boesch, C. (1991b). The effects of leopard predation on grouping patterns in forest chimpanzees. *Behaviour* 117: 220–242.

Boesch, C. (1994). Cooperative hunting in wild chimpanzees. *Animal Behaviour* 48: 653–667.

Boesch, C. (1996). Social grouping in Tai chimpanzees. In McGrew, W. C., Marchant, L. F., and Nishida, T. (eds.), *Great Ape Societies*, Cambridge University Press, New York, pp. 101–113.

Boesch, C. (1997). Evidence for dominant wild female chimpanzees investing more in sons. *Animal Behaviour* 54: 811–815.

Boesch, C. and Boesch, H. (1984). Possible causes of sex differences in the use of natural hammers by wild chimpanzees. *Journal of Human Evolution* 13: 415–440.

Boesch, C. and Boesch-Achermann, H. (2000). *The Chimpanzees of the Taï Forest*. Oxford University Press, New York.

Boesch, C. and Boesch, H. (1989). Hunting behavior of wild chimpanzees in the Taï National Park. *American Journal of Physical Anthropology* 78: 547–573.

Boesch, C. and Tomasello, M. (1998). Chimpanzee and human cultures. *Current Anthropology* 5: 591–604.

Boggess, J. (1984). Infant killing and male reproductive strategies in langurs (*Presbytis entellus*). In Hausfater, G. and Hrdy, S. B. (ed.), *Infanticide: Comparative and Evolutionary Perspectives,* Aldine, New York, pp. 283–310.

Boinski, S. (1987a). Birth synchrony in squirrel monkeys. (*Saimiri oerstedi*). *Behavioral Ecology and Sociobiology* 21: 393–400.

Boinski, S. (1987b). Mating patterns in squirrel monkeys (*Saimiri oerstedi*). *Behavioral Ecology and Sociobiology* 21: 13–21.

Boinski, S. (1994). Affiliation patterns among male Costa Rican squirrel monkeys. *Behaviour* 130: 191–209.

Boinski, S. (1999). The social organizations of squirrel monkeys: Implications for ecological models of social evolution. *Evolutionary Anthropology* 8: 101–112.

Boinski, S. and Chapman, C. A. (1995). Predation on primates: Where are we and what's next? *Evolutionary Anthropology* 4: 1–3.

Boinski, S. and Cropp, S. J. (1999). Disparate data sets resolve squirrel monkey (*Saimiri*) taxonomy: Implications for behavioral ecology and biomedical usage. *International Journal of Primatology* 20: pp. 237–256.

Boinski, S., Quatrone, R. P., and Swartz, H. (2001). Substrate and tool use by brown capuchins in Suriname: ecological contexts and cognitive bases. *American Anthropologist* 102: 741–761.

Borner, M. (1985). The rehabilitated chimpanzees of Rubondo Island. *Oryx* 19: 151–154.

Borries, C. (1997). Infanticide in seasonally breeding multimale groups of Hanuman langurs (*Presbytis entellus*) in Ramnagar (South Napal). *Behavioral Ecology and Sociobiology* 41: 139–150.

Borries, C. (2000). Male dispersal and mating season influxes in Hanuman langurs living in multimale groups. In Kappeler, P. M. (ed.), *Primate Males,* Cambridge University Press, Cambridge, pp. 146–158.

Borries, C., Koenig, A., and Winkler, P. (2001). Variation of life history traits and mating patterns in female langur monkeys (*Semnopithecus entellus*). *Behavioral Ecology and Sociobiology* 50: 391–402.

Borries, C., Launhdart, K., Epplen, C., Epplen, J. T., and Winkler, P. (1999a). DNA analyses support the hypothesis that infanticide is adaptive in langur monkeys. *Proceedings of the Royal Society of London Series B* 266: 901–904.

Borries, C., Launhardt, K., Epplen, C., Epplen, J. T., and Winkler, P. (1999b). Males as infant protectors in Hanuman langurs (*Presbytis entellus*) living in multimale groups—defense pattern, paternity and sexual behaviour. *Behavioral Ecology and Sociobiology* 46: 350–356.

Borries, C., Sommer, V., and Srivastava, A. (1991). Dominance, age, and reproductive success in free-ranging female Hanuman langurs. *International Journal of Primatology* 12: 231–257.

Boubli, J. P. (1999). Feeding ecology of black-headed uacaris (*Cacajao melanocephalus melanocephalus*) in Pico da Neblina National Park, Brazil. *International Journal of Primatology* 20: 719–749.

Boubli, J. P. and Ditchfield, A. D. (2000). The time of divergence between the two species of uacari monkeys: *Cacajao calvus* and *Cacajao melanocephalus. Folia Primatologica* 71: 387–391.

Bowles, I. A., Rice, R. E., Mittermeier, R. A., and da Fonseca, G. A. B. (1998a). Logging and tropical forest conservation. *Science* 280: 1899–1900.

Bowles, I. A., Rice, R. E., Mittermeier, R. A., and Fonseca, G. A. B. (1998b). *Response* (Letters). *Science* 281: 1455–1456.

Box, H. O. (1991). Training for life after release: Simian primates as examples. In Gipps, J. H. W. (ed.), *Beyond Captive Breeding: Re-introducing Endangered Mammals to the Wild,* Clarendon Press, Oxford, pp. 111–123.

Brockelman, W. Y., Reichard, U., Treesucon, U., and Raemakers, J. J. (1998). Dispersal, pair formation and social structure in gibbons (*Hylobates lar*). *Behavioral Ecology and Sociobiology* 42: 329–339.

Brockman, D. K. (1999). Reproductive behavior of female *Propithecus verreauxi* at Beza Mahafaly, Madagascar. *International Journal of Primatology* 20: 375–398.

Brockman, D. K. and Whitten, P. L. (1996). Reproduction in free-ranging *Propithecus verreuxi:* Estrus and the relationship between multiple partner matings and fertilization. *American Journal of Physical Anthropology* 100: 57–69.

Brockman, D. K., Whitten, P. L., Richard, A. F., and Benander, B. (2001). Birth season testosterone levels in male Verreaux's sifaka, *Propithecus verreauxi:* insights into socio-demographic factors mediating seasonal testicular function. *Behavioral Ecology and Sociobiology* 49: 117–127.

Brockman, D. K., Whitten, P. L., Richard, A. F., and Schneider, A. (1998). Reproduction in free-ranging male *Propithecus verreauxi:* The hormonal correlates of mating and aggression. *American Journal of Physical Anthropology* 105: 137–151.

Brockman, D. K., Whitten, P. L., Russell, E., Richard, A. R., and Izard, M. K. (1995). Application of fecal steroid techniques to the reproductive endocrinology of female Verreaux's sifaka, *Propithecus verreauxi. American Journal of Primatology* 36: 313–325.

Bronson, F. H. and Rissman, E. F. (1986). The biology of puberty. *Biological Reviews* 61: 157–195.

Brown, J. L. and Eklund, A. (1994). Kin recognition and the major histocompatibility complex: An integrative review. *American Naturalist* 143: 435–461.

Bruner, A. G., Gullison, R. E., Rice, R. E., and Fonseca, G. A. B. (2001). Effectiveness of parks in protecting tropical biodiversity. *Science* 291: 125–128.

Bshary, R. and Noë, R. (1997). Anti-predation behaviour of red colobus monkeys in the presence of chimpanzees. *Behavioral Ecology and Sociobiology* 41: 321–333.

Buchanan-Smith, H. M. (1999). Tamarin polyspecific associations: Forest utilization and stability of mixed-species groups. *Primates* 40: 233–247.

Buchanan-Smith, H. M. and Jordan, T. R. (1992). An experimental investigation of the pair bond in the callitrichid monkey, *Saguinus labiatus. International Journal of Primatology* 13: 51–72.

Busse, C. D. (1978). Do chimpanzees hunt cooperatively? *American Naturalist* 112: 767–770.

Busse, C. D. (1984). Triadic interactions among male and infant chacma baboons. In Taub, D. M. (ed.), *Primate Paternalism,* Van Nostrand Reinhold, New York, pp. 186–212.

Busse, C. D. and Hamilton III, W. J. (1981). Infant carrying by male chacma baboons. *Science* 212: 1281–1283.

Butlin, R. K. and Ritchie, M. G. (1994). Behaviour and speciation. In Slater, P. J. B. and Halliday, T. R. (eds.), *Behaviour and Evolution,* Cambridge University Press, Cambridge, pp. 43–79.

Byrne, R. W. (1996a). The misunderstood ape: Cognitive skills of the gorilla. In Russon, A. E., Bard, K. A., and Parker, S. T. (eds.), *Reaching into Thought. The Minds of the Great Apes,* Cambridge University Press, Cambridge, pp. 111–130.

Byrne, R. W. (1996b). Relating brain size to intelligence in primates. In Mellars, P. and Gibson, K. (eds.), *Modelling the Early Human Mind,* McDonald Institute for Archaeological Research, Cambridge, pp. 49–56.

Byrne, R. W. (1996c). Machiavellian Intelligence. *Evolutionary Anthropology* 5: 172–180.

Byrne, R. W. (1997a). What's the use of anecdotes? Distinguishing psychological mechanisms in primate tactical deception. In Mitchell, R. W., Thompson, N. S., and Miles, H. L. (eds.), *Anthropomorphism, Anecdotes and Animals,* State University of New York Press, New York, pp. 134–150.

Byrne, R. W. (1997b). The technical intelligence hypothesis: An additional evolutionary stimulus to intelligence? In Whiten, A. and Byrne, R. W. (eds.), *Machiavellian intelligence II: Extensions and*

Evaluations, Cambridge University Press, Cambridge, pp. 289–311.

Byrne, R. W. (1998). Cognition in great apes. In Milner, A. D. (ed.), *Comparative Neuropsychology,* Oxford University Press, Oxford, pp. 228–244.

Byrne, R. W. and Byrne, J. M. E. (1993). Complex leaf-gathering skills of mountain gorillas (*Gorilla g. beringei*): Variability and standardization. *American Journal of Primatology* 31: 241–261.

Byrne, R. W. and Whiten, A. (1988). *Machiavellian Intelligence.* Clarendon Press, Oxford.

Byrne, R. W. and Whiten, A. (1990). Tactical deception in primates: The 1990 database. *Primate Report* 27: 1–101.

Byrne, R. W. and Whiten, A. (1997). Machiavellian intelligence. In Whiten, A. and Byrne, R. W. (ed.), *Machiavellian Intelligence II: Extensions and Evaluations,* Cambridge University Press, pp. 1–23.

Byrne, R. W., Whiten, A., and Henzi, S. P. (1990). Social relationships of mountain baboons: Leadership and affiliation in a non-female-bonded monkey. *American Journal of Primatology* 20: 313–329.

Byrne, R. W., Whiten, A., Henzi, S. P., and McCulloch, F. M. (1993). Nutritional constraints on mountain baboons (*Papio ursinus*): Implications for baboon socio-ecology. *Behavioral Ecology and Sociobiology* 33: 233–246.

Caine, N. G. (1993). Flexibility and co-operation as unifying themes in *Saguinus* social organization and behaviour: The role of pressures. In Rylands, A. B. (ed.), *Marmosets and Tamarins: Systematics, Ecology and Behavior,* Oxford University Press, New York, pp. 200–219.

Campbell, C. J. (2000). Fur rubbing behavior in free-ranging black-handed spider monkeys (*Ateles geoffroyi*) in Panama. *American Journal of Primatology* 51: 205–208.

Campbell, C. J., Shideler, S. E., Todd, H. E., and Lasley, B. L. (2001). Fecal analysis of ovarian cycles in female black-handed spider monkeys (*Ateles geoffroyi*). *American Journal of Primatology* 54: 79–89.

Cannon, C. H., Peart, D. R., and Leighton, M. (1998). Tree species diversity in commercially logged Bornean rainforest. *Science* 281: 1366–1368.

Carlson, A. A. and Isbell, L. A. (2001). Causes and consequences of single-male and multi-male mating in free-ranging patas monkeys (*Erythrocebus patas*). *Animal Behavior* 62: 1047–1058.

Carpenter, C. R. (1934). A field study of the behavior and social relations of howling monkeys. *Comparative Psychology Monographs* 48: 1–168.

Carpenter, C. R. (1964). *Naturalistic Behavior of Nonhuman Primates,* The Pennsylvania State University Press, University Park.

Carson, H. L. and Templeton, A. R. (1984). Genetic revolutions in relation to speciation phenomena: The founding of new populations. *Annual Review of Ecology and Systematics* 15: 97–131.

Cartmill, M. (1972). Arboreal adaptations and the origin of the order Primates. In Tuttle, R. (ed.), *The Functional and Evolutionary Biology of Primates*, Aldine, Chicago, pp. 97–122.

Cartmill, M. (1974). Rethinking primate origins. *Science* 184: 436–443.

Cartmill, M. (1990). Human uniqueness and theoretical content in paleoanthropology. *International Journal of Primatology* 11: 173–192.

Castellanos, H. G. and Chanin, P. (1996). Seasonal differences in food choice and patch preference of long-haired spider monkeys (*Ateles belzebuth*). In Norconk, M. A., Rosenberger, A. L., and Garber, P. A. (eds.), *Adaptive Radiations of Neotropical Primates*, Plenum Press, New York, pp. 451–466.

Censky, E. J., Hodge, K., and Dudley, J. (1998). Overwater dispersal of lizards due to hurricanes. *Nature* 395: 556.

Channell, R. and Lomolino, M. V. (2000). Dynamic biogeography and conservation of endangered species. *Nature* 403: 84–86.

Chapais, B. (2001). Primate nepotism: What is the explanatory value of kin selection? *International Journal of Primatology* 22: 203–229.

Chapais, B. and Gauthier, C. (1993). Early agonistic experience and the onset of matrilineal rank acquisition in Japanese macaques. In Pereira, M. E. and Fairbanks, L. A. (eds.), *Juvenile Primates: Life History, Development, and Behavior*, Oxford University Press, New York, pp. 245–258.

Chapman, C. (1988). Patch use and patch depletion by the spider and howling monkeys of Santa Rosa National Park, Costa Rica. *Behaviour* 105: 99–116.

Chapman, C. A. (1989). Primate seed dispersal: The fate of dispersed seeds. *Biotropica* 21: 148–154.

Chapman, C. A. (1990). Ecological constraints on group size in three species of neotropical primates. *Folia Primatologica* 55: 1–9.

Chapman, C. A. (1995). Primate seed dispersal: Coevolution and conservation implications. *Evolutionary Anthropology* 4: 74–82.

Chapman, C. A. and Balcomb, S. R. (1998). Population characteristics of howlers: Ecological conditions or group history. *International Journal of Primatology* 19: 385–403.

Chapman, C. A. and Chapman, L. J. (1996a). Mixed-species primate groups in the Kibale forest: Ecological constraints on association. *International Journal of Primatology* 17: 31–50.

Chapman, C. A. and Chapman, L. J. (1996b). Frugivory and the fate of dispersed and non-dispersed seeds of six African tree species. *Journal of Tropical Ecology* 12: 491–504.

Chapman, C. A. and Fedigan, L. M. (1990). Dietary differences between neighboring cebus monkey groups: Local tradition or responses to food availability? *Folia Primatologica* 54: 177–186.

Chapman, C. A. and Onderdonk, D. A. (1998). Forests without primates: Primate/Plant codependency. *American Journal of Primatology* 45: 127–141.

Chapman, C. A., White, F. J., and Wrangham, R. W. (1994). Party size in chimpanzees and bonobos: A re-evaluation of theory based on two similarly forested sites. In Wrangham, R. W., Waal, F. B. M. de, and Heltne, P. G. (eds.), *Chimpanzee Cultures*, Harvard University Press, Cambridge, pp. 41–57.

Chapman, C. A., Wrangham, R. W., and Chapman, L. J. (1995). Ecological constraints on group size: An analysis of spider monkey and chimpanzee subgroups. *Behavioral Ecology and Sociobiology* 36: 59–70.

Charles-Dominique, P. (1977). *Ecology and Behaviour of Nocturnal Primates*. Columbia University Press, New York.

Charnov, E. L. and Berrigan, D. (1993). Why do female primates have such long lifespans and so few babies? Or life in the slow lane. *Evolutionary Anthropology* 1: 191–194.

Chazdon, R. L. (1998). Tropical forests—Log 'em or leave 'em? *Science* 281: 1295–1296.

Cheney, D. L. (1987). Interactions and relationships between groups. In Smuts, B. B., Cheney, D. L., Seyfarth, R. M., Wrangham, R. W., and Struhsaker, T. T. (eds.), *Primate Societies*, University of Chicago Press, Chicago, pp. 267–281.

Cheney, D. L. (1992). Intragroup cohesion and intergroup hostility: The relation between grooming distributions and intergroup competition among female primates. *Behavioral Ecology* 3: 334–345.

Cheney, D. L. and Seyfarth, R. M. (1980). Vocal recognition in free-ranging vervet monkeys. *Animal Behaviour* 28: 362–367.

Cheney, D. L. and Seyfarth, R. M. (1982). Recognition of individuals within and between groups of free-ranging vervet monkeys. *American Zoologist* 22: 519–529.

Cheney, D. L. and Seyfarth, R. M. (1983). Nonrandom dispersal in free-ranging vervet monkeys: Social and genetic consequences. *American Naturalist* 122: 392–412.

Cheney, D. and Seyfarth, R. (1985). Vervet monkey alarm calls: Manipulation through shared information. *Behaviour* 94: 150–166.

Cheney, D. L. and Seyfarth, R. M. (1988). Assessment of meaning and the detection of unreliable signals by vervet monkeys. *Animal Behaviour* 36: 477–486.

Cheney, D. and Seyfarth, R. (1990). *How Monkeys See the World.* University of Chicago Press, Chicago.

Cheney, D. L., Seyfarth, R. M., Andelman, S. J., and Lee, P. C. (1988). Reproductive success in vervet monkeys. In Clutton-Brock, T. H. (ed.), *Reproductive Success,* University of Chicago Press, Chicago, pp. 384–402.

Cheney, D. L., Seyfarth, R. M., and Silk, J. B. (1995). The role of grunts in reconciling opponents and facilitating interactions among adult female baboons. *Animal Behaviour* 50: 249–257.

Cheney, D. L., Seyfarth, R. M., and Smuts, B. B. (1986). Social relationships and social cognition in nonhuman primates. *Science* 234: 1361–1366.

Cheney, D. L. and Wrangham, R. W. (1987). Predation. In Smuts, B. B., Cheney, D. L., Seyfarth, R. M., Wrangham, R. W., and Struhsaker, T. T. (eds.), *Primate Societies,* University of Chicago Press, Chicago, pp. 227–239.

Chepko-Sade, B. D. and Sade, D. S. (1979). Patterns of group splitting within matrilineal kinship groups. *Behavioral Ecology and Sociobiology* 5: 67–86.

Chernela, J. M. and Thatcher, V. E. (1989). Comparison of parasite burdens in two native Amazonian populations. *Medical Anthropology* 10: 279–285.

Chism, J. (1991). Ontogeny of behavior in humans and nonhuman primates: The search for common ground. In Loy, J. D. and Peters, C. B. (eds.), *Understanding Behavior: What Primates Studies Tell Us About Human Behavior,* Oxford University Press, New York, pp. 90–120.

Chism, J. (2000). Allocare patterns among cercopithecines. *Folia Primatologica* 71: 55–66.

Chism, J. and Rogers, W. (1997). Male competition, mating success and female choice in a seasonally-breeding primate (*Erythrocebus patas*). *Ethology* 103: 109–126.

Cincotta, R. P., Wisnewski, J., and Engelman, R. (2000). Human population in the biodiversity hotspots. *Nature* 404: 990–992.

Clark, A. B. (1978). Sex ratio and local resource competition in a prosimian primate. *Science* 201: 163–165.

Clark, A. P. (1993). Rank differences in the vocal production of Kibale Forest chimpanzees as a function of social context. *American Journal of Primatology* 31: 159–179.

Clark, A. P. and Wrangham, R. W. (1994). Chimpanzee arrival pant hoots: Do they signify food or status? *International Journal of Primatology* 15: 185–206.

Clark, D. A., Mitra, P. P., and Wang, S. S.-H. (2001). Scalable architecture in mammalian brains. *Nature* 411: 189–193.

Clarke, A. S. and Boinski, S. (1995). Temperament in nonhuman primates. *American Journal of Primatology* 37: 103–125.

Clarke, A. S., Harvey, N. C., and Lindburg, D. G. (1992). Reproductive coordination in a nonseasonally breeding primate species, *Macaca silenus*. *Ethology* 91: 46–58.

Clarke, A. S. and Mason, W. A. (1988). Differences among three macaque species in responsiveness to an observer. *International Journal of Primatology* 9: 347–364.

Clarke, M. R., Glander, K. E., and Zucker, E. L. (1998). Infant–nonmother interactions of free-ranging mantled howlers (*Alouatta palliata*) in Costa Rica. *International Journal of Primatology* 19: 451–472.

Clutton-Brock, T. H. and Harvey, P. H. (1977). Primate ecology and social organization. *Journal of Zoology* 183: 1–39.

Clutton-Brock, T. H. and Harvey, P. (1980). Primates, brains, and ecology. *Journal of Zoology, London* 190: 309–332.

Clutton-Brock, T. H. and Harvey, P. H. (1984). Comparative approaches to investigating adaptation. In Krebs, J. R. and Davies, N. B. (eds.), *Behavioural Ecology: An Evolutionary Approach,* Blackwell Scientific Publications, Oxford, pp. 7–29.

Clutton-Brock, T. H. and Iason, G. R. (1986). Sex ratio variation in mammals. *Quarterly Review of Biology* 61: 339–374.

Coe, C. L., Wiener, S. G., and Levine, S. (1983). Psychoendocrine responses of mother and infant monkeys to disturbance and separation. In Rosenblum, L. A. and Moltz, H. (eds.), *Symbiosis in Parent-Offspring Interactions,* Plenum Press, New York, pp. 189–214.

Colmenares, F. (1991). Greeting, aggression, and coalitions between male baboons: Demographic correlates. *Primates* 32: 453–463.

Constable, J. L., Ashley, M. V., Goodall, J., and Pusey, A. E. (2001). Noninvasive paternity assignment in Gombe chimpanzees. *Molecular Ecology* 10: 1279–1300.

Cooney, D. O. and Struhsaker, T. T. (1997). Adsorptive capacity of charcoals eaten by Zanzibar red colobus monkeys: Implications for reducing dietary toxins. *International Journal of Primatology* 18: 235–246.

Cords, M. (1987). Forest guenons and patas monkeys: Male–male competition in one-male groups. In Smuts, B. B., Cheney, D. L., Seyfarth, R. M., Wrangham, R. W., and Struhsaker, T. T. (eds.), *Primate Societies,* University of Chicago Press, Chicago, pp. 98–111.

Cords, M. A. (1990). Mixed-species association of East African guenons: General patterns or specific examples? *American Journal of Primatology* 21: 101–114.

Cords, M. and Aureli, F. (1993). Patterns of reconciliation among juvenile long-tailed macaques. In Pereira, M. E. and Fairbanks, L. A. (eds.), *Juvenile Primates: Life History, Development, and Behavior,* Oxford University Press, New York, pp. 271–284.

Cords, M. and Aureli, F. (1996). Reasons for reconciling. *Evolutionary Anthropology* 5: 42–45.

Cords, M. and Aureli, F. (2000). Reconciliation and relationship qualities. In Aureli, F. and de Waal, F. B. M. (eds.), *Natural Conflict Resolution,* University of California Press, Berkeley, pp. 117–198.

Coutinho, P. E. G. and Correa, H. K. M. (1995). Polygyny in free-ranging group of buffy tufted-ear marmosets, *Callithrix aurita. Folia Primatologica* 65: 25–29.

Cowlishaw, G. and Dunbar, R. I. M. (1991). Dominance rank and mating success in male primates. *Animal Behaviour* 41: 1045–1056.

Cowlishaw, G. and Dunbar, R. I. M. (2000). *Primate Conservation Biology.* University of Chicago Press, Chicago.

Cox, C. R. and Le Boeuf, B. J. (1977). Female incitation of male competition: A mechanism of mate selection. *American Naturalist* 111: 317–335.

Creel, S. (2001). Social dominance and stress hormones. *Trends in Ecology and Evolution* 16: 491–497.

Crockett, C. M. (1984). Emigration by female red howler monkeys and the case for female competition. In Small, M. F. (ed.), *Female Primates: Studies by Women Primatologists,* Alan R. Liss, Inc., New York, pp. 159–173.

Crockett, C. M. (1996). The relation between red howler monkey (*Alouatta seniculus*) troop size and population growth in two habitats. In Norconk, M. A., Rosenberger, A. L., and Garber, P. A. (eds.), *Adaptive Radiations of Neotropical Primates,* Plenum Press, New York, pp. 489–510.

Crockett, C. M. (1998). Conservation biology of the genus *Alouatta. International Journal of Primatology* 19: 549–578.

Crockett, C. M. and Eisenberg, J. F. (1987). Howlers: Variations in group size and demography. In Smuts, B. B., Cheney, D. L., Seyfarth, R. M., Wrangham, R. W., and Struhsaker, T. T. (eds.), *Pri-*

mate Societies, University of Chicago Press, Chicago, pp. 54–68.

Crockett, C. M. and Pope, T. R. (1993). Consequences of sex differences in dispersal for juvenile red howler monkeys. In Pereira, M. E. and Fairbanks, L. A. (eds.), *Juvenile Primates: Life History, Development, and Behavior,* Oxford University Press, New York, pp. 104–118.

Crockett, C. M. and Rudran, R. (1987). Red howler monkey birth data I: Seasonal variation. *American Journal of Primatology* 13: 347–368.

Crook, J. H. and Gartlan, J. H. (1966). Evolution of primate societies. *Nature* 210: 1200–1203.

Dahl, J. F., Nadler, R. D., and Collins, D. C. (1991). Monitoring the ovarian cycles of *Pan troglodytes* and *P. paniscus:* A comparative approach. *American Journal of Primatology* 24: 195–209.

Davies, C. R., Ayres, J. M., Dye, C., and Deane, L. M. (1991). Malaria infection rate of Amazonian primates increases with body weight and group size. *Functional Ecology* 5: 655–662.

Davies, N. B. (1991). Mating systems. In Krebs, J. R. and Davies, N. B. (eds.), *Behavioural Ecology, Third Edition,* Blackwell Scientific Ltd., Oxford, pp. 263–294.

Deag, J. M. and Crook, J. H. (1971). Social behaviour and "agonistic buffering" in the wild barbary macaque *Macaca sylvana. Folia Primatologica* 15: 183–200.

Delgado, R. A. J. and van Schaik, C. P. (2000). The behavioral ecology and conservation of the orangutan (*Pongo pygmaeus*): A tale of two islands. *Evolutionary Anthropology* 9: 201–218.

Delson, E. (1994). Evolutionary history of the colobine monkeys in paleoenvironmental perspective. In Davies, A. G. and Oates, J. F. (eds.), *Colobine Monkeys: Their Ecology, Behaviour and Evolution,* Cambridge University Press, Cambridge, pp. 11–43.

Demment, M. W. (1983). Feeding ecology and the evolution of body size in baboons. *African Journal of Ecology* 21: 219–233.

DeVore, I. (1962). *The Social Behavior and Organization of Baboon Troops.* Ph.D. Dissertation, University of Chicago.

Di Fiore, A. and Rendall, D. (1994). Evolution of social organization: A reappraisal for primates by using phylogenetic methods. *Proceedings of the National Academy of Science* 91: 9941–9945.

Di Fiore, A. and Rodman, P. S. (2001). Time allocation patterns of lowland woolly monkeys (*Lagothrix lagotricha poeppigii*) in a neotropical *terra firma* forest. *International Journal of Primatology* 22: 449–480.

Dias, L. G. and Strier, K. B. (2000). Agonistic encounters between muriquis, *Brachyteles arachnoides hypoxanthus* (Primates, Cebidae), and other animals at the Estação Biológica de Caratinga, Minas Gerais, Brazil. *Neotropical Primates* 8: 138–141.

Dietz, J. M. and Baker, A. J. (1993). Polygyny and female reproductive success in golden lion tamarins (*Leontopithecus rosalia*). *Animal Behaviour* 46: 1067–1078.

Dietz, J. M., Coimbra-Filho, A. F., and Pessamilio, D. M. (1986). Projeto mico-leao. I. Um modelo para a conservação de especie ameaçada de extinção. In Thiago de Mello, M. (ed.), *A Primatologia no Brasil—2*, Sociedade Brasileira de Primatologia, Campinas, pp. 217–222.

Digby, L. (1995). Infant care, infanticide, and female reproductive strategies in polygynous groups of common marmosets (*Callithrix jacchus*). *Behavioral Ecology and Sociobiology* 37: 51–61.

Digby, L. (2000). Infanticide by female mammals: Implications for the evolution of social systems. In van Schaik, C. P. and Janson, C. H. (eds.), *Infanticide by Males*, Cambridge University Press, Cambridge, pp. 423–446.

Digby, L. J. and Ferrari, S. F. (1994). Multiple breeding females in free-ranging groups of *Callithrix jacchus*. *International Journal of Primatology* 15: 389–397.

Dittus, W. (1979). The evolution of behaviors regulating density and age-specific sex ratios in a primate population. *Behaviour* 69: 265–301.

Dixson, A. F. (1998). *Primate Sexuality*. Oxford University Press, New York.

Dixson, A. F. and George, L. (1982). Prolactin and parental behaviour in a male New World primate. *Nature* 299: 551–553.

Dixson, A. F., Anzenberger, G., Monteiro da Cruz, M. A. O., Patel, I., and Jeffreys, A. J. (1992). DNA fingerprinting of free-ranging groups of common marmosets (*Callithrix jacchus jacchus*) in NE Brazil. In Martin, R. D., Dixson, A. F., and Wickings, E. J. (eds.), *Paternity in Primates: Genetic Tests and Theories*, Karger, Basel, pp. 192–202.

Dolhinow, P. J. (1972). The North Indian langur. In Dolhinow, P. J. (ed.), *Primate Patterns*, Holt, Rinehart and Winston, New York, pp. 181–238.

Dolhinow, P. (1977). Normal monkeys? *American Scientist* 65: 266.

Dolhinow, P. (1999). Play: A critical process in the developmental system. In Dolhinow, P. and Fuentes, A. (eds.), *The Nonhuman Primates*, Mayfield Publishing Company, Mountain View, California, pp. 213–236.

Domb, L. G. and Pagel, M. (2001). Sexual swellings advertise female quality in wild baboons. *Nature* 410: 204–206.

Dominy, N. J. and Lucas, P. W. (2001). Ecological importance of trichromatic vision to primates. *Nature* 410: 363–366.

Dominy, N. J., Lucas, P. W., Osorio, D., and Yamashita, N. (2001). The sensory ecology of primate food perception. *Evolutionary Anthropology* 10: 171–186.

Doran, D. (1997). Influence of seasonality on activity patterns, feeding behavior, ranging, and grouping patterns in Täi chimpanzees. *International Journal of Primatology* 18: 183–206.

Doran, D. M. and McNeilage, A. (1998). Gorilla ecology and behavior. *Evolutionary Anthropology* 6: 120–131.

Dunbar, R. I. M. (1979). Population demography, social organization, and mating strategies. In Bernstein, I. S. and Smith, E. O. (eds.), *Primate Ecology and Human Origins*, Garland Press, New York, pp. 67–88.

Dunbar, R. I. M. (1983). Structure of gelada baboon reproductive units, 2: Social relationships between reproductive females. *Animal Behaviour* 31: 556–564.

Dunbar, R. I. M. (1984). *Reproductive Decisions: An Economic Analysis of Gelada Baboon Social Strategies*. Princeton University Press, Princeton.

Dunbar, R. I. M. (1987a). Habitat quality, population dynamics, and group composition in colobus monkeys (*Colobus guereza*). *International Journal of Primatology* 8: 299–321.

Dunbar, R. I. M. (1987b). Demography and reproduction. In Smuts, B. B., Cheney, D. L., Seyfarth, R. M., Wrangham, R. W., and Struhsaker, T. T. (eds.), *Primate Societies*, University of Chicago Press, Chicago, pp. 240–249.

Dunbar, R. I. M. (1988). *Primate Social Systems*. Cornell University Press, Ithaca.

Dunbar, R. I. M. (1996). Determinants of group size in primates: A general model. *Proceedings of the British Academy* 88: 33–57.

Dunbar, R. (1997). The monkeys' defence alliance. *Nature* 386: 555–557.

Dunbar, R. I. M. (1998). The social brain hypothesis. *Evolutionary Anthropology* 6: 178–190.

Dunbar, R. I. M. (2001). What's in a baboon's behind? *Nature* 410: 158.

Eeley, H. A. C. and Lawes, M. J. (1999). Large-scale patterns of species richness and species range size in anthropoid primates. In Fleagle, J., G., Janson, C. H., and Reed, K. E. (eds.), *Primate Communities*, Cambridge University Press, Cambridge, pp. 191–219.

Eilenberger, U. (1997). Individual, group-specific and ecological influence factors on the status of endoparasites of wild eastern lowland gorillas

(*Gorilla gorilla graueri*) in Zaire. *Primate Report* 47: 89–93.

Eisenberg, J. F., Makenhirn, N. A., and Rudran, R. (1972). The relation between ecology and social structure in primates. *Science* 176: 863–874.

Elowson, A. M., Sweet, C. S., and Snowdon, C. T. (1992). Ontogeny of trill and J-call vocalizations in the pygmy marmoset, *Cebuella pygmaea*. *Animal Behaviour* 42: 703–715.

Emlen, S. T., Emlen, J. M., and Levin, S. A. (1986). Sex-ratio selection in species with helpers-at-the-nest. *American Naturalist* 127: 1–8.

Emlen, S. T. and Oring, L. (1977). Ecology, sexual selection and the evolution of mating systems. *Science* 197: 215–223.

Erhart, E. M., Coelho, A. M. J., and Bramblett, C. A. (1997). Kin recognition by paternal half-siblings in captive *Papio cynocephalus*. *American Journal of Primatology* 43: 147–157.

Erhart, E. M. and Overdorff, D. J. (1998). Infanticide in *Propithecus diadema edwardsi*: An evaluation of the sexual selection hypothesis. *International Journal of Primatology* 19: 73–81.

Erickson, C. J., Nowicki, S., Dollar, L., and Goehring, N. (1998). Percussive foraging: stimuli for prey location by aye-ayes (*Daubentonia madagascariensis*). *International Journal of Primatology* 19: 111–122.

Essock-Vitale, S. and Seyfarth, R. M. (1987). Intelligence and social cognition. In Smuts, B. B., Cheney, D. L., Seyfarth, R. M., Wrangham, R. W., and Struhsaker, T. T. (eds.), *Primate Societies*, University of Chicago Press, Chicago, pp. 452–461.

Estrada, A. and Coates-Estrada, R. (1991). Howler monkeys (*Alouatta palliata*), dung beetles (Scarabaeidae) and seed dispersal: Ecological interactions in the tropical rain forest of Los Tuxtlas, Mexico. *Journal of Tropical Ecology* 7: 459–474.

Fagen, R. (1993). Primate juveniles and primate play. In Pereira, M. E. and Fairbanks, L. A. (eds.), *Juvenile Primates: Life History, Development, and Behavior*, Oxford University Press, New York, pp. 182–196.

Fairbanks, L. A. (1993). Juvenile vervet monkeys: Establishing relationships and practicing skills for the future. In Pereira, M. E. and Fairbanks, L. A. (eds.), *Juvenile Primates: Life History, Development, and Behavior*, Oxford University Press, New York, pp. 211–227.

Fairbanks, L. A. (2000). Maternal investment throughout the life span in Old World monkeys. In Whitehead, P. F. and Jolly, C. J. (eds.), *Old World Monkeys*, Cambridge University Press, Cambridge, pp. 341–367.

Farrell, B. D. (1998). "Inordinate fondness" explained: Why are there so many beetles? *Science* 281: 555–559.

Feder, K. L. and Park, M. A. (1997). *Human Antiquity: An Introduction to Physical Anthropology and Archaeology*, Third Edition. Mayfield Publishing Company, New York.

Fedigan, L. (1982). *Primate Paradigms: Sex Roles and Social Bonds*. Eden Press, Montreal.

Fedigan, L. (1983). Dominance and reproductive success in primates. *Yearbook of Physical Anthropology* 26: 91–129.

Fedigan, L. (1993). Sex differences and intersexual relations in adult white-faced capuchins (*Cebus capucinus*). *International Journal of Primatology* 14: 853–878.

Fedigan, L. M. (1997). Changing views of female life histories. In Morbeck, M. E., Galloway, A., and Zihlman, A. L. (eds.), *The Evolving Female: A Life History Perspective*, Princeton University Press, Princeton, pp. 15–26.

Fedigan, L. M. and Baxter, M. J. (1984). Sex differences and social organization in free-ranging spider monkeys (*Ateles geoffroyi*). *Primates* 25: 279–284.

Fedigan, L. M. and Jack, K. (2001). Neotropical primates in a regenerating Costa Rican dry forest: a comparisons of howler and capuchin population patterns. *International Journal of Primatology* 22: 689–713.

Fedigan, L. M. and Pavelka, M. S. M. (2001). Is there adaptive value to reproductive termination in Japanese macaques? A test of maternal investment hypotheses. *International Journal of Primatology* 22: 109–125.

Fedigan, L. M. and Rose, L. M. (1995). Interbirth interval variation in three sympatric species of neotropical monkey. *American Journal of Primatology* 37: 9–24.

Fedigan, L. M., Rose, L. M., and Avila, R. M. (1998). Growth of mantled howler groups in a regenerating Costa Rican dry forest. *International Journal of Primatology* 19: 405–432.

Fedigan, L. M. and Zohar, S. (1997). Sex differences in mortality of Japanese monkeys. *American Journal of Physical Anthropology* 102: 161–175.

Ferrari, S. F., Correa, H. K. M., and Coutinho, P. E. G. (1996). Ecology of the "southern" marmosets (*Callithrix aurita* and *Callithrix flaviceps*): How different, how similar? In Norconk, M. A., Rosenberger, A. L., and Garber, P. A. (eds.), *Adaptive Radiations of Neotropical Primates*, Plenum Press, New York, pp. 157–171.

Ferrari, S. F. and Digby, L. J. (1996). Wild *Callithrix* groups: Stable extended families? *American Journal of Primatology* 38: 19–27.

Ferrari, S. F. and Strier, K. B. (1992). Exploitation of *Mabea fistulifera* nectar by marmosets (*Callithrix flaviceps*) and muriquis (*Brachyteles arachnoides*) in southeast Brazil. *Journal of Tropical Ecology* 8: 225–239.

Ferris, C. F., Snowdon, C. T., King, J. A., Duong, T. Q., Ziegler, T. E., Ugurbil, K., Ludwig, R., Schultz-Darken, N. J., Wu, Z., Olson, D. P., Sullivan Jr., J. M., Tannenbaum, P. L., and Vaughan, J. T. (2001). Functional imaging of brain activity in conscious monkeys responding to sexually arousing cues. *NeuroReport* 12: 2231–2236.

Finlay, B. L. and Darlington, R. B. (1995). Linked regularities in the development and evolution of mammalian brains. *Science* 268: 1678–1684.

Fleagle, J. G. (1999). *Primate Adaptation and Evolution, Second Edition.* Academic Press, New York.

Fleagle, J. G. and Mittermeier, R. A. (1980). Locomotor behavior, body size and comparative ecology of seven Surinam monkeys. *American Journal of Physical Anthropology* 52: 301–314.

Fleury, M. C. and Gautier-Hion, A. (1997). Better to live with allogenerics than to live alone? The case of single male *Cercopithecus pogonias* in troops of *Colobus satanas*. *International Journal of Primatology* 18: 967–974.

Ford, S. M. and Davis, L. C. (1992). Systematics and body size: Implications for feeding adaptations in New World monkeys. *American Journal of Physical Anthropology* 88: 415–468.

Fossey, D. (1983). *Gorillas in the Mist.* Houghton Mifflin, Boston.

Fouts, R. S. and Fouts, D. H. (1999). Chimpanzee sign language research. In Dolhinow, P. and Fuentes, A. (eds.), *The Nonhuman Primates,* Mayfield Publishing Company, Mountain View, California, pp. 252–256.

Fragaszy, D., Fedigan, L., and Visalberghi, E. (In press). *The Complete Capuchin Monkey.* Cambridge University Press, Cambridge.

Frank, S. A. (1990). Sex allocation theory for birds and mammals. *Annual Review of Ecology and Systematics* 21: 13–55.

Franklin, I. R. (1980). Evolutionary change in small populations. In Soule, M. E. and Wilcox, B. A. (eds.), *Conservation Biology, An Evolutionary–Ecological Perspective,* Sinauer Associates, Sunderland, Massachusetts, pp. 135–149.

Fredrickson, W. T. and Sackett, G. P. (1984). Kin preferences in primates (*Macaca nemestrina*): Relatedness or familiarity? *Journal of Comparative Psychology* 98: 29–34.

Freed, B. Z. (1999). An introduction to the ecology of daylight-active lemurs. In Dolhinow, P. and Fuentes, A. (eds.), *The Nonhuman Primates,* Mayfield Publishing Company, Mountain View, California, pp. 123–132.

Freeland, W. J. (1976). Pathogens and the evolution of primate sociality. *Biotropica* 8: 12–24.

Freeland, W. J. (1980). Mangabey (*Cercocebus albigena*) movement patterns in relation to food availability and fecal contamination. *Ecology* 61: 1297–1303.

Fruth, B. and Hohmann, G. (1996). Nest building behavior in the great apes: The great leap forward? In McGrew, W. C., Marchant, L. F., and Nishida, T. (eds.), *Great Ape Societies,* Cambridge University Press, New York, pp. 225–240.

Fuentes, A. (1998). Re-evaluating primate monogamy. *American Anthropologist* 100: 890–907.

Fuentes, A. (1999). Variable social organization: What can looking at primate groups tell us about the evolution of plasticity in primate societies? In Dolhinow, P. and Fuentes, A. (eds.), *The Nonhuman Primates,* Mayfield Publishing Company, Moutain View, California, pp. 183–188.

Furuichi, T. (1989). Social interactions and the life history of female *Pan paniscus* in Wamba, Zaire. *International Journal of Primatology* 10: 173–197.

Furuichi, T. (1997). Agonistic interactions and matrifocal dominance rank of wild bonobos (*Pan paniscus*) at Wamba. *International Journal of Primatology* 18: 855–875.

Furuichi, T. and Ihobe, H. (1994). Variation in male relationships in bonobos and chimpanzees. *Behavior* 130: 212–228.

Gachot-Neveu, H., Petit, M., and Roeder, J. J. (1999). Paternity determination in two groups of *Eulemur fulvus mayottensis:* Implications for understanding mating strategies. *International Journal of Primatology* 20: 107–119.

Gagneux, P., Woodruff, D. S., and Boesch, C. (1997). Furtive mating in female chimpanzees. *Nature* 387: 358–359.

Galdikas, B. M. F. (1981). Orangutan reproduction in the wild. In Graham, C. E. (ed.), *Reproductive Biology of the Great Apes,* Academic Press, New York, pp. 281–300.

Galdikas, B. M. F. (1985). Adult male sociality and reproductive tactics among orangutans at Tanjung Puting. *Folia Primatologica* 45: 9–24.

Galdikas, B. M. F. (1995a). Social and reproductive behavior of wild adolescent female orangutans. In Nadler, R. D., Galdikas, B. M. F., Sheeran, L. K., and Rosen, N. (eds.), *The Neglected Ape,* Academic Press, New York, pp. 163–182.

Galdikas, B. M. F. (1995b). *Reflections of Eden: My Years with the Orangutans of Borneo.* Little, Brown, Boston.

Ganzhorn, J. U. (1988). Food partitioning among Malagasy primates. *Oecologia* 75: 436–450.

Ganzhorn, J. U. (1995). Low-level forest disturbance effects on primary productivity, leaf chemistry, and lemur populations. *Ecology* 76: 2084–2096.

Ganzhorn, J. U., Wright, P. C., and Ratsimbazafy, J. (1999). Primate communities: Madagascar. In Fleagle, J. G., Janson, C. H., and Reed, K. E. (eds.), *Primate Communities,* Cambridge University Press, Cambridge, pp. 75–89.

Gao, F., Bailes, E., Robertson, D. L., Chen, Y., Rodenburg, C. N., Michael, G. M., Sharp, P. M., and Hahn, B. H. (1999). Origin of HIV-1 in the chimpanzee *Pan troglodytes troglodytes. Nature* 397: 436–441.

Garber, P. A. (1997). One for all and breeding for one: Cooperation and competition as a tamarin reproductive strategy. *Evolutionary Anthropology* 5: 187–199.

Garber, P. A. and Dolins, F. L. (1996). Testing learning paradigms in the field: Evidence for use of spatial and perceptual information and rule-based foraging in wild moustached tamarins. In Norconk, M. A., Rosenberger, A. L., and Garber, P. A. (eds.), *Adaptive Radiations of Neotropical Primates,* Plenum Press, New York, pp. 201–216.

Garber, P. A. and Kitron, U. (1997). Seed swallowing in tamarins: Evidence of a curative function or enhanced foraging efficiency? *International Journal of Primatology* 18: 523–538.

Garland, T. J. and Adolph, S. C. (1994). Why not to do two-species comparative studies: Limitations on inferring adaptation. *Physiological Zoology* 67: 797–828.

Gaulin, S. J. C. (1979). A Jarman/Bell model of primate feeding niches. *Human Ecology* 7: 1–19.

Gautier-Hion, A. (1978). Food niches and coexistence in sympatric primates in Gabon. In Chivers, D. J. and Herbert, J. (eds.), *Recent Advances in Primatology, vol. 1, Behaviour,* Academic Press, New York, pp. 269–286.

Gautier-Hion, A., Gautier, J. P., and Maisels, F. (1993). Seed dispersal versus seed predation: An intersite comparison of two related African monkeys. *Vegetatio* 107/108: 237–244.

Gebo, D. L. and Chapman, C. A. (1995). Positional behavior in five sympatric Old World monkeys. *American Journal of Physical Anthropology* 97: 49–76.

Gerloff, U., Hartung, B., Fruth, B., Hohmann, G., and Tautz, D. (1999). Intracommunity relationships, dispersal pattern and paternity success in a wild living community of Bonobos (*Pan paniscus*) determined from DNA analyses of faecal samples. *Proceedings of the Royal Society of London, Series B* 266: 1189–1195.

Gibbons, A. (1998). A blow to the 'Grandmother Theory'. *Science* 280: 516.

Gibson, K. A. (1986). Cognition, brain size and the extraction of embedded food resources. In Else, J. and Lee, P. C. (eds.), *Primate Ontogeny, Cognition and Social Behavior,* Cambridge University Press, Cambridge, pp. 93–104.

Gilbert, K. A. (1994). Parasitic infection in red howling monkeys in forest fragments. *Neotropical Primates* 2: 10–12.

Glander, K. E. (1978). Howling monkey feeding behavior and plant secondary compounds: A study of strategy. In Montgomery, G. G. (ed.), *The Ecology of Arboreal Folivores,* Smithsonian Institution Press, Washington, D.C., pp. 561–574.

Glander, K. E. (1980). Reproduction and population growth in free-ranging mantled howling monkeys. *American Journal of Physical Anthropology* 53: 25–36.

Glander, K. E. (1992). Dispersal patterns in Costa Rican mantled howling monkeys. *International Journal of Primatology* 13: 415–436.

Glander, K. E. (1994). Nonhuman primate self-medication with wild plant foods. In Etkin, N. L. (ed.), *Eating on the Wild Side: The Pharmacologic, Ecologic, and Social Implications of Using Non-cultigens,* University of Arizona Press, Tucson, pp. 239–256.

Glander, K. E., Wright, P. C., Seigler, D. S., Randrianasolo, V., and Randrianasolo, B. (1989). Consumption of cyanogenic bamboo by a newly discovered species of bamboo lemur. *American Journal of Primatology* 19: 119–124.

Glenn, M. E. (1997). Group size and group composition of the mona monkey (*Cercopithecus mona*) on the island of Grenada, West Indies. *American Journal of Primatology* 43: 167–173.

Glenn, M. E. and Bensen, K. J. (1998). Capture techniques and morphological measurements of the Mona monkey (*Cercopithecus mona*) on the Island of Grenada, West Indies. *American Journal of Physical Anthropology* 105: 481–491.

Godfrey, L. R., Samonds, K. E., Jungers, W. L., and Sutherland, M. R. (2001). Teeth, brains, and primate life histories. *American Journal of Physical Anthropology* 114: 192–214.

Goldberg, T. L. and Wrangham, R. W. (1997). Genetic correlates of social behaviour in wild chimpanzees: Evidence from mitochondrial DNA. *Animal Behaviour* 54: 559–570.

Goldizen, A. W., Mendelson, J., van Vlaardingen, M., and Terborgh, J. (1996). Saddle-back tamarin (*Saguinus fuscicollis*) reproductive strategies: Evidence from a thirteen-year study of a marked population. *American Journal of Primatology* 38: 57–83.

Gomendio, M., Clutton-Brock, T. H., Albon, S. D., Guiness, F. E., and Simpson, M. J. (1990). Mammalian sex ratios and variation in the costs of rearing sons and daughters. *Nature* 343: 260–263.

Gonder, M. K., Oates, J. F., Disotell, T. R., Forstner, M. R. J., Morales, J. C., and Melnick, D. J. (1997). A new west African chimpanzee subspecies? *Nature* 388: 337.

Goodall, J. (1968). The behaviour of free-living chimpanzees in the Gombe Stream Reserve. *Animal Behaviour Monographs* 1: 161–307.

Goodall, J. (1971). *In the Shadow of Man.* Collins, London.

Goodall, J. (1986). *The Chimpanzees of Gombe: Patterns of Behavior.* Harvard University Press, Cambridge.

Gosling, M. and Sutherland, W. J. (2000). Behaviour and Conservation. Cambridge University Press, Cambridge.

Gould, L. (1997). Intermale affiliative behavior in ring-tailed lemurs (*Lemur catta*) at the Beza-Mahafaly Reserve, Madagascar. *Primates* 38: 15–30.

Gould, L. (1999). How female dominance and reproductive seasonality affect the social lives of adult male ringtailed lemurs. In Dolhinow, P. and Fuentes, A. (eds.), *The Nonhuman Primates,* Mayfield Publishing Company, Mountain View, California, pp. 133–139.

Gould, L., Sussman, R. W., and Sauther, M. L. (1999). Natural disasters and primate population: The effects of a two-year drought on a naturally occurring population of ring-tailed lemurs (*Lemur catta*) in southwestern Madagascar. *International Journal of Primatology* 20: 69–84.

Gould, S. J. (1982). Darwinism and the expansion of evolutionary theory. *Science* 216: 380–386.

Gouzoules, S. (1984). Primate mating systems, kin associations, and cooperative behavior: Evidence for kin recognition? *Yearbook of Physical Anthropology* 27: 99–134.

Gouzoules, S. and Gouzoules, H. (1987). Kinship. In Smuts, B. B., Cheney, D. L., Seyfarth, R. M., Wrangham, R. W., and Struhsaker, T. T. (eds.), *Primate Societies,* University of Chicago Press, Chicago, pp. 299–305.

Gouzoules, S., Gouzoules, H., and Marler, P. (1984). Rhesus monkey (*Macaca mulatta*) screams: Representational signalling in the recruitment of agonistic aid. *Animal Behaviour* 32: 182–193.

Gowaty, P. A. and Lennartz, M. R. (1985). Sex ratios of nestling and fledgling redcockaded woodpeckers (*Picoides borealis*) favor males. *American Naturalist* 126: 347–353.

Grant, P. R. and Grant, B. R. (2002). Adaptive radiation of Darwin's finches. *American Scientist* 90: 130–139.

Gray, J. P. (1985). *Primate Sociobiology.* HRAF Press, New Haven.

Green, S. (1975a). Dialects in Japanese monkeys: Vocal learning and cultural transmission of locale-specific vocal behaviour? *Zeitschrift fur Tierpsychologie* 38: 304–314.

Green, S. (1975b). Variation of vocal pattern with social situation in the Japanese monkey (*Macaca fuscata*): A field study. In Rosenblum, L. A. (ed.), *Primate Behavior,* Academic Press, New York, pp. 1–102.

Guimarães, A. (1998). *Comportamento Reprodutivo e Marcação de Cheiro em um Grupo Silvestre de Callithrix flaviceps.* Masters thesis, Universidade Federal de Minas Gerais, Belo Horizonte.

Gursky, S. L. (1994). Infant care in the spectral tarsier (*Tarsius spectrum*) Sulawesi, Indonesia. *International Journal of Primatology* 15: 843–853.

Gursky, S. (1995). Group size and composition in the spectral tarsier, *Tarsius spectrum:* Implications for social organization. *Tropical Biodiversity* 3: 57–62.

Gursky, S. (1998). Conservation status of the spectral tarsier, *Tarsius spectrum:* Population density and home range size. *Folia Primatologica* 69: 191–203.

Gursky, S. (1999). The tarisiidae: Taxonomy, behavior, and conservation status. In Dolhinow, P. and Fuentes, A. (eds.), *The Nonhuman Primates,* Mayfield Publishing Company, Mountain View, California, pp. 140–145.

Gust, D. A., McCaster, T., Gordon, T. P., Gergits, W. F., Casna, N. J., and McClure, H. M. (1998). Paternity in sooty mangabeys. *International Journal of Primatology* 19: 83–94.

Hall, K. R. L. and DeVore, I. (1965). Baboon social behavior. In DeVore, I. (ed.), *Primate Behavior,* Holt, Rinehart and Winston, Inc., New York, pp. 53–110.

Hamilton, W. D. (1964). The genetical evolution of social behaviour, I and II. *Journal of Theoretical Biology* 7: 1–52.

Hannah, A. C. and McGrew, W. C. (1991). Rehabilitation of captive chimpanzees. In Box, H. O. (ed.), *Primate Responses to Environmental Change,* Chapman and Hall, London, pp. 167–186.

Haraway, D. (1989). *Primate Visions: Gender, Race, and Nature in the World of Modern Science.* Routledge, New York.

Harcourt, A. H. (1987). Dominance and fertility among the female primates. *Journal of Zoology* 213: 471–487.

Harcourt, A. H. (1995). Population viability estimates: Theory and practice for a wild gorilla population. *Conservation Biology* 9: 134–142.

Harcourt, A. H. (1996). Sexual selection and sperm competition in primates: What are male genitalia good for? *Evolutionary Anthropology* 4: 121–129.

Harcourt, A. H. (1998). Does primate socioecology need nonprimate socioecology? *Evolutionary Anthropology* 7: 3–7.

Harcourt, A. H. and Schwartz, M. W. (2001). Primate evolution: A biology of Holocene extinction and survival on the southeast Asian Sunda shelf islands. *American Journal of Physical Anthropology* 114: 4–17.

Harcourt, A. H., Stewart, K. J., and Hauser, M. (1993). Functions of wild gorilla 'close' calls. I. Repertoire, context and interspecific comparison. *Behaviour* 124: 89–121.

Harcourt, A. H., Stewart, K. J., and Inaharo, I. M. (1989). Gorilla quest in Nigeria. *Oryx* 23: 7–13.

Harding, R. S. O. and Olson, D. (1986). Patterns of mating among male patas monkeys (*Erythrocebus patas*) in Kenya. *American Journal of Primatology* 11: 343–358.

Harlow, H. F. and Zimmermann, R. R. (1959). Affectional responses in the infant monkey. *Science* 130: 421–432.

Hart, B. L. (1990). Behavioral adaptation to pathogens and parasites: Five strategies. *Neuroscience and Biobehavioral Reviews* 14: 273–294.

Hartwig, W. C. (1994). Patterns, puzzles and perspectives on platyrrhine origins. In Corruccini, R. S. and Ciochon, R. L. (eds.), *Integrative Paths to the Past: Paleoanthropological Advances in Honor of F. Clark Howell*, Prentice-Hall, Englewood Cliffs, New Jersey, pp. 69–93.

Hartwig, W. C. (1996). Perinatal life history traits in New World monkeys. *American Journal of Primatology* 40: 99–130.

Harvey, P. H. and Harcourt, A. H. (1984). Sperm competition, testes size, and breeding systems in primates. In Smith, R. L. (ed.), *Sperm Competition and the Evolution of Animal Mating Systems*, Academic Press, New York, pp. 589–600.

Harvey, P. H. and Krebs, J. R. (1990). Comparing brains. *Science* 249: 140–146.

Hasegawa, T. and Hiraiwa-Hasegawa, M. (1983). Opportunistic and restrictive matings among wild chimpanzees in the Mahale Mountains, Tanzania. *Journal of Ethology* 1: 75–85.

Hashimoto, C., Furuichi, T., and Takenaka, O. (1996). Matrilineal kin relationship and social behavior of wild bonobos (*Pan paniscus*): Sequencing the D-loop region of mitochondrial DNA. *Primates* 37: 305–318.

Hauser, M., Teixidor, P., Field, L., and Flaherty, R. (1993). Food-elicited calls in chimpanzees: Effects of food quantity and divisibility. *Animal Behaviour* 45: 817–819.

Hausfater, G. (1975). *Dominance and Reproduction in Baboons (Papio cynocephalus)*. Karger, Basel.

Hausfater, G. (1984). Infanticide in langurs: Strategies, counterstrategies, and parameter values. In Hausfater, G. and Hrdy, S. B. (eds.), *Infanticide: Comparative and Evolutionary Perspectives,* Aldine, New York, pp. 257–281.

Hausfater, G. and Meade, B. J. (1982). Alteration of sleeping groves by yellow baboons (*Papio cynocephalus*) as a strategy for parasite avoidance. *Primates* 23: 287–297.

Hausfater, G. and Watson, D. F. (1976). Social and reproductive correlates of parasite ova emissions by baboons. *Nature* 262: 688–689.

Hawkes, K., O'Connell, J. F., and Blurton Jones, N. G. (1997). Hadza women's time allocation, offspring provisioning, and the evolution of long postmenopausal life spans. *Current Anthropology* 38: 551–565.

Heinsohn, R. and Packer, C. (1995). Complex cooperative strategies in group-territorial African lions. *Science* 269: 1260–1262.

Heistermann, M., Tari, S., and Hodges, J. K. (1993). Measurement of faecal steroids for monitoring ovarian function in New World primates, Callitrichidae. *Journal of Reproduction and Fertility* 99: 243–251.

Henig, R. M. (2000). *The Monk in the Garden*. Houghlin Mifflin Company, New York.

Henzi, S. P. and Barrett, L. (1999). The value of grooming to female primates. *Primates* 40: 47–59.

Herbinger, I., Boesch, C. and Rothe, H. (2001). Territory characteristics among three neighboring chimpanzee communities in the Täi National Park, Côte d'Ivoire. *International Journal of Primatology* 22: 143–167.

Heymann, E. W. (1995). Sleeping habits of tamarins, *Saguinus mystax* and *Saguinus fuscicollis* (Mammalia; Primates; Callitrichidae), in northeastern Peru. *Journal of Zoology* 237: 211–226.

Hill, D. A. (1994). Affiliative behaviour between adult males of the genus *Macaca*. *Behaviour* 130: 293–308.

Hill, D. A. (1997). Seasonal variation in the feeding behavior and diet of Japanese macaques (*Macaca fuscata yakui*) in lowland forest of Yakushima. *American Journal of Primatology* 43: 305–322.

Hill, D. A. (1999). Effects of provisioning on the social behaviour of Japanese and rhesus macaques: Implications for socioecology. *Primates* 40: 187–198.

Hill, D. A. and Okayasu, N. (1995). Absence of 'youngest ascendancy' in the dominance relations of sisters in wild Japanese macaques (*Macaca fuscata yakui*). *Behaviour* 132: 267–279.

Hill, D. A. and Okayasu, N. (1996). Determinants of dominance among female macaques: Nepotism, demography, and danger. In Fa, J. E. and Lindburg, D. G. (eds.), *Evolution and Ecology of Macaque Societies.*, Cambridge University Press, New York, pp. 459–472.

Hill, D. A. and van Hooff, J. (1994). Affiliative relationships between males in groups of nonhuman primates: A summary. *Behaviour* 130: 143–149.

Hill, K., Boesch, C., Goodall, J., Pusey, A., Williams, J., and Wrangham, R. (2001). Mortality rates among wild chimpanzees. *Journal of Human Evolution* 40: 437–450.

Hill, R. A. and Lee, P. C. (1998). Predation risk as an influence on group size in cercopithecoid primates: Implications for social structure. *Journal of Zoology, London* 245: 447–456.

Hiraiwa-Hasegawa, M. (1993). Skewed birth sex ratios in primates: Should high ranking mothers have daughters or sons? *Trends in Ecology and Evolution* 8: 395–400.

Holekamp, K. E. and Smale, L. (1995). Rapid change in offspring sex ratios after clan fission in the spotted hyena. *American Naturalist* 145: 261–278.

Holenweg, A. K., Noë, R., and Schabel, M. (1996). Waser's gas model applied to associations between red colobus and Diana monkeys in the Täi National Park, Ivory Coast. *Folia Primatologica* 67: 125–136.

Holmes, W. G. and Sherman, P. W. (1983). Kin recognition in animals. *American Science* 71: 46–55.

Höner, O. P., Leumann, L., and Noë, R. (1997). Dyadic associations of red colobus and Diana monkey groups in the Täi National Park, Ivory Coast. *Primates* 38: 281–291.

Hood, L. C. (1994). Infanticide among ringtailed lemurs (*Lemur catta*) at Berenty Reserve, Madagascar. *American Journal of Primatology* 33: 65–69.

van Hooff, J. A. R. A. M. (2000). Relationships among non-human primate males: A deductive framework. In Kappeler, P. M. (ed.), *Primate males: causes and consequences of variation in group composition*, Cambridge University Press, Cambridge, pp. 183–191.

van Hooff, J. A. R. A. M. and van Schaik, C. P. (1992). Cooperation in competition: The ecology of primate bonds. In Harcourt, H. A. and de Waal, F. B. M. (eds.), *Coalitions and Alliances in Humans and Other Animals*, Oxford University Press, Oxford, pp. 357–389.

van Hooff, J. A. R. A. M. and van Schaik, C. P. (1994). Male bonds: Affiliative relationships among non-human primate males. *Behaviour* 130: 309–337.

Horwich, R. H. and Gebhard, K. (1983). Roaring rhythms in black howler monkeys (*Alouatta pigra*) of Belize. *Primates* 24: 290–296.

Hrdy, S. B. (1974). Male–male competition and infanticide among the langurs (*Presbytis entellus*) of Abu, Rajasthan. *Folia Primatologica* 22: 19–58.

Hrdy, S. B. (1976). Care and exploitation of nonhuman primate infants by conspecifics other than the mother. *Advances in the Study of Behavior* 6: 101–158.

Hrdy, S. B. (1977). *The Langurs of Abu*. Harvard University Press, Cambridge.

Hrdy, S. B. (1981). *The Woman That Never Evolved*. Harvard University Press, Cambridge.

Hrdy, S. B. (1995). The primate origins of female sexuality and their implications for the role of non-conceptive sex in the reproductive strategies of women. *Journal of Human Evolution* 10: 131–144.

Hrdy, S. B. and Hausfater, G. (1984). Comparative and evolutionary perspectives on infanticide: An introduction and overview. In Hausfater, G. and Hrdy, S. B. (eds.), *Infanticide: Comparative and Evolutionary Perspectives*, Aldine, Hawthorne, N.Y., pp. xiii–xxxv.

Hrdy, S. B. and Whitten, P. L. (1987). Patterning of sexual activity. In Smuts, B. B., Cheney, D. L., Seyfarth, R. M., Wrangham, R. W., and Struhsaker, T. T. (eds.), *Primate Societies*, University of Chicago Press, Chicago, pp. 370–384.

Hsu, M. J. and Lin, J.-F. (2001). Troop size and structure in free-ranging Formosan macaques (*Macaca cyclopis*) at Mt. Longevity, Taiwan. *Zoological Studies* 40: 49–60.

Hsu, M. J., Moore, J., Lin, J. F., and Agoramoorthy, G. (2000). High incidence of supernumerary nipples and twins in Formosan macaques (*Macaca cyclopis*) at Mt. Longevity, Taiwan. *American Journal of Primatology* 52: 199–205.

Huffman, M. A. (1984). Stone-play of *Macaca fuscata* in Arashiyama B troop: Transmission of a non-adaptive behavior. *Journal of Human Evolution* 13: 725–735.

Huffman, M. A. (1992). Influences of female partner preference on potential reproductive outcome in Japanese macaques. *Folia Primatologica* 59: 77–88.

Huffman, M. A. (1997). Current evidence for self-medication in primates: A multidisciplinary perspective. *Yearbook of Physical Anthropology* 40: 171–200.

Huffman, M. A. and Caton, J. M. (2001). Self-induced increase of gut motility and the control of parasitic infections in wild chimpanzees. *International Journal of Primatology* 22: 329–346.

Huffman, M. A. and Quiatt, D. (1986). Stone handling by Japanese macaques (*Macaca fuscata*). *Primates* 27: 413–423.

Humphrey, N. K. (1976). The social function of intellect. In Bateson, P. P. G. and Hinde, R. A. (eds.), *Growing Points in Ethology*, Cambridge University Press, Cambridge, pp. 303–317.

Ihobe, H. (1992). Male–male relationships among wild bonobos (*Pan paniscus*) at Wamba, Republic of Zaire. *Primates* 33: 163–179.

Imanishi, K. (1966). The purpose and method of our research in Africa. *Kyoto University African Studies* 1: 1–10.

Inagaki, H. and Tsukahara, T. (1993). A method of identifying chimpanzee hairs in lion feces. *Primates* 34: 109–112.

Ingmanson, E. J. (1996). Tool-using behavior in wild *Pan paniscus:* Social and ecological considerations. In Russon, A. E., Bard, K. A., and Parker, S. T. (eds.), *Reaching into Thought: The Minds of the Great Apes,* Cambridge University Press, Cambridge, pp. 190–210.

Insley, S. J. (2000). Long-term vocal recognition in the northern fur seal. *Nature* 406: 404–405.

Isbell, L. A. (1991). Contest and scramble competition: Patterns of female aggression and ranging behavior among primates. *Behavioral Ecology* 2: 143–155.

Isbell, L. A. (1994). Predation on primates: Ecological patterns and evolutionary consequences. *Evolutionary Anthropology* 3: 61–71.

Isbell, L. A. (1998). Diet for a small primate: Insectivory and gummivory in the (large) patas monkey (*Erythrocebus patas pyrrhonotus*). *American Journal of Primatology* 45: 381–398.

Isbell, L. A. and Young, T. (1993). Human presence reduces predation in a free-ranging vervet monkey population in Kenya. *Animal Behaviour* 45: 1233–1235.

IUCN. 1994. *IUCN Red List Categories.* International Union for Conservation of Nature and Natural Resources, Gland, Switzerland.

Jablonski, N. G. and Kelley, J. (1997). Did a major immunological event shape the evolutionary histories of apes and Old World monkeys? *Journal of Human Evolution* 33: 513–520.

Jack, K. M. and Pavelka, M. S. M. (1997). The behavior of peripheral males during the mating season in *Macaca fuscata. Primates* 38: 369–377.

Jacob, S., McClintock, M. K., Zelano, B., and Ober, C. (2002). Paternally inherited HLA alleles are associated with women's choice of male odor. *Nature Genetics* 30: 175–179.

Jalles-Filho, E., Cunha, R. G. T., and Salm, R. A. (2001). Transport of tools and mental representation: Is capuchin monkey tool behaviour a useful model of Plio-Pleistocene hominid technology. *Journal of Human Evolution* 40: 365–377.

Janik, V. M. (2000). Whistle matching in wild bottlenose dolphins (*Tursiops truncatus*). *Science* 289: 1355–1357.

Janson, C. H. (1983). Adaptation of fruit morphology to dispersal agents in a Neotropical forest. *Science* 219: 187–189.

Janson, C. H. (1984). Female choice and mating system of the brown capuchin monkey *Cebus apella* (Primates: Cebidae). *Zeitschrift fur Tierpsychologie* 65: 177–200.

Janson, C. (1985). Aggressive competition and individual food consumption in wild brown capuchin monkeys (*Cebus apella*). *Behavioral Ecology and Sociobiology* 18: 125–138.

Janson, C. H. (1992). Evolutionary ecology primate social structure. In Smith, E. A. and Winterhalder, B. (eds.), *Evolutionary Ecology and Human Behavior,* Aldine de Gruyter, New York, pp. 95–130.

Janson, C. H. (1996). Toward an experimental socioecology of primates: Examples from Argentine brown capuchin monkeys (*Cebus apella nigritus*). In Norconk, M. A., Rosenberger, A. L., and Garber, P. A. (eds.), *Adaptive Radiations of Neotropical Primates,* Plenum Press, New York, pp. 309–325.

Janson, C. H. (1998). Experimental evidence for spatial memory in foraging wild capuchin monkeys, *Cebus apella. Animal Behaviour* 55: 1229–1243.

Janson, C. H. and Chapman, C. A. (1999). Resources and primate community structure. In Fleagle, J. G., Janson, C. H., and Reed, K. E. (eds.), *Primate Communities,* Cambridge University Press, Cambridge, pp. 237–267.

Janson, C. H. and Di Bitetti, M. S. (1997). Experimental analysis of food detection in capuchin monkeys: Effects of distance, travel speed, and resource size. *Behavioral Ecology and Sociobiology* 41: 17–24.

Janson, C. H. and Goldsmith, M. L. (1995). Predicting group size in primates: Foraging costs and predation risks. *Behavioral Ecology* 6: 326–336.

Janson, C. H. and van Schaik, C. P. (1993). Ecological risk aversion in juvenile primates: Slow and steady wins the race. In Pereira, M. E. and Fairbanks, L. A. (eds.), *Juvenile Primates: Life History, Development, and Behavior,* Oxford University Press, New York, pp. 57–74.

Janson, C. H., Terborgh, J., and Emmons, L. H. (1981). Non-flying mammals as pollinating agents in the Amazonian forest. *Biotropica* 13: 1–6.

Janzen, D. H. (1978). Complications in interpreting the chemical defenses of trees against tropical arboreal plant-eating vertebrates. In Montgomery, G. G. (ed.), *The Ecology of Arboreal Folivores,* Smithsonian Institution Press, Washington, D.C., pp. 73–84.

Jarman, P. J. (1974). The social organization of antelope in relation to their ecology. *Behaviour* 48: 215–267.

Jay, P. C. (1968). Studies on variability in species behavior: Comments. In Jay, P. C. (ed.), *Primates: Studies in Adaptation and Variability,* Holt, Rinehart and Winston, New York, pp. 173–179.

Jernvall, J. and Wright, P. C. (1998). Diversity components of impending primate extinctions. *Proceedings of the National Academy of Sciences, USA* 95: 11279–11283.

Joffe, T. H. (1997). Social pressures have selected for an extended juvenile period in primates. *Journal of Human Evolution* 32: 593–605.

Johns, A. D. (1992). Vertebrate responses to selective logging: Implications for the design of logging systems. *Philosophical Transactions of the Royal Society of London* 335: 437–442.

Johns, A. D. and Skorupa, J. P. (1987). Responses of rain-forest primates to habitat disturbance: A review. *International Journal of Primatology* 8: 157–191.

Johnsen, A., Andersen, V., Sunding, C., and Lifjeld, J. T. (2000). Female bluethroats enhance offspring immunocompetence through extra-pair copulations. *Nature* 406: 296–299.

Johnson, C. N. (1988). Dispersal and sex ratio at birth in primates. *Nature* 332: 726–728.

Johnson, R. L. and Kapsalis, E. (1998). Menopause in free-ranging rhesus macaques: Estimated incidence, relation to body condition, and adaptive significance. *International Journal of Primatology* 19: 751–765.

Jolly, A. (1966). Lemur social behaviour and primate intelligence. *Science* 153: 501–506.

Jolly, A. (1988). Madagascar's lemurs: On the edge of survival. *National Geographic* 174: 132–160.

Jolly, A. (1991). "Conscious chimpanzees?" A review of recent literature. In Ristau, C. A. (ed.), *Cognitive Ethology: The Minds of Other Animals. Essays in Honor of Donald R. Griffin*, Lawrence Erlbaum Associates, Inc., Hillsdale, New Jersey, pp. 231–252.

Jolly, A., Caless, S., Cavigelli, S., Gould, L., Pereira, M. E., Pitts, A., Pride, R. E., Rabenandrasana, H. D., Walker, J. D., and Zafison, T. (2000). Infant killing, wounding and predation in *Eulemur* and *Lemur*. *International Journal of Primatology* 21: 21–40.

Jolly, C. J. (1993). Species, subspecies, and baboon systematics. In Kimbel, W. H. and Martin, L. B. (eds.), *Species, Species Concepts, and Primate Evolution*, Plenum Press, New York, pp. 67–107.

Jolly, C. J. and White, R. (1995). *Physical Anthropology and Archaeology*. McGraw-Hill, New York.

Jolly, C. J., Woolley-Barker, T., Beyene, S., Disotell, T. R., and Phillips-Conroy, J. E. (1997). Intergeneric hybrid baboons. *International Journal of Primatology* 18: 597–627.

Jones, C. B. (1980). The functions of status in the mantled howler monkey, *Alouatta palliata* Gray: Intraspecific competition for group membership in a folivorous neotropical primate. *Primates* 21: 389–405.

Jones, C. B. (1994). Injury and disease of the mantled howler monkey in fragmented habitats. *Neotropical Primates* 2: 4–5.

Jones, C. B. (1999). Why both sexes leave: Effects of habitat fragmentation on dispersal behavior. *Endangered Species UPDATE* 15: 70–73.

Kano, T. (1996). Male rank order and copulation rate in a unit-group of bonobos at Wamba, Zaire. In McGrew, W. C., Marchant, L. F., and Nishida, T. (eds.), *Great Ape Societies*, Cambridge University Press, New York, pp. 135–145.

Kano, T. (1997). Comment. *Current Anthropology* 38: 568.

Kaplin, B. A. (2001). Ranging behavior of two species of guenons (*Cercopithecus lhoesti* and *C. mitis doggetti*) in the Nyungwe Forest Rserve, Rwanda. *International Journal of Primatology* 22: 521–548.

Kaplin, B. A. and Moermond, T. C. (1998). Variation in seed handling by two species of forest monkeys in Rwanda. *American Journal of Primatology* 45: 83–101.

Kappeler, P. M. (1996). Causes and consequences of life-history variation among Strepsirhine primates. *American Naturalist* 148: 868–891.

Kappeler, P. M. (1997a). Determinants of primate social organization: Comparative evidence and new insights from Malagasy lemurs. *Biological Reviews of the Cambridge Philosophical Society* 72: 111–151.

Kappeler, P. M. (1997b). Intrasexual selection and testis size in Strepsirhine primates. *Behavioral Ecology* 8: 10–19.

Kawai, M. (1958). On the system of social ranks in a natural group of Japanese monkeys. *Primates* 1: 11–48.

Kawai, M. (1965). On the system of social ranks in a natural troop of Japanese monkeys (1): Basic rank and dependent rank. Primates 1, 111–148. In Imanishi, I. and Altmann, S. A. (eds.), *Japanese monkeys: A collection of translations*, Emory University Press, Atlanta, pp. 66–86.

Kawamura, S. (1958). Matriarchal social order in the Minoo-B Group: A study on the rank system of Japanese macaques. *Primates* 1: 149–156.

Kay, R. F., Ross, C., and Williams, B. A. (1997). Anthropoid origins. *Science* 275: 797–804.

Kay, R. N. B. and Davies, G. A. (1994). Digestive physiology. In Davies, A. G. and Oates, J. F. (eds.), *Colobine Monkeys: Their Ecology, Behaviour and Evolution*, Cambridge University Press, Cambridge, pp. 229–249.

Keller, L. and Reeve, H. K. (1998). Familiarity breeds cooperation. *Nature* 394: 121–122.

Kelley, J. (1998). Noncompetitive replacement of apes by monkeys in the late Miocene of Eurasia. *American Journal of Physical Anthropology (Supplement)* 26: 137–138.

King, B. J. (1991). Social information transfer in monkeys, apes, and hominids. *Yearbook of Physical Anthropology* 34: 97–115.

King, F. A., Yarbrough, C. J., Anderson, D. C., Gordon, T. P., and Gould, K. G. (1988). Primates. *Science* 240: 1475–1482.

Kinzey, W. G. and Cunningham, E. P. (1994). Variability in platyrrhine social organization. *American Journal of Primatology* 34: 185–198.

Kinzey, W. G. and Norconk, M. A. (1990). Hardness as a basis of food choice in two sympatric primates. *American Journal of Physical Anthropology* 81: 5–15.

Kinzey, W. G. and Norconk, M. A. (1993). Physical and chemical properties of fruit and seeds eaten by *Pithecia* and *Chiropotes* in Surinam and Venezuela. *International Journal of Primatology* 14: 207–227.

Kinzey, W. G. and Robinson, J. G. (1983). Intergroup calls, range size, and spacing in *Callicebus torquatus*. *American Journal of Physical Anthropology* 60: 539–544.

Kleiman, D. G. (1996). Reintroduction programs. In Kleiman, D. G., Allen, M. E., Thompson, K. V., and Lumpkin, S. (eds.), *Wild Mammals in Captivity*, University of Chicago Press, Chicago, pp. 297–305.

Kleiman, D. G., Hoage, R. J., and Green, K. M. (1988). The lion tamarins, genus *Leontopithecus*. In Mittermeier, R. A., Rylands, A. B., Coimbra-Filho, A., and Fonseca, G. A. B. (eds.), *Ecology and Behavior of Neotropical Primates*, World Wildlife Fund, Washington, D.C., pp. 299–347.

Knapp, L. A., Cadavid, L. F., and Watkins, D. I. (1998). The MHC-E locus is the most well conserved of all known primate class I histocompatibility genes. *Journal of Immunology* 160: 189–196.

Knapp, L. A., Ha, J. C., and Sackett, G. P. (1996). Parental MHC antigen sharing and pregnancy wastage in captive pigtailed macaques. *Journal of Reproductive Immunology* 32: 73–88.

Knott, C. D. (1998). Changes in orangutan caloric intake, energy balance, and ketones in response to fluctuating fruit availability. *International Journal of Primatology* 19: 1029–1043.

Knott, C. (1999). Orangutan behavior and ecology. In Dolhinow, P. and Fuentes, A. (eds.), *The Nonhuman Primates*, Mayfield Publishing Company, Mountain View, California, pp. 50–57.

Koenig, A. (2000). Competitive regimes in forest-dwelling Hanuman langur females (*Semnopithecus entelllus*). *Behavioral Ecology and Sociobiology* 48: 93–100.

Koenig, A., Beise, J., Chalise, M. K., and Ganzhorn, J. U. (1998). When females should contest food—testing hypotheses about resource density, distribution, size, and quality with Hanuman langurs (*Presbytis entellus*). *Behavioral Ecology and Sociobiology* 42: 225–237.

Koenig, A., Borries, C., Chalise, M. K., and Winkler, P. (1997). Ecology, nutrition, and timing of reproductive events in an Asian primate, the Hanuman langur (*Presbytis entellus*). *Journal of Zoology* 243: 1–21.

Kohn, M. H. and Wayne, R. K. (1997). Facts from feces revisited. *Trends in Ecology and Evolution* 12: 223–227.

Komdeur, J. (1996). Facultative sex ratio bias in the offspring of Seychelles warblers. *Proceedings of the Royal Society of London Series B* 263: 661–666.

Krebs, J. R. and Davies, N. B. (1993). *An Introduction to Behavioural Ecology*. Blackwell Scientific Publications, Oxford.

Kummer, H. (1968). *Social organization of hamadryas baboons*. University of Chicago Press, Chicago.

Kummer, K. (1995). *In Quest of the Sacred Baboon*. Princeton University Press, Princeton.

Kurland, J. A. (1977). *Kin selection in the Japanese monkey*. Karger, Basel.

Lacy, R. C. (1993). VORTEX: A computer simulation model for population viability analysis. *Wildlife Research* 20: 45–65.

Lambert, J. E. (1998). Primate digestion: Interactions among anatomy, physiology, and feeding ecology. *Evolutionary Anthropology* 7: 8–20.

Lambert, J. E. and Garber, P. A. (1998). Evolutionary and ecological implications of primate seed dispersal. *American Journal of Primatology* 45: 9–28.

Lande, R. (1995). Mutation and conservation. *Conservation Biology* 9: 782–791.

Launhardt, K., Borries, C., Hardt, C., Epplen, J. T., and Winkler, P. (2001). Paternity analysis of alternative male reproductive routes among the langurs (*Semnopithecus entellus*) or Ramnagar. *Animal Behaviour* 61: 53–64.

Laurence, W. F. (1998). A crisis in the making: Responses of Amazonian forests to land use and climate change. *Trends in Ecology and Evolution* 13: 411–415.

Lazaro-Perea, C. (2001). Intergroup interactions in wild common marmosets, *Callithrix jacchus*: Territorial defense and assessment of neighbors. *Animal Behaviour* 62: 11–21.

Lazaro-Perea, C., Castro, C. S. S., Harrison, R., Araujo, A., Arruda, M. F., and Snowdon, C. T. (2000). Behavioral and demographic changes following the loss of the breeding female in cooperatively breeding marmosets. *Behavioral Ecology and Sociobiology* 48: 137–146.

Lazaro-Perea, C., Snowdon, C. T., and Arruda, M. F. (1999). Scent-marking behavior in wild groups of common marmosets (*Callithrix jacchus*). *Behavioral Ecology and Sociobiology* 46: 313–324.

Leakey, M. G., Spoor, F., Brown, F. H., Gathogo, P. N., Kiarie, C., Leakey, L. N., and McDougall, I. (2001). New hominin genus from eastern Africa shows diverse middle Pliocene lineages. *Nature* 410: 433–440.

Lee, P. C. (1994). Social structure and evolution. In Slater, P. J. B. and Halliday, T. R. (eds.), *Behaviour and Evolution*, Cambridge University Press, Cambridge, pp. 266–303.

Lee, P. C. (1996). The meanings of weaning: Growth, lactation, and life history. *Evolutionary Anthropology* 5: 87–96.

Lee, P. C., Majiluf, P., and Gordon, I. J. (1991). Growth, weaning and maternal investment from a comparative perspective. *Journal of Zoology, London* 225: 99–114.

Leigh, S. (1994). Growing up to be a primate. *Evolutionary Anthropology* 3: 106–108.

Leigh, S. R. and Terranova, C. J. (1998). Comparative perspectives in bimaturism, ontogeny, and dimorphism in lemurid primates. *International Journal of Primatology* 19: 723–749.

Leighton, D. R. (1987). Gibbons: Territoriality and monogamy. In Smuts, B. B., Cheney, D. L., Seyfarth, R. M., Wrangham, R. W., and Struhsaker, T. T. (eds.), *Primate Societies*, University of Chicago Press, Chicago, pp. 135–145.

Leighton, M. and Leighton, D. R. (1982). The relationship of size of feeding aggregate to size of food patch: Howler monkeys (*Alouatta palliata*) feeding in *Trichilia cipo* fruit trees on Barro Colorado Island. *Biotropica* 14: 81–90.

Lenski, R. E. and Mittler, J. E. (1993). The directed mutation controversy and neo-Darwinism. *Science* 259: 188–194.

Leutenegger, W. (1979). The evolution of litter size in primates. *American Naturalist* 114: 525–531.

Lewin, R. (1996). A growing number of evolutionary biologists think that the interests of groups sometimes supersede those of individuals. *Natural History* 105: 12–17.

Lillehei, R. and Snowdon, C. T. (1978). Individual and situational differences in the vocalizations of young stumptail macaques (*Macaca arctoides*). *Behaviour* 64: 270–281.

Lindburg, D. G. (1987). Seasonality of reproduction in primates. In Mitchell, G. and Erwin, J. (eds.), *Comparative Primate Biology, Volume 2B: Behavior,* *Cognition, and Motivation*, Alan R. Liss, New York, pp. 167–218.

Lippold, L. (1995). Distribution and conservation status of douc langurs in Vietnam. *Asian Primates* 4: 4–6.

Lippold, L. K. (1999). Doing fieldwork among the Doucs in Vietnam. In Dolhinow, P. and Fuentes, A. (eds.), *The Nonhuman Primates,* Mayfield Publishing Company, Mountain View, California, pp. 170–174.

Lovejoy, C. O. (1988). Evolution of human walking. *Scientific American* 256: 118–125.

Lucas, P. W. and Corlett, R. T. (1998). Seed dispersal by long-tailed macaques. *American Journal of Primatology* 45: 29–44.

Lucas, P. W., Beta, T., Darvell, B. W., Dominy, N. J., Essackjee, H. C., Lee, P. K. D., Osorio, D., Ramsden, L., Yamashita, N., and Yuen, T. D. B. (2001). Field kit to characterize physical, chemical and spatial aspects of potential primate foods. *Folia Primatologica* 72: 11–25.

Lynch, J. W. (1998). Mating behavior in wild tufted capuchins (*Cebus apella nigritus*) in Brazil's Atlantic forest. *American Journal of Physical Anthropology* Supplement 26: 153.

Lynch, J. W., Ziegler, T. E., and Strier, K. B. (2002). Individual and seasonal variation in fecal testosterone and cortisol levels of wild tufted capuchin monkeys, *Cebus apella nigritus. Hormones and Behavior* 41.

MacKinnon, J. (1974). The behaviour and ecology of wild orang-utans (*Pongo pygmaeus*). *Animal Behaviour* 22: 3–74.

MacKinnon, J. and MacKinnon, K. (1980). The behavior of wild spectral tarsiers. *International Journal of Primatology* 1: 361–379.

MacKinnon, K. C. (1995). Foraging behavior of the white faced capuchin monkey (*Cebus capucinus*). *American Journal of Physical Anthropology Supplement* 20: 138–139.

MacPhee, R., Beard, K., and Qi, T. (1995). Significance of primate petrosal from the Middle Eocene fissure-fillings at Shanghuang, Jiangsu Province, People's Republic of China. *Journal of Human Evolution* 29: 501–514.

Maggioncalda, A. N., Sapolsky, R. M., and Czekala, N. M. (1999). Reproductive hormone profiles in captive male orangutans: Implications for understanding developmental arrest. *American Journal of Physical Anthropology* 109: 19–32.

Maggioncalda, A. N., Czekala, N. M., and Sapolsky, R. M. (2000). Growth hormone and thyroid stimulating hormone concentrations in captive male orangutans: Implications for understanding developmental arrest. *American Journal of Primatology* 50: 67–76.

Maisels, F., Gautier-Hion, A., and Gautier, J. P. (1994). Diets of two sympatric colobines in Zaire: More evidence on seed-eating in forests on poor soils. *International Journal of Primatology* 15: 681–701.

Manson, J. H. (1994). Mating patterns, mate choice, and birth season heterosexual relationships in free-ranging rhesus macaques. *Primates* 35: 417–433.

Manson, J. H. (1996). Rhesus macaque copulation calls: Re-evaluating the "honest signal" hypothesis. *Primates* 37: 145–154.

Manson, J. H. (1997). Primate consortships: A critical review. *Current Anthropology* 38: 353–374.

Manson, J. H., Perry, S., and Parish, A. R. (1997). Nonconceptive sexual behavior in bonobos and capuchins. *International Journal of Primatology* 18: 767–786.

Marivaux, L., Welcomme, J.-L., Antoine, P.-O., Métais, G., Baloch, I. M., Benammi, M., Chaimanee, Y., Ducrocq, S., and Jaeger, J.-J. (2001). A fossil lemur from the Oligocene of Pakistan. *Science* 294: 587–591.

Marks, J. (1994). Blood will tell (won't it?): A century of molecular discourse in anthropological systematics. *American Journal of Physical Anthropology* 94: 59–79.

Marks, J. (2002). *What It Means to be 98% Chimpanzee: Apes, People, and their Genes.* University of California Press, Berkeley.

Marler, P. and Hobbett, L. (1975). Individuality in a long-range vocalization of wild chimpanzees. *Zeitschrift fur Tierpsychologie* 38: 97–109.

Martin, R. D. (1981). Relative brain size and basal metabolic rate in terrestrial vertebrates. *Nature* 293: 57–60.

Martin, R. D. (1992). Female cycles in relation to paternity in primates societies. In Martin, R. D., Dixson, A. F., and Wickings, E. J. (eds.), *Paternity in Primates: Genetic Tests and Theories,* Karger, Basel, pp. 238–274.

Martin, R. D. (1996). Scaling of the mammalian brain: The maternal energy hypothesis. *New in Physiological Sciences* 11: 149–156.

Martin, R. D. (1998). Comparative aspects of human brain evolution: Scaling, energy costs and confounding variables. In Jablonski, N. G. and Aiello, L. C. (eds.), *The Origin and Diversification of Language,* Memoirs of the California Academy of Sciences, Number 24, Pasadena, pp. 35–68.

Martin, R. D. (2000). Origins, diversity and relationships of lemurs. *International Journal of Primatology* 21: 1021–1049.

Martin, R. D., Dixson, A. F., and Wickings, E. J. (1992). *Paternity in Primates: Genetic Tests and Theories.* Karger, Basel.

Masataka, N. and Fujita, K. (1989). Vocal learning of Japanese and rhesus monkeys. *Behaviour* 109: 191–199.

Mason, W. A. (1993). The nature of social conflict: A psycho-ethological perspective. In Mason, W. A. and Mendoza, S. P. (eds.), *Primate Social Conflict,* SUNY Press, Albany, pp. 13–47.

Mason, W. A. and Mendoza, S. P. (1993). Primate social conflict: An overview of sources, forms, and consequences. In Mason, W. A. and Mendoza, S. P. (eds.), *Primate Social Conflict,* SUNY Press, Albany, pp. 1–11.

Matsuzawa, T. (1996). Chimpanzee intelligence in nature and in captivity: Isomorphism of symbol use and tool use. In McGrew, W. C., Marchant, L. F., and Nishida, T. (eds.), *Great Ape Societies,* Cambridge University Press, New York, pp. 196–209.

McGrew, W. C. (1979). Evolutionary implications of sex differences in chimpanzee predation and tool use. In Hamburg, D. A. and McCown, E. R. (eds.), *The Great Apes,* The Benjamin/Cummings Publishing Company, Menlo Park, California, pp. 441–463.

McGrew, W. C. (1992). *Chimpanzee Material Culture: Implications for Human Evolution.* Cambridge University Press, Cambridge.

McGrew, W. C. (1993). The intelligent use of tools: Twenty propositions. In Gibson, K. R. and Ingold, T. (eds.), *Tools, Language and Cognition in Human Evolution,* Cambridge University Press, Cambridge, pp. 151–170.

McGrew, W. C. (1998). Culture in nonhuman primates? *Annual Review of Anthropology* 27: 301–328.

McGrew, W. C., Ham, R. M., White, L. J. T., Tutin, C. E. G., and Fernandez, M. (1997). Why don't chimpanzees in Gabon crack nuts? *International Journal of Primatology* 18: 353–374.

McGrew, W. C. and Tutin, C. E. G. (1978). Evidence for a social custom in wild chimpanzees. *Man* 13: 234–251.

McGrew, W. C., Marchant, L. F., Scott, S. E., and Tutin, C. E. G. (2001). Intergroup differences in a social custom of wild chimpanzees: The grooming hand-clasp of the Mahale Mountains. *Current Anthropology* 42: 148–153.

McGrew, W. C., Tutin, C. E., Collins, D. A., and File, S. K. (1989). Intestinal parasites of sympatric *Pan troglodytes* and *Papio* spp. at two sites: Gombe (Tanzania) and Mt. Assirik (Senegal). *American Journal of Primatology* 17: 147–155.

McHenry, H. (1975). Fossils and the mosaic nature of human evolution. *Science* 190: 425–431.

McKenna, J. J. (1979). The evolution of allomothering behavior among colobine monkeys: Function and opportunism in evolution. *American Anthropologist* 81: 818–840.

McKey, D. B., Gartlan, J. S., Waterman, P. G., and Choo, G. M. (1981). Food selection by black colobus monkeys (*Colobus satanas*) in relation to plant chemistry. *Biological Journal of the Linnaean Society* 16: 115–146.

McNeil Jr., D. G. (1999). The great ape massacre. *The New York Times Magazine*. May 9, 1999: 54–57.

McRae, M. (1997). Road kill in Cameroon. *Natural History* 106: 36–47.

Meier, B., Albignac, R., Peyriéras, A., Rumpler, Y., and Wright, P. (1987). A new species of *Hapalemur* (Primates) from southeast Madagascar. *Folia Primatologica* 48: 211–215.

Melnick, D. J. and Hoelzer, G. A. (1992). Differences in male and female macaque dispersal lead to contrasting distributions of nuclear and mitochondrial DNA variation. *International Journal of Primatology* 13: 379–393.

Melnick, D. J. and Pearl, M. C. (1987). Cercopithecines in multimale groups: Genetic diversity and population structure. In Smuts, B. B., Cheney, D. L., Seyfarth, R. M., Wrangham, R. W., and Struhsaker, T. T. (eds.), *Primate Societies*, University of Chicago Press, Chicago, pp. 121–134.

Mendes Pontes, A. R. (1997). Habitat partitioning among primates in Maraca Island, Roraima, northern Brazilian Amazonia. *International Journal of Primatology* 18: 131–157.

Menzel, E. W. (1974). A group of young chimpanzees in a one-acre field. In Schrier, A. M. and Stollnitz, F. (eds.), *Behavior of Nonhuman Primates*, Vol. 5, Academic Press, New York, pp. 83–153.

Menzel, E. W. (1991). Chimpanzees (*Pan troglodytes*): Problem seeking versus the bird-in-the-hand, least-effort strategy. *Primates* 32: 497–508.

Michael, R. P., Zumpe, D., Keverne, E. B., and Bonsall, R. W. (1972). Neuroendocrine factors in the control of primate behavior. *Recent Progress in Hormone Research* 28: 665–706.

Miller, G. H., Magee, J. W., Johnson, B. J., Fogell, M. L., Spooner, N. A., McCulloch, M. T., and Ayliffe, L. K. (1999). Pleistocene extinction of *Genyornis newtoni*: Human impact on Australian megafauna. *Science* 283: 205–208.

Miller, R. E. (1971). Experimental studies of communication in the monkey. In Rosenblum, L. A. (ed.), *Primate Behaviour*, Academic Press, New York, pp. 139–175.

Miller, R. E. (1975). Nonverbal expressions of aggression and submission in social groups of primates. In Pliner, P., Krames, L., and Alloway, T. (eds.), *Nonverbal Communication of Aggression*, Plenum Press, New York, pp. 135–160.

Miller, L. E. (1996). The behavioral ecology of wedge-capped capuchin monkeys (*Cebus olivaceus*). In Norconk, M. A., Rosenberger, A. L., and Garber, P. A. (eds.), *Adaptive Radiations of Neotropical Primates*, Plenum Press, New York, pp. 271–288.

Milton, K. (1981). Distribution patterns of tropical plant foods as a stimulus to primate mental development. *American Anthropologist* 83: 534–548.

Milton, K. (1982). Dietary quality and demographic regulation in a howler monkey population. In Leigh, Jr., E. G., Rand, A. S., and Windsor, D. M. (eds.), *The Ecology of a Tropical Forest: Seasonal Rhythms and Long-Term Changes*, Smithsonian Institution Press, Washington, D.C., pp. 273–290.

Milton, K. (1984a). The Role of Food-Processing Factors in Primate Food Choice. In Rodman, P. S. and Cant, J. G. H. (eds.), *Adaptations for Foraging in Nonhuman Primates: Contributions to an Organismal Biology of Prosimians, Monkeys, and Apes*, Columbia University Press, New York, pp. 249–279.

Milton, K. (1984b). Habitat, diet, and activity patterns of free-ranging woolly spider monkeys (*Brachyteles arachnoides*, E. Geoffroy, 1806). *International Journal of Primatology* 5: 491–514.

Milton, K. (1985a). Mating patterns of woolly spider monkeys, *Brachyteles arachnoides*: Implications for female choice. *Behavioral Ecology and Sociobiology* 17: 53–59.

Milton, K. (1985b). Urine washing behavior in the woolly spider monkey (*Brachyteles arachnoides*). *Zeitschrift fur Tierpsychologie* 67: 154–160.

Mitani, J. C. (1985a). Sexual selection and adult male orangutan long calls. *Animal Behaviour* 33: 272–283.

Mitani, J. C. (1985b). Mating behavior of male orangutans in the Kutai Reserve, East Kalimantan, Indonesia. *Animal Behaviour* 33: 392–402.

Mitani, J. C. (1987). Species discrimination of male song in gibbons. *American Journal of Primatology* 13: 413–423.

Mitani, J. C. (1996). Comparative studies of African ape vocal behavior. In McGrew, W. C., Marchant, L. F., and Nishida, T. (eds.), *Great Ape Societies*, Cambridge University Press, New York, pp. 241–254.

Mitani, J. and Gros-Louis, J. (1995). Species and sex differences in the screams of chimpanzees and bonobos. *International Journal of Primatology* 16: 393–411.

Mitani, J. C., Gros-Louis, J., and Manson, J. H. (1996a). Number of males in primate groups: Comparative tests of competing hypotheses. *American Journal of Primatology* 38: 315–332.

Mitani, J. C., Gros-Louis, J., and Richards, A. F. (1996b). Sexual dimorphism, the operational sex ratio, and the intensity of male competition in polygynous primates. *American Naturalist* 147: 966–980.

Mitani, J., Hasegawa, T., Gros-Louis, J., Marler, P., and Byrne, R. (1992). Dialects in wild chimpanzees? *American Journal of Primatology* 27: 233–243.

Mitani, J. C., Hunley, K. L., and Murdoch, M. E. (1999). Geographic variation in the calls of wild chimpanzees: A reassessment. *American Journal of Primatology* 47: 133–151.

Mitani, J. and Nishida, T. (1993). Contexts and social correlates of long-distance calling by male chimpanzees. *Animal Behaviour* 45: 735–746.

Mitani, J. C. and Rodman, P. S. (1979). Territoriality: The relation of ranging patterns and home range size to defendability, with an analysis of territoriality among primate species. *Behavioral Ecology and Sociobiology* 5: 241–251.

Mitani, J. C. and Watts, D. (1997). The evolution of non-maternal caretaking among anthropoid primates: Do helpers help? *Behavioral Ecology and Sociobiology* 40: 213–220.

Mitani, J. C. and Watts, D. P. (1999). Demographic influences on the hunting behavior of chimpanzees. *American Journal of Primatology* 109: 439–454.

Mitani, J. C. and Watts, D. P. (2001). Why do chimpanzees hunt and share meat? *Animal Behaviour* 61: 915–924.

Mitani, J. C., Merriwether, D. A., and Zhang, C. (2000a). Male affiliation, cooperation and kinship in wild chimpanzees. *Animal Behaviour* 59: 885–893.

Mitani, J. C., Struhsaker, T. T., and Lwanga, J. S. (2000b). Primate community dynamics in old growth forest over 23.5 years at Ngogo, Kibale National Park, Uganda: Implications for conservation and census methods. *International Journal of Primatology* 21: 269–286.

Mitani, J. C., Sanders, W. J., Lwanga, J. S., and Windfelder, T. L. (2001). Predatory behavior of crowned hawk-eagles (*Stephanoaetus coronatus*) in Kibale National Park, Uganda. *Behavioral Ecology and Sociobiology* 49: 187–195.

Mitchell, C. L. (1994). Migration alliances and coalitions among adult male South American squirrel monkeys (*Saimiri sciureus*). *Behaviour* 130: 169–190.

Mitchell, C. L., Boinski, S., and van Schaik, C. P. (1991). Competitive regimes and female bonding in two species of squirrel monkeys (*Saimiri oerstedi* and *S. sciureus*). *Behavioral Ecology and Sociobiology* 28: 55–60.

Mitchell, R. W. and Thompson, N. S. (1986). *Deception: Perspectives on Human and Nonhuman Deceit.* State University of New York Press, Albany.

Mittermeier, R. A. (1987). Effects of hunting on rain forest primates. In Marsh, C. W. and Mittermeier, R. A. (eds.), *Primate Conservation in the Tropical Rain Forest,* Alan R. Liss, New York, pp. 109–146.

Mittermeier, R. A. and Cheney, D. L. (1987). Conservation of primates and their habitats. In Smuts, B. B., Cheney, D. L., Seyfarth, R. M., Wrangham, R. W., and Struhsaker, T. T. (eds.), *Primate Societies,* University of Chicago Press, Chicago, pp. 477–490.

Mittermeier, R. A. and Konstant, W. R. (1996/1997). Primate conservation: A retrospective and a look into the 21st century. *Primate Conservation* 17: 7–17.

Mittermeier, R. A., Rylands, A. B., and Konstant, W. R. (1999). Primates of the world: An introduction. In Nowak, R. M. (ed.), *Walker's Primates of the World,* Johns Hopkins University Press, Baltimore, Maryland, pp. 1–52.

Mittermeier, R. A., Rylands, A. B., Konstant, W. R., Eudey, A., Butynski, T., Ganzhorn, J. U., and Rodíguez-Luna, E. (2000). Primate specialist group. *Species* 34: 82–88.

Moffett, M. W. (2000). What's "up?" A critical look at the basic terms of canopy biology. *Biotropica* 32: 569–596.

Molnar, S. (2002). *Human Variation, 5th edition.* Prentice Hall, Upper Saddle River, New Jersey.

Moore, J. (1984). Female transfer in primates. *International Journal of Primatology* 5: 537–589.

Moore, J. (1992a). Dispersal, nepotism, and primate social behavior. *International Journal of Primatology* 13: 361–378.

Moore, J. (1992b). "Savanna" chimpanzees. In Nishida, T., McGrew, W. C., Marler, P., Pickford, M., and de Waal, F. B. M. (eds.), *Topics in Primatology, Vol. i: Human Origins,* University of Tokyo Press, Tokyo, pp. 99–118.

Moore, J. (1993). Inbreeding and outbreeding in primates: What's wrong with 'the dispersing' sex? In Thornhill, N. W. (ed.), *The Natural History of Inbreeding and Outbreeding: Theoretical and Empirical Perspectives,* University of Chicago Press, Chicago, pp. 392–426.

Moore, J. (1996). Savanna chimpanzees, referential models and the last common ancestor. In McGrew, W. C., Marchant, L. F., and Nishida, T. (eds.), *Great Ape Societies,* Cambridge University Press, Cambridge, pp. 275–292.

Moore, J. (1999). Population density, social pathology, and behavioral ecology. *Primates* 40: 1–22.

Moore, J. and Ali, R. (1984). Are dispersal and inbreeding avoidance related? *Animal Behaviour* 32: 94–112.

Moraes, P. L. R., Carvalho Jr., O., and Strier, K. B. (1998). Population variation in patch and party size in muriquis (*Brachyteles arachnoides*). *International Journal of Primatology* 19: 325–337.

Mori, A. (1979). Analysis of population changes by measurement of body weight in the Koshima troop of Japanese monkeys. *Primates* 20: 371–397.

Morin, P. A., Moore, J. J., Chakraborty, R., Jin, L., Goodall, J., and Woodruff, D. S. (1994). Kin selection, social structure, gene flow, and the evolution of chimpanzees. *Science* 265: 1193–1201.

Morin, P. A., Chambers, K. E., Boesch, C., and Vigilant, L. (2001). Quantitative polymerase chain reaction analysis of DNA from noninvasive samples for accurate microsatellite genotyping of wild chimpanzees (*Pan troglodytes verus*). *Molecular Ecology* 10: 1835–1844.

Morin, P. A. and Woodruff, D. S. (1992). Paternity exclusion using multiple hypervariable microsatellite loci amplified from nuclear DNA of hair cells. In Martin, R. D., Dixson, A. F., and Wickings, E. J. (eds.), *Paternity in Primates: Genetic Tests and Theories*, Karger, Basel, pp. 63–81.

Muruthi, P., Altmann, J., and Altmann, S. (1991). Resource base, parity, and reproductive condition affect females' feeding time and nutrient intake within and between groups of a baboon population. *Oecologia* 87: 467–472.

Myers, N., Mittermeier, R. A., Mittermeier, C. G., Fonseca, G. A. B., and Kent, J. (2000). Biodiversity hotspots for conservation priorities. *Nature* 403: 853–858.

Napier, J. R. and Napier, P. H. (1994). *The Natural History of the Primates*. The MIT Press, Cambridge, Massachusetts.

Nash, L. T. (1986). Social organization of two sympatric galagos at Gedi, Kenya. In Else, J. G. and Lee, P. C. (eds.), *Primate Ecology and Conservation*, Cambridge University Press, New York, pp. 125–131.

Nash, L. T. (1993). Juveniles in nongregarious primates. In Pereira, M. E. and Fairbanks, L. A. (eds.), *Juvenile Primates: Life History, Development, and Behavior*, Oxford University Press, New York, pp. 119–137.

Nekaris, K. A. I. (2001). Activity budget of the Mysore slender loris (*Loris tardigradus lydekkerianus*): implications for "slow locomotion." *Folia Primatologica* 72: 228–241.

Nekaris, K. A. I. (2002). Slender in the night. *Natural History* 111(1): 54–59.

Newton, P. N. (1986). Infanticide in an undisturbed forest population of Hanuman langurs (*Presbytis entellus*). *Animal Behaviour* 34: 785–789.

Newton, P. N. and Dunbar, R. I. M. (1994). Colobine monkey society. In Davies, A. G. and Oates, J. F. (eds.), *Colobine Monkeys: Their Ecology, Behaviour and Evolution*, Cambridge University Press, Cambridge, pp. 311–346.

Nickle, D. A. and Heymann, E. W. (1996). Predation on *Orthoptera* and other orders of insects by tamarin monkeys, *Saguinus mystax mystax* and *Saguinus fuscicollis nigrifrons* (Primates: Callitrichidae), in northeastern Peru. *Journal of Zoology* 239: 799–819.

Nicolson, N. A. (1987). Infants, mothers, and other females. In Smuts, B. B., Cheney, D. L., Seyfarth, R. M., Wrangham, R. W., and Struhsaker, T. T. (eds.), *Primate Societies*, University of Chicago Press, Chicago, pp. 330–342.

Nicolson, N. A. (1991). Maternal behavior in human and nonhuman primates. In Loy, J. D. and Peters, C. B. (eds.), *Understanding Behavior: What Primate Studies Tell Us about Human Behavior*, Oxford University Press, New York, pp. 17–50.

Nievergelt, C. M., Digby, L. J., Ramakrishnan, U., and Woodruff, D. S. (2000). Genetic analysis of group composition and breeding systems in a wild common marmoset (*Callithrix jacchus*) population. *International Journal of Primatology* 21: 1–20.

Nikolei, J. and Borries, C. (1997). Sex differential behavior of immature Hanuman langurs (*Presbytis entellus*) in Ramngar, South Nepal. *International Journal of Primatology* 18: 415–437.

Nishida, T. (1979). The social structure of chimpanzees of the Mahale Mountains. In Hamburg, D. A. and McCown, E. R. (eds.), *The Great Apes*, Benjamin/Cummings Publishing, Menlo Park, California, pp. 73–121.

Nishida, T. (1987). Local traditions and cultural transmission. In Smuts, B. B., Cheney, D. L., Seyfarth, R. M., Wrangham, R. W., and Struhsaker, T. T. (eds.), *Primate Societies*, University of Chicago Press, Chicago, pp. 462–474.

Nishida, T. (1990). A quarter century of research in the Mahale Mountains: An overview. In Nishida, T. (ed.), *The Chimpanzees of the Mahale Mountains: Sexual and Life History Strategies*, University of Tokyo Press, Japan, pp. 3–35.

Nishida, T. (1997). Comment. *Current Anthropology* 38: 568–569.

Nishida, T. and Hosaka, K. (1996). Coalition strategies among adult male chimpanzees of the Mahale Mountains, Tanzania. In McGrew, W. C., Marchant, L. F., and Nishida, T. (eds.), *Great Ape Societies*, Cambridge University Press, New York, pp. 114–134.

Nishida, T., Takasaki, H., and Takahata, Y. (1990). Demography and reproductive profiles. In Nishida, T. (ed.), *The Chimpanzees of the Mahale Mountains*, University of Tokyo Press, Tokyo, pp. 63–97.

Noë, R. (1990). A Veto game played by baboons: A challenge to the use of the Prisoner's Dilemma as a paradigm for reciprocity and cooperation. *Animal Behaviour* 39: 78–90.

Noë, R. (1994). A model of coalition formation among male baboons with fighting ability as the crucial parameter. *Animal Behaviour* 47: 211–213.

Noë, R. and Bshary, R. (1997). The formation of red colobus-diana monkey associations under predation pressure from chimpanzees. *Proceedings from the Royal Society of London B* 264: 253–259.

Noë, R. and Sluijter, A. A. (1995). Which adult male savanna baboons form coalitions? *International Journal of Primatology* 16: 77–105.

van Noordwijk, M. A. and van Schaik, C. P. (1985). Male migration and rank acquisition in wild long-tailed macaques (*Macaca fascicularis*). *Animal Behaviour* 33: 849–861.

van Noordwijk, M. A. and van Schaik, C. P. (1987). Competition among female long-tailed macaques, *Macaca fascicularis. Animal Behaviour* 35: 577–589.

van Noordwijk, M. A. and van Schaik, C. P. (1999). The effects of dominance rank and group size on female lifetime reproductive success in wild long-tailed macaques, *Macaca fascicularis. Primates* 40: 105–130.

van Noordwijk, M. A. and van Schaik, C. P. (2000). Reproductive patterns in eutherian mammals: Adaptations against infanticide. In van Schaik, C. P. and Janson, C. H. (eds.), *Infanticide by Males,* Cambridge University Press, Cambridge, pp.322–360.

Norconk, M. A. (1996). Seasonal variation in the diets of white-faced and bearded sakis (*Pithecia pithecia* and *Chiropotes satanas*) in Guri Lake, Venezuela. In Norconk, M. A., Rosenberger, A. L., and Garber, P. A. (eds.), *Adaptive Radiations of Neotropical Primates,* Plenum Press, New York, pp. 403–423.

Norconk, M. A., Grafton, B. W., and Conklin-Brittain, N. L. (1998). Seed dispersal by neotropical seed predators. *American Journal of Primatology* 45: 103–126.

Norconk, M. A., Wertis, C., and Kinzey, W. G. (1997). Seed predation by monkeys and macaws in eastern Venezuela: Preliminary findings. *Primates* 38: 177–184.

Nowak, R. M. (2000). *Walker's Primates of the World.* Johns Hopkins University Press, Baltimore, Maryland.

Nunes, A. and Chapman, C. A. (1997). A re-evaluation of factors influencing the sex ratio of spider monkey populations with new data from Maraca Island, Brazil. *Folia Primatologica* 68: 31–33.

Nunn, C. L. (1999a). The number of males in primate social groups: a comparative test of the socioecological model. *Behavioral Ecology and Sociobiology* 46: 1–13.

Nunn, C. L. (1999b). The evolution of exaggerated sexual swellings in primates and the graded-signal hypothesis. *Animal Behaviour* 58: 229–246.

Nunn, C. L. and Barton, R. A. (2001). Comparative methods for studying primate adaptation and allometry. *Evolutionary Anthropology* 10: 81–98.

Nunn, C. L., Gittleman, J. L., and Antonovics, J. (2000). Promiscuity and the primate immune system. *Science* 2290: 1168–1170.

Nunn, C. L. and Pereira, M. E. (2000). Group histories and offspring sex ratios in ringtailed lemurs (*Lemur catta*). *Behavioral Ecology and Sociobiology* 48: 18–28.

Oates, J. (1977). The guereza and its food. In Clutton-Brock, T. H. (ed.), *Primate Ecology: Studies of Feeding and Ranging Behavior in Lemurs, Monkeys, and Apes,* Academic Press, London, pp. 276–323.

Oates, J. F. (1987). Food distribution and foraging behavior. In Smuts, B. B., Cheney, D. L., Seyfarth, R. M., Wrangham, R. W., and Struhsaker, T. T. (eds.), *Primate Societies,* University of Chicago Press, Chicago, pp. 197–209.

Oates, J. F. (1994). Africa's primates in 1992: Conservation issues and options. *American Journal of Primatology* 34: 61–71.

Oates, J. F. (1996). Habitat alteration, hunting and the conservation of folivorous primates in African forests. *Australian Journal of Ecology* 21: 1–9.

Oates, J. F., Anadu, P. A., Gadsby, E. L., and Werre, J. L. (1992). Sclater's guenon: A rare Nigerian monkey threatened by deforestation. *National Geographic Research* 8: 476–491.

O'Brien, S. J. and Mayr, E. (1991). Bureaucratic mischief: Recognizing endangered species and subspecies. *Science* 251: 1187–1188.

O'Brien, T. G. (1991). Female-male social interactions in wedge-capped capuchin monkeys: Benefits and costs of group living. *Animal Behaviour* 41: 555–568.

O'Brien, T. G. and Robinson, J. G. (1993). Stability of social relationships in female wedge-capped capuchin monkeys. In Pereira, M. E. and Fairbanks, L. A. (eds.), *Juvenile Primates: Life History, Development, and Behavior,* Oxford University Press, New York, pp. 197–210.

Oddie, K. (1998). Sex discrimination before birth. *Trends in Ecology and Evolution* 13: 130–131.

Oftedal, O. T. and Iverson, S. J. (1995). Comparative analysis of nonhuman milks. In Jensen, R. G. (ed.), *Handbook of Milk Composition,* Academic Press, San Diego, pp. 749–788.

Oka, T. and Takenaka, O. (2001). Wild gibbons' parentage tested by non-invasive DNA sampling and PCR-amplified polymorphic microsatellites. *Primates* 42: 67–73.

Olupot, W., Chapman, C. A., Waser, P. M., and Isabirye-Basuta, G. (1997). Mangabey (*Cercocebus albigena*) ranging patterns in relation to fruit availability and the risk of parasite infection in Kibale National Park, Uganda. *American Journal of Primatology* 43: 65–78.

Olupot, W., Waser, P. M., and Chapman, C. A. (1998). Fruit finding by mangabeys (*Lophocebus albigena*): Are monitoring of fig trees and use of sympatric frugivore calls possible strategies? *International Journal of Primatology* 19: 339–353.

Ostro, L. E. T., Silver, S. C., Koontz, F. W., Horwich, R. H., and Brockett, R. (2001). Shifts in social structure of black howler (*Alouatta pigra*) groups associated with natural and experimental variation in population density. *International Journal of Primatology* 22: 733–748.

Ottoni, E. B. and Mannu, M. (2001). Semifree-ranging tufted capuchins (*Cebus apella*) spontaneously use tools to crack open nuts. *International Journal of Primatology* 22: 347–358.

Overdorff, D. J. (1996). Ecological correlates to social structure in two lemur species in Madagascar. *American Journal of Physical Anthropology* 100: 487–506.

Overdorff, D. J. (1998). Are *Eulemur* species pairbonded? Social organization and mating strategies in *Eulemur fulvus rufus* from 1988–1995 in southeast Madagascar. *American Journal of Physical Anthropology* 105: 153–166.

Packer, C. (1977). Reciprocal altruism in *Papio anubis*. *Nature* 265: 441–443.

Packer, C. (1979a). Inter-troop transfer and inbreeding avoidance in *Papio anubis*. *Animal Behaviour* 27: 1–36.

Packer, C. (1979b). Male dominance and reproductive activity in *Papio anubis*. *Animal Behaviour* 27: 37–45.

Packer, C., Collins, D. A., Sindlimwo, A., and Goodall, J. (1995). Reproductive constraints on aggressive competition in female baboons. *Nature* 373: 60–63.

Packer, C., Tatar, M., and Collins, A. (1998). Reproductive cessation in female mammals. *Nature* 392: 807–811.

Pagel, M. D. and Harvey, P. H. (1993). Evolution of the juvenile period in mammals. In Pereira, M. E. and Fairbanks, L. A. (eds.), *Juvenile Primates: Life History, Development, and Behavior*, Oxford University Press, New York, pp. 28–37.

Palombit, R. A. (1993). Lethal territorial aggression in white-handed gibbons. *American Journal of Primatology* 31: 311–318.

Palombit, R. A. (1994). Extra-pair copulations in a monogamous ape. *Animal Behaviour* 47: 721–723.

Palombit, R. A. (1995). Longitudinal patterns of reproduction in wild female siamang (*Hylobates syndactylus*) and white-handed gibbons (*Hylobates lar*). *International Journal of Primatology* 16: 739–760.

Palombit, R. A. (1999). Infanticide and the evolution of pair bonds in nonhuman primates. *Evolutionary Anthropology* 7: 117–129.

Palombit, R. A. (2000). Infanticide and the evolution of male-female bonds in animals. In van Schaik, C. P. and Janson, C. H. (eds.), *Infanticide by Males*, Cambridge University Press, Cambridge, pp. 239–268.

Palombit, R. A., Cheney, D. L., and Seyfarth, R. M. (2001). Female-female competition for male 'friends' in wild chama baboons, *Papio cynocephalus ursinus*. *Animal Behaviour* 61: 1159–1171.

Palombit, R. A., Seyfarth, R. M., and Cheney, D. L. (1997). The adaptive value of "friendships" to female baboons: Experimental and observational evidence. *Animal Behaviour* 54: 599–614.

Panger, M. A. (1998). Hand preferences in free-ranging white-throated capuchins (*Cebus capucinus*) in Costa Rica. *International Journal of Primatology* 19: 133–163.

Panger, M. (1999). Capuchin object manipulation. In Dolhinow, P. and Fuentes, A. (eds.), *The Nonhuman Primates*, Mayfield Publishing Company, Mountain View, California, pp. 115–120.

Parker, S. T. and Gibson, K. R. (1977). Object manipulation, tool use and sensorimotor intelligence as feeding adaptations in *Cebus* monkeys and great apes. *Journal of Human Evolution*. 6: 623–641.

Parker, S. T. and Gibson, K. R. (1990). *"Language" and Intelligence in Monkeys and Apes: Comparative Developmental Perspectives*. Cambridge University Press, New York.

Parnell, R. J. and Buchanan-Smith, H. M. (2001). An unusual social display by gorillas. *Nature* 412: 294.

Parr, L. A. and de Waal, F. B. M. (1999). Visual kin recognition in chimpanzees. *Nature* 399: 647–648.

Parr, L. A., Hopkins, W. D., and de Waal, F. B. M. (1998). The perception of facial expressions by chimpanzees, *Pan troglodytes*. *Evolution of Communication* 2: 1–23.

Partridge, L. and Harvey, P. H. (1988). The ecological context of life history evolution. *Science* 241: 1449–1455.

Paterson, J. D. (2001). *Primate Behavior: An Exercise Workbook*, 2nd Edition. Waveland Press, Prospect Heights, Illinois.

Paul, A. (1999). The socioecology of infant handling in primates: Is the current model convincing? *Primates* 40: 33–46.

Pavelka, M. S. M. (1993). *Monkeys of the Mesquite: The Social Life of the South Texas Snow Monkey.* Kendall/Hunt Publishing Company, Dubuque, Iowa.

Pavelka, M. S. M. (1999). Primate gerontology. In Dolhinow, P. and Fuentes, A. (eds.), *The Nonhuman Primates,* Mayfield Publishing Company, Mountain View, California, pp. 220–224.

Pavelka, M. S. M. and Fedigan, L. M. (1999). Reproductive termination in female Japanese macaques: A comparative life history perspective. *American Journal of Physical Anthropology* 109: 455–464.

Peccei, J. S. (2001). Menopause: Adaptation or epiphenomenon? *Evolutionary Anthropology* 10: 43–57.

Pereira, M. E. (1991). Asynchrony within estrous synchrony among ringtailed lemurs (Primates: Lemuridae). *Physiology and Behavior* 49: 47–52.

Pereira, M. E. (1993a). Juvenility in animals. In Pereira, M. E. and Fairbanks, L. A. (eds.), *Juvenile Primates: Life History, Development, and Behaviour,* Oxford University Press, New York, pp. 17–27.

Pereira, M. E. (1993b). Agonistic interactions, dominance relations, and ontogenetic trajectories in ringtailed lemurs. In Pereira, M. E. and Fairbanks, L. A. (eds.), *Juvenile Primates: Life History, Development, and Behavior,* Oxford University Press, New York, pp. 285–305.

Pereira, M. E. and Fairbanks, L. A. (1993). What are juvenile primates all about? In Pereira, M. E. and Fairbanks, L. A. (eds.), *Juvenile Primates: Life History, Development, and Behavior,* Oxford University Press, New York, pp. 3–12.

Pereira, M. E. and Macedonia, J. M. (1991). Ringtailed lmeur anti-predator calls denote predator class, not response urgency. *Animal Behaviour* 41: 543–544.

Peres, C. A. (1990). Effects of hunting on western Amazonian primate communities. *Biological Conservation* 54: 47–59.

Peres, C. A. (1992). Prey–capture benefits in a mixed-species group of Amazonian tamarins, *Saguinus fuscicollis* and *S. mystax. Behavioral Ecology and Sociobiology* 31: 339–347.

Peres, C. A. (1994). Diet and feeding ecology of gray woolly monkeys (*Lagothrix lagotricha cana*) in central Amazonia: Comparisons with other atelines. *International Journal of Primatology* 15: 333–372.

Peres, C. A. (1996). Use of space, spatial group structure, and foraging group size of gray woolly monkeys (*Lagothrix Lagotricha cana*) at Urucu,

Brazil. In Norconk, M. A., Rosenberger, A. L., and Garber, P. A. (eds.), *Adaptive Radiations of Neotropical Primates,* Plenum Press, New York, pp. 467–488.

Peres, C. A. and Janson, C. H. (1999). Species coexistence, distribution and environmental determinants of neotropical primate richness: A community-level zoogeographic analysis. In Fleagle, J. G., Janson, C. H., and Reed, K. E. (eds.), *Primate Communities,* Cambridge University Press, Cambridge, pp. 55–74.

Perry, S. (1996). Intergroup encounters in wild white-faced capuchins (*Cebus capucinus*). *International Journal of Primatology* 17: 309–330.

Perry, S. (1998a). A case report of a male rank reversal in a group of wild white-faced capuchins (*Cebus capucinus*). *Primates* 39: 51–70.

Perry, S. (1998b). Male–male social relationships in wild white-faced capuchins, *Cebus capucinus. Behaviour* 135: 139–172.

Petrie, M. and Kempenaers, B. (1998). Extra-pair paternity in birds: Explaining variation between species and populations. *Trends in Ecology and Evolution* 13: 52–58.

Phillips-Conroy, J. E. (1986). Baboons, diet, and disease: Food plant selection and schistosomiasis. In Taub, D. M. and King, F. A. (eds.), *Current Perspectives in Primate Social Dynamics,* Van Nostrand and Reinhold, New York, pp. 287–304.

Phillips-Conroy, J. E. and Jolly, C. J. (1981). Sexual dimorphism in two subspecies of Ethiopian baboons (*Papio hamadryas*) and their hybrids. *American Journal of Physical Anthropology* 56: 115–129.

Phillips-Conroy, J. E., Jolly, C. J., and Brett, F. L. (1991). Characteristics of hamadryas-like male baboons living in anubis baboon troops in the Awash hybrid zone, Ethiopia. *American Journal of Physical Anthropology* 86: 353–368.

Phillips-Conroy, J. E., Jolly, C. J., Nystrom, P., and Hemmalin, H. A. (1992). Migration of male hamadryas baboons into anubis groups in the Awash National Park, Ethiopia. *International Journal of Primatology* 13: 455–476.

Pimm, S. L. and Raven, P. (2000). Extinction by numbers. *Nature* 403: 843–845.

Pinder, L. (1986). Projeto mico-leão. III. Avaliação tecnica de translocação em *Leontopithecus rosalia* (Linnaeus, 1766) (Callitrichidae, Primates). In Thiago de Mello, M. (ed.), *A Primatologia no Brasil— 2,* Sociedade Brasileira de Primatologia, Campinas, pp. 235–241.

Pinto, L. P. S., Costa, C. M. R., Strier, K. B., and da Fonseca, G. A. B. (1993). Habitats, density, and group size of primates in the Reserva Biologica Augusto Ruschi (Nova Lombardia), Santa Teresa, Brazil. *Folia Primatologica* 61: 135–143.

Pissinati, A., Coimbra-Filho, A. F., and Rylands, A. B. (1998). Observations on reproduction and behavior of the muriqui, *Brachyteles arachnoides,* in captivity. *Neotropical Primates* 6: 40–45.

Plant, T. M. (1994). Puberty in primates. In Knobil, E. and Neill, J. D. (eds.), *The Physiology of Reproduction,* Second Edition, Raven Press, Ltd., New York, pp. 453–485.

Pope, T. R. (1990). The reproductive consequences of male cooperation in the red howler monkey: Paternity exclusion in multi-male and single-male troops using genetic markers. *Behavioral Ecology and Sociobiology* 27: 439–446.

Pope, T. R. (1992). The influence of dipsersal patterns and mating systems on genetic differentiation within and between populations of the red howler monkey (*Alouatta seniculus*). *Evolution* 46: 1112–1128.

Pope, T. R. (1996). Socioecology, population fragmentation, and patterns of genetic loss in endangered primates. In Avise, J. A. and Hamrick, J. L. (eds.), *Conservation Genetics,* Chapman and Hall, New York, pp. 119–159.

Pope, T. R. (1998). Effects of demographic change on group kin structure and gene dynamics of populations of red howling monkeys. *J Mammalogy* 79: 692–712.

Pope, T. R. (2000). Reproductive success increases with degree of kinship in cooperative coalitions of female red howler monkeys (*Alouatta seniculus*). *Behavioral Ecology and Sociobiology* 48: 253–267.

Popp, J. L. and DeVore, I. (1979). Aggressive competition and social dominance theory: Synopsis. In Hamburg, D. A. and McCown, E. R. (eds.), *The Great Apes,* The Benjamin/Cummings Publishing Company, Menlo Park, California, pp. 317–338.

Porter, L. M. (2001). Benefits of polyspecific associations for the Goeldi's monkey (*Callimico goeldii*). *American Journal of Primatology* 54: 143–158.

Potts, W. K., Manning, C. J., and Wakeland, E. K. (1991). Mating patterns in seminatural populations of mice influenced by MHC genotype. *Nature* 352: 619–621.

Povinelli, D. J., Nelson, K. E., and Boysen, S. T. (1992a). Comprehension of role reversal in chimpanzees: Evidence of empathy? *Animal Behaviour* 43: 633–640.

Povinelli, D. J., Parks, K. A., and Novak, M. A. (1992b). Role reversal by rhesus monkeys but no evidence of empathy. *Animal Behaviour* 44: 269–281.

Power, M. L. (1999). Aspects of energy expenditure of callitrichid primates: Physiology and behavior. In Dolhinow, P. and Fuentes, A. (eds.), *The Nonhuman Primates,* Mayfield Publishing Company, Mountain View, California, pp. 225–230.

Premack, D. and Woodruff, G. (1978). Does the chimpanzee have a theory of mind? *Behavioral and Brain Sciences* 4: 515–526.

Printes, R. C. and Strier, K. B. (1999). Behavioral correlates of dispersal in female muriquis (*Brachyteles arachnoides*). *International Journal of Primatology* 20: 941–960.

Pryce, C. R., Schwarzenberger, F., and Dobeli, M. (1994). Monitoring fecal samples for estrogen excretion across the ovarian cycle in Goeldi's monkey (*Callimico goeldii*). *Zoo Biology* 13: 219–230.

Purvis, A., Agapow, P.-M., Gittleman, J. L., and Mace, G. M. (2000). Nonrandom extinction and the loss of evolutionary history. *Science* 288: 328–330.

Pusey, A. E. and Packer, C. (1987). Dispersal and philopatry. In Smuts, B. B., Cheney, D. L., Seyfarth, R. M., Wrangham, R. W., and Struhsaker, T. T. (eds.), *Primate Societies,* University of Chicago Press, Chicago, pp. 250–266.

Pusey, A. E. and Packer, C. (1997). The ecology of relationships. In Krebs, J. R. and Davies, N. B. (eds.), *Behavioural Ecology,* Fourth Edition, Blackwell Scientific Ltd, Oxford, pp. 254–283.

Pusey, A., Williams, J., and Goodall, J. (1997). The influence of dominance rank on the reproductive success of female chimpanzees. *Science* 277: 828–831.

Quiatt, D. and Reynolds, V. (1993). *Primate Behaviour-Information, Social Knowledge, and the Evolution of Culture.* Cambridge University Press, Cambridge.

Rajpurohit, L. S. and Sommer, V. (1991). Sex differences in mortality among langurs (*Presbytis entellus*) of Jodhpur, Rajasthan. *Folia Primatologica* 56: 17–27.

Rajpurohit, L. S. and Sommer, V. (1993). Juvenile male emigration from natal one-male troops in Hanuman langurs. In Pereira, M. E. and Fairbanks, L. A. (eds.), *Juvenile Primates: Life History, Development, and Behavior,* Oxford University Press, New York, pp. 86–103.

Rasoloharijaona, S., Rakotosamimanana, B., and Zimmermann, E. (2000). Infanticide by a male Milne Edwards' sportive lemur (*Lepilemur edwardsi*) in Ampiljoroa, NW-Madagascar. *International Journal of Primatology* 21: 41–45.

Reed, K. E. (1999). Population density of primates in communities: Differences in community structure. In Fleagle, J. G., Janson, C. H., and Reed,

K. E. (eds.), *Primate Communities,* Cambridge University Press, Cambridge, pp. 116–140.

Reed, K. E. and Fleagle, J. G. (1995). Geographic and climatic control of primate diversity. *Proceedings of the National Academy of Sciences, USA* 92: 7874–7876.

Reichard, U. (1995). Extra-pair copulation in a monogamous gibbon (*Hylobates lar*). *Ethology* 100: 99–112.

Reichard, U. and Sommer, V. (1997). Group encounters in wild gibbons (*Hylobates lar*): Agonism, affiliation, and the concept of infanticide. *Behaviour* 134: 1135–1174.

Remis, M. J. (1997a). Western lowland gorillas (*Gorilla gorilla gorilla*) as seasonal frugivores: Use of variable resources. *American Journal of Primatology* 43: 87–109.

Remis, M. J. (1997b). Ranging and grouping patterns of a western lowland gorilla group at Bai Hokou, Central African Republic. *American Journal of Primatology* 43: 111–133.

Remis, M. J., Dierenfeld, E. S., Mowry, C. B., and Carroll, R. W. (2001). Nutritional aspects of western lowland gorilla (*Gorilla gorilla gorilla*) diet during seasons of fruit scarcity at Bai Hokou, Central African Republic. *International Journal of Primatology* 22: 807–836.

Richard, A. F. (1981). Changing assumptions in primate ecology. *American Anthropologist* 83: 517–533.

Richard, A. F. (1985). *Primates in Nature.* W. H. Freeman, New York.

Richard, A. F. (1992). Aggressive competition between males, female-controlled polygyny and sexual monomorphism in a Malagasy primate, *Propithecus verreauxi. Journal of Human Evolution* 22: 395–406.

Richard, A. F. and Dewar, R. E. (1991). Lemur ecology. *Annual Review of Ecology and Systematics* 22: 145–175.

Richard, A. F., Goldstein, S. J., and Dewar, R. E. (1989). Weed macaques: The evolutionary implications of macaque feeding ecology. *International Journal of Primatology* 10: 569–594.

Ridley, M. (1986). The number of males in a primate troop. *Animal Behaviour* 34: 1848–1858.

Rijksen, H. D. (1974). Orangutan conservation and rehabilitation in Sumatra. *Biological Conservation* 6: 20–25.

Riss, D. C. and Goodall, J. (1977). The recent rise to the alpha rank in a population of free-living chimpanzees. *Folia Primatologica* 27: 134–151.

Robbins, M. M. (1995). A demographic analysis of male life history and social structure of mountain gorillas. *Behaviour* 132: 21–47.

Robbins, M. M. (1996). Male–male interactions in heterosexual and all-male wild mountain gorilla groups. *Ethology* 102: 942–965.

Robbins, M. M. (2001). Variation in the social system of mountain gorillas: The male perspective. In Robbins, M. M., Sicotte, P., and Stewart, K. J. (eds.), *Mountain Gorillas,* Cambridge University Press, Cambridge, pp. 29–58.

Robbins, M. M. and Czekala, N. M. (1997). A preliminary investigation of urinary testosterone and cortisol levels in wild male mountain gorillas. *American Journal of Primatology* 43: 51–64.

Roberts, D. F. (1968). Genetic effects of population size reduction. *Nature* 220: 1084–1088.

Roberts, G. and Sherratt, T. N. (1998). Development of cooperative relationships through increasing investment. *Nature* 394: 175–179.

Robinson, J. G. (1988a). Group size in wedge-capped capuchin monkeys *Cebus olivaceus* and the reproductive success of males and females. *Behavioral Ecology and Sociobiology* 23: 187–197.

Robinson, J. G. (1988b). Demography and group structure in wedge-capped capuchin monkeys, *Cebus olivaceus. Behaviour* 104: 202–232.

Robinson, J. G. and Janson, C. H. (1987). Capuchins, squirrel monkeys, and atelines: Socioecological convergence. In Smuts, B. B., Cheney, D. L., Seyfarth, R. M., Wrangham, R. W., and Struhsaker, T. T. (eds.), *Primate Societies,* University of Chicago Press, Chicago, pp. 69–82.

Rodman, P. S. (1984). Foraging and social systems of orangutans and chimpanzees. In Rodman, P. S. and Cant, J. G. H. (eds.), *Adaptations for Foraging in Nonhuman Primates,* Columbia University Press, New York, pp. 134–160.

Rodman, P. S. and Mitani, J. C. (1987). Orangutans: Sexual dimorphism in a solitary species. In Smuts, B. B., Cheney, D. L., Seyfarth, R. M., Wrangham, R. W., and Struhsaker, T. T. (eds.), *Primate Societies,* University of Chicago Press, Chicago, pp. 146–154.

Rogers, J. (1992). Nuclear DNA polymorphisms in hominoids and cercopithecoids: Applications to paternity testing. In Martin, R. D., Dixson, A. F., and Wickings, E. J. (eds.), *Paternity in Primates: Genetic Tests and Theories,* Karger, Basel, pp. 82–95.

Rogers, M. E., Voysey, B. C., McDonald, K. E., Parnell, R. J., and Tutin, C. E. G. (1998). Lowland gorillas and seed dispersal: The importance of nest sites. *American Journal of Primatology* 45: 45–68.

Roonwal, M. L. and Mohnot, S. M. (1977). *Primates of South Asia: Ecology, Sociology, and Behavior.* Harvard University Press, Cambridge.

van Roosmalen, M. G. M., van Roosmalen, T., Mitter-meier, R. A., and Rylands, A. B. (2000). Two new species of marmoset, genus *Callithrix* Erxleben, 1977 (Callitrichidae, Primates), from the Tapajós/Madeira interfluvium, south Central Amazonia, Brazil. *Neotropical Primates* 8: 2–18.

Rose, K. D. (1995). The earliest primates. *Evolutionary Anthropology* 3: 159–173.

Rose, L. M. (1994). Sex differences in diet and forag-ing behavior in white-faced capuchins (*Cebus capucinus*). *International Journal of Primatology* 15: 95–114.

Rose, L. M. (1997). Vetebrate predation and food-sharing in *Cebus* and *Pan*. *International Journal of Primatology* 18: 727–765.

Rose, L. M. (2001). Meat and the early human diet: In-sights from neotropical primate studies. In Stan-ford, C. B. and Bunn, H. T. (eds.), *Meat Eating and Human Evolution*, Oxford University Press, Ox-ford. pp. 141–159.

Rosenbaum, B., O'Brien, T. G., Kinnaird, M., and Supriatna, J. (1998). Population densities of Su-lawesi crested black macaques (*Macaca nigra*) on Bacan and Sulawesi, Indonesia: Effects of habi-tat disturbance and hunting. *American Journal of Primatology* 44: 89–106.

Rosenberger, A. L. and Kinzey, W. G. (1976). Func-tional patterns of molar occlusion in platyrrhine primates. *American Journal of Physical Anthropol-ogy* 45: 281–298.

Ross, C. (1991). Life history patterns of New World monkeys. *International Journal of Primatology* 12: 481–502.

Ross, C. (2001). Park or ride? Evolution of infant car-rying in primates. *International Journal of Prima-tology* 22: 749–771.

Roush, W. (1997). Chimp retirement plan proposed. *Science* 277: 471.

Rowe, N. (1996). *The Pictorial Guide to the Living Pri-mates*. Pogomias Press, New York.

Rowell, T. E. (1966). Forest living baboons in Uganda. *Journal of the Zoological Society of London* 147: 344–364.

Rowell, T. E. (1974). The concept of social dominance. *Behavioral Biology* 131–154.

Rowell, T. E. (1993). Reification of social systems. *Evolutionary Anthropology* 2: 135–137.

Rowell, T. E. and Mitchell, B. J. (1991). Comparison of seed dispersal of guenons in Kenya and capu-chins in Panama. *Journal of Tropical Ecology* 7: 269–274.

de Ruiter, J. R. and van Hooff, J. A. R. A. M. (1993). Male dominance and reproductive success in primate groups. *Primates* 34: 513–523.

de Ruiter, J. R. and Geffen, E. (1998). Relatedness of matrilines, dispersing males and social groups in long-tailed macaques (*Macaca fascicularis*). *Proceedings of the Royal Society of London, Series B* 265: 79–87.

de Ruiter, J. R., van Hooff, J. A. R. A. M., and Schef-frahn, W. (1994). Social and genetic aspects of paternity in wild long-tailed macaques. *Behav-iour* 129: 203–224.

Rylands, A. B. (1996). Habitat and the evolution of so-cial and reproductive behavior in Callitrichidae. *American Journal of Primatology* 38: 5–18.

Rylands, A. B., Mittermeier, R. A., and Luna, E. R. (1995). A species list for the New World primates (Platyrrhini): Distribution by country, endemism, and conservation status according to the Mace-Land system. *Neotropical Primates* (Supplement) 3: 113–160.

Rylands, A. B., Mittermeier, R. A., and Luna, E. R. (1997). Conservation of neotropical primates: Threatened species and an analysis of primate diversity by country and region. *Folia Primato-logica* 68: 134–169.

Rylands, A., Strier, K., Mittermier, R., Borovansky, J., and Seal, U. S. (1998). *Population and Habitat Viability Assessment Workshop for the Muriqui (Brachyteles arachnoides)*. Captive Breeding Spe-cialist Group/IUCN, Apple Valley, Minnesota.

Sade, D. S., Cushing, K., Cushing, P., Dunaif, J., Figueroa, A., Kaplan, J. R., Lauer, C., Rhodes, D., and Schneider, J. (1976). Population dynamics in relation to social structure on Cayo Santiago. *Yearbook of Physical Anthropology* 20: 253–262.

Sahlins, M. (1976). *The Use and Abuse of Biology: An Anthropological Critique of Sociobiology*. Univer-sity of Michigan Press, Michigan.

Sakura, O. (1994). Factors affecting party size and composition of chimpanzees (*Pan troglodytes verus*) at Bossou, Guinea. *International Journal of Primatology* 15: 167–183.

Samuels, A. and Altmann, J. (1991). Baboons of the Amboseli Basin: Demographic stability and change. *International Journal of Primatology* 12: 1–19.

Samuels, A., Silk, J. B., and Altmann, J. (1987). Conti-nuity and change in dominance relations among female baboons. *Animal Behaviour* 35: 785–793.

Sapolsky, R. M. and Ray, J. C. (1989). Styles of domi-nance and their endocrine correlates among wild olive baboons (*Papio anubis*). *American Journal of Primatology* 18: 1–13.

Sauther, M. L. and Sussman, R. W. (1993). A new in-terpretation of the social organization and mat-ing system of the ringtailed lemur (*Lemur catta*).

In Kappeler, P. M. and Ganzhorn, J. U. (eds.), *Lemur Social Systems and Their Ecological Basis*, Plenum Press, New York, pp. 111–121.

Sauther, M. L., Sussman, R. W., and Gould, L. (1999). The socioecology of ringtailed lemur: Thirty-five years of research. *Evolutionary Anthropology* 8: 120–132.

Savage, A., Giraldo, L. H., Soto, L. H., and Snowdon, C. T. (1996a). Demography, group composition, and dispersal in wild cotton-top tamarin (*Saguinus oedipus*) groups. *American Journal of Primatology* 38: 85–100.

Savage, A., Shideler, S. E., Soto, L. H., Causado, J., Giraldo, L. H., Lasley, B. L., and Snowdon, C. T. (1997). Reproductive events of wild cotton-top tamarins (*Saguinus oedipus*) in Colombia. *American Journal of Primatology* 43: 329–337.

Savage, A., Snowdon, C. T., Giraldo, L. H., and Soto, L. H. (1996b). Parental care patterns and vigilance in wild cotton-top tamarins (*Saguinus oedipus*). In Norconk, M. A., Rosenberger, A. L., and Garber, P. A. (eds.), *Adaptive Radiations of Neotropical Primates*, Plenum Press, New York, pp. 187–199.

Savage, A., Ziegler, T. E., and Snowdon, C. T. (1988). Sociosexual development, pair bond formation, and mechanisms of fertility suppression in female cotton-top tamarins (*Saguinus oedipus oedipus*). *American Journal of Primatology* 14: 345–359.

Savage-Rumbaugh, E. S., Wilkerson, B. J., and Bakeman, R. (1977). Spontaneous gestural communication among conspecifics in the pygmy chimpanzee. In Bourne, G. H. (ed.), *Progress in Ape Research*, Academic Press, New York, pp. 97–116.

van Schaik, C. P. (1983). Why are diurnal primates living in groups? *Behaviour* 87: 120–144.

van Schaik, C. P. (1989). The ecology of social relationships amongst primate females. In Standen, V. and Foley, R. A. (eds.), *Comparative Socioecology: The Behavioural Ecology of Humans and Other Mammals*, Blackwell Scientific, Oxford, pp. 195–218.

van Schaik, C. P. (1999). The socioecology of fission-fusion sociality in orangutans. *Primates* 40: 69–86.

van Schaik, C. P. and Aureli, F. (2000). The natural history of valuable relationships in primates. In Aureli, F. and de Waal, F. B. M. (eds.), *Natural Conflict Resolution*, University of California Press, Berkeley, pp. 307–333.

van Schaik, C. P. and Fox, E. A. (1996). Manufacture and use of tools in wild Sumatran orangutans. *Naturwissenschaften* 83: 186–188.

van Schaik, C. P. and van Hooff, J. A. R. A. M. (1996). Toward an understanding of the orangutan's social system. In McGrew, W. C., Marchant, L. F., and Nishida, T. (eds.), *Great Ape Societies*, Cambridge University Press, New York, pp. 3–15.

van Schaik, C. P. and Hrdy, S. B. (1991). Intensity of local resource competition shapes the relationship between maternal rank and sex ratios at birth in cercopithecine primates. *American Naturalist* 138: 155–162.

van Schaik, C. P. and Kappeler, P. M. (1993). Life history, activity period and lemur social systems. In Kappeler, P. M. and Ganzhorn, J. U. (eds.), *Lemur Social Systems and Their Ecological Basis*, Plenum Press, New York, pp. 241–260.

van Schaik, C. P. and Kappeler, P. M. (1996). The social systems of gregarious lemurs: Lack of convergence with anthropoids due to evolutionary disequilibrium? *Ethology* 102: 915–941.

van Schaik, C. P. and Kappeler, P. M. (1997). Infanticide risk and the evolution of male–female association in primates. *Proceedings of the Royal Society of London, B* 264: 1687–1694.

van Schaik, C. P. and Knott, C. D. (2001). Geographic variation in tool use on *Neesia* fruits in orangutans. *American Journal of Physical Anthropology* 114: 331–342.

van Schaik, C. P. and van Noordwijk, M. A. (1985a). Evolutionary effect of the absence of felids on the social organization of the macaques on the island of Simeulue (*Macaca fascicularis fusca*, Miller 1903). *Folia Primatologica* 44: 138–147.

van Schaik, C. P. and van Noordwijk, M. A. (1985b). Interannual variability in fruit abundance and the reproductive seasonality in Sumatran long-tailed macaques (*Macaca fascicularis*). *Journal of Zoology, London, A* 206: 533–549.

van Schaik, C. P., Deaner, R. O., and Merrill, M. Y. (1999a). The conditions for tool use in primates: Implications for the evolution of material culture. *Journal of Human Evolution* 36: 719–741.

van Schaik, C. P., Hodges, J. K., and Nunn, C. L. (2000). Paternity confusion and the ovarian cycles of female primates. In van Schaik, C. P. and Janson, C. H. (eds.), *Infanticide by Males*, Cambridge University Press, Cambridge, pp. 361–387.

van Schaik, C. P., van Noordwijk, M. A., and Nunn, C. L. (1999b). Sex and social evolution in primates. In Lee, P. C. (ed.), *Primate Socioecology*, Cambridge University Press, Cambridge, pp. 204–240.

van Schaik, C. P., van Noordwijk, M. A., Warsono, B., and Sutriono, E. (1983). Party size early detection of predators in Sumatran forest primates. *Primates* 24: 211–221.

Schilling, A. (1979). Olfactory communication in prosimians. In Dole, G. A. and Martin, R. D.

(eds.), *The Study of Prosimian Behavior,* Academic Press, New York, pp. 461–542.

Schmid, J. (1998). Tree holes used for resting by gray mouse lemurs (*Microcebus murinus*) in Madagascar: Insulation capacities and energetic consequences. *International Journal of Primatology* 19: 797–809.

Schoeninger, M. J., Iwaniec, U. T., and Glander, K. E. (1997). Stable isotope ratios monitor diet and habitat use in New World monkeys. *American Journal of Physical Anthropology* 103: 69–83.

Schoeninger, M. J., Iwaniec, U. T., and Nash, L. T. (1998). Ecological attributes recorded in stable isotope ratios of arboreal prosimian hair. *Oecologia* 113: 222–230.

Schoeninger, M. J., Moore, J., and Sept, J. M. (1999). Subsistence strategies of two 'savanna' chimpanzee populations: The stable isotope evidence. *American Journal of Primatology* 49: 297–314.

Selander, R. K. (1972). Sexual selection and dimorphism in birds. In Campbell, B. (ed.), *Sexual Selection and the Descent of Man, 1871–1971,* Aldine, Chicago, pp. 180–230.

Setchell, J. M. and Dixson, A. F. (2001). Arrested development of secondary sexual adornments in subordinate adult male mandrills (*Mandrillus sphinx*). *American Journal of Physical Anthropology* 115: 245–252.

Setchell, J. M., Lee, P. C., Wickings, J., and Dixson, A. F. (2001). Growth and ontogeny of sexual size dimorphism in the mandrill (*Mandrillus sphinx*). *American Journal of Physical Anthroplogy* 115: 349–360.

Seyfarth, R. M. (1987). Vocal communication and its relation to language. In Smuts, B. B., Cheney, D. L., Seyfarth, R. M., Wrangham, R. W., and Struhsaker, T. T. (eds.), *Primate Societies,* University of Chicago Press, Chicago, pp. 440–451.

Seyfarth, R. and Cheney, D. (1984). Grooming alliances and reciprocal altruism in vervet monkeys. *Nature* 308: 541–542.

Seyfarth, R. M. and Cheney, D. L. (1986). Complexities in the study of vervet monkey grunts. In Taub, D. M. and King, F. A. (eds.), *Current Perspectives in Primate Social Dynamics,* van Nostrand, New York, pp. 378–388.

Seyfarth, R. M., Cheney, D. L., Harcourt, A. H., and Stewart, K. J. (1994). The acoustic features of gorilla double grunts and their relation to behavior. *American Journal of Primatology* 33: 31–50.

Seyfarth, R. M., Cheney, D. L., and Marler, P. (1980). Monkey responses to three different alarm calls: Evidence for predator classification and semantic communication. *Science* 210: 801–803.

Sherman, P. W. (1998). The evolution of menopause. *Nature* 392: 759–761.

Sherman, P. W. and Holmes, W. G. (1985). Kin recognition: Issues and evidence. In Holldobler, B. and Lindauer, M. (eds.), *Experimental Behavioral Ecology and Sociobiology,* Fischer Verlag, Stuttgart, pp. 437–460.

Sherwood, R. J., Ward, S. C., and Hilll, A. (2002). The taxonomic status of the Chemeron temporal (KNM-BD 1). *Journal of Human Evolution* 42: 153–184.

Shettleworth, S. J. (1984). Learning and behavioural ecology. In Krebs, J. R. and Davies, N. B. (eds.), *Behavioural Ecology,* Second Edition, Blackwell Scientific Publications, Oxford, pp. 170–194.

Shideler, S. E., Ortuno, A. M., Moran, F. M., Moorman, E. A., and Lasley, B. L. (1993). Simple extraction and enzyme immunoassays for estrogen and progesterone metabolites in the feces of *Macaca fascicularis* during non-conceptive and conceptive ovarian cycles. *Biology of Reproduction* 48: 1290–1298.

Sicotte, P. (1995). Interpositions in conflicts between males in bi-male groups of mountain gorillas. *Folia Primatologica* 65: 14–24.

Sicotte, P. (2001). Female mate choice in mountain gorillas. In Robbins, M. M., Sicotte, P., and Stewart, K. J. (eds.), *Mountain Gorillas,* Cambridge University Press, Cambridge, pp. 59–87.

Sigg, H., Stolba, A., Abegglen, J. J., and Dasser, V. (1982). Life history of hamadryas baboons: Physical development, infant mortality, reproductive parameters and family relationships. *Primates* 23: 473–487.

Silk, J. B. (1983). Local resource competition and facultative adjustment of sex ratios in relation to competitive abilities. *American Naturalist* 108: 203–213.

Silk, J. B. (1996). Why do primates reconcile? *Evolutionary Anthropology* 5: 39–42.

Silk, J. B. (1997). The function of peaceful post-conflict contacts among primates. *Primates* 38: 265–279.

Silk, J. B., Cheney, D. L., and Seyfarth, R. M. (1996). The form and function of post-conflict interactions between female baboons. *Animal Behaviour* 52: 259–268.

Simons, E. L. (1988). A new species of *Propithecus* (Primates) from northeast Madagascar. *Folia Primatologica* 50: 143–151.

Small, M. F. (1981). Body fat, rank, and nutritional status in a captive group of rhesus macaques. *International Journal of Primatology* 2: 91–96.

Small, M. F. (1988). Female primate sexual behavior and conception. *Current Anthropology* 29: 81–100.

Small, M. F. (1989). Female choice in nonhuman primates. *Yearbook of Physical Anthropology* 32: 103–127.

Small, M. F. (1990). Alloparental behaviour in Barbary macaques, *Macaca sylvanus. Animal Behaviour* 39: 297–306.

Small, M. F. (1992). Female choice in mating: The evolutionary significance of female choice depends on why the female chooses her reproductive partner. *American Scientist* 80: 142–151.

Smith, A. C. (2000). Composition and proposed nutritional importance of exudates eaten by saddleback (*Saguinus fuscicollis*) and mustached (*Saguinus mystax*) tamarins. *International Journal of Primatology* 21: 69–83.

Smith, D. G., Kanthaswamy, S., Disbrow, M., and Wagner, J. L. (1999). Reconstructions of parentage in a band of captive hamadryas baboons. *International Journal of Primatology* 20: 415–429.

Smith, H. J., Newman, J. D., and Symmes, D. (1982). Vocal concomitants of affiliative behavior in squirrel monkeys. In Snowdon, C. T., Brown, C. H., and Petersen, M. (eds.), *Primate Communication,* Cambridge University Press, New York, pp. 30–49.

Smith, R. J. and Jungers, W. L. (1997). Body mass in comparative primatology. *Journal of Human Evolution* 32: 523–559.

Smith, W. J. (1977). *The Behavior of Communicating.* Harvard University Press, Cambridge.

Smuts, B. B. (1985). *Sex and Friendship in Baboons.* Aldine, New York.

Smuts, B. B. (1987a). Gender, aggression, and influence. In Smuts, B. B., Cheney, D. L., Seyfarth, R. M., Wrangham, R. W., and Struhsaker, T. T. (eds.), *Primate Societies,* University of Chicago Press, Chicago, pp. 400–412.

Smuts, B. B. (1987b). Sexual competition and mate choice. In Smuts, B. B., Cheney, D. L., Seyfarth, R. M., Wrangham, R. W., and Struhsaker, T. T. (eds.), *Primate Societies,* University of Chicago Press, Chicago, pp. 385–399.

Smuts, B. B. and Smuts, R. W. (1993). Male aggression and sexual coercion of females in nonhuman primates and other mammals: Evidence and theoretical implications. *Advances in the Study of Behavior.* 22: 1–63.

Smuts, B. B. and Watanabe, J. M. (1990). Social relationships and ritualized greetings in adult male baboons (*Papio cynocephalus anubis*). *International Journal of Primatology* 11: 147–172.

Sniegowski, P. D. (1995). The origin of adaptive mutants: Random or nonrandom? *Journal of Molecular Evolution* 40: 94–101.

Snowdon, C. T. (1986). Vocal communication. In Mitchell, G. and Erwin, J. (eds.), *Comparative Primate Biology,* Alan R. Liss, New York, pp. 495–530.

Snowdon, C. T. (1988). A comparative approach to vocal communication. In Leger, D. W. (ed.), *Comparative Perspectives in Modern Psychology, Nebraska Symposium on Motivation,* University of Nebraska Press, Lincoln, Nebraska, pp. 145–199.

Snowdon, C. T. (1990a). Mechanisms maintaining monogamy in monkeys. In Dewsbury, D. A. (ed.), *Contemporary Issues in Comparative Psychology,* Sinauer Associates, Sunderland, Massachusetts, pp. 225–251.

Snowdon, C. T. (1990b). Language capacities of nonhuman animals. *Yearbook of Physical Anthropology* 33: 215–243.

Snowdon, C. T. (1997). The "nature" of sex differences: Myths of male and female. In Gowaty, P. A. (ed.), *Feminism and Evolutionary Biology: Boundaries, Intersections, and Frontiers,* Chapman and Hall, New York, pp. 276–293.

Snowdon, C. T. and Cleveland, J. (1980). Individual recognition of contact calls by pygmy marmosets. *Animal Behaviour* 28: 717–727.

Snowdon, C. T. and Cleveland, J. (1984). "Conversations" among pygmy marmosets. *American Journal of Primatology* 7: 15–20.

Snowdon, C. T. and Hodun, A. (1981). Acoustic adaptations in pygmy marmoset contact calls: Locational cues vary with distance between conspecifics. *Behavioral Ecology and Sociobiology* 9: 295–300.

Snowdon, C. T. and Pola, Y. V. (1978). Interspecific and intraspecific responses to synthesized marmoset vocalizations. *Animal Behaviour* 26: 192–206.

Sober, E. (1994). Did evolution make us psychological egoists? In Sober, E. (ed.), *From a Biological Point of View: Essays in Evolutionary Philosophy,* Cambridge University Press, Cambridge, pp. 8–27.

Sober, E. and Wilson, D. S. (1998). *Unto Others: The Evolution and Psychology of Unselfish Behavior.* Harvard University Press, Cambridge.

Soltis, J., Mitsunaga, F., Shimizu, K., Nozaki, M., Yanagihara, Y., Domingo-Roura, X., and Takenaka, O. (1997a). Sexual selection in Japanese macaques II: female mate choice and male–male competition. *Animal Behaviour* 54: 737–746.

Soltis, J., Mitsunaga, F., Shimizu, K., Yanagihara, Y., and Nozaki, M. (1997b). Sexual selection in Japanese macaques I: Female mate choice or male sexual coercion? *Animal Behaviour* 54: 725–736.

Soltis, J., Thomsen, R., and Takenaka, O. (2001). The interaction of male and female reproductive strategies and paternity in wild Japanese macaques, *Macaca fuscata. Animal Behaviour* 62: 485–494.

Sommer, V. and Mohnot, S. M. (1985). New observations of infanticide among hanuman langurs (*Presbytis entellus*) near Jodhpur (Rajasthan/India). *Behavioral Ecology and Sociobiology* 16: 245–248.

Sommer, V. and Rajpurohit, L. S. (1989). Male reproductive success in harem troops of Hanuman langurs (*Presbytis entellus*). *International Journal of Primatology* 10: 293–317.

Sommer, V. and Reichard, U. (2000). Rethinking monogamy: The gibbon case. In Kappeler, P. M. (ed.), *Primate males: Causes and consequences of variation in group composition,* Cambridge University Press, Cambridge, pp. 159–168.

Sousa, M. B. C. and Ziegler, T. E. (1998). Diurnal variation on the excretion patterns of fecal steroids in common marmoset (*Callithrix jacchus*) females. *American Journal of Primatology* 46: 105–117.

Southwick, C. H. and Siddiqi, M. F. (1988). Partial recovery and a new population estimate of rhesus monkey populations in India. *American Journal of Primatology* 16: 187–197.

Sprague, D. S. (1991). Mating by non-troop males among the Japanese macaques of Yakushima. *Folia Primatologica* 57: 156–158.

Sprague, D. S., Suzuki, S., Takahashi, H., and Sato, S. (1998). Male life history in natural populations of Japanese macaques: Migration, dominance rank, and troop participation of males in two habitats. *Primates* 39: 351–363.

Sprague, D. S., Suzuki, S., and Tsukahara, T. (1996). Variation in social mechanisms by which males attained the alpha rank among Japanese macaques. In Fa, J. E. and Lindburg, D. G. (eds.), *Evolution and Ecology of Macaque Societies,* Cambridge University Press, Cambridge, pp. 444–458.

Srivastava, A. and Dunbar, R. I. M. (1996). The mating system of Hanuman langurs: A problem in optimal foraging. *Behavioral Ecology and Sociobiology* 39: 219–226.

Stammbach, E. (1987). Desert, forest and montane baboons: Multi-level societies. In Smuts, B. B., Cheney, D. L., Seyfarth, R. M., Wrangham, R. W., and Struhsaker, T. T. (eds.), *Primate Societies,* University of Chicago Press, Chicago, pp. 112–120.

Stanford, C. B. (1991). *The Capped Langur in Bangladesh: Behavioral Ecology and Reproductive Tactics.* Karger, Basel.

Stanford, C. B. (1995). The influence of chimpanzee predation on group size and anti-predator behaviour in red colobus monkeys. *Animal Behaviour* 49: 577–587.

Stanford, C. B. (1998a). The social behavior of chimpanzees and bonobos. *Current Anthropology* 39: 339–407.

Stanford, C. B. (1998b). *Chimpanzee and Red Colobus: The Ecology of Predator and Prey.* Harvard University Press, Cambridge.

Stanford, C. B., Wallis, J., Matama, H., and Goodall, J. (1994). Patterns of predation by chimpanzees on red colobus monkeys in Gombe National Park, 1982–1991. *American Journal of Physical Anthropology* 94: 213–228.

Stanley Price, M. (1986). The reintroduction of the Arabian oryx (*Oryx leucoryx*) into Oman. *International Zoo Yearbook* 24/25: 179–188.

Stanley Price, M. (1989). *Animal Re-introductions: The Arabian Oryx in Oman.* Cambridge University Press, New York.

Staski, E. and Marks, J. (1992). *Evolutionary Anthropology: An Introduction to Physical Anthropology and Archaeology.* Harcourt Brace Jovanovich, Fort Worth, Texas.

Stein, D. (1984). *The Sociobiology of Infant and Adult Male Baboons.* Albex, Norwood, New Jersey.

Stelzner, J. and Strier, K. (1981). Hyena predation on an adult male baboon. *Mammalia* 45: 106–107.

Sterck, E. H. M. (1997). Determinants of female dispersal in Thomas langurs. *American Journal of Primatology* 42: 49–198.

Sterck, E. H. M. (1998). Female dispersal, social organization, and infanticide in langurs: Are they linked to human disturbance? *American Journal of Primatology* 44: 235–254.

Sterck, E. H. M. (1999). Variation in langur social organization in relation to the socioecological model, human habitat alteration, and phylogenetic constraints. *Primates* 40: 199–213.

Sterck, E. H. M., Watts, D. P., and van Schaik, C. P. (1997). The evolution of female social relationships in nonhuman primates. *Behavioral Ecology and Sociobiology* 41: 291–309.

Stern, K. and McClintock, M. K. (1998). Regulation of ovulation by human pheromones. *Nature* 392: 177–179.

Steudel, K. (1996). Limb morphology, bipedal gait, and the energetics of hominid locomotion. *American Journal of Physical Anthropology* 99: 345–356.

Stevenson, P. R. and Castellanos, M. C. (2000). Feeding rates and daily path range of the Colombian woolly monkeys as evidence for between- and within-group competition. *Folia Primatologica* 71: 399–408.

Stevenson, P. R., Quinones, M. J., and Ahumada, J. A. (1994). Ecological strategies of woolly monkeys (*Lagothrix lagotricha*) at Tinigua National Park,

Colombia. *American Journal of Primatology* 32: 123–140.

Stewart, C-B. and Disotell, T. R. (1998). Primate evolution—in and out of Africa. *Current Biology* 8: R582–R588.

Stewart, K. J. (2001). Social relationships of immature gorillas and silverbacks. In Robbins, M. M., Sicotte, P., and Stewart, K. J. (eds.), *Mountain Gorillas,* Cambridge University Press, Cambridge, pp. 183–213.

Strauss, E. (1999). Can mitochondrial clocks keep time? *Science* 283: 1435–1438.

Strier, K. B. (1987a). Activity budgets of woolly spider monkeys, or muriquis (*Brachyteles arachnoides*). *American Journal of Primatology* 13: 385–395.

Strier, K. B. (1987b). Ranging behavior of woolly spider monkeys. *International Journal of Primatology* 8: 575–591.

Strier, K. B. (1989). Effects of patch size on feeding associations in muriquis (*Brachyteles arachnoides*). *Folia Primatologica* 52: 70–77.

Strier, K. B. (1990). New World primates, new frontiers: Insights from the wooly spider monkey, or muriqui (*Brachyteles arachnnoides*). *International Journal of Primatology* 11: 7–19.

Strier, K. B. (1991a). Diet in one group of woolly spider monkeys, or muriquis (*Brachyteles arachnoides*). *American Journal of Primatology* 23: 113–126.

Strier, K. B. (1991b). Demography and conservation in an endangered primate, *Brachyteles arachnoides. Conservation Biology* 5: 214–218.

Strier, K. B. (1992a). *Faces in the Forest: The Endangered Muriqui Monkeys of Brazil.* Oxford University Press, New York.

Strier, K. B. (1992b). Atelinae adaptations: Behavioral strategies and ecological constraints. *American Journal of Physical Anthropology* 88: 515–524.

Strier, K. B. (1992c). Causes and consequences of nonaggression in woolly spider monkeys. In Silverberg, J. and Gray, J. P. (eds.), *Aggression and Peacefulness in Humans and Other Primates,* Oxford University Press, New York, pp. 100–116.

Strier, K. B. (1993a). The animal boundaries of anthropology, or why don't all anthropologists consider themselves primatologists? *Reviews in Anthropology* 22: 165–174.

Strier, K. B. (1993b). Growing up in a patrifocal society: Sex differences in the spatial relations of immature muriquis. In Pereira, M. E. and Fairbanks, L. A. (eds.), *Juvenile Primates: Life History, Development, and Behavior,* Oxford University Press, New York, pp. 138–147.

Strier, K. B. (1993/1994). Viability analyses of an isolated population of muriqui monkeys (*Brachyteles arachnoides*): Implications for primate conservation and demography. *Primate Conservation* 14/15: 43–52.

Strier, K. B. (1994a). Myth of the typical primate. *Yearbook of Physical Anthropology* 37: 233–271.

Strier, K. B. (1994b). Brotherhoods among atelins. *Behaviour* 130: 151–167.

Strier, K. B. (1996a). Male reproductive strategies in New World primates. *Human Nature* 7: 105–123.

Strier, K. B. (1996b). Reproductive ecology of female muriquis. In Norconk, M. A., Rosenberger, A. L., and Garber, P. A. (eds.), *Adaptive Radiations of Neotropical Primates,* Plenum Press, New York, pp. 511–532.

Strier, K. B. (1997a). Behavioral ecology and conservation biology of primates and other animals. *Advances in the Study of Behavior* 26: 101–158.

Strier, K. B. (1997b). Mate preferences of wild muriqui monkeys (*Brachyteles arachnoides*): Reproductive and social correlates. *Folia Primatologica* 68: 120–133.

Strier, K. B. (1997c). Subtle cues of social relations in male muriqui monkeys (*Brachyteles arachnoides*). In Kinzey, W. G. (ed.), *New World Primates: Evolution, Ecology and Behavior,* Aldine de Gruyter, New York, pp. 109–118.

Strier, K. B. (1999a). The atelines. In Dolhinow, P. and Fuentes, A. (eds.), *The Nonhuman Primates,* McGraw Hill, New York, pp. 109–114.

Strier, K. B. (1999b). Why is female kin bonding so rare: Comparative sociality of New World primates. In Lee, P. C. (ed.), *Primate Socioecology,* Cambridge University Press, Cambridge.

Strier, K. B. (1999c). Predicting primate responses to "stochastic" demographic events. *Primates* 40: 131–142.

Strier, K. B. (2000a). From binding brotherhoods to short-term sovereignty: The betwixting dilemma of male Cebidae. In Kappeler, P. M. (ed.), *Primate Males,* Cambridge University Press, Cambridge, pp. 72–83.

Strier, K. B. (2000b). Population viabilities and conservation implications for muriquis (*Brachyteles arachnoides*) in Brazil's Atlantic forest. *Biotropica* 32: 903–913.

Strier, K. B. (2001). Beyond the apes: Reasons to consider the entire primate order. In de Waal, F. B. M. (ed.), *Tree of Origin,* Harvard University Press, Cambridge, Massachusetts, pp. 69–93.

Strier, K. B. (In preparation). Demography and the temporal scale of sexual selection. In Jones, C. B. (ed.), *Sexual Selection and Reproductive Competition in Primates,* American Society of Primatologists: Special Topics in Primatology.

Strier, K. B. and Fonseca, G. A. B. (1996/1997). The endangered muriquis in Brazil's Atlantic forest. *Primate Conservation* 17: 131–137.

Strier, K. B. and Ziegler, T. E. (1994). Insights into ovarian function in wild muriqui monkeys (*Brachyteles arachnoides*). *American Journal of Primatology* 32: 31–40.

Strier, K. B. and Ziegler, T. E. (1997). Behavioral and endocrine characteristics of the reproductive cycle in wild muriqui monkeys, *Brachyteles arachnoides*. *American Journal of Primatology* 42: 299–310.

Strier, K. B. and Ziegler, T. E. (2000). Lack of pubertal influences on female dispersal in muriqui monkeys, *Brachyteles arachnoides*. *Animal Behaviour* 59: 849–860.

Strier, K. B., Dib, L. T., and Figueira, J. E. C. (In press). Social dynamics of male muriquis (*Brachyteles arachnoides hypoxanthus*). *Behaviour*

Strier, K. B., Mendes, S. L., and Santos, R. R. (2001). Timing in births in sympatric brown howler monkeys (*Alouatta fusca clamitans*) and northern muriquis (*Brachyteles arachnoides hypoxanthus*). *American Journal of Primatology* 55: 87–100.

Strier, K. B., Ziegler, T. E., and Wittwer, D. (1999). Seasonal and social correlates of fecal testosterone and cortisol levels in wild male muriquis (*Brachyteles arachnoides*). *Hormones and Behavior* 35: 125–134.

Struhsaker, T. T. (1967a). Ecology of vervet monkeys (*Cercopithecus aethiops*) in the Masai-Amboseli Game Reserve, Kenya. *Ecology* 48: 891–904.

Struhsaker, T. T. (1967b). Auditory communication among vervet monkeys (*Cercopithecus aethiops*). In Altmann, S. A. (ed.), *Social Communication among Primates,* University of Chicago Press, Chicago, pp. 281–324.

Struhsaker, T. T. (1969). Correlates of ecology and social organization among African cercopithecines. *Folia Primatologica* 11: 80–118.

Struhsaker, T. T. (1973). A recensus of vervet monkeys in the Masai-Amboseli Game Reserve, Kenya. *Ecology* 54: 930–932.

Struhsaker, T. T. (1975). *The Red Colobus Monkey.* University of Chicago Press, Chicago.

Struhsaker, T. T. (1978). Food habits of five monkey species in the Kibale Forest, Uganda. In Chivers, D. J. and Herbert, J. (eds.), *Recent Advances in Primatology,* Academic Press, New York, pp. 225–248.

Struhsaker, T. T. (1997). *Ecology of an African Rain Forest. Logging in Kibale and the Conflict Between Conservation and Exploitation.* University Press of Florida, Gainesville, FL.

Struhsaker, T. T., Butynski, T. M., and Lwanga, J. S. (1988). Hybridization between redtail (*Cercopithecus ascanius schmidti*) and blue (*C. m. stuhlmanni*) monkeys in the Kibale Forest, Uganda. In Gautier-Hion, A., Bourliere, F., Gautier, J.-P., and Kingdon, J. (eds.), *A Primate Radiation; Evolutionary Biology of the African Guenons,* Cambridge University Press, Cambridge, pp. 477–497.

Struhsaker, T. T., Cooney, D. O., and Siex, K. S. (1997). Charcoal consumption by Zanzibar red colobus monkeys: Its function and its ecological and demographic consequences. *International Journal of Primatology* 18: 61–72.

Strum, S. C. (1982). Agonistic dominance in male baboons: An alternative view. *International Journal of Primatology* 3: 175–202.

Strum, S. C. (1984). Why males use infants. In Taub, D. M. (ed.), *Primate Paternalism,* Van Nostrand Reinhold, New York, pp. 146–185.

Strum, S. C. (1994). Reconciling aggression and social manipulation as means of competition 1. Life history perspective. *International Journal of Primatology* 15: 739–765.

Strum, S. S. and Latour, B. (1991). Redefining the social link from baboons to humans. In Schubert, G. and Masters, R. D. (eds.), *Primate Politics,* Southern Illinois University Press, Carbondale, Illinois, pp. 73–85.

Stuart, M. D., Greenspan, L. L., Glander, K. E., and Clarke, M. R. (1990). A coprological survey of parasites of wild mantled howling monkeys, *Alouatta palliata palliata. Journal of Wildlife Diseases* 26: 547–549.

Stuart, M. D. and Strier, K. B. (1995). Primates and parasites: A case for a multidisciplinary approach. *International Journal of Primatology* 16: 577–593.

Stuart, M. D., Strier, K. B., and Pierberg, S. M. (1993). A coprological survey of parasites of wild woolly spider monkeys, *Brachyteles arachnoides,* and brown howling monkeys, *Alouatta fusca. Journal of the Helminthological Society* 60: 111–115.

Sugiyama, Y. (1964). Group composition, population density and some sociological observations of hanuman langurs (*Presbytis entellus*). *Primates* 5: 7–37.

Sugiyama, Y. (1997). Social tradition and the use of tool-composites by wild chimpanzees. *Evolutionary Anthropology* 6: 23–27.

Sugiyama, Y. (1999). Socioecological factors of male chimpanzee migration at Bossou, Guinea. *Primates* 40: 61–68.

Sussman, R. W. (1978). Foraging patterns of nonhuman primates and the nature of food preferences in man. *Federation Proceedings* 37: 55–60.

Sussman, R. W. (1991). Primate origins and the evolution of angiosperms. *American Journal of Primatology* 23: 209–223.

Sussman, R. W. (1992a). Male life history and intergroup mobility among ringtailed lemurs (*Lemur catta*). *International Journal of Primatology* 13: 395–413.

Sussman, R. W. (1992b). Smell as a signal. In Jones, S., Martin, R., and Pilbeam, D. (eds.), *The Cambridge Encyclopedia of Human Evolution*, Cambridge University Press, Cambridge, pp. 157–160.

Sussman, R. W. (1999a). *Primate Ecology and Social Structure. Volume 1: Lorises, Lemurs, and Tarsiers*. Pearson Custom Publishing, Needham Heights, Massachusetts.

Sussman, R. W. (1999b). The taxonomy and evolution of primates. In Sussman, R. W. (ed.), *The Biological Basis of Human Behavior: A Critical Review*, Prentice Hall, Upper Saddle River, New Jersey, pp. 26–42.

Sussman, R. W., Cheverud, J. M., and Bartlett, T. Q. (1995). Infant killing as an evolutionary strategy: Reality or myth? *Evolutionary Anthropology*. 3: 149–151.

Sussman, R. W. and Raven, P. H. (1978). Pollination by lemurs and marsupials: An archaic coevolutionary system. *Science* 200: 731–736.

Suzuki, S., Hill, D. A., and Sprague, D. S. (1998). Intertroop transfer and dominance rank structure of nonnatal male Japanese macaques in Yakushima, Japan. *International Journal of Primatology* 19: 703–722.

Symington, M. M. (1987a). Sex ratio and maternal rank in wild spider monkeys: When daughters disperse. *Behavioral Ecology and Sociobiology* 20: 333–335.

Symington, M. M. (1987b). *Ecological and Social Correlates of Party Size in the Black Spider Monkey, Ateles paniscus chamek*. Ph.D. Dissertation, Princeton University.

Symington, M. M. (1990). Fission–fusion social organization in *Ateles* and *Pan*. *International Journal of Primatology* 11: 47–61.

Taberlet, P., Waits, L. P., and Luikart, G. (1999). Noninvasive genetic sampling: Look before you leap. *Trends in Ecology and Evolution* 14: 323–327.

Takahata, Y., Huffman, M. A., Suzuki, S., Koyama, N., and Yamagiwa, J. (1999). Why dominants do not consistently attain high mating and reproductive success: A review of longitudinal Japanese macaque studies. *Primates* 40: 143–158.

Takahata, Y., Sprague, D. S., Suzuki, S., and Okayasu, N. (1994). Female competition, co-existence, and the mating structure of wild Japanese macaques on Yakushima Island, Japan. In Jarman, P. J. and Rossiter, A. (eds.), *Animal Societies: Individuals, Interactions and Organisation*, Kyoto University Press, Kyoto, pp. 163–179.

Takasaki, H. and Takenaka, O. (1991). Paternity testing in chimpanzees with DNA amplification from hairs and buccal cells in wadges: A preliminary note. In Ehara, A., Kimura, T., Takenaka, O., and Iwamoto, M. (eds.), *Primatology Today*, Elsevier, Amsterdam, pp. 613–616.

Takenaka, O., Takasaki, H., Kawamoto, S., Arakawa, M., and Takenaka, A. (1993). Polymorphic microsatellite DNA amplification customized for chimpanzee paternity testing. *Primates* 34: 27–35.

Talmage-Riggs, G., Winter, P., Ploog, D., and Mayer, W. (1972). Effect of deafening on the vocal behavior of the squirrel monkey (*Saimiri sciureus*). *Folia Primatologica* 17: 404–420.

Tattersall, I. (1993). Madagascar's lemurs. *Scientific American* 268: 110–117.

Taub, D. and Mehlman, P. (1991). Primate paternalistic investment: A cross-species view. In Loy, J. D. and Peters, C. B. (eds.), *Understanding Behavior: What Primate Studies Tell Us about Human Behavior*, Oxford University Press, New York, pp. 51–89.

Teleki, G. (1973). *The Predatory Behavior of Wild Chimpanzees*. Bucknell University Press, Lewisburg, Pennsylvania.

Tenaza, R. R. (1976). Songs and related behavior of Kloss' gibbon (*Hylobates klossii*) in Siberut Island, Indonesia. *Zeitschrift fur Tierpsychologie* 40: 37–52.

Terborgh, J. (1983). *Five New World Primates: A Study in Comparative Ecology*. Princeton University Press, Princeton.

Terborgh, J. and Janson, C. H. (1986). The socioecology of primate groups. *Annual Review of Ecology and Systematics* 17: 111–135.

Thoisy, B., Vogel, I., Reynes, J.-M., Pouilquen, J.-F., Carme, B., Kazanji, M., and Vié, J.-C. (2001). Health evaluation of translocated free-ranging primates in French Guiana. *American Journal of Primatology* 54: 1–16.

Tilden, C. D. and Oftedal, O. T. (1997). Milk composition reflects pattern of maternal care in prosimian primates. *American Journal of Primatology* 41: 195–211.

Timmermans, P. J. A. and Vossen, J. M. H. (1996). The influence of rearing conditions on maternal behavior in cynomolgus macaques (*Macaca fascicularis*). *International Journal of Primatology* 17: 259–276.

Tinbergen, N. (1963). On aims and methods of ethology. *Zeitschrift fur Tierpsychologie* 20: 410–433.

Tooby, J. and DeVore, I. (1987). The reconstruction of hominid behavioral evolution through strategic modelling. In Kinzey, W. G. (ed.), *The Evolution of Human Behavior: Primate Models,* SUNY Press, Albany, pp. 183–237.

Torres de Assumpção, C. (1981). *Cebus apella* and *Brachyteles arachnoides* (Cebidae) as potential pollinators of *Mabea fistulifera* (Euphorbiaceae). *Journal of Mammalogy* 62: 386–388.

Treves, A. (1999a). Within-group vigilance in red colobus and redtail monkeys. *American Journal of Primatology* 48: 113–126.

Treves, A. (1999b). Has predation shaped the social systems of arboreal primates? *International Journal of Primatology* 20: 35–67.

Treves, A. and Chapman, C. A. (1996). Conspecific threat, predation avoidance, and resource defense: Implications for grouping in langurs. *Behavioral Ecology and Sociobiology* 39: 43–53.

Trivers, R. L. (1971). The evolution of reciprocal altruism. *Quarterly Review of Biology* 46: 35–57.

Trivers, R. L. (1972). Parental investment and sexual selection. In Campbell, B. (ed.), *Sexual Selection and the Descent of Man 1871–1971,* Aldine, Chicago, pp. 136–179.

Trivers, R. L. (1974). Parent–offspring conflict. *American Zoologist* 14: 249–264.

Trivers, R. L. and Willard, D. E. (1973). Natural selection of parental ability to vary the sex ratio of offspring. *Science* 179: 90–92.

Trut, L. N. (1999). Early canid domestication: The farm-fox experiment. *American Scientist* 87: 160–169.

Turnbaugh, W. A., Jurmain, R., Kilgore, L., and Nelson, H. (2002). *Understanding Physical Anthropology and Archaeology,* 8th Edition. Wadsworth/Thomson, Belmont, California.

Turner, T. R., Weiss, M. L., and Pereira, M. E. (1992). DNA fingerprinting and paternity assessment in Old World monkeys and ringtailed lemurs. In Martin, R. D., Dixson, A. F., and Wickings, E. J. (eds.), *Paternity in Primates: Genetic Tests and Theories,* Karger, Basel, pp. 96–112.

Tutin, C. E. G. (1979). Mating patterns and reproductive strategies in a community of wild chimpanzees (*Pan troglodytes schweinfurthii*). *Behavioral Ecology and Sociobiology* 6: 29–38.

Tutin, C. E. G. (1999). Fragmented living: Behavioural ecology of primates in a forest fragment in the Lopé Reserve, Gabon. *Primates* 40: 249–265.

Tutin, C. E. G. and Fernandez, M. (1984). Nationwide census of gorilla (*Gorilla g. gorilla*) and chimpanzee (*Pan t. troglodytes*) populations in Gabon. *American Journal of Primatology* 6: 313–336.

Tutin, C. E. G. and Fernandez, M. (1993). Composition of the diet of chimpanzees and comparisons with that of sympatric lowland gorillas in the Lope Reserve, Gabon. *American Journal of Primatology* 30: 195–211.

Tutin, C. E. G. and Fernandez, M. (1994). Comparison of food processing by sympatric apes in the Lope Reserve, Gabon. In Thierry, B., Anderson, J. R., Roeder, J. J., and Herrenschmidt, N. (eds.), *Current Primatology, Vol. I: Ecology and Evolution,* University Louis Pasteur, Strasbourg, pp. 29–36.

Tutin, C. E. G. and White, L. (1999). The recent evolutionary past of primate communities, likely environmental impacts during the past three millenia. In Fleagle, J. G., Janson, C. H., and Reed, K. E. (eds.), *Primate Communities,* Cambridge University Press, Cambridge, pp. 220–236.

Tutin, C. E. G., McGrew, W. C., and Baldwin, P. J. (1983). Social organization of savanna-dwelling chimpanzees, *Pan troglodytes verus,* at Mt. Assirik, Senegal. *Primates* 24: 154–173.

Tutin, C. E. G., Williamson, E. A., Rogers, M. E., and Fernandez, M. (1991). A case study of a plant-animal relationship: *Cola lizae* and lowland gorillas in the Lope Reserve, Gabon. *Journal of Tropical Ecology* 7: 181–199.

Tuttle, R. H. (1967). Knuckle-walking and the evolution of hominoid hands. *American Journal of Physical Anthropology* 26: 171–206.

Tuttle, R. H. (1975). Parallelism, brachiation and hominoid phylogeny. In Luckett, W. P. and Szalay, F. S. (eds.), *Phylogeny of the Primates,* Plenum Press, New York, pp. 447–480.

Utami, S. S., Wich, S. A., Sterck, E. H. M., and van Hooff, J. A. R. A. M. (1997). Food competition between wild orangutans in large fig trees. *International Journal of Primatology* 18: 909–927.

Veen, T., Borge, T., Griffith, S. C., Sætre, G.-P., Bures, S., Gustafsson, L., and Sheldon, B. C. (2001). Hybridization and adaptive mate choice in flycatchers. *Nature* 411: 45–50.

Vehrencamp, S. L. (1983). A model for the evolution of despotic versus egalitarian societies. *Animal Behavior* 31: 667–682.

Vick, L. G. and Pereira, M. E. (1989). Episodic targeting aggression and the histories of *Lemur* social groups. *Behavioral Ecology and Sociobiology* 25: 3–12.

Vigilant, L., Hofreiter, M., Siedel, H., and Boesch, C. (2001). Paternity and relatedness in wild chimpanzee communities. *Proceedings of the National Academy of Sciencies USA*, 98: 12890–12895.

Visalberghi, E. and Fragaszy, D. M. (1990). Do monkeys ape? In Parker, S. T. and Gibson, K. R.

(eds.), *Language and Intelligence in Monkeys and Apes,* Cambridge University Press, Cambridge, pp. 247–273.

de Waal, F. B. M. (1982). *Chimpanzee Politics.* Jonathan Cape, London.

de Waal, F. B. M. (1984). Coping with social tension: Sex differences in the effect of food provision to a small rhesus monkey group. *Animal Behaviour* 32: 765–773.

de Waal, F. B. M. (1987). Tension regulation and non-reproductive function of sex in captive bonobos (*Pan paniscus*). *National Geographic Research* 3: 318–335.

de Waal, F. B. M. (1989). *Peacemaking among Primates.* Harvard University Press, Cambridge.

de Waal, F. B. M. (1993). Codevelopment of dominance relations and affiliative bonds in rhesus monkeys. In Pereira, M. E. and Fairbanks, L. A. (eds.), *Juvenile Primates: Life History, Development, and Behavior,* Oxford University Press, New York, pp. 259–270.

de Waal, F. B. M. (1996). Conflict as negotiation. In McGrew, W. C., Marchant, L. F., and Nishida, T. (eds.), *Great Ape Societies,* Cambridge University Press, New York, pp. 159–172.

de Waal, F. B. M. (2000). Primates—a natural heritage of conflict resolution. *Science* 289: 586–590.

de Waal, F. B. M. and Berger, M. L. (2000). Payment for labour in monkeys. *Nature* 404: 563.

de Waal, F. B. M. and Luttrell, L. M. (1988). Mechanisms of social reciprocity in three primate species: Symmetrical relationship characteristics or cognition? *Ethology and Sociobiology* 9: 101–118.

de Waal, F. B. M. and Luttrell, L. M. (1989). Toward a comparative socioecology of the genus *Macaca:* Different dominance styles in rhesus and stumptail monkeys. *American Journal of Primatology* 19: 83–109.

de Waal, F. B. M. and van Roosmalen, A. (1979). Reconciliation and consolation among chimpanzees. *Behavioral Ecology and Sociobiology* 5: 55–66.

Wachter, B., Schabel, M., and Nöe, R. (1997). Diet overlap and polyspecific associations of red colobus and Diana monkeys in the Täi National Park, Ivory Coast. *Ethology* 103: 514–526.

Walker, S. E. (1996). The evolution of positional behavior in the saki-uakaris (*Pithecia, Chiropotes,* and *Cacajao*). In Norconk, M. A., Rosenberger, A. L., and Garber, P. A. (eds.), *Adaptive Radiations of Neotropical Primates,* Plenum Press, New York, pp. 335–367.

Wallis, J. (1995). Seasonal influence on reproduction in chimpanzees of Gombe National Park. *International Journal of Primatology* 16: 435–551.

Wallis, J. (1997). A survey of reproductive parameters in the free-ranging chimpanzees of Gombe National Park. *Journal of Reproduction and Fertility* 109: 297–307.

Wallis, J. and Lee, D. R. (1999). Primate conservation: The prevention of disease transmission. *International Journal of Primatology* 20: 803–826.

Walters, J. R. (1980). Interventions and the development of dominance relationships in female baboons. *Folia Primatologica* 34: 61–89.

Walters, J. R. (1987). Kin recognition in non-human primates. In Fletcher, D. J. C. and Michener, C. D. (eds.), *Kin Recognition in Animals,* John Wiley & Sons Ltd, New York, pp. 359–393.

Wang, M.-H. and vom Saal, F. S. (2000). Maternal age and traits in offspring. *Nature* 407: 469–470.

Ward, S., Brown, B., Hill, A., Kelley, J., and Downs, W. (1999). *Equatorius:* A new hominoid genus from the middle Miocene of Kenya. *Science* 285: 1317.

Waser, P. M. (1977a). Individual recognition, intragroup cohesion, and intergroup spacing: Evidence from sound playback to forest monkeys. *Behaviour* 60: 28–74.

Waser, P. M. (1977b). Feeding, ranging and group size in the mangabey, *Cercocebus albigena.* In Clutton-Brock, T. H. (ed.), *Primate Ecology,* Academic Press, London, pp. 183–222.

Washabaugh, K. and Snowdon, C. T. (1998). Chemical communication of reproductive status in female cotton-top tamarins (*Saguinus oedipus oedipus*). *American Journal of Primatology* 45: 337–349.

Washburn, S. L. and DeVore, I. (1961). The social life of baboons. *Scientific American* 204: 62–71.

Wasser, S. K., Monfort, S. L., and Wildt, D. E. (1991). Rapid extraction of faecal steroids for measuring reproductive cyclicity and early pregnancy in free-ranging yellow baboons (*Papio cynocephalus cynocephalus*). *Journal of Reproductive Fertility* 92: 415–423.

Wasser, S. K., Risler, L., and Steiner, R. A. (1988). Excreted steroids in primate feces over the menstrual cycle and pregnancy. *Biology of Reproduction* 39: 862–872.

Wasser, S. and Starling, A. (1988). Proximate and ultimate causes of reproductive suppression among female yellow baboons at Mikumi National Park, Tanzania. *American Journal of Primatology* 16: 97–121.

Waterman, P. G. and Kool, K. M. (1994). Colobine food selection and plant chemistry. In Davies, A. G. and Oates, J. F. (eds.), *Colobine Monkeys: Their Ecology, Behaviour and Evolution,* Cambridge University Press, Cambridge, pp. 251–284.

Watts, D. P. (1985). Relations between group size and composition and feeding competition in mountain gorilla groups. *Animal Behaviour* 33: 72–85.

Watts, D. P. (1989). Mountain gorilla life histories, reproductive competition, and sociosexual behavior and some implications for captive husbandry. *Zoo Biology* 9: 1–16.

Watts, D. P. (1990). Ecology of gorillas and its relation to female transfer in mountain gorillas. *International Journal of Primatology* 11: 21–45.

Watts, D. P. (1995a). Post-conflict social events in wild mountain gorillas (Mammalia, Hominoidea), I: Social interactions between opponents. *Ethology* 100: 139–157.

Watts, D. P. (1995b). Post-conflict social events in wild mountain gorillas. II. Redirection, side direction and consolation. *Ethology* 100: 158–174.

Watts, D. P. (1996). Comparative socio-ecology of gorillas. In McGrew, W. C., Marchant, L. F., and Nishida, T. (eds.), *Great Ape Societies,* Cambridge University Press, New York, pp. 16–28.

Watts, D. P. (1998). Coalitionary mate guarding by male chimpanzees at Ngogo, Kibale National Park, Uganda. *Behavioral Ecology and Sociobiology* 44: 43–55.

Watts, D. P. (2001). Social relationships of female mountain gorillas. In Robbins, M. M., Sicotte, P., and Stewart, K. J. (eds.), *Mountain Gorillas,* Cambridge University Press, Cambridge, pp. 215–240.

Watts, D. P. and Mitani, J. C. (2001). Boundary patrols and intergroup encounters in wild chimpanzees. *Behaviour* 138: 299–327.

Watts, D. P. and Pusey, A. E. (1993). Behavior of juvenile and adolescent great apes. In Pereira, M. E. and Fairbanks, L. A. (eds.), *Juvenile Primates: Life History, Development, and Behavior,* Oxford University Press, New York, pp. 148–167.

Weiss, R. A. and Wrangham, R. W. (1999). From *Pan* to pandemic. *Nature* 397: 385–386.

Western, D. (1997). *In the Dust of Kilimanjaro.* Island Press/Shearwater Books, Washington, D.C.

Western, D. and van Praet, C. (1973). Cyclical changes in the habitat and climate of an East African ecosystem. *Nature* 241: 104–106.

Westneat, D. F. and Sherman, P. W. (1997). Density and extra-pair fertilizations in birds: A comparative analysis. *Behavioral Ecology and Sociobiology* 41: 205–215.

Wheeler, P. E. (1985). The evolution of bipedality and loss of functional body hair in hominids. In Wind, J. (ed.), *Essays in Human Sociobiology,* Academic Press, London, pp. 91–98.

White, F. J. and Wrangham, R. W. (1988). Feeding competition and patch size in the chimpanzee species *Pan paniscus* and *Pan troglodytes. Behaviour* 105: 148–164.

White, L. J. T. and Tutin, C. E. G. (2001). Why chimpanzees and gorillas respond differently to logging. In Weber, W., White, L. J. T., Vedder, A., and Naughton-Treves, L. (eds.), *African Rain Forest Ecology and Conservation,* Yale University Press, New Haven, pp. 449–462.

Whiten, A. and Boesch, C. (2001). The cultures of chimpanzees. *Scientific American* 284: 60–67.

Whiten, A. and Byrne, R. W. (1997). *Machiavellian Intelligence II: Extensions and Evaluations.* Cambridge University Press, Cambridge.

Whiten, A., Goodall, J., McGrew, W. C., Nishida, T., Reynolds, V., Sugiyama, Y., Tutin, C. E. G., Wrangham, R. W., and Boesch, C. (1999). Culture in chimpanzees. *Nature* 399: 682–685.

Whitten, P. L. (1983). Diet and dominance among female vervet monkeys (*Cercopithecus aethiops*). *American Journal of Primatology* 5: 139–159.

Whitten, P. L. (1987). Infants and adult males. In Smuts, B. B., Cheney, D. L., Seyfarth, R. M., Wrangham, R. W., and Struhsaker, T. T. (eds.), *Primate Societies,* University of Chicago Press, Chicago, pp. 343–357.

Widdig, A., Nürnberg, P., Krawczak, M., Streich, W. J., and Bercovitch, F. B. (2001). Paternal relatedness and age proximity regulate social relationships among adult female rhesus macaques. *Proceedings of the National Academy of Sciences USA* 98: 13769–13773.

Widowski, T. M., Porter, T. A., Ziegler, T. E., and Snowdon, C. T. (1992). The stimulatory effect of males on the initiation but not the maintenance of ovarian cycling in cotton-top tamarins (*Saguinus oedipus*). *American Journal of Primatology* 26: 97–108.

Widowski, T. M., Ziegler, T. E., Elowson, A. M., and Snowdon, C. T. (1990). The role of males in the stimulation of reproductive function in female cotton-top tamarins, *Saguinus o. oedipus. Animal Behaviour* 40: 731–741.

Wikelski, M. and Thom, C. (2000). Marine iguanas shrink to survive El Niño. *Nature* 403: 37–38.

Wilkie, D. S., Sidle, J. G., and Boundzanga, G. C. (1992). Mechanized logging, market hunting, and a bank loan in Congo. *Conservation Biology* 6: 570–580.

Wilson, C. C. and Wilson, W. W. (1975). The influence of selective logging on primates and some other animals in East Kalimantan. *Folia Primatologica* 23: 245–274.

Wilson, D. S. (1997a). Altruism and organism: Disentangling the themes of multilevel selection theory. *American Naturalist (Supplement)* 150: 122–134.

Wilson, D. S. (1997b). Human groups as units of selection. *Science* 276: 1816–1817.

Wilson, D. S., Clark, A. B., Coleman, K., and Dearstyne, T. 1994. Shyness and boldness in humans and other animals. *Trends in Ecology and Evolution* 9: 442–446.

Wilson, D. S. and Sober, E. (1994). Reintroducing group selection to the human behavioral sciences. *Behavioral and Brain Sciences* 17: 585–654.

Wilson, E. O. (1975). *Sociobiology: The New Synthesis.* Harvard University Press, Cambridge.

Wilson, M. L., Hauser, M. D., and Wrangham, R. W. (2001). Does participation in intergroup conflict depend on numerical assessment, range location, or rank for wild chimpanzees? *Animal Behaviour* 61: 1203–1216.

Winter, P., Handley, P., Ploog, D., and Schott, D. (1973). Ontogeny of squirrel monkey calls under normal conditions and under acoustic isolation. *Behaviour* 47: 230–239.

Wolfe, L. D. (1987). *Field Primatology: A Guide to Research.* Garland Publishing, Inc., New York.

Wolfe, L. D. (1991). Human evolution and the sexual behavior of female primates. In Loy, J. D. and Peters, C. B. (eds.), *Understanding Behavior: What Primate Studies Tell Us About Human Behavior,* Oxford University Press, New York pp. 121–151.

Wood, B. (1992). Origin and evolution of the genus *Homo. Nature* 355: 783–790.

Wood, B. and Collard, M. (1999). The human genus. *Science* 284: 65–71.

Wrangham, R. W. (1977). Feeding behaviour of chimpanzees in Gombe National Park, Tanzania. In Clutton-Brock, T. H. (ed.), *Primate Ecology,* Academic Press, New York, pp. 503–538.

Wrangham, R. W. (1979). On the evolution of ape social systems. *Social Science Information* 18: 335–368.

Wrangham, R. W. (1980). An ecological model of female-bonded primate groups. *Behaviour* 75: 262–299.

Wrangham, R. W. (1981). Drinking competition in vervet monkeys. *Animal Behaviour* 29: 904–910.

Wrangham, R. W. (1982). Mutualism, kinship and social evolution. In Kings College. (ed.), *Current Problems in Sociobiology,* Cambridge University Press, Cambridge, pp. 269–289.

Wrangham, R. W. (1987a). The significance of African apes for reconstructing human social evolution. In Kinzey, W. G. (ed.), *The Evolution of Human Behavior: Primate Models,* SUNY Press, Albany, pp. 51–71.

Wrangham, R. W. (1987b). Evolution of social structure. In Smuts, B. B., Cheney, D. L., Seyfarth, R. M., Wrangham, R. W., and Struhsaker, T. T. (eds.), *Primate Societies,* University of Chicago Press, Chicago, pp. 282–296.

Wrangham, R. W. (1999). Evolution of coalitionary killing. *Yearbook of Physical Anthropology* 42: 1–30.

Wrangham, R. W. and Bergmann-Riss, E. (1990). Rates of predation on mammals by Gombe chimpanzees, 1972–1975. *Primates* 31: 157–170.

Wrangham, R. W., Chapman, C. A., and Chapman, L. J. (1994). Seed dispersal for forest chimpanzees. *Journal of Tropical Ecology* 10: 355–368.

Wrangham, R. and Peterson, D. (1996). *Demonic Males: Apes and the Origins of Human Violence.* Houghton Mifflin, Boston.

Wrangham, R. W. and Smuts, B. B. (1980). Sex differences in the behavioral ecology of chimpanzees in the Gombe National Park, Tanzania. *Journal of Reproductive Fertility Supplement* 28: 13–31.

Wright, P. C. (1988). Lemurs lost and found. *Natural History* 97: 56–66.

Wright, P. C. (1990). Patterns of paternal care in primates. *International Journal of Primatology* 11: 89–102.

Wright, P. C. (1994). Ecological disaster in Madagascar and the prospects for recovery. In Chapple, C. K. (ed.), *Ecological Prospects,* SUNY Press, Albany, pp. 11–24.

Wright, P. C. (1995). Demography and life history of free-ranging *Propithecus diadema edwardsi* in Ranomafana National Park, Madagascar. *International Journal of Primatology* 16: 835–854.

Wright, P. C. (1998). Impact of predation risk on the behaviour of *Propithecus diadema edwardsi* in the rain forest of Madagascar. *Behaviour* 135: 1–30.

Wright, P. C. (1999). Lemur traits and Madagascar ecology: Coping with an island environment. *Yearbook of Physical Anthropology* 42: 31–72.

Wright, P. C. and Jernvall, J. (1999). The future of primate communities: A reflection of the present. In Fleagle, J. G., Janson, C. H., and Reed, K. E. (eds.), *Primate Communities,* Cambridge University Press, Cambridge, pp. 295–309.

Wu, H., Holmes, W. G., Medina, S. R., and Sackett, G. P. (1980). Kin preference in infant *Macaca nemestrina. Nature* 285: 225–227.

Wynne-Edwards, V. C. (1962). *Animal Dispersion in Relation to Social Behavior,* Hafner, New York.

Yamagiwa, J. (1983). Diachronic changes in the eastern lowland gorilla groups (*Gorilla gorilla graueri*) in the Mt. Kahuzi region, Zaire. *Primates* 24: 174–183.

Yamagiwa, J. (1987). Male life history and the social structure of wild mountain gorillas (*Gorilla gorilla beringei*). In Kawano, S., Connell, J. H., and Hidaka, T. (eds.), *Evolution and Coadaptation in Biotic Communities,* University of Tokyo Press, Tokyo, pp. 31–51.

Yamagiwa, J. (1999). Socioecological factors influencing population structure of gorillas and chimpanzees. *Primates* 40: 87–104.

Yamagiwa, J., Maruhashi, T., Yumoto, T., and Mwanza, N. (1996). Dietary and ranging overlap in sympatric gorillas and chimpanzees in Kahuzi-Biega National Park, Zaire. In McGrew, W. C., Marchant, L. F., and Nishida, T. (eds.), *Great Ape Societies,* Cambridge University Press, New York, pp. 82–98.

Yamagiwa, J., Mwanza, N., Yumoto, T., and Maruhashi, T. (1994). Seasonal change in the composition of the diet of eastern lowland gorillas. *Primates* 35: 1–14.

Yamakoshi, G. (1998). Dietary responses to fruit scarcity of wild chimpanzees at Bossou, Guinea: Possible implications for ecological importance of tool use. *American Journal of Physical Anthropology* 106: 283–295.

Yamazaki, K., Beauchamp, G. K., Kupniewski, D., Bard, J., Thomas, L., and Boyse, E. A. (1988). Familial imprinting determines H-2 selective mating preferences. *Science* 240: 1331–1332.

Yeager, C. P. and Silver, S. C. (1999). Translocation and rehabilitation as primate conservation tools: Are they worth the cost? In Dolhinow, P. and Fuentes, A. (eds.), *The Nonhuman Primates,* Mayfield Publishing Company, Mountain View, California, pp. 164–169.

Young, A. L., Richard, A. F., and Aiello, L. C. (1990). Female dominance and maternal investment in strepsirhine primates. *American Naturalist* 135: 473–488.

Zeller, A. C. (1987). Communication by sight and smell. In Smuts, B. B., Cheney, D. L., Seyfarth, R. M., Wrangham, R. W., and Struhsaker, T. T. (eds.), *Primate Societies,* University of Chicago Press, Chicago, pp. 433–439.

Ziegler, T. E. (2000). Hormones associated with non-maternal infant care: A review of mammalian and avian studies. *Folia Primatologica* 71: 6–21.

Ziegler, T. E. and Snowdon, C. T. (2001). Preparental hormone levels and parenting experience in male cotton-top tamarins, *Saguinus oedipus. Hormones and Behavior* 38: 159–167.

Ziegler, T. E., Santos, C. V., Pissinatti, A., and Strier, K. B. (1997). Steroid excretion during the ovarian cycle in captive and wild muriquis, *Brachyteles arachnoides. American Journal of Primatology* 42: 311–321.

Ziegler, T. E., Savage, A., Scheffler, G., and Snowdon, C. T. (1987). The endocrinology of puberty and reproductive functioning in female cotton-top tamarins (*Saguinus oedipus*). *Biology of Reproduction* 37: 618–627.

Ziegler, T. E., Wegner, F. H., and Snowdon, C. T. (1996). Hormonal responses to parental and nonparental conditions in male cotton-top tamarins, *Saguinus oedipus,* a New World primate. *Hormones and Behavior* 30: 287–297.

Zimmermann, E. (1990). Differentiation of vocalizations in bushbabies (Galaginae, Prosimiae, Primates) and the significance for assessing phylogenetic relationships. *Zzeitschrift für Zoologische Systematik und Evolutionsforschung* 28: 217–239.

Zimmermann, E., Masters, J., and Rumpler, Y. (2000). Use of vocal fingerprinting for specific discrimination of gray (*Microcebus murinus*) and rufous mouse lemurs (*Microcebus rufus*). *International Journal of Primatology* 21: 837–852.

Zucker, E. L. and Clarke, M. R. (1998). Agonistic and affiliative relationships of adult female howlers (*Alouatta palliata*) in Costa Rica over a 4-year period. *International Journal of Primatology* 19: 433–449.

Zumpe, D. and Michael, R. P. (1996). Social factors modulate the effects of hormones on the sexual and aggressive behavior of macaques. *American Journal of Primatology* 38: 233–261.

GLOSSARY

activity budget   Amount and distribution of time allocated to different activities.

adaptation   The evolutionary process by which populations adjust to their environments; may also refer to a trait that is favored by natural selection.

adaptive   A trait is said to be adaptive if it increases the fitness of the individual who possesses it.

adaptive radiation   The evolutionary process by which a species diversifies to occupy different ecological niches.

affiliative bond   Strong associations among individuals, usually manifested by higher rates of proximity and nonaggressive social interactions.

age-graded   A system by which dominance and status are affected by age.

agonism   Aggressive and submissive interactions.

alkaloid   A class of molecules produced by plants, usually in low quantities, that can pass through an organism's gut and interfere with metabolism.

allele   Variant form of a gene.

alloparental care   Any parenting-type behavior shown toward an infant by an individual other than the infant's biological mother or father.

allometric scaling (allometry)   Proportional changes in one trait as a function of another, often due to developmental processes.

allopatric   Two or more species that are geographically separated from one another.

altricial   Born in an undeveloped state relative to the condition at maturity.

altruistic   Behavior that benefits the fitness of the recipient at a cost to the fitness of the actor.

androgen   Hormone necessary for the development and maintenence of male sexual characteristics.

angiosperm   Flowering plant.

anthelminthic   Possessing antiparasitic properties.

anthropocentric   Human-focused perspective.

anthropoid   The inclusive name for all New World monkeys, Old World Monkeys, and Hominoids.

arboreal   Tree-dwelling.

assemblage   Aggregation of two or more species.

autosomal   Genetic material found in the nonsex-determining chromosomes.

basal metabolic rate (BMR)   The rate at which an organism uses energy in a resting state.

basic rank   The dominance rank that an individual can attain as a result of his or her own competitive abilities.

behavioral adaptation   A behavior that benefits an individual's fitness.

behavioral ecology   The study of behavior from an evolutionary and ecological perspective.

bimaturism   Sex-specific growth periods; may also refer to different developmental pathways that members of the same species follow.

biomass   Total weight; the sum of body weights of all members of a group yields the group biomass.

bipedal   Two-legged locomotion.

brachiator   Organism whose locomotor system involves arm-over-arm propulsion.

bushmeat   The meat of wild animals, which have been hunted.

canine   The tooth located behind the incisors and in front of the premolars; in some primates, canines are bared in aggressive displays and used in fights.

canopy   Plant growth that blocks out sunlight; can also refer to the main layer of the trees where their branches and foliage are most dense. In canopy biology, refers to all above-ground plant organs (Moffett, 2000).

captive setting   A variety of conditions under which the movements of primates are restricted; range from isolated cages in sterile laboratories to large fenced enclosures containing one or more social groups.

carbohydrate   A class of compounds (of carbon, hydrogen, and oxygen) easily converted by the body into metabolizable energy.

catarrhine   The Old World monkeys and hominoids.

cathemeral   Active during both the day and night.

cercopithecine   One of the two major divisions of Old World monkeys, these have cheek pouches.

clade   A taxonomic group including all species that share a common ancestor.

cladistic analysis A method of determining common ancestries among species.

clavicle The bone that connects the sternum to the shoulder joint.

coalition rank The rank that one or more individuals attains when assisted by one or more other individuals.

coalition Two or more individuals who provide one another mutual support in social settings.

codominant alleles Alleles that are equally expressed at a particular locus, and evident as a distinct phenotype.

coevolution The process by which two species are mutually interdependent, and therefore each evolves in response to the selection pressures of the other.

cognitive abilities or cognition Thought processes and reasoning abilities.

cohesiveness The degree to which members of a group stay together; usually measured by the distance between individuals and the coordination of their movement patterns.

colobine One of the two major divisions of Old World monkeys, these have anatomical specializations for digesting leaves.

community Ecological communities include all of the living organisms that occur in an area; chimpanzee communities refer to their social groups.

consort A male and female who maintain an exclusive relationship, highly variable in duration, usually to facilitate mating opportunities.

conspecific A member of the same species as another individual.

contest competition The form of competition that occurs when access to a resource can be monopolized by one or more individuals.

continental drift The movement of continental landmasses that results from shifts in the underlying plates of the earth.

convergent evolution The evolutionary process whereby distantly related species independently evolve similar traits.

core area An area in which one or more individuals spend most of their time and obtain most of their food.

costs and benefits In evolution, these are the losses and gains to individual fitness or inclusive fitness.

critical function A trait that is essential for an organism's survival during discrete periods of time, even if it is not used the majority of time.

cross-fostering Rearing an individual of one species with one or more members of another species.

cultural primatology Study of local traditions that are transmitted from members of groups or populations by social means.

cultural tradition Local behavior that appears to develop from novel innovations that are then socially transmitted.

day range The daily distance traveled. Also called **daily path length.**

degree of relatedness The proportion of genes shared by two individuals through their common descent from one or both parents.

demography The size and composition of groups or populations, as determined by the births, deaths, immigrations, and emigrations of individuals in these groups or populations.

dental formula The number of each tooth type in one-quarter of the mouth.

dependent rank The rank that an individual can attain with support from one or more others.

derived trait Unique trait of a species that is not shared with its ancestor.

developmental arrest Delayed development of secondary sexual characteristics.

diploid Containing two copies.

dispersal Emigration from a social group; can involve emigration from the natal group or, in secondary dispersal, emigration from another group into which the individual has previously immigrated.

diurnal Active during daylight hours.

dominance hierarchy A ranking system among individuals usually established by the outcome of aggressive and submissive interactions.

dominant allele An allele that is expressed in the heterozygote condition.

ecological niche The total of a species's way of living in a particular environment at a particular time.

eco-tourism A brand of tourism that provides opportunities for visitors to see wildlife and habitats; developed in many parts of the world to help bring income into conservation projects.

egalitarian The absence of a hierarchy, or pecking order; access to resources is more likely to be determined by who gets to them first than by any other attributes of individuals.

emergent Tree that towers over the rest of the canopy.

endemism   Species found only in a small region or geographic area.

endoparasite   An organism that lives inside a host for at least some part of the organism's life cycle.

energy maximizer   A species with a lifestyle aimed at obtaining the maximum possible energy.

energy minimizer   A species with a lifestyle aimed at expending the least possible energy.

Eosimias   A group of stem primates whose fossils were recently discovered in Eocene deposits and which may represent ancestral haplorrhines.

estrous, *adj.*(estrus, *n.*)   Pertaining to the period of heightened sexual activity and receptivity exhibited by female mammals, usually around the time of ovulation.

ethnographic   An approach that involves the study of human cultures.

ethogram   The repertory of behaviors exhibited by a species.

evolutionary stable strategy (ESS)   A behavior or suite of behaviors that is the most adaptive solution under a prescribed set of conditions.

evolutionary theory   The combination of scientific laws and hypotheses based on these laws that explain the process of evolution.

extra-pair copulation   Copulation that occurs between a male or female member of a pairbond and a partner of the opposite sex other than the so-called mate. Extra-group copulations involve members of the opposite sex that do not associate in the same social groups.

extra-pair fertilization   Fertilization resulting from extra-pair or extra-group copulations.

feeding party   Individuals that are part of a larger social network, but split off from others for feeding purposes.

feeding strategy   The total activity, locomotor, ranging, grouping, social, and dietary pattern of an individual or a species that pertains to feeding.

female-bonded   Females that remain in their natal groups, with their extended matrilineal kin, and maintain differentiated relationships.

female choice   The selection of one or more mates by a female. Expressed to different degrees in different species.

female-defense polygyny   A form of polygyny in which a male defends two or more females from other males.

fission–fusion   Societies in which individuals split up into smaller feeding parties.

fitness   An individual's reproductive success relative to the fitnesses of other members of the same species.

fixed   The condition in which the frequency of a gene is 1.0 in a population; there are no other alleles in the population when one has become fixed.

folivore   A leaf-eater; traditionally classified as such if leaves constitute over 50 percent of an animal's diet.

food availability   The spatial and temporal presence of food.

food distribution   The location of food resources in space.

food patch   One or more members of the same food species concentrated in a specific area.

food quality   The proportion of readily digestible energy and essential proteins and nutrients in food.

foraging   Feeding and food-related travel activities.

foraging efficiency   The degree to which time and energy expended in feeding and food-related travel is offset by the energy obtained.

founder population   A small initial population, representing a low level of genetic heterogeneity, that colonizes an area or becomes geographically (and genetically) isolated from other populations.

frugivore   A fruit-eater; traditionally classified as such if fruits constitute over 50 percent of an animal's diet.

function   The purpose a trait serves in increasing an individual's fitness.

game theory   In behavior, the most "fit" behavioral response of one individual is dependent on the response of one or more other individuals.

gamete   A sex cell, either sperm or ovum.

gene flow   The movement of genes between populations through the reproductive activities of individuals.

generalized trait   See **primitive trait.**

genetic drift   Evolutionary process of random fluctuations in gene frequencies in a population.

genotype   The genetic composition of an individual.

geophagy   The eating of dirt, soils, sands, or clay.

graded signal   Changes in the size and color of the sexual swelling that signal the probability of ovulation to other group members.

gregarious   Social.

grooming   The removal of dirt, or other objects from the skin or fur, which may be performed by another individual (allogrooming) or by one's self; allogrooming is considered to be a social activity.

group selection Theoretically, an evolutionary process whereby traits that favor the fitness of the group are selected for over time, even if these traits are deleterious to the fitness of individual group members.

growth diet High quality food that can be used to sustain one's self and converted into offspring.

guenon Diverse species of African cercopithecine monkeys.

habituated The point at which animals cease to alter their behavior in the presence of human observers.

Hamilton's rule An equation that predicts when it is to an individual's inclusive fitness benefit to behave altruistically toward a relative by taking the individual fitness costs of the actor, the individual fitness benefits to the recipient, and the degree of relatedness between them into account.

Haplorhini The tarsiers, New World Monkeys, Old World monkeys, and hominoids.

heritable A trait that is transmitted in the genes, and therefore can be passed along from generation to generation in the descendants.

heterogametic Possessing two types of sex chromosomes; in mammals, males are heterogametic (XY).

heterzygote Possessing two different alleles at a locus.

hierarchical A pecking order, usually established through direct contests.

high-quality diet **Growth diet.**

home range The area an individual or group of individuals uses.

hominid Humans and other bipedal primates, among which we are the only living representatives.

hominoid The apes and hominids.

homogametic Possessing one type of sex chromosome; in mammals, females are homogametic (XX).

homology A trait found in two or more species that is shared due to their common ancestry.

homoplasy A trait found in two or more species that has evolved independently in each.

homozygote The same two alleles at a locus.

honest advertisement Signals that are accurate indicators of an individual's condition.

hotspot An area that is high in biodiversity, based on the number of endemic species it supports and the proportion of habitat that has already been lost.

hybrid An offspring produced by parents from different species or genera.

hyoid A bone in the throat that supports the vocal apparatus.

imitation Copying the behavior or gestures of another individual. It requires a level of representational thought that few primates are thought to possess.

inbreeding Reproduction between biological relatives.

inbreeding depression The deleterious genetic effects of inbreeding involving close biological relatives.

incisor The teeth at the front of the mouth, ahead of the canines.

inclusive fitness The sum of an individual's fitness and the fitness of all of the individual's relatives, weighted by their **degree of relatedness.**

indicator species Species with prominent roles in their communities, usually high on the food chain.

infanticide The deliberate killing of infants.

insectivore An insect-eater.

interbirth interval The time interval between successive births; in primates, measured in months or years.

interspecific Refers to comparisons among different species.

intrasexual competition Competition among members of the same sex (e.g., male–male or female–female).

intraspecific Refers to comparisons among different populations of the same species; important for evaluating the significance of interspecific variation.

isometric scaling Refers to a one-to-one variation between two traits.

Jarman/Bell principle A general rule that the nutrient requirements of large-bodied animals are absolutely higher than those of smaller animals, but lower relative to their body size. Therefore, larger animals tend to feed on more abundant, but lower-quality foods than smaller animals.

karyotype The full set of chromosomes individuals of a species tend to carry.

ketone   The product of fat metabolism in the body.

kin recognition   The ability to discriminate biological relatives from unrelated individuals. Usually measured by differential interactions and relationships among kin versus nonkin.

kin selection   A form of natural selection in which an individual's fitness is influenced by the fitness of his or her relatives because kin share a proportion of their genes.

knuckle-walker   A mode of locomotion used by the African apes (gorillas, chimpanzees, and bonobos), which walk on the soles of their feet and the knuckles of their hands.

lactational amenorrhea   A feedback process whereby the stimulus of lactation releases hormones that inhibit ovulation.

last common ancestor (LCA)   The ancestor of two or more living or extinct species.

life history strategy   The total of developmental stages and durations over an individual's lifetime; species with fast life histories tend to reach maturity quickly and have high reproductive rates, while those with slow life histories experience delayed maturation and lower reproductive rates.

life history trait   A trait such as age at first reproduction, gestation length, interbirth interval, and lifespan, which together affect potential lifetime reproductive rates.

lipid   Fat that can be converted to energy through metabolic processes.

local resource competition   Competition among group members over common resources, which can be reduced by producing infants who will disperse instead of infants who will remain in the group.

local resource enhancement   If larger groups have competitive advantages in contests over resources with other groups, it can be advantageous to increase group size by producing offspring who will remain in the natal group and participate in resource defense against other groups.

local tradition   Behavior specific to particular groups or populations that are not always explained by differences in their ecologies.

locomotor   The system by which animals move from one location to another. Among primates, locomotor systems include vertical clinging and leaping, quadrupedality, brachiation, knuckle-walking, and bipedality.

locus   The position of a particular gene and its variant alleles on a chromosome.

low-quality diet   Food with little nutrient value to the organism; usually sufficient for maintaining life, but may result in malnourishment and preclude reproduction over extended periods.

lumper   Taxonomist that tends to minimize the variation exhibited by populations or species, and group them together in the same taxa.

Machiavellian intelligence   A form of intelligence involving tactical deception, whereby individuals perceive the world through their own and others' perspectives, and adjust their behavior to advance their own fitness interests.

major histocompatibility complex (MHC)   A suite of genes involved in the immune system. Some evidence suggests that rodents and primates choose mates with different MHC alleles than their own, to the benefit of their offspring who acquire greater disease resistance.

masseter muscle   One of the major chewing muscles; responsible for lateral movements of the jaw involved in chewing.

mast fruiting   Occurs when many species flower and then fruit in synchrony.

mate guarding   Male defense of female mates from harassment or mating attempts by other males.

mating effort   Time and energy devoted to securing access to a mate.

matriline   Related to one another through maternal descent.

matrilocal   Living in the same group as one's matrilineal kin.

meaning   In communication systems, the way a signal is perceived.

meiosis   The process of cell division responsible for the production of gametes, which contain half of the genetic complement of the parent cell.

Mendelian genetics   The process by which traits from each parent assort independently and recombine during sexual reproduction to result in genetically novel offspring.

mitochondrial DNA (mtDNA)   The DNA found only in the mitochondria of cells; it is only inherited from an individual's mother.

molar   A type of tooth found behind the premolar.

molecular clock   The estimated rate at which genetic mutations accumulate; used to estimate times of divergence between species.

monogamy   Technically speaking, a mating system in which one male reproduces exclusively with one female.

monotypic   A genus represented by a single species.

morphology   Anatomical characteristics.

mosaic nature of evolution   Different functional systems, such as those related to locomotion and those related to feeding, evolve at different rates in response to different pressures.

motivation   In communication, the stimulus for sending a signal.

multiparous   A female who has reproduced more than once.

mutation   Random mistake during the process of DNA replication that can have deleterious, neutral, or positive effects on an individual's fitness.

mutualism   When two or more individuals benefit by cooperating.

natal group   The group into which an individual is born.

natural selection   The evolutionary process that leads to higher fitness in some individuals and lower fitness in others under particular conditions; depends on genetic variation within a population or species to operate.

negative assortative mating   Preferential mating between individuals with phenotypical differences.

neocortex   The region of the brain above and surrounding the cerebral cortex where higher thought processes and reasoning are thought to occur.

neutral mutation   Randomly occurring mutation that has no effects on an individual's fitness, and therefore is invisible to the process of natural selection.

niche divergence   The process by which potentially competitive species reduce competition through separation in some or multiple aspects of their ecologies.

nocturnal   Active at night.

nongovernmental organizations (NGOs)   Private organizations that play an increasingly important role in conservation efforts throughout the world.

ontogeny   The processes and mechanisms involved in development.

operational sex ratio (OSR)   Used to assess levels of reproductive competition; the OSR takes into account both the number of potential breeding males and females and the amount of time that individuals of both sexes are reproductively active.

opposable thumb   A highly mobile thumb that is capable of rotating and touching other fingers; necessary for **precision gripping.**

optimal   The compromise solution that yields the highest fitness differential between benefits and costs for a particular individual at a particular time.

parallel evolution   Evolutionary process by which closely related species evolve similar, derived traits.

parasite   Any animal (or plant) that lives in or on another organism.

parent–offspring conflict   A parent's inclusive fitness is maximized by ceasing to invest in an offspring (for future offspring) sooner than when an offspring's inclusive fitness would be maximized by gaining siblings.

paternity certainty   Certainty as to which male sired an offspring.

patriline   Related to one another through paternal descent.

patrilocal   Living in the same group as one's patrilineal kin.

phenotype   The observed characteristics of an individual, often reflecting the effects of environmental conditions on genotypic expression.

phenotypic matching   Recognizing others with similar phenotypes to oneself.

pheromone   Substance secreted by one animal and detected by another; important in sexual communication for many primates.

philopatric   Individuals that remain in their natal, or birth, groups.

phylogeny   Evolutionary relationships of species to one another.

plate tectonics   The processes by which the plates comprising the earth's crust move apart or together, leading to continental drift.

platyrrhine   The New World monkeys.

plesiadapiform   Mammal dating back to the Paleocene; once thought to be an ancestral primate.

polyandry   A mating system whereby one reproductive female mates with two or more different males.

polygamy   A mating system whereby both males and females mate with two or more different partners.

polygyny   A mating system whereby one male mates with two or more different females.

polygyny threshold   The point at which a female's fitness is enhanced by joining another female on a high quality territory instead of being the sole female on a lower quality territory.

polymorphic   Multiple forms; may refer to a population with multiple phenotypes.

polyspecific association   Association between two or more different species that involves behavioral changes by at least one of the participating species.

population   Individuals of the same species that share a common gene pool.

population density   The number of individuals per unit area.

positive assortative mating   Preferential mating between individuals with similar phenotypes.

postconflict resolution   Reconciliation that occurs following conflicts. Thought to repair relationships.

precision grip   A position of the hand in which two or more digits hold an object.

precocial   Infants are born relatively well developed at birth.

prehensile tail   A tail that is capable of grasping objects or substrates, almost like a third hand.

premolar   A type of tooth behind the canine and in front of the molars.

primary sex ratio   The proportion of males and females conceived.

primiparous   A females who has given birth once.

primitive trait   Trait inherited from an ancestor. Also called a **generalized trait.**

priority of access   The assumed benefits associated with high rank in a pecking order, or **hierarchy.**

Prisoner's dilemma   A "game" that predicts how cooperation can evolve.

prolactin   A hormone with multiple functions, among which is parenting behavior. Prolactin levels of females are affected by the stimulus of suckling, but at least some male primates also show elevated prolactin levels prior to and after offspring are born.

promiscuous   Mating with multiple partners; may be indiscriminate or discriminating.

prosimii   Lemurs, galagos, lorises, and tarsiers.

protein   Building block for bodily growth, reproduction, and function.

provisioned   Primates that obtain all or some of their food from humans.

proximate   The neural and physiological mechanisms that regulate behavior.

puberty   The process of sexual maturation.

quadrumanous   A locomotory style that involves the use of all four limbs; usually associated with slow, deliberate climbing.

quadrupedal   A locomotory style that involves the use of all four limbs.

races   Populations that exhibit variation equivalent to that of subspecies.

rank reversal   Switch in the ranks of two or more individuals, usually as a result of direct challenges by subordinates.

recessive allele   An allele that is only expressed in its homozygote form.

reciprocal altruism   Behaviors that are costly to the actor's fitness and beneficial to the fitness of the recipient and reciprocated by the recipient.

recombination   The process by which alleles get mixed up and later joined in novel combinations; an important source of genetic variation in sexually reproducing organisms.

reconciliation   The process of making up after a conflict; may be initiated by winners or losers, depending on species and the context of the conflict.

referential model   The use of particular species for drawing analogies with others.

refuges   Forests that have contracted in size, fragmenting continuous populations into isolated ones.

reintroduction   Procedure for returning animals that have lived in captivity back to the wild.

reproductive lifespan   The interval between puberty and death, during which individuals can reproduce.

reproductive potential   The maximum number of offspring an individual can produce.

reproductive seasonality   Females of a group give birth at the same time of year.

reproductive strategy   The combination of behaviors and life history traits that affect reproduction.

reproductive success   An individual's genetic contributions to future generations through his or her own offspring.

reproductive synchrony   Females ovulate at similar times; need not be seasonal.

resource-defense polygyny   A form of polygyny in which a male defends resources, such as areas containing food, that attract females.

sacculated stomach   Complex stomach in which digestion is aided by intense microbial action; a specialized adaptation in **colobines.**

safari   When a male and female chimpanzee travel to the periphery of their community's range, usually during or encompassing the female's estrus.

savanna   Tropical grassland.

scramble competition   The form of competition that occurs when resources cannot be easily monopolized or defended, and therefore are distributed on a first-come basis.

secondary compound   Thousands of compounds produced by plants that affect the digestibility, palatability, and toxicity of the plants.

secondary sex ratio   The sex ratio of infants at birth.

secondary sexual characteristic   Trait that affects competitive ability and attractiveness to mates, but not survival.

selfish   Acting on behalf of one's own best fitness interests at a cost to the fitness of others.

semiterrestrial   Primates that spend significant proportions of their time on the ground.

sex skin   The fleshy swelling on the rumps of some female primates that inflates and deflates in response to their phase in the ovulatory cycle.

sexual dimorphism   Morphological differences between the sexes.

sexual monomorphism   Morphological similarities between the sexes (except reproductive organs).

sexual selection   A form of natural selection acting on variation in the ability of individuals to compete with others of their own sex and to attract members of the opposite sex.

sexually receptive   When a female solicits male sexual attention or is responsive to male advances.

signal   In communication, the information that one individual transmits.

social strategy   Behaviors that affect an individual's social relationships and status.

sociobiology   The biological (evolutionary) study of social behavior.

socionomic sex ratio   The ratio of the number of breeding females to males in a group.

solitary   Living alone.

sound spectrogram   Visual representation of the acoustic properties of sound.

specialized trait   Trait that is derived.

speciation   The evolutionary process whereby new species are formed.

species   Individuals that are capable of interbreeding and producing viable, fertile offspring.

species richness   The diversity of species found in ecological communities.

sperm competition   Competition for fertilizations occurring among sperm.

splitter   Taxonomist who recognizes variation by using different names.

stereoscopic vision   Results from partially overlapping fields of vision; important for depth perception.

stochastic   Random processes or randomly occurring events.

strategic model   The use of evolutionary theory to predict differences and similarities among species.

strategy   Behavior or behaviors that increase individual fitness, and therefore are favored by natural selection.

Strepsirhini   The lemurs and lorises.

study group   Social group that is typically the focus of behavioral research.

subsistence food   Survival, or fall-back, low-quality food eaten when higher-quality foods are rare or unavailable.

subspecies   Populations of the same species that can be distinguished from one another by their traits.

supernumerary nipple   Accessory, or greater than two, nipples. Usually occurs at low frequencies in most populations of primates.

suspensory   A locomotor or postural style involving swinging or hanging from the arms.

sustainable forest management   The harvesting of trees or other forest products without destroying the habitat.

sympatric   Two or more species occurring in the same area.

systematic method   Standardized method for collecting data to reduce observer bias.

systematics   The process of classifying organisms into taxonomic groups.

tactical deception   Apparently deliberate dishonest signaling used by primates to deceive one another.

tannin   A form of secondary plant compound that reduces digestibility of food in the gut.

tapetum   A reflective layer in the eye's retina that improves night vision.

taxa   Species, subspecies, and populations that are distinguished taxonomically.

taxonomic classification   The scientific naming of categories of organisms.

temperament   The different personalities that individuals and species exhibit.

temporalis muscle   One of the major chewing muscles; involved in opening and closing the mouth.

terrestrial   Ground-dwelling.

territorial   Defense of an area, which is exclusively used, from other conspecifics.

theory of mind   The ability to perceive how one is perceived by another individual.

tool-composite   The use of two or more objects for different purposes.

torpor   Reduced **BMR** during resting to conserve energy expenditure.

translocation   Procedure for transferring one or more animals from one location to another.

triadic awareness   An individual acts as if he or she understands his or her status and social situation relative to others.

trichromatic vision   The ability to discriminate red-green colors.

ultimate   The adaptive significance of a trait.

understory   Area underneath the canopy, above the forest floor.

variance in reproductive success   The range of differences in the number of surviving offspring individuals produce.

viability   The probability of surviving into the future; often used in assessments of a species or a population's chances of escaping extinction.

woodland   Habitat with continuous tree cover, but less dense than forest.

zoonoses   The interspecific transmission of infectious diseases.

zoopharmacognosy   The scientific study of medicinal plant use by animals.

zygote   A fertilized ovum.

INDEX

Note: Italicized page numbers indicate tables and figures.

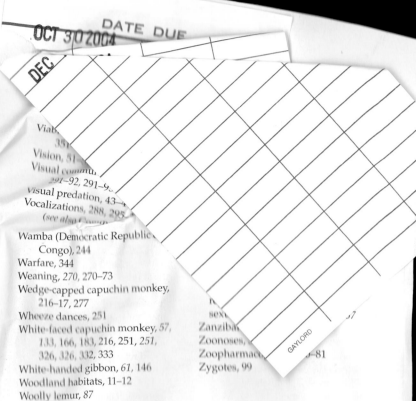

DATE DUE